THE ANALYSIS OF CROSS-CLASSIFIED DATA HAVING ORDERED CATEGORIES

THE ANALYSIS OF CROSS-CLASSIFIED DATA HAVING ORDERED CATEGORIES

Leo A. Goodman

with contributions by Clifford C. Clogg
and a Foreword by Otis Dudley Duncan

Harvard University Press
Cambridge, Massachusetts, and London, England
1984

Library of Congress Cataloging in Pulication Data

Goodman, Leo A.
  The analysis of cross-classified data having ordered categories.

  Includes bibliographical references and index.
  1. Social sciences—Statistical methods.   I. Clogg,
Clifford C.   II. Title.   III. Title: Cross-classified data having ordered
categories.
HA29.G659   1984   300'.1'5195   83-22717
ISBN 0-674-03145-8 (alk. paper)

To Andy and Tom: The Future

CONTENTS

Appendixes

Foreword

Otis Dudley Duncan

This set of articles on the analysis of cross-classified frequency data is the fourth such collection of contributions by Leo Goodman, with various collaborators, to be published in the last half-dozen years. The 1978 book, *Analyzing Qualitative/Categorical Data*, included seven of his articles on log-linear models, with special attention to their use in analyzing survey data, and an additional three papers on latent-structure and scaling models. In 1979 a selection of articles translated into Hungarian was published; its contents overlap those of both the 1978 and the present collection. Also in 1979, Goodman and William Kruskal published a volume containing their four classic pieces on the measurement of association for cross-classifications. Apart from the items in its Appendix, the present collection includes only works originally published in 1979 or later.

Certain shifts of viewpoint and emphasis can be discerned in comparing the later with the earlier work. The more recent papers have a different kind of rationale from that adopted by Goodman and Kruskal when they began their studies of measures of association in the 1950s. That work laid stress on the idea of "operational interpretation" of a measure of association as, for example, in a model of the predictive activity of an investigator interested, say, in predicting, for an individual chosen at random, the category of variable B into which he falls, given his classification according to variable A. The measure of association then serves to assess the predictability of B from A under some proposed prediction rule. The new work is not so much concerned with models of the investigator's activity as with models that pertain to the way in which the data might have been generated. In that context, measures of association may take the form of parameters of a model. This approach, it seems to me, might appropriately be termed "structural," and the distinction between the "operational" and the "structural" points of view in the treatment of categorical data might be seen as parallel, in certain respects, to the distinction between estimation equations and structural equations in the domain of linear regression models.

Another prominent feature of the recent articles is the focus on variables whose categories are ordered. Some earlier work on log-linear models in which order is, in a certain sense, taken into account was published in 1972 (Appendix D); and in the 1978 collection there is one article in which linear and quadratic components of the associations involving a trichotomy are separately tested within the saturated model. But the articles at hand go beyond the earlier expositions to provide a variety of unsaturated models wherein the "structure" is specified or constrained to be linear (or, for that matter, to take some other mathematically explicit form, if that is desired). In this connection it is relevant that, with the exception already noted, all the empirical examples taken up in the 1978 book pertained to dichotomous variables, where the issue of the order of the categories might arise with respect to the substantive interpretation of statistical interactions but did not enter into the specification, estimation, or testing of the model. Indeed, some careless readers surmised that Goodman was only interested in naturally dichotomous or artificially dichotomized variables, even though he was careful to present formal generalizations of the log-linear models to the case in which some or all variables in the two-way or multi-way cross-classification are polytomous.

Furthermore, whereas the 1978 collection emphasized log-linear models (including logit models as a special case), several of the articles in this book deal in whole or in part with log-multiplicative models. It is the first book to give a detailed treatment of this class of models.

The four books I have referred to contain only a fraction of Goodman's writing on methods for studying cross-classifications. There are now about as many uncollected as collected papers on that topic. (Altogether, Goodman's work in this area accounts for not more than half of his writing on statistical methods and quantitative social science, although it is the writing in this area that is perhaps most widely appreciated.) Apart from the series of papers on measures of association, which appeared between 1954 and 1972, Goodman published in the 1960s a number of notable contributions dealing with interactions in contingency tables and related topics, as well as several that suggested models especially well suited to the analysis of mobility tables and similar data. Some of the flavor of this earlier work, carried out prior to Goodman's general exposition of the log-linear model in 1970 (reprinted as chapter 4 of the 1978 collection), is conveyed by Appendixes A and B of this collection. The earlier papers gave much attention to methods that could be applied using only the desk calculator as an aid to computation. The more recent work relies heavily on iterative algorithms that ordinarily are not feasible without access to an electronic computer and programs specially constructed to handle log-linear or log-multiplicative models.

The Contents and Preface make the general plan of this volume explicit. It begins with a clarification of the distinctions and relationships among three classes of models—those concerned, respectively, with joint distributions, dependence, and association of categorical variables. Each of the three papers that follow is devoted to the elaboration of one of these viewpoints. Although the discussion of association models makes up the greater part of the book, I hope readers will not conclude that the material on analyzing joint distributions and dependence can safely be slighted. My own experience suggests that problems one is first tempted to formulate in terms of association models may sometimes be attacked more productively from a different point of view. We must resist the temptation to play Procrustes, forcing all analysis into a common mold for sake of convenience or to honor an outmoded disciplinary convention.

The next two chapters demonstrate hitherto unsuspected connections between models of association and statistical methods based on the assumption of an underlying bivariate normal distribution (Chapter 5) or the notion of canonical correlation (Chapter 6). Just as one must be something of a Hellenist fully to savor the poetry of Euripides, only a statistician will fully appreciate the power and finesse of these contributions to statistical theory. But anyone who has looked at the language of the polemical exchanges between Karl Pearson and G. Udny Yule can marvel that Goodman is able to put the two titans into one tent. And if, like me, you have been somewhat awed by certain formidable applications of the canonical correlation approach in the literature on occupational mobility tables, you will be pleased to learn that canonical correlation can be reconciled with the association models approach that has taken the mobility table as a kind of paradigmatic challenge.

In Chapters 7, 8, and 9—the last two by Goodman's former student and current collaborator, Clifford Clogg—we are shown some interesting applications of association models. The first of these deals with the much-vexed issue of how one should reach decisions about the reduction or collapsing of a contingency table to one with fewer rows and/or columns. (Appendix A contains material relevant to this problem, and might well be read first.) Perhaps the most important message is that this step should be taken in full cognizance of the information that is, or may be, lost in such data reduction. Hitherto, considerations of convenience and rules of expediency have governed the almost wholly intuitive and capricious attitude adopted by most investigators confronted with the problem. Goodman's results make it clear that the classification itself is part of the model specification. Hence it may make little sense to ask, What is "the" relationship between father's and son's occupation? Rather, we must ask, What models are consistent with the data in a cross-classification expressed in terms of the following (explicitly defined) categories? As I have put the matter, I suppose an experienced analyst can only rejoin, Of course! But no amount of raw experience with data will substitute for the explicit consideration of formal criteria for combining categories that Goodman provides.

Clogg's chapters on applications take us into a different domain of subject matter. Whether by preference or by happenstance, the dozen or so cross-classifications Goodman uses for illustrative purpose in the first seven chapters almost all are constructed from relatively objective variables. In Chapters 8 and 9 we plunge into the subjective, making use of respondents' self-assessments of their personal attitudes and feelings. Survey analysts interested in this kind of material will recognize immediately that the new models confront directly a fact typically glossed over in research reports and even in the methodological literature: a large fraction of the questions put to respondents in surveys of subjective phenomena incorporate response categories designed to register degree of attitude intensity, level of personal satisfaction, severity of moral disapproval, and the like. That is, they often take the form of a rating scale, with semantically or numerically ordered categories. Until recently, there was a flourishing debate as to whether "interval" or merely "ordinal" properties could be ascribed to such measures. The popularity of methods based on the Pearsonian correlation statistic strongly encouraged a tacit—or sometimes explicitly defended—choice of the stronger assumption. The debate, in my opinion, is now of only historical interest. Whether intervals between categories are equal is a question that cannot be answered without prior specification and explication of a model that is sensitive in a statistically detectable way to the difference between the two cases. Clogg's articles, although they are surely just the initiation of a large program of work on models having that capability, provide a new vocabulary for rigorous arguments on the properties of rating scales. These two chapters also offer a wealth of examples of three-way cross-classifications and thereby help us greatly to appreciate the potential utility of Goodman's generalizations (Chapters 1 and 4) of association models to the multi-way case.

The Appendix is a welcome bonus. Even readers well acquainted with the 1978 collection may find it useful to begin reading the present work with Appendix A or B, which contain seeds of some of the ideas developed in the preceding chapters. I personally find Appendix C a more reader-friendly introduction to association models than the more formal and comprehensive Chapter 4. My students seem to find the tabular displays featured in Appendix C a valuable aid to understanding models and, as Goodman observes, a convenient "machine" for building models that incorporate effects of possible substantive interest. I cannot recommend Appendix D for introductory reading but am nevertheless pleased at its inclusion. It is a veritable tour de force demonstrating that life in a model-rich environment is more exciting—if also more stressful—than any amount of routine data reduction using conventional descriptive statistics. Goodman has given us a computer program called Everyman's Contingency Table Analyzer. He might have labeled Appendixes C and D Everyman's Model Building Apparatus.

I have tried to ease into the matter of style or rhetoric in these remarks addressed primarily to the less experienced or more timorous reader. Let me emphasize that the intention is to encourage such readers. Some of the shorter papers in this volume admittedly present obstacles for students with less than adequate backgrounds in theoretical statistics. Here we must either seek help or be content to appreciate results only in general terms. The longer expository papers pose a different kind of difficulty. Although they are technically accessible, for the most part, to a reader with modest preparation, they are exceedingly thorough and detailed. Goodman wants to apprise us of the great variety of distinct issues that may arise in the course of analyzing a complex set of data. And it is simply not possible for him, or anyone, to give advice covering all these circumstances that is both sound and succinct. Some matters really are complex in detail even when the principle is straightforward; and Goodman never allows us to relax our responsibility for the fine structure of an analysis in favor of a specious preoccupation with the big picture. Without minimizing the effort that may be required, therefore, I do want to urge the reader to persevere in the study of these remarkable contributions to statistical method. Few efforts will be more richly rewarded.

Preface

This book is concerned primarily with the analysis of *discrete* data (such as counts of various kinds), with *ordered categories* (for example, counts of people in, say, four ordered educational categories or in, say, six ordered socioeconomic status categories), and with *cross-classified* data (such as counts of people who are both in particular educational categories and also in particular socioeconomic status categories). Its general approach can be applied both in the case where the categories are ordered for each of the qualitative (categorical) variables under consideration (for the educational variable and for the socioeconomic status variable, for example), and in the case where the categories are ordered for some (but not all), of the qualitative variables under consideration (for the educational variable and for the socioeconomic status variable but not for, say, a religious affiliation variable with people classified with respect to particular (unordered) religious affiliation categories). The approach can also be applied when the particular ordering of the categories of the variable is specified a priori, or when the ordering of the categories is not specified a priori but is instead determined by an examination of the relationship of the variable to other related variables. For example, with respect to the educational variable, the categories can be ordered a priori from the lower to the higher categories; while with respect to the socioeconomic status variable, the category ordering can be determined by the observed relationship of this variable to other relevant variables, using some of the methods that will be described in this book. Some of the methods to be presented here can even be applied when all of the qualitative variables under consideration have categories that are not ordered, and the observed relationship between the variables can be used to determine an ordering for the categories.

The methods described here are applicable to work in many different fields, such as sociology and other related social sciences, psychology, biology and the biological sciences, marketing and other areas of business, education, political science, medical research. Many different kinds of data can be analyzed, as can be seen by perusing the list below of the cross-classification tables that are used as illustrative examples in this book. Examples from an even wider range of fields could have been used instead.

1. Cross-classification of children according to status as noncarriers or carriers of *Streptococcus Pyogenes* and enlargement level of tonsils (Chapter 1)
2. Cross-classification of women according to right eye grade and left eye grade with respect to unaided distance vision (Chapters 1 and 2)
3. Length of stay in hospital for schizophrenic patients classified by visiting pattern that had been ascribed in the hospital (Chapters 1 and 3)
4. Number of deaths in litters of mice classified by litter size and treatment (Chapter 3)
5. Cross-classification of subjects according to their mental health and their parents' socioeconomic status (Chapter 4)
6. Cross-classification of British male sample according to each subject's occu-

pational status category and his father's occupational status category (Chapters 4, 5, and 7)

7. Cross-classification of Danish male sample according to each subject's occupational status category and his father's occupational status category (Chapter 5)
8. Cross-classification of students according to number of newspapers read carefully and number of newspapers looked at only briefly (Chapter 5)
9. Cross-classification of stature of fathers and daughters (Chapter 5)
10. Cross-classification of periodontal condition and calcium intake level of women (Chapter 6)
11. Cross-classification of eye color and hair color of children in Caithness and in Aberdeen (Chapter 6)
12. Respondent's attitude toward the courts' treatment of criminals as reported in response to question in the General Social Survey, classified by question wording and by amount of schooling of the respondent (Chapter 8)
13. Cross-classification of U.S. sample according to attitude on abortion and attitude on premarital sex (Chapter 8)
14. Level of happiness reported by respondent in U.S. sample, classified by sex of the respondent and by the amount of schooling of the respondent (Chapters 8 and 9)
15. Cross-classification of U.S. sample according to three indicators of satisfaction with life (Chapters 8 and 9)
16. Level of happiness reported by respondent in U.S. sample, classified by the amount of schooling of the respondent and by the number of siblings of the respondent (Chapter 9)

Additional material related to the analysis of the British and Danish samples in cross-classifications 6 and 7 above is included in Appendices B and D; and additional material related to the analysis of the British sample in cross-classification 6 is included in Appendix A, which also includes other illustrative examples not listed above.

The introductory chapter of this book describes three elementary ways to view the analysis of cross-classifications having ordered categories. (This chapter is based on a lecture delivered when I received the Outstanding Statistician of the Year Award for 1978–79 from the American Statistical Association, Chicago Chapter.) The three elementary views considered in Chapter 1 pertain to the use of log-linear models in three different contexts; viz., the analysis of the joint distribution in a cross-classification, the analysis of dependence, and the analysis of association. The three contexts are considered further in Chapters 2, 3, and 4. (Parts of these chapters were included in the Keynote Address delivered by me at the 1981 Symposium on the Analysis of Discrete Data, sponsored by the American Statistical Association, Northern New Jersey Chapter, and in the American Lecture at the 1981 International Meeting on the Analysis of Multidimensional Contingency Tables, at the University of Rome, under the auspices of the Italian Statistical Society.) Chapters 5 and 6 develop further the analysis of association, showing in which ways the models and methods introduced here are preferable to those obtained with the various approaches developed earlier by Karl Pearson, R. A. Fisher, and others. (These chapters were included in the

George W. Snedecor Memorial Lectures which I delivered in 1980, and the topics are developed further in the Henry L. Rietz Memorial Lecture delivered by me, at the invitation of the Institute of Mathematical Statistics, at the 1983 joint meeting of the Institute of Mathematical Statistics, the American Statistical Association, the Biometric Society, and the Statistical Society of Canada.) Chapters 7, 8, and 9 provide additional kinds of applications of association models. Chapter 7 uses these models in the development of criteria for determining whether certain categories in a cross-classification table should be combined; and the criteria are applied, for illustrative purposes, to occupational categories in an occupational mobility table. Chapters 8 and 9, by Clifford C. Clogg, provide additional examples using three-way cross-classifications, and develop further the analysis of multiway cross-classifications, a topic considered also in the final section of Chapter 1 and briefly in Chapter 4. (I thank Clifford Clogg for permission to include his work here.)

Beginning with an overall view of the relevant topics and the main themes introduced in Chapter 1, the volume develops these topics and themes more fully in the subsequent chapters. The volume provides a unified, coherent, and integrated presentation of models and methods for the analysis of ordered categorical data.

Appendixes A through D include some of my earlier work to which reference is made in the body of the text; they are included here for the convenience of the reader. Otis Dudley Duncan, in his Foreword, notes that A and B include material that may be viewed as introductory to the volume as a whole, and Appendix C includes material that may be viewed as introductory to the chapters on association models. (Appendix A was the R. A. Fisher Memorial Lecture presented, at the invitation of the Committee of Presidents of Statistical Societies, at the 1968 joint meeting of the American Statistical Association and the Biometric Society.) Appendixes C and D are concerned with association models, and Duncan has suggested that they be called Everyman's Model Building Apparatus. (Appendix D was a lecture delivered at the Sixth Berkeley Symposium on Mathematical Statistics and Probability in 1970.) To facilitate application of the methods described in the present volume, Appendix E on computer programs is also included.

For the convenience of the reader, a list of Citations, which provides full bibliographical data for the chapters and appendixes in this volume, follows this Preface. In the references at the end of each chapter, an asterisk indicates an article included in the book. (Occasionally the date cited in a reference differs from that in the list of Citations, for example, when an unpublished paper written and cited in 1978 was actually published in 1979.)

This volume includes articles from the *Journal of the American Statistical Association,* the *American Journal of Sociology, Biometrika, Sociological Methodology, Biometrics,* and the *Berkeley Symposium on Mathematical Statistics and Probability.* Like nearly all statistical research, an approach that springs from interest in one kind of phenomena, such as social mobility between generations, may well turn out to be relevant in totally different contexts, such as the relationship between eye color and hair color. Past examples of that kind encourage us to seek even wider relevance for the application of the models and methods developed in this volume.

Acknowledgments

All of the research in this book was prepared with the partial support of the National Science Foundation. The research in Appendix A was supported also by the Army Research Office, the Office of Naval Research, and the Air Force Office of Scientific Research. Much of the work reported in this book has benefited from the helpful comments of O. D. Duncan, S. Haberman, C. Clogg, and R. McCullagh, and it is a pleasure to acknowledge them here. In addition to them, I am also indebted to others for helpful comments on earlier drafts of particular chapters: for Chapter 1, they are D. Andrich and S. Leinhardt; for Chapter 3, J. Whittaker and D. Wallace; for Chapter 4, E. B. Anderson, S. Fienberg, R. Hauser, W. Kruskal, and G. Simon; for Chapter 5, F. Anscombe, R. D. Bock, W. Kruskal, R. Plackett, and J. Wahrendorf; for Chapter 6, M. O'Neil and D. Wallace; and for Chapter 7, R. Hauser, F. Béland, and R. Breiger. For Chapters 8 and 9, Clifford Clogg acknowledges the help of M. C. Chang, S. Presser, J. Shockey, C. Turner, and W. Harkness (in addition to O. D. Duncan and me). For Appendix B, I acknowledge the help of R. Hodge, W. Kruskal, J. Levine, D. McFarland, T. Pullum, and A. Stinchcombe; for Appendix C, R. Hauser; and for Appendix D, R. Fay, S. Fienberg, and T. Pullum. Finally, helpful programming was done by T. Gerling in connection with Chapter 4, and by R. Kuziel in connection with many of the chapters

L.A.G.

Citations

In the references at the end of each chapter, an asterisk appears to the left of articles included in this book. These articles are:

1. "Three Elementary Views of Log-Linear Models for the Analysis of Cross-Classifications Having Ordered Categories," *Sociological Methodology 1981,* pp. 193–239.
2. "Multiplicative Models for Square Contingency Tables with Ordered Categories," *Biometrika,* 1979, 66, pp. 413–418.
3. "The Analysis of Dependence in Cross-Classifications Having Ordered Categories, Using Log-Linear Models for Frequencies and Log-Linear Models for Odds," *Biometrics,* 1983, 39, pp. 149–160. Reproduced with permission from The Biometric Society.
4. "Simple Models for the Analysis of Association in Cross-Classifications Having Ordered Categories," *Journal of the American Statistical Association,* 1979, 74, pp. 537–552.
5. "Association Models and the Bivariate Normal for Contingency Tables with Ordered Categories," *Biometrika,* 1981, 68, pp. 347–355.
6. "Association Models and Canonical Correlation in the Analysis of Cross-Classifications Having Ordered Categories," *Journal of the American Statistical Association,* 1981, 76, pp. 320–334.
7. "Criteria for Determining Whether Certain Categories in a Cross-Classification Table Should Be Combined, with Special Reference to Occupational Categories in an Occupational Mobility Table," *American Journal of Sociology,* 1981, 87, pp. 612–650. Reprinted by permission of The University of Chicago Press. © 1981 by The University of Chicago.
8. "Using Association Models in Sociological Research: Some Examples," C. C. Clogg, *American Journal of Sociology,* 1982, 88, pp. 114–134. Reprinted by permission of The University of Chicago Press. © 1982 by The University of Chicago.
9. "Some Models for the Analysis of Association in Multiway Cross-Classifications Having Ordered Categories," C. C. Clogg, *Journal of the American Statistical Association,* 1982, 77, pp. 803–815.

Appendixes

A. "The Analysis of Cross-Classified Data: Independence, Quasi-Independence, and Interactions in Contingency Tables with or without Missing Entries," *Journal of the American Statistical Association,* 1968, pp. 1091–1131.
B. "How to Ransack Social Mobility Tables and Other Kinds of Cross-Classification Tables," *The American Journal of Sociology,* 1969, 75, pp. 1–40. Reprinted by permission of The University of Chicago Press. © 1969 by The University of Chicago.
C. "Multiplicative Models for the Analysis of Occupational Mobility Tables and Other Kinds of Cross-Classification Tables," *American Journal of Sociology,* 1979, 84, pp. 804–819. Reprinted by permission of The University of Chicago Press. © 1979 by The University of Chicago.
D. "Some Multiplicative Models for the Analysis of Cross-Classified Data," *Proceedings of the Sixth Berkeley Symposium on Mathematical Statistics and Probability,* ed. L. LeCam et al., University of California Press, Berkeley, 1972, pp. 649–696.

1.
Introduction

Three Elementary Views of Log-Linear Models for the Analysis of Cross-Classifications Having Ordered Categories

In analyzing a two-way cross-classification table for two qualitative (dichotomous and/or polytomous) variables, we can use log linear models for three purposes: (1) to examine the joint distribution of the variables, (2) to assess the possible dependence of a response variable upon an explanatory or regressor variable, and (3) to study the association between two response variables. With each of the three uses of log linear models, a different view of the models will be obtained. Each view will highlight a different class of log linear models, and it will provide a particularly appropriate way to describe the models in that class. The three views will illuminate our understanding of the corresponding three classes of log linear models.

We focus here on cross-classification tables in which the categories of each qualitative variable are ordered. For the two-way table, the corresponding two variables will be called variables A and B. We shall consider first the joint bivariate distribution of variables A and B. This distribution can sometimes be expressed conveniently in terms of the following components: a component pertaining to the univariate distribution of variable A, a component pertaining to the univariate distribution of variable B, and a component pertaining to the association between variables A and B. Expressing the joint bivariate distribution of variables A and B this way is useful when the association between the variables is of special interest. When the association between the variables is of interest but their univariate distributions are not, the log linear models for the analysis of association are particularly useful.

Instead of expressing the joint bivariate distribution of variables A and B in terms of the three components just cited, we can sometimes express it more conveniently in terms of the following two components: a component pertaining to the univariate distribution of variable A and a component pertaining to the possible dependence of variable B on variable A. Expressing the joint bivariate distribution this way is useful when the possible dependence of variable B on variable A is of special interest. When this possible dependence is of interest but the univariate distribution of variable A is not, the log linear models for the analysis of dependence are particularly useful.

Log linear models for the analysis of the association between variables A and B cannot be used to shed light (either directly or indirectly) upon the univariate distribution of variable A or variable B. Similarly, log linear models for the analysis of the dependence of variable B on variable A cannot be used to shed light (either directly or indirectly) upon the univariate distribution of variable A; and log linear models for the analysis of the dependence of variable A on variable B cannot be used to shed light (either directly or indirectly) upon the univariate distribution of variable B. When the interest in the joint bivariate distribution of variables A and B is not confined to the

TABLE 1

Cross-Classification of 7,477 Women According to Right Eye Grade and
Left Eye Grade with Respect to Unaided Distance Vision

Right Eye Grade	Left Eye Grade				
	Best (1)	Second (2)	Third (3)	Worst (4)	Total
Best (1)	1,520	266	124	66	1,976
Second (2)	234	1,512	432	78	2,256
Third (3)	117	362	1,772	205	2,456
Worst (4)	36	82	179	492	789
Total	1,907	2,222	2,507	841	7,477

association between the two variables, or to the possible dependence of one of the variables on the other, then other log linear models for the analysis of the joint distribution will be useful.

To illustrate how log linear models can be used to analyze (1) the joint distribution of the qualitative variables, (2) the possible dependence of a qualitative response variable on a qualitative explanatory or regressor variable, and (3) the association between two qualitative response variables, we shall reanalyze three tables.

Table 1 is the classic 4 × 4 table on unaided vision first analyzed by Stuart (1953, 1955). It cross-classifies the right eye grade and the corresponding left eye grade in unaided distance vision (each eye graded in one of four categories from best to worst) for 7,477 women. These data have been discussed and reanalyzed by many statisticians using various models and methods (see, for example, Kendall and Stuart, 1961; Goodman and Kruskal, 1963; Caussinus, 1965; Bhapkar, 1966, 1979; Ireland, Ku, and Kullback, 1969; Grizzle, Starmer, and Koch, 1969; Koch and Reinfurt, 1971; Plackett, 1974; Wedderburn, 1974; Bishop, Fienberg, and Holland, 1975; Tukey, 1977; Gokhale and Kullback, 1978; Mantel and Byar, 1978; McCullagh, 1978; Plackett and Paul, 1978; Agresti, 1980; Anscombe, 1981). By applying an appropriate log-linear model to Table 1 to study the joint distribution of right eye vision and left eye vision, we shall obtain new insight into these data.

Table 2 is a 3 × 3 table describing the length of stay in the hospital for 132 schizophrenic patients classified by the visiting pattern that had been ascribed to the patient and his or her visitors in the hospital. These data were analyzed earlier by Wing (1962), Haberman (1974a), and Fienberg (1977). By applying an appropriate log linear model to study the possible dependence of the patient's length of

TABLE 2

Length of Stay in Hospital for 132 Schizophrenic Patients Classified by Visiting Pattern
That Had Been Ascribed in the Hospital

| | Length of Stay in Hospital | | | |
Visiting Pattern	2–10 Years	10–20 Years	20 Years or More	Total
Received visitors regularly or patient went home	43	16	3	62
Received visitors infrequently; patient did not go home	6	11	10	27
Never received visitors; patient did not go home	9	18	16	43
Total	58	45	29	132

hospital stay on the ascribed visiting pattern, we shall obtain some new results that supplement those presented earlier by Haberman (1974a) and Fienberg (1977).

Table 3 is the classic 2 × 3 table first analyzed by Armitage (1955) on the relationship between streptococcus carrier status (noncarrier or carrier) and tonsil enlargement level for 1,398 children. These data have been discussed and reanalyzed by various statisticians (see, for example, Armitage, 1955, 1971; Cox, 1970; Clayton, 1974; Plackett, 1974; Andrich, 1979; Agresti, 1980; McCullagh, 1980), and the data are also included in Holmes and Williams (1954). By applying an appropriate log linear model to Table 3 to study the association between streptococcus carrier status and level of tonsil enlargement, we shall also obtain some new insight into these data.

These three tables have been previously analyzed using a wide variety of models and methods, and comparison of the results presented

TABLE 3

Cross-Classification of 1,398 Children According to
Status as Noncarriers or Carriers of *Streptococcus
Pyogenes* and Enlargement of Tonsils

| Streptococcus Carrier Status | Tonsil Enlargement Level | | | |
	+	+ +	+ + +	Total
Noncarrier	497	560	269	1,326
Carrier	19	29	24	72
Total	516	589	293	1,398

in the earlier literature with those presented here will help the interested reader to appreciate the various advantages of the models and methods that will be described here. Our analysis of these classic examples will facilitate this comparison. The three tables will be used here for expository and illustrative purposes.

Tables 1, 2, and 3 are two-way cross-classification tables each of which pertains to two qualitative variables.[1] The methods presented here can be applied to two-way cross-classification tables in which each variable is either polytomous or dichotomous, where the classes of each polytomous variable are ordered, and the classes of each dichotomous variable may be either ordered or unordered.

Variables that have classes (categories) which are ordered abound in sociology, in the social sciences more generally, and in other areas of inquiry as well. Some of the models and methods described here have already been applied to the study of such variables as occupational status, socioeconomic status, and mental health status. (The relationship between socioeconomic status and mental health, and the relationship between father's occupational status and son's occupational status were studied, using log linear models for the analysis of association, in Goodman, 1979a, 1980a. See also Duncan, 1979a, 1979b, Duncan and McRae, 1978, and Goodman, 1980b, for related material.)

Log linear models can be used to analyze two-way cross-classification tables where (1) the number of rows and columns is equal and there is a one-to-one relationship between them (as in Table 1), or (2) the number of rows and columns is equal but there is not a one-to-one relationship between them (as in Table 2), or (3) the number of rows and columns differs (as in Table 3). Each of these kinds of cross-classification tables can be studied by using log linear models to accomplish any of the three general purposes mentioned earlier: analysis of the joint distribution, analysis of dependence, and analysis of association.

On the other hand, if the data in the cross-classification table are such that the row and column marginals are considered to be given (or constant) and these marginals need to be fitted exactly by the

---

[1]The two qualitative variables are polytomous in Tables 1 and 2, but in Table 3 one of the variables is polytomous (more specifically, trichotomous) and the other is dichotomous.

model, then only models for the analysis of association (or equivalent models) will be relevant (see, for example, Goodman, 1970, 1979a). Similarly, if the data are such that the row marginal is considered to be given (or constant) and this marginal needs to be fitted exactly by the model, then only models that pertain to the dependence of the column variable on the row variable (or equivalent models) will be relevant. Also, if the data are such that the column marginal is considered to be given (or constant) and this marginal needs to be fitted exactly by the model, then only models that pertain to the dependence of the row variable on the column variable (or equivalent models) will be relevant.

With the three views to be presented here, we shall see that there is a hierarchical perspective: The class of models for the analysis of association is, in a certain sense, included within the class of models for the analysis of dependence, which is in turn included within the class of models for the analysis of the joint distribution. This perspective is discussed later.

Although we focus our attention here primarily on the analysis of two-way cross-classification tables and on the use of log linear models to accomplish the three general purposes mentioned earlier, the models and methods presented here can be extended to the analysis of multi-way cross-classification tables, and the corresponding log linear models can be used to analyze such multiway tables in order to accomplish a corresponding set of general purposes. The extensions to the multiway cross-classification table are considered in the final section.

SOME ELEMENTARY NULL MODELS

In our analysis of Tables 1, 2 and 3, we shall use some elementary "null models" as baselines for comparative purposes. Different null models are appropriate in different contexts. In this section, I describe some of the null models appropriate in the analysis of (1) the joint distribution, (2) dependence, and (3) association. Before doing so, I first introduce the notation we shall need to describe the null models.

For the two-way $I \times J$ contingency table pertaining to the joint distribution of two qualitative variables, say, variables A and B, let f_{ij} denote the observed frequency in cell (i, j) of the table ($i = 1, 2, \ldots, I$;

$j = 1, 2, \ldots, J$), and let F_{ij} denote the corresponding expected frequency under some model. In other words, f_{ij} is the observed frequency at level i on variable A and at level j on variable B, and F_{ij} is the corresponding expected frequency.

In the analysis of the $I \times J$ contingency table, the usual null model employed in the past states that variable A and variable B are statistically independent. Under this null model, the expected frequencies F_{ij} are estimated from the observed frequencies pertaining to the univariate distributions of variable A and variable B, using the usual elementary formula for the null model (see, for example, Goodman, 1970). Since the expected frequencies pertaining to the univariate distributions of variable A and variable B are estimated under the null model to be equal to the corresponding observed frequencies pertaining to these two univariate distributions, this null model cannot be used to shed light upon the two univariate distributions (aside from whatever light may be shed by the observed frequencies pertaining to the corresponding univariate distributions). When the interest in the joint bivariate distribution of variables A and B is not confined to the association between the two variables, then other null models should be used as baselines for comparative purposes.

Null Models for Analysis of the Joint Distribution

In our study of the joint distribution of variables A and B in the two-way $I \times J$ contingency table, we could consider various kinds of null models. For the sake of simplicity, we begin here with the most elementary null model: the model which states that all the expected frequencies F_{ij} ($i = 1, 2, \ldots, I; j = 1, 2, \ldots, J$) are equal. Thus under this model

$$F_{ij} = N/(IJ) \tag{1}$$

where N is the sample size. This model states that the probability that an observation will fall in cell (i, j) of the $I \times J$ contingency table is $1/(IJ)$; that is, all the cells (i, j) (for $i = 1, 2, \ldots, I; j = 1, 2, \ldots, J$) are equiprobable.

A null model is used as a baseline for comparative purposes, and in some situations we might begin the analysis of the data by using a null model that is less elementary than Model (1). In some cases, a less elementary null model could provide a more relevant baseline for comparative purposes. For example, in the analysis of the 4×4 table (Table 1) on unaided vision, the possible asymmetry between right eye and left eye vision is of special interest, so we might begin the analysis of these data using the following null model:

$$F_{ij} = F_{ji} \qquad \text{for } i < j \qquad (2)$$

This model states that the expected frequencies F_{ij} are symmetric. Model (2) is the usual symmetry model in which the expected frequency in cell (i, j) of the table is equal to the expected frequency in cell (j, i) of the table. Let us call Model (2) the "null asymmetry model."[2] We shall apply Model (2) later in our analysis of the joint distribution of the qualitative variables in Table 1.

Models (1) and (2) serve as examples of the various kinds of null models that could be considered in the analysis of the joint distribution. Other examples could also be presented; in order to save space, I shall not do so here.

Null Models for Analysis of Dependence

We shall now consider the two-way $I \times J$ contingency table for variables A and B in the situation where variable A is viewed as an explanatory or regressor variable and variable B is viewed as the response variable. For adjacent classes pertaining to the response variable B (say, classes j and $j + 1$), we define as follows the odds $\Omega_{ij}^{A\bar{B}}$ based on the expected frequencies:

$$\Omega_{ij}^{A\bar{B}} = F_{ij}/F_{i,j+1} \qquad \text{for } j = 1, 2, \ldots, J - 1 \qquad (3)$$

Let $\Psi_{ij}^{A\bar{B}}$ denote the natural logarithm of $\Omega_{ij}^{A\bar{B}}$ (that is, the log-odds). In the present context, the most elementary null model is the following "null log-odds model":

$$\Psi_{ij}^{A\bar{B}} = 0 \qquad \text{for } i = 1, 2, \ldots, I; j = 1, 2, \ldots, J - 1 \qquad (4)$$

Model (4) states that $\Omega_{ij}^{A\bar{B}} = 1$, and this is equivalent to the model which states that the classes of variable B are conditionally equiprobable, given the level of variable A (see, for example, Good-

---

[2]Of course, Model (2) could be called the "symmetry model," but in the present exposition the term "null asymmetry model" turns out to be more felicitous.

man, 1970). This model is the most elementary null model in the present context—that is, analysis of the possible dependence of variable B on variable A.

As we noted earlier, a less elementary null model can sometimes provide a more relevant baseline for comparative purposes. In the present context we also note that a null model less elementary than the null model (4) will sometimes be useful; however, in our analysis of the 3 × 3 table (Table 2) on the possible dependence of length of hospital stay on the ascribed visiting pattern, we shall find that Model (4) can serve as the baseline for comparative purposes. We shall apply it later in our analysis of the dependence in Table 2.

Null Models for Analysis of Association

We shall now consider the two-way $I \times J$ contingency table for variables A and B in the situation where they are viewed as response variables and the association between these variables is of interest. For adjacent classes of variable A (say, classes i and $i + 1$) and adjacent classes of variable B (say, classes j and $j + 1$), we define as follows the odds-ratio Θ_{ij} based on the expected frequencies:

$$\Theta_{ij} = (F_{ij}F_{i+1,j+1})/(F_{i,j+1}F_{i+1,j})$$
$$\text{for } i = 1, 2, \ldots, I - 1; j = 1, 2, \ldots, J - 1 \quad (5)$$

Let Φ_{ij} denote the natural logarithm of Θ_{ij} (that is, the log-odds-ratio). In the present context, the most elementary null model is the following "null association model":

$$\Phi_{ij} = 0 \quad \text{for } i = 1, 2, \ldots, I - 1; j = 1, 2, \ldots, J - 1 \quad (6)$$

Model (6) states that $\Theta_{ij} = 1$, and this is equivalent to the model which states that A and B are statistically independent. This model is the most elementary null model in the present context—that is, analysis of the association between A and B.

In the present context we also note that a null model less elementary than Model (6) will sometimes be useful; but in our analysis of Table 3 on the association between streptococcus carrier status and level of tonsil enlargement, we shall find that Model (6) can serve as the baseline for comparative purposes. We shall apply it later in our analysis of the association in Table 3.

TABLE 4
Chi Square Values for Models Applied to Tables 1, 2, and 3

Model	DF	Goodness-of-Fit Chi Square	Likelihood-Ratio Chi Square
For Table 1: analysis of the joint distribution			
Null asymmetry model (2)	6	19.11	19.25
Fitted asymmetry model	3	0.50	0.50
For Table 2: analysis of dependence			
Null log-odds model (4)	6	44.96	48.24
Fitted log-odds model	5	5.46	5.81
For Table 3: analysis of association			
Null association model (6)	2	7.88	7.32
Fitted association model	1	0.24	0.24

We shall use the null asymmetry model (2), the null log-odds model (4), and the null association model (6) as baselines for comparative purposes in our analysis of Tables 1, 2, and 3, respectively. Each of these models will be applied to the corresponding table, and the observed frequencies in the table will be compared with the expected frequencies estimated under the model using the usual goodness-of-fit and the likelihood-ratio chi-squares. Table 4 gives the chi-square values obtained by using these null models, and it also gives the corresponding chi-square values obtained when the null models are modified in appropriate ways. By using the null models as baselines for comparative purposes, we find that these models can be modified in particularly simple and appropriate ways to obtain models that are more congruent with the observed data and that provide a dramatic improvement in fit.

ANALYSIS OF THE JOINT DISTRIBUTION

In our study of the joint distribution of A and B in the two-way $I \times J$ contingency table, we shall consider models that describe F_{ij} in terms of appropriate multiplicative factors, or equivalently we shall consider models that describe the natural logarithm G_{ij} of F_{ij} in terms of the corresponding additive factors. There are many possible models that could be considered (see, for example, Goodman, 1972, 1979b; Haberman, 1974a, 1974b). Different substantive contexts will suggest

TABLE 5
Rearrangement of Data in Table 1 for Analysis of
Symmetry and Related Phenomena

Right Eye–Left Eye Grade Difference	Entries from Table 1			Total
+1	234	362	179	775
−1	266	432	205	903
+2	117	82		199
−2	124	78		202
+3	36			36
−3	66			66

different factors that may affect the F_{ij} (or the G_{ij}). Our analysis of the joint distribution of right eye vision and left eye vision in Table 1 will serve as an example of how multiplicative models for the F_{ij} (or the equivalent additive models for the G_{ij}) can be used to study the joint distribution of two qualitative variables.

In our analysis of Table 1, we begin with the null asymmetry model (2) as the baseline for comparative purposes. To apply this model to Table 1, we can rearrange the data conveniently as presented in Table 5. We can compare f_{21} with f_{12}, f_{32} with f_{23}, f_{43} with f_{34}, f_{31} with f_{13}, f_{42} with f_{24}, and f_{41} with f_{14} to test the corresponding hypothesis that $F_{21} = F_{12}$, $F_{32} = F_{23}$, and so on. Each hypothesis can be tested by using the usual elementary chi-square test with 1 degree of freedom; moreover, since there are six different hypotheses to be tested, and each of the chi-square statistics is statistically independent (asymptotically), the sum of the six chi-square statistics will be distributed asymptotically as chi-square with 6 degrees of freedom, under Model (2). From the chi-square values (with $DF = 6$) given in Table 4 for Model (2) applied to Table 1, we see that this model does not fit the observed data; however, a dramatic improvement in fit can be obtained with the model we consider next.

Before describing this model, we first express the null asymmetry model (2) as follows:

$$F_{ij} = \rho_{ij} \qquad \text{for } i \neq j \tag{7}$$

where the parameters ρ_{ij} satisfy the condition

$$\rho_{ij} = \rho_{ji} \tag{8}$$

Formula (7) describes the F_{ij} in terms of the symmetry parameters ρ_{ij}.

We now modify Model (7) by introducing into it the diagonals-parameter δ_k for the right eye–left eye grade difference $i - j = k$ (for $k = \pm 1, \pm 2, \pm 3$). Thus we obtain

$$F_{ij} = \rho_{ij}\delta_k \qquad \text{for } i \neq j, k = i - j \tag{9}$$

Although there are six diagonals-parameters δ_k ($k = \pm 1, \pm 2, \pm 3$), without loss of generality we can delete from (9) the three δ_k for $k = -1, -2, -3$; that is, we can set $\delta_k = 1$ for $k = -1, -2, -3$. Having introduced into the null asymmetry model (7) three parameters ($\delta_1, \delta_2, \delta_3$), the number of degrees of freedom for testing Model (9) will be three less than for Model (7). The chi-square values obtained with Model (9) in Table 4 show that introducing these three parameters leads to dramatic results.

Model (9) can be expressed in more elementary terms with the data in Table 1 rearranged as in Table 5. In Table 5, consider the 2×3 table for right eye–left eye grade difference $k = \pm 1$, and the 2×2 table for grade difference $k = \pm 2$. Model (9) applied to Table 1 is equivalent to the model which states that there is statistical independence between the row and column variables in the 2×3 table (for $k = \pm 1$) and also in the 2×2 table (for $k = \pm 2$), in Table 5. To test the hypothesis of statistical independence between the row and column variables in the 2×3 table, the usual chi-square test will have 2 degrees of freedom; the corresponding chi-square test for the 2×2 table will have 1 degree of freedom. The corresponding chi-square statistics for the two tables are statistically independent (asymptotically), and the sum of the two chi-square statistics will be distributed asymptotically as chi-square with $2 + 1 = 3$ degrees of freedom under the null hypothesis. The sum of the chi-square values (with DF = 3) is given in Table 4.

The parameter δ_1 is simply the odds that the right eye–left eye grade difference will be $+1$ rather than -1, and the parameters δ_2 and δ_3 can be defined similarly. These parameters can be estimated directly from the totals column in Table 5. Thus we obtain

$$\hat{\delta}_1 = 0.86 \qquad \hat{\delta}_2 = 0.99 \qquad \hat{\delta}_3 = 0.55 \tag{10}$$

Since $\hat{\delta}_k < 1$ for $k = 1, 2, 3$, a right eye–left eye grade difference of k is estimated to be less likely than a corresponding difference of $-k$; that is, a right eye grade lower than a left eye grade (by k grades) is estimated to be more likely than the reverse.

From the entries in Table 5, in addition to calculating the usual chi-square statistics for testing the hypothesis of statistical independence between the row and column variables in the 2×3 table (for $k = \pm 1$) and for testing the corresponding hypothesis in the 2×2 table (for $k = \pm 2$), as noted above, we can also estimate the expected frequencies under these hypotheses by using the usual elementary formula. Since Model (9) applied to Table 1 is equivalent to the model which states that there is statistical independence between the row and column variables in the 2×3 table ($k = \pm 1$) and the 2×2 table ($k = \pm 2$), the estimated expected frequencies under these hypotheses are also the corresponding estimated expected frequencies under Model (9). These estimates are displayed in Table 6 in a form that facilitates comparison with the observed frequencies in Table 1.

The estimate $\hat{F}_{ij}$ of the expected frequency under Model (9) can also be expressed in terms of the estimate of δ_k ($k = 1, 2, 3$) given in (10) and the corresponding estimate of the symmetry parameter ρ_{ij} in (9). (As was the case for the parameter δ_k, the ρ_{ij} in (9) can be calculated in an elementary way from the entries in Table 5; and it can be easily interpreted in terms of the entries in Table 6.) The asymmetry between right eye and left eye grade, with

$$\hat{F}_{ij} > \hat{F}_{ji} \qquad \text{for } i < j$$

(see Table 6), is a direct consequence of the fact that $\hat{\delta}_k < 1$ (for $k = 1$, 2, 3).

From the $\hat{F}_{ij}$ under Model (9), we can directly calculate the corresponding estimate $\hat{F}_{i.}$ of the expected frequency in the ith row marginal and the estimate $\hat{F}_{.j}$ of the expected frequency in the jth column marginal. (See the totals column and the totals row in Table 6.) The difference between the univariate distribution of the right eye

TABLE 6
Maximum-Likelihood Estimate of Expected Frequencies Obtained
When Model (9) Is Applied to Table 1

Right Eye Grade	Left Eye Grade				
	1	2	3	4	Total
1	1,520.0	269.1	121.4	66.0	1,976.5
2	230.9	1,512.0	427.3	80.6	2,250.8
3	119.6	366.7	1,772.0	206.6	2,464.9
4	36.0	79.4	177.4	492.0	784.8
Total	1,906.5	2,227.2	2,498.1	845.2	7,477.0

grade and the univariate distribution of the left eye grade, with

$$\sum_{t=1}^{x} \hat{F}_{t.} > \sum_{t=1}^{x} \hat{F}_{.t} \qquad \text{for } x = 1, 2, 3$$

(see Table 6), is also a direct consequence of the fact that $\hat{\delta}_k < 1$ (for $k = 1, 2, 3$).

The parameter δ_k in Model (9) may depend on k (where $k = i - j$, the right eye–left eye grade difference), but no prior assumptions were made here about the nature of the dependence. Elementary methods can be used to test the hypothesis that δ_k is independent of k—that is, the hypothesis that

$$\delta_k = \delta \; (k = 1, 2, 3) \tag{11}$$

and similar methods are available for testing other related kinds of hypotheses (see Goodman, 1979c). When δ_k is not independent of k, the dependence may be of a rather simple form—for example,

$$\delta_k = \delta^k \; (k = 1, 2, 3) \tag{12}$$

where the superscript k denotes a specified power. The hypothesis that the dependence is of the form (12) can be tested by using log linear methods, and these methods are available for testing other related kinds of hypotheses as well.

For further discussion of the estimate $\hat{\delta}_k$ of δ_k in Model (9), see Goodman (1979c); there Model (9) is called the diagonals-parameter symmetry model, and it is closely related to the diagonals-parameter model introduced in Goodman (1972). Although Model (9) is closely related to the model in Goodman (1972), the former model pertains to the analysis of the joint distribution, whereas the latter pertains to the analysis of association. We shall discuss this point in more detail later when we compare the results obtained in the present section for the analysis of Table 1 with results obtained when models for the analysis of association are applied to this table.

As we noted earlier, Model (9) applied to Table 1 can help to explain the observed asymmetry between right and left eye vision and the difference between the marginal distributions for right eye vision and left eye vision. This model sheds light on the joint bivariate distribution of the variables in Table 1 and on the corresponding univariate distributions. Models for the analysis of association would not shed light on the corresponding univariate distributions.

Model (9) serves as an example of the various kinds of models that could be considered in the analysis of the joint distribution. We shall take note of other examples later when we comment on the analysis of the joint distribution of the variables in Tables 2 and 3.

ANALYSIS OF DEPENDENCE

In our analysis of the possible dependence of variable B on variable A in the two-way $I \times J$ contingency table, we shall consider models that describe the odds $\Omega_{ij}^{A\bar{B}}$ in terms of appropriate multiplicative factors,[3] or equivalently we shall consider models that describe the log-odds $\Psi_{ij}^{A\bar{B}}$ in terms of the corresponding additive factors. Each model can also be reexpressed as an equivalent multiplicative model for the F_{ij} (and/or an equivalent additive model for the G_{ij}). Our analysis of Table 2 will serve as an example of how these models can be used to study the possible dependence of one qualitative variable on another.

In our analysis of Table 2, we begin with the null log-odds model (4) as the baseline for comparative purposes. This model can be applied to the 3×3 table (Table 2) using the appropriate chi-square statistic for testing the hypothesis of conditional equiprobability (see, for example, Goodman, 1970), with $3 \times 2 = 6$ degrees of freedom. From the chi-square values (with DF = 6) given in Table 4 for the null log-odds model applied to Table 2, we see that this model does not fit the observed data, but we obtain better results with the model we consider next.

Table 7 gives the log-odds based on the observed frequencies f_{ij}, and also the standardized value of these log-odds.[4] The data in Table 7

[3]Although our attention here is focused on the odds $\Omega_{ij}^{A\bar{B}}$ pertaining to adjacent classes (classes j and $j + 1$) of variable B (see Formula 3), we could instead have considered more generally the odds pertaining to any two classes (say, classes j and j') of variable B. The latter odds can be expressed as a product of an appropriate set of $\Omega_{ij}^{A\bar{B}}$; hence any model that describes the Ω_{ij}^{AB} in terms of multiplicative factors will also describe the latter odds in terms of multiplicative factors (see, for example, Goodman, 1979b).

[4]The log-odds in Table 7 are calculated as the natural logarithm of the odds defined by (3), where the expected frequencies in (3) are replaced by a function of the corresponding observed frequencies. The F_{ij} in (3) are replaced by $f_{ij} + \frac{1}{2}$ for reasons explained in, for example, Gart and Zweifel (1967) and Goodman (1970). Each standardized value in Table 7 is calculated by dividing the corresponding log-odds in this table by its estimated standard deviation, where the F_{ij} in the formula for the standard deviation are also replaced by $f_{ij} + \frac{1}{2}$ as in the literature just cited.

TABLE 7
Observed Log-Odds for Adjacent Classes Pertaining to
Response Variable in Table 2

	Length of Stay in Hospital	
	2–10 Years vs.	10–20 Years vs.
Visiting Pattern	10–20 Years	20 Years or More
Received visitors regularly or patient went home	0.97 (3.35)	1.55 (2.63)
Received visitors infrequently; patient did not go home	−0.57 (−1.16)	0.09 (0.21)
Never received visitors; patient did not go home	−0.67 (−1.67)	0.11 (0.34)

NOTE: The standardized value of the observed log-odds is given in paren-theses.

suggest why Model (4) does not fit the data, and they also suggest a remedy. Consider the modified log-odds model defined as follows:

$$\Psi_{1j}^{A\bar{B}} = \psi \qquad \Psi_{2j}^{A\bar{B}} = \Psi_{3j}^{A\bar{B}} = 0 \qquad (13)$$

where ψ is estimated from the data. This model introduces a single parameter into Model (4), and as we have already noted from the results in Table 4, the introduction of this parameter is worthwhile. This model states that the classes of variable B are conditionally equiprobable when variable A is at level 2 or 3; when variable A is at level 1, however, the log-odds $\Psi_{1j}^{A\bar{B}} = \psi$ (for $j = 1, 2$).

Table 8 gives the maximum-likelihood estimate $\hat{F}_{ij}$ of the expected frequencies obtained when Model (13) is applied to Table 2. When variable A is at level 2 and 3, the entries in Table 8 are

TABLE 8
Maximum-Likelihood Estimate of Expected
Frequencies Obtained When Model (13)
Is Applied to Table 2

	Length of Stay in Hospital			
Visiting Pattern	1	2	3	Total
1	44.2	13.6	4.2	62.0
2	9.0	9.0	9.0	27.0
3	14.3	14.3	14.3	43.0[a]
Total	67.5	36.9	27.5	132.0[a]

[a]The entry is equal to the sum of summands having more significant digits than are reported here.

calculated in an elementary way; when variable A is at level 1, the calculation of the entries is not so elementary. (I shall describe how these entries are calculated later.) From the $\hat{F}_{1j}$ under Model (13), we find that the maximum-likelihood estimate of the log-odds parameter ψ is $\hat{\psi} = 1.18$. (All calculations in this chapter were made with more significant digits than are reported here.)

The $\hat{F}_{ij}$ under Model (13) can be expressed in terms of the estimate of the log-odds parameter ψ in (13) and the corresponding observed frequency $f_{i.}$ at the ith level of variable A. (For models that pertain to the dependence of variable B on variable A, the estimate $\hat{F}_{i.}$ is set equal to the corresponding observed frequency $f_{i..}$.) The dependence of variable B on variable A, with

$$\hat{F}_{1j}/\hat{F}_{1,j+1} > \hat{F}_{2j}/\hat{F}_{2,j+1} = \hat{F}_{3j}/\hat{F}_{3,j+1} = 1$$

(see Table 8), is a direct consequence of the fact that the estimate of the parameter ψ in (13) is greater than zero.

From the $\hat{F}_{ij}$ under Model (13), we can calculate directly the corresponding estimate $\hat{F}_{.j}$ of the expected frequency in the jth column marginal (see the totals row in Table 8). The particular shape of the corresponding univariate distribution (the distribution of variable B, the length of stay in hospital), with

$$\hat{F}_{.1} > \hat{F}_{.2} > \hat{F}_{.3}$$

(see Table 8), is also a direct consequence of the fact that the estimate of ψ in (13) is greater than zero.

As we have noted, Model (13) applied to Table 2 can help to explain the particular form of the dependence of variable B on variable A and also the particular shape of the corresponding univariate distribution of variable B. Models for the analysis of association would not shed light on the univariate distribution of variable B (or on the univariate distribution of variable A); and models for the analysis of the dependence of variable B on variable A (such as Model 13) do not shed light on the univariate distribution of variable A.

Model (13) is related to but somewhat different from the model described by Haberman (1974a) and Fienberg (1977) for these data. The development of the model in the earlier literature was expressed in terms somewhat different from those used here; the classes of variable B were not conditionally equiprobable at levels 2 and 3 of variable A in the earlier model; moreover, two more parameters were needed in the earlier model than in Model (13) here. The model presented here is more parsimonious than the model in the earlier literature, and it also fits the data well. We shall discuss the advantages of using the more parsimonious model later in a separate section. (The general method used here to obtain a more parsimonious model that fits the data can also be applied in other related contexts; see, for example, Goodman, 1975, 1978, 1979d.)

Before closing this section, we take note of the fact that the odds $\Omega_{ij}^{A\bar{B}}$ defined by (3) and the corresponding log-odds $\Psi_{ij}^{A\bar{B}}$ take account of the order of the classes of variable B, but not the order of the classes of variable A. When the classes of variable B are ordered, models for the odds $\Omega_{ij}^{A\bar{B}}$ or the corresponding log-odds $\Psi_{ij}^{A\bar{B}}$, can be applied both when the classes of variable A are ordered and when they are unordered. Model (13) takes into account to some extent the order of the classes of variable A, and other methods are also available for taking this into account (see, for example, Goodman, 1979e).

As we noted earlier, with models for the odds $\Omega_{ij}^{A\bar{B}}$ or log-odds $\Psi_{ij}^{A\bar{B}}$ (that is, models that pertain to the dependence of variable B on variable A), the univariate distribution of variable A is set equal to the corresponding observed distribution. However, instead of setting the univariate distribution equal to the corresponding observed distribution, we could introduce a model for the univariate distribution, and test this model by comparing the observed frequencies f_i. with the corresponding expected frequencies estimated under the model. If the model for the univariate distribution of variable A is then combined with a model pertaining to the dependence of variable B on variable A (for example, Model 13), we obtain a combined model for the joint distribution of variables A and B. The combined model can help to explain the particular form of the dependence of variable B on variable A, the particular shape of the corresponding univariate distribution of variable B, and the univariate distribution of variable A. Models of this kind, together with models of the kind described in the preceding section, can serve as examples of models that could be considered in the analysis of the joint distribution.

ANALYSIS OF ASSOCIATION

In our analysis of the association between variables A and B in the two-way $I \times J$ contingency table, we shall consider models that describe the odds-ratio Θ_{ij} in terms of appropriate multiplicative factors,[5] or equivalently we shall consider models that describe the log-odds-ratio Φ_{ij} in terms of the corresponding additive factors. Each model can also be reexpressed as an equivalent multiplicative model for the F_{ij} (and/or an equivalent additive model for the G_{ij}). Our analysis of Table 3 will serve as an example of how these models can be used to study the association between variables A and B.

In our analysis of Table 3, we shall begin with the null association model (6) as the baseline for comparative purposes. This model can be applied to the 2×3 table (Table 3) using the usual chi-square statistic for testing the hypothesis that variables A and B are statistically independent, with $1 \times 2 = 2$ degrees of freedom. From the chi-square values (with DF = 2) given in Table 4 for the null association model applied to Table 3, we see that this model does not fit the data. We consider next the uniform association model, which does fit the data well.

The uniform association model is defined as follows:

$$\Phi_{ij} = \phi \tag{14}$$

where the parameter ϕ is estimated from the data. Model (14) introduces a single parameter into Model (6), and in this simple way we obtain a model that is congruent with the observed data (see Table 4).

To clarify further our understanding of the uniform association model as defined by (14), Table 9 presents the log-odds-ratios based on the observed frequencies f_{ij}, and also the standardized value of these log-odds-ratios.[6] For the 2×3 table (Table 3), there are two observed log-odds-ratios (see Table 9). The difference between them is -0.25

---

[5]Although our attention here is focused on the odds-ratio Θ_{ij} pertaining to adjacent classes of variable A (classes i and $i + 1$) and variable B (classes j and $j + 1$) (see Formula 5), we could instead have considered more generally the odds-ratio pertaining to any two classes of variable A (say, classes i and i′) and variable B (say, classes j and j′). The latter odds-ratio can be expressed as a product of an appropriate set of θ_{ij}; hence any model that describes the θ_{ij} in terms of multiplicative factors will also describe the latter odds-ratio in terms of multiplicative factors (see, for example, Goodman, 1979a, 1979b.)

[6]The log-odds-ratios in Table 9 are calculated as the natural logarithm of the odds-ratios defined by (5), where the expected frequencies in (5) are replaced by a function of the corresponding observed frequencies. Here, too, the F_{ij} are replaced by $f_{ij} + \frac{1}{2}$; see, for example, Goodman (1970). Each standardized value in Table 9 is calculated by dividing the corresponding log-odds-ratio in this table by its estimated standard deviation, where the F_{ij} in the formula for the standard deviation are also replaced by $f_{ij} + \frac{1}{2}$, as in, for example, Goodman (1970).

TABLE 9
Observed Association for Adjacent Rows and Adjacent
Columns in Table 3

Streptococcus Carrier Status	Tonsil Enlargement Level	
	+ vs. + +	+ + vs. + + +
Noncarrier vs. carrier	0.29 (0.99)	0.55 (1.93)

NOTE: The standardized value of the observed association is given in parentheses.

[0.295 − 0.547 = −0.252], and the standardized value of this difference is −0.51.[7] This standardized value is rather close to zero, thus helping to explain why the uniform association model (14) fits the data so well.

In the preceding section, we used the observed log-odds in Table 7 to suggest why Model (13) fits the data in Table 2; in the present section we can use the observed log-odds-ratios in Table 9 to suggest why Model (14) fits the data in Table 3. In addition to the observed log-odds-ratios as presented in Table 9, it will often prove enlightening to calculate contrasts among them, and the corresponding standardized value of the contrasts. A similar remark can also be applied to the observed log-odds presented earlier in Table 7.

Table 10 gives the maximum-likelihood estimate $\hat{F}_{ij}$ of the expected frequencies obtained when Model (14) is applied to Table 3. (I shall describe how these entries are calculated later.) From the $\hat{F}_{ij}$ under Model (14), we find that the maximum-likelihood estimate of the log-odds-ratio parameter ϕ in (14) is $\hat{\phi} = 0.43$. Also, the $\hat{F}_{ij}$ under Model (14) can be expressed in terms of the estimate of ϕ in (14) and the corresponding observed frequency $f_{i.}$ at the ith level of variable A and the observed frequency $f_{.j}$ at the jth level of variable B. (For models that pertain to the association between variables A and B, the $\hat{F}_{i.}$ and $\hat{F}_{.j}$ are set equal to the corresponding observed frequencies $f_{i.}$ and $f_{.j}$, respectively.) The association between variables A and B, with

$$(\hat{F}_{11}\hat{F}_{22})/(\hat{F}_{12}\hat{F}_{21}) = (\hat{F}_{12}\hat{F}_{23})/(\hat{F}_{13}\hat{F}_{22}) > 1$$

[7]The log-odds-ratios in Table 9, and the difference between them, are examples of estimated two-factor interactions in the two-way contingency table. The general formula for the estimated standard deviation of an estimated interaction can be applied here; see, for example, Goodman (1970). The standardized value of the estimated interaction is the ratio of the estimated interaction and its estimated standard deviation.

TABLE 10
Maximum-Likelihood Estimate of Expected Frequencies
Obtained When Model (14) Is Applied to Table 3

Streptococcus Carrier Status	Tonsil Enlargement Level			Total
	1	2	3	
1	498.0	558.0	270.0	1,326.0
2	18.0	31.0	23.0	72.0
Total	516.0	589.0	293.0	1,398.0

(see Table 10), is a direct consequence of the fact that the estimate of ϕ in (14) is greater than zero.

The uniform association model (14) provides a simple description of the association between variables A and B in Table 3. This model is useful in the analysis of the association in Table 3, and it can also shed light on the analysis of these data when variable B is viewed as a response variable with variable A a possible regressor and when variable A is viewed as a response variable with variable B a possible regressor. This topic is discussed more fully later. (See also Duncan 1979a; Goodman, 1979a, 1979b.)

As we noted earlier, with models for the analysis of the association between variables A and B, the univariate distributions of variable A and variable B are set equal to the corresponding observed distributions. On the other hand, these models can be modified in various ways to obtain models that do not set the corresponding univariate and observed distributions equal; and the modified models can help to explain the particular form of the association between variables A and B and the shape of the corresponding univariate distributions. An example of such a model is included in the next section.

SOME COMPARISONS

Analysis of Association vs. Analysis of the Joint Distribution

Each model for the analysis of the association between variables A and B can be rewritten in an equivalent form as a special kind of model for the analysis of the joint distribution between variables A and B. For example, the null association model (6) is equivalent to the model which states that variables A and B are statistically independent; that is,

$$F_{ij} = \alpha_i \beta_j \qquad (15)$$

where α_i and β_j are parameters pertaining to the ith level of variable A and the jth level of variable B, respectively (with $\alpha_i \geq 0$, $\beta_j \geq 0$). Similarly, the uniform association model (14) is equivalent to the model which states that

$$F_{ij} = \alpha_i \beta_j \theta^{ij} \qquad (16)$$

where θ is the odds-ratio parameter (with $\theta > 0$), and the superscripts i and j denote specified powers (see Goodman, 1979a, 1979b). Each model for the analysis of association can be defined as a model for the F_{ij} that includes parameters α_i and β_j pertaining to the ith row and jth column, respectively, in the cross-classification table.

We shall now consider some additional models for the analysis of association defined in these terms, and we shall apply these models to the data in Table 1. The results thus obtained will provide a comparison to the results obtained earlier in the analysis of the joint distribution for Table 1.

As we noted above, Model (15) is the usual model of statistical independence between variables A and B. With respect to Table 1, when the entries on the main diagonal are deleted, the independence model (15) can be modified to obtain the corresponding quasi-independence model:

$$F_{ij} = \alpha_i \beta_j \mu_{ij} \qquad (17)$$

where μ_{ij} is a parameter pertaining to cell (i, j) in the cross-classification table, with $\mu_{ij} = 1$ when $i \neq j$. (More generally, when the entries in any given subset of the cells in the cross-classification table are deleted, the quasi-independence model can be defined by (17) with $\mu_{ij} = 1$ for all cells that are not deleted; see, for example, Goodman, 1968.) Earlier we noted that the usual independence model (15) can be expressed in terms of the log-odds-ratios using the formula for the equivalent model (6); similarly, the quasi-independence model (17) can also be expressed in terms of the log-odds-ratios, but the formula for the corresponding equivalent model is not quite so simple. (The formula for the equivalent model can be obtained by applying to (17) the general method used in Goodman, 1979b.)

Table 11 gives the chi-square values obtained when the usual independence model (15) is applied to Table 1 with no entries deleted, and when the quasi-independence model (17) is applied to the

TABLE 11

Chi-Square Values for Some Association Models Applied to Table 1

Model	DF	Goodness-of-Fit Chi Square	Likelihood-Ratio Chi Square
Independence model (15)	9	8,096.86	6,671.50
Quasi-independence model (17)	5	198.01	199.10
Symmetric association model (18)	3	7.26	7.27
Diagonals-parameter model (22)	1	0.22	0.22

cross-classification with the entries on the main diagonal deleted. From the chi-square values in Table 11 we see that, although there is a dramatic improvement in the fit when the independence model is replaced by the quasi-independence model, the latter model still does not fit the data in Table 1 in a satisfactory way. Additional improvement can be obtained with the other two models listed in Table 11; we shall discuss them now.

The symmetric association model in Table 11 can also be defined in terms of the F_{ij} or the corresponding log-odds-ratio Φ_{ij}. With respect to the F_{ij}, we obtain

$$F_{ij} = \alpha_i \beta_j \rho'_{ij} \qquad \text{for } i \neq j \qquad (18)$$

where the parameters ρ'_{ij} satisfy the condition

$$\rho'_{ij} = \rho'_{ji} \qquad (19)$$

With respect to the corresponding Φ_{ij}, we obtain

$$\Phi_{ij} = \rho^*_{ij} \qquad \text{for } i \neq j \qquad (20)$$

where the parameters ρ^*_{ij} satisfy the condition

$$\rho^*_{ij} = \rho^*_{ji} \qquad (21)$$

Model (20) states that the log-odds-ratios are symmetric, and the equivalent model (18) is the usual quasi-symmetry model (see, for example, Caussinus, 1965; Goodman, 1979a). The final model in Table 11 is the diagonals-parameter model introduced in Goodman (1972):

$$F_{ij} = \alpha_i \beta_j \delta'_k \qquad \text{for } i \neq j; k = i - j \qquad (22)$$

This model too can be expressed in an equivalent form in terms of the log-odds-ratios, by applying the general method used in Goodman (1979b). Model (22) states that, aside from the diagonals parameter in the model and the entries on the main diagonal, there is quasi-independence between variables A and B in the cross-classification table.

For a 4×4 cross-classification table, the symmetric association model (18) is equivalent to a model obtained by imposing certain restrictions on the diagonals-parameter model (22). (This can be shown by applying the general method used in Goodman, 1972, to demonstrate such equivalence.) From the chi-square values for Models (18) and (22) in Table 11, we see that the latter model fits the data in Table 1 well, and it is a statistically significant improvement over the former model.

While the diagonals-parameter model (22) fits the data in Table 1 well, the chi-square values pertaining to this model are tested with 1 degree of freedom in the 4×4 cross-classification table (see Goodman, 1972). A more parsimonious model that also fits the data well would be preferable. I shall now present such a model.

All the models described so far in this section pertain to the association in the cross-classification table. (Each of these models can be expressed as a model for the F_{ij} that includes α_i and β_j pertaining to the ith row and jth column, respectively, in the cross-classification table.) We shall now modify the diagonals-parameter model (22) in a way that changes this model for the analysis of association into a model for the analysis of the joint distribution.

For the square $I \times I$ cross-classification table, let us consider the model obtained when the following restriction is imposed on Model (22):

$$\alpha_i = \beta_i = \rho_i \qquad \text{for } i = 1, 2, \ldots, I \tag{23}$$

This restriction states that α_i for the ith row and the corresponding β_i for the ith column are equal to a common unspecified value—say, ρ_i (with $\rho_i \geq 0$). Model (22) with restriction (23) imposed on it is equivalent to the following model:

$$F_{ij} = \rho_i \rho_j \delta_k' \qquad \text{for } i \neq j; k = i - j \tag{24}$$

Model (24) states that, aside from the diagonals parameter in the model and the entries on the main diagonal, there is quasi-independence between variables A and B in the cross-classification table, and each row parameter is equal to the corresponding column parameter. For a 4×4 cross-classification table, Model (24) is equivalent to the fitted asymmetry model (9) (see Goodman, 1979c). Thus when this model is fitted to the data in Table 1, the chi-square values reported in Table 4 for Model (9) are obtained. This model fits the data well, and it is more parsimonious than the diagonals-parameter model (22).

Model (22) pertains to the analysis of association, whereas Model (24) pertains to the analysis of the joint distribution. Model (22) sheds light on the association in Table 1, but not on the univariate distribution of variable A or the univariate distribution of variable B in the table. Model (24), however, sheds light upon the association in Table 1 and also upon the corresponding univariate distributions. Under Model (22) and under Model (24), the association in the table can be explained by the diagonals parameter in the model and the entries on the main diagonal. In addition, since α_i for the ith row and the corresponding β_i for the ith column are equal in Model (24), the difference between the corresponding univariate distributions under this model can be explained in terms of the diagonals parameter. With the $\hat{F}_{ij}$ under Model (24) and the corresponding estimates $\hat{F}_{i.}$ and $\hat{F}_{.j}$ pertaining to the univariate distributions (see Table 6), the fact that

$$\sum_{t=1}^{x} \hat{F}_{t.} > \sum_{t=1}^{x} \hat{F}_{.t} \qquad \text{for } x = 1, 2, 3$$

can be explained in terms of the diagonals parameter in the model.

Model (24) was obtained from Model (22) by the imposition of Condition (23). This imposition changes a model for the analysis of association into a model for the analysis of the joint distribution. Any model for the analysis of association can be changed into a model for the analysis of the joint distribution by imposing this kind of condition. I have used the change from Model (22) to Model (24) here as an example to illustrate this general method.

Let us consider for a moment the imposition of Condition (23) on, say, the independence model (15). The model thus obtained states that there is independence between variables A and B in the cross-classification table and that each row parameter is equal to the corresponding column parameter. In other words, this model states that there is both independence and symmetry in the cross-classification table. Thus, the model can be called the "independence and symmetry model" or the "null association and null asymmetry model." If Condition (23) is imposed instead upon, say, the quasi-independence model (17), we obtain the "quasi-independence and symmetry model" or the "null association and null asymmetry model" for the entries not on the main diagonal. With the introduction of the diagonals parameter into this model, we obtain Model (24), the "diagonals-parameter quasi-independence and symmetry model."

Instead of using Condition (23), other conditions can be imposed upon the α_i and β_j in a model for the analysis of association to change it into a model for the analysis of the joint distribution. I have also used Condition (23) as an example to illustrate the general method.

In closing this section, we note that the analysis of the association in Table 1 led us to the diagonals-parameter model (22), and by replacing this model for the analysis of association by a related model for the analysis of the joint distribution, we were led to the more parsimonious model (24). The corresponding analysis of the joint distribution in the earlier section led us directly to Model (9), the diagonals-parameter symmetry model in Goodman (1979c), which is equivalent to Model (24) for the 4×4 cross-classification table.

Analysis of Association vs. Analysis of Dependence

Each model for the analysis of the association between variables A and B can be rewritten in an equivalent form as a special kind of model for the analysis of the dependence of variable B on variable A, and in an equivalent form as a special kind of model for the analysis of the dependence of variable A on variable B. For example, the null association model (6) is equivalent to the model which states that the log-odds $\Psi_{ij}^{A\overline{B}}$ is independent of the level i on variable A; that is,

$$\Psi_{ij}^{A\overline{B}} = \psi_j^B \qquad \text{for } i = 1, 2, \ldots, I \qquad (25)$$

where ψ_j^B is a parameter pertaining to the jth level of variable B. Similarly, the uniform association model (14) is equivalent to the model which states that

$$\Psi_{ij}^{A\overline{B}} = \psi_j^B - i\phi \qquad (26)$$

where ϕ is the log-odds-ratio parameter (see Goodman, 1979b). Each model for the analysis of association can be defined as a model for $\Psi_{ij}^{A\overline{B}}$ that includes a parameter ψ_j^B pertaining to the jth column of the cross-classification table. Similarly, with respect to the log-odds $\Psi_{ji}^{B\overline{A}}$

defined as the natural logarithm of

$$\Omega_{ji}^{B\overline{A}} = F_{ij}/F_{i+1,j} \qquad \text{for } i = 1, 2, \ldots, I - 1 \qquad (27)$$

(compare Formula 27 witn Formula 3), each model for the analysis of association can be defined as a model for the $\Psi_{ji}^{B\overline{A}}$ that includes a parameter ψ_i^A pertaining to the ith row of the cross-classification table. We shall now see how the association model (14) applied to Table 3 can be interpreted when it is considered as a model for the dependence of variable B on variable A (see Model 26) and when it is considered as a model for the dependence of variable A on variable B.

Model (26) states that the log-odds $\Psi_{ij}^{A\overline{B}}$ is a linear function of the level i on variable A, and the slope of the linear function is equal to $-\phi$, which is the same for each value of j (for $j = 1, 2, \ldots, J - 1$). When $J = 2$, this model states simply that $\Psi_{i1}^{A\overline{B}}$ is a linear function of the level i on variable A; when $J > 2$, the model states that the lines obtained for the log-odds, $\Psi_{i1}^{A\overline{B}}, \Psi_{i2}^{A\overline{B}}, \ldots, \Psi_{i, J-1}^{A\overline{B}}$, are parallel. Thus Model (26) can be called the "parallel log-odds model," with variable A having a linear effect on $\Psi_{ij}^{A\overline{B}}$. Since $\hat{\phi} = 0.43$ is the maximum-likelihood estimate of ϕ obtained in the earlier section on the analysis of the association in Table 3, the estimated slope is -0.43 in the linear relationship describing the dependence of $\Psi_{ij}^{A\overline{B}}$ on variable A, and also in the linear relationship describing the dependence of $\Psi_{ji}^{B\overline{A}}$ upon variable B. Thus, from the $\hat{F}_{ij}$ in Table 10, we find that the corresponding estimated log-odds satisfy the following relationships:

$$\hat{\Psi}_{2j}^{A\overline{B}} - \hat{\Psi}_{1j}^{A\overline{B}} = -0.43 \qquad \text{for } j = 1, 2$$

$$\hat{\Psi}_{21}^{B\overline{A}} - \hat{\Psi}_{11}^{B\overline{A}} = \hat{\Psi}_{31}^{B\overline{A}} - \hat{\Psi}_{21}^{B\overline{A}} = -0.43$$

Before closing this section, it may be worthwhile to note that the estimates presented by Andrich (1979) in his analysis of the data in Table 3 (where variable B, tonsil enlargement level, was viewed as a response variable and variable A, streptococcus carrier status, was a possible regressor variable) should have turned out to be equal to the corresponding estimates obtained here when the uniform association model (14) or the equivalent parallel log-odds model (26) is applied.[8]

---

[8]Andrich (1979) described his model in different terms from those used here to describe Model (14) or the equivalent model (26), but the estimated expected frequencies for the data in Table 3 under his model (and the estimate of the parameter corresponding to the slope) should have turned out to be equal to the corresponding estimates presented here (see Table 10).

However, this was not so. The estimates presented by Andrich (1979) for the data in Table 3 differ from the corresponding estimates presented here because his method for calculating maximum-likelihood estimates was somewhat inaccurate. His method did not provide estimates that satisfy the maximum-likelihood equations.

Analysis of Dependence vs. Analysis of the Joint Distribution

Each model for the analysis of dependence of variable B on variable A can be rewritten in an equivalent form as a special kind of model for the analysis of the joint distribution of variables A and B. For example, the null log-odds model (4) is equivalent to the model which states that the classes of variable B are conditionally equiprobable, given the level of variable A. In other words, this model states that

$$F_{ij} = \alpha_i \tag{28}$$

where α_i is a parameter pertaining to the ith level of variable A (with $\alpha_i \geq 0$). Similarly, if we consider, say, the simple log-odds model

$$\Psi_{ij}^{A\overline{B}} = \psi \tag{29}$$

then we find that this log-odds model is equivalent to the model which states that

$$F_{ij} = \alpha_i / \omega^j \tag{30}$$

where ω is a parameter pertaining to the odds defined by Formula (3) (with $\omega > 0$), and the superscript j denotes a specified power. (Formula 30 can be obtained by applying to Formula 29 the general method used in Goodman, 1979b.) Each model for the analysis of the dependence of variable B on variable A can be defined as a model for the F_{ij} that includes a parameter α_i pertaining to the ith row of the cross-classification table. We shall now see how the model obtained earlier in the analysis of dependence applied to Table 2 can be interpreted when it is considered as a model for the joint distribution of variables A and B in this table.

Let us first consider the following log-odds model:

$$\Psi_{ij}^{A\overline{B}} = \psi_i \tag{31}$$

Model (13) is a special case of Model (31) in which $\psi_2 = \psi_3 = 0$; Model (29) is a special case in which $\psi_1 = \psi_2 = \psi_3$. Model (31) states that the log-odds satisfy the following condition:

$$\psi_{i1}^{AB} = \psi_{i2}^{AB} = \cdots = \psi_{i,J-1}^{AB} \tag{32}$$

Thus Model (31) can be called the "uniform log-odds model," and Model (29) is a special case of this model in which the effect of variable A on the log-odds is nil.

As was the case with Model (29), we find that Model (31) can be expressed in the following equivalent form:

$$F_{ij} = \alpha_i / \omega_i^j \tag{33}$$

where ψ_i is the natural logarithm of ω_i. With respect to the natural logarithm G_{ij} of the F_{ij}, Model (33) can be expressed as

$$G_{ij} = \alpha_i' - j\psi_i \tag{34}$$

where α_i' is the natural logarithm of α_i. Thus the uniform log-odds model (31) is equivalent to the model which states that G_{ij} is a linear function of the level j of variable B, and the slope is $-\psi_i$. Since $\hat{\psi}_1 = 1.18$ is the maximum-likelihood estimate of the log-odds parameter ψ_1 obtained earlier in the analysis of dependence applied to Table 2 (with $\psi_2 = \psi_3 = 0$), the estimated slope is -1.18 in the linear relationship of G_{1j} on the level j of variable B (see Table 8).

Before closing this section, it might be worthwhile to note that models for the analysis of dependence of variable B on variable A are also models for the conditional distribution of variable B, given the level of variable A. For example, the null log-odds model (4) and the equivalent model (28) state that the classes of variable B are conditionally equiprobable, given the level of variable A; that is, the conditional distribution of variable B is the uniform distribution. Similarly, the uniform log-odds model (31) and the equivalent model (33) state that the conditional distribution of variable B (given the level of variable A) is the truncated geometric distribution. (When the parameter ω_i in Model (33) is greater than or equal to 1, the geometric distribution is defined with the classes of variable B numbered consecutively from $j = 1$ to $j = J$; and when $\omega_i < 1$, the distribution is defined with the classes numbered in reverse order.) Model (29) and the equivalent model (30) state that the conditional distribution of variable B (given the level of variable A) is the truncated geometric distribution, and that the parameter ω_i in this distribution does not depend upon the level i of variable A (that is, $\omega_i = \omega$, for $i = 1, 2, \ldots, I$).

RELATIONSHIPS AMONG MODELS FOR THE ANALYSIS OF ASSOCIATION, DEPENDENCE, AND THE JOINT DISTRIBUTION

We noted earlier that each model for the analysis of the association between variables A and B can be rewritten in an equivalent form as a special kind of model for the analysis of the dependence of variable B on variable A (that is, a model for $\Psi_{ij}^{A\bar{B}}$ that includes the parameter ψ_j^B) and as a special kind of model for the analysis of the dependence of variable A on variable B (that is, a model for $\psi_{ji}^{B\bar{A}}$ that includes the parameter ψ_i^A). Thus these special kinds of models for the analysis of dependence (such as Models 25 and 26) are equivalent to models for the analysis of association. On the other hand, models for the analysis of dependence that are not of this special kind (such as Models 4, 13, 29, 31) are not equivalent to models for the analysis of association.

We also noted earlier that each model for the analysis of the association between variables A and B can be rewritten in an equivalent form as a special kind of model for the analysis of the joint distribution of variables A and B (a model for the F_{ij} that includes the parameters α_i and β_j). Thus, models of this special kind (such as Models 15, 16, 17, 18, 22) are equivalent to models for the analysis of association. On the other hand, models for the analysis of the joint distribution that are not of this special kind (such as Models 1, 2, 7, 9, 24, 28, 30, 33) are not equivalent to models for the analysis of association.

We also noted earlier that each model for the analysis of the dependence of variable B on variable A can be rewritten in an equivalent form as a special kind of model for the analysis of the joint distribution (a model for the F_{ij} that includes the parameter α_i), and each model for the analysis of the dependence of variable A on variable B can be rewritten in an equivalent form as a special kind of model for the analysis of the joint distribution (a model for the F_{ij} that includes the parameter β_j). Thus these special kinds of models for the analysis of the joint distribution (such as Models 15, 16, 17, 18, 22, 28, 30, 33) are equivalent to models for the analysis of dependence. On the other hand, models for the analysis of the joint distribution not of this special kind (for example, Models 1, 2, 7, 9, 24) are not equivalent to models for the analysis of dependence.

The relationships among the models described above are

TABLE 12

Relationships Among Association Models (A Models), Dependence Models (D Models), and
Joint Distribution Models (JD Models)

Model	Association Model (A, D, and JD)	Dependence Model (D and JD)	Joint Distribution Model (JD)
Log-odds-ratio	[6,14,20]		
Log-odds	[25,26]	[4,13,29,31]	
Expected frequency	[15,16,17,18,22]	[28,30,33]	[1,2,7,9,24]

summarized in Table 12 and Figure 1. For additional comparisons
among these models, see also Table 13.

AN OVERVIEW OF THE MODELS

With respect to the two-way $I \times J$ contingency table, there are
four elementary log linear models obtained in the situation where the
order of the rows and the order of the columns are not taken into
account (see, for example, Goodman, 1970):

1. The usual model H' of statistical independence between variables
   A and B

Figure 1. Relationships among association models (A models), dependence models (D
models), and joint distribution models (JD models).

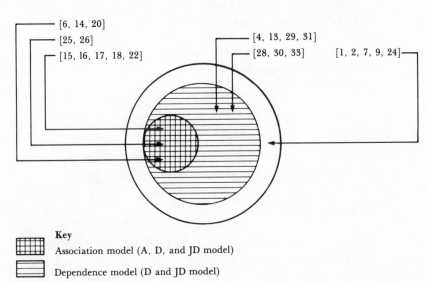

Key

Association model (A, D, and JD model)

Dependence model (D and JD model)

Joint distribution model (JD model)

TABLE 13
Models Pertaining to Two-Way Cross-Classification Table

Association models

Relevant multiplicative function: odds-ratio	Θ_{ij}
Relevant additive function: log-odds-ratio	Φ_{ij}
Relevant multiplicative statistic: observed odds-ratio	θ_{ij}
Relevant additive statistic: observed log-odds-ratio	ϕ_{ij}
Simplest null model: independence model	$\Phi_{ij} = 0$
Fitted marginals include: $\{A\}, \{B\}$	

Dependence models for variable B given A

Relevant multiplicative function: odds	$\Omega^{A\bar{B}}_{ij}$
Relevant additive function: log-odds	$\Psi^{A\bar{B}}_{ij}$
Relevant multiplicative statistic: observed odds	$\omega^{A\bar{B}}_{ij}$
Relevant additive statistic: observed log-odds	$\psi^{A\bar{B}}_{ij}$
Simplest null model: conditional equiprobability	$\Psi^{A\bar{B}}_{ij} = 0$
Fitted marginals include: $\{A\}$	

Dependence models for variable A given B

Relevant multiplicative function: odds	$\Omega^{B\bar{A}}_{ji}$
Relevant additive function: log-odds	$\Psi^{B\bar{A}}_{ji}$
Relevant multiplicative statistic: observed odds	$\omega^{B\bar{A}}_{ji}$
Relevant additive statistic: observed log-odds	$\psi^{B\bar{A}}_{ji}$
Simplest null model: conditional equiprobability	$\Psi^{B\bar{A}}_{ji} = 0$
Fitted marginals include: $\{B\}$	

Joint distribution models

Relevant multiplicative function: expected frequencies	F_{ij}
Relevant additive function: log expected frequencies	G_{ij}
Relevant multiplicative statistic: observed frequencies	f_{ij}
Relevant additive statistic: log observed frequencies	g_{ij}
Simplest null model: equiprobability model	$F_{ij} = N/(IJ)$
Fitted marginals include: sample size	N

2.   The model H'' which states that the J classes of variable B are conditionally equiprobable, given the level of variable A

3.   The model H''' which states that the I classes of variable A are conditionally equiprobable, given the level of variable B

4.   The model H'''' which states that the IJ classes of the joint variable (A, B) are equiprobable.

Model H' can be described by (15); model H'' can be described by (28); model H''' can be described by (28) with α_i replaced by β_j; and model H'''' can be described by (1).

Model H' can be used in the analyses of association (see Model 6), dependence (see, for example, Model 25), and the joint distribution (see Model 15). Models H'' and H''' can be used in the analyses of dependence (see, for example, Model 4) and the joint distribution (see, for example, Model 28), but not in the analysis of association. Model H'''' can be used in the analysis of the joint distribution (see Model 1), but not in the analyses of association or dependence.

With model H', the marginal for variable A and the marginal for variable B are fitted. With model H'', the marginal for variable A is fitted; with model H''', the marginal for variable B is fitted (see, for example, Goodman, 1970).

Each model for the analysis of the joint distribution that takes into account the order of the rows and/or the order of the columns in the cross-classification table can be formed from the null model H'''' by introducing parameters that take this order into account (see, for example, Models 7, 9, 16, 18, 22, 24, 30, 33). Each model for the analysis of dependence that takes into account the order of the rows and/or columns can be formed from the corresponding null models H'' and H''' by introducing parameters that take this order into account (see, for example, Models 16, 18, 22, 30, 33). Each model for the analysis of association that takes into account the order of the rows and/or columns can be formed from the corresponding null model H' by introducing parameters that take this order into account (see, for example, Models 16, 18, 22).

The class of models for the analysis of association is included in the class of models for the analysis of dependence, which is in turn included in the class of models for the analysis of the joint distribution (see Figure 1). Each model for the analysis of association can be expressed as a special kind of model for the analysis of dependence, and each model for the analysis of dependence can be expressed as a special kind of model for the analysis of the joint distribution. With each model for the analysis of association, the marginals for both variable A and variable B are fitted (see, for example, Goodman 1970, 1979a). With each model for the dependence of variable B on variable A, the marginal for variable A is fitted; with each model for the dependence of variable A on variable B, the marginal for variable B is fitted (see, for example, Goodman 1970, 1979b). On the other hand, there are models for the analysis of the joint distribution that fit neither the marginal for variable A nor that for variable B; there are models for the analysis of the dependence of variable B on A that do not fit the marginal for variable B (although they do fit the marginal for variable A); and there are models for the analysis of the dependence of variable A on variable B that do not fit the marginal for variable A (although they do fit the marginal for variable B).

THE ESTIMATION OF THE PARAMETERS
IN THE MODELS

Let us first consider, say, Model (14) for the analysis of association. As we noted earlier, this model is equivalent to Model (16), which is a multiplicative model for the F_{ij}. Model (14) is an example of a more general class of association models that are equivalent to multiplicative models for the F_{ij} (see, for example, Goodman 1979a). The maximum-likelihood estimates of the parameters in the association models, and the corresponding estimates of the F_{ij}, can be obtained by the method presented in Goodman (1979a).

Each of the models considered here for either the analysis of association, the analysis of dependence, or the analysis of the joint distribution is equivalent to a multiplicative model for the F_{ij} and thus to a corresponding additive model for the natural logarithm G_{ij} of the F_{ij}. These are log linear models. The maximum-likelihood estimates of the parameters in these models and the corresponding estimates of the F_{ij} can be obtained by a direct extension of the method presented in Goodman (1979a) or by using general computer programs for log linear models (see, for example, Haberman, 1974a, 1979; Bock, 1975; Nelder, 1975).

For each of the models considered here, the maximum-likelihood estimates can be obtained by the methods described above. However, for some of these models, more elementary methods can be used instead. The methods presented here for the models used in the analysis of the joint distribution for Table 1 serve as an example of this; the methods used with the various null models considered here also serve as an example.

THE MERITS OF PARSIMONIOUS MODELS

Various methods for obtaining parsimonious models that fit the data have been presented here. I shall now comment on some of the advantages of using such models.

Let us first consider, say, the analysis of association. With the models and methods presented here, we obtain asymptotically more powerful methods for testing various hypotheses about the association in the $I \times J$ cross-classification table. For example, with respect to the usual null hypothesis of statistical independence between variables A and B in the $I \times J$ table, if the uniform association model (14) holds true, then instead of using the usual chi-square statistic (with $(I - 1)$ $(J - 1)$ degrees of freedom) to test the null hypothesis, we obtain an asymptotically more powerful test of this hypothesis by using the chi-square statistic (with 1 degree of freedom) pertaining to the hypothesis that the association parameter ϕ in Model (14) is equal to zero. Thus, with respect to the analysis of association presented in Table 4 for the 2×3 cross-classification (Table 3), we see from Table 4 that 7.32 is the numerical value of the likelihood-ratio chi-square (with 2 degrees of freedom) that is obtained in testing the usual null hypothesis of statistical independence in the usual way; but an asymptotically more powerful test of this null hypothesis can be obtained, when the uniform association model (14) holds true, by using the difference between the corresponding chi-squared values—that is, $7.32 - 0.24 = 7.08$, with 1 degree of freedom. This difference provides us with a test of the hypothesis that ϕ in Model (14) is equal to zero (see Goodman, 1979a).

More generally, let us now consider models M and M', where M is more parsimonious than M' (that is, where M can be described in terms of fewer parameters than M'), and M is a special case of M'. (For example, let M be Model 14, and let M' be the usual saturated log linear model for the cross-classification table.) Let H denote a hypothesis within model M' and the equivalent hypothesis within model M. (For example, let H be the usual hypothesis of statistical independence between variables A and B in the saturated log linear model; the equivalent hypothesis within Model 14 is the hypothesis that $\phi = 0$.) The chi-square test of H within the more parsimonious model M will be asymptotically more powerful than the corresponding test of this hypothesis within model M', if model M holds true.

There are also other advantages in using the more parsimonious model M rather than M'. For example, the asymptotic variance of the maximum-likelihood estimates of the parameters in the model M will be less than (or equal to) the asymptotic variance of the corresponding estimates of the same parameters in model M', if model M holds true. (This follows directly from the fact that the maximum-likelihood estimates are fully efficient.) In addition, with respect to the hypothesis that a specified parameter in model M is equal to some specified value (say, zero), the chi-square test of this hypothesis within model M is asymptotically more powerful than the corresponding test of the same hypothesis within model M', if model M is true. (The chi-square tests in the present context are asymptotically equivalent to the usual F tests of linear hypotheses, with an infinite number of degrees of freedom in the denominator; and the usual F tests are uniformly most powerful invariant tests—see Haberman, 1974b, Lehmann, 1959.)

For models M and M' described above, it is preferable to use the more parsimonious model M rather than M' if both models are true. However, it should be noted that if both models are congruent with the observed data, this does not necessarily mean that both models hold true.[9] If more data were obtained, we might find that model M no longer fit the data whereas model M' may continue to fit. With more data, the estimates of the additional parameters in M' (that is, those in M' but not in M) may turn out to be significantly different from zero, and the model that did not include these parameters may no longer suffice. The choice of the more parsimonious model for a given set of data does not imply that the less parsimonious model is dismissed entirely as a possible model for the data (see, for example, Goodman, 1979d).

EXTENSIONS TO MULTIWAY CROSS-CLASSIFICATION TABLES

The models and methods presented here for the two-way table can be extended to the m-way table (for $m = 3, 4, \ldots$), and we can obtain more powerful methods for testing various hypotheses about the m-way table. We shall consider first the $I \times J \times K$ three-way table, in the case where the I levels of variable A, the J levels of variable B, and the K levels of variable C are ordered.

Let f_{ijk} denote the observed frequency in cell (i, j, k) of the three-way table ($i = 1, 2, \ldots, I; j = 1, 2, \ldots, J; k = 1, 2, \ldots, K$),

---

[9]Even if both models are congruent with the observed data, and the fit of model M is not significantly worse than the fit of model M', this does not necessarily mean that both models are true.

and let F_{ijk} denote the corresponding expected frequency under some model. Let us now consider models for the analysis of the three-factor interaction in the three-way table.

For adjacent classes of variable A (say, classes i and $i + 1$), variable B (say, classes j and $j + 1$), and variable C (say, classes k and $k + 1$), we define as follows the odds-ratio-ratio Θ_{ijk} based on the expected frequencies:

$$\Theta_{ijk} = \left(\frac{F_{ijk}F_{i+1,j+1,k}}{F_{i,j+1,k}F_{i+1,j,k}}\right) \Big/ \left(\frac{F_{i,j,k+1}F_{i+1,j+1,k+1}}{F_{i+1,j,k+1}F_{i,j+1,k+1}}\right) \tag{35}$$

(Compare Formula 35 with Formula 5.) Let Φ_{ijk} denote the natural logarithm of Θ_{ijk} (i.e., the log-odds-ratio ratio). In the present context, the most elementary null model is the following:

$$\Phi_{ijk} = 0 \qquad \text{for } i = 1, 2, \ldots, I - 1; j = 1, 2, \ldots, J - 1;$$

$$k = 1, 2, \ldots, K - 1 \tag{36}$$

(Compare Model 36 with Model 6.) Model (36) is equivalent to the model which states that the three-factor interaction in the three-way table is zero (see, for example, Goodman, 1970).

The uniform three-factor interaction model can be defined as follows:

$$\Phi_{ijk} = \phi \tag{37}$$

where the parameter ϕ is estimated from the data. (Compare Model 37 with Model 14.) Model (37) introduces a single parameter into the null model (36).

Each model for the analysis of the three-factor interaction between variables A, B, and C can be rewritten in an equivalent form as a special kind of model for the analysis of the joint distribution between variables A, B, and C. For example, the null model (36) is equivalent to

$$F_{ijk} = \alpha_{ik}\beta_{jk}\gamma_{ij} \tag{38}$$

where α_{ik}, β_{jk}, and γ_{ij} are parameters pertaining to the (i, k) level of the joint variable (A, C), and the (j, k) level of the joint variable (B, C), and the (i, j) level of the joint variable (A, B), respectively (with $\alpha_{ik} \geq 0$, $\beta_{jk} \geq 0$, $\gamma_{ij} \geq 0$). (Compare Model 38 with Model 15.) Similarly, the uniform three-factor interaction model (37) is equivalent to

$$F_{ijk} = \alpha_{ik}\beta_{jk}\gamma_{ij}\theta^{ijk} \tag{39}$$

where θ is the odds-ratio-ratio parameter (with $\theta > 0$), and the superscripts i, j, and k denote specified powers. (Compare Model 39 with Model 16.) Each model for the analysis of the three-factor interaction can be defined as a model for the F_{ijk} that includes parameters α_{ik}, β_{jk}, and γ_{ij} pertaining to the cells (i, k), (j, k), and (i, j) in the two-way marginal tables for the joint variables (A, C), (B, C), and (A, B), respectively, in the three-way cross-classification table.

The null three-factor interaction model (36) can be tested in the usual way by applying Model (38) to the three-way table (see, for example, Goodman, 1970), and the uniform three-factor interaction model (37) can be tested by applying Model (39) to the three-way table, using a generalized form of the method used earlier to test the uniform association model (16) in the two-way table (see Goodman, 1979a).

Consider now the usual null hypothesis that the three-factor interaction in the three-way table is zero. Instead of using the usual chi-square statistic to test this null hypothesis (with $(I - 1)$ $(J - 1)$ $(K - 1)$ degrees of freedom), we can obtain an asymptotically more powerful test of this hypothesis, if the uniform three-factor interaction model (37) holds true. In this case, the null hypothesis can be tested by using the chi-square statistic (with 1 degree of freedom) pertaining to the hypothesis that the three-factor interaction parameter ϕ in Model (37) is equal to zero. To test the latter hypothesis, the appropriate chi-squared statistic (with 1 degree of freedom) is equal to the difference between the corresponding chi-squared statistic for testing the usual hypothesis of zero three-factor interaction and the statistic for testing the uniform three-factor interaction model.

Model (14) is an example of a general class of models pertaining to the association in the two-way table; similarly, Model (37) is an example of a general class of models pertaining to the three-factor interaction in the three-way table (see Goodman, 1979a). Each of the models in this class is equivalent to one formed from the null model (38) by introducing parameters that take into account the order of the rows, and/or the order of the columns, and/or the order of the layers in the three-way table (see, for example, Model 39).

In the overview presented earlier of the models for the two-way table, we noted that each of these models could be viewed as a modification of one of the four elementary log linear models obtained when the order of the rows and the order of the columns are not taken into account. Similarly, each of the corresponding models for the three-way table can be viewed as a modification of one of the 18 log linear models obtained when the order of the rows, the order of the columns, and the order of the layers are not taken into account (see Goodman, 1970, Table 3). The 18 log linear models pertain to the analysis of:

1. The three-factor interaction between variables A, B, and C
2. The conditional association between variables B and C given the level of variable A (there are three models of this general kind obtained by permuting the letters, A, B and C)
3. The association between variable C and the joint variable (A, B) (there are three models of this general kind)
4. The dependence of variable C upon the joint variable (A, B) (there are three models of this general kind)
5. The two-factor interaction (and three-factor interaction) in the three-way table
6. The dependence of variable C upon the joint variable (A, B), and the association between variables A and B (there are three models of this general kind)
7. The dependence of the joint variable (B, C) upon variable A (there are three models of this general kind)
8. The joint trivariate distribution of variables A, B, and C.

Each of these models can be modified by introducing parameters that take into account the order of the rows, and/or the order of the columns, and/or the order of the layers in the three-way table.

The discussion presented earlier in this section pertained to topic 1 in the preceding list. We shall now briefly discuss topic 2. For expository purposes, let us consider the conditional association between variables A and B, given the level of variable C (permuting the letters A, B, and C in the statement of topic 2).

For adjacent classes of variable A (say, classes i and $i + 1$) and variable B (say, classes j and $j + 1$), at level k of variable C, we now define the conditional odds-ratio $\Theta_{ij:k}$ based on the expected frequencies:

$$\Theta_{ij:k} = (F_{ijk}F_{i+1,j+1,k})/(F_{i,j+1,k}F_{i+1,j,k})$$

$$\text{for } i = 1, 2, \ldots, I - 1; j = 1, 2, \ldots, J - 1 \quad (40)$$

(Compare Formula 40 with Formula 5.) Let $\Phi_{ij:k}$ denote the natural logarithm of $\Theta_{ij:k}$ (that is, the conditional log-odds-ratio). In the present context, the most elementary null model is the following:

$$\Phi_{ij:k} = 0 \quad \text{for } i = 1, 2, \ldots, I - 1; j = 1, 2, \ldots, J - 1;$$

$$k = 1, 2, \ldots, K \quad (41)$$

(Compare Model 41 with Model 6.) Model (41) is equivalent to the model which states that variables A and B are conditionally independent, given the level of variable C (see, for example, Goodman, 1970).

The model which states that the conditional association between variables A and B is uniform (given the level of variable C) can be defined as follows:

$$\Phi_{ij:k} = \phi_k \quad (42)$$

where the parameter ϕ_k is estimated from the data. (Compare Model 42 with Model 14.) Model (42) introduces into the null model (41) a single parameter ϕ_k at level k of variable C, for $k = 1, 2, \ldots, K$.

Each model for the analysis of the conditional association between variables A and B (given the level of variable C) can be rewritten in an equivalent form as a special kind of model for the analysis of the joint distribution between variables A, B, and C. For example, the null model (41) is equivalent to

$$F_{ijk} = \alpha_{ik}\beta_{jk} \quad (43)$$

where α_{ik} and β_{ik} are parameters pertaining to the (i, k) level of the joint variable (A, C) and to the (j, k) level of the joint variable (B, C), respectively (with $\alpha_{ik} \geq 0$, $\beta_{jk} \geq 0$). (Compare Model 43 with Model 15.) Similarly, the uniform conditional association model (42) is equivalent to

$$F_{ijk} = \alpha_{ik}\beta_{jk}\theta_k^{ij} \quad (44)$$

where θ_k is the conditional odds-ratio parameter (with $\theta_k > 0$), and the superscripts i and j denote specified powers. (Compare Model 44 with Model 16.) Each model for the analysis of the conditional association between variables A and B, given the level of variable C, can be defined as a model for the F_{ijk} that includes α_{ik} and β_{jk} pertaining to the (i, k)

and (j, k) levels in the two-way marginal tables for the joint variables (A, C) and (B, C), respectively, in the three-way cross-classification table.

The null conditional association model (41) can be tested in the usual way by applying Model (43) to the three-way table (see, for example, Goodman, 1970). Similarly, the uniform conditional association model (42) can be tested by applying Model (44) to the three-way table. To apply Model (44), we simply fit the uniform association model at level k of variable C, for $k = 1, 2, \ldots, K$ (see Goodman, 1979a).

Consider now the usual null hypothesis that variables A and B are conditionally independent, given the level of variable C. Instead of using the usual chi-square statistic to test this null hypothesis (with $(I - 1)(J - 1)K$ degrees of freedom), we can obtain an asymptotically more powerful test if the conditional uniform association model (42) holds true. In this case, the null hypothesis can be tested by using the chi-square statistic (with K degrees of freedom) pertaining to the hypothesis that the conditional association parameter ϕ_k in Model (42) is equal to zero (for $k = 1, 2, \ldots, K$). The method described in the preceding section, for obtaining an asymptotically more powerful test (with 1 degree of freedom) of the null hypothesis that variables A and B are statistically independent, can be applied directly at level k of variable C (for $k = 1, 2, \ldots, K$) to obtain the asymptotically more powerful test (with K degrees of freedom) of the null hypothesis that variables A and B are conditionally independent, given the level of variable C.

Consider now the situation where ϕ_k in Model (42) satisfies the following condition:

$$\phi_k = \phi \qquad \text{for } k = 1, 2, \ldots, K \tag{45}$$

where ϕ is unspecified. In this case, the uniform conditional association models (42) and (44) are replaced by

$$\Phi_{ij \cdot k} = \phi \tag{46}$$

and

$$F_{ijk} = \alpha_{ik} \beta_{jk} \theta^{ij} \tag{47}$$

respectively. These models state that the conditional association between variables A and B (given the level of variable C) is uniform and that the three-factor interaction between variables A, B, and C is zero. In this case, the ϕ in Model (46) pertains to the partial association between variables A and B, given the level of variable C (see, for example, Goodman, 1969, 1970; Clogg, 1980). Models (46) and (47) state that the partial association between variables A and B (given variable C) is uniform.

When Model (42) holds true, we can test the usual null hypothesis of zero three-factor interaction by determining whether Condition (45) is satisfied (with $K - 1$ degrees of freedom). This test can be based on the difference between the corresponding chi-square statistics obtained when Models (47) and (44) are applied. Similarly, when Model (47) holds true, we can test the usual null hypothesis of zero partial association between variables A and B (given the level of variable C) by testing (with 1 degree of freedom) whether ϕ in Model (46) is equal to zero. This test can be based on the difference between the corresponding chi-square statistics obtained when Models (43) and (47) are applied. The tests described here for the hypotheses of zero three-factor interaction and zero partial association are asymptotically more powerful than the usual tests.

The parameter ϕ in Model (46) and the corresponding θ in (47) pertain to the partial association between variables A and B, given variable C. Comparing (47) with (38) we see that the model for uniform partial association between variables A and B (given variable C) replaces the two-factor parameter γ_{ij} pertaining to variables A and B in (38) by θ^{ij} in (47), where the superscripts i and j denote specified powers. Similarly, the model for uniform partial association between variables A and B (given variable C), uniform partial association between variables A and C (given variable B), and uniform partial association between variables B and C (given variable A) can be expressed as

$$F_{ijk} = \alpha_i \beta_j \gamma_k \theta_{AB}^{ij} \theta_{AC}^{ik} \theta_{BC}^{jk} \tag{48}$$

where the superscripts i, j, and k denote specified powers. The parameters θ_{AB}, θ_{AC}, and θ_{BC} in (48) pertain to the partial association between variables A and B (given variable C), between variables A and C (given variable B), and between variables B and C (given variable A), respectively. Model (48) is more parsimonious than Model (47), which is in turn more parsimonious than the usual Model (38) for zero three-factor interaction.

When the three-factor interaction is zero, we can consider the more parsimonious models obtained by replacing one or more of the two-factor parameters in (38) by appropriate terms for the situations where the corresponding partial associations are uniform (as in, for example, Model 47 or 48). Models (47) and (48) are examples of a general class of models pertaining to partial association in the three-way table. In this general class, parameters pertaining to uniform partial association (for example, ϕ in Model 46) can be replaced by more general parameters that can take into account the possible effects of rows, columns, and/or layers on the partial association (see, for example, Clogg, 1980). Similarly, with respect to the general class of models pertaining to conditional association between variables A and B (given variable C), parameters pertaining to uniform conditional association (for example, ϕ_k in Model 42) can be replaced by more general parameters that can take into account the possible effects of rows and/or columns on the conditional association (at level k of variable C).

The methods described in this section for the analysis of the three-factor interaction and the conditional association (and the related partial association) can be developed further (see, for example, Clogg, 1980), and they can be extended in a straightforward way to the analysis of the other relationships listed earlier in the section as topics 3 to 8 in the analysis of the three-way table. These methods for the analysis of the three-way table can be explicated in more detail as we did earlier with respect to the two-way table. The various results presented for the analysis of the two-way and three-way tables can also be extended in a straightforward way to the m-way table.

REFERENCES

AGRESTI, A.
    1980   "Generalized odds ratios for ordinal data." *Biometrics* 36:59–67.
ANDRICH, D.
    1979   "A model for contingency tables having an ordered response classification." *Biometrics* 35:405–415.
ANSCOMBE, F. J.
    1981   *Computing in Statistical Science Through APL*. New York: Springer-Verlag.

ARMITAGE, P.
1955   Tests for linear trends in proportions and frequencies." *Biometrics* 11:375–386.
1971   *Statistical Methods in Medical Research.* Oxford: Blackwell.
BHAPKAR, V. P.
1966   "A note on the equivalence of two test criteria for hypotheses in categorical data." *Journal of American Statistical Association* 61:288–235.
1979   "On tests of marginal symmetry and quasi-symmetry in two and three-dimensional contingency tables." *Biometrics* 35:417–426.
BISHOP, Y., FIENBERG, S. E., AND HOLLAND, P. W.
1975   *Discrete Multivariate Analysis: Theory and Practice.* Cambridge, Mass: M.I.T. Press.
BOCK, D. R.
1975   *Multivariate Statistical Methods in Behavioral Research.* New York: McGraw-Hill.
CAUSSINUS, H.
1965   "Contribution à l'analyse statistique des tableaux de corrélation." *Annales de la Faculté des Sciences de l'Université de Toulouse* 29:77–182.
CLAYTON, D. C.
1974   "Some odds-ratio statistics for the analysis of ordered categorical data." *Biometrika* 61:525–531.
CLOGG, C. C.
* 1980   "Some models for the analysis of association in multiway cross-classifications having ordered categories." Unpublished manuscript.
COX, D. R.
1970   *The Analysis of Binary Data.* London: Methuen.
DUNCAN, O. D.
1979a   "How destination depends on origin in the occupational mobility table." *American Journal of Sociology* 84:793–803.
1979b   "Constrained parameters in a model for categorical data." *Sociological Methods and Research* 8:57–68.
DUNCAN, O. D., AND MCRAE, J. A., JR.
1978   "Multiway contingency analysis with a scaled response or factor." In K. F. Schuessler (Ed.), *Sociological Methodology 1979.* San Francisco: Jossey-Bass.
FIENBERG, S. E.
1977   *The Analysis of Cross-Classified Categorical Data.* Cambridge, Mass: M.I.T. Press.
GART, J. J., AND ZWEIFEL, J. R.
1967   "On the bias of various estimators of the logit and its variance." *Biometrika* 54:181–187.

GOKHALE, D. V., AND KULLBACK, S.
  1978   *The Information in Contingency Tables.* New York: Marcel Dekker.

GOODMAN, L. A.
* 1968   "The analysis of cross-classified data: Independence, quasi-independence, and interactions in contingency tables with or without missing entries." *Journal of American Statistical Association* 69:1091–1131.

  1969   "On partitioning χ^2 and detecting partial association in three-way contingency tables." *Journal of Royal Statistical Society,* series B, 31:486–498.

  1970   "The multivariate analysis of qualitative data: Interactions among multiple classifications." *Journal of American Statistical Association* 65:226–256.

* 1972   "Some multiplicative models for the analysis of cross-classified data." In L. Le Cam and others (Eds.), *Proceedings of Sixth Berkeley Symposium on Mathematical Statistics and Probability.* Berkeley: University of California Press.

  1975   "A new model for scaling response patterns: An application of the quasi-independence concept." *Journal of American Statistical Association* 70:755–768.

  1978   *Analyzing Qualitative/Categorical Data: Log-Linear Models and Latent-Structure Analysis.* Cambridge, Mass.: Abt Books.

* 1979a   "Simple models for the analysis of association in cross-classifications having ordered categories." *Journal of American Statistical Association* 74:537–552.

* 1979b   "Multiplicative models for the analysis of occupational mobility tables and other kinds of cross-classification tables." *American Journal of Sociology* 84:804–819.

* 1979c   "Multiplicative models for square contingency tables with ordered categories." *Biometrika* 66:413–418.

  1979d   "The analysis of qualitative variables using more parsimonious quasi-independence models, scaling models, and latent structures." In R. M. Merton, J. S. Coleman, and P. H. Rossi (Eds.), *Qualitative and Quantitative Social Research: Papers in Honor of Paul F. Lazarsfeld.* New York: Free Press.

* 1979e   "The analysis of dependence in cross-classifications having ordered categories, using log-linear models for frequencies and log-linear models for odds." Unpublished manuscript.

* 1980a   "Association models and the bivariate normal distribution in the analysis of cross-classifications having ordered categories." *Biometrika* 67: in press.

* 1980b   "Association models and canonical correlation in the analysis of
            cross-classifications having ordered categories." *Journal of
            American Statistical Association* 75: in press.

GOODMAN, L. A., AND KRUSKAL, W. H.
  1963   "Measures of association for cross-classifications. III: Approxi-
            mate sampling theory." *Journal of American Statistical Associa-
            tion* 58:310–364.

GRIZZLE, J. E., STARMER, C. F., AND KOCH, G. G.
  1969   "Analysis of categorical data by linear models." *Biometrics*
            25:137–156.

HABERMAN, S. J.
  1974a   "Log-linear models for frequency tables with ordered classifica-
            tions." *Biometrics* 30:589–600.
  1974b   *The Analysis of Frequency Data.* Chicago: University of
            Chicago Press.
  1979   *Analysis of Qualitative Data.* Vol. 2: *New Developments.* New
            York: Academic Press.

HOLMES, M. C., AND WILLIAMS, R. E. O.
  1954   "The distribution of carriers of streptococcus pyogenes among
            2,413 healthy children." *Journal of Hygiene* (Cambridge)
            52:165–179.

IRELAND, C. T., KU, H. H., AND KULLBACK, S.
  1969   "Symmetry and marginal homogeneity of an $r \times r$ contingency
            table." *Journal of American Statistical Association* 64:1323–
            1341.

KENDALL, M. G., AND STUART, A.
  1961   *The Advanced Theory of Statistics.* Vol. 2: *Inference and Rela-
            tionships.* London: Griffin.

KOCH, G. G., AND REINFURT, D. W.
  1971   "The analysis of categorical data from mixed models." *Biomet-
            rics* 27:157–173.

LEHMANN, E. L.
  1959   *Testing Statistical Hypotheses.* New York: Wiley.

MANTEL, M., AND BYAR, D. P.
  1978   "Marginal homogeneity, symmetry, and independence." *Com-
            munications in Statistics: Theory and Methods* A7(10):953–976.

MCCULLAGH, P.
  1978   "A class of parametric models for the analysis of square contin-
            gency tables with ordered categories." *Biometrika* 65:413–418.
  1980   "Regression models for ordinal data." *Journal of Royal Statistical
            Society*, series B, 42:109–142.

NELDER, J.
  1975   *General Linear Interactive Modelling.* Release 2. Oxford: NAG.

PLACKETT, R. L.
1974 *The Analysis of Categorical Data*. London: Griffin.

PLACKETT, R. L., AND PAUL, S. R.
1978 "Dirichlet models for square contingency tables." *Communications in Statistics: Theory and Methods* A7(10):939–952.

STUART, A.
1953 "The estimation and comparison of strengths of association in contingency tables." *Biometrika* 40:105–110.
1955 "A test of homogeneity of the marginal distributions in a two-way classification." *Biometrika* 42:412–416.

TUKEY, J. W.
1977 *Exploratory Data Analysis*. Reading, Mass.: Addison-Wesley.

WEDDERBURN, R. W. M.
1974 "Generalized linear models specified in terms of constraints." *Journal of Royal Statistical Society*, series B, 36:449–454.

WING, J. K.
1962 "Institutionalism in mental hospitals." *British Journal of Social and Clinical Psychology* 1:38–51.

2.
Models for the Joint Distribution
Multiplicative Models for Square Contingency Tables with Ordered Categories

For the analysis of square contingency tables having ordered categories, this paper introduces the diagonals-parameter symmetry model and other related multiplicative models. When these models are applied to the 4×4 table on unaided vision first analysed by Stuart (1953, 1955), a possible explanation is obtained for (i) the 'strange residual pattern' noted by McCullagh (1978), both in his recent analysis of the data using the palindromic symmetry model and in the analysis of the data using the quasisymmetry model as fitted by Plackett (1974, p. 61) and others; (ii) the observed asymmetry in the table; (iii) the inhomogeneity observed between the row marginal, i.e. right eye vision, and the column marginal, left eye vision; and (iv) the observed association between right eye and left eye vision. The models introduced in this paper are included within the general class of multiplicative models considered by Goodman (1972), but they are different from the specific kinds of models considered in that article.

1. INTRODUCTION

The data in Table 1 have been analysed by many statisticians using various statistical models and methods; see, for example, Stuart (1953, 1955), Kendall & Stuart (1961, p. 586), Goodman & Kruskal (1963), Caussinus (1965,) Bhapkar (1966), Ireland, Ku & Kullback (1969), Grizzle, Starmer & Koch (1969), Koch & Reinfurt (1971), Plackett (1974, p. 61), Bishop, Fienberg & Holland (1975, p. 284), Gokhale & Kullback (1978, p. 255) and McCullagh (1978). New insight into these data will be obtained herein with the diagonals-parameter symmetry model and other related multiplicative models. These models are particularly well suited for the analysis of many kinds of square contingency tables having ordered categories.

2. THE DIAGONALS-PARAMETER SYMMETRY MODEL

For the $R \times R$ square contingency table, let π_{ij} denote the probability that an observation will fall in cell (i, j) $(i = 1, ..., R; j = 1, ..., R)$. The usual symmetry model is defined by the condition that

$$\pi_{ij} = \phi_{ij} \quad (i \neq j), \tag{1}$$

where

$$\phi_{ij} = \phi_{ji}. \tag{2}$$

The diagonals-parameter symmetry model will be defined by the condition that

$$\pi_{ij} = \phi_{ij}\delta_k \quad (i \neq j, \ k = i - j), \tag{3}$$

where the ϕ_{ij} satisfy condition (2), and where δ_k denotes a parameter pertaining to the cells

(i, j) for which $i - j = k$, with $k = \pm 1, \ldots, \pm (R - 1)$. Note that the parameter δ_k may depend upon the difference $i - j$, but no prior assumptions are made here about the nature of this dependence. However, without loss of generality, we can delete from (3) the δ_k for $k = -1, \ldots, -(R-1)$; that is, we can set $\delta_k = 1$ for $k = -1, \ldots, -(R-1)$. Thus, the diagonals-parameter symmetry model (3) modifies the usual symmetry model (1) and (2) by intro-ducing $R - 1$ additional parameters, namely, the δ_k for $k = 1, \ldots, R - 1$.

The usual quasisymmetry model also introduced $R - 1$ additional parameters into the symmetry model, and the palindromic symmetry model did this too (McCullagh, 1978). Thus, each of the quasisymmetry, palindromic symmetry, and diagonals-parameter sym-metry models can be tested for goodness of fit by a chi-squared statistic with the same num-ber of degrees of freedom, namely, $\frac{1}{2}(R - 1)(R - 2)$. For the data in Table 1, there are 3 degrees of freedom for testing each of these models, and the chi-squared values obtained, using the likelihood ratio chi-squared statistic, under the three models, are 7·3, 6·2, and 0·50, respectively. The improvement in fit obtained with the model (3) is dramatic.

Table 1. *Unaided distance vision of women: observed frequencies (upper value) and fitted frequencies under the diagonals-parameter symmetry model* (3) *(lower value)*

	Best	Left eye grade		
	Best	Second	Third	Worst
Right eye grade				
Best	1520	266	124	66
	1520·0	269·1	121·4	66·0
Second	234	1512	432	78
	230·9	1512·0	427·3	80·6
Third	117	362	1772	205
	119·6	366·7	1772·0	206·6
Worst	36	82	179	492
	36·0	79·4	177·4	492·0

3. STATISTICAL METHODS FOR THE DIAGONALS-PARAMETER SYMMETRY MODEL

In contrast to the iterative procedures required for the analysis of the quasisymmetry and palindromic symmetry models, the diagonals-parameter symmetry model can be analysed by elementary methods. We next describe these.

With f_{ij} denoting the observed frequency in cell (i, j) of the $R \times R$ table, we introduce now a rectangular table Δ_k defined as follows. The first row of Δ_k consists of $f_{1,1+k}, \ldots, f_{R-k,R}$, and the second row consists of $f_{1+k,1}, \ldots, f_{R,R-k}$. Thus, Δ_k is a $2 \times (R - k)$ table, and there are $R - 2$ such tables, for $k = 1, \ldots, R - 2$. Then the diagonals-parameter symmetry model (3) for the $R \times R$ table is equivalent to the usual model of statistical independence between the row classification and the column classification in each of the two-way tables Δ_k. For the $2 \times (R - k)$ table Δ_k, the usual chi-squared test of independence will have $R - k - 1$ degrees of freedom, and the sum of the corresponding chi-squared statistics, for $k = 1, \ldots, R - 2$, will have $\frac{1}{2}(R - 1)(R - 2)$ degrees of freedom. For the data in Table 1, the chi-squared values obtained for the 2×3 table Δ_1 and the 2×2 table Δ_2 are 0·22 and 0·28, with 2 degrees of freedom and 1 degree of freedom, respectively; and the sum of these chi-squared values is 0·50, with 3 degrees of freedom.

The expected frequencies under the diagonals-parameter symmetry model (3) can also be estimated directly from Δ_k, for $k = 1, \ldots, R - 2$. For the data in Table 1, these estimated expected frequencies are summarized in the table. The 'strange residual pattern' noted by McCullagh (1978), both in his analysis of Table 1 using the palindromic symmetry model and in the analysis using the quasisymmetry model, disappears when the diagonals-parameter symmetry model (3) is used.

The parameter δ_k in the diagonals-parameter symmetry model (3) is simply the odds that an observation will fall in one of the cells (i, j) where $i - j = k$, rather than in one of the cells where $i - j = -k$ for $k = 1, ..., R - 1$. This parameter can be estimated directly from the row marginal of table Δ_k for $k = 1, ..., R - 2$; and δ_{R-1} is estimated simply by f_{R1}/f_{1R}. These are the maximum likelihood estimates of δ_k under the diagonals-parameter symmetry model (3). For the data in Table 1, we obtain $\hat{\delta}_1 = 0 \cdot 86$, $\hat{\delta}_2 = 0 \cdot 99$ and $\hat{\delta}_3 = 0 \cdot 55$.

To test the hypothesis that

$$\delta_k = \delta \quad (k = 1, ..., R - 1), \tag{4}$$

we simply form a $2 \times (R - 1)$ table Δ, with the first row consisting of the numerators used in the calculation of the odds-ratios $\hat{\delta}_k$ and the second row consisting of the corresponding denominators, and we test the usual hypothesis of statistical independence between the row classification and the column classification in table Δ, with $R - 2$ degrees of freedom. For the data in Table 1, there are 2 degrees of freedom in testing hypothesis (4), and the chi-squared value obtained is $6 \cdot 85$. Thus, hypothesis (4) is rejected at the $0 \cdot 05$ level.

The conditional symmetry model considered by McCullagh (1978) and by Bishop et al. (1975, pp. 285–6) is equivalent to the diagonals-parameter symmetry model (3) with condition (4) imposed. For the data in Table 1, we found that condition (4) was rejected, and so the diagonal-parameter symmetry model is also preferable to the conditional symmetry model considered in the earlier literature.

Let X_1 and X_2 denote the row and column variables, respectively. Under the diagonals-parameter symmetry model (3), X_1 is stochastically smaller than X_2 if $\delta_k \leqslant 1$ for every k, X_1 is stochastically larger than X_2 if $\delta_k \geqslant 1$ for every k, and the distribution of X_1 is equal to the distribution of X_2 if $\delta_k = 1$ for every k. Indeed, when $\delta_k = 1$ for all k, we see from (1) and (3) that the symmetry model holds. When some of the δ_k are larger than 1 and some are smaller than 1, then the stochastic ordering between X_1 and X_2, when there is such an ordering, will depend upon the magnitude of the δ_k and ϕ_{ij} in the diagonals-parameter symmetry model (3). For the data in Table 1, we see that $\hat{\delta}_k \leqslant 1$ for every k, and in this case these estimated parameters provide a more detailed explanation for the marginal inhomogeneity and stochastic ordering between X_1 and X_2, a description of how the right eye vision is better than left eye vision. The $\hat{\delta}_k$ can be analysed in the usual ways that odds are analysed; but for brevity we shall not go into these details here.

4. MORE PARSIMONIOUS DIAGONALS-PARAMETER SYMMETRY MODELS

We noted earlier that there were $\frac{1}{2}(R - 1)(R - 2)$ degrees of freedom for testing the diagonals-parameter symmetry model (3); and for that model with condition (4) imposed for every k the number of degrees of freedom will be

$$(R - 2) + \frac{1}{2}(R - 1)(R - 2) = \frac{1}{2}(R + 1)(R - 2).$$

If condition (4) is imposed for a specified subset of the $R - 1$ values of k, where the subset consists of, say, K values for $K \leqslant R - 1$, then the number of degrees of freedom for testing the corresponding model will be

$$(K - 1) + \frac{1}{2}(R - 1)(R - 2) = K + \frac{1}{2}R(R - 3).$$

For example, for the data in Table 1, to test the diagonals-parameter symmetry model with condition (4) imposed for $k = 1$ and 2, the chi-squared value obtained is 2·03, with 4 degrees of freedom. Thus, this more parsimonious diagonals-parameter symmetry model also fits the data well.

When the more parsimonious diagonals-parameter symmetry model described above is applied to Table 1, we obtain the following estimates of the δ_k parameters: $\hat{\delta}_1 = \hat{\delta}_2 = 0.88$, $\hat{\delta}_3 = 0.55$. This model is as easy to interpret as the original diagonals-parameter symmetry model (3), and the interpretation of the parameters δ_k in the original model can be applied here as well. Recall that δ_k is simply the odds that an observation will fall in one of the cells (i, j) where $i - j = k$ rather than in one of the cells where $i - j = -k$ for $k = 1, ..., R-1$.

Instead of imposing on the δ_k conditions of the kind considered earlier in this section, other kinds of conditions could be imposed. Let us consider next, say, the condition that

$$\delta_k = 1, \tag{5}$$

for a specified subset of the $R-1$ values of k, where the subset consists of, say, K values for $K \leqslant R-1$. Then the number of degrees of freedom for testing the diagonals-parameter symmetry model with this condition imposed will be $K + \frac{1}{2}(R-1)(R-2)$. For example, for the data in Table 1, to test the diagonals parameter-symmetry model (3) with condition (5) imposed for $k = 2$, the chi-squared value obtained is 0·52, with 4 degrees of freedom. Thus, this more parsimonious diagonals-parameter symmetry model fits the data well too. When this model is applied to Table 1, we obtain the following estimates of the δ_k parameters: $\hat{\delta}_1 = 0.86$, $\hat{\delta}_2 = 1.00$, $\hat{\delta}_3 = 0.55$.

In closing this section, we note that the kinds of models introduced in the section could be analysed by elementary methods as we did earlier in the analysis of the diagonals-parameter symmetry model (3). The particular numerical results obtained when the more parsimonious models were applied to Table 1 should be interpreted with caution, since the particular conditions imposed were specified after perusal of the data.

5. OTHER RELATED MODELS

The diagonals-parameter symmetry model defined by (3) and (2) did not impose any restrictions on the parameters ϕ_{ij} aside from the symmetry condition (2). Consider next the model defined by the condition that

$$\pi_{ij} = \alpha_i \alpha_j \delta_k \quad (i \neq j, \ k = i - j), \tag{6}$$

where α_i denotes a parameter pertaining to the ith row and the ith column of the $R \times R$ table. Model (6) is a special case of the diagonals-parameter symmetry model in which $\phi_{ij} = \alpha_i \alpha_j$. This model states that, apart from the diagonals parameter in the model, and the entries on the main diagonal, there is 'quasiindependence' between the row classification and column classification in the $R \times R$ table; and each row parameter is equal to the corresponding column parameter. Using methods presented by Goodman (1972), we find that model (6) is more parsimonious than the corresponding diagonals-parameter symmetry model (3) when $R > 4$, but for $R = 4$ and $R = 3$ model (6) and the diagonals-parameter symmetry model (3) are equivalent. Thus, for the data in Table 1, in testing model (6), we obtain the chi-squared value of 0·50, with 3 degrees of freedom.

The result presented above means that the association between right eye vision and left eye vision, which was described in quite different terms by various statisticians analysing these data earlier, can be explained almost entirely by the diagonals parameter in model (6) and the entries on the main diagonal. We noted earlier herein that for these data the asymmetry and marginal inhomogeneity, which was also described in quite different terms by various statisticians, could be explained almost entirely by the diagonals-parameter.

Model (6) is a special case of the diagonals-parameter model introduced by Goodman (1972). That model can be described as follows:

$$\pi_{ij} = \alpha_i \beta_j \delta_k \quad (i \neq j, \ k = i - j), \tag{7}$$

where α_i and β_j denote parameters pertaining to the ith row and the jth column, respectively, of the $R \times R$ table. Model (6) is a special case of model (7) in which $\alpha_i = \beta_i$ for all i.

To test the diagonals-parameter model, the corresponding chi-squared statistic will have $(R^2 - 5R + 5)$ degrees of freedom for $R \geqslant 4$ (Goodman, 1972); and the special case defined by (6) will have $(R-1)(R-3)$ degrees of freedom. When $R = 3$, there will be zero degrees of freedom for testing the diagonals-parameter model (7), and the special case defined by (6) will have 1 degree of freedom. All these models are included within the general class of multiplicative models considered by Goodman (1972), and the statistical methods presented there for the analysis of multiplicative models can be applied to the specific models introduced in the present paper.

Since the diagonals-parameter symmetry model (3) and the model defined by (6) are equivalent when $R = 4$, the results for the analysis of Table 1 can be viewed as an application of the diagonals-parameter model (7) modified by the imposition of the condition $\alpha_i = \beta_i$; and the diagonals-parameter symmetry model (3) can be viewed as a generalized form of this modified diagonals-parameter model (7) when $R > 4$. The relationship between (3) and (7) can be directly extended to the other specific kinds of models introduced by Goodman (1972). Thus, for example, corresponding to the triangle-parameter model of Goodman (1972), we could consider here both the triangle-parameter symmetry model and the model obtained when the condition $\alpha_i = \beta_i$ is imposed upon the triangle-parameter model. We shall not go into these details here. The interested reader is referred to the results of Goodman (1972) pertaining both to specific kinds of multiplicative models and to the general class of multiplicative models, and to related results of, say, Haberman (1974a, p. 215; 1974b).

REFERENCES

BHAPKAR, V. P. (1966). A note on the equivalence of two test criteria for hypotheses in categorical data. *J. Am. Statist. Assoc.* **61**, 228–35.

BISHOP, Y., FIENBERG, S. E. & HOLLAND, P. W. (1975). *Discrete Multivariate Analysis: Theory and Practice.* Cambridge, Mass: Massachusetts Institute of Technology Press.

CAUSSINUS, H. (1965). Contribution à l'analyse statistique des tableaux de corrélation. *Annales de la Faculté des Sciences de l'Université de Toulouse* **29**, 77–182.

GOKHALE, D. V. & KULLBACK, S. (1978). *The Information in Contingency Tables.* New York: Marcel Dekker.

* GOODMAN, L. A. (1972). Some multiplicative models for the analysis of cross classified data. *Proc. 6th Berkeley Symp.* **1**, 649–96.

GOODMAN, L. A. & KRUSKAL, W. H. (1963). Measures of association for cross-classifications. III: Approximate sampling theory. *J. Am. Statist. Assoc.* **58**, 310–64.

GRIZZLE, J. E., STARMER, C. F. & KOCH, G. G. (1969). Analysis of categorical data by linear models. *Biometrics* **25**, 137–56.

HABERMAN, S. J. (1974a). *The Analysis of Frequency Data.* University of Chicago Press.

HABERMAN, S. J. (1974b). Log-linear models for frequency tables with ordered classifications. *Biometrics* **30**, 589–600.

IRELAND, C. T., KU, H. H. & KULLBACK, S. (1969). Symmetry and marginal homogeneity of an $r \times r$ contingency table. *J. Am. Statist. Assoc.* **64**, 1323–41.

KENDALL, M. G. & STUART, A. (1961). *The Advanced Theory of Statistics*, Vol. 2. London: Griffin.

KOCH, G. G. & REINFURT, D. W. (1971). The analysis of categorical data from mixed models. *Biometrics* **27**, 157–73.

MCCULLAGH, P. (1978). A class of parametric models for the analysis of square contingency tables with ordered categories. *Biometrika* **65**, 413–8.

PLACKETT, R. L. (1974). *The Analysis of Categorical Data*. London: Griffin.

STUART, A. (1953). The estimation and comparison of strengths of association in contingency tables. *Biometrika* **40**, 105–10.

STUART, A. (1955). A test for homogeneity of the marginal distributions in a two-way classification. *Biometrika* **42**, 412–6.

3.
Models of Dependence

The Analysis of Dependence in Cross-Classifications Having Ordered Categories, Using Log-Linear Models for Frequencies and Log-Linear Models for Odds

To analyse the dependence of a qualitative (dichotomous or polytomous) response variable upon one or more qualitative explanatory variables, log-linear models for frequencies are compared with log-linear models for odds, when the categories of the response variable are ordered and the categories of each explanatory variable may be either ordered or unordered. The log-linear models for odds express the odds (or log odds) pertaining to adjacent response categories in terms of appropriate multiplicative (or additive) factors. These models include the 'null log-odds model', the 'uniform log-odds model', the 'parallel log-odds model', and other log-linear models for the odds. With these models, the dependence of the response variable (with ordered categories) can be analysed in a manner analogous to the usual multiple regression analysis and related analysis of variance and analysis of covariance. Application of log-linear models for the odds sheds light on earlier applications of log-linear models for the frequencies in contingency tables with ordered categories.

1. Introduction

When the categories of a qualitative (dichotomous or polytomous) response variable are ordered, the odds for adjacent response categories, and how these odds depend upon one or more qualitative explanatory variables, can be of considerable interest. We shall consider models that express these odds in terms of appropriate multiplicative factors pertaining to the joint categories of the qualitative explanatory variables, or, equivalently, models that express the corresponding log odds in terms of appropriate additive factors. These log-linear models for the odds can be applied in situations in which the response categories are ordered and the categories of each explanatory variable may be either ordered or unordered.

The log-linear models for the odds are related to certain log-linear models for the frequencies in contingency tables with ordered categories. Using the models considered here for the odds, we shall reanalyse two sets of data that have been analysed previously with log-linear models used for the frequencies; our findings shed additional light on the earlier analyses and on the data.

The models considered here for the odds can be described in rather simple terms, being somewhat analogous to the usual models used in multiple regression analysis, the analysis of variance and the analysis of covariance. They also give further insight into the meaning of the related log-linear models for the frequencies.

There are a great many log-linear models for the frequencies in contingency tables (see, for example, Goodman, 1970; Haberman, 1974a). With the introduction of odds log-linear models, we exclude from consideration all those frequency log-linear models that are not relevant when one of the variables in the contingency table is a response variable and the other variables are possible explanatory or regressor variables, and we also focus attention

Table 1

Length of stay in hospital for 132 *schizophrenic patients, classified by visiting patterns that had been ascribed in the hospital*

Visiting pattern	Length of stay in hospital			
	2–10 years	10–20 years	20 years or more	Total
Received visitors regularly or patient went home	43	16	3	62
Received visitors infrequently; patient did not go home	6	11	10	27
Never received visitors; patient did not go home	9	18	16	43

upon a particular subset of the relevant log-linear models that is useful in many situations where the categories of the response variable are ordered.

To illustrate how the models considered here can be used, we shall apply them to reanalyse Tables 1 and 2. Table 1 shows the length of stay in hospital for 132 schizophrenic patients classified according to the visiting patterns that had been ascribed in hospital; Table 2 shows the number of deaths in 657 litters of mice classified by litter size and treatment. Table 1 was analysed by Wing (1962), Haberman (1974a) and Fienberg (1977). Table 2 was analysed by Kastenbaum and Lamphiear (1959), Darroch (1962), Plackett (1962), Goodman (1963, 1964), Ku and Kullback (1968), Berkson (1968, 1972), Grizzle, Starmer and Koch (1969), Koch, Tolley and Freeman (1976), Whittaker and Aitkin (1978), Paul (1979), and by P. McCullagh in a paper presented at the 42nd Session of the International Statistical Institute, Manilla, 1979. Some new insights into these data will be obtained here.

In Table 1 we view the patient's length of stay in hospital as the response variable and his/ her visiting pattern as a possible explanatory or regressor variable; in Table 2 the number of deaths in a litter is the response variable and the litter size and treatment are explanatory variables. Table 1 is a two-way cross-classification, and Table 2 is three-way. The models and methods considered here can be applied to an m-way cross-classification ($m = 2, 3, \ldots$) when the categories of the response variable are ordered.

2. Log-Linear Models for Frequencies and Log-Linear Models for Odds

First consider a two-way $I \times J$ contingency table for two qualitative variables, say, A and B, where A is an explanatory variable and B is the response variable. Let f_{ij} denote the observed

Table 2

Number of deaths in 657 *litters of mice classified by litter size and treatment*

Litter size	Treatment	Number of deaths			
		0	1	2 or more	Total
7	A	58	11	5	74
	B	75	19	7	101
8	A	49	14	10	73
	B	58	17	8	83
9	A	33	18	15	66
	B	45	22	10	77
10	A	15	13	15	43
	B	39	22	18	79
11	A	4	12	17	33
	B	5	15	8	28

frequency in the ith category of Variable A and in the jth category of Variable B ($i = 1, 2,$ $\ldots, I$; $j = 1, 2, \ldots, J$), and let F_{ij} denote the corresponding expected frequency under some model. The log-linear models for the F_{ij} state that the F_{ij} are additive in the systematic effects of A, B and their interactions, when measured on a logarithmic scale:

$$\log F_{ij} = \theta + \lambda_i^A + \lambda_j^B + \lambda_{ij}^{AB}, \tag{1}$$

where log denotes the natural logarithm (see, for example, Goodman, 1970). The λ parameters are required to satisfy appropriate constraints to ensure estimability. When the categories of, say, A are ordered, these categories (levels) can sometimes be treated as quantitative, with the corresponding λ parameters, λ_i^A and λ_{ij}^{AB}, expressed as functions of the level i ($i = 1, 2, \ldots,$ I) that can take account of linear, quadratic and higher-order effects (see, for example, Haberman, 1974a). When the categories (levels) of B are ordered, a similar remark applies also to the corresponding λ parameters, λ_j^B and λ_{ij}^{AB}.

The reader will appreciate that when *explanatory* factors have ordered levels there may be advantages in treating the factor levels as quantitative; how to deal with the situation in which *response* variables have ordered levels is less obvious and we shall consider this here. With log-linear models we can directly consider situations in which response variables and/or explanatory variables have ordered levels.

For adjacent categories, say j and $j + 1$, pertaining to the response variable B, we define as follows the odds $\Omega_{ij}^{A\bar{B}}$ based upon the expected frequencies:

$$\Omega_{ij}^{A\bar{B}} = F_{ij}/F_{i,j+1}, \qquad j = 1, 2, \ldots, J - 1; \tag{2}$$

and we let $\Psi_{ij}^{A\bar{B}}$ denote the natural logarithm of $\Omega_{ij}^{A\bar{B}}$ (i.e. the log odds). We next consider three simple models for the log odds $\Psi_{ij}^{A\bar{B}}$, namely, the 'null log-odds model', the 'uniform log-odds model', and the 'parallel log-odds model'. When the categories of B are ordered, use of these simple models will often turn out to be worthwhile in data analysis.

The null log-odds model is

$$\Psi_{ij}^{A\bar{B}} = 0, \qquad j = 1, 2, \ldots, J - 1; \tag{3}$$

the uniform log-odds model is

$$\Psi_{ij}^{A\bar{B}} = \psi_i^A, \qquad j = 1, 2, \ldots, J - 1, \tag{4}$$

where the ψ_i^A parameters are unspecified; and the parallel log-odds model is

$$\Psi_{ij}^{A\bar{B}} = \psi_i^A + \psi_j^B, \qquad j = 1, 2, \ldots, J - 1, \tag{5}$$

where the ψ_j^B parameters satisfy an appropriate constraint. From (1) and (2), we see that Model (3) is equivalent to Model (1) with

$$\lambda_j^B = 0 \quad \text{and} \quad \lambda_{ij}^{AB} = 0, \qquad j = 1, 2, \ldots, J. \tag{6}$$

Similarly, we find that Model (4) is equivalent to Model (1) with

$$\lambda_j^B = \{j - \tfrac{1}{2}(J + 1)\}\mu \quad \text{and} \quad \lambda_{ij}^{AB} = \{j - \tfrac{1}{2}(J + 1)\}\mu_i^A, \qquad j = 1, 2, \ldots, J, \tag{7}$$

where the parameter μ is unspecified and the μ_i^A parameters satisfy an appropriate constraint; and Model (5) is equivalent to Model (1) with

$$\lambda_{ij}^{AB} = \{j - \tfrac{1}{2}(J + 1)\}\mu_i^A, \qquad j = 1, 2, \ldots, J. \tag{8}$$

Restrictions of the kind described by (7) and (8) were introduced in the log-linear model framework by Haberman (1974a), and were also discussed by, for example, Fienberg (1977). With the log-odds models introduced in the present paper, namely Models (3), (4) and (5), we obtain different formulations of the models that may be more easily understood: for example, compare (4) and (7). These formulations will yield some new results for the models, for example, Equation (9) below, and also afford other advantages that will be considered later.

From (3) and (6) we see that the null log-odds model (3) is equivalent to the condition that

$$F_{i1} = F_{i2} = \cdots = F_{iJ}.$$

In other words, (3) states that the categories of Variable B are conditionally equiprobable, when Variable A is in the ith category (Goodman, 1970). We now describe further the uniform and parallel log-odds models (4) and (5).

Model (4) states that the log odds $\Psi_{ij}^{A\bar{B}}$ are equal for $j = 1, 2, \ldots, J - 1$. This is equivalent to the condition that $\Omega_{ij}^{A\bar{B}} = \omega_i^A$ for $j = 1, 2, \ldots, J - 1$, which is, in turn, equivalent to the condition that

$$F_{ij} = F_{i1}(\omega_i^A)^{1-j}, \qquad j = 1, 2, \ldots, J. \tag{9}$$

Thus, the uniform log-odds model (4) states that the conditional probability distribution for B is the truncated geometric, when A is in the ith category. (When $\omega_i^A \geqslant 1$, the geometric distribution is defined with the levels of B numbered consecutively from $j = 1$ to $j = J$; and when $\omega_i^A < 1$, the distribution is defined with the levels numbered in reverse order.) When all $\omega_i^A \geqslant 1$ ($i = 1, 2, \ldots, I$) or all $\omega_i^A \leqslant 1$ ($i = 1, 2, \ldots, I$), if the levels of Variable A are ordered according to the magnitudes of the ω_i^A, the expected frequencies in the $I \times J$ table will be isotropic (see, for example, Yule and Kendall, 1950, p. 57; Goodman, 1979, 1981a).

The parallel log-odds model (5) states that the effect of the ith level of A on the log odds $\Psi_{ij}^{A\bar{B}}$ is the same for each value of j ($j = 1, 2, \ldots, J - 1$). When the levels of A are ordered and the ψ_i^A parameter in (5) is, say, a linear function of the level i with slope α, then the log odds $\Psi_{ij}^{A\bar{B}}$ can be described by parallel lines with slope α. (When $J = 2$, the parallel and uniform log-odds models reduce simply to a model for the $\Psi_{i1}^{A\bar{B}}$.) From Model (5), we obtain as special cases the uniform log-odds model (when $\psi_j^B = 0$, for $j = 1, 2, \ldots, J - 1$), the null log-odds model (when $\psi_i^A = 0$ and $\psi_j^B = 0$), and the usual model of statistical independence between A and B (when $\psi_i^A = \psi$, for $i = 1, 2, \ldots, I$).

With the log odds $\Psi_{ij}^{A\bar{B}}$ defined in terms of adjacent categories for the response variable B, the analysis of these log odds will take into account the ordering of these categories. When the categories of the explanatory variable A are not ordered, we use the usual parameterization of the additive effects as in the usual two-way analysis of variance. When the categories of A are ordered, we can use instead a corresponding set of parameters that will take this ordering into account: for example, parameters that pertain to linear, quadratic and higher-order effects can be used. However, in some situations, such as when there is a plateau effect or some similar effect, these parameters may not be particularly helpful and alternative formulations will then be preferable.

The uniform log-odds model (4) is analogous to a one-way analysis-of-variance model applied to the $\Psi_{ij}^{A\bar{B}}$, with $J - 1$ replications ($j = 1, 2, \ldots, J - 1$) in the ith category of A. Similarly, when the A effect is linear in the uniform log-odds model, then this model is analogous to a corresponding simple linear regression model with $J - 1$ replications at Level i of A. The parallel log-odds model (5) includes the ψ_j^B effect ($j = 1, 2, \ldots, J - 1$) in order to distinguish between the different replications. We could also introduce into Model (5) a row × column interaction effect ψ_{ij}^{AB}, but for the sake of simplicity we postpone consideration of this until later.

The log odds $\Psi_{ij}^{A\bar{B}}$ can be viewed as entries in a $I \times (J - 1)$ two-way table, and a test of the parallel log-odds model (5) is analogous to a test of the hypothesis that the row × column interaction effect is zero in the $I \times (J - 1)$ table. Thus, there will be $(I - 1)(J - 2)$ degrees of freedom (df) in testing this model. Similarly, a test of the uniform log-odds model (4) is analogous to a test of the hypothesis that the $J - 1$ entries $\Psi_{ij}^{A\bar{B}}$ in the ith row are equal to ψ_i^A ($i = 1, 2, \ldots, I$), and so there will be $I(J - 2)$ df in testing this model. Table 3 gives the

Table 3
Degrees of freedom for testing odds models applied to the $I \times J$
contingency table

Odds models	Degrees of freedom
Parallel log-odds models	
With full A effect	$(I-1)(J-2)$
With linear A effect	$IJ-I-J$
With null A effect	$(I-1)(J-1)$
Uniform log-odds models	
With full A effect	$I(J-2)$
With linear A effect	$IJ-I-2$
With null A effect	$IJ-I-1$
Null log-odds model	
At all I levels of A	$I(J-1)$

degrees of freedom used in testing the models considered in this section. Note that there are $J-2$ more degrees of freedom in testing the uniform log-odds models than in testing the corresponding parallel log-odds models; and that the maximum number of degrees of freedom is used in testing the null log-odds model.

The class of log-odds models considered here differs from the class of association models considered by Goodman (1979). The null and uniform log-odds models are not equivalent to association models: the fitted marginal totals for the response variable will usually not equal the corresponding observed marginal totals under the null and uniform log-odds models. On the other hand, Model (5) can be expressed in a form equivalent to the row-effect association model of Goodman (1979); and when the parameter ψ_i^A in Model (5) is a linear function of the level i, the model thus obtained can be expressed in a form equivalent to the uniform association model. (For further details on the relationship between log-odds models and association models, see Goodman, 1981b.) The models given by McCullagh (1980) are different from the log-odds models considered here and the association models of Goodman (1979).

In the analysis of two-way contingency tables, it will often be sufficient to consider log-odds models of the kind described above; and in the analysis of m-way contingency tables ($m = 3, 4, \ldots$), it will often be sufficient to consider straightforward extensions of these simple models. Our analyses of Tables 1 and 2 will provide examples of the use of these models.

3. The Analysis of Table 1

In Table 4 we present the values of the goodness-of-fit chi square and the likelihood-ratio chi square obtained by applying the log-odds models introduced in §2 to the data in Table 1. Additional models referred to in the bottom part of Table 4 will be discussed later in this section.

The models in the first two parts of Table 4 are equivalent to models presented by Haberman (1974a) for these data, but his development of these models was expressed in different terms than those used here: he considered frequency log-linear models, some of which are irrelevant in the present context. Within the class of models applied by Haberman to Table 1, the most parsimonious model that was not rejected yielded a likelihood-ratio chi square value of 3.20, with 3 df; this model is equivalent to the uniform log-odds model (4) with full A effect. This model was also described by Fienberg (1977) in terms similar to those used by Haberman (1974a).

In the third part of Table 4, we consider the null log-odds model applied at all three levels

Table 4

Chi square values for log-odds models applied to the data in Table 1

Odds models	Degrees of freedom	Goodness-of-fit chi square	Likelihood-ratio chi square
Parallel log-odds models			
With full A effect	2	0.02	0.02
With linear A effect	3	7.31	7.12
With null A effect	4	35.17	38.35
Uniform log-odds models			
With full A effect	3	3.26	3.20
With linear A effect	4	8.97	9.48
With null A effect	5	34.51	38.60
Null log-odds models			
At Levels 1, 2, 3 of A	6	44.96	48.24
At Levels 2 and 3 of A	4	4.67	5.00
Additional log-odds models			
Parallel log-odds Model I	3	0.03	0.03
Parallel log-odds Model II	4	0.19	0.19
Uniform log-odds Model I	4	3.27	3.20
Uniform log-odds Model II	5	5.46	5.81

of A, and also the corresponding model applied only at the second and third levels. The improvement in fit obtained with the latter model is dramatic. This model states simply that the classes of the response variable, B, are conditionally equiprobable when the explanatory variable, A, is either at Level 2 or Level 3. The model is parsimonious (with 4 df) and fits the data in Table 1. This model can also be described as follows: it states that (i) the effects of A on the $\Psi_{ij}^{A\bar{B}}$ are equal at Levels 2 and 3, (ii) the $\Psi_{21}^{A\bar{B}}$ and $\Psi_{31}^{A\bar{B}}$ are equal to zero, and (iii) the $\Psi_{22}^{A\bar{B}}$ and $\Psi_{32}^{A\bar{B}}$ are equal to zero. Additional insight into the data in Table 1 can be obtained by applying Conditions (i), (ii) and (iii) separately to the log-odds models considered earlier. Some of the results thus obtained are summarized briefly in the fourth part of Table 4.

Parallel log-odds Models I and II in Table 4 were obtained by applying Conditions (i) and (iii), respectively, to the parallel log-odds model with full A effect; the uniform log-odds Models I and II were obtained similarly from the corresponding uniform log-odds model. The uniform log-odds Model II states simply that the uniform log-odds model applies at Level 1 of Variable A, and the null log-odds model applies at Levels 2 and 3 of A.

From the chi square values in Table 4, we see that there are a number of log-odds models that fit the data in Table 1. Comparison of these chi square values will shed further light on the data. For example, comparison of the chi square value for the uniform log-odds model with full A effect (with 3 df) and the corresponding value for the uniform log-odds Model II (with 5 df) indicates that the former model can be made more parsimonious by using the null log-odds model at Levels 2 and 3 of A. A similar kind of comparison can be made with the parallel log-odds models.

If the A effect in Table 1 is viewed only in terms of the usual polynomial components (i.e. linear and quadratic effects), then the full A effect cannot be simplified further since the quadratic (nonlinear) component cannot be ignored in this case. All of the earlier literature on this topic considered the effects of the explanatory variable (or variables) only in terms of the usual polynomial components. However, our analysis of Table 1 demonstrates that, if we do not limit consideration to these components, then more parsimonious models can be obtained in some cases.

Various methods can be applied to choose among the log-odds models in Table 4 that fit the data; and the conclusions reached will depend upon the particular selection method used and the particular level of significance specified (Goodman, 1971; Haberman, 1974a; Spjøtvoll, 1977; Aitkin, 1980; Atkinson, 1980, and the related literature cited). The method of model selection is still a disputed subject; and for the sake of brevity, we shall not pursue this here. The interested reader will find that Table 4 provides a concise summary of the information used by the various methods of selection.

4. The Analysis of Table 2

Table 1 is a two-way table, and now we shall consider the three-way table, Table 2.

We first introduce appropriate notation. Consider the three-way $I \times J \times K$ contingency table pertaining to three qualitative varibles, say A, B and C, where A and B are explanatory variables and C is a response variable. Let f_{ijk} denote the observed frequency in the ith category of A, the jth category of B, and kth category of C ($i = 1, 2, \ldots, I$; $j = 1, 2. \ldots, J$; $k = 1, 2, \ldots, K$), and let F_{ijk} denote the corresponding expected frequency under some model. The usual log-linear models for the F_{ijk} can be expressed as

$$\log F_{ijk} = \theta + \lambda_i^A + \lambda_j^B + \lambda_k^C + \lambda_{ij}^{AB} + \lambda_{ik}^{AC} + \lambda_{jk}^{BC} + \lambda_{ijk}^{ABC}; \tag{10}$$

see Goodman (1970) and Haberman (1974a).

For adjacent categories, say k and $k + 1$, pertaining to the response variable, C, we define the odds $\Omega_{ijk}^{AB\bar{C}}$ based upon the expected frequencies as

$$\Omega_{ijk}^{AB\bar{C}} = F_{ijk}/F_{i,j,k+1}, \qquad k = 1, 2, \ldots, K - 1, \tag{11}$$

and we let $\Psi_{ijk}^{AB\bar{C}}$ denote the natural logarithm of $\Omega_{ijk}^{AB\bar{C}}$, i.e. the log odds. We next consider simple models for $\Psi_{ijk}^{AB\bar{C}}$.

The parallel log-odds model for $\Psi_{ijk}^{AB\bar{C}}$ is simply

$$\Psi_{ijk}^{AB\bar{C}} = \psi_{ij}^{AB} + \psi_k^C, \qquad k = 1, 2, \ldots, K - 1, \tag{12}$$

where the ψ_{ij}^{AB} parameters are unspecified and the ψ_k^C parameters satisfy an appropriate constraint. [Compare (12) with (5).] From Model (12) we obtain as special cases the uniform log-odds model (when $\psi_k^C = 0$ for $k = 1, 2, \ldots, K - 1$), the null log-odds model (when $\psi_k^C = 0$ and $\psi_{ij}^{AB} = 0$), and the usual model of statistical independence between the response variable, C, and the joint explanatory variable, (A, B) (when $\psi_{ij}^{AB} = \psi$ for $i = 1, 2, \ldots, I$, $j = 1, 2, \ldots, J$). We could also introduce into Model (12) the interaction effects ψ_{ik}^{AC}, ψ_{jk}^{BC} and ψ_{ijk}^{ABC}, but for the sake of simplicity this is considered later.

From (10) and (11), we see that the parallel log-odds model (12) is equivalent to Model (10) with

$$\lambda_{ik}^{AC} = \{k - \tfrac{1}{2}(K + 1)\}\mu_i^A, \quad \lambda_{jk}^{BC} = \{k - \tfrac{1}{2}(K + 1)\}\mu_j^B$$

$$\text{and} \quad \lambda_{ijk}^{ABC} = \{k - \tfrac{1}{2}(K + 1)\}\mu_{ij}^{AB}, \qquad k = 1, 2, \ldots, K, \tag{13}$$

where the μ parameters satisfy appropriate constraints. [Compare (13) with (8).] Similarly, we find that the uniform log-odds model obtained from (12) with $\psi_k^C = 0$ is equivalent to Model (10) with the λ_{ik}^{AC}, λ_{jk}^{BC} and λ_{ijk}^{ABC} parameters satisfying (13) and with the λ_k^C parameter satisfying the additional condition

$$\lambda_k^C = \{k - \tfrac{1}{2}(K + 1)\}\mu, \qquad k = 1, 2, \ldots, K. \tag{14}$$

[Compare (13) and (14) with (7).]

The parallel log-odds model (12) can be rewritten as

$$\Psi_{ijk}^{AB\bar{C}} = \psi + \psi_i^A + \psi_j^B + \psi_{ij}^{AB} + \psi_k^C, \tag{15}$$

where the parameters in (15) satisfy appropriate constraints. Thus, we see that the uniform log-odds model obtained from (15) when $\psi_k^C = 0$ is analogous to a two-way analysis-of-variance model applied to the $\Psi_{ijk}^{AB\bar{C}}$, with $K - 1$ replications ($k = 1, 2, \ldots, K - 1$) in each category of the corresponding two-way table. Similarly, when the categories of A are ordered and the parameters ψ_i^A and ψ_{ij}^{AB} are linear in i, then the uniform log-odds model is analogous to a corresponding analysis-of-covariance model with $K - 1$ replications at Level i of A in the jth category of B. The parallel log-odds model (15) includes the ψ_k^C effect ($k = 1, 2, \ldots$, $K - 1$) in order to distinguish between the different replications.

The log odds $\Psi_{ijk}^{AB\bar{C}}$ can be viewed as entries in an $IJ \times (K - 1)$ two-way table, and a test of the parallel log-odds model (15), with full A, B and $A \times B$ effects, is analogous to a test of the hypothesis that the row $\times$ column interaction is zero in the $IJ \times (K - 1)$ table. Thus, there will be $(IJ - 1)(K - 2)$ df for testing this model. This result for the parallel log-odds model associated with the $I \times J \times K$ contingency table is a direct extension of the corresponding result in Table 3 for the parallel log-odds model (with full A effect) associated with the $I \times J$ contingency table. The other results in Table 3 for the various log-odds models pertaining to the $I \times J$ contingency table can also be directly extended to the log-odds models for the $I \times J \times K$ contingency table.

Table 5 gives the chi square values obtained when some log-odds models are applied to Table 2. In Table 5, the chi square values obtained for the parallel log-odds model M_1 indicate that this model fits the data, and the corresponding values obtained for the uniform log-odds model M_1' indicate that this more parsimonious model also fits these data. The remaining models in Table 5 (viz. $M_2 - M_5$ and $M_2' - M_5'$) are directly analogous to models used in the usual analysis of covariance, with the categories of A viewed as ordered. Since, in Table 2, B is dichotomous, the linear B effect is equivalent to the full B effect. In Table 5, for M_2 and M_2', the slope of the A effect can differ in each category of B since the models include

Table 5

Chi square values for log-odds models applied to the data in Table 2 and in a modified form of Table 2

Odds models	Degrees of freedom	Goodness-of-fit chi square	Likelihood-ratio chi square
For Table 2			
Parallel log-odds models			
M_1: Full A, B and $A \times B$ effects	9	11.15	10.57
M_2: Linear A, B and $A \times B$ effects	15	12.26	12.01
M_3: Linear A and B, and null $A \times B$ effects	16	15.39	15.12
M_4: Linear A, and null B and $A \times B$ effects	17	20.10	20.07
M_5: Null A, B and $A \times B$ effects	18	107.01	107.02
Uniform log-odds models			
M_1': Full A, B and $A \times B$ effects	10	12.02	11.71
M_2': Linear, A, B and $A \times B$ effects	16	13.28	13.21
M_3': Linear A and B, and null $A \times B$ effects	17	16.60	16.43
M_4': Linear A, and null B and $A \times B$ effects	18	21.77	21.57
M_5': Null A, B and $A \times B$ effects	19	119.29	113.64
For modified Table 2			
Parallel log-odds models			
M_1: Full A, B and $A \times B$ effects	8	3.88	3.81
M_2: Linear A, B and $A \times B$ effects	13	4.21	4.22
M_3: Linear A and B, and null $A \times B$ effects	14	7.91	8.24
M_4: Linear A, and null B and $A \times B$ effects	15	12.21	13.01
M_5: Null A, B and $A \times B$ effects	16	87.95	86.72
Uniform log-odds models			
M_1': Full A, B and $A \times B$ effects	9	6.64	6.67
M_2': Linear A, B and $A \times B$ effects	14	7.07	7.10
M_3': Linear A and B, and null $A \times B$ effects	15	11.19	11.35
M_4': Linear A, and null B and $A \times B$ effects	16	16.28	16.40
M_5': Null A, B and $A \times B$ effects	17	105.22	95.84

an $A \times B$ interaction effect; for M_3 and M_3', the slope of the A effect is the same in each category of B since the $A \times B$ interaction effect is null in these models; etc. These models can be used, as in the usual analysis of covariance, to test whether the $A \times B$ interaction is null, whether the B effect is null, etc.

None of the log-odds models in Table 5 are equivalent to any of the models applied to these data by Whittaker and Aitkin (1978), except for the parallel log-odds model with null effects, which is, in turn, equivalent to the model that states that Variable C is statistically independent of the joint variable (A, B). The log-odds models in Table 5 are easy to interpret and are particularly well-suited for the analysis of many kinds of contingency tables. They are also more parsimonious than the corresponding models considered by Whittaker and Aitkin.

The models that were applied by these authors to the data in Table 2 do not take account of the fact that the categories of the response variable in this table are ordered. When this ordering is taken into account, the models considered by Whittaker and Aitkin can be replaced in this case by the log-odds models introduced here, and greater parsimony is obtained.

Further examination of Table 2 would lead some researchers to consider the possibility that entries in the last row of the table (i.e. litter size of 11, Treatment B) may be aberrant, and so we have included in the bottom part of Table 5 a summary of the results obtained when Table 2, modified by the deletion of the last row, is analysed. The difference between the chi square value obtained for, say, the parallel log-odds model (with full effects) applied to Table 2 and the corresponding value obtained with the modified Table 2 can be used to test whether the entries in the last row of Table 2 are significantly different from those expected under the model, with the assumption that the model holds true for the modified table. Using the likelihood-ratio chi square values, we obtain a difference of 6.76 (i.e. 10.57 − 3.81) with 9 − 8 = 1 df. For some different but related results, using models that are different from those introduced here, see McCullagh's 1979 paper presented at Manilla. A test based on the difference in the chi square value obtained with Table 2 and the corresponding value obtained with the modified Table 2 would not have the usual level of statistical significance if the deletion of the last row in Table 2 was data-based. The assessment of this difference should take account of whatever procedure was used in determining the modified form of Table 2.

Some researchers, in examining Table 2, may also wish to consider log-odds models that are more general than the parallel log-odds model (15) [viz. models in which the interaction effects ψ_{ik}^{AC}, ψ_{jk}^{BC} and ψ_{ijk}^{ABC} may be introduced into (15)]; and we shall comment briefly on this now.

The various parallel log-odds models in Table 5 could be compared with the corresponding models obtained when the related ψ interaction effects are inserted into the model in order to see whether the inclusion of the additional interaction effects might lead to a real improvement in the fit of the model to the data. This can be done, in part, by comparing the chi square values presented in Table 5 for these models with the values presented by Whittaker and Aitkin (1978) for the corresponding models that include the additonal effects. These comparisons indicate that the additional effects do not provide a real improvement in fit.

There are a great many log-linear models for the frequencies in a multiway contingency table. In many situations in which the categories of the response variable are ordered, it will be sufficient to consider only those models in which the λ interaction effects between explanatory variables and the response variable are linear with respect to the categories of the response variable, and those models in which the main effect λ for the response variable is also linear [see (13) and (14)]. These models are simply the parallel and uniform log-odds models.

With the approach introduced here, the analysis of the contingency table could begin in some cases with the parallel log-odds model with the full effects of the explanatory variables [see (12)], while in other cases it could begin with a more parsimonious model. For example, in the analysis of Table 1, we could begin with the null log-odds models discussed in §3; and in the analysis of Table 2, we could begin, as with the usual sequence of models tested in the analysis of covariance, by considering in turn, say, Models M_2, M_3, . . . , in Table 5. If the parallel log-odds model with the full effects of the explanatory variables does not fit the data, we would then consider the more general log-odds models obtained by the introduction of additional ψ interaction effects into Model (15) as indicated earlier. Alternatively, we could begin with an analysis of the more general log-odds models, and then determine whether the models thus obtained can be replaced by the more parsimonious parallel or uniform log-odds models. The more general log-odds models will be equivalent to log-linear models in which the λ interaction effects [see (1) and (10)] between the explanatory variables and the response variable are not linear with respect to the categories of the response variable. Even with these more general log-linear models, it may still be illuminating to interpret them in terms of log-odds models pertaining to adjacent categories of the response variable. All of these models can be analysed using general computer programs for log-linear models (Haberman, 1974a, 1974b; Baker and Nelder, 1978).

Before closing this section, we note that, if the general computer program GLIM (Release 3) (Baker and Nelder, 1978) is applied to analyse the models considered in this paper, there are small discrepancies between the generalized Pearson chi square values obtained with GLIM and the corresponding goodness-of-fit chi square values presented in Tables 4 and 5. In this paper, the Pearson goodness-of-fit chi square values were obtained with the usual formula [viz. the sum of the (observed–fitted)^2/fitted], and these values are essentially the same as those obtained by computing the sum of the squared residuals (with the residuals obtained from Program DISPLAY of GLIM 3); but they are slightly different from the generalized Pearson chi square values (computed in Program FITMOD of GLIM 3). Although the GLIM 3 Manual (Baker and Nelder, 1978, p. 6) states that the generalized Pearson chi square is the sum of squares of the standardized residuals, this statement is not, strictly speaking, correct (see Program FITMOD of GLIM 3).

5. The Conditional Distribution of the Response Variable

When the conditional distribution of a polytomous response variable is considered at each joint category of the explanatory variables (with the full effects of the explanatory variables included), in the uniform log-odds model the usual multinomial distribution at each joint category is replaced by a distribution having a single parameter, namely, the truncated geometric distribution, and the parallel log-odds model introduces some additional parameters. For the response variables in Tables 1 and 2, we found that the uniform and parallel log-odds models fit these data well. We shall now comment further on the conditional distribution of the response variable in Table 2.

To describe this conditional distribution, Koch, Tolley and Freeman (KTF) (1976) proposed the binomial model, where the parameter P is the probability that a given mouse will die. They noted that this model did not satisfactorily characterize the data, but they nevertheless used the parameter defined by the model to analyse these data. In this model the usual multinomial distribution for the response variable is replaced by a distribution having a single parameter, and in the uniform log-odds model it is replaced by a different distribution having a single parameter, namely, the truncated geometric. Since there are 10 joint categories for the explanatory variables in Table 2, each of these models can be tested with 10 df. For the KTF model, the likelihood ratio chi square value is 31.59; whereas for the uniform log-odds model, the corresponding value is 11.71. The improvement in fit is dramatic. Additional improvement in fit can be obtained by applying the uniform log-odds model to the modified Table 2; the likelihood-ratio chi square values thus obtained is 6.67, with 9 df.

Whittaker and Aitkin (1978) noted that the fit of the KTF binomial model can be improved somewhat by using instead the Poisson or negative binomial, and Paul (1979) obtained further improvement with a restricted beta–binomial. The latter model introduces an additional parameter to obtain the improvement in fit, whereas the other three models and the uniform log-odds model do not. The uniform log-odds model fits the data much better than the KTF binomial model, the Poisson model, and the negative binomial model; and it also fits the data better than the restricted beta–binomial, achieving this improvement in fit without the need for an additional parameter. For the restricted beta–binomial, the likelihood-ratio chi square value is 12.93 with 9 df, whereas the corresponding value for the uniform log-odds model is 11.71 with 10 df. In addition to the advantages of the uniform log-odds model noted above, the simplicity of this model also adds to its attractiveness.

When the estimated expected frequencies under the restricted beta–binomial are compared with the observed frequencies, we obtain the likelihood ratio chi square value of 12.93 with 9 df, whereas Paul obtained 9.29 by comparing the likelihood estimated under the restricted beta–binomial with that estimated under the unrestricted beta–binomial. Although the latter model is saturated in this case, Paul noted that it actually did not fit the full set of data, and that this complication affected the soundness of his approach. It may also be worth noting that the interaction between litter-size effect and treatment effect is tested in Paul's model with $(I - 1)(J - 1)$ df (4 df in this case), whereas the $A \times B$ interaction effect in Model M_2 or M_2' of Table 5 is tested, as in the usual analysis of covariance, with $J - 1$ df (1 df in this case).

REFERENCES

Aitkin, M. (1980). A note on the selection of log-linear models. *Biometrics* **36**, 173–178.
Atkinson, A. C. (1980). A note on the generalized information criterion for choice of a model. *Biometrika* **67**, 413–418.
Baker, R. J. and Nelder, J. (1978). *The GLIM System. Release* 3. Oxford: Numerical Algorithms Group.
Berkson, J. (1968). Application of minimum logit χ^2 estimate to a problem of Grizzle with a notation on the problem of "no interaction". *Biometrics* **24**, 75–96.
Berkson, J. (1972). Minimum discrimination information, "no interaction" problem and the logistic function. *Biometrics* **28**, 443–468.
Darroch, J. N. (1962). Interactions in multi-factor contingency tables. *Journal of the Royal Statistical Society, Series B* **25**, 179–188.
Fienberg, S. E. (1977). *The Analysis of Cross-Classified Categorical Data.* Cambridge, Massachusetts: MIT Press.
Goodman, L. A. (1963). On Plackett's test for contingency table interactions. *Journal of the Royal Statistical Society, Series B* **25**, 179–188.
Goodman, L. A. (1964). Simple methods for analysing three-factor interactions in contingency tables. *Journal of the American Statistical Association* **59**, 319–352.
Goodman, L. A. (1970). The multivariate analysis of qualitative data: Interactions among multiple classifications. *Journal of the American Statistical Association* **65**, 226–256.
Goodman, L. A. (1971). The analysis of multidimensional contingency tables: Stepwise procedures and direct estimation methods for building models for multiple classifications. *Technometrics* **13**, 33–61.
* Goodman, L. A. (1979). Simple models for the analysis of association in cross-classifications having ordered categories. *Journal of the American Statistical Association* **74**, 537–552.
* Goodman, L. A. (1981a). Association models and canonical correlation in the analysis of cross-classifications having ordered categories. *Journal of the American Statistical Association* **76**, 320–334.
* Goodman, L. A. (1981b). Three elementary views of log-linear models for the analysis of cross-classifications having ordered categories. In *Sociological Methodology* 1981, S. Leinhardt (ed.). San Francisco: Jossey-Bass.
Grizzle, J. E., Starmer, C. F. and Koch, G. G. (1969). Analysis of categorical data by linear models. *Biometrics* **25**, 480–504.
Haberman, S. J. (1974a). Log-linear models for frequency tables with ordered classifications. *Biometrics* **30**, 589–600.
Haberman, S. J. (1974b). *The Analysis of Frequency Data.* Chicago: University of Chicago Press.

Kastenbaum, M. A. and Lamphiear, D. E. (1959). Calculation of chi-square to calculate the no three-factor interaction hypothesis. *Biometrics* **15**, 107–115.

Koch, G. G., Tolley, D. and Freeman, J. L. (1976). An application of the clumped binomial model to the analysis of clustered attribute data. *Biometrics* **32**, 337–354.

Ku, H. H. and Kullback, S. (1968). Interaction in multidimensional contingency tables—an information theoretic approach. *Journal of Research of the National Bureau of Standards B* **72**, 159–199.

McCullagh, P. (1980). Regression models for ordinal data. *Journal of the Royal Statistical Society, Series B* **42**, 109–142.

Paul, S. R. (1979). A clumped beta–binomial for the analysis of clustered attribute data. *Biometrics* **35**, 821–824.

Plackett, R. L. (1962). A note on interaction in contingency tables. *Journal of the Royal Statistical Society, Series B* **24**, 162–166.

Spøtvoll, E. (1977). Alternatives to plotting C_p in multiple regression. *Biometrika* **64**, 1–8.

Whittaker, J. and Aitkin, M. (1978). A flexible strategy for fitting complex log-linear models. *Biometrics* **34**, 487–495.

Wing, J. K. (1962). Institutionalism in mental hospitals. *British Journal of Social and Clinical Psychology* **1**, 38–51.

Yule, G. U. and Kendall, M. G. (1950). *An Introduction to the Theory of Statistics* (14th ed.). New York: Hafner.

4.
Models of Association
Simple Models for the Analysis of Association in Cross-Classifications Having Ordered Categories

A class of models is proposed for the analysis of association in a contingency table with ordered rows and ordered columns. Association is measured in terms of the odds-ratios in 2×2 subtables formed from adjacent rows and adjacent columns. This class includes the null association model, the uniform association model, and models that describe the possible effects of the rows and/or columns on the association. With these models, the association in the table can be analyzed in a manner analogous to the usual two-way analysis of variance, and parsimonious descriptions of this association can be obtained often. Applications are discussed here, some well-known sets of data are reanalyzed, and new insights into these data are obtained.

1. INTRODUCTION

To illustrate how the models proposed in the present article can be used, we apply them to study the association in three different cross-classification tables:

1. A 4×6 table on the relationship between mental health and socioeconomic status (Table 1), studied earlier by Srole et al. (1962) and Haberman (1974a, 1979);

2. A 7×7 table on the relationship between father's occupational status category and son's status category (Table 2), studied earlier by Glass and his co-workers (1954) and by Goodman (1972); and

3. A related 8×8 table (Table 3) based on data in Glass (1954) and on additional special tabulations,

1. Cross-Classification of Subjects According to Their Mental Health and Their Parents' Socioeconomic Status

Mental Health Status	Parents' Socioeconomic Status					
	A	B	C	D	E	F
Well	64	57	57	72	36	21
Mild Symptom Formation	94	94	105	141	97	71
Moderate Symptom Formation	58	54	65	77	54	54
Impaired	46	40	60	94	78	71

published by Miller (1960) and studied by Duncan (1979), Hauser (1980), and McCullagh (1978).

Each of these tables has ordered row categories and ordered column categories. We are concerned here mainly with the analysis of doubly ordered tables (i.e., tables with ordered rows and ordered columns), but we also comment on the analysis of singly ordered tables and on tables in which neither the rows nor the columns is ordered.

Many different kinds of data can be analyzed by using the models and methods presented in this article. Tables 1, 2, and 3 serve well to illustrate a variety of problems that could arise in the analysis of such data, but to suggest the wide range of applicability of these models and methods, examples from more diverse substantive areas could have been used instead.

The models considered in this article are intended for the situation in which row categories and column categories are specified. Results obtained with the specified categories can differ from results obtained when changes are made in these categories, for example, when some rows are combined and/or some columns are combined (e.g., see Sections 3.2 and 3.3).

For a 2×2 contingency table, the association in the table can usually be measured by the odds-ratio or by

2. Cross-Classification of British Male Sample According to Each Subject's Occupational Status Category and His Father's Occupational Status Category, Using Seven Status Categories*

Father's Status	Subject's Status						
	1	2	3	4	5	6	7
1	50	19	26	8	18	6	2
2	16	40	34	18	31	8	3
3	12	35	65	66	123	23	21
4	11	20	58	110	223	64	32
5	14	36	114	185	715	258	189
6	0	6	19	40	179	143	71
7	0	3	14	32	141	91	106

* See addendum at end of article.

some function of the odds-ratio (e.g., see Edwards 1963; Goodman 1965, 1969). For an $I \times J$ contingency table, the total association in the table may be viewed in terms of the association present in each of the 2×2 subtables formed from the full $I \times J$ table (e.g., see Goodman 1969). When the contingency table has ordered rows and ordered columns, analysis of the table should take this ordering into account, and we do so here by focusing our attention on the 2×2 subtables formed from adjacent rows and adjacent columns of the full table. There will be $(I - 1)(J - 1)$ such 2×2 subtables, and we shall refer to them as the basic set of subtables.

The total association in the $I \times J$ table may be viewed in terms of the association present in the basic set of subtables because the association present in any other 2×2 subtable of the full table (where the two rows need not be adjacent and/or the two columns need not be adjacent) can be expressed in terms of the association present in the basic set of subtables (e.g., see Goodman 1969). In other words, local association as measured with the subtables formed from adjacent rows and adjacent columns of the full table (i.e., subtables in the basic set) determines total association in the table.

For, say, the 4×6 cross-classification given here (Table 1), there will be $3 \times 5 = 15$ subtables in the basic set. Because two of the four rows can be chosen in 6 ways and two of the six columns can be chosen in 15 ways, the total number of 2×2 subtables we could have formed from the 4×6 table would have been $6 \times 15 = 90$. But focusing our attention on the basic set of 15 subtables is sufficient because the association present in any of the 90 subtables can be expressed in terms of the association present in the basic set.

By applying the models and methods presented here to Table 1, we shall show that the association present in the 15 subtables is uniform. This association can be described by a single number. Thus, we obtain a simple parsimonious description of the total association in Table 1. Our analysis provides an example of the usefulness of the uniform association model. This model is equivalent to a model presented by Haberman (1974a) for this table, but his development of this model was expressed in terms somewhat different from those used in the present article.

With our analysis of Table 2, we shall provide an example of the usefulness of a modified form of the uniform association model, namely, the quasi-uniform association model. This model provides a more parsimonious description of Table 2 than any of the models used in Goodman (1972).

3. Cross-Classification of British Male Sample According to Each Subject's Occupational Status Category and His Father's Occupational Status Category, Using Eight Status Categories

Father's Status	Subject's Status							
	1	2	3	4	5	6	7	8
1	50	19	26	8	7	11	6	2
2	16	40	34	18	11	20	8	3
3	12	35	65	66	35	88	23	21
4	11	20	58	110	40	183	64	32
5	2	8	12	23	25	46	28	12
6	12	28	102	162	90	554	230	177
7	0	6	19	40	21	158	143	71
8	0	3	14	32	15	126	91	106

With our analysis of Table 3, we shall provide an example of the usefulness of various generalizations of the uniform association model, for example, models that describe the possible effects of the rows and columns on the association in the table. Application of these models to Table 3 yields results that supplement those in Duncan (1979) and Hauser (1980), thereby obtaining a more complete description of the table.

The usual chi-squared statistic (with $(I - 1)(J - 1)$ degrees of freedom) for testing the model of statistical independence between the row categories and the column categories (i.e., the null association model) may be viewed as a test pertaining to the association in the $(I - 1)$ $\times (J - 1)$ subtables in the basic set. With the odds-ratio (or a given function of the odds-ratio) used as the measure of association in each of the $(I - 1)(J - 1)$ subtables in the basic set, these quantities can be displayed as entries in a $(I - 1) \times (J - 1)$ two-way table (with one entry per cell). In a manner analogous to the usual analysis of variance of a two-way $(I-1) \times (J-1)$ table (with one entry per cell), we can analyze the association in a contingency table of the kind considered here. The usual chi-squared statistic pertaining to the total association in the contingency table (and in the $(I - 1)(J - 1)$ subtables in the basic set) can be partitioned into the following components:

1. A chi-squared statistic (with one degree of freedom) pertaining to the general overall level of the association in the basic set of subtables;

2. A chi-squared statistic (with $I - 2$ degrees of freedom) pertaining to row effects on the association;

3. A chi-squared statistic (with $J - 2$ degrees of freedom) pertaining to column effects on the association;

4. A chi-squared statistic (with $(I - 2)(J - 2)$ degrees of freedom) pertaining to other effects.

The usual analysis of variance (ANOVA) table format can be used here to obtain an analysis of association (ANOAS) table.

This approach to the analysis of the $I \times J$ contingency table makes use of simple models, described in Section 2, pertaining to the total association in the table. When any of these models fit the observed data, we obtain simple interpretations of the association in the table.

The class of models presented here may be viewed as an extension and generalization of one of the models proposed by Simon (1974) for the singly ordered contingency table; it is also related to models in Haberman (1974a, 1979), Duncan (1979), Goodman (1979a), Rasch (1966), Fienberg (1968), and Andersen (1979). These relationships will be discussed further later in this article.

The models and methods presented here can be extended to multiway tables and the analysis of higher-order as well as two-factor interactions. These extensions are considered briefly later in the present article.

2. ASSOCIATION MODELS

For the $I \times J$ cross-classification table, let f_{ij} denote the observed frequency in the ith row and jth column of the table $(i = 1, 2, \ldots, I; j = 1, 2, \ldots, J)$, and let F_{ij} denote the corresponding expected frequency under some model. As is the case in the usual statistical analysis of such tables, we assume here that a multinomial distribution applies to the $I \times J$ table. (The methods presented here are also applicable when the multinomial distribution applies independently to each of the I rows in the table, or when this distribution applies independently to each of the J columns, or when the Poisson distribution applies independently to each of the $I \times J$ cells. These different distributional assumptions will not affect the applicability of the statistics presented here to test various models nor will they affect the asymptotic distribution of these statistics under the corresponding null hypotheses, but they will affect the power of the corresponding tests.)

For 2×2 subtables formed from adjacent rows (i.e., rows i and $i + 1$) and adjacent columns (i.e., columns j and $j + 1$), let θ_{ij} denote the corresponding odds-ratio (for $i = 1, 2, \ldots, I - 1$; $j = 1, 2, \ldots, J - 1$) based on the expected frequencies. Thus,

$$\theta_{ij} = (F_{ij}F_{i+1,j+1})/(F_{i,j+1}F_{i+1,j}). \qquad (2.1)$$

With the $(I - 1)(J - 1)$ odds-ratios θ_{ij} defined by (2.1), we can determine the odds-ratio pertaining to any other 2×2 subtable formed from the $I \times J$ table (e.g., see Goodman 1969).

Under the usual model of statistical independence between the row categories and the column categories,

$$\theta_{ij} = 1, \quad \text{for} \quad i = 1, 2, \ldots, I - 1;$$
$$j = 1, 2, \ldots, J - 1. \qquad (2.2)$$

Thus, the usual model of statistical independence can be called the null association model. The usual chi-squared statistic for testing the appropriateness of this model has $(I - 1)(J - 1)$ degrees of freedom.

Instead of condition (2.2), consider the model in which the following condition is satisfied:

$$\theta_{ij} = \theta, \quad \text{for} \quad i = 1, 2, \ldots, I - 1;$$
$$j = 1, 2, \ldots, J - 1 \ , \qquad (2.3)$$

where θ is unspecified. This is the uniform association model. (When $\theta = 1$, we have the null association model.) Because the uniform association model has one more parameter (viz., θ) than the null association model, the number of degrees of freedom for testing the former model will be $(I - 1)(J - 1) - 1 = IJ - I - J$.

Instead of condition (2.2) or (2.3), consider next the model in which the following condition is satisfied:

$$\theta_{ij} = \theta_{i\cdot}, \quad \text{for} \quad i = 1, 2, \ldots, I - 1;$$
$$j = 1, 2, \ldots, J - 1 \ , \qquad (2.4)$$

where $\theta_{i\cdot}$ is unspecified. This is the row-effect association model. This model has $I - 1$ more parameters (viz., $\theta_{i\cdot}$, for $i = 1, 2, \ldots, I - 1$) than the null association

4. Degrees of Freedom for the Association Models Applied to the I × J Table

Association Models	Degrees of Freedom
Null Association	$(I-1)(J-1)$
Uniform Association	$IJ-I-J$
Row-Effect Association	$(I-1)(J-2)$
Column-Effect Association	$(I-2)(J-1)$
Row and Column Effects (I)	$(I-2)(J-2)$
Row and Column Effects (II)	$(I-2)(J-2)$

model, and so the number of degrees of freedom for testing the former model will be $(I-1)(J-1)-(I-1)$ $=(I-1)(J-2)$.

Similarly, in the column-effect association model the following condition is satisfied:

$$\theta_{ij} = \theta_{.j}, \quad \text{for} \quad i = 1, 2, \ldots, I-1;$$
$$j = 1, 2, \ldots, J-1 , \quad (2.5)$$

where $\theta_{.j}$ is unspecified, and the corresponding number of degrees of freedom for testing this model will be $(I-2)(J-1)$.

The number of degrees of freedom for each of the models considered here is summarized in Table 4. The last two lines in Table 4 pertain to two further models, each of which includes the effects of both the rows and columns on the θ_{ij}. The first of these generalizations (Model I) can be described by the following condition:

$$\theta_{ij} = \theta_{i.}\theta_{.j}, \quad \text{for} \quad i = 1, 2, \ldots, I-1;$$
$$j = 1, 2, \ldots, J-1 , \quad (2.6)$$

where $\theta_{i.}$ and $\theta_{.j}$ are unspecified. The second of these generalizations (Model II) can be described by the following condition:

$$\log \theta_{ij} = \phi_{i.}\phi_{.j}, \quad \text{for} \quad i = 1, 2, \ldots, I-1;$$
$$j = 1, 2, \ldots, J-1 , \quad (2.7)$$

where $\phi_i.$ and $\phi._j$ are unspecified and where log denotes the natural logarithm. Both models describe the $(I - 1) \times (J - 1)$ odds-ratios θ_{ij} in terms of row effects and column effects, and both will have $(I - 2)(J - 2)$ degrees of freedom.

In Sections 4 and 5 we shall discuss all these models more fully and we shall describe there the statistical methods used with them. Now we shall illustrate how useful these simple models can be by applying them to the analysis of Tables 1, 2, and 3.

3. ANALYSIS OF ASSOCIATION IN TABLES 1, 2, AND 3

3.1 Analysis of Table 1

Applying the statistical methods described in Sections 4 and 5 to Table 1, we obtain the values of the goodness-of-fit chi-square and the likelihood-ratio chi-square presented in Table 5A for each of the association models. The usual null association model does not fit the data, but all the other association models fit the data very well indeed, and the improvement in fit obtained .with these models is dramatic. Because the uniform association model is the most parsimonious model among those that fit the data, it will serve well as a simple description of the association in Table 1.

Because the uniform association model fit the data so well, we would not have had to consider the other association models following it in Table 5A, but we included the results for all the models for expository purposes and for the sake of completeness.

Table 5B illustrates how the chi-square pertaining to the total association can be partitioned into components pertaining to the general overall level of the association, the effects of the rows and columns on the association, and other effects on the association. Note the dramatic effect of the general overall level of association. For the sake of completeness, we also include in Table 5C the following partitioned components of the chi-square pertaining to the row and column effects on the associa-

5A. Association Models Applied to Table 1

Association Models	Degrees of Freedom	Goodness-of-Fit Chi-Square	Likelihood Ratio Chi-Square
(1) Null Association	15	45.99	47.42
(2) Uniform Association	14	9.73	9.89
(3) Row-Effect Association	12	6.29	6.28
(4) Column-Effect Association	10	6.78	6.83
(5) Row and Column Effects (I)	8	3.06	3.04
(6) Row and Column Effects (II)	8	3.57	3.57

5B. Analysis of Association in Table 1

Effects on Association	Models Used	Degrees of Freedom	Goodness-of-Fit Chi-Square	Likelihood Ratio Chi-Square
General Effect	(1) − (2)	15 − 14 = 1	36.26	37.53
Row and Column Effects	(2) − (5)	14 − 8 = 6	6.67	6.85
Other Effects	(5)	8	3.06	3.04
Total Effects	(1)	15	45.99	47.42

tion: a component pertaining to the row effects on the association and a component pertaining to the column effects on the association. The analysis presented in Tables 5B and 5C confirms our initial impression that the uniform association model suffices to describe the association in Table 1.

Because Models I and II on lines 5 and 6 of Table 5A (see (2.6) and (2.7)) include the effects of the rows and columns on the association (and also the effect of the general level), the corresponding chi-squared values pertain to the other effects on the θ_{ij}, including the effect of the interaction between the row and column effects

5C. Partition of Row and Column Effects on Association in Table 1

Effects on Association	Models Used	Degrees of Freedom	Goodness-of-Fit Chi-Square	Likelihood Ratio Chi-Square
Row Effect	(2) − (3)	14 − 12 = 2	3.44	3.61
Column Effect	(3) − (5)	12 − 8 = 4	3.23	3.24
Row and Column Effects	(2) − (5)	14 − 8 = 6	6.67	6.85

on θ_{ij}. The entry in Table 5B for the other effects on the association could be obtained with either Model I or II. The former model was used there, but we could instead have used the latter one, and the numerical results in Table 5B would have differed only slightly.

Because the uniform association model on line 2 of Table 5A includes the general effect of θ on the association (see (2.3)), the corresponding chi-squared value pertains to all other effects on the θ_{ij}, including the effects of the rows and columns on θ_{ij}. Because the chi-square for the uniform association model pertains to all other effects including the row and column effects and the chi-square for Model I (or Model II) pertains to these other effects excluding the row and column effects, the difference between these two chi-squared values is the entry in Table 5B for the row and column effects on the association.

The null association model on line 1 of Table 5A does not include any effects on the association (see (2.2)), and the corresponding chi-squared value pertains to all effects on the θ_{ij}, including the general effect of θ. Because the chi-square for the null association model pertains to all effects, including the general effect of θ, and the chi-square for the uniform association model pertains to all effects, excluding the general effect of θ, the difference between these two chi-squared values is the entry in Table 5B for the general effect on the association.

When two models, say, M and M', differ only to the extent that model M does not include a given effect on the association but model M' does include the effect, then the difference between the corresponding chi-squared values, $\chi^2(M) - \chi^2(M')$, pertains to the given effect on the association (e.g., see Goodman 1968, 1970). This difference can be used to test the hypothesis that the given effect on the association is nil, under the assumption that model M' holds true. (If this assumption is contradicted by the data, then the test based on the difference between the chi-squares is invalid.) The specific examples in the preceding two paragraphs serve to illustrate the general method described in the present paragraph.

When the likelihood-ratio chi-squared statistics are used in the preceding paragraph for $\chi^2(M)$ and $\chi^2(M')$, then the difference between them, $\chi^2(M) - \chi^2(M')$, is equal to $\chi^2(M\,|\,M')$, the chi-squared statistic based on the likelihood-ratio criterion for testing model M assuming that model M' is true (e.g., see Goodman 1968, 1970). When the goodness-of-fit chi-squared statistics are used, then the corresponding difference between the goodness-of-fit chi-squares for testing models M and M' can serve to test model M assuming that model M' is true, but this difference cannot, in general, be expressed in the usual form of a goodness-of-fit chi-squared statistic.

In Table 5C, the column-effect component was obtained as the difference (with $12 - 8 = 4$ degrees of freedom) between the chi-squares for the row-effect association model and Model I, and the row-effect component was obtained as the difference (with $14 - 12 = 2$ degrees of freedom) between the chi-squares for the uniform association model and the row-effect association model. We could instead have considered a row-effect component obtained as the difference (with $10 - 8 = 2$ degrees of freedom) between the chi-squares for the column-effect association model and Model I and a column-effect component obtained as the difference (with $14 - 10 = 4$ degrees of freedom) between the chi-squares for the uniform association model and the column-effect association model. Had we done so, the numerical results in Table 5C would have differed only slightly. With Table 5C, the hypothesis that the column effect is nil can be tested under the assumption that Model I holds true, and the hypotheses that the row effect is nil can be tested under the assumption that the row-effect association model holds true. We could instead have considered the hypothesis that the row effect is nil under the assumption that Model I holds true and the hypothesis that the column effect is nil under the assumption that the column-effect association model holds true.

The conclusions presented here for the analysis of Table 1 are consistent with results presented in Haberman (1974a, 1979), although the models he describes are expressed in terms somewhat different from those described here.

3.2 Analysis of Table 2

In the analysis of occupational mobility tables of the kind described by Table 2, we have found that the cells on the main diagonal often need to be treated separately from the other cells in the table and that analyzing the table with the cells on the main diagonal deleted is often worthwhile (e.g., see Goodman 1969, 1972; Haberman 1974b). Table 6A gives the values of the chi-squared statistics under each of the association models applied to Table 2 with the main diagonal deleted. The null association model (which is the quasi-independence model in this case) does not fit the data, but all the other association models fit the data very well indeed. From Table 6B we find again the dramatic effect of the general overall level of association. From the analysis presented in Tables 6A through 6C, we see that in describing the association in Table 2 (with the main diagonal deleted) considering only the general overall level of the associa-

6A. Association Models Applied to Table 2 With Main Diagonal Deleted

Association Models	Degrees of Freedom	Goodness-of-Fit Chi-Square	Likelihood Ratio Chi-Square
(1) Null Association	29	522.98	408.37
(2) Uniform Association	28	29.54	30.39
(3) Row-Effect Association	23	24.90	26.29
(4) Column-Effect Association	23	24.81	25.43
(5) Row and Column Effects (I)	18	20.02	21.33
(6) Row and Column Effects (II)	18	20.13	21.49

6B. Analysis of Association in Table 2 With Main Diagonal Deleted

Effects on Association	Models Used	Degrees of Freedom	Goodness-of-Fit Chi-Square	Likelihood Ratio Chi-Square
General Effect	(1) − (2)	29 − 28 = 1	493.44	377.98
Row and Column Effects	(2) − (5)	28 − 18 = 10	9.52	9.06
Other Effects	(5)	18	20.02	21.33
Total Effects	(1)	29	522.98	408.37

6C. Partition of Row and Column Effects on Association in Table 2 With Main Diagonal Deleted

Effects on Association	Models Used	Degrees of Freedom	Goodness-of-Fit Chi-Square	Likelihood Ratio Chi-Square
Row Effect	(2) − (3)	28 − 23 = 5	4.64	4.10
Column Effect	(3) − (5)	23 − 18 = 5	4.88	4.96
Row and Column Effects	(2) − (5)	28 − 18 = 10	9.52	9.06

tion is sufficient, and all other effects (row, column, and still other effects) on the association are negligible.

With respect to the number of degrees of freedom pertaining to each model in Table 6A, because the seven cells on the main diagonal of the 7×7 contingency table were deleted, the correct number of degrees of freedom would be seven less than the number of degrees of freedom pertaining to the corresponding model applied to the full 7×7 table. More generally, for the $I \times I$ table with the cells on the main diagonal deleted, the correct number of degrees of freedom would be I less than the number of degrees of freedom presented in Table 4 for the corresponding model applied to the full table. For contingency tables in which a given subset of the cells are deleted, the meaning of the corresponding association models will be better understood in terms of the perspective introduced in Section 4.5 rather than the the perspective of Section 2.

3.3 Analysis of Table 3

As in the analysis of Table 2, we shall consider Table 3 with the cells on the main diagonal deleted. Table 7A gives the values of the chi-squared statistics under each of the association models applied to Table 3 with the main diagonal deleted. From Tables 7A through 7C we see that, contrary to the results presented earlier for Table 2, we would reject (at the .05 level) the uniform association model (which is, more precisely, the quasi-uniform association model in this case) when applied to Table 3 but accept the other association models following it in Table 7A. Models I and II (on lines 5 and 6 of Table 7A) fit the data quite well. Although the column-effect association model and the row-effect association model are not rejected, they do not fit the data so well as Models I and II. The column-effect association model fits the data somewhat better than the row-effect association model; both the column effect and the row effect are statistically significant, but the row effect is barely statistically significant. In describing the association in Table 3, considering the effects of the columns and rows on the association is sufficient.

Model I provided a slightly better fit than did Model II in the analysis of Table 2, and the reverse is true here for Table 3. Model I was used in Tables 6B and 6C, and we use Model II here in Tables 7B and 7C.

7A. Association Models Applied to Table 3 With Main Diagonal Deleted

Association Models	Degrees of Freedom	Goodness-of-Fit Chi-Square	Likelihood Ratio Chi-Square
(1) Null Association	41	555.12	446.84
(2) Uniform Association	40	55.77	58.44
(3) Row-Effect Association	34	43.13	45.91
(4) Column-Effect Association	34	40.63	42.02
(5) Row and Column Effects (I)	28	29.28	30.52
(6) Row and Column Effects (II)	28	27.97	29.15
(7) Homogeneous Row-Column Effect (I*)	34	32.01	33.39
(8) Homogeneous Row-Column Effect (II*)	34	31.21	32.56
(9) Symmetric Association	21	20.34	22.93

7B. Analysis of Association in Table 3 With Main Diagonal Deleted

Effects on Association	Models Used	Degrees of Freedom	Goodness-of-Fit Chi-Square	Likelihood Ratio Chi-Square
General Effect	(1) − (2)	41 − 40 = 1	499.35	388.40
Row and Column Effects	(2) − (6)	40 − 28 = 12	27.80	29.29
Other Effects	(6)	28	27.97	29.15
Total Effects	(1)	41	555.12	446.84

7C. Partition of Row and Column Effects on Association in Table 3 With Main Diagonal Deleted

Effects on Association	Models Used	Degrees of Freedom	Goodness-of-Fit Chi-Square	Likelihood Ratio Chi-Square
Column Effect	(2) − (4)	40 − 34 = 6	15.14	16.41
Row Effect	(4) − (6)	34 − 28 = 6	12.66	12.87
Row and Column Effects	(2) − (6)	40 − 28 = 12	27.80	29.28

7D. Analysis of Association in Table 3 With Main Diagonal Deleted

Effects on Association	Models Used	Degrees of Freedom	Goodness-of-Fit Chi-Square	Likelihood Ratio Chi-Square
Main Effects	(1) − (6)	41 − 28 = 13	527.14	417.69
Other Effects	(6)	28	27.97	29.15
Total Effects	(1)	41	555.11	446.84

The kinds of remarks made in Section 3.1 pertaining to the partitioning in Tables 5B and 5C apply also to Tables 7B and 7C here. For Table 7C, instead of considering the row-effect component obtained as the difference (with $34 - 28 = 6$ degrees of freedom) between the chi-squares for the column-effect association model and Model II and the column-effect component obtained as the difference (with $40 - 34 = 6$ degrees of freedom) between the chi-squares for the uniform association model and the column-effect association model, we could have considered the column-effect component obtained as the difference (with $34 - 28 = 6$ degrees of freedom) between the chi-squares for the row-

7E. Partition of Row and Column Effects on Association in Table 3 With Main Diagonal Deleted

Effects on Association	Models Used	Degrees of Freedom	Goodness-of-Fit Chi-Square	Likelihood Ratio Chi-Square
Homogeneous Row-Column Effect	(2) − (8)	40 − 34 = 6	24.56	25.87
Row-Column Difference Effect	(8) − (6)	34 − 28 = 6	3.24	3.41
Row and Column Effects	(2) − (6)	40 − 28 = 12	27.80	29.28

7F. Partition of Chi-Square for Model II* With Homogeneous Row-Column Effect on Association in Table 3 With Main Diagonal Deleted

Effects on Association	Models Used	Degrees of Freedom	Goodness-of-Fit Chi-Square	Likelihood Ratio Chi-Square
Row-Column Difference Effect	(8) − (6)	34 − 28 = 6	3.24	3.41
Other Excluded Effects	(6)	28	27.97	29.15
Effects Excluded From Model II*	(8)	34	31.21	32.56

7G. Partition of Chi-Square for Model II* With Homogeneous Row-Column Effect on Association in Table 3 With Main Diagonal Deleted

Effects on Association	Models Used	Degrees of Freedom	Goodness-of-Fit Chi-Square	Likelihood Ratio Chi-Square
Excluded Symmetric Effects	(8) − (9)	34 − 21 = 13	10.87	9.63
All Asymmetric Effects	(9)	21	20.34	22.93
Effects Excluded From Model II*	(8)	34	31.21	32.56

effect association model and Model II and the row-effect component obtained as the difference (with 40 − 34 = 6 degrees of freedom) between the chi-squares for the uniform association model and the row-effect association model. Had we done so, the numerical results in Table 7C would have differed slightly, and the barely statistically significant row effect would have moved slightly from being on one side of the significance cutting point to being on the other side. In testing hypotheses about these effects, the cautionary remark in Section 3.1 about the possible invalidity of the test should be kept in mind when the reader is examining the column-effect component in Table 7C or the row-effect component that would have been obtained had the alternate approach noted in the present paragraph been used.

The cautionary remark in Section 3.1 should also be kept in mind when the reader is examining the general-effect component in Table 7B. In view of this, Table 7B might be replaced by Table 7D in which the general-effect component is combined with the component pertaining to the row and column effects to form a single component for the main effects. Also, Table 7C might be replaced by Table 7E in order to partition the row and column effects on the association. We shall next discuss the partitioning in Table 7E and the related partitioning in Tables 7F and 7G.

Because Table 3 is actually a square contingency table ($I = J = 8$) in which there is a one-to-one correspondence between the row categories and column categories, considering the possibility that the row effects on the association are equal to the corresponding column effects on the association would seem natural. (We could have considered this possibility earlier in our analysis of Table 2, but we did not do so because the row and column effects on the association in Table 2 were negligible.) In our analysis of Table 3, we next consider Models I* and II* obtained by replacing (2.6) and (2.7) by

$$\theta_{ij} = \theta_i \theta_j \qquad (3.1)$$

and

$$\log \theta_{ij} = \phi_i \phi_j \; , \qquad (3.2)$$

where θ_i and ϕ_i are homogeneous row-column effects (for $i = 1, 2, \ldots, I - 1$) in Models I* and II*, respectively. Models I* and II* are special cases of Models I and II, respectively, obtained when the row effects on the association are assumed to be equal to the corresponding column effects on the association. (For further details, see the discussion of (3.8) through (3.11) later.)

The values of the chi-squared statistics obtained when Models I* and II* are applied to Table 3 are given on lines 7 and 8 in Table 7A. The difference between the chi-squares for Models I* and I can be used to test the hypothesis that the row and column effects in Model I are homogeneous (assuming that Model I holds true); a similar difference can be used with Models II* and II. The latter difference is included in Table 7E as the component for the row-column difference effect on the association. Note that this difference is negligible; and the homogeneous row-column effect in Table 7E is dramatic.

Because Models I* and II* include the homogeneous effect of the rows and columns on the association (and also the effect of the general level), the corresponding chi-squared values pertain to the other effects on the θ_{ij}, including the row-column difference effect and the effect of the interaction between the row and column effects on θ_{ij}. This partitioning of the chi-squares for Model II* is presented in Table 7F.

Consider next the symmetric association model, listed on line 9 of Table 7A, which states that

$$\theta_{ij} = \theta_{ji}, \quad \text{for} \quad i = 1, 2, \ldots, I - 1;$$
$$j = 1, 2, \ldots, I - 1 \; . \qquad (3.3)$$

(Models I* and II* and the symmetric association model are for square contingency tables, with $I = J$.) If Model I* or Model II* holds true, then the symmetric association model will also hold true. The difference between the chi-squares for Model I* and the symmetric association model can be used to test the hypothesis that Model I* is true under the assumption that the association is symmetric; a similar difference can be used with Model II* and the symmetric association model. The latter difference is included in Table 7G as the component for the symmetric effects excluded from Model II*. Because Model II* (and Model I*) includes the homogeneous effect of the rows and columns on the association (and also the effect of the general level), the effects excluded from Model II* (and Model I*) are the other symmetric effects (viz., the symmetric effects of the interaction between the homogeneous row and column effects) and all asymmetric effects. Table 7G presents this partitioning of the effects excluded from Model II*.

From Table 7A we see that, although Models I* and II* have the same number of degrees of freedom as the row-effect association model and the column-effect association model, the former models fit the data better. From Tables 7A and 7E through 7G, we see that, although Models I and II and the symmetric association model include more effects on the association than do Models I* and II*, none of these additional effects is statistically significant. Models I* and II* fit the data well, and they have the advantage of being more parsimonious than Models I and II and the symmetric association model. Model II* fits the data slightly better than does Model I*.

Because the homogeneous row-column effect association models have the same number of parameters as the row-effect association model and the column-effect association model, the number of degrees of freedom will also be the same. From Table 4 we see that, when these models are applied to the full $I \times I$ contingency table, the number of degrees of freedom is $(I-1)(I-2)$, and when these models are applied to the table with the cells on the main diagonal deleted, the number of degrees of freedom is $I^2 - 4I + 2$. Also, for the symmetric association model, because there are $(I - 1)(I - 2)/2$

parameters θ_{ij} in the upper-right triangle of the $(I - 1)$ $\times$ $(I - 1)$ table of θ_{ij} (where $i < j$), the number of nonredundant equalities in (3.3) will be $(I-1)(I-2)/2$, which will also be the number of degrees of freedom for the model. (The symmetric association model defined by (3.3) can be shown to be equivalent to the usual quasi-symmetry model defined by Caussinus (1965) for the $I \times I$ contingency table.)

As we have noted, Models I* and II* are more parsimonious than Models I and II and the symmetric association model. We may obtain even more parsimonious models that fit the observed data by considering models in which the homogeneous row-column effects (viz., the θ_i in (3.1) or the ϕ_i in (3.2)) for a specified subset of the possible values of i are set equal to each other. Similarly, Models I and II can be made more parsimonious by considering models in which the row effects (viz., the $\theta_i.$ in (2.6) or the $\phi_i.$ in (2.7)) for a specified subset of the possible values of i are set equal to each other, and/or the column effects (viz., the $\theta_{.j}$ in (2.6) or the $\phi_{.j}$ in (2.7)) for a specified subset of the possible values of j are set equal to each other. Also, we can consider modifications of Models I and II in which a specified subset of row and column effects is homogeneous and the others are heterogeneous. (For examples of this general method of obtaining more parsimonious models that fit the data, using related kinds of models, see Goodman 1975, 1979b.)

The conclusions presented here for the analysis of Table 3 supplement results in Duncan (1979) and Hauser (1980). Duncan considered the uniform association model and the row-effect association model, and Hauser considered the quasi-symmetry model. (McCullagh (1978) analyzed Table 3 by using a model that is quite different from those presented here.)

3.4 Estimated Parameters

Table 8A gives the maximum likelihood estimates for the parameter θ in the uniform association model (see

8A. Maximum Likelihood Estimates of Parameters in Some Association Models Applied to Tables 1, 2, and 3

Association Models	Estimated Association Parameters	
	θ	$\log \theta$
Table 1		
Uniform Association	1.09	.09
Row-Effect Association	1.16, 1.02, 1.15	.15, .02, .14
Column-Effect Association	.99, 1.13, 1.05, 1.15, 1.15	−.01, .13, .05, .14, .14
Table 2		
Uniform Association	1.26	.23
Row-Effect Association	1.09, 1.40, 1.28, 1.27, 1.22, 1.20	.09, .34, .24, .24, .20, .18
Column-Effect Association	1.36, 1.24, 1.37, 1.22, 1.26, 1.14	.31, .21, .31, .20, .23, .13
Table 3		
Uniform Association	1.15	.14
Row-Effect Association	1.06, 1.30, 1.23, 1.07, 1.14, 1.17, 1.11	.06, .26, .21, .07, .13, .15, .10
Column-Effect Association	1.24, 1.20, 1.26, .98, 1.24, 1.15, 1.10	.22, .18, .23, −.02, .22, .14, .09

(2.3)), the parameters θ_i. (for $i = 1, 2, \ldots, I - 1$) in the row-effect association model (see (2.4)), and the parameters $\theta_{\cdot j}$ (for $j = 1, 2, \ldots, J - 1$) in the column-effect association model (see (2.5)), when these models are applied to Tables 1, 2, and 3. (For Tables 1 and 2, the association in these tables could have been summarized simply by $\hat{\theta} = 1.09$ and $\hat{\theta} = 1.26$, respectively, but for didactic purposes we include also the $\hat{\theta}_i$. and $\hat{\theta}_{\cdot j}$ for these tables.) Table 8A also includes the corresponding estimates of $\log \theta$, $\log \theta_i$., and $\log \theta_{\cdot j}$.

To estimate the parameters in the association models with both row and column effects (Models I and II), these models need to be rewritten in terms of identifiable parameters. In the usual ANOVA additive model for the two-way table including both row and column effects, the parameters in the model become identifiable only when certain restrictions are imposed (e.g., the row-effect parameters need to sum to zero, the column-effect parameters need to sum to zero, etc.). In the corresponding association models presented in this article, analogous kinds of restrictions are needed.

Formula (2.6) for Model I can be rewritten as

$$\theta_{ij} = \theta \zeta_{i\cdot} \zeta_{\cdot j}, \tag{3.4a}$$

where

$$\prod_{i=1}^{I-1} \zeta_{i\cdot} = 1 \ , \quad \prod_{j=1}^{J-1} \zeta_{\cdot j} = 1 \ . \tag{3.4b}$$

Formula (3.4a) expresses θ_{ij} in multiplicative form, and it can be rewritten in an equivalent additive form:

$$\log \theta_{ij} = \psi + \eta_{i\cdot} + \eta_{\cdot j}, \tag{3.5a}$$

where $\psi = \log \theta$, $\eta_{i\cdot} = \log \zeta_{i\cdot}$, and $\eta_{\cdot j} = \log \zeta_{\cdot j}$. The $\eta_{i\cdot}$ and $\eta_{\cdot j}$ satisfy the usual kinds of conditions included in additive models:

$$\sum_{i=1}^{I-1} \eta_{i\cdot} = 0 \ , \quad \sum_{j=1}^{J-1} \eta_{\cdot j} = 0 \ . \tag{3.5b}$$

Table 8B gives the maximum likelihood estimates for $\theta, \zeta_{i\cdot}$ $(i = 1, 2, \ldots, I - 1)$, and $\zeta_{\cdot j}$ $(j = 1, 2, \ldots, J - 1)$, and for the corresponding ψ, η_i, and $\eta_{\cdot j}$, under Model I (see (3.4a) and (3.5a)) applied to Tables 1, 2, and 3. Also, for purposes of comparison, we include in Table 8B the corresponding estimated parameters obtained under the row-effect association model and the column-effect association model.

Although the θ_i and $\theta_{\cdot j}$ in the row-effect association model (2.4) and column-effect association model (2.5), respectively, are identifiable, in order to facilitate comparison with the estimates obtained under the association models with both row and column effects, we can rewrite the parameters in (2.4) and (2.5) as follows:

$$\theta_i = \theta \zeta_i. \qquad (3.6a)$$

and

$$\theta_{\cdot j} = \theta \zeta_{\cdot j} , \qquad (3.6b)$$

and the corresponding $\log \theta_i$ and $\log \theta_{\cdot j}$ can be rewritten as

$$\log \theta_i = \psi + \eta_i. \qquad (3.7a)$$

and

$$\log \theta_{\cdot j} = \psi + \eta_{\cdot j} , \qquad (3.7b)$$

where ζ_i and $\zeta_{\cdot j}$ satisfy condition (3.4b) and the η_i and $\eta_{\cdot j}$ satisfy condition (3.5b). From (3.4a), (2.4), and (3.6a), we see that $\zeta_{\cdot j} = 1$ and $\eta_{\cdot j} = 0$ (for $j = 1, 2, \ldots, J - 1$) in the row-effect association model. From (3.4a), (2.5), and (3.6b), we see that $\zeta_i = 1$ and $\eta_i = 0$ (for $i = 1, 2, \ldots, I - 1$) in the column-effect association model. Except for round-off error, the $\hat{\theta}_i$ in Table 8A will satisfy (3.6a) with the corresponding term on the right-hand side of this formula replaced by $\hat{\theta}$ and $\hat{\zeta}_i$ for the row-effect association model in Table 8B. The $\hat{\theta}_{\cdot j}$ in Table 8A will have a similar relationship to the $\hat{\theta}$ and $\hat{\zeta}_{\cdot j}$ for the column-effect association model in Table 8B. Similar remarks also apply to the $\log \hat{\theta}_i$ and $\log \hat{\theta}_{\cdot j}$ in Table 8A and the corresponding estimates for the row-effect association model and column-effect association model, respectively, in Table 8B.

We next consider the estimated parameters in the

homogeneous row-column effect association models introduced in Section 3.3. Under these models, we see, for example, that the parameters in (3.4a) would satisfy the condition that

$$\zeta_{i.} = \zeta_{.i} = \zeta_i, \quad \text{for} \quad i = 1, 2, \ldots, I - 1 \; ; \quad (3.8)$$

and the parameters in (3.5a) would satisfy the condition that

$$\eta_{i.} = \eta_{.i} = \eta_i, \quad \text{for} \quad i = 1, 2, \ldots, I - 1 \; ; \quad (3.9)$$

where $\eta_i = \log \zeta_i$, and the magnitudes of these quantities are unspecified. (The ζ_i and η_i will satisfy conditions corresponding to (3.4b) and (3.5b), respectively.) When conditions (3.8) and (3.9) are satisfied, formulas (3.4a) and (3.5a) for Model I can be replaced by the following formulas for Model I*:

$$\theta_{ij} = \theta \zeta_i \zeta_j \qquad (3.10)$$

and

$$\log \theta_{ij} = \psi + \eta_i + \eta_j \; . \qquad (3.11)$$

Table 8C gives the maximum likelihood estimates for θ and ζ_i (for $i = 1, 2, \ldots, I - 1$) and for the corresponding ψ and η_i (for $i = 1, 2, \ldots, I - 1$) under Model I* applied to Table 3. The estimates $\hat{\zeta}_i$ under Model I* in Table 8C can be compared with the corresponding $\hat{\zeta}_{i.}$ and $\hat{\zeta}_{.i}$ under Model I in Table 8B, and similarly the $\hat{\eta}_i$ in Table 8C can be compared with the $\hat{\eta}_{i.}$ and $\hat{\eta}_{.i}$ in Table 8B.

The preceding comments about Models I and I*, and their estimated parameters, can be extended also to Models II and II* and their estimated parameters. We shall not go into these details here except to note that the specific kind of reparameterization used with Model I (viz., rewriting (2.6) as (3.4a) and (3.4b)) would usually not be used with Model II. Other kinds of reparameterizations would usually be more appropriate for the latter models. For example, (2.7) could be rewritten as

$$\log \theta_{ij} = \phi \xi_{i.} \xi_{.j} \; , \qquad (3.12)$$

8B. Maximum Likelihood Estimates of Parameters in Some Association Models Applied to Tables 1, 2, and 3

Parameters	Association Models					
	Row-Effect Association		Column-Effect Association		Row- and Column-Effect Association	
Table 1						
θ	1.11		1.09		1.11	
ζ 1	1.04	1.00	1.00	.90	1.05	.90
2	.92	1.00	1.00	1.04	.92	1.03
3	1.04	1.00	1.00	.96	1.03	.96
4	—	1.00	—	1.05	—	1.06
5	—	1.00	—	1.05	—	1.05
ψ	.10		.09		.10	
η 1	.04	.00	.00	−.10	.05	−.10
2	−.08	.00	.00	.04	−.08	.03
3	.04	.00	.00	−.04	.03	−.04
4	—	.00	—	.05	—	.05
5	—	.00	—	.05	—	.05
Table 2						
θ	1.24		1.26		1.20	
ζ 1	.88	1.00	1.00	1.08	.86	.98
2	1.13	1.00	1.00	.98	1.13	1.03
3	1.03	1.00	1.00	1.09	1.04	1.10
4	1.02	1.00	1.00	.96	1.04	.99
5	.99	1.00	1.00	1.00	1.04	1.05
6	.97	1.00	1.00	.90	.91	.87
ψ	.21		.23		.18	
η 1	−.13	.00	.00	.08	−.15	−.03
2	.12	.00	.00	−.02	.12	.03
3	.03	.00	.00	.08	.04	.10
4	.02	.00	.00	−.04	.04	−.01
5	−.01	.00	.00	−.00	.04	.05
6	−.03	.00	.00	−.10	−.10	−.14

Table 3

θ	1.15		1.16		1.15	
1	.92	1.00	1.00	1.07	.91	1.00
2	1.13	1.00	1.00	1.03	1.12	1.04
3	1.07	1.00	1.00	1.08	1.08	1.09
ζ 4	.93	1.00	1.00	.84	.93	.84
5	.99	1.00	1.00	1.07	1.00	1.09
6	1.01	1.00	1.00	.99	1.03	1.01
7	.97	1.00	1.00	.94	.96	.95
ψ	.14		.15		.14	
1	−.08	.00	.00	.07	−.10	−.00
2	.12	.00	.00	.03	.11	.04
3	.07	.00	.00	.08	.08	.09
η 4	−.07	.00	.00	−.17	−.08	−.17
5	−.01	.00	.00	.07	−.00	.08
6	.01	.00	.00	−.01	.03	.01
7	−.03	.00	.00	−.06	−.04	−.05

8C. Maximum Likelihood Estimates of Parameters in the Homogeneous Row-Column Effect Association Model Applied to Table 3

Param-eters	Row-Column Effect Association
θ	1.15
1	.95
2	1.08
3	1.09
ζ 4	.88
5	1.05
6	1.02
7	.96
ψ	.14
1	−.05
2	.08
3	.08
η 4	−.13
5	.05
6	.02
7	−.05

but the restrictions imposed on the $\xi_{i\cdot}$ and $\xi_{\cdot j}$ would be different from the kind used in (3.4b). Further comments on these matters will be included in Section 4.3.

4. ASSOCIATION MODELS REVISITED

4.1 Frequencies Expected Under the Models

Models pertaining to the odds-ratios θ_{ij} can be reexpressed in terms of the expected frequencies (see Goodman 1979a). Thus, we find that the two association models that include both row and column effects (Models I and II) can be reexpressed as follows: Under Model I, we obtain

$$F_{ij} = \alpha_i \beta_j \gamma_i{}^j \delta_j{}^i, \quad \text{for all } i, j , \qquad (4.1a)$$

where the superscripts on γ_i and δ_j denote powers, and under Model II we obtain

$$F_{ij} = \alpha_i \beta_j e^{\mu_i \nu_j}, \quad \text{for all } i, j . \qquad (4.1b)$$

From (2.1) and (4.1a), we see that the odds-ratio θ_{ij} can be expressed as

$$\theta_{ij} = (\gamma_{i+1}/\gamma_i)(\delta_{j+1}/\delta_j) \qquad (4.2a)$$

under Model I; from (2.1) and (4.1b) we see that

$$\log \theta_{ij} = (\mu_{i+1} - \mu_i)(\nu_{j+1} - \nu_j) \qquad (4.2b)$$

under Model II.

Note that formula (2.6) for θ_{ij} under Model I and formula (2.7) for $\log \theta_{ij}$ under Model II have the same form as (4.2a) and (4.2b), respectively. From (2.6) and (4.2a), we see that

$$\theta_{i\cdot} = \tau(\gamma_{i+1}/\gamma_i) \quad \text{and} \quad \theta_{\cdot j} = (\delta_{j+1}/\delta_j)/\tau \qquad (4.3a)$$

under Model I, and from (2.7) and (4.2b) we see that

$$\phi_{i\cdot} = \upsilon(\mu_{i+1} - \mu_i) \quad \text{and} \quad \phi_{\cdot j} = (\nu_{j+1} - \nu_j)/\upsilon \qquad (4.3b)$$

under Model II, where τ and υ are unspecified constants.

All the association models considered earlier (except for the symmetric association model presented in Section 3.3) are special cases of Models I and II. Model I can be expressed as a log-linear model, but Model II cannot. We have included both Models I and II in this article because in some cases the former model will be more appropriate and in other cases the latter model will be. The differences between the chi-squares obtained with these models can be large.

4.2 Invariance Properties for the Models

To demonstrate certain invariance properties for some of the models in this article, let us compare, say, Table 1 with the corresponding table obtained by interchanging columns A and B. From Tables 5A and 9A, we see that the chi-squared values were invariant under a change in column order for the null association model, the column-effect model, and Model II, but not for the other models. Similarly, chi-squared values are invariant under a change in row order for the null association model, the row-effect model, and Model II, but not for the other models. Only for the null association model and Model II are the chi-squared values invariant under changes in row order and column order.

For Model II, the i and j appear in formula (4.1b) only as indices, but for Model I, the i and j appear in formula (4.1a) as indices and powers. Thus, the invariance property applied for Model II but not for Model I. For similar reasons, the row-effect model and column-effect model are invariant under changes in row order and column order, respectively.

In the situation in which the row order is specified but the column order is not, under the column-effect model the columns can be ordered so that the estimated odds-ratios $\hat{\theta}_{.j} \geq 1$, for $j = 1, 2, \ldots, J - 1$. For example, from the $\hat{\theta}_{.j}$ in Table 8A, we see that by interchanging columns A and B in Table 1 we would obtain $\hat{\theta}_{.j} > 1$ for $j \geq 1$. (When the kth and $(k + 1)$th columns are interchanged, the $\hat{\theta}_{.k}$ and $\hat{\theta}_{.(k+1)}$ will be equal to $1/\hat{\theta}_{.k}'$ and $\hat{\theta}_{.k}'\hat{\theta}_{.(k+1)}'$, respectively, with $\hat{\theta}_{.k}'$ and $\hat{\theta}_{.(k+1)}'$

9A. Association Models Applied to Table 1 With Columns A and B Interchanged

Association Models	Degrees of Free-dom	Goodness-of-Fit Chi-Square	Likelihood Ratio Chi-Square
(1) Null Association	15	45.99	47.42
(2) Uniform Association	14	9.10	9.21
(3) Row-Effect Association	12	6.02	6.03
(4) Column-Effect Association	10	6.78	6.83
(5) Row and Column Effects (I)	8	3.59	3.59
(6) Row and Column Effects (II)	8	3.57	3.57

obtained from the original table. There is also a corresponding change in $\hat{\theta}._{(k-1)}$ when $k > 1$.) The desired column ordering can also be determined from the estimated δ_j in the column-effect model obtained from (4.1a) with $\gamma_i = 1$ (for $i = 1, 2, \ldots, I$). From (2.5) and (4.2a), we see that $\hat{\theta}._j \geqq 1$ if the columns are arranged in order of increasing (nondecreasing) $\hat{\delta}_j$, for $j = 1, 2, \ldots, J$. Thus, under the column-effect model, with the columns ordered appropriately, the estimated expected frequencies will be isotropic (see Yule and Kendall 1950). This result can be translated directly into a corresponding result for the row-effect model and Model II.

Under the column-effect model, if there is an ordering of the columns for which $\theta._j = \theta$ (for $j = 1, 2, \ldots, J-1$), then this ordering can be determined by the methods just described, and the uniform association model will hold true with the columns ordered appropriately. Also, under the column-effect model, if $\theta._j = 1$ for a specified subset of the values of j, then the column-effect model will hold true for the table obtained by combining certain adjacent columns, namely, the jth and $(j + 1)$th columns for values of j in the specified subset. If $\theta._j = 1$ for the specified subset of values of j and $\theta._j = \theta$ for the values of j not included in the subset, then the uniform association model will hold true for the table modified as just described. These results too can be translated directly into corresponding results for the row-effect model and Model II.

The estimated column effects $\hat{\theta}_{.j}$ presented in Table 8A for Table 1 led us to consider interchanging columns A and B, and the corresponding estimated row effects $\hat{\theta}_{i.}$ in Table 8A would lead us to consider combining rows 2 and 3 in Table 1. Even though the uniform association model fit quite well the data in the original Table 1, some improvement in fit can still be obtained with these modified forms of Table 1 (see Table 9B).

Under Model II the rows and the columns can be ordered so that the estimated odds-ratios $\hat{\theta}_{ij} \geqq 1$ (for $i = 1, 2, \ldots, I - 1$; $j = 1, 2, \ldots, J - 1$), using methods corresponding to those presented earlier in this section. Similarly, the estimated parameters under Model II can be used to determine which (if any) adjacent rows and/or adjacent columns can be combined. For example, with respect to $\xi_{i.}$ and $\xi_{.j}$ in (3.12), if $\xi_{i.} = 0$ and/or $\xi_{.j} = 0$ for a specified subset of the values of i and/or a specified subset of the values of j, respectively, then Model II will hold true for the table obtained by combining certain adjacent rows and/or adjacent columns, namely, the ith and $(i + 1)$th rows and/or the jth and $(j + 1)$th columns, for values of i and j in their respective specified subsets. Furthermore, if $\xi_{i.} = 0$ for a specified subset of the values of i and $\xi_{i.} = \xi$ for the values of i not included in the subset, then the column-effect model will hold true for the table modified as just described. A similar result applies when $\xi_{.j} = 0$ for a specified subset of the values of j.

For square contingency tables having a one-to-one correspondence between the row and column categories, we would usually not consider reordering the rows without reordering the columns in the same way. For such tables, the results for Model II in the preceding paragraph can be translated directly into corresponding results for Model II*.

The results pertaining to the ordering of the rows and

9B. Uniform Association Model Applied to Table 1 and to Modified Forms of Table 1

Form of Table 1	Degrees of Freedom	Goodness-of-Fit Chi-Square	Likelihood Ratio Chi-Square
Unmodified	14	9.73	9.89
Columns A and B Interchanged	14	9.10	9.21
Rows 2 and 3 Combined	9	3.99	4.00
Columns A and B Interchanged; Rows 2 and 3 Combined	9	3.88	3.92
Columns A and B Combined; Rows 2 and 3 Combined	7	1.80	1.79

columns for Models II and II* can be applied to contingency tables with entries deleted in certain specified cells, as long as the set of deleted entries remains unaffected by changes in the row and/or column order. The results pertaining to the combining of adjacent rows and/or adjacent columns cannot be applied to tables with entries deleted in certain specified cells, unless the particular combining of adjacent rows and/or adjacent columns does not affect the set of deleted entries. (These entries will be affected by such changes in the rows and/or columns, when the deleted cells are, say, those on the main diagonal.)

4.3 The Parameters Identified Under the Models

As we noted in Section 3.4, the parameters θ, $\theta_i.$, and $\theta._j$ in the uniform association model, the row-effect association model, and the column-effect association model are identifiable, and Models I and II can be rewritten in terms of identifiable parameters. From (2.6) and (3.4a), we see that

$$\theta_i. = \theta \zeta_i.\kappa , \quad \text{and} \quad \theta._j = \zeta._j/\kappa , \qquad (4.4a)$$

under Model I; and from (2.7) and (3.12) we see that

$$\phi_i. = \phi \xi_i.\lambda, \quad \text{and} \quad \phi._j = \xi._j/\lambda , \qquad (4.4b)$$

under Model II, where κ and λ are unspecified constants. Because the parameters $\zeta_i.$, $\zeta._j$, $\xi_i.$, and $\xi._j$ are identifiable, we see from (4.4a) and (4.4b) that the corresponding parameters $\theta_i.$, $\theta._j$, $\phi_i.$, and $\phi._j$ in Models I and II would be identifiable except for unspecified multiplicative constants. For some purposes, estimating the parameters that would be identifiable (with the unspecified multiplicative constant ignored) is sufficient, and we do not have to estimate the identifiable parameters themselves. For example, in the preceding section where Model II was used to determine row order and/or column order, the estimated $\phi_i.$ and $\phi._j$ could be used (ignoring the unspecified multiplicative constant) instead of the corresponding estimated $\xi_i.$ and $\xi._j$, since these quantities are used only to determine whether $\hat{\xi}_{i.} \geqq 0$ and $\hat{\xi}_{.j} \geqq 0$ (for $i = 1, 2, \ldots, I - 1$; $j = 1, 2, \ldots, J - 1$).

The preceding remarks about the parameters in Models I and II as defined by (2.6) and (2.7) can be translated into corresponding remarks about the parameters in these models as defined by (4.1a) and (4.1b). The latter formulas can be rewritten in terms of identifiable parameters. By rewriting (4.1a) and (4.1b) as

$$F_{ij} = \alpha_i \beta_j \theta^{ij} \gamma_i{}^j \delta_j{}^i, \quad \text{for all } i, j \qquad (4.5a)$$

and

$$F_{ij} = \alpha_i \beta_j e^{\phi \mu_i \nu_j}, \quad \text{for all } i, j , \qquad (4.5b)$$

respectively (with the superscripts on θ, γ_i, and δ_j in (4.5a) denoting powers), we find from (2.1) that

$$\theta_{ij} = \theta (\gamma_{i+1}/\gamma_i)(\delta_{j+1}/\delta_j) \qquad (4.6a)$$

and

$$\log \theta_{ij} = \phi(\mu_{i+1} - \mu_i)(\nu_{j+1} - \nu_j) \qquad (4.6b)$$

under Models I and II, respectively. Note that (4.6a) and (4.6b) have the same form as (3.4a) and (3.12), respectively.

Restrictions imposed on the parameters in (3.4a) and (3.12) can be imposed also on the corresponding quantities in (4.6a) and (4.6b). For example, restriction (3.4b) is equivalent to the restriction that

$$\gamma_1 = \gamma_I = 1, \quad \delta_1 = \delta_J = 1 , \qquad (4.7)$$

for the parameters in (4.5a).

Since Model II as defined by (4.5b) is invariant under changes in row order and/or column order, introducing parameter restrictions for this model that are also invariant in this way would be preferable in some cases. For example, we could consider the following restrictions:

$$\sum_{i=1}^{I} \mu_i = 0 , \quad \sum_{i=1}^{I} \mu_i^2 = 1 ,$$

$$\sum_{j=1}^{J} \nu_j = 0 , \quad \sum_{j=1}^{J} \nu_j^2 = 1 \qquad (4.8)$$

for the parameters in (4.5b). Model II expressed in the
form (4.5b) and (4.8) is considered by Andersen
(1979), and it is also related to models discussed by
Rasch (1966) and Fienberg (1968).

4.4 The Odds Described by the Models

The models described in terms of expected frequencies
F_{ij} view the row and column variables as response variables, but we may also describe these models by viewing
the row variable as a response or dependent variable
and the column variable as an explanatory factor, and
vice versa. Let $\Omega_{ij}{}^{A\bar{B}}$ denote the odds that an observation
will fall in column j rather than in column $j + 1$,
given that it is in row i, and let $\Omega_{ji}{}^{B\bar{A}}$ denote the odds
that an observation will fall in row i rather than in row
$i + 1$, given that it is in column j. Thus

$$\Omega_{ij}{}^{A\bar{B}} = F_{ij}/F_{i,j+1} ,$$

and a similar formula can be obtained for $\Omega_{ji}{}^{B\bar{A}}$. From
(4.1a) we see that

$$\Omega_{ij}{}^{A\bar{B}} = (\beta_j/\beta_{j+1})\{(\delta_j/\delta_{j+1})^i/\gamma_i\} \qquad (4.9)$$

under Model I, and a similar formula can be obtained
for $\Omega_{ji}{}^{B\bar{A}}$. (Under Model II, the term in braces in (4.9)
is replaced by $\exp[\mu_i(\nu_j - \nu_{j+1})]$.) For, say, the row-
effect association model with $\delta_j = 1$(for $j = 1, 2, \ldots, J$)
under Model I, we obtain

$$\Omega_{ij}{}^{A\bar{B}} = (\beta_j/\beta_{j+1})/\gamma_i , \qquad (4.10)$$

and the corresponding formula for $\Omega_{ji}{}^{B\bar{A}}$ is

$$\Omega_{ji}{}^{B\bar{A}} = (\alpha_i/\alpha_{i+1})(\gamma_i/\gamma_{i+1})^j . \qquad (4.11)$$

Formulas (4.10) and (4.11) describe the row-effect association model in terms that show that it is equivalent
to Simon's (1974) formulation A for the singly ordered
table. Models I and II are generalizations of Simon's
model.

In a similar way, we can show how the models considered herein are related to various models in Haberman
(1974a, 1979).

4.5 Models for Tables With Deleted Entries

We next comment briefly on association models for contingency tables in which the entries in certain cells have been deleted (e.g., the cells (i, j) contained in a given set S). Models defined for the full contingency table can be redefined in a straightforward manner for tables with entries deleted. Thus, model (4.1a) for the full table would be redefined as follows:

$$
\begin{aligned}
F_{ij} &= \alpha_i \beta_j \gamma_i{}^j \delta_j{}^i, \quad \text{for } (i, j) \notin S \\
&= \tau_{ij}, \qquad\quad \text{for } (i, j) \in S \ ,
\end{aligned}
\tag{4.12}
$$

where the τ_{ij} are unspecified parameters. The association model defined in terms of the θ_{ij} for the full contingency table (e.g., model (2.6)) is first translated into an equivalent model defined in terms of the F_{ij} (e.g., model (4.1a)), and then this model is redefined for the table with entries deleted (e.g., model (4.12)). The methods used to analyze the full contingency table can be modified in a straightforward way to obtain appropriate methods for tables with deleted entries (see Goodman 1968, 1972).

In our analysis of Tables 2 and 3 in Section 3.2 and 3.3, the set S consisted of the cells on the main diagonal. With this particular set, when the model for the full table was rewritten in terms of identifiable parameters, these parameters remained identifiable in the model for the table with entries deleted, and the parameters could not be divided into separable subsets in the table with entries deleted. We consider here only sets S that have this property. In this case, when there are σ cells in the set S, the number of degrees of freedom for testing a model in the table with set S deleted will be σ less than the corresponding number for the full table.

5. MAXIMUM LIKELIHOOD ESTIMATES

Consider first Model I. Because this model can be expressed as a multiplicative (or log-linear) model (see (4.1a)), the usual methods for calculating the maximum

likelihood estimates for such models can be applied here
(see Darroch and Ratcliff 1972 and Haberman 1974b,
1979). The maximum likelihood estimate $\hat{F}_{ij}$ of the expected frequency F_{ij} under (4.1a) will satisfy the following system of equations:

$$\hat{F}_{i\cdot} = f_{i\cdot} , \qquad (5.1a)$$

$$\hat{F}_{\cdot j} = f_{\cdot j} , \qquad (5.1b)$$

$$\sum_j j\hat{F}_{ij} = \sum_j jf_{ij} , \qquad (5.1c)$$

and

$$\sum_i i\hat{F}_{ij} = \sum_i if_{ij} , \qquad (5.1d)$$

where $f_{i\cdot}$ and $f_{\cdot j}$ denote the corresponding observed row
and column marginals and $\hat{F}_{i\cdot}$ and $\hat{F}_{\cdot j}$ denote the corresponding marginals for the table of $\hat{F}_{ij}$'s. Formulas
(5.1a) and (5.1b) pertain to the parameters α_i and β_j,
respectively, in formula (4.1a), and (5.1c) and (5.1d)
pertain to the γ_i and δ_j, respectively. These equations
can be solved by using the algorithm in Darroch and Ratcliff (1972), but the algorithm converges very slowly for
models of the kind considered here, so we shall propose
in the present article a different iterative procedure that
converges more rapidly in the examples we have considered.

Using circumflexes to denote maximum likelihood
estimates of the corresponding parameters, from (4.1a)
we obtain the following:

$$\hat{F}_{ij} = \hat{\alpha}_i\hat{\beta}_j\hat{\gamma}_i{}^j\hat{\delta}_j{}^i, \quad \text{for all } i, j . \qquad (5.2)$$

At any given stage in the iterative procedure, with the
trial values for the parameter estimates at that stage
denoted by $\alpha_i{}^*$, $\beta_j{}^*$, $\gamma_i{}^*$, $\delta_j{}^*$, a given parameter-estimate
trial value, say $\alpha_i{}^*$, can be replaced by a new trial value,
say $\alpha_i{}^{**}$, defined as follows:

$$\alpha_i{}^{**} = \alpha_i{}^* f_{i\cdot}/F_{i\cdot}{}^* , \qquad (5.3a)$$

where $F_{i\cdot}{}^*$ denotes the row marginal for the table of
$F_{ij}{}^*$'s calculated as in (5.2) by using the corresponding
trial values for the parameter estimates on the right-

hand side of (5.2). With the new trial value replacing $\alpha_i{}^*$, we recalculate $F_{ij}{}^*$, and then another parameter-estimate trial value, say $\beta_j{}^*$, can be replaced by a new trial value, say $\beta_j{}^{**}$, defined as follows:

$$\beta_j{}^{**} = \beta_j{}^* f_{\cdot j}/F_{\cdot j}{}^* , \qquad (5.3b)$$

where $F_{\cdot j}{}^*$ denotes the corresponding column marginal for the table of recalculated $F_{ij}{}^*$'s. With the new trial value replacing $\beta_j{}^*$, we again recalculate $F_{ij}{}^*$, and then another parameter-estimate trial value, say $\gamma_i{}^*$, can be replaced by a new trial value, say $\gamma_i{}^{**}$, defined as follows:

$$\gamma_i{}^{**} = \gamma_i{}^*\{1 + [\sum_j \sigma_j(f_{ij} - F_{ij}{}^*)]/[\sum_j \sigma_j{}^2 F_{ij}{}^*]\} , \quad (5.3c)$$

where $\sigma_j = j - (J + 1)/2$. With the new trial value replacing $\gamma_j{}^*$, we again recalculate $F_{ij}{}^*$, and then another parameter-estimate trial value, say $\delta_j{}^*$, can be replaced by a new trial value, say $\delta_j{}^{**}$, defined as follows:

$$\delta_j{}^{**} = \delta_j{}^*\{1 + [\sum_i \rho_i(f_{ij} - F_{ij}{}^*)]/[\sum_i \rho_i{}^2 F_{ij}{}^*]\} , \quad (5.3d)$$

where $\rho_i = i - (I + 1)/2$. This procedure is repeated until the trial values $F_{ij}{}^*$ for the $\hat{F}_{ij}$ satisfy conditions (5.1a) through (5.1d). The order in which the parameter-estimate trial values are replaced affects the speed of convergence, and we have found that the replacement of $\alpha_i{}^*$, $\delta_j{}^*$, $\beta_j{}^*$, and $\gamma_i{}^*$ in turn, recalculating $F_{ij}{}^*$ each time a replacement is made, led to satisfactory results.

Although the parameters on the right-hand side of (4.1a) are not identifiable in the form presented there, they still can be used to calculate the maximum likelihood estimates $\hat{F}_{ij}$ subject to the restrictions (5.1a) through (5.1d), using the procedure just described. The parameters can be made identifiable by imposing restrictions of the kind described in Section 4.3.

The iterative procedure described here was obtained by applying successively Newton's elementary (unidimensional) method of approximation (see Appendix A). This procedure converges more rapidly than the Darroch-Ratcliff algorithm in the cases considered here. An alternate method could be based on the usual (multi-dimensional) Newton-Raphson method in Haberman (1974b, 1979) or on related methods for the analysis of general log-linear models, but these methods are not so easy to apply as the iterative procedure proposed here.

The preceding procedure applied to Model I, and for special cases of this model straightforward modifications in the procedure can be made. For the row-effect association model, the parameter δ_j is deleted and the corresponding formulas (5.1d) and (5.3d) are deleted. Similar modifications are made for the column-effect association model. (With the latter model, the preferred order of replacement of parameter-estimate trial values is $\alpha_i{}^*$, $\delta_j{}^*$, $\beta_j{}^*$; and with the former model, it is $\beta_j{}^*$, $\gamma_i{}^*$, $\alpha_i{}^*$.) For the null association model, both δ_j and γ_i are deleted, and the corresponding (5.1c) and (5.1d) and (5.3c) and (5.3d) are deleted, thus giving the usual estimates for this model. For the uniform association model, we replace (5.1c) and (5.1d) by

$$\sum_{i,j} ij\hat{F}_{ij} = \sum_{i,j} ijf_{ij} , \qquad (5.4)$$

(see Goodman 1979a), the right-hand side of (4.1a) is replaced by $\alpha_i\beta_j\theta^{ij}$, and formulas (5.3c) and (5.3d) are replaced by

$$\theta^{**} = \theta^*\{1 + [\sum_{i,j} \rho_i\sigma_j(f_{ij} - F_{ij}{}^*)]/[\sum_{i,j} (\rho_i\sigma_j)^2 F_{ij}{}^*]\} .$$
$$(5.5)$$

We next consider Model II. Comparing (4.1b) with (4.1a), we see that Model II is a modification of Model I in which the power j in (4.1a) is replaced by ν_j with δ_j deleted, or the power i in (4.1a) is replaced by μ_i with γ_i deleted. Because of this similarity between Models I and II, the maximum likelihood estimate $\hat{F}_{ij}$ of the F_{ij} under Model II will satisfy (5.1a), (5.1b), and the following equations:

$$\sum_{j} \hat{\nu}_j\hat{F}_{ij} = \sum_{j} \hat{\nu}_jf_{ij} \qquad (5.6a)$$

$$\sum_{i} \hat{\mu}_i\hat{F}_{ij} = \sum_{i} \hat{\mu}_if_{ij} . \qquad (5.6b)$$

Compare (5.6a) and (5.6b) with (5.1c) and (5.1d). The iterative estimation procedure described here for Model I can be modified to obtain a corresponding procedure for Model II (see Appendix B).

Although Model II is not a multiplicative (log-linear) model, if the μ_i and/or ν_j in (4.1b) are specified, the model becomes multiplicative. Thus, the usual methods for the analysis of such multiplicative models can be applied in this case. Model II could be analyzed by first viewing the μ_i as specified in order to estimate the corresponding ν_j, then viewing the estimated ν_j thus obtained as specified to estimate the corresponding μ_i. The iterative estimation procedure continues in this alternating fashion until convergence is achieved.

When the μ_i or the ν_j in (4.1b) are specified, we obtain a generalization of the column-effect association model (with the rows not necessarily equidistant) or a generalization of the row-effect association model (with the columns not necessarily equidistant), respectively. When the μ_i and ν_j are specified, we obtain a corresponding generalization of the uniform association model. For these generalizations, we can modify in a straightforward way the methods presented earlier in this section for Model I.

The methods for Model I can also be modified in a straightforward way to obtain corresponding methods for Model I*, and methods for Model II* can be obtained too. With respect to the symmetric association model, because this model is equivalent to the usual quasi-symmetry model, the usual methods for the analysis of the latter model can be applied in this case (see Caussinus 1965; Bishop, Fienberg, and Holland 1975).

6. SOME EXTENSIONS

The models and methods presented in this article for the two-way table can be extended to the m-way table ($m = 3, 4, \ldots$). Let us consider, say, an $I \times J \times K$ three-way table with the I rows and the J columns ordered. This table can be viewed as a set of K $I \times J$ tables, and each of the K tables can be analyzed by using the methods developed here. Thus, for example, if the uniform association model holds true in the kth table ($k = 1, 2, \ldots, K$), then we can test the usual hypothesis of independence between the row and column classifications in this table by using the chi-squared statistic (with one degree of freedom) pertaining to the hypothesis that the general overall level of association in the table is nil (see the general effect component in Tables 5B, 6B, and 7B). Summing this chi-squared statistic for the K tables, we obtain a chi-squared statistic (with K degrees of freedom) for testing the hypothesis of conditional independence between the row and column classifications, given the level of the third classification in the three-way table, under the assumption that the conditional uniform association model holds true. Similarly, if the uniform association model holds true for each of the K two-way tables, we can test the hypothesis of zero three-factor interaction in the three-way table by using a chi-squared statistic (with $K - 1$ degrees of freedom) pertaining to the hypothesis that the overall level of association in each of the K tables is the same. The methods introduced earlier can be directly extended to do this.

Let us consider next the $I \times J \times K$ table with the I rows, the J columns, and the K layers ordered. For this table, a basic set of $2 \times 2 \times 2$ subtables can be formed from adjacent rows, adjacent columns, and adjacent layers of the full table. There will be $(I - 1)(J - 1) \times (K - 1)$ such subtables. The three-factor interaction in the full table can be measured in terms of the odds-ratio-ratios in the $2 \times 2 \times 2$ subtables. Corresponding to the uniform association model for the two-way table, we now have a uniform three-factor interaction model for the three-way table. If this model holds true, then we can test the usual hypothesis of zero three-factor interaction by using a chi-squared statistic (with one degree of freedom) pertaining to the hypothesis that the overall level of the three-factor interaction is nil. The methods introduced earlier can be directly extended to do this too.

To analyze further the three-factor interaction in the three-way contingency table, the odds-ratio-ratios in the $2 \times 2 \times 2$ subtables can be displayed as entries in a three-way $(I - 1) \times (J - 1) \times (K - 1)$ table format, and the usual three-way analysis of variance viewpoint can be applied to obtain corresponding models for the analysis of these odds-ratio-ratios.

These remarks can be extended in a straightforward way to the analysis of the m-way contingency table.

APPENDIX A: THE ITERATIVE PROCEDURE FOR MODEL I

We consider here Model I expressed in the more general form

$$F_{ij} = \alpha_i \beta_j \gamma_i^{\sigma_j} \delta_j^{\rho_i} , \qquad (A.1)$$

where the superscripts σ_j and ρ_i denote specified powers. For this model, the maximum likelihood equations can be rewritten as

$$f_{i \cdot} - \hat{F}_{i \cdot} = 0 , \quad f_{\cdot j} - \hat{F}_{\cdot j} = 0 , \quad \sum_j \sigma_j (f_{ij} - \hat{F}_{ij}) = 0 ,$$

$$\sum_i \rho_i (f_{ij} - \hat{F}_{ij}) = 0 . \quad (A.2)$$

With α_i^*, β_j^*, γ_i^*, and δ_j^* denoting the parameter-estimate trial values at a given stage in the iterative procedure, and F_{ij}^* denoting the corresponding trial value for $\hat{F}_{ij}$, we can view α_i^* as an approximate root in the equation $f_{i \cdot} - F_{i \cdot}^* = 0$ obtained from (A.2), and we can apply Newton's elementary (unidimensional) method to this equation to replace the approximate root α_i^* by α_i^{**} defined by (5.3a). Similarly, by viewing β_j^*, γ_i^*, and δ_j^* as approximate roots in the corresponding equations obtained from the three other equations in (A.2), we can derive (5.3b), (5.3c), and (5.3d). The corresponding iterative procedure will have the same convergence properties for Model (A.1) (a log-linear model) as the usual (multidimensional) Newton-Raphson procedure, except that the rate of convergence will be slower in the former case (see Haberman 1974b).

APPENDIX B: THE ITERATIVE PROCEDURE FOR MODEL II

We consider here Model II expressed in the form

$$F_{ij} = \alpha_i \beta_j e^{\rho_i \sigma_j} , \qquad (B.1)$$

where $\rho_i = \mu_i - \bar{\mu}$, $\sigma_j = \nu_j - \bar{\nu}$, $\bar{\mu} = \sum_i \mu_i / I$, $\bar{\nu} = \sum_j \nu_j / J$, and where the exponents ρ_i and σ_j now denote parameters. The iterative procedure presented here for Model I can be modified for Model II by replacing (5.2) by

$$\hat{F}_{ij} = \hat{\alpha}_i \hat{\beta}_j e^{\hat{\rho}_i \hat{\sigma}_j} , \qquad (B.2)$$

and by replacing (5.3c) and (5.3d) by

$$\mu_i^{**} = \mu_i^* + \left[\sum_j \sigma_j^* (f_{ij} - F_{ij}^*) \right] / \left[\sum_j \sigma_j^{*2} F_{ij}^* \right] ,$$

$$\nu_j^{**} = \nu_j^* + \left[\sum_i \rho_i^* (f_{ij} - F_{ij}^*) \right] / \left[\sum_i \rho_i^{*2} F_{ij}^* \right] ,$$

where $\rho_i^* = \mu_i^* - \bar{\mu}^*$, $\sigma_j^* = \nu_j^* - \bar{\nu}^*$, $\rho_i^{**} = \mu_i^{**} - \bar{\mu}^{**}$, $\sigma_j^{**} = \nu_j^{**} - \bar{\nu}^{**}$, with $\bar{\mu}^* = \sum_i \mu_i^* / I$, and with $\bar{\nu}^*$, $\bar{\mu}^{**}$, and $\bar{\nu}^{**}$ defined similarly. The specified values used for ρ_i and σ_j in (5.3c) and (5.3d) are now used as initial values for the corresponding ρ_i^* and σ_j^* in the iterative procedure. (In other words, as initial values for the corresponding μ_i^* and ν_j^* in the iterative procedure, we now take $\mu_i^* = i$ and $\nu_j^* = j$.) For Model II, we have found that the replacement of α_i^*, ρ_i^*, β_j^*, σ_j^* in turn, recalculating F_{ij}^* each time a replacement is made, led to satisfactory results.

* Addendum: The entry in cell (5,5) of Table 2 was given as 714 in the earlier literature that used the data in Glass (1954); but for the sake of consistency with the results given by Miller (1960), we have changed the number to 715. This change does not affect the analysis presented here.

REFERENCES

Andersen, E.B. (1979), *Discrete Statistical Models With Social Science Applications*, Amsterdam: North-Holland Publishing Co.

Bishop, Y.M., Fienberg, S.E., and Holland, P.W. (1975). *Discrete Multivariate Analysis: Theory and Practice*, Cambridge, Mass.: MIT Press.

Caussinus, H. (1965), "Contribution à l'analyse statistique des tableaux de corrélation," *Annales de la Faculté des Sciences de l'Université de Toulouse*, 29, 77–182.

Darroch, J.N., and Ratcliff, D. (1972), "Generalized Iterative Scaling for Log-Linear Models," *Annals of Mathematical Statistics*, 43, 1470–1480.

Duncan, O.D. (1979), "How Destination Depends on Origin in the Occupational Mobility Table," *American Journal of Sociology*, 84, 793–803.

Edwards, A.W.F. (1963), "The Measure of Association in a 2 × 2 Table," *Journal of the Royal Statistical Society*, Ser. A, 126, 109–114.

Fienberg, S.E. (1968), "The Estimation of Cell Probabilities in Two-Way Contingency Tables," unpublished Ph.D. thesis, Dept. of Statistics, Harvard University.

Glass, D.V. (ed.) (1954), *Social Mobility in Britain*, Glencoe, Ill.: Free Press.

Goodman, Leo A. (1965), "On the Multivariate Analysis of Three Dichotomous Variables," *American Journal of Sociology*, 71, 290–301.

* ———— (1968), "The Analysis of Cross-Classified Data: Independence, Quasi-Independence, and Interactions in Contingency Tables With or Without Missing Entries," *Journal of the American Statistical Association*, 63, 1091–1131.

* ———— (1969), "How to Ransack Social Mobility Tables and Other Kinds of Cross-Classification Tables," *American Journal of Sociology*, 75, 1–39.

———— (1970), "The Multivariate Analysis of Qualitative Data: Interactions among Multiple Classifications," *Journal of the American Statistical Association*, 65, 226–256.

* ———— (1972), "Some Multiplicative Models for the Analysis of Cross-Classified Data," in *Proceedings of the Sixth Berkeley Symposium on Mathematical Statistics and Probability*, eds. L. Le Cam et al., Berkeley: University of California Press.

———— (1975), "A New Model for Scaling Response Patterns: An Application of the Quasi-Independence Concept," *Journal of the American Statistical Association*, 70, 755–768.

* ———— (1979a), "Multiplicative Models for the Analysis of Occupational Mobility Tables and Other Kinds of Cross-Classification Tables," *American Journal of Sociology*, 84, 804–819.

———— (1979b), "The Analysis of Qualitative Variables Using More Parsimonious Quasi-Independence Models, Scaling Models, and Latent Structures that Fit the Observed Data," in *Qualitative and Quantitative Social Research: Papers in Honor of Paul F.*

Lazarsfeld, ed. R.M. Merton, J.S. Coleman, and P.H. Rossi, New York : Free Press.

Haberman, S.J. (1974a), "Log-Linear Models for Frequency Tables With Ordered Classifications," *Biometrics*, 30, 589–600.

—— (1974b), *The Analysis of Frequency Data*, Chicago : University of Chicago Press.

—— (1979), *Analysis of Qualitative Data: Vol. 2. New Developments*, New York : Academic Press.

Hauser, R.M. (1980), "Some Exploratory Methods for Modeling Mobility Tables and Other Cross-Classified Data," in *Sociological Methodology 1980*, ed. Karl F. Schuessler, San Francisco : Jossey-Bass.

McCullagh, P. (1978), "The Analysis of Matched Pairs With Qualitative Data," Technical Report No. 75, Department of Statistics, University of Chicago.

Miller, S.M. (1960), "Comparative Social Mobility," *Current Sociology*, 9, 1–89.

Rasch, G. (1966), *Statistikkens Teori*, Lecture notes compiled by U. Christiansen in Danish, University of Copenhagen.

Simon, Gary (1974), "Alternative Analyses for the Singly-Ordered Contingency Table," *Journal of the American Statistical Association*, 69, 971–976.

Srole, L., Langner, T.S., Michael, S.T., Opler, M.K., and Rennie, T.A.C. (1962), *Mental Health in the Metropolis: The Midtown Manhattan Study*, New York : McGraw-Hill Book Co.

Yule, G.U., and Kendall, M.G. (1950), *An Introduction to the Theory of Statistics* (14th ed.), New York : Hafner.

5.
Association Models Revisited: I
Association Models and the Bivariate Normal for Contingency Tables with Ordered Categories

Association models considered by Goodman (1979) for contingency tables with ordered categories are presented here in a somewhat different form to facilitate comparison with the bivariate normal. Association models can be applied when an underlying bivariate normal is assumed and also under more general conditions, and they provide alternatives to tetrachoric and polychoric correlation. These models agree more closely with the bivariate normal than does Plackett's model (1965), when the row and column classifications arise from underlying univariate normal distributions. The general utility of the association models is illustrated here.

1. INTRODUCTION

For the analysis of two-way contingency tables, Karl Pearson (1900) proposed, among other things, an approach based on the bivariate normal. This approach has been developed further over the years; see, for example, Tallis (1962), Lancaster & Hamdan (1964), Lancaster (1969, p. 199), Kirk (1973) and Divgi (1979). The approach assumes that the row and column classifications arise from underlying continuous random variables having a bivariate normal distribution, so that the sample contingency table comes from a discretized bivariate normal. In many contexts, this assumption is invalid, and a more general approach is needed.

In the present paper, association models are used to provide a more general approach. These models can be applied to estimate, say, the correlation ρ in the underlying bivariate normal distribution when that distribution obtains, and they can also be applied to estimate a related coefficient under more general circumstances.

Pearson's approach using the bivariate normal appears wholly different from Yule's (1912) approach to contingency table analysis; but by use of association models here, I shall obtain a kind of reconciliation between them. In a commentary on Yule's work, Pearson & Heron (1913, p. 159) stated, for example, that

if Mr Yule's views are accepted, irreparable damage will be done to the growth of modern statistical theory.

And Yule (1912, p. 640) stated, for example, that the value of Pearson's method

depends entirely on the empirical truth of the assumptions made . . . . These assumptions were never adequately tested [by Pearson] . . ., and the few tests which I applied . . . sufficed to show that they were, to say the least, of exceedingly doubtful validity . . . .

The reader may be surprised that any reconciliation is possible.

The association models considered here were presented in a somewhat different form by Goodman (1979); see also related literature cited there. We compare the association models with the bivariate normal in the same situation that Plackett (1965) used to compare his class of bivariate distributions with the bivariate normal. We find that the association models agree more closely with the bivariate normal than does Plackett's model, when the row and column classifications arise from underlying univariate normal distributions.

Plackett's model was called the distribution with 'constant Yulean association' by Pearson (1913). One of the association models considered by Goodman (1979), namely the uniform association model, can be called the distribution with 'constant local association'. We find that the distribution with constant local association, and the other association models considered here, agree more closely with the bivariate normal than does the distribution with constant Yulean association.

Pearson & Heron (1913, p. 315) stated that

no frequency surfaces in actual practice exhibit, as far as we are aware, . . . constant Yulean association.

Nevertheless, the distribution with constant Yulean association has been applied in actual practice (Wahrendorf, 1980; Anscombe, 1981, chapter 12). We shall compare this distribution in some examples with the distribution with constant local association and the other association models considered here.

2. ASSOCIATION MODELS AND THE BIVARIATE NORMAL

For an $I \times J$ contingency table with ordered rows and ordered columns, let f_{ij} denote the observed frequency in the ith row and jth column of the table ($i = 1, ..., I; j = 1, ..., J$), and let F_{ij} denote the corresponding expected frequency under some model. We assume as usual that a multinomial distribution applies to the $I \times J$ table, although some of the methods presented here can be applied in other situations as well (Goodman, 1979).

Consider as a model for the expected frequencies

$$F_{ij} = \alpha_i \beta_j e^{\phi \mu_i \nu_j}, \qquad (2\cdot1)$$

where α_i, β_j, μ_i, ν_j and ϕ are parameters. The meaning of these parameters is clarified by (2·3) and (2·5) below, and by further comments by Goodman (1979, 1981). For 2×2 subtables formed from adjacent rows, rows i and $i+1$, and adjacent columns, columns j and $j+1$, in the $I \times J$ table, let Θ_{ij} denote the corresponding odds ratio based on the expected frequencies:

$$\Theta_{ij} = (F_{ij} F_{i+1,j+1})/(F_{i,j+1} F_{i+1,j}) \quad (i = 1, ..., I-1; j = 1, ..., J-1). \qquad (2\cdot2)$$

From (2·1) and (2·2) we obtain

$$\log \Theta_{ij} = \phi(\mu_i - \mu_{i+1})(\nu_j - \nu_{j+1}). \qquad (2\cdot3)$$

From (2·3) we see that the 'uniform association model' is obtained when

$$\mu_i - \mu_{i+1} = \Delta \quad (i = 1, ..., I-1), \quad \nu_j - \nu_{j+1} = \Delta' \quad (j = 1, ..., J-1), \qquad (2\cdot4)$$

where Δ and Δ' are unspecified; and the 'row-effect association model' and 'column-effect association model' can be defined in similar terms (Goodman, 1979, 1981). Model (2·1) includes both row and column effects on the association. When $\phi = 0$ in (2·1), the 'null association model' is obtained.

The μ_i in (2·1) can be viewed as a score or a location pertaining to the ith row; the ν_j in (2·1) can be viewed similarly for the jth column. We compare the joint distribution of the scores μ_i and ν_j with the bivariate normal.

Consider now random variables X and Y having a joint bivariate normal distribution with, say, zero means and unit variances. To facilitate our comparison, we standardize μ_i and ν_j similarly:

$$\sum_{i=1}^{I} \mu_i P_{i.} = 0, \quad \sum_{i=1}^{I} \mu_i^2 P_{i.} = 1, \quad \sum_{j=1}^{J} \nu_j P_{.j} = 0, \quad \sum_{j=1}^{J} \nu_j^2 P_{.j} = 1, \quad (2\cdot5)$$

where $P_{i.} = \Sigma_j P_{ij}, P_{.j} = \Sigma_i P_{ij}, P_{ij} = F_{ij}/N, N = \Sigma F_{ij}$. The correlation between X and Y is $\rho = E(XY)$, and the corresponding correlation between μ_i and ν_j is

$$\rho^* = \sum_{i=1}^{I} \sum_{j=1}^{J} \mu_i \nu_j P_{ij}. \quad (2\cdot6)$$

The bivariate normal density at $X = x$ and $Y = y$ includes $xy\rho/(1-\rho^2)$ in the exponent, whereas the corresponding term in (2·1) is $\mu_i \nu_j \phi$. To facilitate our comparison, express ϕ in (2·1) as

$$\phi = \tau/(1-\tau^2); \quad (2\cdot7a)$$

thus, for $\phi > 0$,

$$\tau = (1+\eta^2)^{\frac{1}{2}} - \eta, \quad (2\cdot7b)$$

with $\eta = (2\phi)^{-1}$ and $0 < |\tau| < 1$. Formula (2·7a) expresses ϕ in terms of τ, and (2·7b) expresses τ in terms of $\eta = (2\phi)^{-1}$. When $\phi < 0$, the negative square root is taken in (2·7b). By replacing ϕ by $\tau/(1-\tau^2)$, we see that model (2·1) for the scores μ_i and ν_j is related to the bivariate normal; but the α_i and β_j in (2·1) are more general in form than the corresponding functions in the bivariate normal.

When the row and column scores, μ_i and ν_j, in the $I \times J$ table pertain to underlying continuous random variables, say, U and V, respectively, then all values of U that are in the ith row are treated in (2·6) as if they were concentrated at μ_i, and all values of V that are in the jth column are treated as if they were concentrated at ν_j. In this context, the variance calculated from such 'grouped data' can be corrected for the grouping effect by Sheppard's correction (Yule & Kendall, 1950, p. 133); the correlation can be adjusted accordingly. Thus, since the variances calculated from the grouped data are equal to one in (2·5), the corrected variances for the underlying row and column variables would be $1 - \delta_\mu^2/12$ and $1 - \delta_\nu^2/12$, respectively, where δ_μ and δ_ν are the widths of the corresponding row and column categories; and the corrected correlation would be

$$\rho_S = \rho^* \{(1 - \delta_\mu^2/12)(1 - \delta_\nu^2/12)\}^{-\frac{1}{2}}. \quad (2\cdot8)$$

The δ_μ and δ_ν in (2·8) are taken equal to $|\Delta|$ and $|\Delta'|$, respectively, when (2·4) is satisfied; and more generally, we take $\delta_\mu = |(\mu_I - \mu_1)/(I-1)|$ and $\delta_\nu = |(\nu_J - \nu_1)/(J-1)|$, when the rows and the columns are in their appropriate order. When (2·4) is not satisfied, to apply (2·8) the row widths should not vary excessively, and neither should the column widths. Since ρ^* in (2·6) is a product moment correlation, and ρ_S in (2·8) is the corrected correlation, the usual interpretations of such correlations can be applied directly to ρ^* and ρ_S.

Since the parameter τ in model (2·1) for the 'grouped data' can be related to the correlation ρ in an underlying bivariate normal, a corrected τ will sometimes be of interest:

$$\tau_S = \tau\{(1 - \delta_\mu^2/12)(1 - \delta_\nu^2/12)\}^{-\frac{1}{2}}. \quad (2\cdot9)$$

Sheppard's correction can be made by division as in (2·9) or (2·8), or by multiplication by $\{(1 + \delta_\mu^2/12)(1 + \delta_\nu^2/12)\}^{\frac{1}{2}}$.

3. The bivariate normal, the uniform association model and Plackett's model

Table 1 compares the discretized bivariate normal for $\rho = \frac{1}{2}$ with two related models. From this table we see that the corresponding uniform association model agrees more closely with the bivariate normal than does Plackett's model.

The bivariate normal entries for $\rho = \frac{1}{2}$ were calculated from National Bureau of Standards tables (1959); the Plackett model entries were obtained from his 1965 article; and the entries for the uniform association model can be obtained by either of two methods:

(i) calculate μ_i and ν_j from (2·4) and (2·5) using the discretized univariate normal; calculate ϕ from (2·7a) with τ obtained from (2·9) with $\tau_S = \frac{1}{2}$; calculate (2·1) using μ_i, ν_j and ϕ with margins fitted iteratively to the discretized univariate normal;

(ii) use the iterative procedure of Goodman (1979) for the uniform association model applied to the discretized bivariate normal frequencies. This iterative procedure can provide the corresponding entries in Table 1 and scores μ_i and ν_j, which we can then standardize using (2·5).

All numerical results pertaining to association models in the present article were obtained by the methods introduced by Goodman (1979) and by straightforward modifications of those methods.

For the uniform association model in Table 1, the ρ_S and τ_S in (2·8) and (2·9) were $\frac{1}{2}$, the ρ^* and τ in (2·6) and (2·7) were 0·49, and ϕ in (2·1) was 0·65; see (2·7a) and (2·7b). All calculations were carried out to more significant digits than are reported here. To the present order of accuracy, ρ_S and τ_S agree in numerical value, and so do ρ^* and τ, but this will usually not be the case if the width of the row and column categories is much broader than in Table 1, and/or if the underlying model is not the bivariate normal. The correlation ρ_S will usually agree more closely with the correlation coefficient in the underlying bivariate normal than will τ_S. Thus, use of ρ_S is recommended when an underlying bivariate normal is assumed. On the other hand, when this assumption is invalid, choice between ρ_S and τ_S can be based on whether attention is focused upon the correlation between the random variables in the underlying distribution or upon a parameter in the underlying distribution that is more directly related to ϕ in (2·1) or τ in (2·7). Sheppard's correction replacing ρ^* by ρ_S can be justified even when the underlying continuous distribution is not bivariate normal (Yule & Kendall, 1950, p. 231), but a corresponding justification is not available in this case for the replacement of τ by τ_S.

The uniform association model, rather than the more general (2·1), was used in Table 1 because consecutive row categories in this table could be treated as if they were, in a certain sense, equidistant, and consecutive column categories could be treated similarly; see (2·4). When the categories cannot be treated this way, model (2·1) can be used instead. This model will agree even more closely with the bivariate normal than does the uniform association model.

The particular Plackett's model in our Table 1 was compared with the bivariate normal for $\rho = \frac{1}{2}$ by Pearson (1913), Plackett (1965), and above; but it was compared with the bivariate normal for $\rho = 0·45$ by Mardia (1967) and for $\rho = 0·6$ by Anscombe (1981,

Table 1. *Bivariate normal distribution with ρ = 0·5, first entry, compared with the corresponding uniform association model, second entry, and Plackett's model, third entry. Probability = entry/10⁴*

y\x	0·0	0·5	1·0	1·5	2·0	2·5
	6	11	14	13	9	7
	6·5	11·4	14·3	13·1	8·6	5·4
2·5	11	12	14	7	5	1
	23	35	37	29	16	9
	23·4	34·7	37·2	29·0	16·4	8·6
2·0	27	36	33	23	8	5
	79	99	90	60	29	13
	78·4	99·3	90·7	60·2	29·0	13·1
1·5	76	97	88	52	24	6
	191	205	160	90	37	14
	190·7	205·9	160·4	90·7	37·2	14·3
1·0	180	210	165	88	32	15
	336	309	205	99	35	11
	336·9	310·0	205·9	99·3	34·7	11·4
0·5	340	331	210	97	36	12
	429	336	191	79	23	6
	429·5	336·9	190·7	78·4	23·4	6·5
0·0	458	340	180	77	26	11
	396	266	129	45	12	2
	396·5	265·2	128·0	44·9	11·4	2·7
−0·5	397	239	115	49	17	6
	266	152	63	19	4	1
	265·2	151·1	62·2	18·6	4·0	0·8
−1·0	238	131	64	26	10	3
	129	63	22	6	1	0
	128·0	62·2	21·8	5·6	1·0	0·2
−1·5	116	63	30	14	4	2
	45	19	6	1	0	0
	44·9	18·6	5·6	1·2	0·2	0·0
−2·0	49	27	13	5	2	1
	12	4	1	0	0	0
	11·4	4·0	1·0	0·2	0·0	0·0
−2·5	17	9	5	2	1	0
	2	1	0	0	0	0
	2·7	0·8	0·2	0·0	0·0	0·0
	6	3	2	0	1	0

Chapter 12). Comparison now of the discretized bivariate normal for $\rho = 0\cdot45$ and $\rho = 0\cdot6$ with the related models shows, as was the case in Table 1, that the corresponding uniform association models agree more closely with the bivariate normal distributions than does Plackett's model.

Plackett's model did not agree so well with the bivariate normal because of the skewness of the conditional distributions obtained with this model and the nonlinearity of its regressions (Pearson, 1913), and because Yulean association is constant in Plackett's model but not in the bivariate normal (Mosteller, 1968).

4. FREQUENCY SURFACES IN ACTUAL PRACTICE

Pearson (1913) thought that no frequency surfaces in actual practice could be described by Plackett's model. Since Pearson was the first to study this model, it could be called the Pearson–Plackett model, but Pearson might have objected to this. It could also be called the Yule–Plackett model since Yulean association is constant in it, or the model with 'constant quadrant association'. We shall now briefly compare results obtained when this model is applied in actual practice, as for example, by Wahrendorf (1980), with results that can be obtained using the association models.

We reanalyse the data considered by Wahrendorf. For earlier analyses of some of these data, see, for example, Goodman (1972) and the literature cited there. The data are given in Table 2. Table 3 gives the value of the likelihood ratio chi-squared obtained when the null association model and the uniform association model are applied to Table 2(a) and to Tables 2(b) and 2(c) with main diagonal deleted. Table 3 includes also results for Table 2(b) with the original entry in cell (5, 1); the original entry was given as 0 by Glass (1954, p.

Table 2. *Three cross-classifications analysed by Wahrendorf* (1980)

(a). *Cross-classification of students according to number of newspapers read carefully and number of newspapers looked at only briefly*

Number read carefully	Number looked at only briefly			
	0	1	2	3 +
0	77	75	19	13
1	179	136	65	37
2	86	70	45	22
3 +	23	25	15	11

(b) and (c). *Cross-classification of British and Danish male samples according to each subject's occupational status category and his father's occupational status category. Upper entry. British; lower entry Danish*

Father's status	Subject's status				
	1	2	3	4	5
1	50	45	8	18	8
	18	17	16	4	2
2	28	174	84	154	55
	24	105	109	59	21
3	11	78	110	223	96
	23	84	289	217	95
4	14	150	185	714	447
	8	49	175	348	198
5	3	42	72	320	411
	6	8	69	201	246

183), not 3 as in the table used by Wahrendorf. Table 3 shows that a dramatic improvement in fit is obtained when the uniform association model is applied to each of the cross-classifications. Note that additional improvement in fit can be obtained for the 5×5 tables with some of the other association models considered here and by Goodman (1979). In contrast, Wahrendorf noted that Plackett's model was congruent with Table 2(a) but not with Tables 2(b) and 2(c). Plackett's model is not congruent with Tables 2(b) and (c) when the main diagonal is not deleted; and when it is deleted, application of this model in its present form is not meaningful. Somewhat similar results can be obtained with the three cross-classifications analyzed by Goodman (1979).

Table 3. *Association models applied to Tables* 2(a), (b) *and* (c)

Association model	Degrees of freedom	Likelihood ratio chi-squared
(a). *For Table* 2(a)		
Null association	9	16·29
Uniform association	8	7·37
(b). *For Table* 2(b) *with main diagonal deleted*		
Null association	11	235·78
Uniform association	10	14·08
(c). *For Table* 2(c) *with main diagonal deleted*		
Null association	11	248·70
Uniform association	10	15·40
(d). *For Table* 2(b) *with main diagonal deleted and original* (5, 1) *entry*		
Null association	11	249·43
Uniform association	10	19·30

5. POLYCHORIC CORRELATION AND THE ρ_S CORRELATION

Pearson (1900) introduced the tetrachoric series to estimate the correlation in the 2×2 contingency table, and Lancaster & Hamdan (1964) introduced the more general polychoric series to estimate the correlation in the $I \times J$ table for $I > 2$ and/or $J > 2$. Lancaster & Hamdan applied their method to estimate the correlation of heights of fathers and daughters in a classic set of data, using three different 8×8 tables, and two smaller tables, obtained by grouping in various ways the row categories, daughter's height, and the column categories, father's height, in the original data. In Table 4 we compare the polychoric estimates with the corresponding values obtained by estimating ρ_S in (2·8) under the uniform association model and association model (2·1), using the 8×8

Table 4. *Estimate of correlation coefficient of stature of fathers and daughters, calculated from* 8×8 *and* 3×3 *cross-classifications*

	Cross-classification	
	8×8	3×3
Pearson contingency method	0·473	0·381
Lancaster–Hamdan polychoric	0·504	0·497
ρ_S for uniform association	0·523	0·494
ρ_S for association model (2·1)	0·529	0·492

and 3×3 tables based on a 'natural' grouping of rows and of columns, neighbouring classes being pooled. Since Lancaster & Hamdan also considered Pearson's contingency method estimates, we include them too in Table 4.

The 8×8 and 3×3 cross-classifications used in Table 4 were obtained by Lancaster & Hamdan from their 18×18 version of the original data. The product moment correlation is 0·517, with Sheppard's correction, in their 18×18 table, not 0·5157 as stated by them, and so the estimates in Table 4 should be compared with this value. From Table 4 Pearson's contingency method is less satisfactory than the other methods, and the polychoric method and the ρ_S method give somewhat similar results. The latter method is a bit better when the uniform association model is applied to the 8×8 table, and the former method is a bit better when applied to the 3×3 table. The ρ_S method is better for the 8×8 table than for the 3×3 table because the association models are more directly related to the bivariate normal density function than to the corresponding bivariate normal probabilities.

The estimates of ρ_S in Table 4 were obtained by applying to the 8×8 and 3×3 cross-classifications the iterative procedure of Goodman (1979). The estimates of μ_i and ν_j thus obtained were standardized using (2·5), and the ρ^* and ρ_S were estimated using (2·6) and (2·8), replacing the terms on the right-hand side of these formulae by their estimates. In contrast to this, Lancaster–Hamdan estimates are calculated as the solutions of polychoric series equations.

REFERENCES

ANSCOMBE, F. J. (1981). *Computing in Statistical Science through APL*. New York: Springer-Verlag.

DIVGI, D. R. (1979). Calculation of the tetrachoric correlation coefficient. *Psychometrika* **44**, 169–72.

GLASS, D. V. (editor) (1954). *Social Mobility in Britain*. Glencoe, Illinois: Free Press.

* GOODMAN, L. A. (1972). Some multiplicative models for the analysis of cross classified data. *Proc. 6th Berkeley Symp.* **1**, 649–96.

* GOODMAN, L. A. (1979). Simple models for the analysis of cross-classifications having ordered categories. *J. Am. Statist. Assoc.* **74**, 537–52.

* GOODMAN, L. A. (1981). Association models and canonical correlation in the analysis of cross-classifications having ordered categories. *J. Am. Statist. Assoc.* **76**. To appear.

KIRK, D. B. (1973). On the numerical approximation of the bivariate normal (tetrachoric) correlation coefficient. *Psychometrika* **38**, 259–68.

LANCASTER, H. O. (1969). *The Chi-squared Distribution*. New York: Wiley.

LANCASTER, H. O. & HAMDAN, M. A. (1964). Estimation of the correlation coefficient in contingency tables with possibly nonmetrical characters. *Psychometrika* **29**, 383–91.

MARDIA, K. V. (1967). Some contributions to contingency-type bivariate distributions. *Biometika* **54**, 235–49.

MOSTELLER, F. (1968). Association and estimation in contingency tables. *J. Am. Statist. Assoc.* **63**, 1–28.

NATIONAL BUREAU OF STANDARDS (1959). *Tables of the Bivariate Normal Distribution Function and Related Functions*, Applied Mathematics Series 50. Washington, D.C.: U.S. Government Printing Office.

PEARSON, K. (1900). Mathematical contribution to the theory of evolution VII: On the correlation of characters not quantitatively measurable. *Phil. Trans. R. Soc. Lond.* **195** A, 1–47.

PEARSON, K. (1913). Note on the surface of constant association. *Biometrika* **9**, 534–7.

PEARSON, K. & HERON, D. (1913). On theories of association. *Biometrika* **9**, 159–315.

PLACKETT, R. L. (1965). A class of bivariate distributions. *J. Am. Statist. Assoc.* **60**, 516–22.

TALLIS, G. M. (1962). The maximum likelihood estimation of correlation from contingency tables. *Biometrics* **18**, 342–53.

WAHRENDORF, J. (1980). Inference in contingency tables with ordered categories using Plackett's coefficient of association for bivariate distributions. *Biometrika* **67**, 15–21.

YULE, G. U. (1912). On the methods of measuring association between two attributes. *J. R. Statist. Soc.* **75**, 579–642.

YULE, G. U. & KENDALL, M. G. (1950). *An Introduction to the Theory of Statistics*, 14th edition. London: Griffin.

6.
Association Models Revisited: II

Association Models and Canonical Correlation in the Analysis of Cross-Classifications Having Ordered Categories

The association models considered in Goodman (1979a) for the analysis of cross-classifications having ordered categories are presented in a somewhat different form in the present article to facilitate comparison of the results obtained using these models with those obtained using the earlier canonical correlation approach. Both the association models and the canonical correlation approach can provide meaningful scores for the row and column categories, and these scores can be used to partition into relevant components the usual chi-squared statistic for testing the null hypothesis of statistical independence between the row classification and column classification. However, while the usual procedure for testing the statistical significance of chi-squared components is invalid when these components are based on the canonical correlations, a corresponding procedure is valid when these components are obtained with the association models. The components of association obtained with the association models can be tested in a straightforward manner.

1. INTRODUCTION

For the analysis of the two-way $I \times J$ cross-classification table having ordered row categories and ordered column categories, Fisher (1940) applied the canonical correlation approach, which was then developed further by Maung (1941), Williams (1952), Lancaster (1957; 1969, p. 248), Kendall and Stuart (1961, p. 568), and others.

This approach provides a method for estimating scores for the I row categories and J column categories of the cross-classification table, and a corresponding partitioning of the usual chi-squared goodness-of-fit statistic for testing the null hypothesis of statistical independence between the row classification and the column classification in the table. The partitioning expresses the usual chi-squared statistic (with $(I - 1)(J - 1)$ degrees of freedom (df)) as a sum of components pertaining to the product moment correlations (the canonical correlations) between the row scores and column scores.

When a chi-squared statistic is partitioned into components, in order to evaluate the magnitude of the components, the research worker will usually wish to compare the numerical value of each component with the percentiles of the corresponding tabulated chi-squared distribution. However, this procedure, as usually applied, is incorrect in the present context where the components pertain to the canonical correlations since the chi-squared asymptotic distribution theory can not be applied in the usual way to this particular kind of component. (The usual chi-squared procedure was proposed by Kendall and Stuart (1961, p. 574) in the present context; it was criticised by Lancaster (1963), and the defect in the proposed procedure was then noted in Kendall and Stuart (1967, p. 575).)

In this article, we shall show how to use association models to obtain estimated scores for the row categories and column categories of the cross-classification table, and a corresponding partitioning of the usual chi-squared statistic (with $(I - 1)(J - 1)$ df) into the components obtained with this approach. In contrast to the components obtained with the canonical correlation approach, we shall show here that the components of association obtained with the association models can be tested in a straightforward manner using the usual chi-squared procedure for analyzing chi-squared components.

Some of the association models that will be considered here were presented in a somewhat different form in Goodman (1979a), and some are generalizations of the models in that article. These association models are also related, in one way or another, to models in Birch (1965), Rasch (1966), Haberman (1974a; 1979, p. 371), Plackett (1974, p. 66), Simon (1974), Duncan (1979), Goodman (1979b), and Andersen (1980, p. 210).

The canonical correlation approach to the analysis of cross-classification tables began with the work of R.A. Fisher (1940), as we noted earlier, and the association models approach can be traced back, in a certain sense, to the work of G. Udny Yule and others (see, e.g., Yule 1906). Fisher's approach using canonical correlation appears wholly different from Yule's approach; but with the further development of the association models in the

Table 1. Three Cross-Classification Tables Analyzed in Earlier Literature Using the Canonical Correlation Approach

a. Periodontal Condition and Calcium Intake Level of 135 Women

Periodontal Condition	Calcium Intake Level			
	1	*2*	*3*	*4*
A	5	3	10	11
B	4	5	8	6
C	26	11	3	6
D	23	11	1	2

b. Eye Color and Hair Color of 5,387 Children in Caithness

Eye Color	Hair Color				
	Fair	*Red*	*Medium*	*Dark*	*Black*
Blue	326	38	241	110	3
Light	688	116	584	188	4
Medium	343	84	909	412	26
Dark	98	48	403	681	85

c. Eye Color and Hair Color of 22,361 Children in Aberdeen

Eye Color	Hair Color				
	Fair	*Red*	*Medium*	*Dark*	*Black*
Blue	1,368	170	1,041	398	1
Light	2,577	474	2,703	932	11
Medium	1,390	420	3,826	1,842	33
Dark	454	255	1,848	2,506	112

present article, I shall obtain a kind of reconciliation between them.

To illustrate the comparison of the association models approach developed in this article with the canonical correlation approach, we shall apply the former approach to reanalyze data studied earlier by Fisher (1940), Maung (1941), Williams (1952), Lancaster (1958), and Kendall and Stuart (1961, p. 586) using the latter approach. Three cross-classification tables will be considered, and it will turn out to be convenient to consider these cross-classification tables in the order presented in Table 1. The first cross-classification table (Table 1a) was analyzed earlier by Williams (1952) and Kendall and Stuart (1961, p. 586);[1] the second cross-classification table (Table 1b) was analyzed by Fisher (1940) and Maung (1941); and the third cross-classification table (Table 1c) was analyzed by Maung (1941) and Lancaster (1958).[2] New insights into these data will be obtained.

Many different kinds of data can be analyzed using the association models approach developed in the present article. The analyses of Tables 1a, 1b, and 1c serve well to illustrate a variety of problems that can arise in the analysis of such data and in the interpretation of results that can be obtained when these models are applied. However, to suggest the wide range of applicability of the association models, examples from more diverse areas could have been used instead.

We shall compare our association models with the canonical correlation approach later in this article, but before closing this introductory section we include some additional references to the latter approach. Hotelling (1936) introduced canonical correlation for the analysis of sets

---

[1] Table 1a was also considered by Treloar (1939, p. 228), but not using the canonical correlation approach.

[2] The entry in cell (4, 4) of Table 1c differs from the corresponding entry in Maung (1941). This entry was incorrect in Maung's table, but his numerical results agree with those obtained when the correct entry is used.

of continuous variates. For canonical correlation analysis of discrete variates, in addition to the references cited earlier in this section, see also related work by, for example, Hirschfeld (1935), Guttman (1941, 1950, 1953), Burt (1950), and Hayashi (1951). With respect to asymptotic distribution theory for canonical correlation analysis of contingency tables, see, for example, Corsten (1976), O'Neill (1978a, 1978b), and Haberman (1981).

2. ASSOCIATION MODELS

For the $I \times J$ cross-classification table, let f_{ij} denote the observed frequency in the ith row and jth column of the table $(i = 1, 2, \ldots, I; j = 1, 2, \ldots, J)$, and let F_{ij} denote the corresponding expected frequency under some model. As is the case in the usual statistical analysis of such tables, we assume here that a multinomial distribution applies to the $I \times J$ table. (The methods presented here are also applicable when the multinomial distribution applies independently to each of the I rows in the table, or when this distribution applies independently to each of the J columns, or when the Poisson distribution applies independently to each of the $I \times J$ cells; see, for example, Goodman 1979a.)

Consider now the following model for the expected frequencies F_{ij},

$$F_{ij} = \alpha_i \beta_j e^{\phi \mu_i \nu_j}, \qquad (2.1)$$

where α_i, β_j, μ_i, ν_j, and ϕ are parameters in the model. The meaning of these parameters is clarified by (2.3), (2.5), and (2.7) in this section, and by further comments later in this article and in Goodman (1979a, 1981). For the 2×2 subtables formed from adjacent rows (i.e., rows i and $i + 1$) and adjacent columns (i.e., columns j and $j + 1$) in the $I \times J$ cross-classification table, let Θ_{ij} denote the corresponding odds-ratio (for $i = 1, 2, \ldots, I - 1$; $j = 1, 2, \ldots, J - 1$) based upon the expected frequencies. Thus

$$\Theta_{ij} = (F_{ij} F_{i+1,j+1})/(F_{i,j+1} F_{i+1,j}); \qquad (2.2)$$

and from (2.1) and (2.2) we obtain

$$\log \Theta_{ij} = \phi(\mu_i - \mu_{i+1})(v_j - v_{j+1}), \qquad (2.3)$$

where log denotes the natural logarithm.

From (2.3) we see that the "uniform association model" is obtained from model (2.1) when the first difference in the μ's is constant and the first difference in the v's is constant; that is, when

$$\mu_i - \mu_{i+1} = \Delta, \quad \text{for } i = 1, 2, \ldots, I - 1, \qquad (2.4a)$$

and

$$v_j - v_{j+1} = \Delta', \quad \text{for } j = 1, 2, \ldots, J - 1, \qquad (2.4b)$$

where Δ and Δ' are unspecified (see Goodman 1979a, 1981). Similarly, we see from (2.3) that the "column-effect association model" is obtained from model (2.1) when (2.4a) is satisifed, and the "row-effect association model" is obtained when (2.4b) is satisfied. When $\phi = 0$ in model (2.1), the "null association model" is obtained.

For the null association model, uniform association model, row-effect association model, and column-effect association model, we shall use the symbols O, U, R, and C, respectively. The symbol RC will denote model (2.1).

From (2.3) we see that the RC model (2.1) includes both row and column effects on the association. This model was referred to as Model II in Goodman (1979a). (Model I of the 1979a article will be considered in Sections 7 and 8.)

The parameter μ_i in the RC model (2.1) can be viewed as a score (or a location) pertaining to the ith row category; the parameter v_j in this model can be viewed similarly for the jth column category; and the differences, $\mu_i - \mu_{i+1}$ and $v_j - v_{j+1}$, can be viewed as distances between consecutive categories. Thus, the R association model is obtained from the RC model when consecutive columns are equidistant (as in (2.4b)); the C association model is obtained when consecutive rows are equidistant (as in (2.4a)); and the U association model is obtained when consecutive rows are equidistant and consecutive columns are equidistant.

The meaning of the μ_i and v_j in the RC model (2.1) will be clarified further in the next section (and also in Section 5) when we compare these quantities with the corresponding scores x_i and y_j obtained using the canonical correlation method. Additional clarification can also be obtained by the comparison of the μ_i and v_j in the RC model with the corresponding row and column category levels in the situation where there is an underlying bivariate normal distribution (see Goodman 1981).

The RC model (2.1) can also be expressed in the following equivalent form:

$$\log F_{ij} = \gamma + \gamma_{i.} + \gamma_{.j} + \phi\mu_i v_j, \qquad (2.5)$$

where $\gamma + \gamma_{i.} = \log \alpha_i$ and $\gamma_{.j} = \log \beta_j$. (For models somewhat similar to (2.5) in the analysis of a two-way array with continuous data, see, for example, Mandel (1971), Johnson and Graybill (1972), Tukey (1977, p. 421).) From (2.5) we see that the parameters μ_i, v_j, and ϕ pertain to the two-factor (row-by-column) interaction in the model for $\log F_{ij}$. By comparing the ith row with the i'th row (for $i \neq i'$), we see from (2.5) that $\log(F_{ij}/F_{i'j})$ is a linear function of the parameter v_j; and similarly by comparing the jth column with the j'th column (for $j \neq j'$), we see that $\log(F_{ij}/F_{ij'})$ is a linear function of the parameter μ_i. The parameter ϕ in (2.5) pertains to the general level of the two-factor interaction; when $\phi = 0$ this interaction in (2.5) is null, and equivalently the association in (2.1) is null (see (2.3)).

We noted earlier that the μ_i and v_j in the RC model can be viewed as scores pertaining to the ith row and jth column, respectively; and an alternative set of scores, say, x_i and y_j, can be obtained using the canonical correlation method. With the usual canonical correlation approach, some restrictions are imposed upon the canonical scores x_i and y_j in order to make these scores identifiable; and similarly some restrictions need to be imposed upon the parameters μ_i and v_j in order to make these parameters identifiable. To facilitate comparison of the μ_i and ν_j in the RC model with the canonical scores x_i and y_j, we shall impose restrictions on the μ_i and ν_j that are somewhat similar to the restrictions imposed on the x_i and y_j. As we shall see, these restrictions can be imposed without loss of generality.

With the usual canonical correlation method, the scores x_i and y_j that are obtained satisfy the following restrictions.

$$\sum_{i=1}^{I} x_i p_{i\cdot} = 0, \quad \sum_{i=1}^{I} x_i^2 p_{i\cdot} = 1,$$

$$\sum_{i=1}^{J} y_j p_{\cdot j} = 0, \quad \sum_{j=1}^{J} y_j^2 p_{\cdot j} = 1,$$

$$(2.6)$$

where

$$p_{i\cdot} = f_{i\cdot}/N, \quad p_{\cdot j} = f_{\cdot j}/N,$$

and

$$f_{i\cdot} = \sum_{j=1}^{J} f_{ij}, \quad f_{\cdot j} = \sum_{i=1}^{I} f_{ij},$$

$$N = \sum_{i=1}^{I} \sum_{j=1}^{J} f_{ij}.$$

Since the absolute value of the product moment correlation (the canonical correlation) between the scores x_i and y_j remains unchanged when the scores are replaced by linear functions of the x_i and y_j, respectively, the restrictions (2.6) have no effect upon the generality of the results obtained in the canonical correlation analysis. Similarly, since the general form of the RC model (2.1) remains unchanged when the parameters μ_i and ν_j are replaced by linear functions of the μ_i and ν_j, respectively, the following restrictions can be imposed upon these parameters without loss of generality.

$$\sum_{i=1}^{I} \mu_i P_{i\cdot} = 0, \quad \sum_{i=1}^{I} \mu_i^2 P_{i\cdot} = 1,$$

$$\sum_{j=1}^{J} \nu_j P_{\cdot j} = 0, \quad \sum_{j=1}^{J} \nu_j^2 P_{\cdot j} = 1,$$

$$(2.7)$$

where

$$P_{i\cdot} = F_{i\cdot}/N, \quad P_{\cdot j} = F_{\cdot j}/N,$$

and

$$F_{i\cdot} = \sum_{j=1}^{J} F_{ij}, \quad F_{\cdot j} = \sum_{i=1}^{I} F_{ij},$$

$$N = \sum_{i=1}^{I} \sum_{j=1}^{J} F_{ij}.$$

(Compare (2.7) with (2.6).) We introduce condition (2.7) to facilitate comparison of the results that we shall obtain using the RC model with those obtained using the canonical correlation approach. (A somewhat different but related condition is presented in Goodman (1979a) and Andersen (1980, p. 210).)

Since the general form of (2.5) remains unchanged when the parameters μ_i and ν_j are replaced by linear functions of the μ_i and ν_j, respectively, without any loss of generality we can impose any restrictions upon the location and scale of the μ_i and ν_j in (2.5); and similarly, we can impose a corresponding restriction upon the location of the additive row and column effects in (2.5). For the $I \times J$ table of $\log F_{ij}$, the number of independent parameters in (2.5) will be

$$1 + (I - 1) + (J - 1) + 1 + (I - 2) + (J - 2) \tag{2.8}$$
$$= 2(I + J - 2),$$

and so the number of df used in testing this model would be

$$IJ - 2(I + J - 2) = (I - 2)(J - 2). \tag{2.9}$$

Since (2.5) is equivalent to the RC model (2.1), the number of df used in testing this model is $(I - 2)(J - 2)$.

The method used in the preceding paragraph, for calculating the number of degrees of freedom pertaining to the RC association model (2.1), differs somewhat from the corresponding method used in Goodman (1979a). We include the calculation (2.8) and (2.9) in the present article because it will facilitate a corresponding calculation presented later for some more general association models (see (7.7) and (7.8)). The method used above to calculate the number of df can be applied to all the association models discussed in this section and also to the association models that will be introduced in Section 7. For the sake of convenience the corresponding results are listed in Table 2. (The association models on lines (6) to (10) of Table 2 will be considered in Section 7.)

The formulas for the df in Table 2 should be interpreted with caution. There are actually zero df when a formula in Table 2 yields either zero or a negative value. (In the special case of the 2×2 cross-classification table ($I = J = 2$), the formula on line (9) is inapplicable; there are actually zero df in this case too.) Thus when $I = J = 2$ there are zero df for each association model in Table 2 except for the usual null association model. (When $I = J = 2$, each of those association models is equivalent to the usual saturated log-linear model.) Similarly, when $I = 2$ and $J > 2$, there are zero df for the C model and the models on lines (5) to (10) in Table 2; and when $J = 2$

Table 2. Degrees of Freedom for the Association Models Applied to the $I \times J$ Table

Association Models	Degrees of Freedom
(1) O	$(I - 1)(J - 1)$
(2) U	$IJ - I - J$
(3) R	$(I - 1)(J - 2)$
(4) C	$(I - 2)(J - 1)$
(5) RC	$(I - 2)(J - 2)$
(6) U + RC	$IJ - 2I - 2J + 3$
(7) R + RC	$(I - 2)(J - 3)$
(8) C + RC	$(I - 3)(J - 2)$
(9) R + C + RC	$(I - 3)(J - 3)$
(10) R + C	$(I - 2)(J - 2)$

NOTE: When $I = 2$ and/or $J = 2$, see relevant comments in Section 2.

and $I > 2$, there are zero df for the R model and the models on lines (5) to (10). (When $I = J = 3$, there are zero df for the models on lines (6) to (9); when $I = 3$ and $J > 3$, there are zero df for the models on lines (8) and (9); when $J = 3$ and $I > 3$, there are zero df for the models on lines (7) and (9).) Note that there are zero df for the RC model when $I = 2$ and/or $J = 2$.

We shall next examine the relationship between the RC model and the canonical correlation approach. In order to do so we shall first need to discuss briefly the scores x_i and y_j obtained with the canonical correlation approach and then the maximum likelihood estimates of the parameters μ_i and ν_j in the RC model.

3. THE RC ASSOCIATION MODEL AND THE CANONICAL CORRELATION METHOD

As we noted earlier the row score x_i and the column score y_j obtained with the usual canonical correlation method will satisfy condition (2.6). In addition, these scores will also satisfy the following equations:

$$\sum_{j=1}^{J} y_j p_{ij} = \lambda p_{i.} x_i \qquad (3.1a)$$

$$\sum_{i=1}^{I} x_i p_{ij} = \lambda p_{.j} y_j, \qquad (3.1b)$$

where $p_{ij} = f_{ij}/N$ (see, for example, Kendall and Stuart 1961, p. 570). Formula (3.1a) is analogous to the corresponding statement, in linear regression analysis, that the conditional expected value of y is linear in x; and (3.1b) is analogous to the corresponding statement that the conditional expected value of x is linear in y. More specifically, formula (3.1a) states that the weighted average of the y's at the ith row is proportional to x_i (when the weights at the ith row are $p_{ij}/p_{i.}$, for $j = 1, 2, \ldots, J$); and (3.1b) states that the weighted average of the x's at the jth column is proportional to y_j (when the weights at the jth column are $p_{ij}/p_{\cdot j}$, for $i = 1, 2, \ldots, I$). Thus, we can rewrite (3.1a) and (3.1b) as follows.

$$E_p\{y \mid i\} = \lambda x_i \qquad (3.2a)$$

$$E_p\{x \mid j\} = \lambda y_j, \qquad (3.2b)$$

where $E_p\{y \mid i\} = \sum_{j=1}^{J} y_j p_{ij}/p_{i\cdot}$ and $E_p\{x \mid j\} = \sum_{i=1}^{I} x_i p_{ij}/p_{\cdot j}$.

From (2.6) and (3.1) we see that

$$\sum_{i=1}^{I} \sum_{j=1}^{J} x_i y_j p_{ij} = \lambda. \qquad (3.3)$$

In other words, the λ in (3.1) and (3.2) is equal to the product moment correlation (the canonical correlation) between the x's and y's.

The canonical scores x_i and y_j that maximize the product moment correlation (3.3) are related to the maximum likelihood estimates of the parameters μ_i and ν_j in the RC association model (2.1).[3] In order to examine this relationship, we shall now need to discuss briefly the maximum likelihood estimates of the parameters in the RC associaton model.

Using circumflexes to denote maximum likelihood estimates of the corresponding parameters, the estimate $\hat{F}_{ij}$ of the expected frequency F_{ij} under model (2.1) can be written as

$$\hat{F}_{ij} = \hat{\alpha}_i \hat{\beta}_j e^{\hat{\phi}\hat{\mu}_i\hat{\nu}_j}; \qquad (3.4)$$

and the $\hat{F}_{ij}$ will satisfy the following equations:

$$\hat{F}_{i\cdot} = f_{i\cdot}, \qquad (3.5a)$$

$$\hat{F}_{\cdot j} = f_{\cdot j}, \qquad (3.5b)$$

$$\sum_{j=1}^{J} \hat{\nu}_j \hat{F}_{ij} = \sum_{j=1}^{J} \hat{\nu}_j f_{ij}, \qquad (3.5c)$$

---

[3] We shall be concerned here only with the canonical scores that maximize the product moment (canonical) correlation (3.3). This canonical correlation will sometimes be referred to as the principal canonical correlation.

$$\sum_{i=1}^{I} \hat{\mu}_i \hat{F}_{ij} = \sum_{i=1}^{I} \hat{\mu}_i f_{ij}, \tag{3.5d}$$

where $\hat{F}_{i\cdot} = \sum_{j=1}^{J} \hat{F}_{ij}$ and $\hat{F}_{\cdot j} = \sum_{i=1}^{I} \hat{F}_{ij}$ (see, e.g., Goodman 1979a). From (3.5a) and (3.5b), we see that (3.5c) and (3.5d) can be replaced by the following equations:

$$E_{\hat{P}}\{\hat{v} \mid i\} = E_p\{\hat{v} \mid i\} \tag{3.6a}$$

$$E_{\hat{P}}\{\hat{\mu} \mid j\} = E_p\{\hat{\mu} \mid j\}, \tag{3.6b}$$

where

$$E_{\hat{P}}\{\hat{v} \mid i\} = \sum_{j=1}^{J} \hat{v}_j \hat{F}_{ij} / \hat{F}_{i\cdot},$$

$$E_{\hat{P}}\{\hat{\mu} \mid j\} = \sum_{i=1}^{I} \hat{\mu}_i \hat{F}_{ij} / \hat{F}_{\cdot j},$$

$$E_p\{\hat{v} \mid i\} = \sum_{j=1}^{J} \hat{v}_j f_{ij} / f_{i\cdot},$$

$$E_p\{\hat{\mu} \mid j\} = \sum_{i=1}^{I} \hat{\mu}_i f_{ij} / f_{\cdot j}.$$

Formula (3.6a) states that, when the weights at the ith row are $\hat{F}_{ij}/\hat{F}_{i\cdot}$ (for $j = 1, 2, \ldots, j$), the weighted average of the $\hat{v}$'s is equal to the corresponding weighted average when the weights are $f_{ij}/f_{i\cdot}$ (for $j = 1, 2, \ldots, J$); and (3.6b) states that, when the weights at the jth column are $\hat{F}_{ij}/\hat{F}_{\cdot j}$ (for $i = 1, 2, \ldots, I$), the weighted average of the $\hat{\mu}$'s is equal to the corresponding weighted average when the weights are $f_{ij}/f_{\cdot j}$ (for $i = 1, 2, \ldots, I$).

When condition (2.7) is imposed upon the parameters μ_i and v_j, the corresponding maximum likelihood estimates will satisfy the following condition:

$$\sum_{i=1}^{I} \hat{\mu}_i \hat{P}_{i\cdot} = 0, \quad \sum_{i=1}^{I} \hat{\mu}_i^2 \hat{P}_{i\cdot} = 1,$$

$$\sum_{j=1}^{J} \hat{v}_j \hat{P}_{\cdot j} = 0, \quad \sum_{j=1}^{J} \hat{v}_j^2 \hat{P}_{\cdot j} = 1, \tag{3.7}$$

where

$$\hat{P}_{i\cdot} = \hat{F}_{i\cdot}/N \quad \text{and} \quad \hat{P}_{\cdot j} = \hat{F}_{\cdot j}/N.$$

(Compare (3.7) with (2.7) and (2.6).) From (3.5a), (3.5b), and (3.7) we see that the following condition is satisfied:

$$\sum_{i=1}^{I} \hat{\mu}_i p_{i\cdot} = 0, \quad \sum_{i=1}^{I} \hat{\mu}_i^2 p_{i\cdot} = 1,$$

$$\sum_{j=1}^{J} \hat{\mu}_j p_{\cdot j} = 0, \quad \sum_{j=1}^{J} \hat{v}_j^2 p_{\cdot j} = 1. \tag{3.8}$$

From (2.6) and (3.8) we see that the maximum likelihood estimates $\hat{\mu}_i$ and $\hat{v}_j$ will satisfy the same restrictions as the corresponding canonical scores x_i and y_j.

From (3.5c) and (3.5d) we see that

$$\sum_{i=1}^{I}\sum_{j=1}^{J} \hat{\mu}_i \hat{v}_j \hat{P}_{ij} = \sum_{i=1}^{I}\sum_{j=1}^{J} \hat{\mu}_i \hat{v}_j p_{ij}, \tag{3.9}$$

where $\hat{P}_{ij} = \hat{F}_{ij}/N$ and $p_{ij} = f_{ij}/N$. From (3.7), (3.8), and (3.9) we see that (3.9) describes an equality between product moment correlations. Formula (3.9) states that, when the distribution $\hat{P}_{ij}$ is used, the product moment correlation of the $\hat{\mu}$'s and $\hat{v}$'s is equal to the corresponding product moment correlation when the distribution p_{ij} is used. We can rewrite (3.9) as

$$E_{\hat{P}}\{\hat{\mu}\hat{v}\} = E_p\{\hat{\mu}\hat{v}\}. \tag{3.10}$$

Although we have used the same notation to describe the equations that are satisfied by the estimates $\hat{\mu}_i$ and $\hat{v}_j$ and the equations that are satisfied by the canonical scores x_i and y_j, the equations (3.6) are actually quite different from the corresponding equations (3.2). Under what conditions will the estimates $\hat{\mu}_i$ and $\hat{v}_j$ turn out to be equal to the corresponding canonical scores x_i and y_j? We shall now provide some answers to this question.

Let us consider first the situation where the $\hat{\mu}_i$ and $\hat{v}_j$ satisfy the following condition:

$$E_{\hat{P}}\{\hat{v} \mid i\} = \lambda'\hat{\mu}_i \qquad (3.11a)$$

$$E_{\hat{P}}\{\hat{\mu} \mid j\} = \lambda'\hat{v}_j, \qquad (3.11b)$$

where λ' is unspecified. (The λ' in (3.11) will turn out to be equal to the product moment correlation $E_P\{\hat{\mu}\hat{v}\}$ between the $\hat{\mu}$'s and $\hat{v}$'s.) From (3.6) and (3.11) we find that

$$E_p\{\hat{v} \mid i\} = \lambda'\hat{\mu}_i \qquad (3.12a)$$

$$E_p\{\hat{\mu} \mid j\} = \lambda'\hat{v}_j. \qquad (3.12b)$$

Comparing (3.12) with (3.2), we see that the estimates $\hat{\mu}_i$ and $\hat{v}_j$ will be canonical scores when (3.12) is satisfied. Thus these estimates will be canonical scores when (3.11) is satisfied.

From (3.4) we see that (3.11) can be rewritten as

$$\sum_{j=1}^{J} \hat{v}_j\hat{\beta}_j e^{\hat{\phi}\hat{\mu}_i\hat{v}_j} = \lambda'\hat{\mu}_i \sum_{j=1}^{J} \hat{\beta}_j e^{\hat{\phi}\hat{\mu}_i\hat{v}_j} \qquad (3.13a)$$

$$\sum_{i=1}^{I} \hat{\mu}_i\hat{\alpha}_i e^{\hat{\phi}\hat{\mu}_i\hat{v}_j} = \lambda'\hat{v}_j \sum_{i=1}^{I} \hat{\alpha}_i e^{\hat{\phi}\hat{\mu}_i\hat{v}_j}. \qquad (3.13b)$$

Thus, when (3.11a) is satisfied, the $\hat{\beta}_j$ in (3.4) will satisfy (3.13a); and when (3.11b) is satisfied, the $\hat{\alpha}_i$ will satisfy (3.13b). The $\hat{\mu}_i$ and $\hat{v}_j$ will be canonical scores when $\hat{\beta}_j$ and $\hat{\alpha}_i$ satisfy (3.13a) and (3.13b).

In the preceding two paragraphs, we considered the situation where (3.11) or the equivalent (3.13) is satisfied. There are, of course, situations where this condition is not satisfied.

To gain additional insight into the circumstances under which the $\hat{\mu}_i$ and $\hat{v}_j$ will be equal (approximately) to the canonical scores, consider for a moment canonical correlation analysis applied to random variables X and Y having a joint bivariate normal distribution with, say, zero means, unit variances, and correlation ρ. In this case, with respect to the principal canonical correlation, the corresponding canonical variables (scores) are X and Y (see, e.g., Lancaster 1957, and Kendall and Stuart 1961, p. 568). Similarly, when the bivariate normal is discretized to form a cross-classification table (with the row and column scores pertaining to the corresponding levels of variables X and Y, respectively), the discretized distribution can be approximated by model (2.1), and the μ_i and ν_j in (2.1) will be approximately equal to the corresponding row and column scores (see Goodman 1981). (This is a consequence of the fact that model (2.1) is related in form to the bivariate normal density at $X = x$ and $Y = y$, with μ_i, ν_j, and ϕ in (2.1) corresponding to x, y, and $\rho/(1 - \rho^2)$, respectively.) Thus, when a sample cross-classification table arises from an underlying bivariate normal, the row and column scores and the corresponding estimates $\hat{\mu}_i$ and $\hat{\nu}_j$ will be approximately equal, and they will also be approximately equal to the corresponding scores obtained in a canonical correlation analysis.

The comments in the preceding paragraph apply also under more general conditions than those considered there. Consider now canonical correlation analysis applied to random variables X' and Y' having a joint bivariate distribution that is not necessarily normal, but where separate transformations of these variables can be made so that the transformed variables, say, X and Y, have a joint bivariate normal distribution. In this case, too, with respect to the principal canonical correlation, the canonical variables (scores) are X and Y (see, e.g., Lancaster 1957). Similarly, when the bivariate distribution of X' and Y' is discretized, the μ_i and ν_j in (2.1) will be approximately equal to row and column scores pertaining to the corresponding levels of the transformed variables X and Y, respectively. Thus, when a sample cross-classification table arises from an underlying bivariate distribution that can be transformed (as previously described) into a bivariate normal, the estimates $\hat{\mu}_i$ and $\hat{\nu}_j$ will be approximately equal to the corresponding canonical scores.

Table 3. Canonical Scores x_i and y_j Compared With Estimates $\hat{\mu}_i$ and $\hat{\nu}_j$ in RC Association Model, Applied to Data in Table 1

	Table 1a		Table 1b		Table 1c	
	Canonical Score	RC Model Estimate	Canonical Score	RC Model Estimate	Canonical Score	RC Model Estimate
Correlation	.56	.56	.45	.44	.38	.38
Row						
1	-1.39	-1.34	-.90	-.94	-1.19	-1.20
2	-1.06	-1.06	-.99	-1.00	-.90	-.90
3	.60	.46	.08	.13	.21	.21
4	1.00	1.14	1.57	1.54	1.55	1.54
Column						
1	.84	.85	-1.22	-1.34	-1.34	-1.42
2	.48	.44	-.52	-.40	-.29	-.19
3	-1.58	-1.62	-.09	.04	-.00	.08
4	-1.14	-1.08	1.32	1.22	1.36	1.28
5	—	—	2.45	2.38	2.83	2.87

We next compare the canonical scores for Tables 1a, 1b, and 1c presented in the earlier literature with the corresponding estimates $\hat{\mu}_i$ and $\hat{\nu}_j$ obtained with the RC association model. From Table 3 we see that the canonical correlation agrees (to two decimal places) with the corresponding product moment correlation of the estimates $\hat{\mu}_i$ and $\hat{\nu}_j$ in Tables 1a and 1c; and the canonical correlation differs from the corresponding product moment correlation by one digit in the second decimal place in Table 1b. We also note from Table 3 how similar the canonical scores are to the estimates $\hat{\mu}_i$ and $\hat{\nu}_j$ obtained with the RC association model. The meaning of the canonical scores and the estimates $\hat{\mu}_i$ and $\hat{\nu}_j$ in Table 3 will be discussed further in Section 5.

The estimates $\hat{\mu}_i$ and $\hat{\nu}_j$ in Table 3 were obtained by applying the iterative procedure presented in Goodman (1979a) for calculating maximum likelihood estimates under the RC association model, and then imposing the appropriate restrictions upon the location and scale of these estimates (see (3.7) and (3.8)). All of the numerical results that will be presented in the present article were obtained by straightforward modifications and/or extensions of the methods introduced in Goodman (1979a). This applies to the numerical results that will be presented using the association models described in Section 2 above (these models are equivalent to association models considered in Goodman 1979a), and also to the numerical results that will be presented using the more general association models introduced later in Section 7.

Before closing this section, we note that under conditions described in Goodman (1981) the product moment correlation of the estimates $\hat{\mu}_i$ and $\hat{\nu}_j$ can be modified in a simple way to provide an estimate of the correlation ρ in an underlying bivariate normal distribution when that distribution obtains, and this modified product moment correlation can also be applied to estimate a related coefficient when the underlying bivariate normal does not necessarily hold true. The corresponding canonical correlation can be modified in a similar way.

4. CANONICAL CORRELATION COMPONENTS AND ASSOCIATION COMPONENTS

One of the purposes of canonical correlation analysis was to provide a method for partitioning into components the usual chi-squared statistic (with $(I - 1)(J - 1)$ df) for testing the null hypothesis of statistical independence between the row classification and the column classification in the cross-classification table. Since the usual chi-squared procedure for analyzing chi-squared components cannot be applied to the components obtained with the canonical correlation approach, it will be of special interest to see that these methods can be applied in a straightforward manner using the closely related association models. In order to analyze some cross-classification tables (e.g., Table 1a), it will be sufficient to apply the association models that were described earlier in Section 2; but for other cross-classification tables (e.g., Tables 1b and 1c), we will need to introduce some more general association models. For expository purposes, we shall first apply the association models in Section 2 to Table 1a; and we shall introduce some more general association models later in Section 7.

Table 4a gives the values of the goodness-of-fit chi-square and the likelihood-ratio chi-square obtained when the association models are applied to Table 1a. (Lines (1) to (5) in Table 4a pertain to models described in Section 2, while the remaining lines pertain to association models that will be considered in Section 7.) From Table 4a we obtain the components of association presented in Tables 4b, 4c, and 4d. From these tables we see that the association model that takes into account both the row effect and the column effect on the association (viz., the RC association model in line (5) of Table 4a) fit the data in Table 1a very well; but the row effect was not statistically significant, and so the RC model could be replaced by the association model that does not include the row effect. The model thus obtained (viz., the C association model in line (4) of Table 4a) also fits the data very well,

Table 4. Analysis of Association (ANOAS) in Table 1a

a. Association Models Applied to Table 1a

Association Models	Degrees of Freedom	Goodness-of-Fit Chi-Square	Likelihood-Ratio Chi-Square
(1) O	9	44.34	46.89
(2) U	8	11.13	11.86
(3) R	6	9.29	9.88
(4) C	6	4.29	4.35
(5) RC	4	1.76	1.74
(6) U + RC	3	1.62	1.60
(7) R + RC	2	1.51	1.49
(8) C + RC	2	.01	.01
(9) R + C + RC	1	.00	.00
(10) R + C	4	2.85	2.81

b. Components of Association in Table 1a

Components	Models Used	Degrees of Freedom	Goodness-of-Fit Chi-Square	Likelihood-Ratio Chi-Square
General effect	(1)–(2)	9 – 8 = 1	33.21	35.03
Row and column effects	(2)–(5)	8 – 4 = 4	9.37	10.12
Other effects	(5)	4	1.76	1.74
Total effects	(1)	9	44.34	46.89

c. Components of Row and Column Effects on Association in Table 1a

Components	Models Used	Degrees of Freedom	Goodness-of-Fit Chi-Square	Likelihood-Ratio Chi-Square
Column effect	(2)–(4)	8 – 6 = 2	6.84	7.51
Row effect	(4)–(5)	6 – 4 = 2	2.53	2.61
Row and column effects	(2)–(5)	8 – 4 = 4	9.37	10.12

d. Components of Association in Table 1a

Components	Models Used	Degrees of Freedom	Goodness-of-Fit Chi-Square	Likelihood-Ratio Chi-Square
General effect and column effect	(1)–(4)	9 – 6 = 3	40.05	42.54
Row effect	(4)–(5)	6 – 4 = 2	2.53	2.61
Other effects	(5)	4	1.76	1.74
Total effects	(1)	9	44.34	46.89

and it is more parsimonious than the RC model.

The association models in lines (1) to (4) of Table 4a are examples of log-linear models (see, e.g., Goodman 1979a), and so the asymptotic chi-squared distribution theory developed for such models can be applied here (see, e.g., Haberman 1974b, p. 97). The asymptotic chi-squared distribution theory in Birch (1964) can be applied to the RC association model in line (5) of Table 4a when the parameter $\phi \neq 0$ in (2.1). (When $\phi = 0$ a different asymptotic distribution is required; see Haberman 1981.)

The components of association presented in Table 4b, 4c, and 4d were obtained by the following general method. When two models, say, M and M', differ only to the extent that model M does not include a given effect on the association but model M' does include the effect, then the difference between the corresponding chi-squared values, $\chi^2(M) - \chi^2(M')$, pertains to the given effect on the association (see, e.g., Goodman 1968, 1970). This difference can be used to test the hypothesis that the given effect on the association is nil, under the assumption that model M' holds true. If this assumption is contradicted by the data, then the test based on the difference between the chi-squares is invalid as a test of the hypothesis that the given effect is nil. (On the other hand, for some models M and M', the test based on the difference between the chi-squares turns out to be equivalent to a test of a hypothesis that does not depend upon whether M' holds true; and in this case, the test based on the difference will be valid as a test of that hypothesis (see, e.g., Goodman 1971).)

When the RC association model is assumed to hold true, then the test based on the difference between the chi-squares is valid, when model M is taken as the R association model, the C associaton model, or the U association model; but it will not be valid when model M is taken as the O association model since the asymptotic chi-squared distribution theory for the RC model does not apply when the parameter $\phi = 0$ in (2.1).

From our analysis of the data in Table 1a, we found

Table 5. Canonical Scores x_i and y_j Compared With Estimates $\hat{\mu}_i$ and $\hat{v}_j$ in Association Models Applied to Table 1a and Modified Table 1a

	Canonical Score	Association Models			
		RC	C	R	U
Table 1a					
Correlation	.56	.56	.54	.51	.49
Row					
1	−1.39	−1.34	−1.53	−1.38	−1.53
2	−1.06	−1.06	−.62	−1.01	−.62
3	.60	.46	.30	.49	.30
4	1.00	1.14	1.21	1.10	1.21
Column					
1	.84	.85	.83	.96	.96
2	.48	.44	.51	.09	.09
3	−1.58	−1.62	−1.53	−.78	−.78
4	−1.14	−1.08	−1.19	−1.65	−1.65
Modified Table 1a					
Correlation	.56	.55	.54	.53	.51
Row					
1	−1.41	−1.37	−1.53	−1.37	−1.53
2	−1.02	−1.01	−.62	−1.07	−.62
3	.59	.45	.30	.59	.30
4	1.01	1.14	1.21	1.01	1.21
Column					
1	.84	.86	.83	1.05	1.05
2	.49	.45	.51	−.09	−.09
3	−1.36	−1.35	−1.36	−1.23	−1.23

that the RC model could be replaced by the C model, and so we would then also replace the estimates $\hat{\mu}_i$ and $\hat{v}_j$ in the RC model by the corresponding estimates under the C model. (Recall that under the C model the μ_i parameters will satisfy condition (2.4a); and the corresponding estimates $\hat{\mu}_i$ will also satisfy the corresponding condition.) Table 5 gives the estimates $\hat{\mu}_i$ and $\hat{v}_j$ under the C model, and under the other models that we have considered, when these models are applied to Table 1a and to a modified form of Table 1a. (The results for the modified Table 1a will be discussed in Section 6.) From the estimates for Table 1a we find that both the RC model and the C model lead to results that are quite similar to those obtained earlier with the canonical correlation approach, but the R model and the U model do not. In particular, the change of trend in the estimated column scores at column 4 of Table 1a, which was first noted using canonical correlation analysis (see Williams 1952, Kendall and Stuart 1961, p. 587), is also present in the RC model and the C model; but the R model and the U model do not allow for this possibility. Further comments on this change of trend will be included in Sections 5 and 6.

5. CANONICAL SCORES, THE CORRESPONDING ASSOCIATION MODEL ESTIMATES, AND ISOTROPY

In canonical correlation analysis, no assumption is introduced as to the order of the row categories, the order of the column categories, or both. If the order of the row categories or the order of the column categories is changed, the canonical correlation will remain invariant, and the magnitude of the canonical score pertaining to each particular category will also remain invariant. (If, say, the position of two row categories is interchanged, the corresponding position of the canonical scores will also be interchanged but their magnitudes will remain invariant.) The magnitude of the canonical score x_i for the ith row category ($i = 1, 2, \ldots, I$) can be used to determine the order of the row categories, and the magnitude of the canonical score y_j for the jth column category ($j = 1, 2, \ldots, J$) can be used to determine the order of the column categories. On the other hand, if there is an a priori prescribed order for the row categories or for the column categories, then a comparison of this prescribed order and the order determined by the canonical scores will be of interest.

Similarly with respect to the RC model, if the order of row categories or the order of the column categories is changed, the magnitude of the estimates $\hat{\mu}_i$ and $\hat{\nu}_j$ pertaining to the particular row and column categories will remain invariant (see Goodman 1979a). The magnitude of the estimate $\hat{\mu}_i$ for the ith row category can be used to determine the order of the row categories, and the magnitude of the estimate $\hat{\nu}_j$ for the jth column category can be used to determine the order of the column categories. Also, if there is an a priori prescribed order for the row categories or for the column categories, then a comparison of this prescribed order and the order determined by the $\hat{\mu}_i$ and $\hat{\nu}_j$ under the RC model will be of interest.

Both the canonical correlation approach and the RC association model can be applied in the situation where there is an a priori prescribed order for the row categories or for the column categories and also in the situation where this is not the case. (The U association model can be applied when the order of the rows and the order of the columns is specified, the R association model can be applied when the order of the columns is specified (but the order of the rows need not be specified), and the C association model can be applied when the order of rows is specified (but the order of the columns need not be specified); see Goodman (1979a).)

With respect to Table 1a, when we compared the prescribed order of the rows and columns with the order determined by the canonical scores (and also by the $\hat{\mu}_i$ and $\hat{\nu}_j$ under the RC model), we found in the preceding section that there was a change of trend in the column scores at column 4 in this table, while the trend in the row scores did not change. (From Table 3 we also see that there was a change of trend in the row scores in Table 1b, while the trend in the column scores in that table did not change.) From (3.2) we see that the change in the canonical score trend in Table 1a can be interpreted as follows: the weighted average of the row canonical scores (for periodontal condition) at the jth column (the jth calcium intake level) changed in trend at $j = 4$. While this result concerning the change of trend seems at first sight to depend upon the actual row canonical scores that are used, we shall see later in this section that, under certain conditions, the result will remain true even if the row scores are replaced by any monotonic transformation of them.

From Table 3 we also note that the canonical score for the ith row in Table 1a increases with i, while the canonical score for the jth column in this table generally decreases with j, with the exception noted above at $j = 4$. (From Table 3 we also see that the canonical score for the ith row in Tables 1b and 1c generally increases with i, and the canonical score for the jth column in these tables increases with j.) The decrease in the column canonical scores in Table 1a reflects the generally negative relationship between the row classification (periodontal condition) and the column classification (calcium intake level) in this table. (The increase in the column canonical scores in Tables 1b and 1c reflects the generally positive relationship between the row and column classifications in these tables.) If the canonical scores for the columns in Table 1a are multiplied by -1, then these scores will generally increase with j, and the corresponding correlation between these column scores and the row scores will actually be negative (see Table 1a). While this result concerning the generally negative relationship between the row and column classifications in Table 1a seems at first sight to depend upon the actual canonical scores that are used, we shall see later in this section that, under certain conditions, the result will hold true without reference to the actual canonical scores.

As we noted earlier, the row and column canonical scores in Table 3 were very similar to the corresponding estimates $\hat{\mu}_i$ and $\hat{\nu}_j$ obtained with the RC model. From (2.3) we see that the logarithm Φ_{ij} of the odds-ratio Θ_{ij} can be expressed in terms of the $\mu_i - \mu_{i+1}$ and $\nu_j - \nu_{j+1}$; and the corresponding maximum likelihood estimate $\hat{\Phi}_{ij}$ of the Φ_{ij} can be expressed in terms of the $\hat{\mu}_i - \hat{\mu}_{i+1}$ and $\hat{\nu}_j - \hat{\nu}_{j+1}$. From Table 3 we see that $(\hat{\mu}_i - \hat{\mu}_{i+1})(\hat{\nu}_j - \hat{\nu}_{j+1})$ is generally negative in Table 1a (corresponding to the generally negative relationship previously noted for this table), and the estimated log-odds-ratio $\hat{\Phi}_{ij}$ will also be generally negative (except for $j = 3$ due to the change in trend for the $\hat{v}_j$ at $j = 4$). (We also see from Table 3 that $(\hat{\mu}_i - \hat{\mu}_{i+1})(\hat{v}_j - \hat{v}_{j+1})$ is generally positive in Tables 1b and 1c, corresponding to the positive canonical correlation in these tables; and the estimated log-odds-ratio $\hat{\Phi}_{ij}$ will also be generally positive in these tables.)

If the rows are arranged in order so that the $\hat{\mu}_i$ increase with i and the columns are arranged in order so that the $\hat{v}_j$ increase with j, then from (2.3) we see that the estimated $\hat{\Phi}_{ij}$ will be positive for all i, j. Thus, under the RC model, with the rows and the columns ordered appropriately, the estimated expected frequencies will be isotropic (see, e.g., Yule and Kendall 1950, p. 57, and Goodman 1979a).

Yule (1906) defined a distribution to be isotropic if the rows and the columns could be ordered in such a way that the odds-ratio $\Theta_{ij} \geqq 1$ for all i, j. He also showed that when the row and the columns are ordered appropriately in an isotropic distribution for the $I \times J$ cross-classification table, then for the 2×2 subtables formed from rows i and i' (with $i' > i$) and columns j and j' (with $j' > j$) in the $I \times J$ table, the corresponding odds-ratio $\Theta_{ij,i'j'}$ would also have the property that $\Theta_{ij,i'j'} \geqq 1$. When $\Theta_{ij} \geqq 1$ (for $j = 1, 2, \ldots, J - 1$), the following inequality can be obtained from (2.2):

$$\frac{F_{ij}}{F_{i+1,j}} \geqq \frac{F_{i,j'}}{F_{i+1,j'}}, \quad \text{for } j' > j. \tag{5.1}$$

The appropriate order of the columns can be determined by the inequality (5.1) pertaining to the odds $F_{ij}/F_{i+1,j}$ (for $j = 1, 2, \ldots, J$) for adjacent rows (i.e., rows i and $i + 1$). When $\Theta_{ij} \geqq 1$ (for $i = 1, 2, \ldots, I - 1; j = 1, 2, \ldots, J - 1$), then (5.1) can be replaced by

$$\frac{F_{ij}}{F_{i'j}} \geqq \frac{F_{ij'}}{F_{i'j'}}, \quad \text{for } j' > j \text{ and } i' > i. \tag{5.2}$$

Thus, the appropriate order of the columns can be determined by the inequality (5.2) pertaining to the odds $F_{ij}/F_{i'j}$ (for $j = 1, 2, \ldots, J$) for any pair of rows (say, rows i and i'). In a similar way, the appropriate order of the rows can be determined by a corresponding inequality pertaining to the odds $F_{ij}/F_{ij'}$ (for $i = 1, 2, \ldots, I$) for any pair of columns (say, columns j and j').

Let $P_{ij}/P_{i\cdot}$ (for $j = 1, 2, \ldots, J$) denote the conditional distribution in the ith row of the $I \times J$ table, and let $Y_{(i)}$ denote the corresponding random variable pertaining to the ith row. Thus,

$$\Pr\{Y_{(i)} = j \mid i\} = P_{ij}/P_{i\cdot}. \qquad (5.3)$$

When condition (5.2) is satisfied, we find that the random variable $Y_{(i)}$ is stochastically smaller than the random variable $Y_{(i')}$, for $i' > i$. Similarly, if we let $X_{(j)}$ denote the random variable pertaining to the jth column, then we find that $X_{(j)}$ is stochastically smaller than $X_{(j')}$ (for $j' > j$), when the rows and the columns are ordered appropriately.

Let $E\{Y_{(i)} \mid i\}$ denote the expected value of the random variable $Y_{(i)}$. From (5.3) we see that

$$E\{Y_{(i)} \mid i\} = \sum_{j=1}^{J} jP_{ij}/P_{i\cdot}. \qquad (5.4)$$

From (5.4) we see that we can use the symbol $E\{j \mid i\}$ for $E\{Y_{(i)} \mid i\}$. When the random variable $Y_{(i)}$ is stochastically smaller than the random variable $Y_{(i')}$, then

$$E\{j \mid i\} \leqq E\{j \mid i'\}, \qquad (5.5)$$

and the following more general inequality also holds true:

$$E\{y_j{}^* \mid i\} \leqq E\{y_j{}^* \mid i'\}, \qquad (5.6)$$

for any column scores $y_j{}^*$ (for $j = 1, 2, \ldots, J$) that are monotonically increasing with j. Thus, when the columns are appropriately ordered in an isotropic distribution, the weighted average of the column scores $y_j{}^*$ at the ith row (when the weights at the ith row are $P_{ij}/P_{i\cdot}$, for $j = 1, 2, \ldots, J$) will reflect the appropriate ordering of the rows. Similarly, when the rows are appropriately ordered in an isotropic distribution, for any row scores $x_i{}^*$ (for $i = 1, 2, \ldots, I$) that are monotonically increasing with i, the weighted average of the row scores x_i^* at the jth column (when the weights at the jth column are $P_{ij}/P_{\cdot j}$, for $i = 1, 2, \ldots, I$) will reflect the appropriate ordering of the columns.

With any isotropic distribution, the rows and the columns can be ordered appropriately so that $\Theta_{ij} \geqq 1$; the inequalities pertaining to the odds $F_{ij}/F_{i'j}$ (for $j = 1, 2, \ldots, J$) and the odds $F_{ij}/F_{ij'}$ (for $i = 1, 2, \ldots, I$) will then hold true (see, e.g., (5.2)), and the corresponding stochastic inequalities noted above will also hold true. With the RC association model, a parameterization of the Θ_{ij} is obtained, and the estimated parameters μ_i and ν_j can be used to quantify both the inequalities pertaining to the odds and also the corresponding stochastic inequalities noted above.

We noted at the beginning of this section that the RC association model and the canonical correlation approach could be applied both in the situation where neither the rows nor the columns are ordered a priori and also in the situation where the rows or the columns are so ordered. Similarly, the concept of isotropy is applicable in both these situations. In the former situation, the isotropic property can be used to determine an appropriate order for the rows and the columns; while in the latter situation, a comparison of the a priori order and the order determined by the isotropic property will be of interest. As we noted earlier, this was also the case when the RC association model or the canonical correlation approach are applied.

Before closing this section, we comment briefly on the relationship between the isotropy concept and some other concepts pertaining to association and/or dependence. Lehmann (1966) showed that "positive likelihood ratio dependence" implies "positive regression dependence," which implies in turn "positive quadrant dependence." Positive likelihood ratio dependence occurs if and only if the bivariate density is "totally positive of order 2" (see, e.g., Karlin 1968, p. 11). In any isotropic distribution with the rows and columns ordered so that $\Theta_{ij} \geq 1$(log

$\Theta_{ij} \geq 0$), this condition is equivalent to positive likelihood ratio dependence and thus to the condition that the dependence is totally positive of order 2. The results presented earlier in this section (e.g., (5.6)), and other related results, can be viewed as consequences of the relationships noted above (see, e.g., Alam and Wallenius 1976). Also, in view of these relationships, the uniform association model can be called the model with "constant local association," or "constant local likelihood ratio dependence," or "constant local dependence of order 2"; whereas the corresponding model considered by Plackett (1965) can be called the model with "constant quadrant association" (see Goodman 1981).

6. A SIMPLE TEST FOR PARAMETER DIFFERENCES IN THE RC MODEL

We noted in the preceding section (and also in earlier sections) that the parameter differences $\mu_i - \mu_{i+1}$ and $\nu_j - \nu_{j+1}$ affected the Θ_{ij}. In particular, when $\mu_i - \mu_{i+1} = 0$, then $\log \Theta_{ij} = 0$ for $j = 1, 2, \ldots, J - 1$; and when $\nu_j - \nu_{j+1} = 0$, then $\log \Theta_{ij} = 0$ for $i = 1, 2, \ldots, I - 1$ (see (2.3)). We shall now provide a simple test of whether a particular parameter difference in the RC model is equal to zero.

For illustrative purposes, consider again the data in Table 1a and the hypothesis H that, say, $\nu_3 = \nu_4$ in model (2.1). From (2.1) and (2.3) we see that, if hypothesis H is true, then (a) there is statistical independence between the rows and columns in the $I \times 2$ population subtable formed from columns 3 and 4, and (b) model (2.1) holds true also for the $I \times (J - 1)$ population table formed from the $I \times J$ table by combining columns 3 and 4. We can test (a) using the usual chi-squared test of statistical independence in the $I \times 2$ table, with $(I - 1)(2 - 1) = I - 1$ df; and we can test (b) using the chi-squared test for the RC model applied to the $I \times (J - 1)$ table, with $(I - 2)(J - 3)$ df (see Goodman 1979a). We can test that both (a) and (b) are true using the sum of the chi-squared statistics pertaining to (a) and (b), with

$$(I - 1) + (I - 2)(J - 3) = (I - 2)(J - 2) + 1$$

df. This chi-squared test is equivalent to a test of the hypothesis that model (2.1) holds true for the $I \times J$ table and that hypothesis H is true (viz., that $v_3 = v_4$). The difference between the chi-squared statistic thus obtained (with $(I - 2)(J - 2) + 1$ df) and the chi-squared statistic for testing model (2.1) in the $I \times J$ table (with $(I - 2)(J - 2)$ df) will provide a test of hypothesis H under the assumption that (2.1) holds true for the $I \times J$ table.

For the 4×2 subtable formed from columns 3 and 4 of Table 1a, with respect to (a) the usual test of statistical independence applied to this subtable, the likelihood-ratio chi-square is 1.50 (and the corresponding goodness-of-fit chi-square is 1.48), with 3 df. For the 4×3 table formed from Table 1a by combining columns 3 and 4, with respect to (b) the RC model applied to this table, the likelihood-ratio chi-square is 1.18 (and the corresponding goodness-of-fit chi-square is 1.20), with 2 df. Focusing attention on, say, the likelihood ratio chi-squares, the sum of the (a) and (b) quantities is 1.50 + 1.18 = 2.68, with 3 + 2 = 5 df. Since the corresponding quantity obtained with model (2.1) applied to Table 1a is 1.74, with 4 df (see Table 4a), we calculate the difference 2.68 − 1.74 = .94, with 5 − 4 = 1 df. Thus, we do not reject the hypothesis H that $v_3 = v_4$, under the assumption that (2.1) holds for Table 1a. Also, model (2.1) with $v_3 = v_4$ fits the data very well.

When the population conditional distributions in columns 3 and 4 are the same (see (a)), our attention is then drawn to Table 1a, modified by combining columns 3 and 4. Thus we present in Table 6 an analysis of the association in this modified Table 1a (compare Table 6 with Tables 4a and 4d), and we included in Table 5 the canonical scores and estimates $\hat{\mu}_i$ and $\hat{v}_j$ for the modified table as well as for the original data.

In closing the present section, we note that the methods presented in the section can be extended in a straightforward way to test the hypothesis that a given subset of the parameters $v_j(j = 1, 2, \ldots, J)$ are equal to each other, or the hypothesis that a given subset of the $\mu_i(i = 1, 2, \ldots, I)$ are equal to each other.

7. MORE GENERAL ASSOCIATION MODELS

With respect to the association models included in this article, we have discussed so far the RC model (2.1) and various special cases of this model. (The association models O, U, R, and C were special cases of (2.1).) Consider next an association model defined as follows:

$$F_{ij} = \alpha_i \beta_j e^{\phi_1 \mu_{1i} v_{1j} + \phi_2 \mu_{2i} v_{2j} + \phi_3 \mu_{3i} v_{3j}}, \qquad (7.1)$$

where μ_{1i} and v_{1j} are linear functions of i and j, respectively; and where v_{2j} and μ_{3i} are linear functions of j and i, respectively. (With respect to μ_{2i} and v_{3j} in (7.1), no assumptions are made here about how these quantities are related to i and j, respectively.) For the 2×2 subtables formed from adjacent rows (i.e., rows i and $i + 1$) and adjacent columns (i.e., columns j and $j + 1$) in the $I \times J$ cross-classification table, the corresponding logarithm of the odds-ratio Θ_{ij} can be expressed as follows under model (7.1):

$$\log \Theta_{ij} = \sum_{k=1}^{3} \phi_k(\mu_{ki} - \mu_{k,i+1})(v_{kj} - v_{k,j+1}) \quad (7.2)$$

(Compare (7.2) with (2.3).) Because of the linear restrictions imposed upon μ_{1i}, v_{1j}, v_{2j}, and μ_{3i}, formula (7.2) can also be expressed as follows:

$$\log \Theta_{ij} = \phi_1' + \phi_2'(\mu_{2i} - \mu_{2,i+1}) \qquad (7.3)$$
$$+ \phi_3'(v_{3j} - v_{3,j+1}),$$

where

$$\phi_1' = \phi_1(\mu_{1i} - \mu_{1,i+1})(v_{1j} - v_{1,j+1}),$$
$$\phi_2' = \phi_2(v_{2j} - v_{2,j+1}), \qquad (7.4)$$
$$\phi_3' = \phi_3(\mu_{3i} - \mu_{3,i+1}).$$

Table 6. Analysis of Association (ANOAS) in Modified Table 1a

a. Association Models Applied to Modified Table 1a

Association Models	Degrees of Freedom	Goodness-of-Fit Chi-Square	Likelihood-Ratio Chi-Square
(1) O	6	42.86	45.39
(2) U	5	7.87	7.70
(3) R	3	4.33	4.51
(4) C	4	3.11	3.29
(5) RC	2	1.20	1.18
(6) U + RC	1	.01	.01
(7) R + RC	0	.00	.00
(8) C + RC	1	.01	.01
(9) R + C + RC	0	.00	.00
(10) R + C	2	.39	.38

b. Components of Association in Modified Table 1a

Components	Models Used	Degrees of Freedom	Goodness-of-Fit Chi-Square	Likelihood-Ratio Chi-Square
General effect and column effect	(1)–(4)	6 − 4 = 2	39.75	42.10
Row effect	(4)–(5)	4 − 2 = 2	1.91	2.11
Other effects	(5)	2	1.20	1.18
Total effects	(1)	6	42.86	45.39

(Note that ϕ_1', ϕ_2', and ϕ_3' do not depend on the subscripts i and j because of the linear restrictions imposed on μ_{1i}, ν_{1j}, ν_{2j}, and μ_{3i}.) From (7.3) we see that the uniform association model is obtained from model (7.1) when $\phi_2 = \phi_3 = 0$, the row-effect association model is obtained when $\phi_3 = 0$, and the column-effect association model is obtained when $\phi_2 = 0$. (Note also that the U model is obtained from (7.3) when μ_{2i} and ν_{3j} are linear functions of i and j, respectively; the R model is obtained when ν_{3j} is a linear function of j; and the C model is obtained when μ_{2i} is a linear function of i.)

Since the μ_i and ν_j in the RC model (2.1) are not subject to the linear restrictions imposed in (7.1) upon μ_{1i}, ν_{1j}, ν_{2j}, and μ_{3i}, model (2.1) is not a special case of (7.1). From (7.3) we see that the association model (7.1) includes both row effects and column effects on the association, but these effects in (7.1) are different in form from the corresponding effects in the RC model. (Compare (7.3) with (2.3).) Since the effects in (7.3) are additive, we shall call the association model (7.1) the R + C model. This model is equivalent to the first model introduced in Goodman (1979a) in order to take into account the effect of the rows and columns on the association, and it was referred to as Model I there. (As we noted earlier, the RC model (2.1) was called Model II in the 1979a article.)

For simplicity, we can rewrite (7.3) in the following more usual form:

$$\log \Theta_{ij} = \psi + \psi_{i\cdot} + \psi_{\cdot j}, \qquad (7.5)$$

where the $\psi_{i\cdot}$ and $\psi_{\cdot j}$ are row and column effects. These effects are additive in (7.5), and the corresponding effects in (2.3) were multiplicative.

We next introduce a generalization of (2.3) and (7.5); namely,

$$\log \Theta_{ij} = \psi + \psi_{i\cdot} + \psi_{\cdot j} + \phi \xi_{i\cdot} \xi_{\cdot j}. \qquad (7.6)$$

When $\psi = \psi_{i\cdot} = \psi_{\cdot j} = 0$, we see that (7.6) is equivalent to (2.3); and when $\phi = 0$ we obtain (7.5). Since the general form of (7.6) will remain unchanged when the parameters $\xi_{i\cdot}$ and $\xi_{\cdot j}$ are replaced by linear functions of the $\xi_{i\cdot}$ and $\xi_{\cdot j}$, respectively, without loss of generality we can impose restrictions upon the location and scale of the $\xi_{i\cdot}$ and $\xi_{\cdot j}$ in (7.6). Similarly, we can impose a corresponding restriction upon the location of the additive row and column effects in (7.6).

For the $(I - 1) \times (J - 1)$ table of $\log \Theta_{ij}$, the number of independent parameters in (7.6) will be

$$1 + (I - 2) + (J - 2) + 1 + (I - 3) + (J - 3) \\ = 2(I + J - 4), \qquad (7.7)$$

and so the number of df used in testing this model would be

$$(I - 1)(J - 1) - 2(I + J + 4)$$

$$= (I - 3)(J - 3). \quad (7.8)$$

(Compare (7.7) and (7.8) with (2.8) and (2.9).)

Model (2.1) could be expressed in the equivalent form (2.3); and model (7.1) could be expressed in the equivalent form (7.2). Similarly, we can rewrite (7.6) in the following equivalent form:

$$F_{ij} = \alpha_i \beta_j \exp \left(\sum_{k=1}^{4} \phi_k \mu_{ki} v_{kj} \right), \quad (7.9)$$

where the μ_{1i}, v_{1j}, v_{2j}, and μ_{3i} satisfy the same linear restrictions imposed in (7.1). Under model (7.9) the logarithm of the odds-ratio Θ_{ij} can be expressed as follows:

$$\log \Theta_{ij} = \phi_1' + \phi_2'(\mu_{2i} - \mu_{2,i+1})$$
$$+ \phi_3'(v_{3j} - v_{3,j+1}) \quad (7.10)$$
$$+ \phi_4(\mu_{4i} - \mu_{4,i+1})(v_{4j} - v_{4,j+1}),$$

where ϕ_1', ϕ_2', and ϕ_3' are defined by (7.4). Note that (7.10) is of the same general form as (7.6).

Since the logarithm of Θ_{ij} under model (7.9) takes the form (7.10), we shall call this model the R + C + RC model. We noted that there were $(I - 2)(J - 2)$ df used in testing the RC model (see (2.9)), and there are $(I - 3)(J - 3)$ df used in testing the R + C + RC model (see (7.8)). When $\phi_3 = 0$ in (7.9) and (7.10), we obtain the R + RC model; when $\phi_2 = 0$ we obtain the C + RC model; and when $\phi_2 = \phi_3 = 0$ we obtain the U + RC model. (Note also that the R + RC model is obtained when v_{3j} is a linear function of j; the C + RC model is obtained when μ_{2i} is a linear function of i; and the U + RC model is obtained when μ_{2i} and v_{3j} are linear functions of i and j, respectively.) The corresponding number of df used in testing each of these models was included in Table 2.

The R + C + RC model (7.9) and the other association models introduced in the preceding paragraph are generalizations of the RC model. The iterative procedure introduced in Goodman (1979a) for calculating the maximum likelihood estimates under the RC model can be directly extended to these more general association models. For example, with respect to the R + C + RC model, the maximum likelihood estimates will satisfy the system of equations (5.1) and (5.6) in the 1979a article, and Appendix B there can be extended to provide the estimated parameters under the model.

The more general association models can be used to obtain chi-squared components pertaining to effects that are not included in the RC model. The RC model included multiplicative row and column effects on the association, and the more general association models include additive effects as well. The additive effects in, say, the R + C + RC model can be assessed in a more complete analysis of the components of association. Table 7 presents an analysis of this kind for the data in Table 1a and in the modified Table 1a. For Table 1a we include in Table 7 a partitioning of the effects not included in the RC model into (a) a component pertaining to the additive row and column effects in the R + C + RC model, and (b) other effects. And for the modified Table 1a we include in Table 7 a partitioning of the effects not included in the RC model into (a) a component pertaining to the additive general effect in the U + RC model, and (b) other effects.

Since the RC model fits the data in Table 1a and in the modified Table 1a very well, there was no real need to apply more general association models in this case. (The more general models were used in Table 7 to obtain a more complete analysis of the components of association, and we include this table here also for the convenience of those readers who may wish to compare the components of association that are obtained using the association models and the corresponding components that were obtained in the canonical correlation analysis of these data presented in the earlier literature.) The RC associ-

Table 7. Components of Association in Table 1a and Modified Table 1a

Components	Models Used	Degrees of Freedom	Goodness-of-Fit Chi-Square	Likelihood-Ratio Chi-Square
Table 1a				
General effect and column effect in C model	(1)–(4)	9 − 6 = 3	40.05	42.54
Row effect in RC model	(4)–(5)	6 − 4 = 2	2.53	2.61
Additive row and column effects in R + C + RC model	(5)–(9)	3	1.76	1.74
Other effects	(9)	1	.00	.00
Total effects	(1)	9	44.34	46.89
Modified Table 1a				
General effect and column effect in C model	(1)–(4)	6 − 4 = 2	39.75	42.10
Row effect in RC model	(4)–(5)	4 − 2 = 2	1.91	2.11
Additive general effect in U + RC model	(5)–(6)	2 − 1 = 1	1.19	1.17
Other effects	(6)	1	.01	.01
Total effects	(1)	6	42.86	45.39

ation model did not fit the data in Tables 1b and 1c so well, and the more general association models are more useful in the analysis of these data.

Table 8a gives the values of the goodness-of-fit chi-square and the likelihood-ratio chi-square obtained when the association models are applied to Tables 1b and 1c. From Table 8a we see that the R + C + RC association model fits the data in Tables 1b and 1c. In addition, the more parsimonious R + RC association model also fits the data in Table 1b but not the data in Table 1c. The corresponding components of association are presented in Table 8b.

From Tables 8a and 8b we see that the unexplained

variation represented by the chi-squared value obtained
for the null association model (i.e., the usual model of
statistical independence between the row variable (eye
color) and column variable (hair color)) can be greatly
reduced by the introduction of the various association
models considered here. For example, the U model
(which includes a general effect on the association) and
the RC model (which includes row and column effects,
as well as the general effect, on the association) greatly
reduce the chi-square. But these two models do not include all the statistically significant effects on the association between the row and column variables in Table
1b and in Table 1c. Thus, when we apply, say, the RC

Table 8. Analysis of Association (ANOAS) in Tables 1b and 1c

a. Association Models Applied to Tables 1b and 1c			
Association Models	Degrees of Freedom	Goodness-of-Fit Chi-Square	Likelihood-Ratio Chi-Square
Table 1b			
(1) O	12	1,240.04	1,218.31
(2) U	11	265.03	262.20
(3) R	9	102.59	101.91
(4) C	8	236.22	201.72
(5) RC	6	65.28	64.62
(6) U + RC	5	40.49	40.34
(7) R + RC	4	7.28	7.74
(8) C + RC	3	36.42	36.34
(9) R + C + RC	2	4.25	4.26
(10) R + C	6	83.25	82.45
Table 1c			
(1) O	12	3,683.88	3,606.21
(2) U	11	523.76	523.88
(3) R	9	291.04	291.34
(4) C	8	383.93	355.42
(5) RC	6	157.69	156.12
(6) U + RC	5	108.58	111.87
(7) R + RC	4	26.24	28.33
(8) C + RC	3	83.66	83.66
(9) R + C + RC	2	5.08	5.20
(10) R + C	6	187.65	186.27

b. Components of Association in Tables 1b and 1c

Components	Models Used	Degrees of Freedom	Goodness-of-Fit Chi-Square	Likelihood-Ratio Chi-Square
		Table 1b		
General effect in U model	(1)–(2)	12 − 11 = 1	1,175.01	956.11
Row and column effects in RC model	(2)–(5)	11 − 6 = 5	199.75	197.58
Additive row effect in R + RC model	(5)–(7)	6 − 4 = 2	58.00	56.88
Additive column effect in R + C + RC model	(7)–(9)	4 − 2 = 2	3.03	3.48
Other effects	(9)	2	4.25	4.26
Total effects	(1)	12	1,240.04	1,218.31
		Table 1c		
General effect in U model	(1)–(2)	12 − 11 = 1	3,160.12	3,082.33
Row and column effects in RC model	(2)–(5)	11 − 6 = 5	366.07	367.76
Additive row and column effects in R + C + RC model	(5)–(9)	6 − 2 = 4	152.61	150.92
Other effects	(9)	2	5.08	5.20
Total effects	(1)	12	3,683.88	3,606.21

model to these tables, the corresponding estimates $\hat{\mu}_i$ and $\hat{v}_j$ and their correlation (or the related canonical scores x_i and y_j and their correlation), which were presented earlier in Table 3, do not fully describe this association. The estimates $\hat{\mu}_i$ and $\hat{v}_j$ in the RC model pertain only to multiplicative row and column effects on the association (see (2.3)). In contrast to the RC model, we include in the R + C + RC model additive row and column effects in addition to the multiplicative effects (see (7.10)). Since the R + C + RC model fits the data in Tables 1b and 1c, the association in these tables can be described in terms of the various effects included in the model, or in terms of the parameters estimated under the model. Since the more parsimonious R + RC model also fits the data in

Table 1b (but not the data in Table 1c), the additive column effect in the R + C + RC model can be ignored in this case (see Table 8b).

8. THE R + C MODEL AND RELATED ASSOCIATION MODELS

Our attention in this article has been focused so far on the RC model, special cases of it (viz., the U, R, and C models), and generalizations of it (viz., the U + RC, R + RC, C + RC, and R + C + RC models). We also described a close relationship between some results obtained with the RC model and corresponding results obtained with the canonical correlation approach. (For a description of the close relationship between results obtained with the RC model and those obtained in the situation where there is an underlying bivariate normal distribution, see Goodman (1981).) The R + C model was discussed only briefly in the preceding section (see (7.1) through (7.5)), and we shall now comment further on this model.

We noted in the preceding section that the U, R, and C models were also special cases of the R + C model (as well as special cases of the RC model), and the R + C + RC was also a generalization of the R + C model (see (7.6)). We consider next the relationship between the U + RC model and the R + C model.

From (7.6) we see that the U + RC model can be written as

$$\log \Theta_{ij} = \psi + \phi \xi_{i \cdot} \xi_{\cdot j}. \qquad (8.1)$$

This model can also be expressed in the following equivalent form:

$$\log \Theta_{ij} = \psi' + \xi_{i \cdot}' + \xi_{\cdot j}' + \phi' \xi_{i \cdot}' \xi_{\cdot j}' \qquad (8.2)$$

where

$$\psi' = \psi + \phi, \qquad \phi' = \phi^{-1}, \qquad (8.3)$$
$$\xi_{i \cdot}' = (\xi_{i \cdot} - 1)\phi, \quad \xi_{\cdot j}' = (\xi_{\cdot j} - 1)\phi.$$

(For a related result in the analysis of a two-way array with continuous data, see the discussion of Tukey's test for additivity in, for example, Tukey 1977, p. 421.) Model (8.2) is a special case of the R + C + RC model in which the multiplicative effects $\xi_i.'$ and $\xi_{.j}'$ in (8.2) are equal to the corresponding additive effects in the model. Thus, the U + RC model can also be viewed as this kind of special case of the R + C + RC model, and consequently as a generalization of the R + C model.

The results in the preceding paragraph can be extended directly to the R + RC and C + RC models. The former model can be expressed in the equivalent form

$$\log \Theta_{ij} = \psi' + \psi_i.' + \xi_{.j}' + \phi'\xi_i.'\xi_{.j}', \qquad (8.4)$$

and the latter model can be expressed in the equivalent form

$$\log \Theta_{ij} = \psi' + \xi_i.' + \psi_{.j}' + \phi'\xi_i.'\xi_{.j}', \qquad (8.5)$$

where $\psi_i.' = \psi_i. + \xi_i.'$ and $\psi_{.j}' = \psi_{.j} + \xi_{.j}'$. Model (8.4) is a special case of the R + C + RC model in which the multiplicative effect $\xi_{.j}'$ in (8.4) is equal to the corresponding additive effect in the model; and (8.5) is a special case of the R + C + RC model in which the multiplicative effect $\xi_i.'$ in (8.5) is equal to the corresponding additive effect in the model. Thus, the R + RC and C + RC models can also be viewed as these kinds of special cases of the R + C + RC model, and consequently as generalizations of the R + C model.

The analysis of components of association considered earlier (see, e.g., Tables 7 and 8b) were based upon the RC model, special cases of it, and generalizations of it. A similar kind of analysis could have been based upon the R + C model. This is presented in Table 9 for the data in Table 1a and in the modified Table 1a. Since the R + C model can be very different from the RC model, results obtained with these models can differ greatly. (For the data considered in Table 9, both the R + C model and the RC model fit the data well, and so in this case the results are similar.)

Table 9. Components of Association in Table 1a and Modified Table 1a

Components	Models Used	Degrees of Freedom	Goodness-of-Fit Chi-Square	Likelihood-Ratio Chi-Square
Table 1a				
General effect and column effect in C model	(1)–(4)	9 − 6 = 3	40.05	42.54
Row effect in R + C model	(4)–(10)	6 − 4 = 2	1.44	1.54
Multiplicative row and column effects in R + C + RC model	(10)–(9)	3	2.85	2.81
Other effects	(9)	1	.00	.00
Total effects	(1)	9	44.34	46.89
Modified Table 1a				
General effect and column effect in C model	(1)–(4)	6 − 4 = 2	39.75	42.10
Row effect in R + C model	(4)–(10)	4 − 2 = 2	2.72	2.91
Miltiplicative general effect in model (8.2)	(10)–(6)	2 − 1 = 1	.38	.37
Other effects	(6)	1	.01	.01
Total effects	(1)	6	42.86	45.39

Before closing this section, we include a final brief comment on the relationship between the RC model and the generalizations of the R + C model considered here. From (8.1) through (8.3) we see that the RC model can be expressed in the equivalent form

$$\log \Theta_{ij} = \phi + \xi_{i\cdot}' + \xi_{\cdot j}' + \phi'\xi_{i\cdot}'\xi_{\cdot j}', \qquad (8.6)$$

where $\phi = 1/\phi'$. Thus, when the general additive effect ψ' in model (8.2) turns out to be equal to the general multiplicative effect in model (8.1), the RC model is obtained.

REFERENCES

ALAM, K., and WALLENIUS, K.T. (1976), "Positive Dependence and Monotonicity in Conditional Distributions," *Communications in Statistics*, A5, 525–534.

ANDERSEN, E.B. (1980), *Discrete Statistical Models With Social Science Applications*, Amsterdam: North-Holland.

BIRCH, M.W. (1964), "A New Proof of the Pearson-Fisher Theorem," *Annals of Mathematical Statistics*, 35, 718–824.

────── (1965), "The Detection of Partial Association, II: The General Case," *Journal of the Royal Statistical Society*, Ser. B, 27, 111–124.

BURT, C. (1950), "The Factorial Analysis of Qualitative Data," *British Journal of Psychology, Statistical Section*, 3, 166–185.

CORSTEN, L.C.A. (1976), "Matrix Approximation, A Key to Application of Multivariate Methods," *Proceedings of the Ninth International Biometric Conference*, 1, 61–77.

DUNCAN, O.D. (1979), "How Destination Depends on Origin in the Occupational Mobility Table," *American Journal of Sociology*, 84, 793–803.

FISHER, R.A. (1940), "The Precision of Discriminant Functions," *Annals of Eugenics, London*, 10, 422–429.

* GOODMAN, L.A. (1968), "The Analysis of Cross-Classified Data: Independence, Quasi-Independence, and Interactions in Contingency Tables With or Without Missing Entries," *Journal of the American Statistical Association*, 63, 1091–1131.

────── (1970), "The Multivariate Analysis of Qualitative Data: Interactions Among Multiple Classifications," *Journal of the American Statistical Association*, 65, 226–256.

────── (1971), "Partitioning of Chi-Square, Analysis of Marginal Contingency Tables, and Estimation of Expected Frequencies in Multidimensional Contingency Tables," *Journal of the American Statistical Association*, 66, 339–344.

* ────── (1979a), "Simple Models for the Analysis of Association in Cross-Classifications Having Ordered Categories," *Journal of the American Statistical Association*, 74, 537–552.

* ────── (1979b), "Multiplicative Models for the Analysis of Occupational Mobility Tables and Other Kinds of Cross-Classification Tables," *American Journal of Sociology*, 84, 804–819.

* ────── (1981), "Association Models and the Bivariate Normal for Contingency Tables With Ordered Categories," *Biometrika*, 68.

GUTTMAN, L. (1941), "The Quantification of a Class of Attributes," in *The Prediction of Personal Adjustment*, eds. P. Horst et al., New York: Social Science Research Council, 319–348.

────── (1950), "The Principal Components of Scale Analysis," in *Measurement and Prediction, Studies in Social Psychology in World War II, Vol. IV*, eds. S.A. Stouffer et al., Princeton, N.J.: Princeton University Press, 312–361.

────── (1953), "A Note on Sir Cyril Burt's Factorial Analysis of Qualitative Data," *British Journal of Statistical Psychology*, 6, 1–4.

HABERMAN, S.J. (1974a), "Log-Linear Models for Frequency Tables With Ordered Classifications," *Biometrics*, 30, 589–600.

———— (1974b), *The Analysis of Frequency Data*, Chicago: University of Chicago Press.

———— (1979), *Analysis of Qualitative Data: Vol. 2. New Developments*, New York: Academic Press.

———— (1981), "Tests for Independence in Two-Way Contingency Tables Based on Canonical Correlation and on Linear-by-Linear Interaction," *Annals of Statistics*, 9.

HAYASHI, C. (1951), "On the Prediction of Phenomena from Qualitative Data and the Quantification of Qualitative Data from the Mathematico-Statistical Point of View," *Annals of the Institute of Statistical Mathematics* (Tokyo), 3, 69–98.

HIRSCHFELD, H.O. (1935), "A Connection Between Correlation and Contingency," *Proceedings of the Cambridge Philosophical Society*, 31, 520–524.

HOTELLING, H. (1936), "Relations Between Two Sets of Variates," *Biometrika*, 28, 321–377.

JOHNSON, D.E., and GRAYBILL, F.A. (1972), "An Analysis of a Two-Way Model With Interaction and No Replication," *Journal of the American Statistical Association*, 67, 862–868.

KARLIN, S. (1968), *Total Positivity*, Stanford, Calif.: Stanford University Press.

KENDALL, M.G., and STUART, A. (1961), *The Advanced Theory of Statistics: Vol. 2. Inference and Relationship*, London: Griffin.

———— (1967), *The Advanced Theory of Statistics: Vol. 2. Inference and Relationship* (2nd ed.), London: Griffin.

LANCASTER, H.O. (1957), "Some Properties of the Bivariate Normal Distribution Considered in the Form of a Contingency Table," *Biometrika*, 44, 289–292.

———— (1958), "The Structure of Bivariate Distributions," *Annals of Mathematical Statistics*, 29, 719–736.

———— (1963), "Canonical Correlations and Partitions of χ^2," *Quarterly Journal of Mathematics*, 14, 220–224.

———— (1969), *The Chi-Squared Distribution*, New York: John Wiley.

LEHMANN, E.L. (1966), "Some Concepts of Dependence," *Annals of Mathematical Statistics*, 37, 1137–1153.

MANDEL, J. (1971), "A New Analysis of Variance Model for Nonadditive Data," *Technometrics*, 13, 1–18.

MAUNG, K. (1941), "Measurement of Association in a Contingency Table With Special Reference to the Pigmentation of Hair and Eye Colour of Scottish School Children," *Annals of Eugenics, London*, 11, 189–205.

O'NEILL, M.E. (1978a), "Asymptotic Distributions of the Canonical Correlations from Contingency Tables," *Australian Journal of Statistics*, 20, 75–82.

———— (1978b), "Distributional Expansions for Canonical Correlations From Contingency Tables," *Journal of the Royal Statistical Society*, Ser. B, 40, 303–312.

PLACKETT, R.L. (1965), "A Class of Bivariate Distributions," *Journal of the American Statistical Association*, 60, 516–522.

———— (1974), *The Analysis of Categorical Data*, New York: Hafner.

RASCH, G. (1966), *Statistikkens Teori*, Lecture notes compiled by U. Christiansen in Danish, University of Copenhagen.

SIMON, G. (1974), "Alternative Analyses for the Singly-Ordered Contingency Table," *Journal of the American Statistical Association*, 69, 971–976.

TRELOAR, A.E. (1939), *Elements of Statistical Reasoning*, New York: John Wiley.

TUKEY, J.W. (1977), *Exploratory Data Analysis*, Reading, Mass.: Addison-Wesley.

WILLIAMS, E.J. (1952), "Use of Scores for the Analysis of Association in Contingency Tables," *Biometrika*, 39, 274–280.

YULE, G.U. (1906), "On a Property Which Holds Good for All Groupings of a Normal Distribution of Frequency for Two Variables, With Applications to the Study of Contingency-Tables for the Inheritance of Unmeasured Qualities," *Proceedings of the Royal Society* (Vol. A), 77, 324–336.

YULE, G.U., and KENDALL, M.G. (1950), *An Introduction to the Theory of Statistics* (14th ed.), New York: Hafner.

7.
Applications of Association Models: I

Criteria for Determining Whether Certain Categories in a Cross-Classification Table Should Be Combined, with Special Reference to Occupational Categories in an Occupational Mobility Table

This article considers two kinds of criteria for determining whether certain rows in a two-way cross-classification table should be combined and/or whether certain columns in the table should be combined. These criteria pertain to homogeneity and structure. When these criteria are applied to the classic cross-classification on British occupational mobility recently studied by Duncan, Goodman, Hauser, and Clogg, new insights into these data are obtained. The application of these criteria in the present article also helps to clarify the meaning of the criteria considered here and related terms recently discussed by Breiger.

The utility of the criteria discussed herein will be illustrated by applying them to the classic occupational mobility data of Glass (1954) and Miller (1960) recently studied by Duncan (1979), Goodman (1979b), Hauser (1979), and Clogg (1981).[1] Table 1A gives these data in the form presented by Miller (1960), table 1B gives them in the form presented by Glass (1954),[2] and table 1C gives them in still another form. Duncan (1979), Hauser (1979), and Clogg (1981) discussed the analysis of table 1A, and Goodman (1979b) considered tables 1A and B. In the present article we shall discuss the analysis of table 1C and use our analysis of this table, together with some additional results on the analysis of tables 1A and B, to further illuminate these data.

The occupational mobility table presented by Glass (1954) (table 1B) can be obtained from table 1A by combining occupational categories 5 and 6

[1] With the first set of criteria, the models of independence (null association) and quasi-independence will be applied to appropriate cross-classification tables; and with the second set of criteria, other association models will be applied; see, e.g., Goodman 1968, 1979.

[2] The entry in cell (V,V) of table 1B was given as 714 in the earlier literature that used the occupational mobility data in Glass (1954); but for the sake of consistency with the results given by Miller (1960), we have changed this number to 715. (This change will not affect the analysis presented here.)

in the latter table, while table 1C is obtained from table 1A by combining occupational categories 5 and 4. Glass's table (table 1B) combined in a single category routine grades of nonmanual occupations and skilled manual occupations, whereas our table 1C combines in a single category routine grades of nonmanual occupations and those nonmanual occupations classified immediately above the routine grades. With our analysis of tables 1A,

TABLE 1

OCCUPATIONAL MOBILITY TABLES

A. CROSS-CLASSIFICATION OF BRITISH MALE SAMPLE ACCORDING TO EACH
SUBJECT'S OCCUPATIONAL STATUS CATEGORY AND HIS FATHER'S OCCU-
PATIONAL STATUS CATEGORY, USING EIGHT STATUS CATEGORIES

FATHER'S STATUS	SUBJECT'S STATUS							
	1	2	3	4	5	6	7	8
1.........	50	19	26	8	7	11	6	2
2.........	16	40	34	18	11	20	8	3
3.........	12	35	65	66	35	88	23	21
4.........	11	20	58	110	40	183	64	32
5.........	2	8	12	23	25	46	28	12
6.........	12	28	102	162	90	554	230	177
7.........	0	6	19	40	21	158	143	71
8.........	0	3	14	32	15	126	91	106

B. CROSS-CLASSIFICATION OBTAINED FROM TABLE 1A BY COMBINING
STATUS CATEGORIES 5 AND 6

FATHER'S STATUS	SUBJECT'S STATUS						
	I	II	III	IV	V	VI	VII
I...............	50	19	26	8	18	6	2
II..............	16	40	34	18	31	8	3
III.............	12	35	65	66	123	23	21
IV.............	11	20	58	110	223	64	32
V..............	14	36	114	185	715	258	189
VI.............	0	6	19	40	179	143	71
VII............	0	3	14	32	141	91	106

C. CROSS-CLASSIFICATION OBTAINED FROM TABLE 1A BY COMBINING
STATUS CATEGORIES 4 AND 5

FATHER'S STATUS	SUBJECT'S STATUS						
	I	II	III	IV	V	VI	VII
I...............	50	19	26	15	11	6	2
II..............	16	40	34	29	20	8	3
III.............	12	35	65	101	88	23	21
IV.............	13	28	70	198	229	92	44
V..............	12	28	102	252	554	230	177
VI.............	0	6	19	61	158	143	71
VII............	0	3	14	47	126	91	106

B, and C, we shall see that, by applying the two kinds of criteria considered here, we obtain good reasons for replacing the eight occupational categories considered by Miller (table 1A) by a system of seven categories. Our replacement by the system of seven categories introduced in table 1C meets the standards set by both kinds of criteria considered here, whereas the replacement by the system of seven categories in Glass's table fails to meet the standards set by one of the kinds of criteria.

The classic British occupational mobility data will be used here for expository and illustrative purposes, but we could have used instead other examples of occupational mobility data that might be more interesting to some of our readers. We decided to use these classic data (despite their limitations) because they have been analyzed by various earlier writers using a wide variety of methods (see, e.g., literature cited in Goodman [1972] and Haberman [1974]), and we thereby facilitate comparison of the results that will be presented in the present article with the results presented by the various earlier writers.

The criteria and methods discussed in the present article can be applied to occupational mobility tables and also to other kinds of cross-classification tables. For an $I \times J$ cross-classification table, these criteria and methods can be used to determine whether certain rows in the table should be combined and/or whether certain columns in the table should be combined. We can consider cross-classification tables in which (1) the number of rows equals the number of columns $(I = J)$ and there is a one-to-one correspondence between the row categories and the column categories (as in the occupational mobility table), or (2) the number of rows equals the number of columns but there is not a one-to-one correspondence between them, or (3) the number of rows does not equal the number of columns $(I \neq J)$. The criteria and methods presented here can be applied to each of these types of cross-classification tables.

The two kinds of criteria that will be considered here are homogeneity criteria and structural criteria. The homogeneity criteria will be discussed next.

HOMOGENEITY CRITERIA

In his discussion of a somewhat related topic, Breiger (1981) defined and applied the term "internal homogeneity," but we shall see that in the present context his particular definition and application of the term are not helpful. Some other homogeneity criteria will be presented here, and these criteria will be applied in the present context to obtain additional insight into the occupational mobility tables (tables 1A, B, and C).

Let us consider whether the eight occupational categories in table 1A should be replaced by the system of seven "classes" obtained from this table when, say, categories 4 and 5 are combined (see table 1C). If Breiger's definition of the term "internal homogeneity" were applied in the present context, the boundaries between the seven "classes" would be used to form $7 \times 7 = 49$ rectangular subtables from the entries in the 8×8 table (table 1A), and each of these rectangular subtables would then be used to test the usual null hypothesis of statistical independence between the corresponding rows and columns of the subtable. However, each of the 49 subtables is either a 1×1 table (consisting of only one entry),[3] or a 1×2 table (consisting of two entries in only one row),[4] or a 2×1 table (consisting of two entries in only one column),[5] or a single 2×2 table.[6] Since the usual null hypothesis of statistical independence is meaningless in a 1×1 table, or a 1×2 table, or a 2×1 table, the only subtable among the 49 subtables that could possibly be used to test this hypothesis is the single 2×2 table noted above. But this particular 2×2 table includes two entries that were on the main diagonal of table 1A (the entries [4,4] and [5,5]),[7] and all the entries on the main diagonal were deleted in Breiger's application of the term "internal homogeneity." Thus, this particular definition and application of the term are not helpful in the present context. Some other homogeneity criteria will be presented next.

To determine whether rows 4 and 5 in the 8×8 table (table 1A) are "homogeneous," let us consider first the 2×8 subtable formed from the two rows (rows 4 and 5) and the eight columns. This particular subtable is presented here as table 2A. with the corresponding "occupational inheritance" entries deleted.[8] To examine whether the two rows of table 2A are homogeneous, we can perform the usual test of the hypothesis of quasi-

---

[3] Each 1×1 table can be described by a single entry (i,j) obtained from the ith row and jth column of the 8×8 table (table 1A), with $i \neq 4$ or 5 and $j \neq 4$ or 5. (Thus, the value of i here can be 1, 2, 3, 6, 7, or 8; and similarly for j.)

[4] Each 1×2 table can be described by a set of two entries $(i,4)$ and $(i,5)$, with $i \neq 4$ or 5.

[5] Each 2×1 table can be described by a set of two entries $(4,j)$ and $(5,j)$, with $j \neq 4$ or 5.

[6] The single 2×2 table can be described by the set of four entries (4,4), (4,5), (5,4), and (5,5).

[7] See n. 6 above.

[8] For occupational mobility tables of the kind described by table 1A, we have found that the entries on the main diagonal often need to be treated separately from the other cells in the table (owing to "occupational inheritance" and related factors), and that analyzing the table with the entries on the main diagonal deleted is often worthwhile (see, e.g., Goodman 1969, 1972; Haberman 1974). Similarly, we delete these "occupational inheritance" entries in the analysis of a given subtable of the occupational mobility table, e.g., the entries in table 2A corresponding to (4,4) and (5,5) in table 1A. For other kinds of cross-classification tables, there may be good reasons for deleting a set of entries different from the set usually deleted in the occupational mobility context, or there may be no need to delete any entries at all.

TABLE 2

SUBTABLES OF TABLE 1A USED IN APPLYING HOMOGENEITY CRITERIA
TO STATUS CATEGORIES 4 AND 5

			A. Applied to Rows 4 and 5				
11	20	58	. . .	40	183	64	32
2	8	12	23	. . .	46	28	12

			B. Applied to Columns 4 and 5				
8	18	66	. . .	23	162	40	32
7	11	35	40	. . .	90	21	15

			C. Applied to Rows 4 and 5 and to Columns 4 and 5				
. . .	. . .	. . .	8	7	. . .	. . .	. . .
. . .	. . .	. . .	18	11	. . .	. . .	. . .
. . .	. . .	. . .	66	35	. . .	. . .	. . .
11	20	58	. . .	40	183	64	32
2	8	12	23	. . .	46	28	12
. . .	. . .	. . .	162	90	. . .	. . .	. . .
. . .	. . .	. . .	40	21	. . .	. . .	. . .
. . .	. . .	. . .	32	15	. . .	. . .	. . .

independence in table 2A.[9] This test yields a χ^2 value of 6.61, with 5 df.[10] Thus, the two rows of table 2A are judged to be homogeneous, and the corresponding rows 4 and 5 of table 1A are also judged to be homogeneous.

To determine whether columns 4 and 5 in table 1A are homogeneous, we can apply to these columns a procedure similar to the one described in the preceding paragraph for rows 4 and 5. This procedure now yields table 2B (rather than table 2A), and the corresponding test applied to table 2B now yields a χ^2 value of 1.20, with 5 df. Thus, the two rows of table 2B are judged to be homogeneous, and the corresponding columns 4 and 5 of table 1A are also judged to be homogeneous.

Tables 2A and B have in common only the entries (4,5) and (5,4) from table 1A.[11] Since the χ^2 tests described above for tables 2A and B did not actually take into account those two entries,[12] the χ^2 test for table 2A and the corresponding test for table 2B are statistically independent (asymptotically). The sum of the two χ^2 values can be used to test the hypothesis that rows 4 and 5 are homogeneous and columns 4 and 5 are homogeneous,

[9] The test of quasi-independence in table 2A is equivalent to the usual test of independence in the 2×6 subtable formed from table 2A by deleting cols. 4 and 5 (see, e.g., Goodman 1968). For the 2×6 table, there will be $1 \times 5 = 5$ df in testing the usual hypothesis of independence.

[10] For the sake of brevity, we shall report in the text of this article only the values of the χ^2 statistic pertaining to the likelihood-ratio.

[11] The occupational inheritance entries (4,4) and (5,5) were deleted in tables 2A and B.

[12] The χ^2 test for table 2A was equivalent to a χ^2 test obtained when the entries (4,5) and (5,4) from table 1A are deleted in table 2A (see n. 9), and a similar remark applies to the corresponding test for table 2B.

ignoring entries (4,5) and (5,4) from table 1A. We thus obtain the sum 6.61+ 1.20 = 7.81, with 5 + 5 = 10 df. This hypothesis of homogeneity is thereby accepted.

We next show how to test this hypothesis without ignoring entries (4,5) and (5,4) from table 1A. To examine the hypothesis that rows 4 and 5 are homogeneous and columns 4 and 5 are homogeneous, we now consider the 8 × 8 table formed from table 1A by deleting all entries that are not in one of the two given rows or in one of the two given columns. This particular subtable is presented here as table 2C, with the corresponding occupational inheritance entries deleted.[13] The usual test of quasi-independence in table 2C does not ignore entries (4,5) and (5,4). When this test is applied to table 2C, we obtain a χ^2 value of 7.87, with 11 df. Thus, this hypothesis of homogeneity is also accepted.

To examine in more detail this hypothesis of homogeneity, we can partition the χ^2 statistic from table 2C into its relevant components.[14] These components can be described in terms of the subtables included in tables 3 and 4. The subtables in table 3 were formed from the entries in table 2C as follows: table 3A was formed from rows 4 and 5 and columns 1, 2, and 3 of table 2C; table 3B was formed from rows 4 and 5 and columns 6, 7, and 8. table 3C was formed from columns 4 and 5 and rows 1, 2, and 3; and table 3D was formed from columns 4 and 5 and rows 6, 7, and 8. (The subtables in table 4 will be described later.)

Since tables 3A–D are 2 × 3 tables, there will be 1 × 2 = 2 df in testing the usual hypothesis of independence in each of these tables. The corresponding χ^2 values (each with 2 df) are 1.73, 4.19, 0.82, and 0.26, for tables 3A, B, C, and D, respectively. The sum of these four χ^2 values can be used to test the hypothesis of independence in the four tables (tables 3A–D). We thus obtain the sum 1.73 + 4.19 + 0.82 + 0.26 = 7.00, with 4 × 2 = 8 df. Thus, this hypothesis of homogeneity is also accepted.

To show how the χ^2 values obtained from the subtables in table 3 are related to the χ^2 values obtained for tables 2A, B, and C, we next consider tables 4A, B, and C. Table 4A is a 2 × 2 table formed from the entries in rows 4 and 5 of table 2C by combining columns 1, 2, and 3 into a single column and combining columns 6, 7, and 8 into a single column (with the

[13] Note that table 2C is a combination of tables 2A and B.

[14] The general method for partitioning the χ^2 statistic described in, e.g., Goodman (1968, 1970, 1978) can be applied here. The χ^2 statistic for testing the hypothesis of "homogeneity" in, for example, a 3 × 2 table (with 2 × 1 = 2 df) can be partitioned into two components: (a) a component (with 1 df) to test the hypothesis of homogeneity in the 2 × 2 subtable formed from, say, rows 1 and 2 of the 3 × 2 table (deleting row 3 of the table); and (b) a component (with 1 df) to test the hypothesis of homogeneity in the 2 × 2 table formed from the 3 × 2 table by combining the corresponding entries in rows 1 and 2. The general method applied in this simple example will be applied in a similar way now to table 2C and later to other tables considered in this article.

TABLE 3

SUBTABLES OF TABLE 2C USED IN
APPLYING HOMOGENEITY CRITERIA

A. Applied to Rows 4 and 5 in Columns
1, 2, and 3

11	20	58
2	8	12

B. Applied to Rows 4 and 5 in Columns
6, 7, and 8

183	64	32
46	28	12

C. Applied to Columns 4 and 5 in Rows
1, 2, and 3

8	18	66
7	11	35

D. Applied to Columns 4 and 5 in Rows
6, 7, and 8

162	40	32
90	21	15

TABLE 4

TABLES FORMED FROM TABLE 2C
AND TABLE 3 USED IN APPLYING
HOMOGENEITY CRITERIA

A. Applied to Rows 4 and 5 in Columns
1+2+3 and 6+7+8

89	279
22	86

B. Applied to Columns 4 and 5 in Rows
1+2+3 and 6+7+8

92	234
53	126

C. Applied to Rows 4 and 5 in Columns 4, 5,
and 1+2+3+6+7+8 and to Columns 4
and 5 in Rows 4, 5, and 1+2+3+6+7+8

. . .	40	368
23	. . .	108
326	179	. . .

entries [4,5] and [5,4] deleted);[15] table 4B is a 2×2 table formed from the entries in columns 4 and 5 of table 2C by combining rows 1, 2, and 3 into a single row and combining rows 6, 7, and 8 into a single row (with entries [4,5] and [5,4]) deleted);[16] and table 4C is a 3×3 table (with the main diagonal deleted) formed from table 2C by combining columns 1, 2, 3, 6, 7, and 8 into a single column and combining rows 1, 2, 3, 6, 7, and 8 into a single row.[17] Since tables 4A and B are 2×2 tables, there will be a $1 \times 1 = 1$ df in testing the usual hypothesis of independence in each of these tables. Also, since table 4C is a 3×3 table with three cells deleted, there will be $2 \times 2 - 3 = 1$ df in testing the hypothesis of quasi-independence in this table. The corresponding χ^2 values (each with 1 df) are 0.69, 0.11, and 0.06, for tables 4A, B, and C, respectively. The sum of these three χ^2 values is $0.69 + 0.11 + 0.06 = 0.86$, with $3 \times 1 = 3$ df.

The sum of the χ^2 values pertaining to the subtables in table 3 was 7.00 with 8 df, and the sum of the χ^2 values in the preceding paragraph was 0.86 with 3 df. The sum of these two sums is $7.00 + 0.86 = 7.87$[18] (with $8 + 3 = 11$ df), which is equal to the corresponding χ^2 value obtained in the analysis of table 2C presented above.

We have partitioned above the χ^2 value (with 11 df) obtained in the homogeneity test pertaining to table 2C into a component pertaining to homogeneity tests in table 3 (with 8 df) and a component pertaining to homogeneity tests in table 4 (with 3 df). The component pertaining to table 3 was also partitioned into four subcomponents (each with 2 df),[19] and the component pertaining to table 4 was partitioned into three subcomponents (each with 1 df).

Table 5A summarizes the partitioning of the homogeneity test pertaining to table 2C into components pertaining to homogeneity tests in tables 3

[15] Note that table 4A can also be formed from the row totals of table 3A and of table 3B.

[16] Note that table 4B can also be formed from the row totals of table 3C and of table 3D.

[17] The general method for partitioning the χ^2 statistic illustrated in the simple example in n. 14 was applied successively to table 2C to obtain the components pertaining to tables 2A and B and 4C (see also nn. 9 and 12), with the components pertaining to tables 2A and B partitioned further to obtain subcomponents pertaining to tables 3A and B and 4A and tables 3C and D and 4B, respectively. Table 4C is obtained when the homogeneity criteria are applied to entries (4,5) and (5,4) in table 2C. Note that table 4C can also be formed from the entries (4,5) and (5,4) in table 2C, the row totals of table 4A, and the row totals of table 4B. The row totals of table 4A are equal to the corresponding totals for rows 4 and 5 in table 2C, with entries (4,5) and (5,4) deleted; and the row totals of table 4B are equal to the corresponding totals for columns 4 and 5 in table 2C with the same two entries deleted. (See also the corresponding row totals from table 2A, and the corresponding row totals from table 2B, with the same two entries deleted in each case.)

[18] The sum is 7.87 (rather than 7.86), with summands having more significant digits than are reported here.

[19] Each subcomponent (with 2 df) can be partitioned into two sub-subcomponents, each with 1 df. The general method for partitioning the χ^2 statistic illustrated in the simple example in n. 14 can be applied here to each subcomponent.

TABLE 5

COMPONENTS OF HOMOGENEITY CRITERIA APPLIED
TO STATUS CATEGORIES 4 AND 5

Component	df	Likelihood-Ratio χ^2
A. For Homogeneity Criteria Applied in Tables 3 and 4		
1. Table 3A	2	1.73
2. Table 3B	2	4.19
3. Table 4A	1	.69
4. Table 3C	2	.82
5. Table 3D	2	.26
6. Table 4B	1	.11
7. Table 4C	1	.06
Total	11	7.87*
B. For Homogeneity Criteria Applied in Tables 2A and B and 4C		
1. Table 2A	5	6.61
2. Table 2B	5	1.20
3. Table 4C	1	.06
Total	11	7.87

* See n. 18.

and 4; and table 5B provides a somewhat different partitioning of that homogeneity test into components pertaining to homogeneity tests in tables 2A and B and 4C.[20] Note that the χ^2 value obtained for table 2A (with 5 df) is equal to the sum of the χ^2 values obtained for tables 3A and B and 4A; and the χ^2 value obtained for table 2B (with 5 df) is equal to the sum of the χ^2 values obtained for tables 3C and D and 4B.[21] Thus, the homogeneity tests in tables 3 and 4A and B can be used to partition into components the homogeneity tests in tables 2A and B.

The results presented above demonstrate that occupational categories 4 and 5 in table 1A pass the various homogeneity tests introduced in this section. These results provide justification for the system of seven categories in table 1C.

A somewhat similar set of homogeneity tests can also be applied to examine whether occupational categories 5 and 6 in table 1A should be combined. Table 6 summarizes the results thus obtained. Compare table 6 with table 5. The total χ^2 value on the bottom line in tables 6A and B was obtained by applying a homogeneity test directly to a table somewhat

[20] With respect to the homogeneity tests in tables 2A and B, see nn. 9 and 12. The general method for partitioning χ^2 illustrated in the simple example in n. 14 can be applied successively to obtain the partitionings in tables 5B and 5A and also the other partitionings noted next in this paragraph.

[21] This equality holds with summands having more significant digits than are reported here.

similar in form to table 2C. (The corresponding total χ^2 value on the bottom line in tables 5A and B was obtained by applying a homogeneity test directly to table 2C.) The total χ^2 value on the bottom line in tables 6A and B was obtained from the 8×8 table formed from table 1A by deleting all entries that are not in one of the two relevant rows (rows 5 and 6 in this case) or in one of the two relevant columns (cols. 5 and 6 in this case), with the corresponding occupational inheritance entries deleted. The general method for partitioning the χ^2 statistic illustrated in the simple example in footnote 14 was then applied to the 8×8 table described above to obtain a component pertaining to a 2×6 table (with 5 df, on line 1 of table 6B) formed from the entries in the two relevant rows, and a component pertaining to a 6×2 table (with 5 df, on line 2 of table 6B) formed from the entries in the two relevant columns, and a component pertaining to a 3×3 table with the main diagonal deleted (with 1 df, on line 3 of table 6B) formed from the 8×8 table by combining all the columns in the 2×6 table above into a single column and combining all the rows in the 6×2 table above into a single row.[22]

TABLE 6

COMPONENTS OF HOMOGENEITY CRITERIA APPLIED
TO STATUS CATEGORIES 5 AND 6

Component	df	Likelihood-Ratio χ^2
A. For Homogeneity Criteria Applied in Tables Similar to Tables 3 and 4		
1.	3	3.03
2.	1	2.81
3.	1	3.17
4.	3	10.05
5.	1	.09
6.	1	18.75
7.	1	.07
Total	11	37.97
B. For Homogeneity Criteria Applied in Tables Similar to Tables 2A and B and 4C		
1.	5	9.01
2.	5	28.89
3.	1	.07
Total	11	37.97

[22] See nn. 9, 12, 14, 17, and 20. By applying the same general method for partitioning the χ^2 statistic, the components pertaining to the foregoing 2×6 table and 6×2 table (on lines 1 and 2 of table 6B) were partitioned further to obtain the subcomponents in table 6A on lines 1, 2, and 3 and on lines 4, 5, and 6, respectively. With respect to, say, the 2×6 table, the corresponding subcomponents (on lines 1, 2, and 3 of table 6A) were obtained by applying the homogeneity criteria to (1) the 2×4 table formed from the relevant rows

From table 6 we see that occupational categories 5 and 6 in table 1A fail the homogeneity tests.[23] These results indicate that the system of seven categories in table 1B (Glass's table) cannot be justified when the homogeneity criteria are applied.[24]

The total χ^2 values on the bottom lines in tables 5 and 6 were partitioned in these tables into sets of χ^2 components and subcomponents that would be relevant in the present context. These total χ^2 values could also have been partitioned into sets of χ^2 components and subcomponents different from the particular sets presented here. (See the general methods of partitioning χ^2 in, e.g., Goodman [1968, 1970, 1971].) In other contexts, different sets of components and/or subcomponents may be more relevant.

The results presented in this section show that Glass (1954) combined in table 1B two occupational categories that had heterogeneous distributions, whereas we combined in our table 1C two categories that had homogeneous distributions. When the definition of these occupational categories is taken into account, the results presented here are not altogether unexpected. (See the definition of the occupational categories included in, e.g., the introductory section of the present article.) The definition of the various occupational categories can sometimes serve as a partial guide, directing the research worker toward the pairs of categories that might possibly pass the homogeneity tests. Later in this article we shall provide a different technique that can also serve this purpose. The research worker can use this technique along with information culled from the definition of the categories to obtain additional partial guidance on this matter.

---

in the columns below the two relevant columns in the 8×8 table, (2) the 2×2 table formed from the relevant rows in the columns above the two relevant columns in the 8×8 table, and (3) the 2×2 table formed from the relevant rows by combining into a single column the entries in the columns below the two relevant columns and combining into a single column the entries in the columns above the two relevant columns. Each subcomponent that has more than 1 df can also be partitioned further using the same general method (see, e.g., n. 19).

[23] From the bottom line in tables 6A and B, we see that the total χ^2 is 37.97, with 11 df. Thus, this homogeneity test in table 6 was failed. From table 6B, we see that this failure was due to the fact that the distributions in cols. 5 and 6 of table 1A were heterogeneous (see, e.g., line 2 in table 6B). (The distributions in rows 5 and 6 of table 1A were not heterogeneous; see, e.g., line 1 in table 6B.) The heterogeneity with respect to cols. 5 and 6 can be described in more detail using the results given on lines 4, 5, and 6 in table 6A. (The components tested on lines 4 and 6 of table 6A were heterogeneous, and the component tested on line 5 was not.)

[24] In some contexts, the homogeneity test based upon the total χ^2 in tables 6A and B might be replaced by a weaker test obtained by deleting some specified components in the total. For example, we could consider here the deletion of the component on line 7 of table 6A and on line 3 of table 6B. If this deletion is made, the corresponding total χ^2 becomes 37.90, with 10 df (rather than 37.97, with 11 df.) This homogeneity test was also failed. (The test of "internal homogeneity" in Breiger [1981] can be viewed as a test constructed from certain homogeneity components; but in the present context his particular definition and application of this term would correspond to the deletion of all the relevant homogeneity components.)

For the sake of simplicity, we have focused our attention in this section on methods for determining whether a given set of two rows in the cross-classification table are homogeneous and/or whether a given set of two columns in the table are homogeneous.[25] Similar methods can be applied directly to determine whether a given set of r rows in the $I \times J$ table are homogeneous and/or whether a given set of c columns in the table are homogeneous, with $2 \leq r \leq I$ and $2 \leq c \leq J$. The general approach to homogeneity criteria presented here can also be extended to the situation in which the I rows are partitioned into subsets of rows and/or the J columns are partitioned into subsets of columns, and the homogeneity criteria are applied to each subset of rows and/or to each subset of columns. (The extension of this general approach will be presented in the final section of this article.)

Having provided in the present section some discussion of the homogeneity criteria, we next consider structural criteria.

STRUCTURAL CRITERIA

To illustrate how structural criteria can be applied in the present context, and to demonstrate how these criteria differ from the kind discussed in the preceding section, we shall now apply the structural criteria to examine the same general question considered in the preceding section; viz., whether the eight occupational categories in table 1A should be replaced by the system of seven classes in table 1B or by the system of seven classes in table 1C.

The structure of the association between father's occupational category and son's occupational category was described for tables 1A and B in Goodman (1979*b*) using association models, and we now include here a similar description for table 1C.[26] Table 7 gives the values of the χ^2 statistics obtained under the association models applied to tables 1A, B, and C.[27]

[25] In the occupational mobility context, where the cross-classification table is square (i.e., where $I = J$ in the $I \times J$ table), and there is a one-to-one relationship between the rows and columns, the given set of two columns would usually correspond to the given set of two rows. But for cross-classification tables where there is not a one-to-one relationship between the rows and columns, there would usually be no need to introduce a correspondence between the given set of two columns and the given set of two rows.

[26] In the analysis of tables 1A and B, the entries on the main diagonal were deleted in Goodman (1979*b*); and a similar deletion is made in the analysis of table 1C here. The association models applied here will be discussed briefly in the present section; they will be discussed further in the next section and the penultimate section of this article.

[27] The χ^2 values in tables 7A and B were included in the analysis of tables 1A and B in Goodman (1979*b*) (except for the values on line 5 of table 7B). Table 7C gives similar results for the analysis of table 1C. The association models on lines 5 and 6 of table 7 are Models II* and II, respectively, defined in Goodman (1979*b*). (To save space, we shall not consider here the related Models I* and I defined in the 1979*b* article. With respect

From the bottom line (line 6) in tables 7A, B, and C,[28] we see that, in describing the association in tables 1A, B, and C, it is sufficient to consider the effects of the rows and the columns on the association in each of the occupational mobility tables. Thus, we find that it is not necessary to introduce any kind of interaction between these row and column effects in

TABLE 7

ASSOCIATION MODELS APPLIED TO TABLES 1A, B, AND C

Association Models	df	Goodness-of-Fit χ^2	Likelihood-Ratio χ^2
A. For Table 1A			
1. Null association	41	555.12	446.84
2. Uniform association	40	55.77	58.44
3. Row-effect association	34	43.13	45.91
4. Column-effect association	34	40.63	42.02
5. Homogeneous row-column effect	34	31.21	32.56
6. Row and column effects	28	27.97	29.15
B. For Table 1B			
1. Null association	29	522.98	408.37
2. Uniform association	28	29.54	30.39
3. Row-effect association	23	24.90	26.29
4. Column-effect association	23	24.81	25.43
5. Homogeneous row-column effect	23	21.47	22.98
6. Row and column effects	18	20.13	21.49
C. For Table 1C			
1. Null association	29	544.82	437.43
2. Uniform association	28	38.32	38.48
3. Row-effect association	23	31.43	31.24
4. Column-effect association	23	28.30	28.80
5. Homogeneous row-column effect	23	23.41	24.72
6. Row and column effects	18	21.42	22.83

to the kinds of questions considered in the present article [e.g., questions about homogeneity], various complications arise with Model I [and Model I*] that do not arise with Model II [and Model II*]. See, e.g., discussion of Model II in the 1979b article [p. 547] and in Goodman [1981b].)

[28] The χ^2 values on the bottom line in these tables were obtained using the iterative procedure for Model II in appendix B of Goodman (1979b); and straightforward modifications of this iterative procedure were used to obtain the results presented for the other association models in table 7. (The other association models can be viewed as special cases of Model II; see, e.g., Goodman [1979b, 1981b].) For each of the other association models, the appropriate modified form of the iterative procedure for Model II turns out to be preferable, in the analysis of some kinds of data, to the corresponding modified form of the iterative procedure for Model I described by (5.2)–(5.3) and appendix A in Goodman (1979b). (Indeed, the iterative procedure for Model I described by [5.2]–[5.3] can be improved upon, in the analysis of some kinds of data, by replacing [5.2] by

$$\hat{F}_{ij} = \hat{\alpha}_i \hat{\beta}_j \exp\left[\sigma_j \hat{\mu}_i + \rho_i \hat{\nu}_j\right],$$

with σ_j and ρ_i defined as in [5.3c] and [5.3d], and by replacing [5.3c] and [5.3d] for γ^{**}_i and δ^{**}_j by the corresponding two formulae for μ^{**}_i and ν^{**}_j in appendix B, with σ^*_j and ρ^*_i in the latter two formulae replaced by the σ_j and ρ_i as used in [5.3c] and [5.3d].)

describing the association in each of these tables. The structure of the association in each occupational mobility table can be described by the association models.

In addition to the association model on the bottom line in tables 7A, B, and C, there are also other association models in table 7 that serve to describe the association in the occupational mobility tables. From table 7 we see that the null association model (on line 1 of tables 7A, B, and C) does not fit the data,[29] but the other association models in table 7 fit the data much better. We would reject (at the .05 level) the uniform association model applied to table 1A (see line 2 of table 7A), but accept the other association models following it in table 7A.[30] With respect to tables 1B and C, we would accept (at the .05 level) the uniform association model and the other association models following it in tables 7B and C.[31]

The fact that the uniform association model was rejected for table 1A but accepted for tables 1B and C might appear at first sight to provide some justification for the replacement of table 1A by table 1B or C. Association in tables 1B and C could be described more simply than association in table 1A. On the other hand, table 1A includes more information than tables 1B and C, and so it should not be surprising that the table which includes more information might need a more complicated model to describe this information.[32] The next section will discuss in somewhat more detail the relationship between results obtained when association models are applied to tables in which some rows are combined and/or some columns are combined (e.g., tables 1B and C) and corresponding results obtained when the association models are applied to the table in which no rows are combined and no columns are combined (e.g., table 1A).

Some of the information about the association between father's occupational category and son's occupational category in table 1A is lost when this table is replaced by table 1B or C; but, in a certain sense, less information about this association is lost with table 1C than with table 1B. Note

[29] Since the entries on the main diagonal are deleted, the null association model is equivalent to the quasi-independence model with the main diagonal deleted.

[30] For further details, see Duncan (1979) and Goodman (1979*b*). The models on lines 2 and 3 of table 7A were considered in both of those articles. For related material, see also Goodman (1979*a*).

[31] For further details with respect to table 1B, see Goodman (1979*b*). (In that article and also in the present article, the level of statistical significance reported for a given test is applicable in the classic context of hypothesis testing, where the given test is considered on its own. Problems associated with sequential and/or simultaneous statistical inference and with the effects of scanning and/or ransacking a body of data are important, but they would take us too far afield; for discussion of somewhat related matters, see, for example, Goodman [1969].)

[32] In table 1B, the separate data in rows 5 and 6 of table 1A are combined, and the separate data in cols. 5 and 6 of this table are combined. Also, with the deletion of entries on the main diagonal in table 1B, the data in cells (5,6) and (6,5) of table 1A are omitted (as well as the data in cells [5,5] and [6,6] of table 1A).

that the χ^2 values for the null association model applied to table 1A are closer to the corresponding values for table 1C than for table 1B (cf. line 1 in tables 7A, B, and C).[33] Since table 1C contains more information about the association in table 1A than does table 1B, caution must be exercised when comparing tables 1B and C with respect to the χ^2 values obtained for a given association model (e.g., the uniform association model).[34]

As noted earlier in this section, with respect to tables 1B and C, we would accept the uniform association model and the other association models following it in tables 7B and C. However, the results in tables 7B and C indicate that these association models fit the data in table 1B somewhat better than they fit the data in table 1C.[35] This difference between tables 1B and C is due, to some extent, to the difference in the total association in the two tables.

We have discussed in this section the application of structural criteria to tables 1B and C. With respect to these two tables, we had noted in the preceding section that the homogeneity criteria were not satisfied by the data relevant to the formation of table 1B (i.e., the data in the rows and the columns of table 1A that were combined in table 1B), but they were satisfied by the data relevant to the formation of table 1C (see tables 5 and 6). In the next section, we shall discuss the relationship between the homogeneity criteria considered in the preceding section and the structural criteria considered above.

Before closing the present section, we take note of the fact that the structural criteria were applied here using the class of association models de-

[33] This relationship between the χ^2 values on line 1 in tables 7A, B, and C is essentially a consequence of results obtained in the preceding section with some of the homogeneity tests in tables 5 and 6. The sum of the corresponding χ^2 values on lines 1 and 2 of table 5B and line 1 of table 7C is equal to the corresponding value that would be obtained on line 1 of table 7A if entries (4,5) and (5,4) were deleted together with the entries on the main diagonal of table 1A; and the sum of the corresponding χ^2 values on lines 1 and 2 of table 6B and line 1 of table 7B is equal to the corresponding value that would be obtained on line 1 of table 7A if entries (5,6) and (6,5) were deleted together with the entries on the main diagonal. The relationship between results in tables 5, 6, and 7 will be discussed further in the following sections.

[34] When comparing tables 1B and C with respect to the χ^2 values obtained for, say, the uniform association model, we should take into account the fact that the total association is different in the two tables (see, e.g., line 1 in tables 7B and C).

[35] With respect to table 1C, we do not reject the uniform association model at the .05 level, but we would at the .10 level (see line 2 of table 7C). Also, comparison of lines 2 and 4 in table 7C indicates that the column effect on the association in table 1C is not statistically significant at the .05 level but would be statistically significant at the .10 level. And comparison of lines 2 and 5 in table 7C indicates that a homogeneous row-column effect on the association in table 1C is significant at the .05 level. (This summary of results in table 7C was obtained using the likelihood-ratio χ^2s in this table. If the goodness-of-fit χ^2s in table 7C are used instead, a slightly different summary would be obtained.) With respect to table 1B, the results in table 7B indicate that the uniform association model fits the data well, and the row and column effects on the association are negligible (see Goodman 1979b).

scribed in Goodman (1979*b*).[36] Structural criteria can also be applied in the situation in which other kinds of models may be of interest. The models of interest can be used instead of the association models in the application of the structural criteria. The association models were used in the present section to illustrate the application of these criteria. These criteria could be described in more general terms, but we shall not go into these matters here.

HOMOGENEITY AND STRUCTURAL CRITERIA

In the preceding sections, our attention was focused primarily on the analysis of some occupational mobility tables, but the methods applied there in the analysis of these tables could be extended and applied more generally to other kinds of cross-classification tables as well. In the present section, the exposition will be facilitated by first considering the analysis of a general two-way $I \times J$ cross-classification table; then we shall show how to apply the results developed here for the general two-way table to the occupational mobility tables.

For the $I \times J$ cross-classification table, let f_{ij} denote the observed frequency in the ith row and jth column of the cross-classification ($i = 1$, $2, \ldots, I; j = 1, 2, \ldots, J$), and let F_{ij} denote the corresponding expected frequency under some model. For 2×2 subtables formed from adjacent rows (rows i and $i + 1$) and adjacent columns (cols. j and $j + 1$), let Θ_{ij} denote the corresponding odds-ratio (for $i = 1, 2, \ldots, I - 1; j = 1, 2, \ldots$, $J - 1$) based on the expected frequencies:

$$\Theta_{ij} = (F_{ij}F_{i+1\ j+1})/(F_{i,j+1}F_{i+1,j}) . \tag{1}$$

Under the usual model of statistical independence between the row categories and the column categories in the $I \times J$ cross-classification,

$$\Theta_{ij} = 1 , \quad \text{for } i = 1, 2, \ldots, I - 1 ; j = 1, 2, \ldots, J - 1 . \tag{2}$$

The odds-ratios Θ_{ij} can be displayed in an $(I - 1) \times (J - 1)$ table. Model (2) states that all the Θ_{ij} in this $(I - 1) \times (J - 1)$ table are equal to 1. This model is equivalent to the usual model of statistical independence between the row categories and the column categories in the $I \times J$ cross-classification; and the usual χ^2 statistic used to test the latter model (with $[I - 1][J - 1]$ df) serves also as a test of the equivalent model (2).

Consider next the model which states that the distributions in two specified adjacent rows (say, rows i' and $i' + 1$) are homogeneous. This model is equivalent to the usual model of statistical independence between the row categories and the column categories in the $2 \times J$ cross-classification formed as a subtable of the $I \times J$ cross-classification by considering only the two specified rows (rows i' and $i' + 1$) in the cross-classification. For

[36] For related material, see, e.g., Duncan (1979) and Goodman (1979*a*).

the two specified rows, this model is equivalent to the model which states
that

$$\Theta_{i'j} = 1 , \quad \text{for } j = 1, 2, \ldots, J - 1 . \tag{3}$$

Model (3) states that the $\Theta_{i'1}, \Theta_{i'2}, \ldots, \Theta_{i',J-1}$ are equal to 1. The usual
χ^2 statistic used to test the model of statistical independence between the
row categories and the column categories in the $2 \times J$ cross-classification
described above (with $[2 - 1][J - 1] = J - 1$ df) serves also as a test of the
equivalent model (3).

Consider now the cross-classification obtained from the $I \times J$ cross-
classification by combining the corresponding entries in the two specified
adjacent rows. We thus obtain a $(I - 1) \times J$ cross-classification. If the
distributions in the two specified adjacent rows (rows i' and $i' + 1$) of the
$I \times J$ cross-classification are homogeneous, we find that (a) condition (3)
will be satisfied for the specified $\Theta_{i'j}$ (for $j = 1, 2, \ldots, J - 1$) obtained from
the $I \times J$ cross-classification, and (b) the other odds-ratios Θ_{ij} (with $i \neq i'$)
obtained from the $I \times J$ cross-classification will be equal to the corresponding odds-ratios obtained from the $(I - 1) \times J$ cross-classification. Thus
we can partition into two components any given hypothesis H about the
odds-ratios Θ_{ij} in the $I \times J$ cross-classification which states, in part, that
condition (3) is true for the specified $\Theta_{i'j}$ (for $j = 1, 2, \ldots, J - 1$): the
first component of H states that the distributions in the two specified
adjacent rows (rows i' and $i' + 1$) are homogeneous; and the second component of H states that the hypothesis about the other odds-ratios Θ_{ij} (with
$i \neq i'$) holds true for the corresponding odds-ratios obtained from the
$(I - 1) \times J$ cross-classification.[37]

Consider now, say, the row-effect association model applied to the $I \times J$
cross-classification. This model states that

$$\Theta_{ij} = \theta_{i\cdot} , \quad \text{for } j = 1, 2, \ldots, J - 1 , \tag{4}$$

where $\theta_{i\cdot}$ is unspecified (for $i = 1, 2, \ldots, I - 1$). We can estimate the
parameters $\theta_{i\cdot}$ in this model, and test various hypotheses about them,
using the general methods described in Goodman (1979b). Consider, for
example, the hypothesis H' that model (4) holds true and that

$$\theta_{i'\cdot} = 1 , \tag{5}$$

for a specified value i'.[38] Since one of the parameters $\theta_{i\cdot}$ in model (4) is not
estimated under hypothesis H' (namely, the specified parameter $\theta_{i'\cdot}$ in [5]),

[37] The general results described above can be illustrated by considering, say, the special
case in which $I = J = 3$, $i' = 1$, and the particular hypothesis H about the odds-ratios
Θ_{ij} states that condition (2) is satisfied. The general result can be applied also when the
given hypothesis H about the Θ_{ij} is different from the hypothesis that condition (2) is
satisfied (as long as the given hypothesis H states, in part, that condition (3) is true for
the specified $\Theta_{i'j}$). This general result is applied later in this article and in, e.g. Goodman
(1981b).

[38] Note that if condition (5) is satisfied, then condition (3) will be satisfied under model (4).

there will be one less parameter to estimate under H′ than under model (4); and thus there will be one more degree of freedom in testing H′ than in testing model (4). Since there are $(I - 1)(J - 2)$ df used in testing model (4),[39] the number of degrees of freedom used in testing hypothesis H′ will be

$$(I - 1)(J - 2) + 1 . \tag{6}$$

From the comments at the end of the preceding paragraph, we see that hypothesis H′ can be partitioned into two components: the first component states that the distributions in the two specified rows i' and $i' + 1$ are homogeneous; the second component states that the row-effect association model holds true for the $(I - 1) \times J$ cross-classification obtained by combining the corresponding entries in rows i' and $i' + 1$.

To test the first component in the $2 \times J$ subtable formed from rows i' and $i' + 1$, there will be $(J - 1)$ df; and to test the second component in the $(I - 1) \times J$ cross-classification, there will be $(I - 2)(J - 2)$ df.[40] The χ^2 statistics can be calculated for each component, and the sum of the corresponding χ^2 components can serve as a test of hypothesis H′. The number of degrees of freedom pertaining to the sum of the two components will be

$$(J - 1) + (I - 2)(J - 2) = (J - 2)(I - 1) + 1 . \tag{7}$$

The number of degrees of freedom in (7) turns out to be equal to the number in (6), since hypothesis H′ could be partitioned into the two components described above.

Consider next, say, the column-effect association model applied to the $I \times J$ cross-classification. This model states that

$$\Theta_{ij} = \theta_{.j} , \quad \text{for } i = 1, 2, \ldots, I - 1 , \tag{8}$$

where $\theta_{.j}$ is unspecified (for $j = 1, 2, \ldots, J - 1$). Methods similar to those described above to test hypothesis H′ can be applied also to test the hypothesis H* that model (8) holds true and that

$$\theta_{.j*} = 1 , \tag{9}$$

for a specified value of j^*. Since there are $(I - 2)(J - 1)$ df used in testing model (8),[41] the number of degrees of freedom used in testing hypothesis H* will be

$$(I - 2)(J - 1) + 1 . \tag{10}$$

The first component of hypothesis H* states that the distributions in the two specified columns j^* and $j^* + 1$ are homogeneous; and the second component of H* states that the column-effect association model holds true

[39] See, e.g., line 3 in table 4 of Goodman (1979b).

[40] This follows from the formula on line 3 in table 4 of Goodman (1979b) applied to the $(I - 1) \times J$ cross-classification.

[41] See, e.g., line 4 in table 4 of Goodman (1979b).

for the $I \times (J - 1)$ cross-classification obtained by combining the corresponding entries in columns j^* and $j^* + 1$.

To test the first component in the $I \times 2$ subtable formed from columns j^* and $j^* + 1$, there will be $(I - 1)$ df; and to test the second component in the $I \times (J - 1)$ cross-classification, there will be $(I - 2)(J - 2)$ df. Note that the number of degrees of freedom pertaining to the sum of the two components will be

$$(I - 1) + (I - 2)(J - 2) = (I - 2)(J - 1) + 1 \, , \qquad (11)$$

which turns out to be equal to the number in (10).

Consider next, say, the association model that includes both row effects and column effects on the association in the $I \times J$ cross-classification.[42] This model states that

$$\log \Theta_{ij} = \phi_{i.}\phi_{.j} \, , \quad \text{for } i = 1, 2, \ldots, I - 1 ; j = 1, 2, \ldots, J - 1 , \quad (12)$$

where $\phi_{i.}$ and $\phi_{.j}$ are unspecified and where log denotes the natural logarithm.[43] Methods similar to those described earlier in this section to test hypothesis H$'$ can be applied now to test the hypothesis M$'$ that model (12) holds true and that

$$\phi_{i'.} = 0 \, , \qquad (13)$$

for a specified value of i'.[44] Since there are $(I - 2)(J - 2)$ df used in testing model (12),[45] the number of degrees of freedom used in testing hypothesis M$'$ will be

$$(I - 2)(J - 2) + 1 \, . \qquad (14)$$

The first component of hypothesis M$'$ states that the distributions in the two specified rows i' and $i' + 1$ are homogeneous; and the second component of M$'$ states that the association model which includes both row effects and column effects holds true for the association in the $(I - 1) \times J$ cross-classification obtained by combining the corresponding entries in rows i' and $i' + 1$.

To test the first component in the corresponding $2 \times J$ subtable, there will be $(J - 1)$ df; to test the second component in the $(I - 1) \times J$ cross-classification, there will be $(I - 3)(J - 2)$ df. Note that the number of degrees of freedom pertaining to the sum of the two components will be

$$(J - 1) + (I - 3)(J - 2) = (J - 2)(I - 2) + 1 \, , \qquad (15)$$

which turns out to be equal to the number in (14).

[42] We consider here Model II defined in Goodman (1979b). For some comments pertaining to the use of this model in the present article, see parenthetical remark at the end of n. 28.

[43] See, e.g., Goodman 1979b, 1981a, 1981b.

[44] Note that if condition (13) is satisfied, then condition (3) will be satisfied under model (12).

[45] See, e.g., line 6 in table 4 of Goodman (1979b).

Methods similar to those described above to test hypothesis M′ can also be applied to test the hypothesis M* that model (12) holds true and that

$$\phi_{.j*} = 0 , \tag{16}$$

for a specified value of j^*. Similar methods can also be applied to test the hypothesis M′* that model (12) holds true and that conditions (13) and (16) are satisfied for a specified value of i' and a specified value of j^*, respectively.

The results described earlier in this section for hypotheses H′ and M′ indicate that we can examine certain kinds of hypotheses about the $I \times J$ cross-classification by (a) applying homogeneity criteria to the $2 \times J$ subtable formed from rows i' and $i' + 1$, and (b) applying structural criteria to the $(I - 1) \times J$ cross-classification obtained by combining corresponding entries in rows i' and $i' + 1$. The corresponding results for hypotheses H* and M* indicate that we can examine certain kinds of hypotheses about the $I \times J$ cross-classification by (a) applying homogeneity criteria to the $I \times 2$ subtable formed from columns j^* and $j^* + 1$, and (b) applying structural criteria to the $I \times (J - 1)$ cross-classification obtained by combining corresponding entries in columns j^* and $j^* + 1$. In a similar way, the corresponding results for hypothesis M′* indicate that we can also examine certain kinds of hypotheses about the $I \times J$ cross-classification by (a) applying homogeneity criteria to the table formed from the $I \times J$ cross-classification by deleting all entries that are not in either row i' or $i' + 1$ or in column j^* or j^*+1, and (b) applying structural criteria to the $(I-1) \times (J - 1)$ cross-classification obtained by combining rows i' and $i' + 1$ and by combining columns j^* and $j^* + 1$.

The results presented so far in this section pertain to the analysis of an $I \times J$ cross-classification in which none of the entries are deleted on a priori grounds. These results can be extended to the analysis of an $I \times J$ cross-classification in which a given set of entries are deleted on a priori grounds. We illustrate this extension now by reexamining the analysis of the 8×8 cross-classification (table 1A) and the related 7×7 cross-classifications (tables 1B and C).

From lines 1 and 2 of table 5B, we saw that the homogeneity criteria yielded a χ^2 value of 6.61 (with 5 df) when applied to rows 4 and 5 of table 1A, and a χ^2 value of 1.20 (with 5 df) when applied to columns 4 and 5.[46] When these criteria were applied both to rows 4 and 5 and to columns 4 and 5, we obtained a χ^2 value of $6.61 + 1.20 = 7.81$, with $5 + 5 = 10$ df.[47]

[46] The entries in cells (4,4) and (5,5) of table 1A were deleted in the calculation of the χ^2 values throughout this article.

[47] For the sake of simplicity, we focus now on the case in which the entries in cells (4,5) and (5,4) of table 1A are deleted (as well as the entries in cells [4,4] and [5,5] of the table). When the entries in cells (4,5) and (5,4) are not deleted, we obtain instead a χ^2 value of 7.87, with 11 df (see the bottom line of table 5B).

This χ^2 value can be viewed as the first component (the homogeneity component) obtained in an analysis of the 8×8 cross-classification (table 1A). We next consider the corresponding second component (the structural component) obtained in this analysis.

From line 6 of table 7C, we see that the χ^2 value is 22.83 (with 18 df) when the association model which includes row and column effects is applied to table 1C. This χ^2 value can be viewed as the second component in the present analysis of table 1A. The sum of the first and second components is

$$7.81 + 22.83 = 30.64 , \tag{17}$$

with $10 + 18 = 28$ df. The sum in (17) serves to test the hypothesis that the association model which includes row and column effects holds true for table 1A, and that the odds-ratio parameters pertaining to the cells in rows 4 and 5, and to the cells in columns 4 and 5, are equal to one.[48] From (17) we see that this hypothesis is congruent with the data.[49]

The preceding paragraph showed how to combine structural criteria applied to table 1C and homogeneity criteria applied to a relevant subset of the data in table 1A in order to analyze a corresponding hypothesis about table 1A. In a similar way, we can combine structural criteria applied to table 1B and homogeneity criteria applied to a relevant subset of the data in table 1A in order to analyze a corresponding hypothesis about table 1A. Thus, from lines 1 and 2 of table 6B, we see that the corresponding homogeneity component yields a χ^2 value of $9.01 + 28.89 = 37.90$, with $5 + 5 = 10$ df;[50] and from line 6 of table 7B we see that the corresponding structural component yields a χ^2 value of 21.49, with 18 df. The sum of the first and second components is

$$37.90 + 21.49 = 59.39 , \tag{18}$$

with $10 + 18 = 28$ df. The sum in (18) serves to test the hypothesis that the association model which includes row and column effects holds true for table 1A, and that the odds-ratio parameters pertaining to the cells in rows 5 and 6, and to the cells in columns 5 and 6, are equal to one.[51] From (18) we see that this hypothesis is not congruent with the data.

The results in this section show that, when the homogeneity and struc-

---

[48] The sum in (17) is obtained when this hypothesis is applied to table 1A with the entries deleted on the main diagonal and in cells (4,5) and (5,4).

[49] This hypothesis and some other related hypotheses will be discussed further in a later section.

[50] For the sake of simplicity, we focus our attention now on the case in which the entries in cells (5,6) and (6,5) of table 1A are deleted (as well as the entries in cells [5,5] and [6,6] of the table). When the entries in cells (5,6) and (6,5) are not deleted, we obtain instead a χ^2 value of 37.97, with 11 df (see the bottom line of table 6B).

[51] The sum in (18) is obtained when this hypothesis is applied to table 1A with the entries deleted on the main diagonal and in cells (5,6) and (6,5).

tural components are combined in the way described here, justification can be found for the replacement of table 1A by table 1C but not by table 1B.

We noted in an earlier section that the definition of the various occupational categories can sometimes provide partial guidance in directing the research worker toward the pairs of categories that might possibly pass the homogeneity tests. From the results presented in the present section, we can obtain a different technique that can also serve this purpose. This technique will be described next.

For two specified adjacent rows (say, rows i' and $i' + 1$), we noted earlier that the condition of homogeneity was equivalent to condition (3) pertaining to the relevant odds-ratios $\Theta_{i'j}$ (for $j = 1, 2, \ldots, J - 1$). Similarly, with respect to two specified adjacent columns (say, columns j^* and $j^* + 1$), the condition of homogeneity is equivalent to a condition similar to condition (3) pertaining to the relevant odds-ratios Θ_{ij^*} (for $i = 1, 2, \ldots, I - 1$). Thus, the estimated odds-ratio parameters pertaining to the cells in adjacent rows, and to the cells in adjacent columns, can provide partial guidance with respect to the possible outcome of the corresponding homogeneity tests.[52] If the estimated odds-ratio parameter pertaining to adjacent rows is quite different from one, then the corresponding adjacent rows will usually not be homogeneous (see [5]); and if the estimated odds-ratio parameter pertaining to adjacent columns is quite different from one, then the corresponding adjacent columns will usually not be homogeneous (see [9]). The magnitudes of the estimated odds-ratio parameters obtained for table 1A[53] are concordant with the overall results on homogeneity reported earlier in this article. When considering which pairs of occupational categories might possibly pass the homogeneity tests, the magnitudes of the estimated odds-ratio parameters could have been used by the research worker to direct him away from the pair of categories combined by Glass (1954) and toward the pair of categories combined in the present article in table 1C.

The results presented in this section can be viewed from the perspective of the partitioning of the total association in a cross-classification in terms of the possible component effects on the association. For an $I \times J$ cross-classification, the χ^2 statistic for testing the usual hypothesis of null association (with $[I - 1][J - 1]$ df) can be partitioned into a homogeneity component applied to a specified subtable of the $I \times J$ table and a component related to the structure of association in a corresponding table of smaller dimension. For the 8×8 cross-classification (table 1A), the usual χ^2

[52] The odds-ratio parameters in the association models considered here can be estimated using the methods introduced in Goodman (1979*b*).

[53] See, e.g., the estimated parameters in table 8A of Goodman (1979*b*). Estimates obtained under the association models on lines 5 and 6 of table 7 in the present article (Models II* and II in the 1979*b* article) can be helpful in the situation in which these models are needed to describe the association in the cross-classification.

statistic with $7 \times 7 = 49$ df can be partitioned into a homogeneity component pertaining to, say, occupational categories 4 and 5 (with 13 df),[54] and a component (with $6 \times 6 = 36$ df) related to the structure of association in a corresponding 7×7 table (table 1C).[55] Each of these two components can be partitioned further into appropriate subcomponents. If the relevant homogeneity subcomponents are negligible, then the total association in the $I \times J$ table can be described simply in terms of the subcomponents pertaining to the structure of association in the table of smaller dimension.[56] On the other hand, if the relevant homogeneity subcomponents are not negligible, the total association in the $I \times J$ table cannot be described simply in terms of the association in the table of smaller dimension.

The general perspective described above provides justification for the replacement of the 8×8 table (table 1A) by the 7×7 table (table 1C), and it can be applied further, using the homogeneity and structural criteria, to replace in turn the 7×7 table (table 1C) by a table of still smaller dimension. To save space, we leave this exercise for the interested reader.[57]

In the present section, we have shown how application of the homogeneity criteria and structural criteria can be combined in the analysis of the association in an $I \times J$ cross-classification. In some situations, application of the two kinds of criteria will lead to the same general conclusion; but in other situations, this will not be the case. We shall now briefly examine the possible conflict that can arise in situations in which the two kinds of criteria may not lead to the same general conclusion.

HOMOGENEITY CRITERIA VERSUS STRUCTURAL CRITERIA

When the general perspective described in the preceding section is applied in the analysis of the association in, say, an 8×8 cross-classification, we noted that the usual χ^2 statistic (with $7 \times 7 = 49$ df) for testing the hy-

[54] The χ^2 statistic applied to table 2C had 11 df (see the bottom line in tables 5A and B); but it would have had $11 + 2 = 13$ df if the entries in cells (4,4) and (5,5) of table 1A had not been deleted.

[55] The χ^2 statistic for testing the usual hypothesis of null association in the corresponding 7×7 table has $6 \times 6 = 36$ df; but the corresponding χ^2 in table 7C had $36 - 7 = 29$ df because the seven entries on the main diagonal of table 1C were deleted there.

[56] With respect to the replacement of table 1A by table 1C, the homogeneity subcomponent pertaining to occupational inheritance in cells (4,4) and (5,5) in table 1A needs to be taken into account. For table 1A with the entries deleted on its main diagonal and in cells (4,5) and (5,4), the application of the homogeneity criteria in the preceding section (see, e.g., n. 33) indicates that this table can be replaced by table 1C with the entries deleted on its main diagonal; none of the homogeneity subcomponents need to be taken into account in this case. (The case in which the entries on the main diagonal of table 1A are deleted but those in cells [4,5] and [5,4] are not will be discussed further in a later section.)

[57] For related material, see, e.g., Goodman (1968, 1979b) and Hauser (1979).

pothesis of null association in the cross-classification can be partitioned into a homogeneity component (with 13 df) and a component related to the structure of the association in a corresponding 7×7 table (with $6 \times 6 = 36$ df). The first component pertains to the association in a certain kind of subtable of the 8×8 table,[58] and the second component pertains to the association in a corresponding 7×7 table. To focus our attention now on the difference between these two components, let us consider two situations that are, in a certain sense, extreme opposites: (I) the situation in which the first component is negligible, and (II) the situation in which the second component is negligible.

In situation (I), the association in the 8×8 table can be described solely in terms of the association in the corresponding 7×7 table, since the association pertaining to the first component is negligible. In situation (II), the association in the 8×8 table can be described solely in terms of the association in the subtable of the 8×8 table,[59] since the association pertaining to the second component is negligible. In situation (I), attention can be focused on the analysis of the association in the corresponding 7×7 table; and in situation (II), attention can be focused on the analysis of the association in the subtable of the 8×8 table. Thus, in situation (I), the homogeneity test is passed by the subtable of the 8×8 table, but the structural criteria may or may not be satisfied in the analysis of the association in the corresponding 7×7 table; and in situation (II), an extreme test based on the structural criteria is passed by the corresponding 7×7 table,[60] but the homogeneity criteria may or may not be satisfied in the analysis of the association in the subtable of the 8×8 table.[61]

In some contexts, we may wish to combine categories in the 8×8 table in order to obtain a situation similar to situation (I); in other contexts, we may wish to obtain a situation similar to situation (II). In the former situation, the absence of association in the subtable of the 8×8 table and the kind of association present in the corresponding 7×7 table may be of

---

[58] The subtable would be similar in form to, say, table 2C when the entries in cells (4,4) and (5,5) are not deleted. (See related comment in n. 54.)

[59] See n. 58.

[60] The test based upon the null association model is passed by the 7×7 table. Since the null association test is equivalent to a test of homogeneity applied to the 7×7 table, we see that the 7×7 table would pass a "homogeneity test". (For expository purposes, we use the term "homogeneity" in this article only in the analysis of the subtable of the 8×8 table [not in the analysis of the corresponding 7×7 table], but we need not limit usage of the term in this way.)

[61] The association in the subtable of the 8×8 table can be analyzed using homogeneity criteria, but in some cases it may be preferable to apply association models (and/or other kinds of models) in the analysis of the subtable. In such cases we could apply "structural criteria" to the subtable. (For expository purposes, we use the term "structural criteria" in this article only in the analysis of the corresponding 7×7 table [not in the analysis of the subtable of the 8×8 table], but we need not limit usage of the term in this way.)

substantive interest; in the latter situation, the absence of association in the corresponding 7×7 table and the kind of association present in the subtable of the 8×8 table may be of substantive interest.

The analysis of the association in the 8×8 cross-classification is simplified by the absence of association in the subtable of the 8×8 table or in the corresponding 7×7 table; and the absence of either of these two forms of association may be of substantive interest. On the other hand, when these two forms of association are present, the simplification noted above cannot be achieved. In this case, some simplification of the analysis may still be possible if either of the two forms of association can be described in relatively simple terms (e.g., in terms of the uniform association model or one of the other association models considered here); and this description of either of the two forms of association may be of substantive interest.

The foregoing comment leads now to the following more general version of an earlier statement in this section: in some contexts, categories in the 8×8 table would be combined in order to obtain a situation analogous to situation (I), where now the association in the subtable of the 8×8 table has some specified property; and in other contexts, categories in the 8×8 table would be combined in order to obtain a situation analogous to situation (II), where now the association in the corresponding 7×7 table has some specified property.

The results described in this section were expressed in terms of the 8×8 table, but they could have been expressed more generally in terms of the $I \times J$ table. We did not consider in this section the situation in which certain entries in the cross-classification are deleted, but the results presented here can be extended to that situation. The results presented in the earlier sections for the situation in which certain entries in the cross-classification are deleted can contribute to the development presented in the present section.

ASSOCIATION IN THE $I \times J$ CROSS-CLASSIFICATION TABLE AND IN THE TABLE OF SMALLER DIMENSION

As we noted earlier, certain kinds of hypotheses about the association in the $I \times J$ cross-classification can be analyzed by applying (a) homogeneity criteria to a relevant subset of the data in the $I \times J$ table, and (b) structural criteria to a corresponding table of smaller dimension. We shall now discuss further models for the $I \times J$ table that constrain parameters in such a way as to take account of the hypothesized homogeneity in the relevant subset of the $I \times J$ table while conveying the hypothesized structure of association as it would appear in the table of smaller dimension.

For the sake of simplicity, we shall first consider again the model of null association in the 8×8 table (table 1A) with the entries deleted on the main diagonal. This model states that the expected frequencies F_{ij} can be described as follows:[62]

$$F_{ij} = \alpha_i \beta_j v_{ij} , \tag{19}$$

where

$$v_{ij} = \begin{cases} v_i , & \text{for } i = j , \\ 1 , & \text{otherwise} , \end{cases} \tag{20}$$

and where α_i, β_j, and v_{ij} are unspecified positive constants, with the v_{ij} satisfying condition (20). This model can be tested using the χ^2 value on line 1 of table 7A. Next consider table 1A with the entries deleted on the main diagonal and in cells (4,5) and (5,4). The corresponding model states that the expected frequencies F_{ij} can be described by (19) with the v_{ij} satisfying the following condition:

$$v_{ij} = \begin{cases} v_i , & \text{for } i = j , \\ v_{45} , & \text{for } i = 4 , j = 5 , \\ v_{54} , & \text{for } i = 5 , j = 4 , \\ 1 , & \text{otherwise} . \end{cases} \tag{21}$$

This model can be tested using the same general method that was used in the calculation of the χ^2 value on line 1 of table 7A (but with the entries in cells [4,5] and [5,4] included now in the deleted set). On the other hand, since this model can be partitioned into (*a*) a component pertaining to homogeneity in a relevant subset of the 8×8 table (see lines 1 and 2 of table 5B), and (*b*) a component pertaining to the structure of association in a corresponding table of smaller dimension (see line 1 of table 7C), the χ^2 value for testing the model will be equal to the sum of the corresponding component χ^2 values:[63]

$$7.81 + 437.43 = 445.24 , \tag{22}$$

with $10 + 29 = 39$ df.

The model considered above includes two more parameters (v_{45} and v_{54}) than the model on line 1 of table 7A.[64] Thus, the number of degrees of freedom (namely, 39) for testing the former model was two less than the corresponding number (namely, 41) for testing the latter model. We shall consider next a model that includes only one more parameter than the model on line 1 of table 7A.

Let us consider now model (19) with the parameters v_{ij} satisfying condition (21) and with the following additional condition also satisfied:

$$v_{45} = v_{54} = v , \tag{23}$$

[62] See, e.g., Goodman 1968, 1979*b*.

[63] See, e.g., n. 33.

[64] Cf. (21) with (20). The introduction of the two parameters v_{45} and v_{54} in (21) led to the deletion of the entries in cells (4,5) and (5,4) in the homogeneity test applied to table 2C and to the deletion of these two entries (together with the entries in cells [4,4] and [5,5]) in the corresponding diagonal cell, which was formed from the four cells, in table 1C.

where v is an unspecified positive constant. In this case, the v_{ij} will satisfy the following condition:

$$v_{ij} = \begin{cases} v_i, & \text{for } i = j, \\ v, & \text{for } (i,j) = (4,5) \text{ and } (5,4), \\ 1, & \text{otherwise}. \end{cases} \quad (24)$$

This model is included within the general class of multiplicative models,[65] and the general methods developed for the analysis of these models can be applied here. On the other hand, since this model can be partitioned into (a) a component pertaining to homogeneity (see lines 1, 2, and 3 of table 5B), and (b) a component pertaining to structure (see line 1 of table 7C), the χ^2 value for testing the model will be equal to the sum of the corresponding component χ^2 values:

$$7.87 + 437.43 = 445.30, \quad (25)$$

with $11 + 29 = 40$ df.

The model considered above includes one less parameter than model (19) with the v_{ij} satisfying (21), and it includes one more parameter than the model on line 1 of table 7A.[66] Thus, in testing the model considered above, the corresponding number of degrees of freedom (namely, 40) was one more than the corresponding number (namely, 39) for testing model (19) with the v_{ij} satisfying (21), and it was one less than the corresponding number (namely, 41) for testing the model on line 1 of Table 7A.

The models considered so far in this section were quasi-independence models (see [19], [20], and [21]) and a simple modification of a quasi-independence model (see [19], [23], and [24]). We shall now consider the corresponding association models that include row effects and column effects on the association. These models can be obtained from model (19) by introducing into (19) additional parameters that pertain to the row effects and column effects on the association:

$$F_{ij} = \alpha_i \beta_j v_{ij} e^{\mu_i \nu_j}, \quad (26)$$

where μ_i and ν_j are the additional parameters.[67]

[65] See, e.g., Goodman 1972. This particular model can serve as a simple example of a multiplicative model, and the quasi-independence models described above by (19) and (20) and by (19) and (21) can serve as still simpler examples.

[66] Cf. (24) with (21), and then (24) with (20). In contrast to the introduction of v_{45} and v_{54} in (21) (see n. 64), the introduction of v in (24) does *not* affect the homogeneity test applied to table 2C (it does *not* lead to the deletion of the entries in cells [4,5] and [5,4] in this homogeneity test); but it does lead to the deletion of the sum of the entries in these two cells (together with the entries in cells [4,4] and [5,5]) in the corresponding diagonal cell, which was formed from the four cells, in table 1C.

[67] See, e.g., Goodman 1979b, 1981b. When the v_{ij} in (26) are all equal to 1, model (26) is equivalent to model (12).

When the v_{ij} in (26) satisfy condition (20), the entries on the main diagonal are deleted in the cross-classification (table 1A) analyzed using the association model that includes row effects and column effects on the association. In this case, the model can be tested using the χ^2 value on line 6 of table 7A. We shall next compare this model with a related model considered earlier: the model tested using the χ^2 value (17).

As noted earlier, the χ^2 value (17) serves to test the hypothesis that the association model (26) holds true and that the odds-ratios pertaining to the cells in rows 4 and 5, and to the cells in columns 4 and 5, are equal to one, in the case where the entries are deleted on the main diagonal and in cells (4,5) and (5,4).[68] Under model (26), with the particular set of deleted entries noted above, the v_{ij} in (26) will satisfy condition (21); and when the particular set of odds-ratios noted above are equal to one, the parameters μ_i and ν_j in (26) will satisfy the following two constraints:[69]

$$\mu_4 = \mu_5 , \tag{27}$$

and

$$\nu_4 = \nu_5 . \tag{28}$$

Thus, the χ^2 value (17) serves to test the hypothesis that model (26) holds true with the v_{ij} satisfying condition (21) and the μ_i and ν_j satisfying the two constraints (27) and (28).

The model considered above includes two more v_{ij} parameters (v_{45} and v_{54}) than the model on line 6 of table 7A (model [26] with the v_{ij} satisfying [20]),[70] and the parameters in the former model are subject to the two additional constraints (27) and (28). The two additional parameters in the former model would decrease the number of degrees of freedom by two, and the two additional constraints in the former model would increase the number of degrees of freedom by two. Thus, the number of degrees of freedom in the former model is equal to the number (namely, 28) in the latter model. We shall consider next a model that includes only one more parameter than the model on line 6 of table 7A, and thus one less parameter than the model considered above.

Let us consider now model (26) with the parameters v_{ij} satisfying condition (24) and with the μ_i and ν_j satisfying (27) and (28). This model modifies the model tested using the χ^2 value (17) by replacing condition (21) with (24). The same kind of replacement was made earlier when the model tested using the χ^2 value (22) was modified to obtain the model tested using the χ^2 value (25). In a similar way, instead of using the χ^2 value (17), the model

[68] See, e.g., n. 48.

[69] See, e.g., Goodman 1979b, 1981b. Note that conditions (27) and (28) are equivalent to (13) and (16), respectively, with $i' = 4$ and $j^* = 4$.

[70] Cf. (21) with (20).

considered now can be tested using the sum of its corresponding component χ^2 values:[71]

$$7.87 + 22.83 = 30.70 , \tag{29}$$

with $11 + 18 = 29$ df.

The χ^2 values (17) and (29) will be equal to the corresponding χ^2 values obtained by applying the general methods developed for the analysis of association models to the corresponding models considered here.[72] These general methods can also be applied when these models are modified by the replacement of conditions (21) and (24) by condition (20). In this case, we obtain a χ^2 value of

$$30.71 , \tag{30}$$

with 30 df.[73]

The three models tested using the χ^2 values (17), (29), and (30) are modifications of the model on line 6 of table 7A. Similar kinds of modifications can also be made in the models on lines 2 through 5 in table 7A.[74] For example, by modifying the model on line 5 of table 7A, the three modified models thus obtained can be tested using the following χ^2 values:

$$7.81 + 24.72 = 32.53 , \tag{31}$$

$$7.87 + 24.72 = 32.59 , \tag{32}$$

---

[71] Cf. (22) and (25) with (17) and (29), respectively.

[72] The iterative procedures described, e.g., in Goodman (1979b) can be extended in a straightforward way for the analysis of models in which restrictions of the kind exemplified by (27) and (28) are imposed upon the μ_i and ν_j parameters, and restrictions of the kind exemplified by (23) are imposed upon the ν_{ij}. Similar kinds of extensions were made, e.g., in Goodman (1972, 1974), where these kinds of restrictions were imposed in the models considered there. With respect to, say, restrictions (27) and (28) imposed in model (26) for the 8×8 table, the extension would consist of (1) modifying the eight equations in (5.6a) in Goodman (1979b) by deleting the equations for $i = 4$ and 5, replacing the two deleted equations by a single equation that equates the sum of the left sides of the two deleted equations and the sum of the right sides of these two equations, (2) modifying the eight equations in (5.6b) in a similar way, and (3) making a related kind of modification in the iterative procedure for estimating μ_i and ν_j described in appendix B of Goodman (1979b).

[73] This model is tested with one more degree of freedom than is the model tested using (29) because the latter model includes one more ν_{ij} parameter (namely, ν) than does the former model (cf. [24] with [20]). The former model is tested with two more degrees of freedom than is the model on line 6 of table 7A because the parameters in the former model are subject to the two additional restrictions (27) and (28).

[74] Modifications of the model on line 1 of table 7A were considered earlier in this section, and they could be tested using the χ^2 values (22) and (25). The models on lines 1 through 4 of table 7A, and the modified forms of these models, are all examples of loglinear models, and the general methods developed for loglinear models can be applied here; but the models on lines 5 and 6 of table 7A, and the modified forms of those models, are not loglinear (see, e.g., Goodman 1979b).

and

$$32.59,[75] \tag{33}$$

with $10 + 23 = 33$ df, $11 + 23 = 34$ df, and 35 df, respectively.[76]

SOME FURTHER RESULTS ON THE HOMOGENEITY CRITERIA

As we noted earlier, application of the homogeneity criteria could be based upon the total χ^2 value obtained in testing homogeneity in the relevant subtable of the $I \times J$ cross-classification; but in some contexts this test might be replaced by a weaker test obtained by deleting some specified component in the total χ^2.[77] With respect to the 8×8 table (table 1A), to determine whether, say, occupational categories 4 and 5 are homogeneous, the relevant total χ^2 value would be tested with 13 df; but we delete two components when the occupational inheritance entries in cells (4,4) and (5,5) are deleted, thereby obtaining a total χ^2 value that would be tested with 11 df.[78] None of the components of the latter χ^2 value (with 11 df), and none of the components of the former χ^2 value (with 13 df), pertain to the term "internal homogeneity" as defined and applied by Breiger (1981).[79] On the other hand, if the entries on the main diagonal had not been deleted in Breiger's application of this term, one of the components (with 1 df) of the former χ^2 value (with 13 df) would have pertained to this term.[80] In the present context, the term "internal homogeneity" would pertain to one of the components (with 1 df) in the homogeneity criteria as defined herein, and the other components (with 12 df in total) in the homogeneity criteria would not pertain to this term.

A simple example will further illustrate the relationship noted above.

[75] The χ^2 values (30) and (33) were obtained by applying the general methods mentioned earlier (see, e.g., n. 72). The model tested using (30) is tested with one more degree of freedom than is the model tested using (29), and similarly the model tested using (33) is tested with one more degree of freedom than is the model tested using (32) (see, e.g., n. 73). The χ^2 value (30) is larger than the corresponding value (29), and similarly the χ^2 value (33) would be larger than the corresponding value (32), but to the order of accuracy reported in this article the two latter values turn out to be equal to each other.

[76] The model using (33) is tested with one more degree of freedom than is the model on line (5) of table 7A because the parameters in the former model are subject to one more restriction than are the parameters in the latter model. (Since the row and column effects are homogeneous in the model on line 5 of table 7A, the restrictions [27] and [28] are equivalent under this model; see, e.g., Goodman [1979*b*].)

[77] See, e.g., n. 24. Also, compare the homogeneity component in (17), (22), and (31) with the corresponding component (29), (25), and (32), respectively.

[78] See the bottom line in tables 5A and B, and also n. 54.

[79] See the introductory comments in the section on homogeneity criteria earlier in the present article.

[80] See nn. 6 and 7.

Consider the 4 × 4 cross-classification in table 8A with the homogeneity criteria applied to, say, categories 1 and 2. In this case, table 8B is the subtable of table 8A used in applying the homogeneity criteria. Table 8B can be partitioned into tables 9A through E when the entries on the main

TABLE 8

TABLES USED IN THE ANALYSIS OF THE
HOMOGENEITY CRITERIA
A. A 4 × 4 CROSS-CLASSIFICATION

	COLUMN CATEGORY			
ROW CATEGORY	1	2	3	4
1...............	a	b	c	d
2...............	e	f	g	h
3...............	i	j	k	l
4...............	m	n	o	p

B. SUBTABLE OF TABLE 8A USED IN APPLYING
HOMOGENEITY CRITERIA TO CATEGORIES 1 AND 2

	COLUMN CATEGORY			
ROW CATEGORY	1	2	3	4
1...............	a	b	c	d
2...............	e	f	g	h
3...............	ı	j	...	...
4...............	m	n	...	...

C. A 3 × 3 CROSS-CLASSIFICATION OBTAINED BY
COMBINING CATEGORIES 1 AND 2 IN TABLE 8A

	COLUMN CATEGORY		
ROW CATEGORY	1+2	3	4
1+2..................	a+b+e+f	c+g	d+h
3.....................	i+j	k	l
4.....................	m+n	o	p

D. SUBTABLE OF TABLE 8C USED IN APPLYING
HOMOGENEITY CRITERIA TO CATEGORIES 3 AND 4

	COLUMN CATEGORY		
ROW CATEGORY	1+2	3	4
1+2..................	...	c+g	d+h
3.....................	i+j	k	l
4.....................	m+n	o	p

TABLE 9

TABLES FORMED FROM TABLE 8B USED IN APPLYING
HOMOGENEITY CRITERIA

A. Applied to Rows 1 and 2 in Cols. 1 and 2 and to Cols. 1
and 2 in Rows 1 and 2

a	b
e	f

B. Applied to Rows 1 and 2 in Cols. 3 and 4

c	d
g	h

C. Applied to Cols. 1 and 2 in Rows 3 and 4

i	j
m	n

D. Applied to Rows 1 and 2 in Cols. 1+2 and 3+4

a+b	c+d
e+f	g+h

E. Applied to Cols. 1 and 2 in Rows 1+2 and 3+4

a+e	b+f
i+m	j+n

F. Applied to Rows 1 and 2 in Cols. 1, 2, and 3+4 and to
Cols. 1 and 2 in Rows 1, 2, and 3+4

. . .	b	c+d
e	. . .	g+h
i+m	j+n	. . .

diagonal of table 8B are not deleted;[81] and it can be partitioned into tables 9B, C, and F when the entries on the main diagonal of table 8B are deleted.[82] When the main diagonal is not deleted, there will be five components each with 1 df; and when the main diagonal is deleted, there will be three components each with 1 df. In the former case, the term "internal homogeneity"

[81] The general method for partitioning the χ^2 statistic illustrated in the simple example in n. 14 can be applied successively to table 8B to obtain the components presented here both in the case when the entries on the main diagonal are not deleted and in the case when they are deleted. The usual mathematical symbols used to denote the entries in a cross-classification table were replaced in tables 8 and 9 by a somewhat simpler notation to facilitate exposition here. The 16 lowercase letters, a–p, denote the 16 entries in the 4 × 4 cross-classification table 8A. (In particular, the lowercase letters i and j denote here particular entries in this table. These symbols as used here should not be confused with the subscripts i and j used to denote the ith row category and ith column category in the $I \times J$ cross-classification. A similar remark applies also to the lowercase letters k and l as used here in contrast to the subscripts k and l used later in this article to denote the kth row class and lth column class in a $K \times L$ cross-classification.)

[82] Table 9F is obtained when the homogeneity criteria are applied to entries (1,2) and (2,1) in table 8B with the entries deleted on the main diagonal. Note that table 9F can

would be limited to one of the components (the component for table 9A), and the other four components in the homogeneity criteria would not pertain to this term. In the latter case, none of the three components would pertain to this term.

Consider now table 8A with the homogeneity criteria applied to categories 1 and 2 in the situation where categories 3 and 4 may also be combined. In this case, with respect to the homogeneity of categories 1 and 2, table 8B is still the relevant subtable of table 8A, and this subtable can be partitioned as described above. However, in this situation in which categories 3 and 4 may also be combined, the term "internal homogeneity" would pertain to a somewhat different set of components than in the situation considered in the preceding paragraph. In the situation in which categories 3 and 4 may also be combined, the term "internal homogeneity" would pertain to the components for tables 9B and C, as well as to the component for table 9A. Thus, when the main diagonal is not deleted, this term would pertain to three of the components; and when the main diagonal is deleted, the term would pertain to two of the components.

By applying to table 8A the general perspective (which was described in an earlier section) pertaining to the partitioning of the total association in a cross-classification, we see that the usual χ^2 statistic for testing the hypothesis of null association in the 4×4 cross-classification (with $3 \times 3 = 9$ df) can be partitioned into a homogeneity component (with 5 df) to test the homogeneity of, say, categories 1 and 2,[83] and a component (with $2 \times 2 = 4$ df) to test the association in the 3×3 cross-classification (table 8C) obtained when the corresponding categories (categories 1 and 2) are combined. The homogeneity component can be calculated directly from table 8B (or from the corresponding tables 9A through E), or it can be calculated as the difference between the usual χ^2 value obtained in testing the hypothesis of null association in the 4×4 cross-classification (table 8A) and the corresponding χ^2 value obtained in testing this hypothesis in the 3×3 cross-classification (table 8C).

Having now applied the general perspective described in the earlier section to table 8A with the homogeneity component pertaining to categories 1 and 2, we shall next apply this perspective in the situation considered

---

be formed from the latter table by combining cols. 3 and 4 into a single column and combining rows 3 and 4 into a single row. When the entries on the main diagonal in table 8B are deleted, the homogeneity component for tables 9A, D, and E cannot be calculated, but the information in these three tables can be combined to provide the homogeneity component for table 9F. A similar kind of interpretation could have been given earlier for the homogeneity component for table 4C.

[83] As noted in the earlier section, in this case the homogeneity criteria are applied to table 8B, and this table can be partitioned into tables 9A through E when the entries on the main diagonal of table 8A are not deleted. For the sake of simplicity, we focus attention now and in the following discussion on the situation in which the main diagonal in table 8A is not deleted.

earlier in the present section in which categories 1 and 2 may be combined and categories 3 and 4 may also be combined in table 8A. When categories 1 and 2 are combined, this perspective can be applied to the corresponding 3×3 cross-classification (table 8C) to test the homogeneity of categories 3 and 4. In this case, table 8D is the subtable of table 8C used in applying the homogeneity criteria to categories 3 and 4.[84] The usual χ^2 statistic for testing the hypothesis of null association in the 3×3 cross-classification table 8C (with $2 \times 2 = 4$ df) can be partitioned into a homogeneity component (with 3 df) to test the homogeneity in table 8D, and a component (with 1 df) to test the association in the 2×2 cross-classification obtained when the corresponding categories (categories 3 and 4) are combined in table 8C. Thus, the usual χ^2 statistic for testing the hypothesis of null association in the 4×4 cross-classification table 8A (with $3 \times 3 = 9$ df) can be partitioned into a homogeneity component (with $5 + 3 = 8$ df) to test the homogeneity of categories 1 and 2 and the homogeneity of categories 3 and 4,[85] and a component (with 1 df) to test the association in the 2×2 cross-classification obtained when the corresponding categories are combined. The homogeneity component can be calculated directly from tables 8B and D (or from the corresponding partitioning of these tables), or it can be calculated as the difference between the usual χ^2 value obtained in testing the hypothesis of null association in the 4×4 cross-classification (table 8A) and the corresponding χ^2 value obtained in testing this hypothesis in the 2×2 cross-classification.

In calculating the homogeneity component directly from table 8B, the pattern of deleted cells in this table is such that the expected frequencies under the homogeneity model can be estimated by explicit formula without iteration.[86] This comment on the estimation of the expected frequencies also holds true in calculating the homogeneity component directly from table 8D. In testing the homogeneity of categories 1 and 2 and the homogeneity of categories 3 and 4, the corresponding total homogeneity component (with 8 df) can be partitioned into a subcomponent (with 5 df) calculated directly from table 8B and a subcomponent (with 3 df) calculated directly from table 8D, with the expected frequencies estimated by explicit formula in each subcomponent. Alternatively, this total homogeneity component can be calculated directly (not using the partitioning noted above) with the expected frequencies also estimated by explicit formula under this homoge-

[84] The χ^2 value obtained in testing homogeneity in table 8D can be partitioned into three components each with 1 df (see, e.g., Goodman 1968).

[85] The homogeneity component here is the sum of the corresponding components obtained from tables 8B and D.

[86] See, e.g., Goodman 1968. As noted in the last sentence of n. 83, we are concerned here with the situation in which the main diagonal in table 8A is not deleted. In this situation, when testing the homogeneity of categories 1 and 2, the pattern of deleted cells is as noted in table 8B.

neity model. We shall now describe this explicit formula, first introducing some additional notation and terminology that will be used in the description.

In the 4×4 cross-classification of row categories and column categories (table 8A), when categories 1 and 2 are combined the 3×3 table thus obtained (table 8C) can be viewed as a 3×3 cross-classification of row "classes" and column "classes." Similarly, when categories 1 and 2 are combined and categories 3 and 4 are combined in the 4×4 cross-classification, the 2×2 table thus obtained can be viewed as a 2×2 cross-classification of row "classes" and column "classes." In the former case, the four categories were replaced by three classes; in the latter case, the four categories were replaced by two classes. More generally, in the $I \times J$ cross-classification of I row categories and J column categories, the I row categories can be partitioned into K row classes (where each row class combines the categories in a given subset of the row categories), and the J column categories can be partitioned into L column classes (where each column class combines the categories in a given subset of the column categories). From the $I \times J$ cross-classification of row categories and column categories, we thus obtain a $K \times L$ cross-classification of K row classes and L column classes (see, e.g., tables 10A and B).

For the $I \times J$ cross-classification, let f_{ij} denote the observed frequency in the ith row category and jth column category $(i = 1, 2, \ldots, I; j = 1, 2, \ldots, J)$; and for the $K \times L$ cross-classification, let f^*_{kl} denote the corresponding frequency in the kth row class and lth row class $(k = 1, 2, \ldots, K; l = 1, 2, \ldots, L)$. Each f^*_{kl} is a sum of a given set of f_{ij}, and each f_{ij} is a summand in a given f^*_{kl} (see, e.g., table 10B). Let $f_{ij,kl}$ denote the observed frequency in the ith row category and jth column category, and in the kth row class and lth column class (see, e.g., table 10C). The additional subscript k simply indicates that the ith row category is included in the kth row class, and the additional subscript l indicates similarly that the jth column category is included in the lth column class. Let $F_{ij,kl}$ denote the expected value of $f_{ij,kl}$ under some model.

Using the same general methods applied in, for example, Goodman (1968, 1970) to obtain explicit formulae for the maximum-likelihood estimate of the expected frequency (in cases where iteration is not necessary), we see that, under the homogeneity model considered in the present article, the $F_{ij,kl}$ can be estimated by the following formula:[87]

$$\hat{F}_{ij,kl} = f_{i.}f_{.j}f^*_{kl}/(f^*_{k.}f^*_{.l}) , \tag{34}$$

[87] The homogeneity model considered in the present article will be discussed further later in this section both for the situation in which none of the cells in the $I \times J$ cross-classification are deleted and for the situation in which some of the cells are deleted. Formula (34), and the corresponding formulae (39) and (40), pertain to the former situation. Formula (34) for the former situation is also presented in Béland (1978).

where

$$f_{i\cdot} = \sum_{j=1}^{J} f_{ij}, \quad f_{\cdot j} = \sum_{i=1}^{I} f_{ij},$$

$$f^*_{k\cdot} = \sum_{l=1}^{L} f^*_{kl}, \quad f^*_{\cdot l} = \sum_{k=1}^{K} f^*_{kl}.$$

(35)

With this explicit formula for $\hat{F}_{ij,kl}$, we can see how $\hat{F}_{ij,kl}$ is related to the usual estimate $\hat{F}_{ij}$ of the expected value of f_{ij} under the hypothesis of null association in the $I \times J$ cross-classification, and to the estimate $\hat{F}^*_{kl}$ of the expected value of f^*_{kl} under the hypothesis of null association in the $K \times L$ cross-classification. Under the hypothesis of null association in the $I \times J$ cross-classification, the expected value of f_{ij} can be estimated simply by the usual formula

$$\hat{F}_{ij} = f_{i\cdot}f_{\cdot j}/N,$$

(36)

TABLE 10

TABLES USED IN APPLYING HOMOGENEITY CRITERIA TO
CATEGORIES 1 AND 2 AND TO CATEGORIES 3 AND 4

A. A 4 × 4 CROSS-CLASSIFICATION OF CATEGORIES

	COLUMN CATEGORY			
ROW CATEGORY	1	2	3	4
1.....................	f_{11}	f_{12}	f_{13}	f_{14}
2.....................	f_{21}	f_{22}	f_{23}	f_{24}
3.....................	f_{31}	f_{32}	f_{33}	f_{34}
4.....................	f_{41}	f_{42}	f_{43}	f_{44}

B. A 2 × 2 CROSS-CLASSIFICATION OF CLASSES

	COLUMN CLASS	
ROW CLASS	1	2
1........	$f^*_{11}=f_{11}+f_{12}+f_{21}+f_{22}$	$f^*_{12}=f_{13}+f_{14}+f_{23}+f_{24}$
2........	$f^*_{21}=f_{31}+f_{32}+f_{41}+f_{42}$	$f^*_{22}=f_{33}+f_{34}+f_{43}+f_{44}$

C. A CROSS-CLASSIFICATION OF CATEGORIES WITHIN A
CROSS-CLASSIFICATION OF CLASSES

	COLUMN CLASS	
ROW CLASS	1	2
1.....................	$\begin{cases} f_{11,11} & f_{12,11} \\ f_{21,11} & f_{22,11} \end{cases}$	$\begin{array}{cc} f_{13,12} & f_{14,12} \\ f_{23,12} & f_{24,12} \end{array}$
2.....................	$\begin{cases} f_{31,21} & f_{32,21} \\ f_{41,21} & f_{42,21} \end{cases}$	$\begin{array}{cc} f_{33,22} & f_{34,22} \\ f_{43,22} & f_{44,22} \end{array}$

where

$$N = \sum_{i=1}^{I} \sum_{j=1}^{J} f_{ij} ; \qquad (37)$$

and under the hypothesis of null association in the $K \times L$ cross-classification, the expected value of f^*_{kl} can be estimated by

$$\hat{F}^*_{kl} = f^*_{k\cdot} f^*_{\cdot l} / N . \qquad (38)$$

From (34), (36), and (38), we see that

$$\hat{F}_{ij,kl} = \hat{F}_{ij} f^*_{kl} / \hat{F}^*_{kl} , \qquad (39)$$

and

$$\hat{F}_{ij} = \hat{F}_{ij,kl} / (f^*_{kl} / \hat{F}^*_{kl}) . \qquad (40)$$

With the χ^2 statistic for testing the hypothesis of null association in the $I \times J$ cross-classification, the observed frequency f_{ij} is compared with the estimated expected frequency $\hat{F}_{ij}$ given simply by (36). If the $\hat{F}_{ij}$ in the usual formula for the likelihood-ratio χ^2 statistic is replaced by the equivalent term on the right side of (40), this χ^2 statistic can then be partitioned directly into a component comparing the observed frequency $f_{ij,kl}$ with $\hat{F}_{ij,kl}$, and a component comparing f^*_{kl} with $\hat{F}^*_{kl}$. The first component can be used to test the homogeneity model, and the second component can be used to test the hypothesis of null association in the $K \times L$ cross-classification. Thus the likelihood-ratio χ^2 statistic for testing the hypothesis of null association in the $I \times J$ cross-classification can be partitioned into a component to test the homogeneity model, and a component to test the hypothesis of null association in the $K \times L$ cross-classification. The homogeneity component can be calculated directly comparing the observed frequency $f_{ij,kl}$ with $\hat{F}_{ij,kl}$, or it can be calculated as the difference between the χ^2 value obtained in testing the hypothesis of null association in the $I \times J$ cross-classification and the corresponding χ^2 value obtained in testing this hypothesis in the $K \times L$ cross-classification.[88]

From formula (34) we see that $\hat{F}_{ij,kl}$ is a product of three factors: (1) a factor pertaining to the ith row category (namely, $f_{i\cdot}$), (2) a factor pertaining to the jth column category (namely, $f_{\cdot j}$), and (3) a factor pertaining to the kth row class and lth column class (namely, $f^*_{kl} / [f^*_{k\cdot} f^*_{\cdot l}]$). This is a consequence of the fact that the homogeneity model considered in this article, when expressed in the terminology of the present section, states that the expected frequency $F_{ij,kl}$ is a product of a row category factor, a

[88] We also find that the number of degrees of freedom for testing the homogeneity model can be calculated as the corresponding difference $(I - 1)(J - 1) - (K - 1)(L - 1)$. This formula pertains to the situation in which none of the cells in the $I \times J$ cross-classification are deleted. (For the situation in which some of the cells are deleted, see nn. 89 and 90.) The above difference formula for the former situation is also presented in Béland (1978) and Béland and Fortier (1981).

column category factor, and a factor pertaining to the row class and column class:

$$F_{ij,kl} = \alpha_i \beta_j \gamma_{kl} . \qquad (41)$$

Model (41) is included within the general class of multiplicative models introduced in Goodman (1972), and the general techniques presented in that article can be applied directly to this model. (This model was also considered in Breiger [1981], but he preferred a different one.) When none of the cells in the $I \times J$ cross-classification are deleted, formula (34) can be used to calculate $\hat{F}_{ij,kl}$ under this model; but this formula cannot be used when some of the cells are deleted (e.g., the cells on the main diagonal). When some of the cells are deleted, the $\hat{F}_{ij,kl}$ can be calculated using the general iterative procedure described in Goodman (1972).[89] In this case, the results presented in the present section pertaining to the partitioning of χ^2 also need to be modified.[90]

Before closing this section, we mention again that the application of the homogeneity criteria could be based upon the total χ^2 value obtained in testing homogeneity, but in some contexts this test might be replaced by a weaker test obtained by deleting some specified components in the total χ^2.[91] We also remind the reader that, in the earlier section on homogeneity criteria versus structural criteria, when considering whether the I row categories and J column categories would be replaced by K row classes and L column classes, respectively, we noted that in some contexts the replacement would be made in order to obtain a situation in which the association in the $I \times J$ table (or in an appropriate subtable of the $I \times J$ table) has some specified property (e.g., the association would fit the homogeneity

---

[89] When some of the cells are deleted, the number of degrees of freedom for testing the homogeneity model can be calculated by modifying the formula in n. 88. The term $(I - 1)(J - 1)$ in this formula would be reduced to take account of the deleted cells, subtracting from this term the number of cells deleted in the case in which the pattern of the deleted cells in the $I \times J$ cross-classification table does not make the table separable (see, e.g., Goodman [1968] for discussion of both the inseparable and separable case); and the term $(K - 1)(L - 1)$ in the formula in n. 88 would also be reduced to take account of the effect of the deleted cells on the dimensionality of the row $\times$ column interaction term γ_{kl} (for $k = 1, 2, \ldots, K; l = 1, 2, \ldots, L$) in model (41).

[90] The partitioning results presented in this section for the case in which none of the cells are deleted (see, e.g., formulae [39] and [40] and the paragraph directly following these formulae) can be extended directly to the case in which some of the cells are deleted, when row category i and column category j are in row class k and column class l, respectively, and the pattern of deleted cells is such that, if cell (i,j) is deleted in the $I \times J$ table, then all the other cells in this table that are in cell (k,l) in the $K \times L$ table are also deleted in the $I \times J$ table. (See, e.g., the discussion of the χ^2 value [22] in the earlier section.) When the pattern of deleted cells is as described above, the formula in n. 88 for the number of degrees of freedom can also be extended directly. When the pattern of deleted cells is not as described above, the partitioning results need to be modified further (see, e.g., the earlier discussion of the χ^2 value [25]); and the number of degrees of freedom can be calculated as in n. 89.

[91] See, e.g., nn. 24 and 77.

model considered in this article or a specified generalization of this model); and in other contexts, the $I \times J$ table would be replaced by a $K \times L$ table in order to obtain a situation in which the association in the $K \times L$ table has some specified property.

REFERENCES

Béland, F. 1978. *L'Indépendance régionale: La Réduction des catégories dans les tableaux de contingence*. Ph.D. dissertation. Université Laval.
Béland, F., and Fortier, J. J. 1981. "The Reduction of Categories of Variables in Contingency Table Analysis: A Model." Unpublished manuscript.
Breiger, R. L. 1981. "The Social Class Structure of Occupational Mobility." *American Journal of Sociology*, in this issue.
Clogg, C. C. 1981. "Latent Structure Models of Mobility." *American Journal of Sociology* 86 (January): 836–68.
Duncan, O. D. 1979. "How Destination Depends on Origin in the Occupational Mobility Table." *American Journal of Sociology* 84 (January): 793–803.
Glass, D. V. 1954. *Social Mobility in Britain*. Glencoe, Ill.: Free Press.
* Goodman, L. A. 1968. "The Analysis of Cross-classified Data: Independence, Quasi-Independence, and Interactions in Contingency Tables With or Without Missing Entries. *Journal of the American Statistical Association* 63 (December): 1091–1131.
* ———. 1969. "How to Ransack Social Mobility Tables and Other Kinds of Cross-Classification Tables." *American Journal of Sociology* 75 (July): 1–39.
———. 1970. "The Multivariate Analysis of Qualitative Data: Interactions among Multiple Classifications." *Journal of the American Statistical Association* 65 (March): 226–56.
———. 1971. "Partitioning of Chi-Square, Analysis of Marginal Contingency Tables, and Estimation of Expected Frequencies in Multidimensional Contingency Tables." *Journal of the American Statistical Association* 66 (June): 339–44.
* ———. 1972. "Some Multiplicative Models for the Analysis of Cross-classified Data." Pp. 649–96 in *Proceedings of the Sixth Berkeley Symposium on Mathematical Statistics and Probability*, edited by L. Le Cam, J. Neyman and E. L. Scott. Berkeley and Los Angeles: University of California Press.
———. 1974. "The Analysis of Systems of Qualitative Variables When Some of the Variables Are Unobservable. I. A Modified Latent Structure Approach." *American Journal of Sociology* 79 (March): 1179–1259.
———. 1978. *Analyzing Qualitative/Categorical Data*. Cambridge, Mass.: Abt.
* ———. 1979a. "Multiplicative Models for the Analysis of Occupational Mobility Tables and Other Kinds of Cross-Classification Tables." *American Journal of Sociology* 84 (January): 804–19.
* ———. 1979b. "Simple Models for the Analysis of Association in Cross-Classifications Having Ordered Categories." *Journal of the American Statistical Association* 74 (September): 537–52.
* ———. 1981a. "Association Models and the Bivariate Normal for Contingency Tables with Ordered Categories." *Biometrika* 68 (2): 347–55.
* ———. 1981b. "Association Models and Canonical Correlation in the Analysis of Cross-Classifications Having Ordered Categories." *Journal of the American Statistical Association* 76 (June): 320–40.
Haberman, S. J. 1974. *The Analysis of Frequency Data*. Chicago: University of Chicago Press.
Hauser, R. M. 1979. "Some Exploratory Methods for Modeling Mobility Tables and Other Cross-classified Data." Pp. 413–58 in *Sociological Methodology 1980*, edited by Karl F. Schuessler. San Francisco: Jossey-Bass.
Miller, S. M. 1960. "Comparative Social Mobility." *Current Sociology* 9 (1): 1–89.

8.
Applications of Association Models: II
Using Association Models in Sociological Research: Some Examples

This paper discusses the log-multiplicative association model and demonstrates how it can be used in a variety of research situations in which ordinal variables are encountered. The examples pertain to (*a*) reconciling response distributions that differ because of question wording (or other context effects), (*b*) assigning a metric to an ordinal variable, (*c*) assigning scale scores to response patterns which arise from a Guttman-type model, and (*d*) analyzing multiple (ordinal) indicators. The log-multiplicative model presents a unified framework for analyzing each of these problems.

This paper considers some suggestive applications of the log-multiplicative association model recently presented by Goodman (1979; also see Andersen 1980). This model does not appear to have been utilized thus far in social research, even though a similar log-linear model has been used rather frequently (see Goodman 1981c). However, the log-multiplicative model has a rich potential for sociological application, and the objective of this paper is to present examples which suggest some uses the model might ultimately have.[1]

The chief advantage of the log-multiplicative model, at least for the examples considered here, is that it provides information about intervals between categories of ordinal variables. Each example considered stresses this aspect of the model, and the assumptions necessary to "scale" ordinal variables are explicitly stated and critically discussed. First I consider how response distributions obtained from two similar questions on attitudes toward the courts can be reconciled by appealing to the association model. An interesting feature of this application consists of discerning the proper placement of the response, don't know, along the underlying scale of the attitude. The second example pertains to the "general happiness" item used

---

[1] For other applications of this model, see, e.g., Goodman (1981a, 1981b).

in the General Social Survey, as well as in other surveys. This item elicits one of three possible ordered responses (not too happy, pretty happy, very happy); it is a simple example of an ordinal variable. By means of a certain conditional association model, it is estimated that the actual distance between the first two categories ("not too happy" and "pretty happy") is three times the distance between the second two categories ("pretty happy" and "very happy"). The third example deals with three items on the attitude toward legal abortion. By assuming that a Guttman-type model underlies the observed responses to these items, both the scale-response patterns and the error-response patterns are assigned scale scores. These scale scores could be used to construct an interval-level variable for use in causal models involving the attitude on abortion. The final example pertains to a cross-classification of three ordinal indicators of satisfaction with life, data that would be analyzed conventionally with the common-factor model. The partial association model applied to these data shows conclusively that (a) the assumption of equal intervals can be rejected, (b) the joint distribution of the variables cannot be the trivariate normal distribution, and (c) an accounting for "consistent responses" (see Duncan 1979) must be made in order to describe the joint distribution of these three items. Outwardly the four examples appear quite different from one another, and distinct bodies of methodology have been developed which purport to deal with each problem area from which the examples are taken. Because the log-multiplicative association model presents a unified framework within which these varied problems can be studied, it should be seriously considered as a competitor with other methods of analyzing ordinal data (see Kim [1975] and references cited there). Before the examples are presented, the model will be formulated and briefly discussed.

THE LOG-MULTIPLICATIVE ASSOCIATION MODEL

Suppose that a discrete ordinal variable with I categories is cross-classified with an ordinal variable with J categories, producing an $I \times J$ contingency table. Let the observed frequencies in this table be denoted by f_{ij}, and let the expected frequencies under some model be denoted by F_{ij}, for $i = 1, \ldots, I; j = 1, \ldots, J$. The log-multiplicative model of interest here can be described in a variety of ways, and it is instructive to consider at least some of these alternatives in order to gain understanding of the uses to which the model can be put. The first formulation is

$$F_{ij} = \tau\tau_i^R\tau_j^C e^{\phi\mu_i\nu_j} ,\tag{1}$$

where ϕ, μ_i, and ν_j are powers of e, the base of natural logarithms.[2] The τ_i^R pertain to "row effects" on the F_{ij}, and they correspond to "fitting" the

[2] The notation used here differs slightly from that used in Goodman (1979).

row marginal in the table of the F_{ij} (i.e., these parameters ensure that $\hat{F}_{i.} = f_{i.}$). Similarly, the τ_j^C pertain to the "column effects" on the F_{ij}, and τ pertains to fitting the sample size n. The τ, τ_i^R, and τ_j^C themselves are of no interest here; the focus is on the "interaction" or "association" between the two variables which is captured by the terms that appear as powers of e in equation (1).

Taking logarithms of equation (1) gives

$$\log F_{ij} = \lambda + \lambda_i^R + \lambda_j^C + \phi \mu_i \nu_j , \qquad (2)$$

where $\lambda = \log \tau$, $\lambda_i^R = \log \tau_i^R$, and $\lambda_j^C = \log \tau_j^C$. If the μ_i and the ν_j are constants, not to be estimated from the data, and if they depict the category scores for the row variable and the column variable, respectively, then the model is identical to Haberman's (1974) model of linear-by-linear interaction. The product of the scores ($\mu_i \nu_j$) defines a linear-by-linear inter-action term, and ϕ would be the coefficient describing its effect on the log F_{ij}. If the μ_i and the ν_j are given, the model is log-linear in the unknown parameters, λ, λ_i^R, λ_j^C, and ϕ, and standard methods of dealing with log-linear models can be directly applied to it (Bock and Yates 1973; Haberman 1979; Goodman 1979).

There is an element of indeterminacy regarding both the row scores μ_i and the column scores ν_j: only the ratios of distances between scores have any importance for the model. Consider for a moment the row-category scores $\mu_1, \ldots, \mu_I$, scores that can be assigned to the categories of the ordinal row variable which would perforce make it an interval variable. Let the distance between the first two categories be $d_1 = \mu_2 - \mu_1$, let the distance between the second two categories be $d_2 = \mu_3 - \mu_2$, and let their ratio be $d = d_2/d_1$. Clearly, if the location of the μ_i is changed by subtracting a constant, that is, $\mu_i^* = \mu_i - a$, the first and second intervals still have distances d_1 and d_2, respectively. The model in equation (2) is not altered by a location change in the μ_i; it can be shown that ϕ would still be the proper interaction parameter. If the location and the scale of the μ_i are changed by taking $\mu_i^* = (\mu_i - a)/b$, then the first distance $\mu_2^* - \mu_1^* = d_1/b \neq d_1$, and the second distance $\mu_3^* - \mu_2^* = d_2/b \neq d_2$. However, the ratio of distances is $(d_2/b)/(d_1/b) = d_2/d_1 = d$, being unaffected by location and scale changes. The model in equation (2) is unaffected by a scale change in the μ_i, except that $\phi^* = b\phi$ would be the relevant interaction parameter.

Now suppose that the μ_i and the ν_j are taken as parameters to be esti-mated, instead of constants chosen a priori to depict the category scores in question. The model of equations (1)–(2) is not in this case a log-linear model, and methods discussed by Goodman (1979) or Clogg (1982) are required to estimate its parameters. Inspection of equation (2) makes it clear that the parameters μ_i and ν_j can be regarded as category scores con-sistent with a model of linear-by-linear interaction. Thus, if the model were true, and if it had been assumed that the association between the variables could be described by linear-by-linear interaction, the parameters μ_i and ν_j could be used to scale the two variables in question, recognizing that only ratios of distances are identifiable.

An alternative way to describe the model in equation (1) is obtained by considering the odds ratios

$$\theta_{ij} = (F_{ij}F_{i+1,j+1})/(F_{i,j+1}F_{i+1,j}) , \tag{3}$$

for $i = 1, \ldots, I - 1; j = 1, \ldots, J - 1$. Each odds ratio measures the association between the row and column variables in a particular region of the table, namely, the association in the 2×2 subtable formed by taking adjacent rows i and $i + 1$ and adjacent columns j and $j + 1$. The full set of $(I - 1) \times (J - 1)$ such odds ratios can be regarded as containing all the information about the association between the variables, and so a model that explains the variability in this set of odds ratios is desired. Using equations (2) and (3), we obtain

$$\log \theta_{ij} = \phi(\mu_{i+1} - \mu_i)(\nu_{j+1} - \nu_j) . \tag{4}$$

Thus, the model is log multiplicative in terms of the association indexes θ_{ij}, and the "distances" appear explicitly as multipliers of ϕ. We note that, if the ordering of the row variable is correct, then $\mu_1 \leq \ldots \leq \mu_I$, and the distances $\mu_{i+1} - \mu_i$ will all be nonnegative, with a similar statement applying to the ν_j. The product $(\mu_{i+1} - \mu_i)(\nu_{j+1} - \nu_j)$ will be nonnegative everywhere, if the correct ordering of categories is used for each variable, and the association will be positive, negative, or nil according to whether ϕ is positive, negative, or nil. The parameter ϕ can be regarded as the "overall" association between the row and column variables, and only the distances between adjacent categories are assumed to account for differences among regions in the association actually observed. For example, consider the case in which j is fixed and let $d_i = \mu_{i+1} - \mu_i$. Then we could write $\log \theta_{ij} = \phi_j d_i$, where $\phi_j = \phi(\nu_{j+1} - \nu_j)$. In the first set of adjacent row categories, the association would be described by $\phi_j d_1$, while in the second set of adjacent row categories the association would be described by $\phi_j d_2$. The differing distances (d_1 vs. d_2) are assumed to account entirely for differences in $\log \theta_{1j}$ and $\log \theta_{2j}$ under the model. Thus, if only the estimates of the row variable scores μ_i are of interest and the column variable scores ν_j are not relevant, the model can be regarded as allowing curvilinearity in the association between the row and column variables, with the ϕ_j describing the association for different levels of the column variable.

An interesting and useful property of the model being discussed is that it is invariant under switches in the categories of the row and/or column categories (Goodman 1979). This means that (a) the χ^2 statistics measuring the fit of the model to data are not altered by switching categories, (b) the parameter ϕ is unchanged (in absolute value) when categories are switched, and (c) relative distances (and orderings) between row scores and between column scores are unchanged when categories are switched. To illustrate the last point, suppose that distances between row categories 1 and 2 and between row categories 2 and 3 are of interest. Under the model, parameters μ_1, μ_2, and μ_3 would convey the information about these distances, and the quantity $d = (\mu_2 - \mu_1)/(\mu_3 - \mu_2)$ is the ratio of the distances. If categories 1 and 2 were switched, the scores would appear in the model in the order 2, 1, 3, and the parameters could be written as μ_2^*, μ_1^*, μ_3^*. The quantity $d^* = (\mu_2^* - \mu_1^*)/(\mu_3^* - \mu_2^*)$ will equal d, the relative distance measure obtained for the original ordering. This is a very important property of the log-multiplicative model, and it is a property that is not satisfied with the log-linear model (the linear-by-linear interaction model) that has been used frequently to analyze the cross-classification of ordinal variables.

THE EFFECTS OF QUESTION WORDING ON RESPONSE DISTRIBUTIONS

Table 1 presents responses to two similar questions on the fairness of the courts' treatment of criminals. The source is the 1974 General Social Survey (Davis 1978), in which a randomization technique was used to determine which individuals would be given which question. There is no other apparent difference between the contexts in which each question was used, implying that the observed differences in the response distributions can be

TABLE 1

ATTITUDE TOWARD TREATMENT OF CRIMINALS BY THE
COURTS, 1974 GENERAL SOCIAL SURVEY

| | QUESTION WORDING | | | |
| | A* | | B† | |
RESPONSE	N	Percentage	N	Percentage
Too harshly..........	42	5.6	33	4.5
About right..........	72	9.6	44	6.0
Not harshly enough...	580	76.9‡	436	59.7‡
Don't know§.........	51	6.8	210	28.7
No answer...........	8	1.1	8	1.1
Total.............	753	100.0	731	100.0

* The question asked was, "In general, do you think the courts in this area deal too harshly or not harshly enough with criminals?"

† The question asked was, "In general, do you think the courts in this area deal too harshly, or not harshly enough with criminals, or don't you have enough information about the courts to say?"

‡ Percentage adjusted to ensure sum = 100.

§ For wording B, the "don't know" should be replaced by "not enough information to say."

attributed solely to question wording, apart from considerations of sampling error. The actual questions used appear in the notes to table 1; a careful reading of them indicates that the response, don't know (DK), was probably discouraged by the first wording but encouraged by the second. The second wording (form B) appears to encourage the DK response in much the same way as the "filter" design discussed by Schuman and Presser (1978), while the first wording (form A) is consistent with standard techniques of survey design. The differences in the two response distributions are dramatic, with the first estimating the proportion of the population who think the courts are "not harsh enough" at 77%, while the second estimates the same proportion at 60%. The DK response is 7% in the first and 29% in the second.

A variety of statistical methods can be used to reconcile the two observed distributions (see Clogg 1980). The approach taken here is to assume that there is an underlying continuum on the attitude in question, and that each question performs differently in locating points on that continuum. An association model that takes these assumptions into account seems appropriate, and the strategy followed consists in the following steps. (1) Delete the response, no answer (NA), from consideration, but retain the DK. The NA response does not appear to represent a source of discrepancy between the two distributions (each wording received 1.1% of NA responses). However, the DK is very important and should somehow be included in an attempt to reconcile the two distributions. (2) Assume that the points along the underlying continuum of the attitude can be represented by scores μ_1, μ_2, μ_3, μ_4, the last quantity referring to the score for the DK. The assumption here is that the DK is somehow a measure of the strength of the attitude—it does not represent a "nonattitude."[3] (3) Assume that each question wording yields a different set of scores $\mu_1, \ldots, \mu_4$, and that the differences in the scores can be attributed solely to the difference in the wording. (4) Choose a "criterion" variable, or "instrument," with which the attitude variable can be cross-classified. The schooling variable was used for this example; it was coded as less than 12, 12, 13–15, 16, and 17 or more years, yielding a five-category ordinal variable.[4] (5)

[3] That the percentage of DK responses differs so widely from one form to the other (7% vs. 29%) lends some credence to the view that the DK response represents something other than a nonattitude.

[4] Since years of schooling is an interval-level variable, we are not interested in estimating distances between categories of this variable. Since the category scores of only one variable are of interest, the model of eq. (1), (2), or (4) can be interpreted as allowing the association between the attitude variable and the schooling variable to depend on the level of schooling (allowing curvilinearity), but once proper category scores for the attitude variable are assigned, this association does not depend on the level of attitude. Stanley Presser notes (personal communication) that a different categorization of the schooling item could lead to a different inference.

Apply a conditional association model (Clogg 1982) which constrains the schooling effects on the association (the v_j of the preceding section) to be identical in each cross-classification, but allows the response variable scores (the μ_i) to differ. The assumption is that schooling is a proper instrument, which implies that the association of the response with the schooling variable is adequately described by linear-by-linear interaction. (This last assumption is critical, and although we can use data in some cases to reject it, no completely convincing empirical test of its validity can be made. Further comments on the rationale for choosing instruments are presented in the final section.)

Using statistical methods described in Goodman (1979) or Clogg (1982), we find that the log-multiplicative association model just described has a likelihood-ratio χ^2 statistic $L^2 = 18.13$ on 15 degrees of freedom, certainly an acceptable fit. The scores obtained for the response variable are reported in table 2, where certain constraints have been used to interpret the differences in scores that result. For question-form A, I set $\hat{\mu}_1$ at zero and obtained $\hat{\mu}_2 = .183$, $\hat{\mu}_3 = .290$, and $\hat{\mu}_4$ (for the DK) $= .288$. The distances $\hat{d}_i = \hat{\mu}_{i+1} - \hat{\mu}_i$ are thus .183, .107, $-.002$, showing that the DK is virtually indistinguishable from the response, not harshly enough, for this wording. (Perhaps the DKs for this wording were leaning toward the response, not harshly enough, but for whatever reason did not wish to commit themselves to this "conservative" response.) The scale of the estimated scores was not further modified; the zero restriction for $\hat{\mu}_1$ was the only restriction imposed. The ratios of distances $r_i = d_{i+1}/d_i$ were estimated at .58 and $-.02$, and I hasten to add that these two quantities would be invariant under any location or scale change in the scores.

For question-form B, an altogether different pattern emerges. To render the scores for this form comparable to those for the first, a location restric-

TABLE 2

ESTIMATED CATEGORY INTERVALS FOR THE
ATTITUDE VARIABLE IN TABLE 1

RESPONSE	QUESTION WORDING	
	A	B
Too harsh.............	.000*	$-.266$
About right...........	.183	.025
Not harshly enough.....	.290	.464
Don't know...........	.288	$-.021$
Mean†................	.26	.26

* The value .000 is arbitrary. See text for explanation.

† Category scores for wording B were adjusted to ensure that equal means would be obtained. Calculations were carried out to more digits than are reported.

tion was first employed. Since both questions measure the same attitude, albeit in different ways, it seems reasonable to expect that the mean score (the actual weighted mean) should be identical for each form. The scores for question-form B were adjusted, while preserving differences, so that the mean for each form was $\bar{X} = .26$. This yields $\hat{\mu}_1 = -.266$, $\hat{\mu}_2 = .025$, $\hat{\mu}_3 = .464$, $\hat{\mu}_4 = -.021$ as the estimated category scores for form B. Thus, the DK response here falls between "too harsh" and "about right," being closer to about right. For this wording, then, it would be reasonable to place the DKs with the neutral response, about right, whereas such a placement would be entirely unacceptable for the first form. Note that the range of the scores is greater for question-form B ($-.266$ to $.464$, for a range of $.730$) than for question-form A ($.290$), implying that the response, too harsh, is further to the left on the continuum for form B than for form A, with a corresponding statement applying to the response, not harshly enough. For form B, the distances between the responses, too harsh and about right, and between about right and not harshly enough (d_1, d_2) are estimated at $.291$ and $.439$, with the ratio being $.439/.291 = 1.51$ (as compared with $.58$ for form A); this ratio shows in different terms how the responses to form B are spread out along the underlying continuum of the attitude.[5]

In sum, the DK response appears to be indistinguishable from the conservative response, not harshly enough, in form A, but it appears to be nearly the same as the neutral response, about right, in form B. Form B yields a set of scores with greater range (more variance). The very different response distributions in table 1 can be reconciled using the log-multiplicative model, and the scores in table 2 could be used to construct an interval-level variable for further substantive analysis. All of these deductions are valid only to the extent that (a) the schooling variable is a proper instrument, implying that (b) the relationship between the attitude and schooling is adequately described by the linear-by-linear interaction model of equation (1) or (2). I defer a critical appraisal of these assumptions until other examples are discussed.

[5] The reader will notice that only one restriction was used for each set of $\hat{\mu}_i$ in table 2; the $\hat{\mu}_i$ for question-form A were restricted by setting $\hat{\mu}_1 = 0$, and the $\hat{\mu}_i$ for question-form B were restricted by adjusting the scores so that their mean was equal to that obtained for the $\hat{\mu}_i$ of question-form A. However, the algorithm used to obtain the results began with identical initial values of $\hat{\mu}_i$ for each wording. Thus, the final values for $\hat{\mu}_i$ for both groups (the maximum-likelihood estimates) are comparable across groups with just one restriction imposed on each set. If $\hat{\mu}_1$ is set at zero for the first form, the calculated value of $\hat{\mu}_1$ for the second form ($= -.266$) can be said to indicate a position on the underlying continuum $.266$ units less than the arbitrary score $\hat{\mu}_1 = 0$ for the first form. Similar comments apply to the other $\hat{\mu}_i$ when compared across question wordings. Such a strategy appears much more fruitful than arbitrarily imposing scale and location restrictions on both sets of estimates. A referee notes that confidence intervals on the distance measures would be useful at this point, but unfortunately the necessary standard errors are difficult to come by.

ASSIGNING A METRIC TO AN ORDINAL VARIABLE:
THE HAPPINESS ITEM

A question that has always appeared on the General Social Survey is the "overall happiness" item, which elicits the ordered responses, not too happy, pretty happy, and very happy. We suspect that many researchers assume that scores 1, 2, and 3 can be used for these response categories, and they then proceed in their statistical analysis as if this arbitrarily scored variable were a proper interval-level variable. Table 3 cross-classifies this trichotomy by sex and schooling for the 1977 General Social Survey, using a slightly different categorization of the schooling variable than was used previously. These data were studied in Clogg (1982) from the point of view of conditional association models, and the reader is referred to this source for a detailed analysis using a variety of different models. The schooling variable is used as an instrument once again, and sex is used as a group variable in order to validate partially the inferences drawn about the scores of the happiness item. The responses to the happiness question do not appear to have different meanings for the sexes; I can think of no compelling reasons why the response, not too happy, for example, would indicate different levels of happiness for males than for females, even though there may indeed be different overall levels of happiness associated with each sex.

The model of conditional independence (happiness independent of schooling for each sex) yields $L^2 = 48.88$ on 12 df, a very significant result. The model allowing schooling scores to differ across sexes (allowing the happiness-schooling association to depend on the level of schooling in different ways for each sex), but retaining homogeneous happiness scores, gives $L^2 = 6.15$ on 5 df. To obtain some sense of how different the happiness scores might be across the sexes, a model allowing these scores to differ as well

TABLE 3

CROSS-CLASSIFICATION OF U.S. SAMPLE ACCORDING TO
REPORTED HAPPINESS AND YEARS OF SCHOOLING,
BY SEX, 1977 GENERAL SOCIAL SURVEY

REPORTED HAPPINESS	YEARS OF SCHOOL COMPLETED			
	<12	12	13–16	17+
	Males			
Not too happy	40	21	14	3
Pretty happy	131	116	112	27
Very happy	82	61	55	27
	Females			
Not too happy	62	26	12	3
Pretty happy	155	156	95	15
Very happy	87	127	76	15

was fitted, yielding the negligibly different L^2 of 5.91 on 4 df. If the model with heterogeneous happiness scores had provided a significant improvement in fit, the improvement would have indicated that the original model could not be used to estimate category scores for the happiness item. The absence of such an improvement adds credibility to the model and to the happiness scores obtained from it.

The model arrived at can be described in terms of equation (4) as

$$\log \theta_{ij}{}^m = \phi^m(\mu_{i+1} - \mu_i)(\nu_{j+1}{}^m - \nu_j{}^m) ,$$

$$\log \theta_{ij}{}^f = \phi^f(\mu_{i+1} - \mu_i)(\nu_{j+1}{}^f - \nu_j{}^f) ,$$

in obvious notation. Note that the level of overall association between schooling and happiness is allowed to differ between the sexes (ϕ^m vs. ϕ^f), and the association is allowed to depend as well on the level of schooling in different ways for the sexes (since the $\nu_j{}^m$ are allowed to differ from the $\nu_j{}^f$). But the happiness scores are constrained to be homogeneous across sex groups, and it is arguable that this should be the case. The reader should note that the application of the log-multiplicative association model in the present example differs from that in the previous one. The chief difference is the use of the sex variable as a means of strengthening the inferences drawn, giving more opportunity to reject the model as a device for estimating happiness scores.

The estimates of the μ_i for the happiness scores appear in table 4, and the estimated distances are $\hat{\mu}_2 - \hat{\mu}_1 = .79$ and $\hat{\mu}_3 - \hat{\mu}_2 = .26$.[6] The distance between the responses, not too happy and pretty happy, is about three times the distance between the responses, pretty happy and very happy ($.79/.26 = 3$). These scores, or any others that preserve the estimated ratio of distances, could, under the truth of this model, be used to scale the

TABLE 4

CATEGORY SCORES FOR THE HAPPINESS VARI-
ABLE IN TABLE 3, OBTAINED FROM THE
CONDITIONAL ASSOCIATION MODEL WITH
HOMOGENEOUS ROW EFFECTS AND HETER-
OGENEOUS COLUMN EFFECTS

Response	Category Score $\hat{\mu}_i$	$\hat{\mu}_{i+1} - \hat{\mu}_i$
Not too happy......	1.35	
Pretty happy.......	2.14	.79
Very happy.........	2.41	.26

[6] No restrictions were imposed on these parameter estimates. The reader should bear in mind that only the ratios of distances are invariant under various parameterizations of the model.

happiness variable. It can be noted that the hypothesis of equal intervals between the happiness scores gives $L^2 = 11.64$ on 6 df. The difference $11.64 - 6.15 = 5.49$, a single degree-of-freedom χ^2 variate under the hypothesis of equal spacing, is statistically significant. This implies that the ratio 3 ($= .79/.26$) is significantly different from one. Suffice it to say that the estimated distances between the categories of the happiness variable appear credible, and the somewhat more involved statistical analysis of rival models (see Clogg 1982) does not give reason to question the results. A technique like that used here can be used to scale any ordered variable that appears in sample surveys, given proper instruments with which these ordinal variables can be calibrated.

ESTIMATING SCALE SCORES FOR GUTTMAN-TYPE RESPONSE PATTERNS

Guttman scaling procedures have been an accepted part of sociological research for three decades. A variety of statistical methods can be used to assess the conformity of data to the Guttman model (Goodman 1975; Clogg and Sawyer 1981; Lazarsfeld and Henry 1968), although convincing methods of assigning scores to response patterns obeying a Guttman model, or one of its stochastic variants, have not been so easy to develop. Lazarsfeld's latent distance model (Lazarsfeld and Henry 1968) is one approach by which scale scores have occasionally been constructed, but most available software packages merely form summated scales (summing up the items) to arrive at an "interval" variable for substantive analysis. The log-multiplicative association model represents an alternative method by which scale scores can be assigned, although, as in the previous examples, the validity of the scale scores so obtained depends on the availability of a suitable instrument.

To illustrate this technique, three items on the attitude toward legal abortion were considered. The items pertained to whether abortion should be legal for a woman who is poor (POOR), for a woman who is single (SINGLE), or for a woman who wants no more children (NOMORE). Assuming that these items indicate different points along an underlying continuum of the attitude in question, Guttman's model predicts that the four response patterns ([1,1,1], [1,1,2], [1,2,2], [2,2,2]) would contain all respondents.[7] (The ordering of items was POOR, SINGLE, and NOMORE,

[7] No test of the conformity of the data to Guttman's model was performed. The test described by Goodman (1975) for his probabilistic variant of the Guttman model cannot be directly applied to the 2^3 table. However, Goodman's parameter π_0, measuring the proportion of respondents "intrinsically unscalable," has an estimate of .32 (Goodman 1975, eq. [A.7]). This index of scalability is reasonably small, especially in comparison with the values obtained for this quantity in other applications of the Goodman scale model (Clogg and Sawyer 1981). We shall assume that these three items are Guttman scalable, implying that they measure a unidimensional attitude.

and 1 refers to the yes response). In the $2 \times 2 \times 2$ class-classification of these items, error responses were found, and in circumstances like these it can be difficult to defend any procedure for assigning scale scores. However, an application of the log-multiplicative association model produces scores that can be defended in terms of the model, and the required assumptions for its use appear to be no more stringent than those used implicitly to construct scale scores by conventional ad hoc methods.

Consider the fivefold variable with one category for each of the four scale-response patterns and an additional category denoting error-response patterns.[8] The exact ordering of the categories of this variable is open to dispute, particularly since it is not clear where the error-response patterns should be placed. What is needed is an instrument with which this fivefold variable can be cross-classified, producing a contingency table that exhibits linear-by-linear interaction. The instrument chosen here was the item measuring the attitude on premarital sex, the assumption being that the abortion attitude should be associated with this variable in a way that can be described adequately by this model.

Table 5 presents the cross-classification of interest; the notes describe the items used. Note that no other variable (e.g., sex) is used here to "validate" results. This 5×4 table can be studied directly with the techniques in Goodman (1979). The independence model yields $L^2 = 236.34$ on 12 df, while the log-multiplicative association model yields a near perfect fit, $L^2 = 5.55$ on 6 df. Table 6 presents the log-odds-ratios observed and predicted

TABLE 5

CROSS-CLASSIFICATION OF ABORTION ATTITUDE BY ATTITUDE ON
PREMARITAL SEX, 1977 GENERAL SOCIAL SURVEY

ABORTION ATTITUDE RESPONSE PATTERNS*	PREMARITAL SEX†				
	1	2	3	4	TOTAL
0. Error responses...	44	11	38	62	155
1. (1,1,1)..........	59	41	147	293	540
2. (1,1,2)..........	23	11	13	27	74
3. (1,2,2)..........	27	8	16	27	78
4. (2,2,2)..........	258	57	105	110	530
Total...........	411	128	319	519	1,377

* The three abortion items were as follows. Should legal abortion be available to a woman: "if she is married and does not want any more children?" (NOMORE); "if the family has a very low income and cannot afford any more children?" (POOR); "if she is not married and does not want to marry the man?" (SINGLE). The Guttman-scale ordering for these items, based on inspection of the single-item marginals, was POOR-SINGLE-NOMORE; a response pattern of (1,1,2) corresponds to a "yes" for both POOR and SINGLE and a "no" for NOMORE.

† The question was, "Do you think [premarital sex] is always wrong, almost always wrong, wrong only sometimes, or not wrong at all?" The responses are coded 1–4, respectively.

8 All the error-response patterns were condensed into one category, but the methods discussed here do not require this condensation.

under the model, showing in different terms how well the model fits. (There do appear to be some log-odds-ratios that are not predicted well under the model, but the reader should bear in mind that the counts in some of the 2×2 subtables are rather small.)

Table 7 presents the scale scores estimated under the model, including a score for the error-response patterns.[9] If the five categories are denoted by 0, 1, 2, 3, 4, then the suggested ordering is 1, 0, 2, 3, 4. The error-response patterns are estimated to indicate a position somewhere between the $(1,1,1)$ and the $(1,1,2)$ patterns. Given these category scores, the numbers .507, .049, −.064, −.101, and −.391 could be used to create an interval-level attitudinal variable, with imputed distances of .458, .113, .037, and .290. The ratios of these distances are $.458/.113 = 4.05$, $.113/.037 = 3.05$, and $.037/.290 = .13$. Under the model, it would be entirely inappro-

TABLE 6

OBSERVED AND EXPECTED LOG-ODDS-RATIOS
FOR TABLE 5

ABORTION ATTITUDE RESPONSE PATTERNS	PREMARITAL SEX		
	1 vs. 2	2 vs. 3	3 vs. 4
0 vs. 1	1.02	.04	.20
	(.57)	(.36)	(.30)
1 vs. 2	−.37	−1.11	.04
	(−.71)	(−.46)	(−.37)
2 vs. 3	−.48	.53	−.21
	(−.05)	(−.03)	(−.02)
3 vs. 4	−.29	−.08	−.48
	(−.36)	(−.23)	(−.19)

NOTE.—Estimated expected log-odds-ratios are shown in parentheses.

TABLE 7

ESTIMATED SCALE SCORES FOR
THE ABORTION ATTITUDE
RESPONSE PATTERNS

Abortion Attitude Response Pattern	Scale Score*
0. Error	.049
1. (1,1,1)	.507
2. (1,1,2)	−.064
3. (1,2,2)	−.101
4. (2,2,2)	−.391

* Scores constrained to sum to zero.

[9] A location restriction was imposed on the $\hat{\mu}_i$ in table 7 by restricting $\Sigma_i \hat{\mu}_i = 0$.

priate to use scores that reflected an assumption of equal intervals (even disregarding the error-response patterns). Once again it must be noted that these inferences are only as good as the model, and the application of the model to obtain category scores depends on the suitability of the instrument (premarital sex) used.

For completeness, it can be noted that the estimates of the v_j, $j =$ 1, . . . , 4, were $-.280$, $-.048$, $.102$, and $.225$, respectively. If it had been decided to use the association in table 5 to calibrate the premarital sex item, these scores could have been used for this purpose. However, a somewhat stronger assumption would have to be made: that the entire bivariate relationship could be simply described by linear-by-linear interaction. It is interesting to examine the model applied to the table with some categories switched. For example, if categories 3 and 4 of the premarital sex item are switched, the log-multiplicative model applied to this modified table still gives $L^2 = 5.55$. The estimates of the premarital sex scores are now $\hat{v}_1 = -.448$, $\hat{v}_2 = -.076$, $\hat{v}_4 = .361$, and $\hat{v}_3 = .164$. These estimates are different from those obtained for the original table, but the relative distances between categories are still the same. For example, $(\hat{v}_3 - \hat{v}_2)/(\hat{v}_4 - \hat{v}_3) = 1.22$ for either set of estimates. This is a demonstration of the invariance property discussed early in this paper (see Goodman 1979), and similar comments apply to other types of category switches.

ANALYSIS OF ORDINAL INDICATORS

Table 8, obtained once again from the 1977 General Social Survey, is a three-way cross-classification of ordinal indicators of satisfaction with life. The specific indicators used pertain to satisfaction with residence, family, and hobbies, and a fourfold categorization of responses was used. These data would be conventionally approached from the framework of the common-factor model (see, e.g., Jöreskog and Sörbom 1979), but they might be approached as well from the latent class framework (Clogg 1979). Here they will be studied from the point of view of the log-multiplicative association model, and the partial association models of Clogg (1982) become relevant. Let R, C, and L denote the three variables under consideration, and let i, j, and k denote the category indexes, ranging from 1 through 4. To describe the partial association between R and C, the partial odds ratios $\theta_{ij(k)}{}^{RC} = (F_{ijk}F_{i+1,j+1,k})/(F_{i,j+1,k}F_{i+1,j,k})$ are relevant, and similar partial odds ratios can be defined for the R-L and C-L partial association. The approach begins by assuming that each variable is a measure of an underlying continuum (e.g., satisfaction with residence), and we let μ_i, v_j, and ξ_k denote the category scores for each variable. (Note that we have not made the assumption that each indicator is somehow a fallible measure of

TABLE 8

CROSS-CLASSIFICATION OF U.S. SAMPLE ACCORDING TO
THREE INDICATORS OF SATISFACTION WITH LIFE,
1977 GENERAL SOCIAL SURVEY

$L =$,	$R =$	$C = 1$	$C = 2$	$C = 3$	$C = 4$
1,	1......	76	14	15	4
1,	2......	32	17	7	3
1,	3......	64	23	28	15
1,	4......	41	11	27	16
2,	1......	15	2	7	4
2,	2......	27	20	9	5
2,	3......	57	31	24	15
2,	4......	27	9	22	16
3,	1......	13	6	13	5
3,	2......	12	13	10	6
3,	3......	46	32	75	20
3,	4......	54	26	58	55
4,	1......	7	6	7	6
4,	2......	7	2	3	6
4,	3......	12	11	31	15
4,	4......	52	36	80	101

NOTE.—Variables L, R, and C refer to satisfaction with hobbies, family,
and residence, respectively. Variable codes are 1 (a fair amount, some, a
little, or none), 2 (quite a bit), 3 (a great deal), and 4 (a very great deal).

a "common" factor.) The model of interest can be expressed in terms of
the partials as

$$\log \theta_{ij(k)}{}^{RC} = \phi^{RC}(\mu_{i+1} - \mu_i)(\nu_{j+1} - \nu_j) ,$$

$$\log \theta_{i(j)k}{}^{RL} = \phi^{RL}(\mu_{i+1} - \mu_i)(\xi_{k+1} - \xi_k) ,$$

$$\log \theta_{(i)jk}{}^{CL} = \phi^{CL}(\nu_{j+1} - \nu_j)(\xi_{k+1} - \xi_k) .$$

Note that the overall levels of partial association are allowed to differ between pairs of variables. Note in addition that the model is positing linear-
by-linear, first-order interaction between pairs of variables, subject to the
appropriate scores being assigned to the response categories. Finally, note
that the μ_i in the first and second equations are identical, the ν_j in the first
and third equations are identical, and the ξ_k in the second and third equations are identical. The model is described in Clogg (1982) as the homogeneous row-, column-, and layer-effects partial association model, and
a more general model would not constrain the category scores to be homogeneous across types of partials. (E.g., the μ_i of the first equation could be
allowed to differ from the μ_i of the second equation.)

Attempts to apply the model described by the three equations immediately above to the data in table 8 were unsuccessful. In fact, a model that
allowed the category scores to differ across types of partials gave an L^2 of
123.59 on 54 df, suggesting that the more restrictive model would also fail

to fit. However, with the consistent responses ([1,1,1], [2,2,2], [3,3,3], [4,4,4]) blanked out, satisfactory results were obtained.[10] The model for the incomplete table so constructed gave $L^2 = 49.31$ on 41 df, certainly an acceptable fit. The conclusion must certainly be that an appropriate model for the association of these ordinal indicators has to take account of the fact that far too many respondents answer all items consistently, invalidating any model which does not take this information into account. Results of Goodman (1981a) indicate that, if the data were adequately described by the (trivariate) normal distribution, the model for the complete table just discussed would provide an acceptable fit. But the model provides an adequate description of the data only when the incomplete table is used. Moreover, the hypothesis of equal intervals can be rejected (even when the consistent responses are deleted), since $L^2 = 103.95$ on 47 df for this model. The common-factor model which assumes equal intervals and multivariate normality, and which makes no allowance for response consistency, simply cannot be defended for these data. I suspect that similar conclusions would be reached if these models were applied to similar survey items on satisfaction indicators (see, e.g., Andrews and McKennell 1980).

The category scores estimated for these three items appear in table 9. No attempt was made to impose scale or location restrictions on these estimates, but nevertheless an anomalous finding was uncovered for the estimated distance between the first and second responses to the family variable (pertaining to "a fair amount, some, a little, or none" and "quite a bit"). The estimates indicate that the position of these two categories must be switched, and this is admittedly a perplexing result. In circumstances like

TABLE 9

PARAMETER ESTIMATES UNDER THE HOMOGENEOUS ROW-, COLUMN-, AND LAYER-EFFECTS MODEL APPLIED TO TABLE 8
(with Consistent Response Patterns Deleted)

Parameters	Maximum Likelihood Estimate						
Row effects........	$-.19$		-1.11		$-.32$		1.62
		$(-.92)$		$(.78)$		(1.95)	
Column effects.....	-1.09		$-.77$		$.43$		1.43
		$(.32)$		(1.20)		(1.00)	
Layer effects.......	$-.92$		$-.89$		$.29$		1.51
		$(.03)$		(1.17)		(1.23)	

NOTE.—Figures in parentheses are differences.

[10] Actually, for some models applied to this table it suffices to "blank out" only the extreme response consistency patterns ([1,1,1], [4,4,4]). Inferences drawn here would not be markedly different with this alternative formulation of the model.

these, the model must be called into question, but as an expedient we might simply average the anomalous scores.[11]

In order to use the scores in table 9 for substantive work, it is necessary to impose some restrictions on them. Table 10 presents one such attempt, in which the score for the fourth category ("a very great deal") is set arbitrarily at one for each item. Because of the anomalous finding (cf. table 9) for the first-category score on the family item, this score was arbitrarily adjusted as well, setting it and the second score to the mean of these two scores. It can be noted that the distances between the first two categories are, on the whole, much smaller than the distances between either the second and third or the third and fourth categories. A "summated scale" of the three items might be constructed by using the appropriate sums of scores in table 10, or these scores might be used in a factor-analytic model to obtain a composite index of a different sort. This is by no means a final solution to the problem of ordinal indicators, but the association models used here are at least suggestive of the potential worth of pursuing the subject further.

DISCUSSION

The four examples considered briefly in this paper were intended to illustrate several problems to which the log-multiplicative association model could be applied. Each situation demanded a slightly different type of model, and it is instructive to consider the way that these different models were formulated and utilized. The first example pertained to reconciling two different question wordings measuring the same attitude (viz., the attitude toward the courts' treatment of criminals). It was assumed that (*a*) schooling should be associated with the attitude in the same way for each question wording, given an appropriate accounting for category scores; (*b*)

TABLE 10

CATEGORY SCORES FOR THE ORDINAL INDICATORS IN TABLE 8

| ITEM | SCORE FOR CATEGORY | | | |
	1	2	3	4
Family........	−1.27*	−1.27*	−.95	1.00†
Residence.....	−1.52	−1.20	.00	1.00†
Hobbies.......	−1.43	−1.40	−.23	1.00†

* Arbitrarily set equal to the mean score for categories 1 and 2.
† Arbitrarily set equal to one.

[11] Techniques described in Goodman (1981*b*) could be extended to the three-variable situation in order to examine whether the switch in categories is statistically significant. To save space, these matters will not be discussed here.

schooling could serve as an instrument with which the category scores could be estimated; and (c) the mean score for the attitude measured should be the same for each question wording. These assumptions led to an association model which produced plausible category scores for each response distribution. The model posited heterogeneous attitude-variable scores (across question wordings), and homogeneous schooling effects on the association (across question wordings). The model allowed "curvilinearity" in the association across levels of schooling.

The second example pertained to the trichotomous happiness item, and the schooling variable was once again chosen as an instrument with which to calibrate the ordinal variable in question. A third variable (sex group) was also introduced, giving more opportunity to reject the model as a device for estimating category intervals. The association between happiness and schooling was allowed to depend on sex, and it was also allowed to depend on the level of schooling. But the happiness item scores were assumed to be the same for each sex, an assumption that is tantamount to claiming that the response, very happy, indicates the same level of happiness for each sex. The model posited homogeneous happiness scores (across sex groups), and heterogeneous schooling effects on the association (across sex groups). This model was compared with one alternative, thereby strengthening the inferences drawn.

The third example pertained to an ordered variable that naturally arises from a Guttman scaling situation. For this problem, one instrument (the attitude on premarital sex) was employed to estimate category scores, using the log-multiplicative model for the two-way table. The necessary specification was that the association between the ordinal variable and the instrument should not depend on the level of the ordinal variable, once a proper adjustment for category intervals is made. The association could depend on the level of the attitude toward premarital sex (the instrument). Satisfactory results were obtained, and plausible scores were assigned to the response patterns that arose from the Guttman model.

The fourth example pertained to an analysis of three ordinal variables, considered in terms of their partial relationships with each other. For this situation, no external instrument was brought into the analysis, and the specification of linear-by-linear first-order association was used to calibrate each ordinal variable. An anomalous result occurred for one of the category scores for one of the variables, casting doubt on the model. But the analysis nevertheless showed conclusively that (a) an assumption of equal intervals could be rejected, (b) the assumption of trivariate normality could be rejected, and (c) an accounting for "response consistency" was required before the association among the variables could be described.

Since three of the examples utilized an "instrumental" variable in order to estimate the desired category intervals, it is appropriate to provide some criteria for the selection of instruments. Of course, if several different instruments were available, it would be prudent to utilize all of them, thereby acquiring some sense of how the estimated category scores depend on the particular instrument chosen. But some criteria can be helpful in deciding which of the available instruments should be used. Even though there is no completely convincing empirical test of the suitability of an instrument, there are several conditions that must be met for the instrument to be valid.

Suppose that the row variable R is the ordinal variable to be calibrated, and the column variable C is the instrument chosen for the application of the model. (If additional variables are also available and relevant—see the first two examples—additional considerations can also be used.) First, there must be association between R and C. If the instrument C is not associated with R, no information is available with which to estimate the category intervals. To see why this is so, consider the expression in equation (4). The case where there is no association between R and C can be equivalently described by saying that $\phi = 0$, or by saying that all the differences $\mu_{i+1} - \mu_i = 0$; thus, there is no way that distances between the categories of R can be estimated.[12] Second, the model must produce estimated category scores which do not violate known ordinality requirements. That is, if it is known a priori that the first I^* of the I categories are naturally ordered from $1, 2, \ldots, I^*$, then the estimated category scores corresponding to these categories must satisfy the relationship $\mu_1 \leq \mu_2 \leq \ldots \leq \mu_{I^*}$. Third, the model used must fit the data to an acceptable degree. If the model does not fit the data, the association between R and C is more complicated than that which can be described by Goodman's row- and column-effects association models, and the calculation of category scores for the R variable would be wholly unjustified. Fourth, the instrument must be chosen with the best substantive and/or theoretical information available about how the R variable is associated with it. If there are serious theoretical reasons why the relationship between R and C cannot be described by linear-by-linear interaction, this information by itself should force the researcher to cast the instrument aside, even if the first three criteria are satisfied. Finally, it may be advisable to exploit information from more than one in-

---

[12] A related topic of some importance is testing whether $\phi = 0$ under the model of eq. (2). The test statistic for this situation has a rather anomalous sampling distribution (Haberman 1982; Goodman 1981b). As an expedient, I recommend that researchers test initially for association of the row and column variables using the conventional χ^2 test of independence. While this test does not exploit the log-multiplicative model, it does appear to be suitable for practical use. If the researcher does not find strong evidence for association using the conventional χ^2 test, then he or she should be skeptical about the use of the particular instrument to calibrate the ordinal variable. On the other hand, if there is strong evidence for association as judged by application of the conventional test, the researcher can be reasonably assured that (a) ϕ is nonzero and (b) the differences $\mu_{i+1} - \mu_i$ are not all zero. Condition (b) implies that the relevant distances can be estimated.

strumental variable or to exploit a group variable in order to strengthen the inferences. If more than one instrument were available, partial association models could be used to include all the information contained in the complete table describing the (partial) association among items. If a group variable were available, defined so that each group possessed homogeneous category scores on the ordinal variable to be calibrated, this information should certainly be exploited. Such a procedure would allow more opportunity to reject the model and would, thus, strengthen the inferences drawn about distances. Note that the latter strategy was used in the example dealing with the happiness item.

The uses of the log-multiplicative association model surveyed in this paper are only as valid as the assumptions necessary to apply them, and I have tried to address these assumptions explicitly and carefully throughout. Only further work with these methods, involving extensive application to other data, can ultimately attest to the practical utility of the model. I do not believe that the assumptions required for the application of the model are any more stringent than assumptions made in the selection of instrumental variables in causal modeling (e.g., in choosing instrumental variables to identify reciprocal effects, or to identify causal effects of unobservable variables measured with error). I do believe that these methods are a clear improvement over the popular "method" of assuming that ordinal variables are interval level with equal intervals, and it appears that these methods might allow a rapprochement between contingency-table methods for discrete data and linear-model methods for quantitative data.

REFERENCES

Andersen, E. B. 1980. *Discrete Statistical Models with Social Science Applications.* Amsterdam: North-Holland.
Andrews, Frank M., and Aubrey C. McKennell. 1980. "Measures of Self-reported Well-being: Their Affective, Cognitive, and Other Components." *Social Indicators Research* 8:127–55.
Bock, R. Darrell, and George Yates. 1973. *Multiqual: Log-Linear Analysis of Nominal or Ordinal Data by the Method of Maximum Likelihood.* Chicago: National Educational Resources.
Clogg, Clifford C. 1979. "Some Latent Structure Models for the Analysis of Likert-Type Data." *Social Science Research* 8:287–301.
———. 1980. "Some Statistical Models for Analyzing Why Surveys Disagree." Paper prepared for the Panel on the Survey Measurement of Subjective Phenomena of the National Academy of Science, Washington, D.C.
* ———. 1982. "Some Models for the Analysis of Association in Multi-Way Cross-Classifications Having Ordered Categories." *Journal of the American Statistical Association,* forthcoming.
Clogg, Clifford C., and Darwin O. Sawyer. 1981. "A Comparison of Alternative Models for Analyzing the Scalability of Response Patterns." Pp. 240–80 in *Sociological Methodology 1981,* edited by Samuel Leinhardt. San Francisco: Jossey-Bass.
Davis, James A. 1978. *General Social Surveys, 1972–1978: Cumulative Codebook.* Chicago: National Opinion Research Center.

Duncan, Otis Dudley. 1979. "Indicators of Sex Typing: Traditional and Egalitarian, Situational and Ideological Responses." *American Journal of Sociology* 85:251-60.

Goodman, Leo A. 1975. "A New Model for Scaling Response Patterns: An Application of the Quasi-Independence Concept." *Journal of the American Statistical Association* 70:755-68.

* ———. 1979. "Simple Models for the Analysis of Association in Cross-Classifications Having Ordered Categories." *Journal of the American Statistical Association* 74: 537-52.

* ———. 1981a. "Association Models and the Bivariate Normal for Contingency Tables with Ordered Categories." *Biometrika* 68:347-55.

* ———. 1981b. "Association Models and Canonical Correlation in the Analysis of Cross-Classifications Having Ordered Categories." *Journal of the American Statistical Association* 76:320-34.

* ———. 1981c. "Three Elementary Views of Log-Linear Models for the Analysis of Cross-Classifications Having Ordered Categories." Pp. 193-239 in *Sociological Methodology 1981*, edited by Samuel Leinhardt. San Francisco: Jossey-Bass.

Haberman, Shelby J. 1974. "Log-Linear Models for Frequency Tables with Ordered Classifications." *Biometrics* 30:589-600.

———. 1979. *Analysis of Qualitative Data*. Vol. 2, *New Developments*. New York: Academic Press.

———. 1982. "Tests for Independence in Two-Way Contingency Tables Based on Canonical Correlation and on Linear-by-Linear Interaction." *Annals of Statistics* 9:1178-86.

Jöreskog, Karl F., and Dag Sörbom. 1979. *Advances in Factor Analysis and Structural Equation Models*. Cambridge, Mass.: Abt Books.

Kim, Jae-On. 1975. "Multivariate Analysis of Ordinal Variables." *American Journal of Sociology* 81:261-89.

Lazarsfeld, Paul F., and Neil W. Henry. 1968. *Latent Structure Analysis*. Boston: Houghton Mifflin.

Schuman, Howard, and Stanley Presser. 1978. "The Assessment of 'No Opinion' in Attitude Surveys." Pp. 241-75 in *Sociological Methodology 1979*, edited by Karl F. Schuessler. San Francisco: Jossey-Bass.

9.
Applications of Association Models: III

Some Models for the Analysis of Association in Multiway Cross-Classifications Having Ordered Categories

Goodman recently presented a class of models for the analysis of association between two discrete, ordinal variables. The association was measured in terms of the odds ratios in 2×2 subtables formed from adjacent rows and adjacent columns of the cross-classification, and models were devised that allowed the odds ratios to depend on an overall effect, on row effects, on column effects, and on other effects. This article presents some generalizations of this approach appropriate for multiway cross-classifications, including (a) models for the analysis of conditional association, (b) models for the analysis of partial association, and (c) models for the analysis of symmetric association. Three cross-classifications are analyzed with these models and methods, and rather simple interpretations of the association in each are provided.

1. INTRODUCTION

Goodman (1979) recently considered a general class of models for the analysis of association between two discrete, ordinal variables. The approach consisted of constructing a basic set of odds ratios from 2×2 subtables formed from adjacent rows and adjacent columns of the cross-classification. This basic set of odds ratios was then studied from a two-way analysis-of-variance framework, and models were considered which allowed the odds ratios to depend on an overall effect, on row effects, on column effects, and on other effects. This "analysis of association" (ANOAS) approach is related to previous work of Williams (1952), Goodman (1971), Haberman (1974a,b, 1979), Simon (1974), Bock (1975), Fienberg (1980), and Andersen (1980). For some applications of similar models and methods to social science data, see Duncan and McRae (1978), Duncan (1979a), and Clogg (1979a, ch. 6).

The new approach contrasts with the more traditional approach that has the objective of constructing an optimal index of association for the doubly ordered contingency table (e.g., see Clayton 1974; Agresti 1980; Goodman and Kruskal 1979). Instead of assuming that a single index of association is sufficient or desirable for every conceivable cross-classification, the new approach considers the association as something that should be studied within the context of a class of models. A researcher using this modeling procedure might find that a single index is sufficient to describe the association, but might also find that a set of indexes, rather than a single index, is required.

Goodman (1979, pp. 550–551) briefly considered some extensions of his method to the m-way cross-classification ($m = 3, 4, \ldots$). One of these pertained to the analysis of the association in a set of K cross-classifications, each $I \times J$. For the case where the association in each $I \times J$ table could be assumed to be "uniform," for example, he described a chi-squared test of conditional independence that has K degrees of freedom. In this article models are considered that cover other situations of interest in the multivariate case. The topics discussed here are: (a) the analysis of conditional association in a set of K two-way tables, (b) the analysis of partial association in the three-way table, and (c) the analysis of symmetric association (and related concepts) in the three-way table. All of these models generalize without difficulty to the m-way table ($m = 4, 5, \ldots$), but for ease of exposition only three-way tables are considered explicitly herein.

Table 1. Cross-Classification of U.S. Sample According to Their Reported Happiness and Their Years of Schooling, by Sex

	Years of School Completed			
Reported Happiness	<12	12	13–16	17+
Males				
Not too Happy	40	21	14	3
Pretty Happy	131	116	112	27
Very Happy	82	61	55	27
Females				
Not too Happy	62	26	12	3
Pretty Happy	155	156	95	15
Very Happy	87	127	76	15

To illustrate how the models can be used, we apply them to three sets of data taken from the General Social Survey (Davis 1977):

1. A set of two 3 × 4 cross-classifications (Table 1) on the relationship between reported happiness (not too happy, pretty happy, very happy) and completed years of schooling (less than 12, 12, 13–16, 17 or more), by sex of respondent. This table is used to illustrate various models of conditional association.

2. A three-way cross-classification (Table 2) on the relationship among reported happiness, completed years of schooling, and number of siblings (0–1, 2–3, 4–5, 6–7, 8 or more). This example illustrates how models of partial association can be used to obtain a parsimonious description of the association in a rather complex (3 × 4 × 5) contingency table.

3. A three-way cross-classification (Table 3) on the relationship among indicators of satisfaction with life. The three indicators are satisfaction with residence, hobbies, and family, and the category codes are 1 (a fair amount, some, a little, or none), 2 (quite a bit), 3 (a great deal), and 4 (a very great deal). Our models will exploit the special structure of this table in worthwhile ways. For example, the consistent responses (Duncan 1979b)

Table 2. Cross-Classification of U.S. Sample
According to Their Reported Happiness, Years of
Schooling, and Number of Siblings

Years of School Completed	Number of Siblings				
	0–1	2–3	4–5	6–7	8+
Not too Happy					
<12	15	34	36	22	61
12	31	60	46	25	26
13–16	35	45	30	13	8
17+	18	14	3	3	4
Pretty Happy					
<12	17	53	70	67	79
12	60	96	45	40	31
13–16	63	74	39	24	7
17+	15	15	9	2	1
Very Happy					
<12	7	20	23	16	36
12	5	12	11	12	7
13–16	5	10	4	4	3
17+	2	1	2	0	1

will be singled out for special treatment using models for incomplete tables, and the similarity of the category codes of different variables will be exploited.

2. ASSOCIATION MODELS FOR THE $I \times J$ TABLE

To facilitate later generalization, we briefly review the association models for the two-way cross-classification of ordinal variables. Let f_{ij} denote the observed frequency in the ith row and jth column of the table ($i = 1, \ldots, I; j = 1, \ldots, J$), and let F_{ij} denote the corresponding expected frequency under some model. We assume that the overall multinomial distribution describes the variability in the f_{ij}, but some other kinds of sampling models could be assumed as well (such as row or column "product" multinomial models). For 2×2 subtables formed from adjacent rows (rows i and $i + 1$) and

Table 3. Cross-Classification of U.S. Sample
According to Three Indicators of Satisfaction With
Life

L =	R =	C = 1	C = 2	C = 3	C = 4
1	1	76	14	15	4
1	2	32	17	7	3
1	3	64	23	28	15
1	4	41	11	27	16
2	1	15	2	7	4
2	2	27	20	9	5
2	3	57	31	24	15
2	4	27	9	22	16
3	1	13	6	13	5
3	2	12	13	10	6
3	3	46	32	75	20
3	4	54	26	58	55
4	1	7	6	7	6
4	2	7	2	3	6
4	3	12	11	31	15
4	4	52	36	80	101

NOTE: Variables L, R, and C refer to satisfaction with hobbies, family, and residence, respectively. Variable codes are 1 (a fair amount, some, a little, or none), 2 (quite a bit), 3 (a great deal), and 4 (a very great deal).

adjacent columns (columns j and $j + 1$), let

$$\theta_{ij} = (F_{ij}F_{i+1,j+1})/(F_{i,j+1}F_{i+1,j}) \qquad (2.1)$$

denote the corresponding odds ratio. This set of $(I - 1)(J - 1)$ odds ratios is referred to as the *basic set*. Note that the θ_{ij} exploit the ordinal character of the variables, and note that all other odds ratios can be computed from them. See Goodman (1969) and Altham (1970). There are certainly other ways that ordinality can be taken into account (see Plackett 1965; Altham 1970; Fienberg 1980), but the mathematical tractability of this procedure of forming the θ_{ij} appears to be a definite advantage. Each θ_{ij} describes the association present in a particular region of the $I \times J$ table; the θ_{ij} thus measure the local association between the row and column variables.

The models presented by Goodman (1979) are all special cases of two models for the F_{ij}:

$$F_{ij} = \tau_{1(i)}\tau_{2(j)}\alpha_i^j\beta_j^i \qquad (2.2)$$

and

$$F_{ij} = \tau_{1(i)}\tau_{2(j)}\exp(\mu_i \nu_j). \qquad (2.3)$$

For the model in (2.2) we find

$$\theta_{ij} = (\alpha_{i+1}/\alpha_i)(\beta_{j+1}/\beta_j), \qquad (2.4)$$

and for the model in (2.3) we find

$$\log \theta_{ij} = (\mu_{i+1} - \mu_i)(\nu_{j+1} - \nu_j). \qquad (2.5)$$

Model (2.4) can be written as

$$\theta_{ij} = \theta_{i\cdot}\theta_{\cdot j}, \qquad (2.6)$$

a multiplicative row and column effects association model. The model of (2.5) can be written as

$$\log \theta_{ij} = \phi_{i\cdot}\phi_{\cdot j}, \qquad (2.7)$$

producing a different kind of row and column effects association model. While the model in (2.6) is loglinear, the model (2.7) is not, and Goodman referred to the two types as Model I and Model II, respectively. Special cases of the models in (2.6) and (2.7) were described by Goodman (1979). For example, the row effects association model is obtained when $\theta_{\cdot j} = 1$ for all j in (2.6), or when $\phi_{\cdot j} = 1$ for all j in (2.7). Similar comments apply to the column effects model.

Another special case of the models arises in the following way. If in (2.4) $\alpha_{i+1}/\alpha_i = \delta^*$ for all i, $\beta_{j+1}/\beta_j = \delta^{**}$ for all j, then $\theta_{ij} = \delta^* \delta^{**} = \theta$. This is the "uniform" association model, which says that the local association is the same in all regions of the table. This model is equivalent to the model

$$F_{ij} = \tau_{1(i)}\tau_{2(j)}\theta^{ij} \qquad (2.8)$$

for the expected frequencies. The uniform association model is obtained from (2.5) when $\mu_{i+1} - \mu_i = \epsilon^*$ for all i, and $\nu_{j+1} - \nu_j = \epsilon^{**}$ for all j.

An alternative way of writing (2.3) is instructive, namely,

$$F_{ij} = \tau_{1(i)}\tau_{2(j)}\exp(\phi\mu_i\nu_j). \qquad (2.9)$$

We could write $\theta = \epsilon^{\phi}$ and regard the μ_i, ν_j as exponents of θ. In particular, if $\mu_i = i$, $\nu_j = j$, then the uniform association model of (2.8) is obtained. More generally, if the μ_i, ν_j are taken as scores that depict the category intervals of the row and column variable (assumed known), and if the row and column marginals each pertain to discretized univariate normal distributions, then the model bears close resemblance to the discretized bivariate normal distribution (Goodman 1981b). The parameter ϕ in this case can be linked up in a direct way to the correlation coefficient that describes the association between two variables that follow the bivariate normal. When the μ_i, ν_j are regarded as parameters, (2.9) can be taken as a generalization of the bivariate normal. Conditional on the μ_i and ν_j of (2.9), treated as category scores, the association is described by linear-by-linear interaction; conversely, conditional on the hypothesis that the association is described by linear-by-linear interaction, the μ_i, ν_j provide estimates of the category scores (and thus category intervals) that are consistent with this hypothesis. For further details concerning these models, see Goodman (1979, 1981a;b,c), Agresti (1981), and Clogg (1981b).

3. CONDITIONAL ASSOCIATION

3.1. The Models

We now consider models for the association in a cross-classification of two ordinal variables, observed for each K groups. Let f_{ijk} denote the observed frequency in the (i, j) cell of the kth table, and let F_{ijk} denote the corresponding expected frequency, for $i = 1, \ldots, I; j = 1, \ldots, J; k = 1, \ldots, K$. We assume that interest focuses partly on the possible sources of between-group heterogeneity in the association (see, e.g., Fleiss 1972; Goodman 1973; Mantel 1963; Kritzer 1977) and that models are considered which represent various cases of interest and which exploit the ordering of variable categories. The relevant sampling model could now be taken as the product-multinomial, appropriate for the situation where K different IJ-dimensional multinomials are considered. We let

$$\theta_{ij(k)} = (F_{ijk}F_{i+1,j+1,k})/(F_{i,j+1,k}F_{i+1,j,k}), \quad (3.1)$$

for $i = 1, \ldots, I - 1, j = 1, \ldots, J - 1, k = 1, \ldots,$ K, denote the basic set of $K(I - 1)(J - 1)$ conditional odds ratios. The models that we shall consider for the $\theta_{ij(k)}$ are related to the expected frequencies F_{ijk} in the following two ways:

$$F_{ijk} = \tau_{13(ik)}\tau_{23(jk)}\alpha_{i(k)}^{j}\,\beta_{j(k)}^{i} \quad (3.2)$$

or

$$F_{ijk} = \tau_{13(ik)}\tau_{23(jk)}\exp\{\mu_{i(k)}\nu_{j(k)}\}. \quad (3.3)$$

Under (3.2) we find

$$\theta_{ij(k)} = (\alpha_{i+1,(k)}/\alpha_{i(k)})(\beta_{j+1,(k)}/\beta_{j(k)}) \quad (3.4)$$

and under (3.3) we find

$$\log \theta_{ij(k)} = (\mu_{i+1,(k)} - \mu_{i(k)})(\nu_{j+1,(k)} - \nu_{j(k)}). \quad (3.5)$$

(Compare (3.2)–(3.5) with (2.2)–(2.5).) We can rewrite (3.4) as

$$\theta_{ij(k)} = \theta_{i\cdot(k)}\,\theta_{\cdot j(k)} \quad (3.6)$$

and we can rewite (3.5) as

$$\log \theta_{ij(k)} = \phi_{i\cdot(k)}\,\phi_{\cdot j(k)}. \quad (3.7)$$

(In (3.6) and (3.7) the subscripted dots denote that the particular parameters do not depend on the value of the subscripts that they replace. For example, $\theta_{i\cdot(k)}$ is a quantity that does not depend on the subscript j (column level). Similar comments apply to the dot notation used elsewhere in this article.)

Model (3.6) then says that there are row effects on the association that differ by group and that there are column effects on the association that differ by group. We describe this as the *heterogeneous row and column effects* conditional association model. Similar comments apply to (3.5) and (3.7). To differentiate the loglinear model of (3.6) from the model of (3.7), we refer to them as Model I and Model II, respectively. Each of the models that are now enumerated is a special case of (3.2)–(3.3), but for ease of exposition we express them in terms of the $\theta_{ij(k)}$, using parameters like those in (3.6) and (3.7).

The *null conditional association* model is obtained when

$$\theta_{ij(k)} = 1 \qquad\qquad (3.8)$$

for $i = 1, \ldots I - 1; j = 1, \ldots, J - 1; k = 1, \ldots, K$. This model is equivalent to the model of conditional independence, and it has $K(I - 1)(J - 1)$ degrees of freedom. A *homogeneous uniform association* model is obtained when

$$\theta_{ij(k)} = \theta. \qquad\qquad (3.9)$$

This model says that the association in each table is uniform and that this uniform association is homogeneous across groups. A model of *heterogeneous uniform association* is obtained when

$$\theta_{ij(k)} = \theta_{..(k)}. \qquad\qquad (3.10)$$

In considering models with heterogeneous effects on the association, of which (3.10) shall be our simplest example, we have left the heterogeneous effects unrestricted. For example, in (3.10) the $\theta_{..(k)}$ are not restricted in any way; we do not consider cases where, for example, $\theta_{..(k)} = 1$ for some (but not all) k.

A *homogeneous row effect* model is obtained when

$$\theta_{ij(k)} = \theta_{i..}, \qquad\qquad (3.11)$$

which says that there are only row effects on the association, and that these row effects are the same for each of the K groups. This model can be obtained from (3.3) or (3.5) by assuming that the differences $(\nu_{j+1,(k)} - \nu_{j(k)})$ are constant for all j and k, and that the differences

$(\mu_{i+1,(k)} - \mu_{i(k)})$ do not depend on k. A model related to (3.11) is

$$\theta_{ij(k)} = \theta_{\cdot\cdot(k)}\theta_{i\cdot\cdot}, \qquad (3.12)$$

which we designate as the *simple heterogeneous row effect* model. In comparing (3.12) and (3.11), we see that the difference between the homogeneous row effect model and the simple heterogeneous row effect model is that the overall effect on the association is different in each of the K tables with the model in (3.12).

A model related to both (3.11) and (3.12) is the *heterogeneous row effect* model, namely,

$$\theta_{ij(k)} = \theta_{i\cdot(k)}. \qquad (3.13)$$

Model (3.13) allows for heterogeneity both in the overall effects on the association and in the row effects on the association, distinguishing it from the models of (3.11) and (3.12).

Continuing in a similar manner, we arrive at other models of conditional association described in Table 4. For the row-column effects models in lines 5a–5d of Table 4, generalization of Goodman's Model II can be considered as well; for example, the model in line 5a has a counterpart in the model

$$\log \theta_{ij(k)} = \phi_{i\cdot\cdot}\theta_{\cdot j\cdot}.$$

The degrees of freedom for each of the models are also presented in Table 4. These quantities were calculated by subtracting the number of nonredundant θ parameters in the models from $K(I - 1)(J - 1)$, the number of $\theta_{ij(k)}$ in the basic set of conditional odds ratios.

It is interesting to consider the relationship between the models just surveyed and other methods for analyzing conditional association. The hierarchical loglinear models that can be expressed in terms of the fitting of marginals constitute one alternative (see Bishop, Fienberg, and Holland 1975; Goodman 1970, 1973). If R, C, and G refer to the row, column, and group variables, respectively, consider model H_1 fitting marginals $[(RC)\ (RG)\ (CG)]$

Table 4. Degrees of Freedom and Logical Implications of Some Conditional Association Models Applied to a Set of K $I \times J$ Cross-Classifications

Effects on the $\theta_{ij(k)}$		Description	Degrees of Freedom $K(I-1)(J-1)$ minus:	Special Case of Models
1.	1	Null	0	2a–5d
2a.	θ	Homogeneous Uniform	1	2b–5d
2b.	$\theta_{..(k)}$	Heterogeneous Uniform	K	3b–3c, 4b–4c, 5b–5d
3a.	$\theta_{i.}$	Homogeneous Row	$(I-1)$	3b–3c, 5a–5d
3b.	$\theta_{..(k)}\theta_{i..}$	Simple Heterogeneous Row	$K+(I-2)$	3c, 5b–5d
3c.	$\theta_{i.(k)}$	Heterogeneous Row	$K+K(I-2)$	5b, 5d
4a.	$\theta_{.j.}$	Homogeneous Column	$(J-1)$	4b–4c, 5a–5d
4b.	$\theta_{..(k)}\theta_{.j.}$	Simple Heterogeneous Column	$K+(J-2)$	4c, 5b–5d
4c.	$\theta_{.j(k)}$	Heterogeneous Column	$K+K(J-2)$	5c–5d
5a.	$\theta_{i.}, \theta_{.j.}$	Homogeneous Row and Column Effects	$1+(I-2)+(J-2)$	5b–5d
5b.	$\theta_{i.(k)}\theta_{.j.}$	Heterogeneous Row, Homogeneous Column	$K+K(I-2)+(J-2)$	5d
5c.	$\theta_{i.}\theta_{.j(k)}$	Homogeneous Row, Heterogeneous Column	$K+(I-2)+K(J-2)$	5d
5d.	$\theta_{i.(k)}\theta_{.j(k)}$	Heterogeneous Row, Heterogeneous Column	$K+K(I-2)+K(J-2)$	—

and model H_2 fitting marginals $[(RG)\ (CG)]$. Model H_1, which has $(I - 1)(J - 1)(K - 1)$ degrees of freedom, is the model of no three-factor interaction, which is a model of homogeneity. Models with homogeneous effects (models 1, 2a, 3a, 4a, 5a in Table 4) imply that H_1 will be true. Models with heterogeneous effects (models 2b, 3b, 3c, 4b, 4c, 5b, 5c, 5d in Table 4) imply that H_1 will be false. Model H_2, which has $K(I - 1)(J - 1)$ degrees of freedom, is the null conditional association or conditional independence model. The goodness of fit of these two models is often all that is used to assess (a) whether there is association between R and C, unspecified in character (H_2 false), and (b) whether this association is homogeneous (H_1 true) or heterogeneous (H_1 false) across groups. When the categories of the R and C variables are ordered, and when this ordering is taken into account in a way like that of the present section, a much richer approach is obtained.

3.2 Analysis of Table 1

The conditional association models of Section 3.1 were each applied to Table 1 using statistical methods discussed in Section 6. Table 5 presents the corresponding goodness-of-fit and likelihood-ratio chi-squared statistics. The homogeneous row effects model (3a) fits the data quite well, with a likelihood-ratio chi-square of 15.08 on 10 degrees of freedom. The homogeneous row and column effects, row-column effects model (I) fits the data approximately as well (5a), with a likelihood-ratio chi-square of 12.12 on 8 degrees of freedom. The heterogeneous column effects, row-column effects model (I) fits the data remarkably well (5c), with a likelihood-ratio chi-square of 3.67 on 5 degrees of freedom. The difference in chi-squared statistics of these last two models (12.12 − 3.67 = 8.45, 3 df) appears to indicate some heterogeneity in the column effects.

The model that is suggested from Table 5 is (5c), in which $\theta_{ij(k)} = \theta_{i..}\theta_{.j(k)}$. In order to interpret results obtained with this model, we consider the additive form:

Table 5. Conditional Association Models Applied to Table 1

Conditional Association Model	Degrees of Freedom	Goodness-of-Fit Chi-Squared	Likelihood-Ratio Chi-Squared
(1) Null	12	49.70	48.88
(2) Uniform			
(2a) Homogeneous	11	23.68	23.68
(2b) Heterogeneous	10	20.92	20.91
(3) Row Effects			
(3a) Homogeneous	10	15.33	15.08
(3b) Simple Heterogeneous	9	13.36	12.31
(3c) Heterogeneous	8	13.40	12.30
(4) Column Effects			
(4a) Homogeneous	9	19.96	19.98
(4b) Simple Heterogeneous	8	17.31	17.31
(4c) Heterogeneous	6	11.52	11.64
(5) Row and Column Effects (I)			
(5a) Homogeneous	8	12.72	12.12
(5b) Heterogeneous Row	6	10.95	9.27
(5c) Heterogeneous Column	5	3.98	3.67
(5d) Heterogeneous Row and Column	4	3.74	3.40
(6) Row and Column Effects (II)			
(6a) Homogeneous	8	12.16	12.03
(6b) Heterogeneous Row	6	7.52	7.24
(6c) Heterogeneous Column	5	6.16	6.15
(6d) Heterogeneous Row and Column	4	5.93	5.91

$\log \theta_{ij(k)} = \log \theta_{i\cdot\cdot} + \log \theta_{\cdot j(k)} = \lambda_i + \lambda_{j(k)}$. To render the parameters of this model identifiable, we consider the parameterization

$$\log \theta_{ij(k)} = \lambda_{(k)}{}^* + \lambda_i{}^* + \lambda_{j(k)}{}^*,$$

where $\lambda_i{}^* = \lambda_i - \bar{\lambda}_\cdot$, $\lambda_{j(k)}{}^* = \lambda_{j(k)} - \bar{\lambda}_{\cdot(k)}$, and $\lambda_{(k)}{}^* = \bar{\lambda}_\cdot + \bar{\lambda}_{\cdot(k)}$. When this is done, we obtain the following parameter estimates:

overall effects: $\hat{\lambda}_{(1)}{}^* = .32;\ \hat{\lambda}_{(2)}{}^* = .29$
row effects: $\hat{\lambda}_1{}^* = .18;\ \hat{\lambda}_2{}^* = -.18$
male column effects: $\hat{\lambda}_{1(1)}{}^* = -.19;\ \hat{\lambda}_{2(1)}{}^* = -.19;$
$\hat{\lambda}_{3(1)}{}^* = .38$
female column effects: $\hat{\lambda}_{1(2)}{}^* = .31;\ \hat{\lambda}_{2(2)}{}^* = -.15;$
$\hat{\lambda}_{3(2)}{}^* = -.15.$

The association between reported happiness and years of schooling can thus be described in the following way: (a) The association tends to be greatest in the "not too happy" vs. "pretty happy" regions of the table, regardless of sex ($\hat{\lambda}_1{}^* = .18$). (b) For males, the association is the highest when considering the regions "13–16" vs. "17+" on the schooling variable ($\hat{\lambda}_{3(1)}{}^* = .38$), and there appears to be little difference between the "< 12" vs. "12" and the "12" vs. "13–16" schooling contrasts ($\lambda_{1(2)}{}^* = \lambda_{2(1)}{}^* = -.19$, to two decimal places). Thus, for males the most positive relationship between happiness and schooling appears to arise from a contrast between college education and graduate education. (c) For females, the association is the highest when considering the "< 12" vs. "12" contrast on the schooling variable ($\hat{\lambda}_{1(2)}{}^* = .31$), and there appears to be little difference between the regions "12" vs. "13–16" and "13–16" vs. "17+" ($\hat{\lambda}_{2(2)}{}^* = \hat{\lambda}_{3(2)}{}^* = -.15$, to two decimal places).

Line (6c) of Table 5 suggests that the heterogeneous column effects, row-column effect model (II) is also acceptable for these data. Table 6 presents the maximum likelihood estimates of the $\mu_{i(k)}$ and the $\nu_{j(k)}$ under this model. Since row effects on the association are homogeneous under this model, we have $\hat{\mu}_{i(1)} = \hat{\mu}_{i(2)}$ for all i. The differences $\hat{\mu}_{i+1.(k)} - \hat{\mu}_{i(k)}$ can be regarded as the estimates of the distance between categories $i + 1$ and i of the happiness variable, and the model says that these distances do not depend on sex. Thus, there is an estimated distance of .79 between the "not too happy" and the "pretty happy" categories, and there is an estimated distance of .26 between the "pretty happy" and the "very happy" categories. The distance between the first two

Table 6. Parameter Estimates for the Heterogeneous Column Effects, Row-Column Effects Model (II), Applied to Table 1

Parameter	Maximum Likelihood Estimate			
	Males (k = 1)		Females (k = 2)	
$\mu_{1(k)}$	1.35		1.35^a	
$\mu_{2(k)}$	2.14		2.14	
$\mu_{3(k)}$	2.41		2.41	
$\mu_{2(k)} - \mu_{1(k)}$		.79		.79
$\mu_{3(k)} - \mu_{2(k)}$		.26		.26
$\nu_{1(k)}$	2.09		1.78	
$\nu_{2(k)}$	2.45		2.95	
$\nu_{3(k)}$	2.70		3.17	
$\nu_{4(k)}$	3.74		3.04	
$\nu_{2(k)} - \nu_{1(k)}$		.36		1.18
$\nu_{3(k)} - \nu_{2(k)}$		.25		.22
$\nu_{4(k)} - \nu_{3(k)}$		1.04		−.13

[a] Under the model, $\hat{\mu}_{i(1)} = \hat{\mu}_{i(2)}$ for all i.

categories is therefore roughly three times that between the second two categories ($.79/.26 \doteq 3$).

The chi-squared statistics for the models in Table 5 can be used to construct tables that decompose the association into its sources (see Goodman 1973, 1979). If H and H^* are two conditional association models such that H^* includes all of the parameters in H (as well as some others), then $X^2(H) - X^2(H^*)$ provides a measure of the contribution of the additional parameters included in H^* (relative to H), $X^2(H^*)$ is a measure of residual variability, and $X^2(H)$ is a measure of variability to be explained. A sequence of models may be used in the same fashion, so long as the models are properly nested. Table 7a partitions the likelihood-ratio chi-square under models that assume homogeneity in effects to define the first three components. The general effect accounts for 52 percent of the total chi square, and the homogeneous row effects account for another 18 percent. Table 7b presents a similar analysis based on models that allow for heter-

Table 7. Analysis of Conditional Association in Table 1

Effects on Association	Models Used	Degrees of Freedom	Likelihood-Ratio Chi-Squared	Proportion of Total
a. Models With Homogeneous Effects				
General Effect	(1)–(2a)	12 – 11 = 1	25.20	.52
Row Effects	(2a)–(3a)	11 – 10 = 1	8.60	.18
Column Effects, Given Row Effects	(3a)–(5a)	10 – 8 = 2	2.96	.06
Heterogeneous Row and Column Effects	(5a)–(5d)	8 – 4 = 4	8.72	.18
Other Effects	(5d)	4	3.40	.07
Total Effects	(1)	12	48.88	1.01[a]
b. Models With Heterogeneous Effects				
General Effects	(1)–(2b)	12 – 10 = 2	27.97	.57
Row Effects	(2b)–(3c)	10 – 8 = 2	8.63	.18
Column Effects, Given Row Effects	(3c)–(5d)	8 – 4 = 4	8.88	.18
Other Effects	(5d)	4	3.40	.07
Total Effects	(1)	12	48.88	1.00
c. Models With Homogeneous and Heterogeneous Effects				
General Effect	(1)–(2a)	12 – 11 = 1	25.20	.52
Heterogeneous General Effects	(2a)–(2b)	11 – 10 = 1	2.77	.06
Homogeneous Row Effects, Given Heterogeneous General Effects	(2b)–(3b)	10 – 9 = 1	8.60	.18
Heterogeneous Row Effects, Given Homogeneous Row and Heterogeneous General Effects	(3b)–(3c)	9 – 8 = 1	.03	.00
Homogeneous Column Effects, Given Homogeneous Row Effects	(3c)–(5b)	8 – 6 = 2	3.01	.06
Heterogeneous Column Effects, Given Homogeneous Column and Heterogeneous Row Effects	(5b)–(5d)	6 – 4 = 2	5.87	.12
Other Effects	(5d)	4	3.40	.07
Total Effects	(1)	12	48.88	1.01[a]

[a] Total does not equal 1.00 owing to round-off.

ogeneous effects. Here we find that the general effects account for 57 percent of the total association, that row effects account for 18 percent, and that column effects (given row effects) account for another 18 percent. A more detailed table appears in Table 7c, where both the homogeneous-type and the heterogeneous-type models are used. We see that the general (homogeneous) effect accounts for 52 percent of the total association, that homogeneous row effects account for 18 percent, and that heterogeneous column effects account for another 12 percent. It can be noted that results of Tables 7A–7C would lead us to consider the heterogeneous column effects, row-column effect model as a plausible model for these data.

4. PARTIAL ASSOCIATION

4.1 The Models

For the three-way cross-classification of ordinal variables, let f_{ijk} and F_{ijk} denote the observed frequencies and the expected frequencies under some model in cell (i, j, k), for $i = 1, \ldots, I; j = 1, \ldots, J; k = 1, \ldots, K$. To describe the partial association between the row and the column variables, we consider quantities

$$\theta_{ij(k)} = (F_{ijk} F_{i+1,j+1,k})/(F_{i,j+1,k} F_{i+1,j,k}), \quad (4.1)$$

the set of $K(I - 1)(J - 1)$ odds ratios formed from adjacent row and adjacent column categories, for each layer k. Formally, this is identical to (3.1). Sets of quantities $\theta_{i(j)k}$ and $\theta_{(i)jk}$ are defined similarly, pertaining to the row-layer and the column-layer partial association, respectively. We first consider partial association models that are generalizations of Goodman's Model I. Consider a model where

$$F_{ijk} = \tau_{1(i)}\tau_{2(j)}\tau_{3(k)}\alpha_i{}^j\bar{\alpha}_i{}^k\beta_j{}^i\bar{\beta}_j{}^k\gamma_k{}^i\bar{\gamma}_k{}^j. \quad (4.2)$$

Under this model, we find

$$\theta_{ij(k)} = (\alpha_{i+1}/\alpha_i)(\beta_{j+1}/\beta_j), \quad (4.3a)$$

$$\theta_{i(j)k} = (\bar{\alpha}_{i+1}/\bar{\alpha}_i)(\gamma_{k+1}/\gamma_k), \qquad (4.3b)$$

$$\theta_{(i)jk} = (\bar{\beta}_{j+1}/\bar{\beta}_j)(\bar{\gamma}_{k+1}/\bar{\gamma}_k). \qquad (4.3c)$$

These equations can be expressed as

$$\theta_{ij(k)} = \theta_{i..}{}^{RC}\theta_{.j.}{}^{RC}, \qquad (4.4a)$$

$$\theta_{i(j)k} = \theta_{i..}{}^{RL}\theta_{..k}{}^{RL}, \qquad (4.4b)$$

$$\theta_{(i)jk} = \theta_{.j.}{}^{CL}\theta_{..k}{}^{CL}. \qquad (4.4c)$$

Note that the $\theta_{i..}{}^{RC}$, proportional to (α_{i+1}/α_i), pertain to row effects on the partial association between the row and the column variables, while the $\theta_{i..}{}^{RL}$, proportional to $(\bar{\alpha}_{i+1}/\bar{\alpha}_i)$, pertain to row effects on the partial association between the row and layer variables. If the α_i and the $\bar{\alpha}_i$ are not restricted in some way, then the two sets of row effects are allowed to differ. Similar comments apply to the $\theta_{.j.}{}^{RC}$ and the $\theta_{.j.}{}^{CL}$ and to the $\theta_{..k}{}^{RL}$ and the $\theta_{..k}{}^{CL}$. Model (4.2) is a generalization of Goodman's Model I appropriate for the $I \times J \times K$ table, and it is also directly related to the models considered by Haberman (1974b). (For related material, see Landis, Heyman, and Koch 1978). A variety of special cases of the model seems particularly worthwhile; in this section models will be considered that are relevant to studies of partial association, and in Section 5 models will be considered that have symmetric effects.

The null partial association model, equivalent to the model of independence of the row, column, and layer variables, is obtained when all

$$\theta_{ij(k)} = 1, \qquad (4.5a)$$

$$\theta_{i(j)k} = 1, \qquad (4.5b)$$

$$\theta_{(i)jk} = 1. \qquad (4.5c)$$

Several types of uniform partial association models can be considered, and the one where each type of partial association is uniform is obtained when

$$\theta_{ij(k)} = \theta^{RC}, \qquad (4.6a)$$

$$\theta_{i(j)k} = \theta^{RL}, \qquad (4.6b)$$

$$\theta_{(i)jk} = \theta^{CL}. \qquad (4.6c)$$

If in these equations $\theta^{RL} = 1$, $\theta^{CL} = 1$, with θ^{RC} unspecified, we would have the RC-uniform model (with RL and CL partials being null). If $\theta^{CL} = 1$, but θ^{RC} and θ^{RL} were unspecified, we would have the RC- and RL-uniform model (with the CL partial being null).

Various models can now be considered, and we provide several examples. A model with row effects on the RC partials and row effects on the RL partials (with the CL partial being uniform) is

$$\theta_{ij(k)} = \theta_{i\cdot\cdot}{}^{RC}, \qquad (4.7a)$$

$$\theta_{i(j)k} = \theta_{i\cdot\cdot}{}^{RL}, \qquad (4.7b)$$

$$\theta_{(i)jk} = \theta^{CL}. \qquad (4.7c)$$

Similar comments apply to models involving column effects or layer effects on the relevant partial associations.

A model with row effects on the RC and RL partials and with column effects on the RC and CL partials is

$$\theta_{ij(k)} = \theta_{i\cdot\cdot}{}^{RC}\, \theta_{\cdot j\cdot}{}^{RC}, \qquad (4.8a)$$

$$\theta_{i(j)k} = \theta_{i\cdot\cdot}{}^{RL}, \qquad (4.8b)$$

$$\theta_{(i)jk} = \theta_{\cdot j\cdot}{}^{CL}. \qquad (4.8c)$$

The model with row effects, column effects, and layer effects on all relevant partials is the model described by (4.4a)–(4.4c). There are a variety of ways that models could be used in a sequential manner to isolate the sources of the partial association, but we shall assume that these will be obvious at this point. The degrees of freedom associated with some partial association models are presented in Table 8. The degrees of freedom for any special case of the models we have considered can be calculated in a straightforward manner.

Generalization of Goodman's Model II will be consid-

*Table 8. Degrees of Freedom for Some Partial
Association Models Applied to the $I \times J \times K$ Table*

Partial Association Model[a]	Degrees of Freedom ($IJK - I - J - K + 2$ minus)
(1) Null	0
(2) Uniform	
(2a) RC	1
(2b) RC, RL	2
(2c) RC, RL, CL	3
(3) Row Effects and Uniform Effects	
(3a) Row Effects on RC	$(I - 1) + 2$
(3b) Row Effects on RL	$(I - 1) + 2$
(3c) Row Effects on RC, RL	$2(I - 1) + 1$
(4) Column Effects and Row Effects and Uniform Effects	
(4a) Column Effects on RC	$3 + 2(I - 2) + (J - 2)$
(4b) Column Effects on CL	$3 + 2(I - 2) + (J - 2)$
(4c) Column Effects on RC, CL	$3 + 2(I - 2) + 2(J - 2)$
(5) Layer Effects and Row and Column Effects	
(5a) Layer Effects on RC	$3 + 2(I - 2) + 2(J - 2) + (K - 2)$
(5b) Layer Effects on CL	$3 + 2(I - 2) + 2(J - 2) + (K - 2)$
(5c) Layer Effects on RC, CL	$3 + 2(I - 2) + 2(J - 2) + 2(K - 2)$

[a] Models (3a) and (3b) are not nested: neither is a special case of the other, but both are special cases of model (3c) and all models below this one. The same kind of comment applies to models (4a) and (4b) and to models (5a) and (5b).

ered next. The general model will be expressed in terms of the F_{ijk} as

$$F_{ijk} = \tau_{1(i)}\tau_{2(j)}\tau_{3(k)}$$
$$\times \exp(\phi_1\mu_i\nu_j + \phi_2\bar{\mu}_i\xi_k + \phi_3\bar{\nu}_j\bar{\xi}_k). \quad (4.9)$$

Under this model, we find

$$\log\theta_{ij(k)} = \phi_1(\mu_{i+1} - \mu_i)(\nu_{j+1} - \nu_j), \quad (4.10a)$$

$$\log\theta_{i(j)k} = \phi_2(\bar{\mu}_{i+1} - \bar{\mu}_i)(\xi_{k+1} - \xi_k), \quad (4.10b)$$

$$\log \theta_{(i)jk} = \phi_3(\bar{\nu}_{j+1} - \bar{\nu}_j)(\bar{\xi}_{k+1} - \bar{\xi}_k), \quad (4.10c)$$

and the parameters on the right side can be reexpressed in a way similar to that of (4.3a)–(4.3c). For purposes of calculation, it turns out to be preferable to use the parameters ϕ_1, ϕ_2, ϕ_3, but we need not have incorporated these into the expressions. It can be noted that when the differences $(\mu_{i+1} - \mu_i)$, $(\nu_{j+1} - \nu_j)$, . . . , $(\bar{\xi}_{k+1} - \bar{\xi}_k)$ do not depend on i, j, or k, the parameters ϕ_1, ϕ_2, ϕ_3 can be rescaled, and we arrive at the uniform-type model

described by (4.6a)–(4.6c) with $\theta_{ij(k)} = e^{\phi_1}$, $\theta_{i(j)k} = e^{\phi_2}$, and $\theta_{(i)jk} = e^{\phi_3}$.

4.2 Analysis of Table 2

Some of the models of Section 4.1 were applied to Table 2, where for convenience R, C, and L will refer to the schooling, siblings, and happiness variables, respectively. Results appear in Table 9. We see that the model of row (5b), with all possible row and column effects and with layer effects on CL, fits the data well. A model obtained by a standard "stepwise" procedure is provided in row (7), and has only row effects on RC, layer effects on CL, and uniform RL association. With a likelihood-ratio chi-square of 52.33 on 44 degrees of freedom, the model in row (7) appears to be adequate; introducing other effects in this model does not reduce chi-square much more than the reduction in degrees of freedom, so we conclude that this model is acceptable. Thus, a model where

$$\theta_{ij(k)} = \theta_{i\cdot\cdot}{}^{\text{RC}},$$

$$\theta_{i(j)k} = \theta^{\text{RL}},$$

$$\theta_{(i)jk} = \theta_{\cdot\cdot k}{}^{\text{CL}}.$$

is suggested for these data. By expressing parameters in additive form and coding effects in a way similar to that used previously in the analysis of Table 1, we find the following results. For the schooling-sibling partial asso-

Table 9. Some Partial Association Models Applied to Table 2

Partial Association Model	Degrees of Freedom	Goodness-of-Fit Chi-Squared	Likelihood-Ratio Chi-Squared
(1) Null	50	328.56	323.65
(2) Uniform			
(2a) RC	49	104.79	98.46
(2b) RC, RL	48	80.03	73.84
(2c) RC, RL, CL	47	79.60	73.55
(3) Row Effects and Uniform Effects			
(3a) Row Effects on RC	45	63.47	64.49
(3b) Row Effects on RL	45	76.05	69.28
(3c) Row Effects on RC, RL	43	60.00	60.35
(4) Row and Column Effects and Uniform Effects			
(4a) Column Effects on RC	40	57.33	56.99
(4b) Column Effects on CL	40	57.35	57.75
(4c) Column Effects on RC, CL	37	54.21	53.73
(5) Row, Column, and Layer Effects			
(5a) Layer Effects on RL	36	50.11	45.33
(5b) Layer Effects on CL	36	42.08	41.65
(5c) Layer Effects on RL, CL (I)	35	40.87	38.54
(5d) Layer Effects on RL, CL (II)	35	39.70	38.29
(6) Zero Three-Factor Interaction	24	24.30	24.88
(7) Row Effects on RC, Layer Effects on CL, Uniform RL	44	51.70	52.33

ciation, $\log \hat{\theta}_{ij(k)} = \hat{\lambda}^{RC} + \hat{\lambda}_{i}{}^{RC}$, and $\hat{\lambda}^{RC} = -.30$, $\hat{\lambda}_{1..}{}^{RC} = -.16$, $\hat{\lambda}_{2..}{}^{RC} = .03$, $\hat{\lambda}_{3..}{}^{RC} = .13$. The partial association is negative overall, with the strongest relationship in the "< 12" vs. "12" schooling contrast. For the schooling-happiness partial association, $\log \hat{\theta}_{i(j)k} = \hat{\lambda}^{RL}$, with $\hat{\lambda}^{RL} = -.21$. This partial association is thus negative. For the siblings-happiness partial association,

$\log \theta_{(i)jk} = \hat{\lambda}^{CL} + \hat{\lambda}_{..k}^{CL}$, with $\hat{\lambda}^{CL} = .06$, $\hat{\lambda}_{..1}^{CL} = -.14$, $\hat{\lambda}_{..2}^{CL} = +.14$. Thus, this partial association is negative when considering the "not too happy" vs. "pretty happy" contrast on the happiness variable, but positive when considering the "pretty happy" vs. "very happy" contrast on the happiness variable.

The models of partial association can be used in a variety of ways to partition the chi-squared statistic of the null model into components that reflect the sources of the association. Table 10 presents one such analysis of partial association. We see that the uniform effects account for the largest share of the association (77 percent) and inspection of Table 9 indicates that the largest share of this part is accounted for by the RC (schooling-sibling) uniform association.

Generalizations of Goodman's Model II were also considered for Table 2, but in order to save space only one of the those models is considered in Table 9. The chi-squared statistics reported in row (5d) pertain to the model with all possible row, column, and layer effects on the partial association (see (4.9) and (4.10a)–(4.10c), and we see that the model fits the data quite well.

4.3 Partial Association Analysis of Table 3

Table 3 is an example of a cross-classification of ordinal indicators (Clogg 1979b, 1981a) and data of this kind are ubiquitous in social research. In applying partial association models to this table, it is worthwhile to blank out the consistent response patterns $\{(1,1,1), (2,2,2), (3,3,3), (4,4,4)\}$. (The null model applied to the complete table yields a likelihood-ratio chi-square of 544.36 on 54 degrees of freedom, while the null model applied to the incomplete table obtained in this way has a likelihood-ratio chi square of 254.72 on 50 degrees of freedom. Similar reductions in the chi-squared statistics are noted for most of the models that we considered when the incomplete form of Table 3 is used.) The partial association models can be applied to tables with certain cells blanked

Table 10. Analysis of Partial Association in Table 2, Using Some Models in Table 9

Effects on Partial Association	Models Used	Degrees of Freedom	Likelihood-Ratio Chi-Squared	Proportion of Total
Uniform Effects	(1)–(2c)	50 − 47 = 3	250.10	.77
Row Effects, Given Uniform Effects	(2c)–(3c)	47 − 53 = 4	13.20	.04
Column Effects, Given Row Effects	(3c)–(4c)	43 − 37 = 6	6.62	.02
Layer Effects, Given Row and Column Effects	(4c)–(5c)	37 − 35 = 2	15.19	.06
Other Partial Effects	(5c)–(6)	35 − 24 = 11	13.66	.04
Three-Factor Interaction	(6)	24	24.88	.08
Total Effects	(1)	50	323.65	1.01[a]

[a] Total does not equal 1.00 owing to round-off.

out, and standard methods of dealing with the incomplete tables that result can be extended to deal with them (Goodman 1968, 1979a; Bishop, Fienberg, and Holland 1975).

Some of the results obtained by applying the partial association models to Table 3 (with consistent responses deleted) appear in Table 11. The model with only uniform effects produces a dramatic reduction in chi-square relative to the null model, and the model with row effects on the RC and RL partials also seems to be useful. When considering the model with row and column effects and the model with row, column, and layer effects, it is evident that Model II provides a better fit than Model I in each case. The model with all possible row, column, and layer effects (II) yields a likelihood-ratio chi-square of 37.67 on 35 degrees of freedom, and this model would probably be selected as a plausible description of the partial association in Table 3.

5. MODELS FOR SYMMETRIC PARTIAL ASSOCIATION

5.1 The Models

In analyzing the association in square (two-way) tables, in cases where there is a one-to-one correspondence between the row and column categories, the model of quasi-symmetry is often useful. This model says that $\theta_{ij} = \theta_{ji}$. Goodman (1979a) presented two special cases of the quasi-symmetry (or symmetric association) model:

Model I*: $\theta_{ij} = \theta_i \theta_j$

Model II*: $\log \theta_{ij} = \phi_i \phi_j.$

Various types of symmetry and quasi-symmetry models have also been presented for the three-way table (see Bishop, Fienberg, and Holland 1975, pp. 299–309), and in this section some models that are related to these will be discussed. We consider results only for the case of

Model I (see (4.2) and (4.3)); results for Model II follow without difficulty.

Let us consider the model that is described by (4.4a)–(4.4c), a model that allows for row, column, and layer effects on the partial association. In this model, the $\theta_{i..}{}^{RC}$ pertain to the row effects on the RC partial, and the $\theta_{i..}{}^{RL}$ pertain to the row effects on the RL partial. The first model that we consider equates the two kinds of row effects, so that

$$\theta_{i..}{}^{RC} = \theta_{i..}{}^{RL} = \theta_{i..}{}^{R}. \qquad (5.1)$$

We refer to this model as the *homogeneous row effects* model. Note that to define this model it is not necessary for the number of rows to equal the number of columns or the number of layers; there is no need to restrict the model of (5.1) solely to cases where there is a one-to-one

Table 11. *Some Partial Association Models Applied to Table 3, With the Consistent Response Patterns Deleted*

Partial Association Model	Degrees of Freedom	Goodness-of-Fit Chi-Squared	Likelihood-Ratio Chi-Squared
(1) Null	50	273.73	254.72
(2) Uniform Effects	47	103.51	103.95
(3) Row Effects and Uniform Effects	43	68.26	69.64
(4) Column Effects and Row Effects			
(4a) Model I	39	62.24	64.48
(4b) Model II	39	56.52	59.13
(5) Layer Effects and Row and Column Effects			
(5a) Model I	35	55.08	58.27
(5b) Model II	35	37.33	37.67
(6) Zero Three-Factor Interaction	24	21.40	21.93

correspondence between row and column categories or between row and column categories or between row and layer categories. Models of homogeneous column effects and homogeneous layer effects follow immediately, and the model with homogeneous row, column, and layer effects is obtained when each of the following equations is satisfied:

$$\theta_{ij(k)} = \theta_{i\cdot\cdot}{}^{R}\, \theta_{\cdot j\cdot}{}^{C}, \qquad (5.2a)$$

$$\theta_{i(j)k} = \theta_{i\cdot\cdot}{}^{R}\, \theta_{\cdot\cdot k}{}^{L}, \qquad (5.2b)$$

$$\theta_{(i)jk} = \theta_{\cdot j\cdot}{}^{C}\, \theta_{\cdot\cdot k}{}^{L}. \qquad (5.2c)$$

The model described by (5.2a)–(5.2c) is of course merely an extension of the previous models. It is a natural starting place from which to consider models for tables in which there is a one-to-one correspondence between row and column categories, between row and layer categories, and between column and layer categories.

Models of symmetric partial association can be easily devised. A symmetric row-column effects model, defined when $I = J$, is obtained when $\theta_{i\cdot\cdot}{}^{RC} = \theta_{\cdot j\cdot}{}^{RC} = \theta_{i}{}^{RC}$, and for this situation the RC partials can be written as

$$\theta_{ij(k)} = \theta_{i}{}^{RC}\theta_{j}{}^{RC}. \qquad (5.3)$$

Models of symmetric row-layer or symmetric column-layer partial association can be described in an analogous manner. The model with all partials symmetric can be described by

$$\theta_{ij(k)} = \theta_{i}{}^{RC}\theta_{j}{}^{RC}, \qquad (5.4a)$$

$$\theta_{i(j)k} = \theta_{i}{}^{RL}\theta_{k}{}^{RL}, \qquad (5.4b)$$

$$\theta_{(i)jk} = \theta_{j}{}^{CL}\theta_{k}{}^{CL}. \qquad (5.4c)$$

We could, of course, consider the case where $\theta_{i}{}^{RC} = \theta_{i}{}^{RL} = \theta_{i}{}^{R}$, and so on, for this model, combining features of the models (5.1) and (5.2) with those in (5.4).

Continuing in a similar fashion, a model of complete

symmetry can be obtained, where $\theta_{i..}{}^{RC} = \theta_{i..}{}^{RL} = \theta_{.j.}{}^{RC}$ $= \cdots = \theta_{..j}{}^{CL} = \theta_i$. Thus,

$$\theta_{ij(k)} = \theta_i \, \theta_j, \qquad (5.5a)$$

$$\theta_{i(j)k} = \theta_i \, \theta_k, \qquad (5.5b)$$

$$\theta_{(i)jk} = \theta_j \, \theta_k, \qquad (5.5c)$$

describes the model of complete symmetry in the context of the partial-association models of this article. A wide range of possible symmetry-type models can be defined, using the special cases that we have here discussed to motivate other possibilities.

5.2 Symmetric Partial-Association Models Applied to Table 3

We first consider the analysis of Table 3 using models with homogeneous row, column, and/or layer effects (see (5.1) and (5.2)). Since the Model II form appears to be most suitable for these data (see Table 11) we confine our attention to models of this general kind. To justify the consideration of these models, note that the several variants of Model II that we have considered provide information about the category intervals that are necessary to yield linear-by-linear interaction. It appears natural to assume, for example, that estimates of the category intervals of the row variable should be the same when considering the RC partial as when considering the RL partial, and this implies that models with homogeneous row effects should be entertained for this purpose. (Of course, the model should fit the data before it is used to assess category intervals.) Similar comments apply to the estimation of category intervals for the column and layer variables.

Table 12 presents the chi-squared statistics for various kinds of homogeneous row, column, and/or layer effects models, all of which are applied to a model with all possible row, column, and layer effects on the partial association. We find modest evidence for heterogeneous column effects (see row (3)), but the model with all

Table 12. *Some Symmetric Row, Column, and Layer Effects Models (II) Applied to Table 3 (With consistent response patterns deleted)*

Model	Degrees of Freedom	Goodness-of-Fit Chi-Squared	Likelihood-Ratio Chi-Squared
(1) Asymmetric Row, Column, and Layer Effects	35	37.33	37.67
(2) Homogeneous Row Effects	37	38.10	38.31
(3) Homogeneous Column Effects	37	45.96	47.14
(4) Homogeneous Layer Effects	37	38.29	39.16
(5) Homogeneous Row and Column Effects	39	46.63	47.85
(6) Homogeneous Row and Layer Effects	39	38.99	39.76
(7) Homogeneous Column and Layer Effects	39	47.09	48.50
(8) Homogeneous Row, Column, and Layer Effects	41	47.84	49.31
(9) Complete Symmetry	45	75.94	80.55

NOTE: Line (1) here corresponds to line (5b) of Table 11.

homogeneous effects performs adequately (see row (8)). We shall use this model in the next section to develop estimates of the category intervals of the variables in Table 3.

The chi-squared statistics of the model of complete symmetry described by (5.5a)–(5.5c) appears in row (9) of Table 12. Many other variants of these models could, of course, be estimated and tested for the data in Table 3.

5.3 Estimated Category Intervals for the Variables of Table 3

In the previous section, it was found that a model with homogeneous row, column, and layer effects adequately described Table 3, and now we use the parameter estimates from this model to obtain estimates of the category intervals. Note that we are assuming that the data in

Table 3 can be described by linear-by-linear (partial) association (with the consistent responses blanked out), and the estimates of category intervals that we shall obtain are conditional on this hypothesis holding true. Table 13 presents the relevant parameter estimates, where each set of estimates is rescaled to have mean zero and variance one. The parameters ϕ_1, ϕ_2, ϕ_3 were estimated at .17, .33, .22, respectively.

For the residence variable the estimated distance between the first two categories is .32, which is about one-fourth the estimated distance between the second and third categories (1.20) and about one-third the distance between the third and fourth categories (1.00). For the hobbies variable, the estimated distance between the first two categories is nearly zero (.03), while the estimated distances between the second and third categories and between the third and fourth categories are 1.17 and 1.23, respectively. For each of these variables, the estimated distance between the first category (referring to "a fair amount, some, a little, or none") and the second category ("quite a bit") is thus much smaller in magnitude than the other two estimated distances.

For the row variable, referring to satisfaction with family, an apparent anomaly arises in the estimation of category intervals. We find that the estimated distance between the first two categories is *negative* ($-.92$), implying that categories 1 and 2 must be switched. The category codes indicate that this is not feasible. Note that (a) all of these inferences are based on the assumption that the partial association is described by linear-by-linear interaction, given an appropriate determination of category scores, and (b) the analysis is based on the *incomplete* table formed by blanking out consistent responses. See Clogg (1982) for further discussion of these findings.

6. MAXIMUM LIKELIHOOD ESTIMATES

Consider first the conditional association models that are generalizations of Goodman's Model I (see Section

Table 13. Parameter Estimates Under the
Homogeneous Row, Column, and Layer Effects
Model Applied to Table 3 (with Consistent Response
Patterns Deleted)

Parameters	Maximum Likelihood Estimate			
Row (Family) Effects	−.19	−1.11	−.32	1.62
Differences		−.92	.78	1.95
Column (Residence)				
Effects	−1.09	−.77	.43	1.43
Differences		.32	1.20	1.00
Layer (Hobbies)				
Effects	−.92	−.89	.29	1.51
Differences		.03	1.17	1.23

3). The general model can be written as

$$F_{ij(k)} = \tau_{13(ik)} \, \tau_{23(jk)} \, \alpha_{i(k)}{}^{\sigma_j} \, \beta_{j(k)}{}^{\rho_i}, \qquad (6.1)$$

where $\rho_i = i - (I + 1)/2$ and $\sigma_j = j - (J + 1)/2$ denote powers. Since this model is loglinear, the generalized iterative scaling procedure of Darroch and Ratcliff (1972) or the Newton-Raphson method discussed by Haberman (1974a,b, 1979) can be used to obtain maximum likelihood estimates. (Computer programs based on the Newton-Raphson method include MULTIQUAL (Bock and Yates 1973), GLIM (Baker and Nelder 1978), and FREQ (Haberman 1979).) The algorithm that we present is a generalization of the one considered by Goodman (1979); it is based on a successive application of Newton's (one-dimensional) numerical method. Properties of this algorithm that recommend it are: (a) it is faster than the Darroch-Ratcliff algorithm, (b) it requires less computer memory than the Newton-Raphson algorithm, (c) it requires many fewer calculations per cycle than the Newton-Raphson algorithm, and (d) for tables of large dimension, convergence to a solution will generally require less computer time than the Newton-Raphson algorithm.
    The relevant portion of the log-likelihood function is

$$\sum_{i,j,k} f_{ij(k)} \log F_{ij(k)},$$

and the projection theorems described by Haberman (1974b) imply the following system of likelihood equations:

$$f_{i \cdot (k)} - \hat{F}_{i \cdot (k)} = 0, \qquad (6.2a)$$

$$f_{\cdot j(k)} - \hat{F}_{\cdot j(k)} = 0, \qquad (6.2b)$$

$$\sum_j \sigma_j (f_{ij(k)} - \hat{F}_{ij(k)}) = 0, \qquad (6.2c)$$

$$\sum_i \rho_i (f_{ij(k)} - \hat{F}_{ij(k)}) = 0, \qquad (6.2d)$$

where $f_{i \cdot (k)} = \sum_j f_{ij(k)}$, $f_{\cdot j(k)} = \sum_i f_{ij(k)}$, $\hat{F}_{ij(k)}$ denotes the maximum likelihood estimate of $F_{ij(k)}$, $\hat{F}_{i \cdot (k)} = \sum_j \hat{F}_{ij(k)}$, and $\hat{F}_{\cdot j(k)} = \sum_i \hat{F}_{ij(k)}$. Using circumflexes to denote maximum likelihood estimates, from (6.1) we obtain

$$\hat{F}_{ij(k)} = \hat{\tau}_{13(ik)} \, \hat{\tau}_{23(jk)} \, \hat{\alpha}_{i(k)}{}^{\sigma_j} \, \hat{\beta}_{j(k)}{}^{\rho_i}. \qquad (6.3)$$

At any given cycle in the iterative procedure, let $\tau_{13(ik)}{}^*$, $\tau_{23(jk)}{}^*$, $\alpha_{i(k)}{}^*$, $\beta_{j(k)}{}^*$ denote trial values. The iterative procedure produces new trial values in the following manner. First, the $\tau_{13(ik)}{}^*$ are replaced by new trial values by calculating

$$\tau_{13(ik)}{}^{**} = \tau_{13(ik)}{}^* \, f_{i \cdot (k)} / F_{i \cdot (k)}{}^*, \qquad (6.4a)$$

where $F_{i \cdot (k)}{}^* = \sum_j F_{ij(k)}{}^*$ and where the $F_{ij(k)}{}^*$ are calculated by using a formula like (6.3), with the quantities on the right side replaced by the corresponding trial values. With the $\tau_{13(ik)}{}^{**}$ replacing the original trial values $\tau_{13(ik)}{}^*$, the $F_{ij(k)}{}^*$ are recalculated, and new trial values for the $\tau_{23(jk)}{}^*$ are obtained by calculating

$$\tau_{23(jk)}{}^{**} = \tau_{23(jk)}{}^* \, f_{\cdot j(k)} / F_{\cdot j(k)}{}^*. \qquad (6.4b)$$

The $F_{\cdot j(k)}{}^*$ are computed in a manner similar to that used to compute $F_{i \cdot (k)}{}^*$. The $F_{ij(k)}{}^*$ are recalculated using the new trial values $\tau_{23(jk)}{}^{**}$ (replacing $\tau_{23(jk)}{}^*$), and new trial values for $\alpha_{i(k)}{}^*$ are calculated using

$$\alpha_{i(k)}{}^{**} = \alpha_{i(k)}{}^* \{1 + [\sum_j \sigma_j (f_{ij(k)} - F_{ij(k)}{}^*)]/$$

$$[\sum_j \sigma_j^2 F_{ij(k)}{}^*]\}. \quad (6.4c)$$

The $F_{ij(k)}^*$ are now recalculated (replacing the $\alpha_{i(k)}^*$ by the $\alpha_{i(k)}^{**}$), and new trial values for the $\beta_{j(k)}^*$ are calculated using

$$\beta_{j(k)}^{**} = \beta_{j(k)}^* \{1 + [\sum_i \rho_i (f_{ij(k)} - F_{ij(k)}^*)]/$$

$$[\sum_i \rho_i^2 F_{ij(k)}^*]\}. \quad (6.4d)$$

With this step completed, the $F_{ij(k)}^*$ are recalculated (replacing the $\beta_{j(k)}^*$ by the $\beta_{j(k)}^{**}$), and the cycle described by (6.4a)–(6.4d) is repeated. This procedure is continued until the $F_{ij(k)}^*$ satisfy the likelihood equations (6.2a)–(6.2d).

This iterative procedure is an application of Newton's one-dimensional iterative procedure. To see why this is the case, consider the likelihood equation (6.2c), pertaining to $\hat{\alpha}_{i(k)}$, and the corresponding equation (6.4c), which provides an improved solution for the root $\hat{\alpha}_{i(k)}$ of this equation, given trial values $\alpha_{i(k)}^*$. Substituting (6.3) into (6.2c) and taking the first derivative with respect to $\hat{\alpha}_{i(k)}$ yields ($\sum_j \sigma_j^2 \hat{F}_{ij(k)}$)/$\hat{\alpha}_{i(k)}$, and this derivative would be approximated by substituting $F_{ij(k)}^*$ for $\hat{F}_{ij(k)}$ and $\alpha_{i(k)}^*$ for $\hat{\alpha}_{i(k)}$. The inverse of this approximation to the derivative appears in Newton's algorithm, and this explains how the denominator of (6.4c) is obtained. Each of the equations (6.4a)–(6.4d) was derived in an analogous manner.

The iterative procedure in the form just discussed provides maximum likelihood estimates for the heterogeneous row and column effects model. To consider the homogeneous row effects model, (6.4c) is replaced by

$$\alpha_i^{**} = \alpha_i^* \{1 + [\sum_{j,k} \sigma_j (f_{ij(k)} - F_{ij(k)}^*)]/$$

$$[\sum_{j,k} \sigma_j^2 F_{ij(k)}^*]\}. \quad (6.5)$$

A similar kind of modification is made for the $\beta_{j(k)}^{**}$ in (6.4d) when the homogeneous column effects model is considered. To consider models with uniform effects on the conditional association, it is desirable to reparameterize the model being considered. For example, the model with heterogeneous uniform effects can be written as

$$F_{ij(k)} = \tau_{13(ik)}\tau_{23(jk)}\theta_{\cdot\cdot(k)}{}^{p_i r_j}.$$

and the model with homogeneous uniform effects can be written in the same way with $\theta_{\cdot\cdot(k)} = \theta$ for all k. With the model written in this form, a straightforward modification of the iterative procedure can be made.

The conditional association models that are generalizations of Goodman's Model II can be considered with an iterative procedure analogous to the one presented here (see Goodman 1979a). It should be noted that Model II, as well as all of the various generalizations of it that we have considered, is not loglinear. This means that Haberman's projection theorems cannot be directly applied in order to obtain the likelihood equations. However, results of Birch (1965) can be applied to obtain these equations.

A generalization of the iterative procedure to contingency tables of any size follows without difficulty. Suppose that a multiplicative model for the expected frequencies contains a term $\alpha_r{}^{g(s)}$, where α_r is some set of parameters, r is some set of indexes of the variables of the table, and $g(s)$ is some power (dependent on some set s of indexes of the table). The likelihood equation for α_r would be of the general form

$$\sum_{s^*} g(s)(f_q - \hat{F}_q) = 0, \tag{6.6}$$

where q represents the full set of indexes of the variables in the table, and $s \subseteq s^*$. The first derivative of this expression with respect to $\hat{\alpha}_r$ is

$$-[\sum_{s^*} (g(s))^2 \hat{F}_q]/\hat{\alpha}_r \tag{6.7}$$

whenever r is not contained in s^*, and so Newton's method would lead us to calculate

$$\alpha_r^{**} = \alpha_r^* + \alpha_r^* \{[\sum_{s^*} g(s)(f_q - F_q^*)]/$$

$$[\sum_{s^*} (g(s))^2 F_q^*]\}, \quad (6.8)$$

where α_r^* is some trial value, F_q^* is the trial value of $\hat{F}_q$ calculated by using α_r^* (as well as the trial values for other parameters in the model), and α_r^{**} denotes the new trial value. If the power $g(s)$ of $\alpha_r^{g(s)}$ is equal to one, then (6.8) reduces to

$$\alpha_r^{**} = \alpha_r^* (\sum_{s^*} f_q)/(\sum_{s^*} F_q^*), \quad (6.9)$$

which is a general expression for one of the iterative procedures discussed by Goodman (1972), analogous in most respects to the Deming-Stephan algorithm (Goodman 1970; Haberman 1974b). To estimate the $\alpha_{i(k)}$ of (6.1) for the homogeneous row effects model (where $\alpha_{i(k)} = \alpha_i$), we have $s = \{j\}$, $g(s) = \sigma_j$, $s^* = \{(j, k)\}$, and $q = \{(i, j, k)\}$. (See (6.5).) The general expression (6.8) can be used to derive the complete iterative procedure for all of the models that we have considered, including the partial association and the symmetric partial association models (if these models are in the form of Goodman's Model I). It can be used as well, when modified in straightforward ways, to derive an iterative procedure for models that are in the form of Model II.

REFERENCES

AGRESTI, ALAN (1980), "Generalized Odds Ratios for Ordinal Data," *Biometrics*, 36, 59–67.

―――― (1981), "A Survey of Strategies for Modelling Cross-Classifications Having Ordinal Categories," unpublished manuscript.

ALTHAM, P.M.E. (1970), "The Measurement of Association of Rows and Columns for an R × C Contingency Table," *Journal of the Royal Statistical Society*, Ser. B, 32, 63–73.

ANDERSEN, E.B. (1980), *Discrete Statistical Models With Social Science Applications*, Amsterdam: North-Holland.

BAKER, R.J., and NELDER, J.A. (1978), *General Linear Interactive Modeling*, Release 3, Oxford: Numerical Algorithms Group.

BIRCH, M.W. (1965), "The Detection of Partial Association, II: The General Case," *Journal of the Royal Statistical Society*, Ser. B, 27, 111–124.

BISHOP, Y., FIENBERG, S., and HOLLAND, P. (1975), *Discrete Multivariate Analysis*, Boston: MIT Press.

BOCK, R.D. (1975), *Multivariate Statistical Methods in Behavioral Research*, New York: McGraw-Hill.

BOCK, R.D., and YATES, G. (1973), *MULTIQUAL: Log-Linear Analysis of Nominal or Ordinal Qualitative Data by the Method of Maximum Likelihood*, Chicago: National Educational Resources.

CLAYTON, D.G. (1974), "Some Odds Ratio Statistics for the Analysis of Ordered Categorical Data," *Biometrika*, 61, 525–531.

CLOGG, C.C. (1979a), *Measuring Underemployment: Demographic Indicators for the United States*, New York: Academic Press.

——— (1979b), "Some Latent Structure Models for the Analysis of Likert-Type Data," *Social Science Research*, 8, 287–301.

——— (1981a), "New Developments in Latent Structure Analysis," in *Factor Analysis and Measurement in Sociological Research*, eds. D.M. Jackson and E.F. Borgatta, Beverly Hills: Sage Publications, 215–246.

——— (1981b), "Some Statistical Models for Analyzing Why Surveys Disagree," Paper prepared for the Panel on the Survey Measurement of Subjective Phenomena, National Research Council, National Academy of Science.

* ——— (1982), "Using Association Models in Sociological Research: Some Examples," *American Journal of Sociology*, 88, 114–134.

DARROCH, J.N., and RATCLIFF, D. (1972), "Generalized Iterative Scaling for Log-Linear Models," *Annals of Mathematical Statistics*, 43, 1470–1480.

DAVIS, J.A. (1977), *Codebook for the 1977 General Social Survey*, Chicago: National Opinion Research Center.

DUNCAN, O.D. (1979a), "How Destination Depends on Origin in the Occupational Mobility Table," *American Journal of Sociology*, 84, 793–803.

——— (1979b), "Indicators of Sex Typing: Traditional and Egalitarian, Situational and Ideological Responses," *American Journal of Sociology*, 85, 251–260.

DUNCAN, O.D., and McRAE, J.A. (1978), "Multiway Contingency Analysis With a Scaled Response or Factor," in *Sociological Methodology 1979*, ed. K.F. Schuessler, San Francisco: Jossey-Bass, 66–85.

FIENBERG, S.E. (1980), *The Analysis of Cross-Classified Categorical Data* (2nd ed.), Cambridge, Mass.: MIT Press.

FLEISS, J.L. (1972), *Statistical Methods for Rates and Proportions*, New York: John Wiley.

*GOODMAN, L.A. (1968), "The Analysis of Cross-Classified Data: Independence, Quasi-Independence, and Interactions in Contingency Tables With or Without Missing Entries," *Journal of the American Statistical Association*, 63, 1091–1131.

* ——— (1969), "How to Ransack Social Mobility Tables and Other

Kinds of Cross-Classifications," *American Journal of Sociology*, 75, 1-39.

——— (1970), "The Multivariate Analysis of Qualitative Data: Interactions Among Multiple Classifications," *Journal of the American Statistical Association*, 65, 226-256.

——— (1971), "The Analysis of Multidimensional Contingency Tables: Stepwise Procedures and Direct Estimation Methods for Building Models for Multiple Classifications," *Technometrics*, 13, 33-61.

*——— (1972), "Some Multiplicative Models for the Analysis of Cross-Classified Data," in *Proceedings of the Sixth Berkeley Symposium on Mathematical Statistics and Probability*, eds. L. Le Cam et al., Berkeley: University of California Press.

——— (1973), "Guided and Unguided Methods for the Selection of Models for a Set of T Multidimensional Contingency Tables," *Journal of the American Statistical Association*, 68, 165-175.

*——— (1979), "Simple Models for the Analysis of Association in Cross-Classifications Having Ordered Categories," *Journal of the American Statistical Association*, 74, 537-552.

*——— (1981a), "Association Models and Canonical Correlation in the Analysis of Cross-Classifications Having Ordered Categories," *Journal of the American Statistical Association*, 76, 320-334.

*——— (1981b), "Association Models, the Bivariate Normal, and Yule-Plackett Association in the Analysis of Cross-Classifications Having Ordered Categories," *Biometrika*, 68, 347-355.

*——— (1981c), "Three Elementary Views of Log-Linear Models for the Analysis of Cross-Classifications Having Ordered Categories," in *Sociological Methodology 1981*, ed. S. Leinhardt, San Francisco: Jossey-Bass, 193-239.

GOODMAN, L.A., and KRUSKAL, W.H. (1979), *Measures of Association for Cross-Classifications*, New York: Springer-Verlag.

HABERMAN, S.J. (1974a), "Log-Linear Models for Frequency Tables With Ordered Classifications," *Biometrics*, 30, 589-600.

——— (1974b), *The Analysis of Frequency Data*, Chicago: University of Chicago Press.

——— (1979), *Analysis of Qualitative Data: Vol. 2. New Developments*, New York: Academic Press.

KRITZER, H.M. (1977), "Analyzing Measures of Association Derived from Contingency Tables," *Sociological Methods and Research*, 5, 387-418.

LANDIS, J.R., HEYMAN, E.R., KOCH, G.G. (1978), "Average Partial Association in Three-Way Tables: A Review and Discussion of Alternative Tests," *International Statistical Review*, 46, 237-254.

MANTEL, N. (1963), "Chi-Square Tests With One Degree of Freedom: Extensions of the Mantel-Haenszel Procedure," *Journal of the American Statistical Association*, 58, 690-700.

PLACKETT, R.L. (1965), "A Class of Bivariate Distributions," *Journal of the American Statistical Association*, 60, 516-522.

SIMON, GARY (1974), "Alternative Analyses for the Singly-Ordered Contingency Table," *Journal of the American Statistical Association*, 69, 971-976.

WILLIAMS, E.J. (1952), "Use of Scores for the Analysis of Association in Contingency Tables," *Biometrika*, 39, 274-289.

APPENDIX A
Independence Models
The Analysis of Cross-Classified Data:
Independence, Quasi-Independence, and
Interactions in Contingency Tables with or
without Missing Entries

1. INTRODUCTION AND SUMMARY

LET ME begin this lecture on the analysis of cross-classified data, in commemoration of Sir Ronald Fisher, by noting that this is a topic to which Fisher made important contributions at various times during a span of forty years, as early as 1922 and as late as 1962, three months before his death (see, e.g., [17] to [24]). Since Fisher's interest in contingency tables arose in the early days of his statistical career and continued to the end of his life, it would seem particularly appropriate to devote a Memorial Lecture to this topic. Having gained much from Fisher's work, I shall look at this topic from a point of view that is different from, though not inconsistent with, his point of view.

261

I shall distinguish between two different kinds of contingency tables: (A) "truncated" contingency tables in which the entries (frequencies) in some of the cells of the table are omitted from the analysis (because they are either missing, unreliable, void, or restricted in certain ways); and (B) the more usual contingency tables in which none of the cells of the table are omitted. For examples of truncated tables, which I shall discuss more fully later, see Tables 1, 7, 10; for a non-truncated table, see Table 3.

We shall see that various methods which are suited to the analysis of the more usual non-truncated tables will lead (when appropriately modified) to methods suited to the analysis of truncated tables, and that, conversely, various methods which are suited to the analysis of truncated tables will lead (when appropriately extended) to methods suited to the analysis of non-truncated tables. The study of truncated contingency tables might appear at first sight to be a topic of rather limited interest, but we shall see that these kinds of tables can arise in a rather wide range of contexts, and more importantly that their analysis leads us to some new proposals for the analysis of the more usual non-truncated contingency tables.

For the usual $R \times C$ non-truncated contingency table (i.e., the non-truncated contingency table with R rows and C columns), it is common practice to calculate Karl Pearson's chi-square statistic for testing the null hypothesis of independence in the table, using the appropriate number of degrees of freedom first suggested by Fisher [19]; viz., $(R-1)(C-1)$. It will, however, often prove worthwhile to supplement or replace this overall test of independence by a variety of more detailed kinds of analyses (see, e.g., Cochran [12, 13], Goodman [33, 34]). To the presently available methods, I shall now add some new methods of analysis, one of which is the following two-step procedure (which will be described at this point in the lecture only in general terms, to be clarified by the end of the lecture). As the first step in this procedure, on the basis of prior considerations, the researcher might remove from the $R \times C$ table the entries in certain cells for which he suspects either row-column affinities or disaffinities (affinities leading possibly to unusually high values in those cells, or disaffinities leading possibly to unusually low values), and then he might analyze the table thus truncated by methods suited to truncated tables. As a second step, assuming that the cells that might exhibit row-column affinities or disaffinities had been removed from the table at the first step (an assumption which is tested at the first step), the researcher might then focus attention on the analysis of the suspected affinities and disaffinities (or a subset of them) which he had removed from the table at the first step, analyzing them by methods which take into account information gained in the first-step analysis of the truncated table. (If all the suspected affinities and disaffinities which were removed in step one were not considered in step two, the researcher might proceed (in some cases) to a third step in which the remaining suspected affinities and disaffinities (or a subset of them) are analyzed. Et cetera.)

In order to clarify what I have in mind, I shall begin at the beginning, with a definition of the usual concept of "independence" in an $R \times C$ population cross-classification table. This concept can be defined in various ways, and for our present development of the subject it will be convenient to proceed as follows. Let p_{ij} be the proportion of individuals in the $R \times C$ population table that fall in the ith row and jth column ($i = 1, 2, \cdots, R$; $j = 1, 2, \cdots, C$) of the table. Then the row and column classifications of the table are defined as "independent" if the proportions p_{ij} can be written as

$$p_{ij} = a_i b_j \qquad \text{(for } i = 1, 2, \cdots, R; j = 1, 2, \cdots C), \qquad (1.1)$$

for a set of positive constants a_i (for $i = 1, 2, \cdots, R$) and b_j (for $j = 1, 2, \cdots, C$). When (1.1) is satisfied, the a_i can be interpreted as the proportion of individuals who are in the ith row of the population table (when the a_i have been normalized so that $\Sigma_i a_i = 1$), and a similar interpretation can be given to the b_j. (If some rows or columns are empty, we consider the table consisting of the non-empty rows and columns.) I shall now present a modification or generalization of the concept of independence.

In the preceding definition, (1.1) applied to the $R \times C$ proportions $p_{ij}(i = 1, 2, \cdots, R; j = 1, 2, \cdots, C)$; i.e., it applied to all $R \times C$ cells in the table. Let us now consider a given subset S of the $R \times C$ cells; e.g., (a) all cells except one particular cell, or (b) all cells except those in the main diagonal (that is, all non-diagonal cells), or (c) all cells except those above the main diagonal, etc. For the subset S, the row and column classifications of the table are defined as "quasi-independent" (or "S-independent") if the proportions p_{ij} can be written as

$$p_{ij} = a_i b_j \qquad \text{(for all cells } (i, j) \text{ in } S), \qquad (1.2)$$

for a set of positive constants a_i and b_j.

This concept of "quasi-independence" is useful in analyzing tables for which some of the cells are truncated (viz., the cells not included in S); and also in analyzing the more usual kinds of cross-classification tables since it leads to methods that focus attention in turn on various subsets of the entire table, making possible a more detailed analysis of the association between the row and column classifications in the table.

To return for a moment to the usual test of independence (i.e., the test of (1.1) with $(R-1)(C-1)$ degrees of freedom), we see that it attempts to answer a single question which can (and often should) be divided into a sequence of questions which could be answered in turn. For example, this single question (do the proportions p_{ij} satisfy (1.1) for all $R \times C$ cells in the table?) can be divided into the following two parts: (a) Do the proportions p_{ij} satisfy (1.2) for a given subset S of the cells in the table, and if so what are the numerical values of the constants a_i and b_j that are obtained? (b) Given that the p_{ij} satisfy (1.2) for the cells in S, do the p_{ij} satisfy (1.2) for the cells that are not included in S, using the constants obtained in answering question (a)? In a similar way, the question pertaining to independence in the $R \times C$ table can be divided into a sequence of three or more questions.

Question (a) can be answered by methods suited to the analysis of contingency tables that are truncated so as to include only the cells in the subset S. I shall illustrate the various methods presented in this lecture for analyzing truncated contingency table by reexamining the different kinds of examples that have appeared in the literature.

Two of our examples first appeared in a dispute between Karl Pearson [60, 61] and J. Arthur Harris [42, 43, 44] concerning contingency tables. Pearson [60] replied to two earlier articles by Harris [42, 43], who then replied [44] to Pearson, who in turn replied in a postscript [61], which then stood unanswered due to the untimely death of Professor Harris. The methods which I shall present for analyzing the kinds of examples cited in this debate differ from both those advocated by Pearson and those advocated by Harris. (Some of my criticisms of Pearson's methods for analyzing truncated tables are similar in point of view, though not in detail, to Fisher's criticism ([17]–[21]) of Pearson's methods for analyzing non-truncated tables. Considering Fisher's various criticisms of Pearson's remarkable work, isn't it appropriate that we should find in a Fisher Memorial Lecture that still another set of methods proposed by Pearson requires emendation?) In addition to the examples cited by Pearson and Harris. I shall also re-examine the kinds of examples considered earlier by Watson [65] and Kastenbaum [48], and shall introduce some alternative methods of analysis which are somewhat simpler to apply than those presented by these earlier writers.

After discussing the particular kinds of examples that have appeared in the literature, I shall then consider more generally the analysis of quasi-independence in truncated contingency tables. For the more general case, in order to calculate the expected frequencies in the cells under the null hypothesis of quasi-independence, different iterative techniques have been proposed by Watson [65], Goodman [30, 32], and Caussinus [9]. More recently, not knowing of Caussinus' work [9], Fienberg [16] has proposed the same iterative technique as Caussinus. The iterative method which I shall present here is essentially the same as that given in my earlier article [32] (except that the starting point for the iterations will, in some cases, be slightly different from my earlier starting point). This method requires less arithmetic calculations than the Caussinus-Fienberg method, and it is also easier to apply in the general case than the Watson [65] method.

The simpler methods presented here might encourage researchers to raise questions concerning quasi-independence with respect to row and column classifications in substantive fields of research in which the question has not come up heretofore. I shall give here only one example (although there are many) of such fields of research, for which the question of quasi-independence should have substantive meaning; viz., the study of the effects of birth-order on the incidence of a condition, say a disease condition.

Various techniques have been developed for the study of birth-order effects in the case where the researcher has ascertained the birth-order and sibship-size (number of siblings in the family) for a random sample of affected individuals (see, e.g., Mantel and Halperin [56]). In this case, the data obtained form a truncated contingency table where the rows and columns of the table denote birth-order and sibship-size, respectively. (The truncated table is triangular since an individual's birth-order cannot exceed his sibship-size.) The techniques which are used at present for studying birth-order effects analyze this kind of truncated table in order to determine if the incidence of a disease condition is affected by the birth-order of the individuals; but these particular techniques cannot be used to determine (in cases where a birth-order effect is noted) if the effect of birth-order is itself "independent," in a certain sense, of the sibship size (i.e., if there is no "interaction" between the effects of birth-order and the effect of sibship size). In studying disease conditions in which there are birth-order effects, the methods we shall present could be used to re-examine truncated tables of this kind in order to determine if birth-order and sibship-size are "quasi-independent."

For other examples of fields of research for which the concepts and methods presented here are (or could be) of value, see, e.g., Batschelet [5], Blumen, Kogan and McCarthy [8], Caussinus [9], Chen, Crittenden, Mantel and Cameron [11], Goodman [29, 30, 37, 38], Kastenbaum [48], Savage and Deutsch [62], Waite [64], and White [66].

For the non-truncated cross-classification table, if the rows and columns are not independent, it will often be of interest to estimate what are the kinds of interaction or association present in the table, and what are their magnitudes. Similarly, for the truncated table, if the rows and columns are not quasi-independent, it will also be of interest to estimate what are the kinds of interaction present in the table, and what are their magnitudes. I shall include in this lecture some discussion of the estimation of the interactions present in such truncated and non-truncated tables.

Most of the methods presented here can be applied to the analysis of "quasi-homogeneity" among R multinomial populations as well as to the analysis of "quasi-independence" in $R \times C$ cross-classification tables. In order to see what I mean by "quasi-homogeneity," let us for the moment consider the $R \times C$ population cross-classification table as a set of R multinomial populations. Each of the R rows of the table will be considered as a multinomial population in which there are C classes. For the ith multinomial population $(i = 1, 2, \cdots, R)$, the proportion of individuals in the jth class $(j = 1, 2, \cdots, C)$ is

$$P_{ij} = p_{ij}/p_{i\cdot}. \tag{1.3}$$

where $p_{i\cdot} = \sum_j p_{ij}$. Note that $\sum_j P_{ij} = 1$, for $i = 1, 2, \cdots, R$. When there is independence in the cross-classification table (i.e., when (1.1) is satisfied), then

$$P_{ij} = b_j / \sum_{k=1}^{c} b_k, \qquad \text{for } i = 1, 2, \cdots, R. \tag{1.4}$$

Thus, when there is independence, the b_j can be interpreted as the proportion of individuals in the jth class of the ith population (once the b_j have been normalized so that $\sum_j b_j = 1$), and the same proportion applies to each of the R multinomial populations $(i = 1, 2, \cdots, R)$. In other words, when there is independence, the R multinomial populations are "homogeneous," as is well-known.

Let us now consider the situation in which there is independence in the population $R \times C$ table, but the proportions of individuals in certain cells in the table cannot be ascertained. Considering only the subset S of cells for which the corresponding proportions of individuals can be ascertained (making void the cells not contained in S), we see from (1.2) and (1.3) that

$$P_{ij} = \delta_{ij} b_j / \sum_k \delta_{ik} b_k, \qquad \text{for } i = 1, 2, \cdots, R, \tag{1.5}$$

where $\delta_{ij} = 1$ for all cells (i, j) in the subset S, and $\delta_{ij} = 0$ otherwise. Thus, when there is quasi-independence with respect to S, the b_j can be interpreted as the hypothetical proportion of individuals in the jth class of the ith population (when the b_j have been normalized so that $\sum_j b_j = 1$) in the hypothetical situation in which none of the classes in the ith population needs to be void, and the same hypothetical proportion applies to each of the R multinomial populations ($i = 1, 2, \cdots, R$). The R multinomial populations will be defined as "quasi-homogeneous" (with respect to S) when (1.5) applies. With this definition we see that when there is quasi-independence in the $R \times C$ cross-classification, the R multinomial populations will be quasi-homogeneous.

The methods presented here can be used to test the null hypothesis that the R multinomial populations are quasi-homogeneous, and they can also be used to estimate the hypothetical proportions b_j (for $j = 1, 2, \cdots, C$). In the case of quasi-homogeneity, the estimated value of b_j estimates what the proportion in the jth class would have been if none of the classes had been void and if the populations had been homogeneous (see, e.g., Sec. 2.3). Similarly, in analyzing the $R \times C$ cross-classification table, the methods presented here can be used to test the null hypothesis of quasi-independence, and (in the case of quasi-independence) they can also be used to estimate what the hypothetical proportion would have been in the ith row and jth column of the table if none of the cells had been void, and if the rows and columns of the table had been independent (see, e.g., Sec. 2.3 below, and [38]).

The methods which I shall present are appropriate for the case where neither the row marginals nor the column marginals are fixed (i.e., where a simple random sample is drawn from a cross-classified population), and they are also appropriate (except where indicated) for the case where either the row marginals or the column marginals (but not both) are fixed (i.e., sampling from the populations that correspond to either the rows or the columns).

I shall also consider, in passing, the analysis of cross-classification tables in which the entries in certain neighboring cells of the table have been combined or "mixed-up." We shall see that one of the methods presented here (for analyzing non-truncated tables and certain kinds of truncated tables) can also be used to simplify the analysis of the tables (with combined or mixed-up entries) that have been discussed in the earlier literature on this topic (see Sec. 3 below).

The preceding remarks pertain to the analysis of a given $R \times C$ table (or a given set of R (or C) multinomial populations). I shall also comment briefly in this lecture on the analysis and comparison of two (or more) $R \times C$ cross-classification tables.

2. SOME EXAMPLES OF TRUNCATED TABLES

In this section I shall re-examine the various examples of truncated tables that have appeared in the literature. For each kind of example I shall describe some of the methods of analysis that seem to me to be particularly appropriate. In so doing, three different methods of analysis will be illustrated:

(a) A method based upon the partitioning of the truncated table into appropriate subtables (see, e.g., Tables 4, 4A–C; Tables 5, 5A–C; Tables 6, 6A–C; Tables 9, 9A–C; Tables 10, 10A–D); (b) a method based upon the estimation of the expected frequencies in the truncated table calculated under the assumption of quasi-independence in the table (see, e.g., formulas (2.1), (2.2), (2.12), (2.17), (2.18)–(2.20)); and (c) a method based upon the estimation of certain interactions in the truncated table (see, e.g., formulas (2.8)–(2.9), (2.11), (2.26)–(2.28)). The relationships between these methods will be discussed later.

2.1 *Separable Subtables*

Our first example is the following 4×9 table presented by Harris [43]. Half the cells in this table are void because of *a priori* considerations, since the first and fourth locular composition (i.e., 0 even − 3 odd and 3 even − 0 odd) cannot occur when the radial-symmetry coefficient is .47, .82, 1.25, 1.41, 1.70; and the second and third locular composition (i.e., 1 even − 2 odd and 2 even − 1 odd) cannot occur when the radial-symmetry coefficient is .00, .94, 1.63, 1.89.

TABLE 1. RELATIONSHIP BETWEEN RADIAL ASYMMETRY AND LOCULAR COMPOSITION IN STAPHYLEA (SERIES A)

Locular-Composition	Coefficient of Radial Symmetry								
	.00	.47	.82	.94	1.25	1.41	1.63	1.70	1.89
3 even 0 odd	462	—	—	130	—	—	2	—	1
2 even 1 odd	—	614	138	—	21	14	—	1	—
1 even 2 odd	—	443	95	—	22	8	—	5	—
0 even 3 odd	103	—	—	35	—	—	1	—	0

For this table, Harris [43] calculated among other things the usual chi-square statistic (with 24 degrees of freedom) for testing independence in the cross-classification table, and the corresponding contingency coefficient (i.e., the chi-square statistic divided by the sample size). He noted that since half the cells in the table were void because of *a priori* considerations these statistics could not be the correct ones to use, thus exhibiting a "limitation in the applicability" of the usual chi-square statistic and the contingency coefficient. In reply, Pearson [60] argued that "there is no real order or continuity in locular composition and no continuity in the coefficient of asymmetry," and he then rearranged Table 1 as follows:

TABLE 2. RELATIONSHIP BETWEEN RADIAL ASYMMETRY AND LOCULAR COMPOSITION IN STAPHYLEA (SERIES A)

Locular-Composition	Coefficient of Radial Symmetry							
	.00	.94	1.63–1.89	.47	.82	1.25	1.41	1.70
3 even 0 odd	462	130	3	—	—	—	—	—
0 even 3 odd	103	35	1	—	—	—	—	—
2 even 1 odd	—	—	—	614	138	21	14	1
1 even 2 odd	—	—	—	443	95	22	8	5

(We have combined the columns pertaining to radial symmetry 1.63 and 1.89 because of the small number of observations in those columns.) Pearson then noted that this table consisted of two separable subtables, and he calculated a combined coefficient of contingency for the two subtables, which he then compared with the "standard error for zero contingency."

Pearson's method of analysis is incorrect for the following three reasons: (a) His calculation of the standard error for the combined coefficient was based on the assumption that the two subtables (a 2×3 subtable and 2×5 subtable in the modified form of Table 2) have a total of $6 + 10 - 1 = 15$ degrees of freedom; but in fact they have a total of $2 + 4 = 6$ degrees of freedom. (b) Even if the correct number of degrees of freedom had been used, Pearson's comparison of the observed coefficient with its standard error assumes (implicitly) that the expected value of the ratio of the coefficient and its (correct) standard error would be zero (when the samples are large) under the null hypothesis of zero contingency (i.e., the hypothesis of quasi-independence); but in fact this ratio has an expected value of $6/\sqrt{2 \times 6} = \sqrt{3}$ for the particular subtables considered here (when the samples are large). (c) Even if the correct expected value and the correct standard error had been applied, the comparison of the difference between an observed coefficient and its expected value under the null hypothesis, using the standard error as a gauge, assumes (implicitly) that this difference divided by the standard error will be approximately normally distributed (when the samples are large); but in fact the distribution is skewed in the same way that a χ^2 distribution with 6 degrees of freedom is skewed. We shall now present a method for analyzing these data which is different from the methods suggested by Pearson and those suggested by Harris.

Since this paper is concerned with the analysis of contingency tables in which the particular order of the rows (and/or columns) is irrelevant, we shall follow Pearson in replacing Table 1 by Table 2. (We shall not discuss here the substantive question of whether the order of the particular row and column classes is irrelevant.) The usual chi-square statistic for testing for independence in the 4×8 contingency table given as Table 2 is inapplicable as noted by Harris [43], since some of the cells in the table are *a priori* void. However, considering only the subset of cells which are not *a priori* void, we can test the hypothesis that the row and column classifications in the 4×8 table are "quasi-independent." From our definition of quasi-independence, we see that this hypothesis can be separated into the following two hypotheses: (1) The hypothesis H_1 that the subset S_1 consisting of the 6 cells in the left three columns and upper two rows are "quasi-independent," which is equivalent in this particular case to the hypothesis of independence for the 2×3 subtable S_1; and (2) the hypothesis H_2 that the subset S_2 consisting of the 10 cells in the right five columns and lower two rows are "quasi-independent," which is equivalent in this particular case to the hypothesis of independence in the 2×5 subtable S_2. Calculating the usual chi-square statistic for testing for independence in the subtable, we obtain $X_2^2 = .8$ for subtable S_1 and $X_4^2 = 6.1$ for subtable S_2, with a sum of $X_{*6}^2 = 6.9$ (Note that the same result would have been obtained if the order of the rows (and/or columns) in either subtable of Table 2 had been permuted in any way.) Under the null hypothesis of quasi-independence in Table 2, these three statistics will have asymptotic χ^2 distributions with 2, 4, and 6 degrees of freedom, respectively. (The chi-square statistics (X_2^2 and X_4^2) calculated for the two subtables are asymptotically independent.) The sum X_{*6}^2 can be used to test the null hypothesis of quasi-independence in Table 2.

We shall use the symbol X_d^2 throughout this paper to denote the usual chi-square statistic for testing for independence in a non-truncated $R \times C$ table (or in a non-truncated $R \times C$ subtable), with degrees of freedom $d = (R-1)(C-1)$; while the symbol χ_d^2 will refer to the tabular chi-square distribution with d, degrees of freedom. When the chi-square statistics X_d^2 calculated for two or more non-truncated tables (or non-truncated subtables) are asymptotically independent, we shall also use the symbol $X_{*d'}^2$ to denote their sum, with d' the corresponding symbol for their degrees of freedom.

In many situations, the research worker will not be content to test the null hypothesis of quasi-independence. He will also want to estimate the amount of interaction there is (if any) between the rows and columns of the table. Since Table 2 consists of two separable subtables, it should be analyzed by first considering separately the separable subtables. Simultaneous confidence intervals could be obtained for all interactions (or a subset of these interactions) in each subtable applying the methods developed by the author in [33], and the intervals thus obtained could be used to provide simultaneous confidence intervals (at an appropriate level of confidence) for the interactions in the truncated table (Table 2). In situations where particular measures of association of the kind described by Goodman and Kruskal [39, 40] are appropriate, the methods of analysis in [41] could be applied to each subtable.

Note that each of the subtables considered above was non-truncated, while the table of which they are a part (Table 2) was truncated. We shall see later herein that the methods for obtaining simultaneous confidence intervals for the interactions, which were developed earlier in [33], can be applied to any kind of truncated table (or truncated subtable), as well as to non-truncated tables (or subtables). Similarly, many of the measures proposed by Goodman and Kruskal [39, 40] can be applied to truncated tables (or subtables) as well as to non-truncated tables (or subtables); see [40, Sec. 2.1, 4.13].

Before closing this section, we comment briefly on the differences between (I) a truncated table (such as Table 2) which consists of two separable subsets S_1 and S_2 (where each non-truncated cell in the table is included in either S_1 or S_2, and where S_1 and S_2 have no rows and no columns in common), and (II) a truncated table which does not consist of separable subsets. If (1.2) is satisfied for the p_{ij} in the non-truncated cells in a table of type II, then the a_i and b_j satisfying (1.2) are unique (when they have been normalized so that $\sum_i a_i = 1$ and $\sum_j b_j = 1$); but this is not the case for a table of type I. On the other hand, if the subset S_1 of a table of type I does not itself consist of separable subsets (i.e., if the subset S_1 is itself a table of type II), then the preceding remark implies that, if (1.2) is satisfied for the p_{ij} in the non-truncated cells in S_1, then the a_i and b_j satisfying (1.2) are unique for the rows and columns of S_1 (when the a_i and b_j for these rows and columns have been normalized); and a similar remark applies to the subset S_2. If the subset S_1 (or S_2) of a table of type I consists of separable subsets, then the preceding remark applies to each of these subsets of S_1 (or S_2).

A table of type I should be analyzed by first considering separately each of its separable subsets of type II. For the analysis of a table of type I, the appropriate number of degrees of freedom is the sum of degrees of freedom calculated for each of its separable subsets of type II. (The methods given later for calculating degrees of freedom for tables of type II will lead to incorrect results if applied directly to a table of type I, rather than to each of its separable subsets of type II.)

2.2 *Deletion of a Cell, or a Block of Cells, or Some Cells in a Given Row, or Some Cells in a Given Column of the $R \times C$ Table*

The analysis of an $R \times C$ table in which a cell is deleted was discussed by Watson [65] and Caussinus [9], who proposed special tests of the null hypothesis of quasi-independence for this particular case. In this section we shall present a more elementary method for testing this null hypothesis, and we shall show how this method can be applied more generally to the case where a block of cells, or several cells in a given row, or several cells in a given column of the $R \times C$ table are deleted. To illustrate the case in which a single cell is deleted, we shall examine the following table considered earlier by Goodman [37] based on data in Glass [26]. (The data in this table were obtained by a kind of stratified random sampling, but for our present exposition we view this table as a contingency table; i.e., as if simple random sampling had been used.)

TABLE 3. CROSS-CLASSIFICATION OF A SAMPLE OF BRITISH MALES ACCORDING TO EACH SUBJECT'S STATUS CATEGORY AND HIS FATHER'S STATUS CATEGORY

Father's Status	Subject's Status		
	Upper	Middle	Lower
Upper	588	395	159
Middle	349	714	447
Lower	114	320	411

Calculating the usual X_d^2 statistic for testing the hypothesis of independence in this 3×3 table, we obtain $X_4^2 = 505.5$. Obviously, the row and column classifications of this table are not independent. With the concept of quasi-independent, we might ask the following question: If we were for the moment to exclude from consideration those upper-status subjects whose fathers also were upper-status, would the row and column classifications (namely, the subject's status and father's status classifications) then be quasi-independent? We shall now present a simple method for answering this question.

In order to study the question, we replace Table 3 with Table 4.

TABLE 4. CROSS-CLASSIFICATION OF A SAMPLE OF BRITISH MALES
ACCORDING TO EACH SUBJECT'S STATUS CATEGORY AND HIS
FATHER'S STATUS CATEGORY, EXCLUDING UPPER-STATUS
SUBJECTS HAVING UPPER-STATUS FATHERS

Father's Status	Subject's Status		
	Upper	Middle	Lower
Upper	—	395	159
Middle	349	714	447
Lower	114	320	411

For the population cross-classification corresponding to Table 4, the hypothesis of quasi-independence, as defined here (see (1.2)), can be partitioned into hypotheses concerning the population subtables corresponding to the following three subtables formed from Table 4:

TABLE 4A

Father's Status	Subject's Status	
	Middle	Lower
Middle	714	447
Lower	320	411

TABLE 4B

Father's Status	Subject's Status	
	Upper	Not Upper
Middle	349	1161
Lower	114	731

TABLE 4C

Father's Status	Subject's Status	
	Middle	Lower
Upper	395	159
Not Upper	1034	858

We shall now make use of some methods for partitioning the chi-square statistic into single degrees of freedom (see Irwin [46], Lancaster [53], Cochran [12, 13], Kimball [50], and Kastenbaum [49]). (These methods have not heretofore been applied to truncated contingency tables, although, as we shall see here, they are particularly well suited for this purpose.) We find that, under the null hypothesis of "quasi-independence" in the population table corresponding to Table 4, each of the three X_1^2 statistics used to test for independence in the three 2×2 subtables (Tables 4A, 4B, and 4C) will have an asymptotic χ_1^2 distribution and the three statistics will be asymptotically independent. Thus, the sum X_{*3}^2 of the three statistics will have an asymptotic χ_3^2 distribution. Note that the number of degrees of freedom for the sum X_{*3}^2 can be calculated (in the usual way) simply by adding up the number of degrees of freedom pertaining to the separate terms in the sum ($1+1+1$ in this case), or equivalently by subtracting the number of truncated cells in Table 4 (one cell in this case) from the number of degrees of freedom there would have been for testing for independence in this table if none of the cells had been *a priori* truncated (see Table 3). The sum X_{*3}^2 can be used to test the hypothesis of quasi-independence in Table 4. For Table 4, we obtain X_1^2 values of 56.9 (Table 4A), 31.8 (Table 4B), and 48.9 (Table 4C), with $X_{*3}^2 = 137.6$.

The method described above can be viewed as a partitioning of the 4 degrees of freedom in Table 3, in which one of the degrees of freedom was ignored. The degree of freedom which was ignored corresponds to the X_1^2 statistic for testing for independence in the following table:

TABLE 3A

Father's Status	Subject's Status	
	Upper	Not Upper
Upper	588	554
Not Upper	463	1892

For this table, we obtain $X_1^2 = 370.6$. This value can be used to test the null[1] hypothesis that there is no "association" between upper-status subjects and upper-status fathers. More complicated formulae for testing this hypothesis were presented by Caussinus [10], but the application of his formulae will lead to a test that is asymptotically equivalent (under the null hypothesis) to the more elementary method presented here; viz., the usual test of independence applied to the appropriate 2×2 subtable (Table 3A).

The difference between X_4^2 obtained earlier for Table 3 and X_1^2 obtained for Table 3A is 134.9, which is similar to the corresponding sum X_{*3}^2 calculated from Tables 4A, 4B, and 4C. Under the null hypothesis of independence in the population table corresponding to Table 3, the difference $X_4^2 - X_1^2$ calculated from Tables 3 and 3A will be asymptotically equivalent to the sum X_{*3}^2 calculated from Tables 4A, 4B, and 4C. (Further insight into the relationship between the various quantities considered here will be obtained in Sec. 5.)

The method of partitioning a contingency table, which we applied above (Table 3 partitioned into Tables 3A, 4A, 4B, 4C), is based upon the successive application of the following fact. A test of homogeneity of the R rows in an $R \times C$ table (which is equivalent to a test of independence in the $R \times C$ table) can be partitioned into two asymptotically independent tests: (1) a test of homogeneity of the first R' rows (with $R' < R$); and (2) a test of homogeneity of the remaining rows (the rows $R'+1$, $R'+2$, $\cdots$, R) and a row obtained by combining the corresponding entries in the first R' rows. Test (1) studies a $R' \times C$ subtable with degrees of freedom $d_1 = (R'-1)(C-1)$; and test (2) studies a $(R-R'+1) \times C$ subtable with $d_2 = (R-R')(C-1)$. By applying this method of partitioning in turn to the subtables obtained for tests (1) and (2) (applying the method to the columns as well as to the rows), we obtain the partitioning of Table 3 given above.

Note that the partitioning of the truncated Table 4 was obtained from the partitioning of the non-truncated Table 3 simply by omitting one subtable (Table 3A) corresponding to the deleted cell. Of course, this partitioning of Table 4 could have been obtained from the corresponding partitioning of any hypothetical non-truncated 3×3 table which had the same frequencies as Table 4 had in its non-deleted cells. The partitioning which we shall give later for other truncated tables, which lead (as with Table 4) to tests based on the X_1^2 statistics, can also be obtained by applying the method of partitioning presented in the preceding paragraph to a hypothetical non-truncated table and then omitting certain subtables corresponding to the particular cells that are actually deleted in the table.

The method suggested here for the analysis of quasi-independence in Table 4 (namely, calculating the sum of the X_1^2 statistics for Tables 4A, 4B, and 4C), and the method presented in the preceding section, can be applied by the reader using only the usual X_d^2 statistic for testing for independence (in various subtables) in order to obtain a test of quasi-independence for the original table. We shall now present an alternative method for testing for quasi-independence in Table 4 which requires a modification of the usual chi-square statistic.

Table 4 can be written in the following form:

—	x
y	Z

where x is a row vector $\{x_1, x_2\}$, y is a column vector $\{y_1, y_2\}'$, and Z is a 2×2 matrix $\{z_{ij}\}$. Let $x_. = \sum_i x_i$, $y_. = \sum_i y_i$, $z_{i.} = \sum_j z_{ij}$, $z_{.j} = \sum_i z_{ij}$, and $z_{..} = \sum_i z_{i.}$ $= \sum_j z_{.j} = \sum_{i,j} z_{ij}$. Then the table of estimated expected frequencies under the null hypothesis of quasi-independence can be obtained by replacing the x_i, y_i, and z_{ij} in the above table by the corresponding quantities given below.

$$\hat{x}_j = x_.(x_j + z_{.j})/(x_. + z_{..}), \qquad \hat{y}_i = y_.(y_i + z_{i.})/(y_. + z_{..}),$$
$$\hat{z}_{ij} = (y_i + z_{i.})(x_j + z_{.j})z_{..}/(y_. + z_{..})(x_. + z_{..}). \tag{2.1}$$

There are various ways to see that (2.1) gives the maximum likelihood estimates of the expected frequencies under the null hypothesis of quasi-independence. (Note that the form of (2.1) is somewhat similar to the usual form of the estimated expected frequencies in the non-truncated contingency table.) A general method for checking such formulae (which can be applied also to the formulae for the maximum likelihood estimates which we shall give later for other truncated tables) is to note that (a) the row and column marginals of the table of estimated expected frequencies are equal to the corresponding observed marginals, and (b) the estimated expected proportions can be expressed in the multiplicative form (1.2). This method of checking is sufficient as can be proved from the following facts: (1) The observed marginals are the maximum likelihood estimates of the corresponding expected marginals (as can be seen by an extension of the corresponding result in Goodman [30] or Birch [6]); (2) The row and column marginals in a table of the maximum likelihood estimates of the expected frequencies will be equal to the maximum likelihood estimates of the corresponding expected marginals; (3) We see from (1) and (2) that the row and column marginals in a table of the maximum likelihood estimates of the expected frequencies will be equal to the observed marginals; (4) The uniqueness of the maximum likelihood estimates of the expected frequencies follows from (3) and the fact that the estimated expected proportions are of the form (1.2) (see, e.g., [63], [7]). For some related matters, see Sec. 4 below.

With the estimated expected frequencies (2.1), we can now calculate the usual chi-square goodness-of-fit statistic by comparing the observed frequencies in Table 4 with the corresponding estimated expected frequencies. Under the null hypothesis of quasi-independence, this statistic will have an asymptotic χ^2 distribution with $4-1=3$ degrees of freedom, and it will be asymptotically equivalent to the sum X^2_{*3} calculated above from Tables 4A, 4B, and 4C. (One degree of freedom was subtracted from the usual four degrees of freedom there would have been for testing for independence the 3×3 table (Table 4) if none of the cells had been *a priori* void.) For Table 4, using the estimated expected frequencies (2.1), we obtain $X^2_{G3} = 143.4$ for the chi-square goodness-of-fit statistic.

We shall use the symbol X^2_{Gd} throughout this paper to denote the chi-square goodness-of-fit statistic, with d degrees of freedom, obtained by comparing the observed frequencies with the estimated expected frequencies calculated under the assumption of quasi-independence. Note that the statistic X^2_d presented earlier will be equal to the corresponding statistic X^2_{Gd} for a non-truncated table whenever the estimated expected frequencies are calculated under the assumption of independence.

The preceding methods of analysis presented in this section (which were based upon X^2_{*3} and X^2_{G3}) were applicable to the case where a single entry in the table is deleted. Let us now extend these methods to the case where a rectangular block of entries is deleted. In this case, our table can be written in the following form:

TABLE 5

	X
Y	Z

where $X = \{x_{ij}\}$, $Y = \{y_{ij}\}$, and $Z = \{z_{ij}\}$ are $r'\times c$, $r\times c'$, and $r\times c$ matrices, respectively. Let $x_{i.} = \sum_j x_{ij}$, $x_{.j} = \sum_i x_{ij}$, $x_{..} = \sum_i x_{i.} = \sum_j x_{.j} = \sum_{i,j} x_{ij}$, etc.

Let z_* denote the column vector $\{z_1., z_2., \cdots, z_r.\}'$, and let $z._*$ denote the row vector $\{z._1, z._2, \cdots, z._c\}$.

For the population table corresponding to Table 5, the hypothesis of quasi-independence (as defined here) can be partitioned into hypotheses concerning the population subtables corresponding to the following three subtables formed from Table 5:

TABLE 5A   TABLE 5B   TABLE 5C

$\{z_{ij}\}$

Y	z_*

X
$z._*$

Under the null hypothesis of quasi-independence in the population cross-classification corresponding to Table 5, each of the X_d^2 statistics used to test for independence in the $r \times c$ subtable (Table 5A), the $r \times (c'+1)$ subtable (Table 5B), and the $(r'+1) \times c$ subtable (Table 5C) will have an asymptotic χ_d^2 distribution with d equal to $(r-1)(c-1)$, $(r-1)c'$, and $r'(c-1)$, respectively; and their sum $X_{*d'}^2$ will have a $\chi_{d'}^2$ distribution with $d' = (r-1)(c-1)+(r-1)c' +r'(c-1) = (r+r'-1)(c+c'-1)-r'c'$. The sum $X_{*d'}^2$ will be asymptotically equivalent to the $X_{Gd'}^2$ statistic calculated by comparing the observed frequencies in Table 5 with the following estimated expected frequencies:

$$\hat{x}_{ij} = x_i.(x._j + z._j)/(x.. + z..), \qquad \hat{y}_{ij} = y._j(y_i. + z_i.)/(y.. + z..),$$
$$\hat{z}_{ij} = (y_i. + z_i.)(x._j + z._j)z../(y.. + z..)(x.. + z..). \tag{2.2}$$

The preceding results pertain to the case where a block of entries is deleted. If several entries (not necessarily a block of them) in a single row (or a single column) are deleted, then the methods presented above can be applied since the columns (or rows) can be rearranged so that the missing entries in the row (or column) then form a block.

Let us now examine briefly the case in which a particular entry in the table is excluded and so are several other entries in the same row (and/or same column) as the particular entry. In this case, our table can be written in the following more general form:

TABLE 6

—	—	U
—	V	X
W	Y	Z

were $U = \{u_{ij}\}$, $X = \{x_{ij}\}$, $Z = \{x_{ij}\}$, $V = \{v_{ij}\}$, $Y = \{y_{ij}\}$, and $W = \{w_{ij}\}$ are $r'' \times c$, $r' \times c$, $r \times c$, $r' \times c'$, $r \times c'$, and $r \times c''$ matrices, respectively. Let $x_i.$, $x._j$, $x..$, x_*, $x._*$, etc. be defined as above. For the population corresponding to Table 6, the hypothesis of quasi-independence can be partitioned into hypotheses concerning the population subtables corresponding to the following three subtables formed from Table 6:

TABLE 6A   TABLE 6B   TABLE 6C

V	X
Y	Z

W	$y_{*.}+z_{*.}$

U
$x_{.*}+z_{.*}$

Table 6A, 6B, and 6C are $(r+r')\times(c+c')$, $r\times(c''+1)$, and $(r''+1)\times c$ tables, respectively. Under the null hypothesis, the sum $X^2_{*d'}$ of the three X^2_d statistics calculated for these subtables will have an asymptotic $\chi^2_{d'}$ distribution with $d'=(r+r'-1)(c+c'-1)+(r-1)c''+r''(c-1)=(r+r'+r''-1)(c+c'+c''-1)-r''(c'+c'')-r'c''$. The sum $X^2_{*d'}$ will be asymptotically equivalent to the $X^2_{Gd'}$ statistic calculated by comparing the observed frequencies in Table 6 with the corresponding estimated expected frequencies which can be determined by methods similar to those used to obtain (2.2). We shall comment further on Table 6 in Sec. 2.4.

Before closing this section we note that the methods presented above were concerned only with the problem of testing the null hypothesis of quasi-independence. We shall now comment briefly on methods for estimating the interactions in tables of the kind considered here. These methods can be applied to any of the tables in this section, but for expository purposes we shall focus attention on Tables 3 and 4.

Let p_{ij} denote the proportion of individuals in the ith row and jth column of the population table corresponding to Table 3. When there is independence in this table (see (1.1)), then we note for example that

$$p_{22}p_{33}/p_{32}p_{23} = 1, \tag{2.3}$$

which can also be written as

$$L = 0 \tag{2.4}$$

where

$$L = \log p_{22} + \log p_{33} - \log p_{32} - \log p_{23}, \tag{2.5}$$

and where $\log x$ denotes the natural logarithm of x. The interaction L defined by (2.5) is of the form

$$L(\alpha) = \sum_{i,j} \alpha_{ij} \log p_{ij}, \tag{2.6}$$

where

$$\sum_i \alpha_{ij} = 0, \qquad \sum_j \alpha_{ij} = 0. \tag{2.7}$$

Any set of numbers α_{ij} satisfying (2.7) can be used to define an interaction $L(\alpha)$ for Table 3. As in [33], this interaction can be estimated by

$$L(\alpha) = \sum_{i,j} \alpha_{ij} \log f_{ij}, \tag{2.8}$$

where f_{ij} is the observed frequency in the ith row and jth column of the sample contingency table; the variance of $\hat{L}(\alpha)$ can be estimated by

$$S^2(\alpha) = \sum_{i,j} \alpha_{ij}^2 g_{ij}, \qquad (2.9)$$

where

$$g_{ij} = 1/f_{ij}; \qquad (2.10)$$

and simultaneous confidence intervals can be calculated for all interactions $L(\alpha)$ or for any given subset of these interactions. (For simplicity we assume here that $f_{ij} > 0$.) The simultaneous confidence intervals for all interactions in Table 3 will be based upon the four degrees of freedom in this table (see [33]).

It may be worthwhile to remark here on the relationship between the interactions defined above by (2.6) and (2.7) and the more usual definition of interaction effects in a linear model in which, in the present context, the $\log p_{ij}$ are written as a sum of row effects, column effects, row-column interaction effects, and an overall effect which is, in the present context, a function of the preceding effects (see, e.g., [6], [55]). It is easy to see that the set of interactions defined by (2.6) and (2.7) includes as special cases the row-column interaction effects in the linear model, and that the null hypothesis that all the interactions defined above (by (2.6) and (2.7)) are zero is equivalent to the null hypothesis that the row-column interaction effects are zero. It may also be of interest to note that the set of interactions defined above includes the row-column interaction effects that were considered relevant in a Bayesian analysis of contingency tables when the prior distribution of the parameters was of a certain type (see [54]). The preceding remarks concerning the relationship between the set of interactions $L(\alpha)$ (which were defined above for the analysis of non-truncated contingency tables (e.g., Table 3)) and the corresponding row-column interaction effects can be extended to the analysis of truncated tables (e.g., Table 4).

When we considered Table 4 earlier, we noted that one degree of freedom was lost from Table 3, leaving three degrees of freedom for Table 4. Since $p_{11} = 0$ in Table 4, we can continue to use the interactions $L(\alpha)$ defined by (2.6) and (2.7) for all α_{ij} for which

$$\alpha_{11} = 0. \qquad (2.11)$$

The methods developed by the author in [33] can be applied to Table 4 in order to calculate simultaneous confidence intervals for all interactions $L(\alpha)$ satisfying (2.7) and (2.11), or for any given subset of these interactions. The simultaneous confidence intervals for all interactions in Table 4 will be based upon the three degrees of freedom in this table. Following [33], this method of analysis has been applied by Caussinus [9] in the present context.

2.3 Deletion of Some Cells in the $2 \times C$ Table, or of Two Separable Blocks of Cells in the $R \times C$ Table

The analysis of a $2 \times C$ table in which the entry in a single cell in the first row and a single cell in the second row were *a priori* void was discussed by Kastenbaum [48]. In the present section we shall present a simpler approach to this subject than was used by Kastenbaum (in part of his article), and we shall show how to generalize the method presented here so that it will be applicable to the case where several cells in the first row and several cells in the second row of the $2 \times C$ table are deleted. We shall also show how to generalize this method to the case where two particular separable blocks of cells in the $R \times C$ table are deleted.

Let us begin by reconsidering Kastenbaum's example [48] based on data in Novitski and Sandler [58].

TABLE 7. NUMBERS OF PROGENY FROM MATING TRANSLOCATION-
BEARING MALES TO ATTACHED-X FEMALES

Female Type	Male Sperm Type			
	AB	$A'B'$	$A'B$	AB'
Female with a Y Chromosome	1413	1029	lethal	2240
Female with Proximal Segment of the Translocation	lethal	548	346	1287

By permuting the order of the columns of Table 7, we obtain the following table:

TABLE 8. NUMBERS OF PROGENY FROM MATING TRANSLOCATION-
BEARING MALES TO ATTACHED-X FEMALES

Female Type	Male Sperm Type			
	$A'B$	AB	$A'B'$	AB'
Female with a Y Chromosome	lethal	1413	1029	2240
Female with Proximal Segment of the Translocation	346	lethal	548	1287

In order to test the null hypothesis of quasi-independence in Table 8, we simply apply the usual chi-square test of independence to the following 2×2 subtable of Table 8:

TABLE 8A

Female Type	Male Sperm Type	
	$A'B'$	AB'
Female with a Y Chromosome	1029	2240
Female with Proximal Segment of the Translocation	548	1287

Under the null hypothesis of quasi-independence in Table 8, the usual X_1^2 statistic calculated from the 2×2 subtable (Table 8A) will have an asymptotic X_1^2 distribution. Note that the number of degrees of freedom for our test (one in this case) can also be calculated by subtracting the number of deleted cells in Table 8 (two cells in this case) from the number of degrees of freedom there would have been for testing for independence in this table if none of the cells had been *a priori* void. From Table 8A we obtain $X_1^2 = 1.4$. (The method presented above is actually equivalent to the technique used by Kastenbaum [48], but the reader of his article might not be aware of the fact that the test applied there is the usual test of independence for the 2×2 subtable 8A.)

In the preceding section we showed how to estimate the expected frequencies for the cells that were not deleted (see (2.1) and (2.2)), under the null hypothesis of quasi-independence. For the example considered in the present section, the expected frequencies for the cells in columns $A'B'$ and AB' of Table 8 are simply the usual expected frequencies calculated from the 2×2 subtable 8A; and the expected frequencies for the (non-deleted) cells in columns $A'B$ and AB are taken as the corresponding observed frequencies. Although the expected frequencies are zero in the deleted cells, it may sometimes be of interest to estimate what the hypothetical expected frequencies would have been in these cells if they had not been deleted and if the rows and columns of the table had been independent. We shall now illustrate how to do this for the present example. The method can be applied more generally to all of the cases considered in this paper. (For a different illustration of the application and utility of this general method, see [38].)

Table 8 can be written in the following form:

—	v	h_{11}	h_{12}
w	—	h_{21}	h_{22}

Let $h_{i\cdot} = \sum_j h_{ij}$, $h_{\cdot j} = \sum_i h_{ij}$, $h_{\cdot\cdot} = \sum_i h_{i\cdot} = \sum_j h_{\cdot j} = \sum_{i,j} h_{ij}$. We noted above that the table of estimated expected frequencies could be written as follows:

—	v	$h_{1\cdot}h_{\cdot 1}/h_{\cdot\cdot}$	$h_{1\cdot}h_{\cdot 2}/h_{\cdot\cdot}$
w	—	$h_{2\cdot}h_{\cdot 1}/h_{\cdot\cdot}$	$h_{2\cdot}h_{\cdot 2}/h_{\cdot\cdot}$

Thus, for the cells that are not truncated, the expected frequency $\hat{f}_{ij}$ in the ith row and the jth column can be written as

$$f_{ij} = \hat{\alpha}_i \hat{\beta}_j, \tag{2.12}$$

where in this particular case $\hat{\alpha}_i = h_{i\cdot}/h_{\cdot\cdot}$ (for $i = 1, 2$); and $\hat{\beta}_1 = w/\hat{\alpha}_2$, $\hat{\beta}_2 = v/\hat{\alpha}_1$, $\hat{\beta}_3 = h_{\cdot 1}$, and $\hat{\beta}_4 = h_{\cdot 2}$. If the cells in which frequencies are missing had not been *a priori* void and if the rows and columns of the table had been independent, then the expected frequencies could be calculated from (2.12) for all cells in the table. Thus, for the missing cell in the first column we would have obtained

$$f_{11} = \hat{\alpha}_1 \hat{\beta}_1 = h_{1\cdot}w/h_{2\cdot}, \tag{2.13}$$

and for the missing cell in the second column we would have obtained

$$\hat{f}_{22} = \hat{\alpha}_2 \hat{\beta}_2 = h_{2\cdot}v/h_{1\cdot}. \tag{2.14}$$

From Table 8, we obtain $\hat{f}_{11} = 616.39$ and $\hat{f}_{22} = 793.16$. It may be worth noting that these numerical values agree to the nearest whole number with the corresponding values presented by Kastenbaum [48] which he obtained by an application of Watson's iterative technique [65]. The method presented here is simpler to apply than the iterative technique.

Having now indicated how to estimate the expected frequencies $\hat{f}_{ij}$ for all cells in the table (with the missing frequencies replaced by hypothetical estimated expected frequencies calculated under the hypothesis of independence in the manner prescribed above), it is possible to give estimates of the corresponding hypothetical expected marginal proportions in the rows or the columns of the table (under the hypothesis of independence) simply by calculating the corresponding proportions from the expected frequencies. Thus, the estimate of the hypothetical expected marginal proportion π_i. in the ith row is

$$\hat{\pi}_{i.} = \hat{\alpha}_i / \sum_k \hat{\alpha}_k \qquad \text{(for } i = 1, 2), \tag{2.15}$$

which in our particular case is simply $\hat{\alpha}_i$; and the estimate of the hypothetical expected marginal proportion $\pi_{.j}$ in the jth column is

$$\hat{\pi}_{.j} = \hat{\beta}_j / \sum_k \hat{\beta}_k \qquad \text{(for } j = 1, 2, 3, 4). \tag{2.16}$$

We began this section by considering the problem of testing the null hypothesis of quasi-independence in Table 8 and of estimating the expected frequencies (for the non-deleted cells) under this null hypothesis. We then noted that, in analyzing any cross-classification table of the kind considered in this paper, once the expected frequencies for the non-deleted cells had been estimated, these estimated expected frequencies could be put in the form (2.12), which could then be used to estimate the hypothetical expected frequencies for the deleted cells under the assumption of independence. We shall now return to the problem of testing the null hypothesis of quasi-independence and of estimating the expected frequencies for the non-deleted cells, but we shall consider the following more general table of which Table 8 is a special case:

TABLE 9

—	V	X
W	—	Z

where $X = \{x_{ij}\}$, $Z = \{z_{ij}\}$, $V = \{v_{ij}\}$, and $W = \{w_{ij}\}$ are $r' \times c$, $r \times c$, $r' \times c'$, and $r \times c''$ matrices, respectively. Note that each row in Table 9 is included either in one or in the other (but not in both) of the two blocks of excluded cells. The methods which we shall present below can also be applied directly to the case where each row in the table is included in at least one of the two blocks of excluded cells. (However, the case where some of the rows are not included in either one of the two blocks of excluded cells, while other rows are included in at least one of these two blocks, requires the more general methods developed in Sec. 4.)

Let $x_{i.}$, $x_{.j}$, $x_{..}$, $x_{*.}$, $x_{.*}$, etc. be defined as in the preceding section. Then the null hypothesis of quasi-independence can be partitioned into hypotheses concerning the following three subtables:

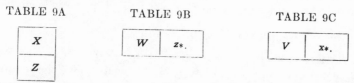

TABLE 9A   TABLE 9B   TABLE 9C

Under the null hypothesis of quasi-independence in Table 9, we find that each of the X_d statistics used to test for independence in the $(r+r')\times c$ subtable (Table 9A), the $r\times(c''+1)$ subtable (Table 9B), and the $r'\times(c'+1)$ subtable (Table 9C) will have an asymptotic χ_d^2 distribution with d equal to $(r+r'-1)(c-1)$, $(r-1)c''$, and $(r'-1)\times c'$, respectively; and their sum $X_{*d'}^2$ will have a $\chi_{d'}^2$ distribution with $d'=(r+r'-1)(c-1)+(r-1)c''+(r'-1)c'$ $=(r+r'-1)(c+c'+c''-1)-r'c''-rc'$. The sum $X_{*d'}^2$ will be asymptotically equivalent to the $X_{Gd'}^2$ statistic calculated by comparing the observed frequencies in Table 9 with the following estimated expected frequencies:

$$\hat{v}_{ij} = v_{.j}(v_{i.} + x_{i.})/(v_{..} + x_{..}), \qquad \hat{w}_{ij} = w_{.j}(w_{i.} + z_{i.})/(w_{..} + z_{..}),$$
$$\hat{x}_{ij} = (v_{i.} + x_{i.})(z_{.j} + x_{.j})x_{..}/(v_{..} + x_{..})(z_{..} + x_{..}), \tag{2.17}$$
$$\hat{z}_{ij} = (w_{i.} + z_{i.})(x_{.j} + z_{.j})z_{..}/(w_{..} + z_{..})(x_{..} + z_{..}).$$

Note that Table 9 is a generalization of Table 5, and equations (2.17) are a generalization of (2.2). By permuting the columns of Table 9, we also obtain a table of the following form:

—	X	V
W	Z	—

This table can be viewed as an example of a set of R "chained" multinomial samples (with $R=r+r'$), with each sample incomplete in the sense that some of the C classes of each multinomial population (with $C=c+c'+c''$) are not available. (In the first r multinomial samples, the first c'' classes are unavailable; in the final r' multinomial samples, the final c' classes are unavailable.) Asano [2] studied this case under the assumption that each of the R samples comes from the same multinomial populations; i.e., the assumption of "quasi-homogeneity." For the general case of "chained" multinomial samples, Asano [2] gives a method for estimating the hypothetical proportion $\pi_{.j}$ in the jth class of the multinomial population, under the assumption of quasi-homogeneity; but he does not consider the problem of testing whether the assumption of quasi-homogeneity is true. A test of this assumption can be based upon the comparison of observed and expected frequencies in the corresponding $R\times C$ table under the assumption of quasi-independence, estimating the expected frequencies by an extension of formulae (2.17), or by the methods of Sec. 4 herein, or by applying Asano's method to estimate the hypothetical proportions which can then serve as a first step in estimating the expected frequencies.

Before closing this section, we note that the method of obtaining simultaneous confidence intervals for all interactions in Table 4, or for a given subset of these interactions, which was presented in the preceding section, can be applied also to the tables in the present section and in the following one.

2.4 *Triangular Table of Cells, or of Blocks of Cells*

In this section we shall consider the following 6×6 truncated table cited by Pearson [60] from a paper by Waite [64]. The cells above the main diagonal are void in this table because the sum of the number of small loops and the number of whorls can not exceed 5 in finger-prints of the right hand.

TABLE 10. RELATIONSHIP BETWEEN SMALL LOOPS AND WHORLS IN FINGER-PRINTS OF THE RIGHT HAND

Whorls	Small Loops					
	0	1	2	3	4	5
5	50	—	—	—	—	—
4	104	26	—	—	—	—
3	125	33	7	—	—	—
2	130	92	55	15	—	—
1	106	153	126	80	32	—
0	78	144	204	211	179	45

The usual chi-square statistic (with 25 degrees of freedom) for testing for independence in the cross-classification table (Table 10) is inapplicable as noted by Harris [42]. A correct method for estimating the expected frequencies in the non-void cells (under the null hypothesis of quasi-independence) was applied by Waite [64], but the analysis presented there was limited because "no correction for the number of cells has been applied to the contingency coefficients in this type of table as we have, at present, no appreciation of what it should be." That is, they did not know how to calculate the number of degrees of freedom for this type of table. We shall introduce below a different approach to this subject which will clarify how the degrees of freedom are calculated, and will provide an alternative method of analysis based only on the use of the usual X_d^2 statistic calculated for testing for independence in subtables of Table 10. In addition, we shall provide a more explicit and simpler set of formulae for estimating the expected frequencies in Table 10 under the null hypothesis of quasi-independence.

Are the rows and columns of Table 10 quasi-independent? This question can be answered by considering the following subtables formed from Table 10:

TABLE 10A

Whorls	Small Loops				
	0	1	2	3	4
1	106	153	126	80	32
0	78	144	204	211	179

TABLE 10B

Whorls	Small Loops			
	0	1	2	3
2	130	92	55	15
Less than 2	184	297	330	291

TABLE 10C

Whorls	Small Loops		
	0	1	2
3	125	38	7
Less than 3	314	389	385

TABLE 10D

Whorls	Small Loops	
	0	1
4	104	26
Less than 4	439	427

Calculating the usual X_a^2 statistic for testing for independence in each of these tables (Tables 10A, 10B, 10C, 10D), we obtain $X_4^2 = 118.9$, $X_3^2 = 143.9$, $X_2^2 = 138.0$, $X_1^2 = 39.2$, respectively. The sum of these values is $X_{*10}^2 = 440.0$. Note that the number of degrees of freedom for this sum can be calculated in the usual way (namely, $4+3+2+1$), or by subtracting the number of deleted cells in Table 10 (namely, 15) from the number of degrees of freedom where there would have been for testing for independence in Table 10 if none of the cells had been *a priori* deleted. For the triangular $R \times R$ table, the number of degrees of freedom will be $(R-1)^2 - R(R-1)/2 = (R-1)(R-2)/2$.

We shall now present some explicit formulae for the estimated expected frequency $\hat{f}_{ij}$ for the ith row and jth column ($i \geq j$) of the triangular $R \times R$ table. Let $F = \{f_{ij}\}$ denote the observed frequencies in the triangular table with $f_{ij} = 0$ for $i < j$; and let $\hat{F} = \{\hat{f}_{ij}\}$ with $\hat{f}_{ij} = 0$ for $i < j$. Let

$$f_{i.} = \sum_j f_{ij}, \quad f_{.j} = \sum_i f_{ij}, \quad s_i = \sum_{j=1}^{i} (f_{.j} - f_{j.}),$$

$$x_i = f_{.(i+1)}/s_i, \quad \text{and} \quad y_{i+1} = \prod_{j=1}^{i} (1 + x_j)$$

with $y_1 = 1$. Then the expected frequencies (for $i \geq j$ can be estimated as follows:

$$\hat{f}_{ij} = \hat{\alpha}_i \hat{\beta}_j, \tag{2.18}$$

with

$$\hat{\alpha}_i = f_{i.}/y_i, \qquad \text{for } i = 1, 2, \cdots, R, \tag{2.19}$$

and

$$\hat{\beta}_j = x_{j-1} y_{j-1}, \qquad \text{for } j = 2, 3, \cdots, R, \tag{2.20}$$

with $\hat{\beta}_1 = 1$.

To check that (2.18)–(2.20) give the maximum likelihood estimates of the expected frequencies, we proceed in three steps: First, we note that $\hat{f}_{1.} = \hat{\alpha}_1\hat{\beta}_1 = f_{1.}$, and that for $i > 1$

$$f_i = \hat{\alpha}_i \sum_{j=1}^{i} \hat{\beta}_j = f_i \left[\left(1 + \sum_{j=2}^{i} x_{j-1}y_{j-1} \right) \Big/ y_i \right], \qquad (2.21a)$$

which is equal to f_i. since the term in brackets is equal to one (as can be seen by induction on i). Second, we note that for $j > 1$

$$f_{.j} = \hat{\beta}_j \sum_{i=j}^{R} \hat{\alpha}_i = f_{.j} \left[y_{j-1} \left(\sum_{k=j}^{R} f_k / y_k \right) \Big/ s_{j-1} \right], \qquad (2.21b)$$

which is equal to $f_{.j}$ since the term in brackets is equal to one (as can be seen by reverse induction on i). Third, we note that

$$f_{.1} = \sum_{i=1}^{R} \hat{\alpha}_i = f_1 + \sum_{i=2}^{R} f_i / y_i = f_1 + s_1 = f_{.1}. \qquad (2.21c)$$

Formulas (2.18)–(2.20) provide a more explicit and simpler set of formulas for estimating the expected frequencies than the step-by-step method applied in [64]. The step-by-step method presented more recently in [7] is the same as the method in [64].

Comparing the expected frequencies estimated by (2.18) with the corresponding observed frequencies in Table 10, we obtain $X^2_{G10} = 399.7$. Under the null hypothesis of quasi-independence, the statistic X^2_{G10} is asymptotically equivalent to the statistic X^2_{*10} presented earlier in this section. Further insight into the relationship between these statistics will be obtained in Sec. 5.

Let us define $\hat{\Pi}_{i.}$ as follows:

$$\hat{\pi}_{i.} = \hat{\alpha}_i / f_{.1}. \qquad (2.22)$$

From (2.21c) we see that $\sum_{i=1}^{R} \hat{\Pi}_{i.} = 1$. Thus the quantity $\hat{\Pi}_{i.}$ can be interpreted as the estimate of the hypothetical expected proportion of observations there would have been in the ith row of the table had no entries in the table been missing and had there been independence between rows and columns. A somewhat different (but similar) method for calculating the $\hat{\Pi}_{i.}$ was given by Caussinus [9] in a more general context.

In order to estimate the hypothetical expected proportion $\Pi_{.j}$ of observations there would have been in the jth column of the table had no entries in the table been missing and had there been independence between rows and columns, the following two methods are available: (a) The rows and columns of the table could be interchanged, and the order of the rows and columns permuted, so that the application of formula (2.22) to the modified table would give the desired result pertaining to the original table. (b) The quantities $\hat{\Pi}_{.j}$ could be calculated directly from (2.20) and (2.16).

The method of partitioning Table 10 into subtables which we presented above is somewhat similar to the method we presented earlier for Table 6. We may view Table 6 as a 3×3 triangular table of blocks of cells. (Note that Tables 4 and 5 can also be viewed as triangular tables of blocks of cells.) The methods which we have presented in the present section for the $R \times R$ triangular table of cells can be extended in a straightforward manner to the analysis of an $R \times R$ triangular table of blocks of cells. The analysis of such tables using the partitioning method described in the present article does not seem to have been presented in the earlier literature on this subject. In this literature (Asano [2], Batschelet [4, 5,] Geppert [25]), these $R \times R$ tables of blocks are viewed as a set of "nested" multinomial samples, in which the multinomial samples are truncated (i.e., in the ith multinomial sample $(i = 1, 2, \cdots, R)$, the first j_i classes from the multinomial population are unavailable, with j_i a non-increasing function of i), and it is assumed there that each of the R samples comes from the same multinomial population. This assumption of "quasi-homogeneity" can be tested using the methods presented herein; see related comments in Sec. 2.3.

It should be noted that the triangular tables discussed in this section are different from the "folded" contingency tables (the "intraclass" tables) considered earlier by Good [28], Okamoto and Ishii [59], Ishii [47], Chen, Crittenden, Mantel and Cameron [11]. It should also be noted that, because of the historical interest in analyzing Table 10 from the point of view of quasi-independence, we have used this table for illustrative purposes in this section; but a different mode of analysis of the fingerprint data, based upon a trivariate generalization of the hypergeometric distribution, actually leads to more interesting findings pertaining to these data. These findings will be discussed in a separate report.

2.5 *Deletion of Diagonal Cells*

In the present section we shall re-examine Table 3 excluding from consideration the three diagonal cells. We obtain the following table:

TABLE 11. CROSS-CLASSIFICATION OF A SAMPLE OF BRITISH MALES ACCORDING TO EACH SUBJECT'S STATUS CATEGORY AND HIS FATHER'S STATUS CATEGORY, EXCLUDING SUBJECTS HAVING THE SAME STATUS AS THEIR FATHERS

Father's Status	Subject's Status		
	Upper	Middle	Lower
Upper	—	395	159
Middle	349	—	447
Lower	114	320	—

The methods applied in the preceding sections to test the null hypothesis of quasi-independence can not be directly applied in a simple fashion to Table 11. We shall describe here a different method for testing the null hypothesis based upon the simultaneous confidence interval approach to which we referred in Sec. 2.1 and 2.2.

Let p_{ij} denote the proportion of individuals in the ith row and jth column $(i \neq j)$ of the population cross-classification corresponding to Table 11. The hypothesis of quasi-independence (see 1.2)) in the present context can be expressed by the equation

$$p_{12}p_{23}p_{31}/p_{13}p_{32}p_{21} = 1, \qquad (2.23)$$

which can also be written as

$$L = 0, \qquad (2.24)$$

where

$$L = \log p_{12} + \log p_{23} + \log p_{31} - \log p_{13} - \log p_{32} - \log p_{21}. \qquad (2.25)$$

As in [33], the quantity L is defined as a first-order interaction in the 3×3 population table, and it is estimated by

$$L = \log f_{12} + \log f_{23} + \log f_{31} - \log f_{13} - \log f_{32} - \log f_{21}. \qquad (2.26)$$

The variance of $\hat{L}$ is estimated by

$$S^2 = g_{12} + g_{23} + g_{31} + g_{13} + g_{32} + g_{21}, \qquad (2.27)$$

where g_{ij} is defined by (2.10). For Table 11 we obtain $\hat{L} = .125$ and $S^2 = .0258$. To test the hypothesis of quasi-independence in the present context (see (2.24)), we calculate the chi-square statistic

$$X_{I1}^2 = \hat{L}^2/S^2, \qquad (2.28)$$

which will have an asymptotic χ_1^2 distribution under the null hypothesis. For Table 11 we obtain $X_{I1}^2 = .6$. Note that confidence intervals for the interaction L can also be calculated by the usual methods using the estimator $\hat{L}$ and its standard error S.

For Table 11, our chi-square test was based upon one degree of freedom. Note that the number of degrees of freedom could have been calculated by subtracting the number of deleted cells (three in this case) from the number of degrees of freedom there would have been for testing for independence in Table 11 if none of the cells had been deleted. More generally, in the $R \times R$ table in which the diagonal entries are deleted, the number of degrees of freedom will be $(R-1)^2 - R = R^2 - 3R + 1$.

The method described earlier herein for calculating simultaneous confidence for all the interactions $L(\alpha)$ in Table 4, or for a subset of them, can be applied to $R \times R$ tables of the kind considered in the present section. As we noted above, the degrees of freedom in these tables will be $R^2 - 3R + 1$, and condition (2.11) will be replaced by

$$\alpha_{ii} = 0, \qquad \text{for } i = 1, 2, \cdots, R. \qquad (2.29)$$

In addition, the method presented in [33] for testing the null hypothesis that all the interactions in the table are zero can also be applied to $R \times R$ tables of the kind considered in this section (see also [9]).

3. SOME REMARKS ON PARTITIONING INTO SUBTABLES

In Sec. 2.2 we gave a general method for partitioning a (non-truncated) table into a set of subtables for which the corresponding X_d^2 statistics were asymptotically independent. For each of the truncated tables considered in Sec. 2.1–2.4, the set of subtables presented there were obtained by an adaptation of this method. By various straightforward applications of this method of partitioning, each of the truncated tables could also have been partitioned into other sets of subtables (for which the corresponding X_d^2 statistics would have been asymptotically independent). The particular sets of subtables presented herein were chosen for expository purposes only. Different sets of subtables will be of interest in different substantive contexts.

As noted in Sec. 2.2, the general method of partitioning a table into subtables is based upon the simple partitioning of an $R \times C$ table (or subtable) into a $R' \times C$ subtable and a $(R - R' + 1) \times C$ subtable. The X_d^2 statistic for the $R' \times C$ subtable will have an asymptotic χ_d^2 distribution (with $d = (R' - 1)(C - 1)$) under the null hypothesis of independence in the $R' \times C$ subtable, regardless of whether there is independence in the $R \times C$ table. Similarly, the X_d^2 statistic for the $(R - R' + 1) \times C$ subtable will also have an asymptotic χ_d^2 distribution (with $d = (R - R')(C - 1)$) under the null hypothesis of independence in the $(R - R' + 1) \times C$ subtable, regardless of whether there is independence in the $R \times C$ table, if the row marginals of the $R' \times C$ table are not fixed. This remark can be applied to each subtable in the set of subtables obtained by the general method of partitioning described in Sec. 2.2.

The partitioning method presented here, which we have found particularly suited for the analysis of the truncated tables in Sec. 2.1–2.4, does not appear to have been applied to such tables before. A somewhat different (but related) kind of table, for which the partitioning method would also be suited is the table in which the frequencies in certain neighboring cell have been combined or "mixed-up"; and again we find that the partitioning method does not appear to have been applied to such tables in the earlier literature on this subject (see Craig [14], Watson [65]). The particular partitioning that would be applied would depend upon the particular pattern of sets of cells for which the frequencies have been combined. For each of the patterns considered in the earlier literature (except for the final more complicated pattern discussed in Craig [14]), the partitioning method would provide a simple tool for analyzing the table. We shall illustrate this point briefly by considering only one of these patterns.

Let us consider for a moment an $R \times C$ table for which the entries in an $r' \times c'$ rectangular block of cells have been combined. The $R \times C$ table would then be of the same form as Table 5 above, except that we now know the sum $v_{..}$ of the entries in the deleted block of Table 5. In this case, we would partition the $R \times C$ table into Tables 5A, 5B, 5C, and the 2×2 table

TABLE 5D

$v.$	$x_{..}$
$y.$	$z_{..}$

A test for independence in the $R \times C$ table, would be based upon the sum X_{*d}^2 of the X_d^2 statistic for Tables 5A, 5B, 5C and 5D. In this case,

$d' = (R-1)(C-1) - r'c' + 1$. Thus, the analysis of this $R \times C$ table is the same as the analysis of Table 5 except that one degree of freedom has been added by Table 5D (i.e., by our knowledge of $v_{..}$).

4. TRUNCATED CONTINGENCY TABLES IN THE GENERAL CASE

We noted in Sec. 2.1 that a truncated table consisting of separable subsets should be analyzed by first considering separately each of the subsets. It will therefore be sufficient to consider here tables that are not separable.

For the $R \times C$ table, let $\delta_{ij} = 1$ if the entry in the ith row and jth column is not deleted, and let $\delta_{ij} = 0$ otherwise. Let p_{ij} denote the proportion of individuals in the ith row and jth column of the population cross-classification (excluding the deleted cells), and let $p_{i.} = \sum_j p_{ij}$ and $p_{.j} = \sum_i p_{ij}$. We assume throughout this section that $p_{ij} > 0$ for the non-deleted cells, and that the corresponding observed frequencies $f_{ij} > 0$ for the non-deleted cells. Under the null hypothesis of quasi-independence, we see that

$$p_{ij} = a_i b_j \tag{4.1}$$

for the non-deleted cells, and that

$$p_{i.} = a_i \sum_j \delta_{ij} b_j, \qquad p_{.j} = b_j \sum_i \delta_{ij} a_i. \tag{4.2}$$

Estimating the $p_{i.}$ and $p_{.j}$ by the corresponding observed proportions $\hat{p}_{i.}$ and $\hat{p}_{.j}$, an estimate of the expected proportion $\tilde{p}_{ij}$ in the ith row and jth column (for the non-deleted cells) under the null hypothesis of quasi-independence is obtained from

$$\tilde{p}_{ij} = \hat{a}_i \hat{b}_j, \tag{4.3}$$

where the $\hat{a}_i$ and $\hat{b}_j$ satisfy the following equations corresponding to (4.2):

$$\hat{p}_{i.} = \hat{a}_i \sum_j \delta_{ij} \hat{b}_j, \qquad \hat{p}_{.j} = \hat{b}_j \sum_i \delta_{ij} \hat{a}_i. \tag{4.4}$$

We shall now present a simple iterative method for calculating the $\hat{a}_i$ and $\hat{b}_j$. This method was first presented by the author in [32] (except that the starting point for the iterations is, in some cases, slightly different from the one proposed earlier).

At the first step (that is, the starting point), calculate the R trial values for $\hat{a}_i (i = 1, 2, \cdots, R)$:

$$\hat{a}_i^0 = \hat{p}_{i.} / \sum_i \delta_{ij}. \tag{4.5}$$

At the $2m$th step ($m \geq 1$), calculate the C trial values for $\hat{b}_j$ ($j = 1, 2, \cdots, C$):

$$\hat{b}_j^{2m-1} = \hat{p}_{.j} / \sum_i \delta_{ij} \hat{a}_i^{2m-2}. \tag{4.6}$$

At the $(2m+1)$th step, calculate the R trial values for $\hat{a}_i$ $(i=1, 2, \cdots, R)$:

$$\hat{a}_i^{2m} = \hat{p}_{i.} / \sum_j \delta_{ij} \hat{b}_i^{2m-1}. \tag{4.7}$$

The iterative steps are continued (for $m=1, 2, \cdots$) until the desired accuracy is obtained. Then for the non-deleted cells the $\tilde{p}_{ij}$ are calculated from (4.3). Note that the estimated expected frequencies $\hat{f}_{ij}$ can be calculated directly by replacing $\hat{p}_{i.}$, $\hat{p}_{.j}$ and $\tilde{p}_{ij}$ in (4.5)–(4.7) and (4.3) by $f_{i.}$ and $f_{.j}$ and $\hat{f}_{ij}$, respectively.

The iterative method presented above is different from the iterative method suggested by Caussinus [9] and Fienberg [16]. With the latter method, the following $R \times C$ trial values for $\tilde{p}_{ij}$ are taken at the first step:

$$\tilde{p}_{ij}^0 = \delta_{ij}. \tag{4.8}$$

At the $2m$th step $(m \geq 1)$, the following $R \times C$ trial values are taken:

$$\tilde{p}_{ij}^{2m-1} = \tilde{p}_{ij}^{2m-2} \hat{p}_{i.} / \sum_j \tilde{p}_{ij}^{2m-2}. \tag{4.9}$$

At the $(2m+1)$-th step, the following $R \times C$ trial values are taken:

$$\tilde{p}_{ij}^{2m} = \tilde{p}_{ij}^{2m-1} \hat{p}_{.j} / \sum_i \tilde{p}_{ij}^{2m-1}. \tag{4.10}$$

The iterative steps are continued (for $m=1, 2, \cdots$) until the desired accuracy is obtained.

It is easy to prove that

$$\tilde{p}_{ij}^{2m} = \delta_{ij} \hat{a}_i^{2m-2} \hat{b}^{2m-1} \tag{4.11}$$

and

$$\tilde{p}_{ij}^{2m+1} = \delta_{ij} \hat{a}_i^{2m} \hat{b}_j^{2m-1}, \tag{4.12}$$

for $m=1, 2, 3, \cdots$. Thus, the trial values for $\hat{a}_i$ and $\hat{b}_j$ obtained by the iterative method suggested herein (viz., (4.5)–(4.7)) could have been used (by applying (4.11)–(4.12)) in order to calculate the same numerical values as those obtained by the Caussinus-Fienberg method (viz., (4.8)–(4.10)) at each iterative step after the first two steps. But by applying directly the method suggested here (i.e., by applying (4.5)–(4.7) and (4.3)) we avoid the calculation of the $R \times C$ trial values (for $\tilde{p}_{ij}$) at each iterative step; we calculate instead either R trial values (for $\hat{a}_i$) or C trial values (for $\hat{b}_j$).

The iterative calculation of the $\tilde{p}_{ij}$ using (4.8)–(4.10) will converge to the desired values as has been noted in [16]. Thus, from equations (4.11)–(4.12) we find that the $\tilde{p}_{ij}$ obtained using the iterative method suggested herein (viz., (4.5)–(4.7) and (4.3)) will also converge. Furthermore, if the iterative method suggested herein is applied, we also find that normalized values of the $\hat{a}_i$ and $\hat{b}_j$ (i.e., $\hat{a}_i / \sum_k \hat{a}_k$ and $\hat{b}_j / \sum_k \hat{b}_k$) will converge, assuming (as we do in this section) that $f_{ij} > 0$ for all non-deleted cells. (This convergence can be proved from the following two facts: (1) the $\tilde{p}_{ij}$ calculated by (4.11)–(4.12) are convergent; and (2) for cross-classification tables of the kind considered in this section (i.e., for tables that are not separable and that do not have rows or columns that are completely deleted), the set of $\hat{a}_i$ and $\hat{b}_j$ which satisfy (4.3) for a given set of $\tilde{p}_{ij}$ is unique when the $\hat{a}_i$ are normalized, as has been noted in [9].)

The normalized values of the $\hat{a}_i$ and $\hat{b}_i$ are equivalent to the normalized values of the corresponding quantities $\hat{\alpha}_i$ and $\hat{\beta}_j$ obtained when the estimated expected frequencies $\hat{f}_{ij}$ (rather than the $\tilde{p}_{ij}$) are calculated (see, e.g., (2.12)). As noted in Sec. 2.3, these normalized values estimate what proportion of the observations would have been in the ith row and in the jth column, respectively, of the table in the hypothetical situation in which (1) none of entries in the table needs to be void, and (2) the row classification and the column classification are independent (see (2.15) and (2.16)). Examples in which these normalized values are of substantive interest in themselves can be found, e.g., in Sec. 2.3 and in [38]. In comparing the iterative method suggested herein with the Caussinus-Fienberg method, we see that the normalized values are calculated more directly from the former method than from the latter method. (Recall that the former method also had the advantage that it required the calculation of only R trial values or C trial values at each iterative step, whereas the latter method required the calculation of $R \times C$ trial values at each iterative step.)

It should perhaps be noted that the iterative procedure recommended by Watson [65] for estimating expected frequencies in truncated tables also calculates $R \times C$ trial values at each iterative step. For the general case considered in this section, the iterative method suggested herein (see (4.5)–(4.7)) is easier to apply than the Watson method [65].

Having estimated the expected proportions or the expected frequencies under the null hypothesis of quasi-independence, the usual chi-square goodness-of-fit statistic for comparing observed and expected frequencies can then be used. It will have $(R-1)(C-1) - T$ degrees of freedom, where T is the number of deleted cells, with $T < (R-1)(C-1)$.

If $T \geq (R-1)(C-1)$, an examination of the cross-classification table with its deleted cells will show that either (a) some of the rows and/or columns are completely deleted, or (b) the expected frequencies in the non-deleted cells can be estimated in a trivial way from the observed marginal frequencies yielding a perfect fit between the observed and estimated expected frequencies. Of course, in all calculations, R (or C) should be taken as the number of rows (or columns) in the cross-classification table that are not completely deleted.

As we noted earlier, the discussion in this section is limited to contingency tables that are not separable. In particular, the results presented in the preceding two paragraphs apply only to such tables. For tables consisting of separable subsets, these results can be applied separately to each subset that is itself not separable.

The methods for estimating the expected frequencies presented in Sec. 2.1–2.4 (see, e.g., formula (2.1)) are simpler than those presented in the present section. For tables of the kind considered in Sec. 2.1–2.4, the numerical values for the estimated expected frequencies obtained by the methods given there will be the same as those obtained by the iterative method of the present section. (This is true even for the separable table in Sec. 2.1, although the degrees of freedom must be calculated as indicated there.) Thus, the statistics X^2_{Gd} calculated in the earlier sections will give the same result as the chi-square goodness-of-fit statistic suggested earlier in the present section.

As we noted earlier, each of the X^2_{*d} statistics (based upon the method of partitioning into subtables) presented in Sec. 2.2–2.4 differed somewhat from the corresponding X^2_{Gd} statistic, but they were asymptotically equivalent under the null hypothesis of quasi-independence in the truncated table. Further insight into the relationship between these statistics will be obtained in Sec. 5.

The methods of the present section can be applied more generally in cases where explicit formulae cannot be obtained for the estimated expected frequencies and/or the method of partitioning into subtables cannot be applied. The truncated 3×3 table (Table 11) considered in Sec. 2.5 is an example of such a case. With the methods of the present section, the expected frequencies can be estimated for Table 11, and a chi-square goodness-of-fit statistic X^2_{G1} can be calculated. Under the null hypothesis of quasi-independence in the truncated table, the statistic X^2_{G1} will be asymptotically equivalent to the statistic X^2_{I1} considered in Sec. 2.5. For Table 11, we obtain $X^2_{G1} = .6$, which agrees in this case (to the order of accuracy reported here) with the value of X^2_{I1} given earlier.

To further illustrate the application of the method presented in the present section, let us re-examine Table 11 before all three diagonal cells were truncated (see Table 3). We shall now consider the hypothesis of quasi-independence when only two of the diagonal cells in Table 3 have been truncated.

Under the null hypothesis of quasi-independence in the population corresponding to Table 12, the chi-square goodness-of-fit statistic, which is obtained by the methods suggested in the present section, will have an asymptotic χ^2 distribution with $2\times2 - 2=2$ degrees of freedom. Applying this method to Table 12, we obtain $X^2_{G2} = 20.2$. We shall return to the analysis of this table in Sec. 6.

Before closing this section, we note that the methods presented in Sec. 2.5, which were quite different from those discussed in the present section, can also be directly extended to the more general $R\times C$ table in which T cells are deleted. As we pointed out above, the number of degrees of freedom for the $R\times C$ table in the general case will be $(R-1)(C-1)-T$. As earlier, we can calculate simultaneous confidence intervals for all interactions $L(\alpha)$ in the table, using (2.6) and (2.7) as our definition of $L(\alpha)$ with (2.11) and (2.29) replaced now by

$$\alpha_{ij} = 0, \qquad \text{for all deleted cells } (i, j). \tag{4.13}$$

Similarly, a test of the null hypothesis that all these interactions are zero can be based upon the corresponding $\hat{L}(\alpha)$ defined by (2.8) with the α_{ij} satisfying (2.7) and (4.13) (see Goodman [31], Caussinus [9]). This null hypothesis is equivalent to the null hypothesis of quasi-independence in the population corresponding to the truncated $R\times C$ table. Under this null hypothesis, the test

TABLE 12. CROSS-CLASSIFICATION OF BRITISH MALE SAMPLE
ACCORDING TO EACH SUBJECT'S STATUS CATEGORY AND HIS
FATHER'S STATUS CATEGORY, EXCLUDING UPPER-STATUS
AND LOWER-STATUS SUBJECTS HAVING THE SAME
STATUS AS THEIR FATHERS

Father's Status	Subject's Status		
	Upper	Middle	Lower
Upper	—	395	159
Middle	349	714	447
Lower	114	320	—

based upon the $\hat{L}(\alpha)$ will be asymptotically equivalent to the test based upon
the chi-square goodness-of-fit statistic suggested earlier in the present section.

5. LIKELIHOOD-RATIO STATISTICS AND TABLES FOR
THE ANALYSIS OF ASSOCIATION

In the earlier sections we used the usual chi-square goodness-of-fit statistic
for comparing the observed frequencies f_{ij} in the non-deleted cells with the
corresponding estimated expected frequencies $\hat{f}_{ij}$ calculated under a given
null hypothesis; i.e.,

$$X_{Gd}^2 = \sum_{i,j} (f_{ij} - \hat{f}_{ij})^2 / \hat{f}_{ij}. \tag{5.1}$$

In (5.1) (and in (5.2)–(5.3) below) the symbol $\sum_{i,j}$ denotes summation only
over the non-deleted cells. (Note that the statistic X_d^2, which we considered
earlier for testing for independence in a non-truncated table (or non-truncated
subtable), is a special case of (5.1) applied to the non-truncated table (or subtable)). Instead of the statistic (5.1) we could have used the corresponding
chi-square statistic X_{Ld}^2 based upon the likelihood-ratio pertaining to the given
null hypothesis (see, e.g., Wilks [67]). For the contingency table (with or without deleted cells), the X_{Ld}^2 statistic can be written as

$$X_{Ld}^2 = 2 \sum_{i,j} f_{ij} [\log (f_{ij}/\hat{f}_{ij})], \tag{5.2}$$

or equivalently as

$$X_{Ld}^2 = 2 \left[\sum_{i,j} f_{ij} \log f_{ij} - \sum_i f_{i.} \log \hat{\alpha}_i - \sum_j f_{.j} \log \hat{\beta}_j \right], \tag{5.3}$$

where $\hat{f}_{ij} = \hat{\alpha}_i \hat{\beta}_j$ for the non-deleted cells. Formula (5.3) can be calculated
more directly than (5.2) from the R terms $\hat{\alpha}_i$ and the C terms $\hat{\beta}_j$, thus avoiding
the calculation of the $R \times C$ terms $\hat{f}_{ij}$.

The exposition in the earlier sections made use of the usual goodness-of-fit
statistics X_{Gd}^2 (and X_d^2), rather than the statistic X_{Ld}^2, because the former statistics are more familiar to many readers of this Journal. On the other hand, the

statistic X_{Ld}^2 has certain advantages for our present purposes. For example, while (as we noted earlier) the statistic X_{Gd}^2 calculated from (5.1) can differ from the corresponding statistic X_{*d}^2 (i.e., the sum of the X_d^2 statistics which are calculated to test for independence within each subtable of the set into which the table has been partitioned), the statistic X_{Ld}^2, calculated from (5.2) will be equal to the corresponding statistic X_{*Ld}^2 obtained as the sum of the X_{Ld}^2 statistics (i.e., the chi-square statistics based upon the likelihood-ratios) which are calculated to test for independence within each subtable of the set into which the table has been partitioned. For other comments on (5.1) and (5.2), see Neyman [57], Anderson and Goodman [1], Good [27], Bahadur [3], Hoeffding [45].

For convenience, all chi-square statistics presented below and in the following section will be based upon the corresponding likelihood-ratios rather than the statistics used earlier herein. Some of the results obtained with the X_{Ld}^2 statistics will be summarized in tables for the analysis of association which are analogous to Fisher's tables for the analysis of variance. These tables are particularly suited for the presentation of results obtained when an $R \times C$ contingency table (truncated or non-truncated) is partitioned into subtables by the general method described in Sec. 2.2 (applied with the X_{Ld}^2 statistics).

Tables for the analysis of association could be given corresponding to the partitioning of the truncated Tables 2, 4, and 10; here Table 4 will serve to illustrate the procedure. For some different (but related) tables, see Cochran [13], Kullback, Kupperman and Ku [51, 52], Snedecor and Cochran [62a].

We had noted earlier that the particular set of subtables into which the truncated table was partitioned was chosen for expository purposes only, and

TABLE 13. ANALYSIS OF ASSOCIATION IN TABLE 4

Component Due To	Chi-Square	Degrees of Freedom
Table 4A	56.9	1
Table 4B	33.2	1
Table 4C	50.5	1
Total	140.6	3

that other sets (obtained also by the method described in Sec. 2.2) may lead to more interesting results. We shall not explore this point here, except to note that a different (and more interesting) partitioning of the 3 degrees of freedom of Table 4 will be presented as part of Table 16.

6. NON-TRUNCATED CONTINGENCY TABLES

Testing for independence in the non-truncated Table 3, we obtain X_{L4}^2 =499.6. Table 14 tells us how much of this chi-square value is due to the "association" between upper-status subjects and upper-status fathers (i.e., the entry in the (U, U) cell), and how much is due to the other cells (Table 4). The component due to the entry in the (U, U) cell can be calculated from Table 3A using the chi-square statistic based on the likelihood-ratio test for independence in the 2×2 table. The component due to the other cells (Table 4) can be obtained by subtracting the component due to Table 3A from the total, or by the direct analysis of Table 4 using the methods of Sec. 2.2, applied now with the chi-square statistics based on the likelihood-ratios. From Table 14, we see that a rather large part of the total chi-square for Table 3 is due to the entry in the (U, U) cell (with its one degree of freedom). (The numerical results presented in this article were calculated to more decimal places than reported here, which led to the apparent discrepancy in the final digit of the reported total chi-square in Table 14 and elsewhere.) Note that the chi-square in the first row of Table 14 pertains simply to Table 3A.

TABLE 14. ANALYSIS OF ASSOCIATION IN TABLE 3

Component Due to	Chi-Square	Degrees of Freedom
Entry in (U, U) cell (Table 3A)	358.9	1
Other cells (Table 4)	140.6	3
Total	499.6	4

The methods used to obtain Table 14 can be applied directly to assess how much of the total chi-square statistic X^2_{Ld} for testing for independence in a non-truncated $R \times C$ table is due to the entry in any given cell, and how much is due to the other cells.

Table 15 tells us how much of the chi-square statistic X^2_{L4} for Table 3 is due to the non-diagonal cells (Table 11). It also tells us how much of the X^2_{L4} is due to the diagonal cells (relative to the marginals of Table 11), assuming that there is quasi-independence (Q-I) within Table 11. The component due to the diagonal cells is the chi-square statistic based on the likelihood-ratio for testing for independence in Table 3 assuming quasi-independence within the non-diagonal cells. This component is a function of the entries in the diagonal cells and the marginals of Table 11. (Given the marginals, the component due to the diagonal cells is independent of the actual entries in Table 11.) This component can be obtained by subtracting the component due to the non-diagonal cells from the total. From Table 15, we see that the total chi-square for Table 3 is due almost entirely to the entries in the diagonal cells.

The method used here to obtain Table 15 can be applied directly to assess

TABLE 15. ANALYSIS OF ASSOCIATION IN TABLE 3

Component Due to	Chi-Square	Degrees of Freedom
Non-diagonal cells (Table 11)	0.6	1
Diagonal cells (Assuming Q-I in Table 11)	499.0	3
Total	499.6	4

how much of the total chi-square statistic X_{Ld}^2 for testing for independence in a non-truncated $R \times C$ table is due to a given subset S of cells (e.g., the non-diagonal cells). If S does not include any cells for which there are suspected affinities or disaffinities (see related comments in Sec. 1), then we can also assess how much of the total X_{Ld}^2 is due to the other cells (those not included in S) relative to the marginals of S.

Tables 14 and 15 can be combined to give Table 16. This table tells us, among other things, how much of the X_{L4}^2 for Table 3 is due to the cells (M, M) and (L, L) (relative to the marginals of Table 11), assuming quasi-independence in Table 11. The component due to the two cells is the chi-square statistic based on the likelihood-ratio for testing for independence in Table 4 assuming quasi-independence within the non-diagonal cells. This component is a function of the entries in the two cells and the marginals of Table 11. (Given these marginals, this component is independent of the actual entries in Table 11.) This component can be obtained by subtraction. From Table 16, we see that the total chi-square for Table 3 is due almost entirely to the entries in the diagonal cells, that a rather large part of this chi-square is due to the entry in the (U, U) cell (with its one degree of freedom), and that a smaller part of the total chi-square is due to the (M, M) and (L, L) cells (with their 2 degrees of freedom).

TABLE 16. ANALYSIS OF ASSOCIATION IN TABLE 3

Component Due To	Chi-Square	Degrees of Freedom
Entry in (U, U) cell (Table 3A)	358.9	1
Non-diagonal cells (Table 11)	0.6	1
(M, M) and (L, L) cells (Assuming Q-I in Table 11)	140.0	2
Total	499.6	4

The analysis in Table 16 was made in three steps: (I) Table 3 was partitioned to form Table 4 and Table 3A; (II) Table 4 was truncated to form Table 11; and (III) attention was focused on the cells in Table 4 that were not in Table 11. The methods used to obtain Table 16 can be applied directly to an $R \times C$ table in three steps: (1) The non-truncated $R \times C$ table (e.g., Table 3) can be partitioned into subtables (e.g. Tables 4A–C and Table 3A) using the general method of partitioning given in Sec. 2.2, or into subtables and truncated tables obtained by combining appropriately some of the partitioned subtables (e.g., Table 3A and Table 4, with Table 4 viewed as a combination of Tables 4A–C); (2) for each subtable or truncated table thus obtained (e.g., Table 4), a subset S of its cells (e.g., the non-diagonal cells), for which there are no suspected row-column affinities or disaffinities, can be considered; and (3) for each subtable or truncated table considered at step (2), attention can be focused on the cells in the subtable or truncated table that were not considered at step (2) (i.e., the cells not included in S). (As noted in Sec. 3, each subtable (or truncated table) obtained at step (1) can be tested for independence (or quasi-independence) even when there is dependence in the non-truncated $R \times C$ table, if the marginals of the $R \times C$ table are not fixed.)

The methods used to carry out step (1) above can be applied to an $R \times C$ table without applying steps (2) and (3). For particular illustrations of these general methods, see Table 14 (in which step (1) was applied to a non-truncated $R \times C$ table) and Table 13 (in which step (1) was applied to a truncated table). The methods used to carry out steps (2) and (3) above can also be applied to an $R \times C$ table without applying step (1). For particular illustrations of these general methods, see Table 15 (in which steps (2) and (3) were applied to a non-truncated $R \times C$ table) and Table 17 below (in which steps (2) and (3) are applied to a truncated table).

For a different example of the application of step (1), consider a non-truncated $R \times C$ table in which the following three tests of homogeneity are made: (a) A test of homogeneity of the first R' rows ($R' < R$); (b) a test of homogeneity of the remaining $R - R'$ rows; (c) a test of homogeneity of a row obtained by combining the corresponding entries in the first R' rows and a row obtained by combining the entries in the remaining $R - R'$ rows. (If $R' = R - 1$, then test (b) can be ignored.) Similarly, for a different example of the application of the kind of analysis described by steps (2) and (3), consider a non-truncated or a truncated $R \times C$ table in which the following three tests of quasi-independence are made based upon the division of the non-deleted cells of the $R \times C$ table into two mutually exclusive and exhaustive subsets S and S': (a) A test of quasi-independence of the cells in S; (b) a test of quasi-independence of the cells in S'; (c) a test of quasi-independence of the non-deleted cells of the $R \times C$ table, assuming both quasi-independence in S and quasi-independence in S'. Test (c) is actually a test of whether the parameter values pertaining to S (assuming quasi-independence in S) are equal to the corresponding values (if any) pertaining to S'. (Using the definition of separability given in Sec. 2.1, if the $R \times C$ table is separable into S and S', then test (c) can be ignored.)

TABLE 17. ANALYSIS OF ASSOCIATION IN TABLE 12

Component Due To	Chi-Square	Degrees of Freedom
Non-diagonal cells (Table 11)	0.6	1
Entry in (M, M) cell (Assuming Q-I in Table 11)	20.0	1
Total	20.6	2

Table 17 tells us how much of the statistic X_{L2}^2 for testing for quasi-independence in Table 12 is due to the (M, M) cell (relative to the marginals of Table 11), assuming quasi-independence in Table 11. This component is the chi-square statistic based on the likelihood-ratio for testing for quasi-independence in Table 12, assuming quasi-independence within the non-diagonal cells (see [37]). It is a function of the entry in the (M, M) cell and the marginals of Table 11; and it can be obtained simply by subtraction. The methods used to obtain Table 17 can be applied directly to the analysis of a given subset (e.g., Table 12) of an $R \times C$ table consisting of (1) a set S of cells (e.g., the non-diagonal cells) and (2) some other cells not included in S (e.g., the (M, M) cell), excluding from the set S those cells that are suspected of having row-column affinities and/or disaffinities.

Since Table 12 does not include the entries in the (U, U) and (L, L) cells, the direct effects of these two diagonal cells are ignored in the analysis presented in Table 17. Thus, Table 17 includes a component due to the effects of the entry in the (M, M) cell, aside from the effects of the (U, U) and (L, L) cells. The component in Table 15 due to the diagonal cells includes the effects of all three diagonal cells, while a component in Table 16 includes the effects of cells (M, M) and (L, L), aside from the effects of the (U, U) cell.

The second and third lines of Table 16 provide an analysis of the three degrees of freedom in the truncated Table 4 (which is different from the earlier analysis in Table 13). Similarly, Table 17 provides an analysis of the two degrees of freedom in the truncated Table 12. The methods which we have used in the present section to analyze these truncated tables can be applied more generally to analyze other $R \times C$ truncated tables (e.g., Table 10) as well as non-truncated tables.

7. THE ANALYSIS OF TWO OR MORE CONTINGENCY TABLES

Having indicated in Sec. 4 (and in Sec. 2.2, 2.5) how to estimate the interactions $L(\alpha)$ in an $R \times C$ table in which T cells are deleted, it is also possible to provide methods for comparing the interactions in two different $R \times C$ tables each having some deleted cells. If the two tables do not have the same deleted cells, then we can modify each of these tables by deleting all cells which are deleted in at least one of the tables. To these two modified tables, we can now apply the methods presented by Goodman [33, 35, 36] and Caussinus [9] for obtaining simultaneous confidence intervals for all the differences between the corresponding interactions in the two tables, or for a subset of these differences, and we can test the null hypothesis that these differences are all zero. In comparing the two modified tables, each having T deleted cells, the number of degrees of freedom will be $(R-1)(C-1)-T$, if each table does not consist of separable subtables.

In order to compare K different $R \times C$ tables $(K \geq 2)$ each having the same deleted cells, the general methods provided in the literature cited above can be applied. If each table has T deleted cells and is not separable, the number of degrees of freedom in comparing the K tables will be $(K-1)[(R-1)(C-1)-T]$. In the case where the K different tables do not have the same deleted cells, these methods could be applied directly to a set of K modified tables (each modified table is obtained by deleting all cells which are deleted in at least one of the tables); but when $K > 2$ the comparison of the K modified tables (rather than the original tables) will not be fully efficient.

To test the null hypothesis that the corresponding interactions in K different $R \times C$ tables (i.e., the original tables) are all equal, we can apply a test of the null hypothesis that the three-factor interactions in the corresponding $R \times C \times K$ table are all zero. Even when the original tables (rather than the modified tables) are used, the general method for testing this null hypothesis, which was given in [31], can be directly applied to the corresponding $R \times C \times K$ table.

The calculation of the appropriate number of degrees of freedom for testing the null hypothesis of no three-factor interaction in the $R \times C \times K$ table is somewhat more complicated in the general case (when some of the cells are deleted) than was the corresponding calculation for the $R \times C$ table. Recall that, for a $R \times C$ table in which a subset S of the cells are not deleted and the other T cells are deleted, the estimated expected frequencies are of the form

$$f_{ij} = \hat{\alpha}_i \hat{\beta}_j \qquad \text{(for all cells } (i, j) \text{ in } S), \tag{7.1}$$

and the number of degrees of freedom are $(R-1)(C-1) - T = R \times C - 1 - T - [(R-1) + (C-1)]$, if the table is not separable; i.e., if S is such that the $\hat{\alpha}_i$ and $\hat{\beta}_j$ satisfying (7.1) are unique (when they have been normalized). Similarly, for a $R \times C \times K$ table in which a subset σ of the cells are not deleted and the other τ cells are deleted, the estimated expected frequencies are of the form

$$f_{ijk} = \hat{\alpha}_{ij} \hat{\beta}_{jk} \hat{\gamma}_{ki} \qquad \text{(for all cells } (i, j, k) \text{ in } \sigma); \tag{7.2}$$

and if σ is such that the $\hat{\alpha}_{ij}$, $\hat{\beta}_{jk}$, and $\hat{\gamma}_{ki}$ satisfying (7.2) are unique (when they have been normalized so that $\sum_j \hat{\alpha}_{ij} = 1$, $\sum_k \hat{\beta}_{jk} = 1$, $\sum_i \hat{\gamma}_{ki} = 1$), then the number of degrees of freedom will be as follows:

$$R \times C \times K - 1 - \tau - [R(C-1) - \tau_{RC} + C(K-1) - \tau_{CK} + K(R-1) \tag{7.3}$$

$$- \tau_{KR}] = (R-1)(C-1)(K-1) - \tau - \tau_{**},$$

where τ_{RC}, τ_{CK}, and τ_{KR} are the number of truncated cells in the $R \times C$, the $C \times K$ and the $K \times R$ marginal tables, respectively; and $\tau_{**} = \tau_{RC} + \tau_{CK} + \tau_{KR}$. Of course, in all calculations, the R, C, and K should be taken as the number of rows, columns, and layers, respectively, that are not completely deleted. (Formula (7.3) can also be obtained by an extension to the truncated case of the formulation for the non-truncated case in [6], with the quantity in brackets in (7.3) interpreted as the total number of estimated first-order and second-order interactions.)

From (7.1), or the corresponding (4.3), we obtained the set of equations (4.4) which were then used to construct the iterative procedure (4.5)–(4.7). Similarly, from (7.2) we obtain the following set of equations:

$$\hat{f}_{ij.} = \hat{\alpha}_{ij} \sum_k \delta_{ijk} \hat{\beta}_{jk} \hat{\gamma}_{ki}, \qquad f_{.jk} = \hat{\beta}_{jk} \sum_i \delta_{ijk} \hat{\alpha}_{ij} \hat{\gamma}_{ki}, \tag{7.4}$$

$$f_{i.k} = \hat{\gamma}_{ki} \sum_j \delta_{ijk} \hat{\alpha}_{ij} \hat{\beta}_{jk},$$

where $\delta_{ijk} = 1$ for cell (i, j, k) in σ, and $\delta_{ijk} = 0$ otherwise. From (7.2), an iterative procedure for calculating $\hat{\alpha}_{ij}$, $\hat{\beta}_{jk}$, $\hat{\gamma}_{ki}$, which is directly analogous to the procedure (4.5)–(4.7) proposed here (and in [32]), can be constructed. (This procedure also provides an extension to the truncated case of a procedure developed for the non-truncated case in [15].) With this procedure for calculating $\hat{\alpha}_{ij}$, $\hat{\beta}_{jk}$, $\hat{\gamma}_{ki}$, we can then use (7.2) to calculate the estimated expected frequencies $\hat{f}_{ijk}$. These frequencies can also be calculated by an extension of the Caussinus-Fienberg iterative method which we discussed in Sec. 4 above (see also [9]). For an illustration of the application of the methods discussed in the present section, see [38].

REFERENCES

[1] Anderson, T. W. and Goodman, L. A., "Statistical inference about Markov chains," *Annals of Mathematical Statistics*, *28* (1957), 89–109.

[2] Asano, C., "On estimating multinomial probabilities by pooling incomplete samples," *Annals of the Institute of Statistical Mathematics*, *17* (1965), 1–13.

[3] Bahadur, R. R., "Rates of convergence of estimates and test statistics," *Annals of Mathematical Statistics*, *38* (1967), 303–24.

[4] Batschelet, E., "Über eine Kontingenztafel mit fehlenden Daten," *Biometrische Zeitschrift*, *2* (1960), 236–43.

[5] Batschelet, E., "Auslesfreie Verteilung des Manifestationsalters mit einer Anwendung auf die Resperationsatopien," *Biometrische Zeitschrift*, *2* (1960), 244–56.

[6] Birch, M. W., "Maximum likelihood in three-way contingency tables," *Journal of the Royal Statistical Society, Series B*, *25* (1963), 220–33.

[7] Bishop, Y., and Fienberg, S., "Incomplete two-dimensional contingency tables," unpublished manuscript.

[8] Blumen, I., Kogan, M., and McCarthy, P. J., *The Industrial Mobility of Labor as a Probability Process*. Cornell Studies of Industrial and Labor Relations, Vol. 4. Ithaca, N.Y.: Cornell University, 1955.

[9] Caussinus, H., "Contribution à l'analyse statistique des tableaux de corrélation," *Annales de la Faculté des Sciences de l'Université de Toulouse*, *29* (1965), 77–182.

[10] Caussinus, H., "Sur un problemè d'analyse de la corrèlation de deux caractères qualitatifs," *Comptes Rendus de l'Académie des Sciences*, *255* (1962), 1688–90.

[11] Chen, W. Y., Crittenden, L. B., Mantel, N. and Cameron, W. R., "Site distribution of cancer deaths in husband-wife and sibling pairs," *Journal of the National Cancer Institute*, *27* (1961), 875–92.

[12] Cochran, W. G., "The χ^2 test of goodness of fit," *Annals of Mathematical Statistics*, *23* (1952), 315–45.

[13] Cochran, W. G., "Some methods for strengthening the common χ^2 tests," *Biometrics*, *10* (1954), 417–52.

[14] Craig, C. C., "Combination of neighboring cells in contingency tables," *Journal of the American Statistical Association*, *48* (1953), 104–112.

[15] Darroch, J. N., "Interactions in multi-factor contingency tables," *Journal of the Royal Statistical Society, Series B*, *24* (1962), 251–63.

[16] Fienberg, S. E., "Preliminary graphical analysis and local independence for two-way contingency tables," unpublished manuscript.

[17] Fisher, R. A., "On the interpretation of χ^2 from contingency tables, and the calculation of P," *Journal of the Royal Statistical Society*, *85* (1922), 87–94.

[18] Fisher, R. A., "Statistical tests of the agreement between observation and hypothesis," *Economica*, *8* (1923), 1–9.

[19] Fisher, R. A., "The conditions under which χ^2 measures the discrepancy between observation and hypothesis," *Journal of the Royal Statistical Society*, *87* (1924), 442–50.

[20] Fisher, R. A., "On a distribution yielding the error functions of several well known statistics," *Proceedings of the International Mathematical Congress, Toronto* (1924), 805–13.

[21] Fisher, R. A., "On a property connecting the χ^2 measure of discrepancy with the method of maximum likelihood," *Atti del Congresso Internazionale dei Mathematici, Bologna, 7* (1928), 95–100.

[22] Fisher, R. A., *Statistical Methods for Research Workers*, 5th and subsequent editions. Edinburg: Oliver and Boyd Ltd., 1934; Section 21.02.

[23] Fisher, R. A., "The logic of inductive inference," *Journal of the Royal Statistical Society, 98* (1935), 39–54.

[24] Fisher, R. A., "Confidence limits for a cross-product ratio," *Australian Journal of Statistics, 4* (1962), 41.

[25] Geppert, M. P., "Erwartungstreue plausibelste Schätzer ans dreieckig gestutzten Kontingenztafeln," *Biometrische Zeitschrift, 3* (1961), 54–67.

[26] Glass, D. V. (ed.), *Social Mobility in Britain*. Glencoe, Illinois: Free Press, 1954.

[27] Good, I. J., "Saddle-point methods for the multinomial distribution," *Annals of Mathematical Statistics, 28* (1957), 861–81.

[28] Good, I. J., *The Estimation of Probabilities*. Cambridge, Mass.: Massachusetts Institute of Technology Press, 1965.

[29] Goodman, L. A., "Statistical methods for the mover-stayer model," *Journal of the American Statistical Association, 56* (1961), 841–68.

[30] Goodman, L. A., "Statistical methods for the preliminary analysis of transaction flows," *Econometrica, 31* (1963), 197–208.

[31] Goodman, L. A., "On Plackett's test for contingency table interactions," *Journal of the Royal Statistical Society, Series B, 25* (1963), 179–88.

[32] Goodman, L. A., "A short computer program for the analysis of transaction flows," *Behavioral Science, 9* (1964), 176–86.

[33] Goodman, L. A., "Simultaneous confidence limits for cross-product ratios in contingency tables," *Journal of the Royal Statistical Society, Series B, 26* (1964), 86–102.

[34] Goodman, L. A., "Simultaneous confidence intervals for contrasts among multinomial populations," *Annals of Mathematical Statistics, 35* (1964), 716–25.

[35] Goodman, L. A., "Simple methods for analyzing three-factor interaction in contingency tables," *Journal of the American Statistical Association, 59* (1964), 319–352.

[36] Goodman, L. A., "Interactions in multidimensional contingency tables," *Annals of Mathematical Statistics, 35* (1964), 632–46.

[37] Goodman, L. A., "On the statistical analysis of mobility tables," *American Journal of Sociology, 70* (1965), 564–585.

*[38] Goodman, L. A., "How to ransack social mobility tables and other kinds of cross-classification tables," *American Journal of Sociology, 75* (1969).

[39] Goodman, L. A. and Kruskal, W. H., "Measures of association for cross classifications," *Journal of the American Statistical Association, 49* (1954), 732–64.

[40] Goodman, L. A. and Kruskal, W. H., "Measures of association for cross classifications. II: Further discussion and references," *Journal of the American Statistical Association, 54* (1959), 123–63.

[41] Goodman, L. A., and Kruskal, W. H., "Measures of association for cross classifications. III: Approximate sampling theory," *Journal of the American Statistical Association, 58* (1963), 310–64.

[42] Harris, J. A. and Treloar, A. E., "On a limitation in the applicability of the contingency coefficient," *Journal of the American Statistical Association, 22* (1927), 460–72.

[43] Harris, J. A. and Chi Tu, "A second category of limitations in the applicability of the contingency coefficient," *Journal of the American Statistical Association, 24* (1929), 367–75.

[44] Harris, J. A., Treloar, A. E., and Wilder, M., "Professor Pearson's note on our papers on contingency," *Journal of the American Statistical Association, 25* (1930), 323–7.

[45] Hoeffding, W., "Asymptotically optimal tests for multinomial distributions," *Annals of Mathematical Statistics, 36* (1965), 369–408.

[46] Irwin, J. O., "A note on the subdivision of χ^2 into components," *Biometrika, 36* (1949), 130–4.

[47] Ishii, G., "Intraclass contingency tables," *Annals of the Institute of Statistical Mathematics, 12* (1960), 161–207.

[48] Kastenbaum, M. A., "Estimation of relative frequencies of four sperm types in Drosophila Melanogaster," *Biometrics, 14* (1958), 223–8.

[49] Kastenbaum, M. A.. "A note on the additive partitioning of chi-square in contingency tables," *Biometrics, 16* (1960), 416–22.

[50] Kimball, A. W., "Short-cut formulas for the exact partition of χ^2 in contingency tables," *Biometrics, 10* (1954), 452–8.

[51] Kullback, S., Kupperman, M., and Ku, H. H., "Tests for contingency tables and Markov chains," *Technometrics, 4* (1962), 573–608.

[52] Kullback, S., Kupperman, M., and Ku, H. H., "An application of information theory to the analysis of contingency tables, with a table of $2n \log n$, $n = 1$ (1) 10,000," *Journal of Research of the National Bureau of Standards, 66B* (1962), 217–43.

[53] Lancaster, H. O., "The derivation and partition of χ^2 in certain discrete distributions," *Biometrika, 36*, (1949), 117–29.

[54] Lindley, D. V., "The Bayesian analysis of contingency tables," *Annals of Mathematical Statistics, 35* (1964). 1622–43.

[55] Mantel, N., "Models for complex contingency tables and polychotomous dosage response curves," *Biometrics, 22* (1966), 83–95.

[56] Mantel, N. and Halperin, M., "Analyses of birth-rank data," *Biometrics 19* (1963), 324–40.

[57] Neyman, J., "Contributions to the theory of the χ^2 test," *Proceedings of the Berkeley Symposium on Mathematical Statistics and Probability.* Berkeley and Los Angeles: University of California Press, 1949; pp. 239–73.

[58] Novitski, E. and Sandler, I., "Are all products of spermatogenesis regularly functional?", *Proceedings of the National Academy of Sciences, 43* (1957), 318–24.

[59] Okamoto, M. and Ishii, G., "Tests of independence in interclass 2×2 tables," *Biometrika, 45* (1961), 181–90.

[60] Pearson, K., "On the theory of contingency. I. Note on Professor J. Arthur Harris' paper on the limitation in the applicability of the contingency coefficient," *Journal of the American Statistical Association, 25* (1930), 320–3.

[61] Pearson, K., "Postscript," *Journal of the American Statistical Association, 25* (1930), 327.

[62] Savage, I. R., and Deutsch, K. W., "A statistical model for the gross analysis of transaction flows," *Econometrica, 28* (1960), 551–72.

[62a] Snedecor, G. W., and Cochran, W. G., *Statistical Methods*, Sixth Edition. Ames, Iowa: The Iowa State University Press, 1967; pp. 252–3.

[63] Thionet, P., "Note sur le remplissage d'un tableau à double entrée," *Journal de la Societe de Statistique de Paris, 10–12* (1964), 228–247.

[64] Waite, H., "Association of finger-prints," *Biometrika, 10* (1915), 421–78.

[65] Watson, G. S., "Missing and 'mixed-up' frequencies in contingency tables," *Biometrics, 12* (1956), 47–50.

[66] White, H. C., "Cause and effect in social mobility tables," *Behavioral Sciences, 7* (1963), 14–27.

[67] Wilks, S. S., *Mathematical Statistics.* New York: John Wiley and Sons, Inc., 1962.

Everyman's Interaction (Association) Analyzer

How to Ransack Social Mobility Tables and Other Kinds of Cross-Classification Tables

This article presents (1) methods for examining every part of a social mobility table in search of the various possible relationships between an individual's status category and his father's status category that are congruent with the data in the table; (2) methods for comparing two (or more) social mobility tables by examining the corresponding parts of each of the tables in search of the differences between the corresponding relationships in the tables; and (3) conceptual tools that can be used by the research worker to assist and stimulate him to conceive of a wide variety of possible relationships between an individual's status category and his father's status category, which could then be checked with the data. These tools and methods can also be applied to other kinds of cross-classification tables to assist in the conception and analysis of the various possible relationships between the column classification and the row classification of each table, and in studying the differences between the corresponding relationships in two (or more) such tables.[1] The techniques presented here for studying the possible relationships between two qualitative variables (the column classification and the row classification) were obtained, in part, by adapting, for qualitative variables, some of the multiple-comparison ideas developed earlier in the analysis of variance context. To illustrate the application of the conceptual tools and methods proposed here, we reanalyze data on intergeneration social mobility in Britain and in Denmark. We find, for example, with the introduction of a new concept of "intrinsic status inheritance and status disinheritance," that there is a statistically significant amount of intrinsic status disinheritance in the middle status category in Britain and in Denmark, as well as statistically significant amounts of intrinsic status inheritance in the upper and lower status categories. (This result concerning status disinheritance is an apparent contradiction of all earlier findings based on the more usual methods of analysis.) Furthermore, there is more intrinsic status inheritance in the upper status category than in the lower, and the difference is statistically significant in both countries. Also, in contrast to all earlier findings, we find that the relationship between a subject's status and his father's status in the British study differs from the corresponding relationship in the Danish study in statistically significant ways which we describe in some detail.

---

[1] The relationships between column and row classifications can be expressed in terms of the interaction (association) in the table(s).

In analyzing a given body of data, many of us have been taught that we should formulate the hypotheses which we might wish to test before we examine the data upon which the test is to be based, and that hypotheses which are suggested to us by a scanning of the data cannot then be tested using the same data. We have been warned (or we should have been warned) that the methods usually used for testing hypotheses can lead us astray if the particular hypotheses selected for testing are determined by first scanning the body of data to be tested. In the present article, we shall provide relatively simple methods for analyzing a given body of data, which are different from the usual methods, and which can be used by the research worker to test hypotheses which might be suggested to him by scanning the data, as well as hypotheses which he might have formulated beforehand. The methods presented here can be used when the body of data to be scanned, and later analyzed, consists of a cross-classification table or a set of cross-classification tables (e.g., a social mobility table for a given country or a set of social mobility tables for various countries).

A research worker cannot be expected to formulate beforehand (i.e., before scanning the data) all the hypotheses which he might later conceive of and which he might then wish to test. Indeed, the research worker's ability to conceive of hypotheses in the course of scanning a body of data is an important asset which he would do well to develop. In the present article, we shall also provide a general conceptual tool which can be used by the research worker to assist and stimulate him to *conceive* of hypotheses which he might then wish to test. In the analysis of a given cross-classification table, this tool can be used to assist in the formulation of a variety of hypotheses pertaining to the various relationships between the column classification of the table and the row classification (e.g., between an individual's status category and his father's status category as represented by the columns and rows, respectively, in an intergeneration social mobility table). In the analysis of a set of two (or more) cross-classification tables, this tool can be used to assist in the formulation of a variety of hypotheses pertaining to the difference between the tables with respect to the corresponding relationships between the column classification and the row classification of each table; for example, the difference between two (or more) countries with respect to the corresponding relationships between an individual's status category and his father's status category in each country.

As we have noted, the methods referred to above can be applied, for instance, to intergeneration social mobility tables in which the columns denote the possible status categories of the individuals (the respondents) and the rows denote the corresponding status categories for their fathers. These methods can also be applied to quite different kinds of cross-classification tables. In order to apply these methods, the number of columns in the table need not be equal to the number of rows in the table, and the column and row classifications can pertain to quite different variables (e.g., education and race). In social mobility tables, the column and row classifications pertain to the same kind of variable (e.g., status—subject's status and father's status), and the tables are usually square (i e., there are an equal number of columns and rows).

In this paper, we shall not discuss all the possible relationships between the column and row classifications of the table that may be of interest, but only some of the ones that appear to be relevant to the particular kind of cross-classification tables under study. For other kinds of cross-classification tables, the general conceptual tool presented here can lead to the formulation of quite different possible relationships between the column and row classifications of the table, which could then be checked with the data using the statistical methods here proposed.

The techniques proposed here were obtained, in part, by adapting, for qualitative variables, some of the multiple-comparison ideas proposed earlier in the analysis of variance context. This adaptation for the analysis of qualitative variables was carried out in an earlier series of articles by the present author (Goodman 1964b–e, 1965a) in which simultaneous confidence intervals and multiple-test procedures were developed for the simultaneous analysis of a variety of questions pertaining to a given qualitative variable or to a given set of qualitative variables.[2] In the present paper, we shall use some of the techniques introduced in this earlier series of articles together with a quite different set of techniques that were developed for the analysis of cross-classified data in which the entries in certain cells of the cross-classification table are omitted from the analysis because they are either missing, unreliable, void, or restricted in certain ways (see e.g., Goodman 1961b, 1963, 1964a, 1965b, 1968, and the literature cited there). We shall see how these two quite different kinds of contributions to our battery of methods for the analysis of qualitative variables can be brought together to shed further light on a single body of data.

The multiple-test procedures proposed herein for the analysis of qualitative variables can be used to overcome some of the methodological problems described by Stinchcombe (1964, p. 196) pertaining to the use of the same material in both the exploratory analysis and in the final survey, and they can also be used to perform some of the data-dredging functions described by Selvin and Stuart (1966) for survey analysis. These techniques provide a flexible yet systematic way to study a given qualitative variable or a given set of qualitative variables. It should, however, be noted that there are certain limits to the flexibility of these techniques. For example, in this article, our analysis of a given cross-classification table will be limited to the study of the various possible "multiplicative interactions" between the column and row classifications (i.e., between the status categories for the individuals and the status categories for their fathers). We shall consider a wide variety of multiplicative interactions between the column and row classifications, and we could, in principle, consider all such multiplicative interactions. But we will not consider here other kinds of interactions (between the column and row classifications) that need not be of the multi-

[2] For a discussion of multiple-comparison techniques in various contexts and for some historical perspective on the development of this field, see Miller 1966, and the literature cited there.

plicative kind.[3] The techniques described herein can be used to freely ransack cross-classification tables in order to search for the multiplicative interactions that are congruent with the data.[4]

It should also be noted that the methods presented here can be applied (1) when the cross-classified data describe either a simple random sample of individuals from a given population, or (2) when the data describe a stratified random sample in which the column categories (or the row categories) of the table form the strata that are sampled. These methods are approximate in the same sense that the usual χ^2 test for independence is approximate (i.e., justification for its use is based upon large-sample theory); and they involve the same order of approximation as does the usual χ^2 test. Application of the methods proposed herein can provide a much more thorough analysis of the data than is obtained with the usual χ^2 test.

THE INTERACTION IN EACH 2 × 2 SUBTABLE

For expository purposes, we shall use table 1 to illustrate the methods that we propose in this section. This table is based upon data obtained by Glass and his co-workers (1954).[5] It provides a cross-classification of a sample of 3,497 males in Britain according to each subject's occupational status category and his father's occupational status category.

We shall sometimes refer to the row and column categories in table 1 as the status categories pertaining to a subject's "origin" and "destination," respectively (see Duncan 1966). Looking at table 1, a research worker might select, as worthy of special attention, the particular 2 × 2 subtable obtained when, for example, we consider only U or M origins and U or M destinations (i.e., when we exclude from consideration all subjects whose origin category is L, and also all subjects whose destination category is L). This subtable is table 2.

From table 2, we see that the observed odds are 395 to 588 (i.e., 0.67 to 1.00) that an individual whose origin is U will have destination M rather than destination U; and that the observed odds are 714 to 349 (i.e., 2.05 to 1.00) that an individual whose origin is M will have destination M rather than destination U. The observed "risk" of having destination M (rather than destination U) is 0.67 for those whose origin is U, and it is 2.05 for

[3] Multiplicative kinds of interactions arise naturally with models that describe the expected entries in the cross-classification table as being affected in a multiplicative way by "row effects" (related to the row marginals), "column effects" (related to the column marginals), and "row × column interaction effects"; whereas other kinds of interactions between the column and row classifications arise with other kinds of models. For multiplicative interactions, see Goodman (1964b–d); for others kinds of interactions and related matters, see Goodman (1961a, 1964e, 1965a, c).

[4] These techniques could also be used to search simultaneously for the row effects and the column effects, as well as the interaction effects in the multiplicative model. For further details, see my article (1964d).

[5] The upper-, middle-, and lower-status categories in table 1 correspond to the occupational status categories 1–4, 5, 6–7, respectively, as defined by Glass. Table 1 was studied earlier by White (1963) and Goodman (1965b).

those whose origin is M.[6] The ratio of the risks is $2.05/0.67 = 3.05$.[7] Thus, comparing those whose origin is M with those whose origin is U, the observed "relative risk" of having destination M (rather than destination U) is 3.05 to 1.00. In other words, the observed risk is 3.05 times as great for those whose origin is M than for those whose origin is U. Since the relative

TABLE 1

CROSS-CLASSIFICATION OF A SAMPLE OF BRIT-
ISH MALES ACCORDING TO EACH SUBJECT'S
STATUS CATEGORY AND HIS FATHER'S STA-
TUS CATEGORY

FATHER'S STATUS	SUBJECT'S STATUS		
	U	M	L
U............	588	395	159
M............	349	714	447
L............	114	320	411

NOTE.—This table referred to as British Sample in
following tables.

TABLE 2

CROSS-CLASSIFICATION OF SAMPLE OF
BRITISH MALES: SUBJECT'S STA-
TUS CATEGORY, U OR M; FATHER'S
STATUS CATEGORY, U OR M

FATHER'S STATUS	SUBJECT'S STATUS	
	U	M
U..............	588	395
M..............	349	714

risk calculated above is actually the ratio of the observed odds (i.e., $2.05/0.67$), we refer to it as the "odds-ratio."

For those readers whose understanding is facilitated by an exposition using mathematical notation, we include the following remarks: If we let f_{ij} denote the observed frequency in the ith row ($i = 1,2$) and jth column ($j = 1,2$) of table 2, then the observed risk is f_{12}/f_{11} for those whose origin is U, and the observed risk is f_{22}/f_{21} for those whose origin is M. The observed

[6] The term "risk" as used here is synonymous with the odds of having destination M rather than U (see, for example, Gart 1962). This term has been used sometimes in the statistics literature to denote other things with which the usage here should not be confused.

[7] All numerical results presented in this article were carried out to more significant digits than are reported here. The results were then rounded off to fewer digits for the sake of of simplicity of exposition.

relative risk (i.e., the odds-ratio) is $(f_{22}/f_{21})/(f_{12}/f_{11})$, which is equal to $(f_{11}f_{22})/(f_{12}f_{21})$. The odds-ratio compares the relative magnitudes of the odds (f_{22}/f_{21}) with the odds (f_{12}/f_{11}), the odds (f_{11}/f_{12}) with the odds (f_{21}/f_{22}), the odds (f_{11}/f_{21}) with the odds (f_{12}/f_{22}), the odds (f_{22}/f_{12}) with the odds (f_{21}/f_{11}). Note that the odds-ratio is not influenced by either the absolute or relative sizes of the row marginal totals or by either the absolute or relative sizes of the column marginal totals.[8] Note also that the odds-ratio would remain unchanged if the 2×2 table was changed by relabeling the rows as columns and vice versa.[9]

If the column classification had been independent of the row classification for the 2×2 population table corresponding to table 2, then the odds-ratio (i.e., the relative risk) would have been 1 for this population, and the logarithm of the odds-ratio would have been zero. The logarithm of the observed odds-ratio (3.05) is actually 1.11.[10] We shall call the logarithm of the observed odds-ratio the "interaction" between the column and row classifications of the 2×2 table, and we shall use the symbol G to denote this interaction (see Goodman 1964b). In order to test the null hypothesis that the column classification is independent of the row classification in the 2×2 population table corresponding to table 2 (i.e., the null hypothesis that the interaction between the column and row classifications is zero for the 2×2 population table), we can compare the observed interaction G with zero, using the standard error of G as a gauge.

Again for those readers whose understanding is facilitated by the use of mathematical notation, we include the following: If we let g_{ij} denote the logarithm of f_{ij}, then the logarithm G of the observed odds-ratio is

$$G = \log \left[(f_{11} f_{22})/(f_{12} f_{21}) \right]$$
$$= g_{11} + g_{22} - g_{12} - g_{21} . \tag{1}$$

Since the odds-ratio tells us what is the relative magnitude of one odds (say, f_{22}/f_{21}) compared with another odds (say, f_{12}/f_{11}) in a 2×2 table, when we compare the odds-ratios calculated for different 2×2 tables it would seem natural to examine the relative magnitudes of these odds-

---

[8] In other words, suppose that in the 2×2 table we make a transformation on the cell entries f_{ij} ($i = 1,2; j = 1,2$) of the form

$$f_{ij} \rightarrow a_i b_j f_{ij} ,$$

where a_i and b_j are any positive numbers ($i = 1,2; j = 1,2$). Then the odds-ratio calculated for the transformed table will be equal to the odds-ratio for the original table.

[9] For the 2×2 table, if a measure of association between the column and row classifications is a function of the proportion of the observations in the first row of the table that fall also in the first column and of the proportion of observations in the second row that fall also in the first column, *and* if this measure is invariant when the rows are relabeled as columns and vice versa, then the measure must be a function of the odds-ratio (see Edwards 1963, Goodman 1965c).

[10] Natural logarithms will be used throughout this article. For some tables of natural logarithms, see, for example, Fisher and Yates (1953) and Pearson and Hartley (1954).

ratios. An examination of the relative magnitudes of odds-ratios is facilitated by the calculation of the logarithms of the odds-ratios (i.e., by the calculation of the interactions) since differences between interactions reflect the relative magnitudes of the corresponding odds-ratios (i e., the difference between two interactions is equal to the logarithm of the relative magnitude of the corresponding odds-ratios). If the difference between two interactions remains unchanged, the corresponding relative magnitudes of the odds-ratios will remain unchanged.[11] Since we are interested in the relative magnitudes of odds ratios, we use the logarithmic scale of measurement; that is, we use the corresponding interactions.[12] We also note that the standard error S of the interaction G is of a particularly simple form, namely,[13]

$$S = (h_{11} + h_{22} + h_{12} + h_{21})^{1/2} , \qquad (2)$$

where $h_{ij} = 1/f_{ij}$ for $i = 1, 2; j = 1, 2$.

Applying formula (2) to table 2, we see that the standard error S of the observed interaction G is[14]

$$S = \left[\tfrac{1}{588} + \tfrac{1}{395} + \tfrac{1}{349} + \tfrac{1}{714} \right]^{1/2} = 0.09 . \qquad (3)$$

Thus, if we divide the observed interaction G by its standard error S, we obtain a value of

$$Z = G/S = 12.08 , \qquad (4)$$

which is statistically significant when compared with the usual percentiles of the standardized normal distribution. (For a two-sided test at the 5 percent level of significance, the absolute value of Z would be compared with the constant 1.96, which is the 97.5th percentile of the standard

---

[11] The reader familiar with differential calculus will also recall that

$$d \log x = (dx)/x ;$$

i.e., if a small change occurs in x, then the relative change in x is equal to the change in the logarithm of x.

[12] As we noted earlier, the interactions defined in this paper also arise naturally with models that consider the expected frequencies in the cross-classification table as being affected in a multiplicative way by "row effects" (related to the row marginals), "column effects" (related to the column marginals), and "row $\times$ column interaction effects" (see Birch 1963, Goodman 1964d).

[13] The statistic (2) is an estimate of the standard deviation of G. Of course, other estimates of this standard deviation could also be considered, but we shall not do so here. Some comments on different estimates of the standard deviation appear in my article (1964d).

[14] As we noted in the preceding section, the methods presented here (formula [2] in particular) can be applied to data obtained by simple random sampling or by stratified random sampling of the kind described there. We use it here as an approximate gauge even though the data in table 1 were actually obtained by a kind of stratified sampling different from that described in the preceding section. For further discussion of this point, see my article (1965b).

normal distribution.) We shall call Z the standardized value of the interaction G.[15]

Using the constant 1.96, we also obtain the following 95 percent confidence interval for the interaction in the population 2×2 table corresponding to table 2:

$$G^+ = G + 1.96S = 1.29$$
$$G^- = G - 1.96S = 0.93 \;.$$

$$(5)$$

The confidence interval for this interaction is from 0.93 to 1.29. Corresponding to this confidence interval, we obtain (with the aid of the table of natural logarithms) the following confidence interval for the odds-ratio in the population 2×2 table corresponding to table 2:[16]

$$R^+ = 3.65$$
$$R^- = 2.54 \;.$$

$$(6)$$

Recall that the observed value of the odds-ratio was $R = 3.05$.[17] Note that the confidence interval for the interaction (in the population 2×2 table) did not include zero, and the corresponding confidence interval for the odds-ratio (in the population 2×2 table) did not include 1.0.[18]

If we had decided to use table 2 (in order to test the null hypothesis that the column classification was independent of the row classification) before we had actually looked at the data in table 2 (or in the larger table 1), then the procedures described above would be legitimate. On the other hand, if we had actually selected the 2×2 subtable (table 2) from the larger 3×3 table (table 1) by noting which subtables of the 3×3 table would appear, at first sight, to provide strong evidence for the rejection of this null hypothesis, then the procedures described above would be illegitimate. In judging the statistical significance of the Z value (12.08) obtained for the 2×2 subtable, it would be necessary to take into account the fact that

---

[15] The term "standardized value" of a statistic is used here to mean the ratio of the statistic and its standard error (as in formula [4]). The same or similar words have also been used elsewhere to denote other things with which the usage here should not be confused.

[16] We would use here the natural-logarithm table in, so to speak, inverted order (or equivalently a table of the exponential function) when we calculate R^+ and R^- from L^+ and L^-, respectively. For example, from the natural-logarithm table we find that 3.65 is the number which is such that its natural logarithm is 1.29. Some comments on other methods for calculating confidence intervals for the odds-ratios in the population 2×2 table appear in my article (1964b).

[17] We use the symbol R at this point in our article to denote the observed value of the odds-ratio, and we let R^+ and R^- denote the upper and lower confidence limits, respectively. This particular notation at this point in the article should not be confused with our use of the symbol R elsewhere in the article to denote the number of rows in the $R \times C$ cross-classification table.

[18] The confidence interval for this interaction will include zero (and the corresponding confidence interval for the odds-ratio will include 1) if and only if the absolute value of Z calculated by (4) is smaller than 1.96.

the subtable which was actually used was selected by an examination of the larger 3×3 table (table 1), and that other Z values (corresponding to the interactions in the other subtables of the 3×3 table) might have been considered too. If a test at the 5 percent level of significance is desired, it would not be correct to compare the Z value with the usual constant (viz., 1.96). We shall now indicate what is the correct constant with which to compare the Z value.

This problem was considered in my article (1964b) where I showed that either one of two constants would be appropriate. The first constant (which we shall present in the following paragraph) is appropriate when we cannot determine beforehand how many interactions may be of possible interest. The second constant (which we shall present in the second paragraph below) is appropriate when we can determine beforehand the interactions that may be of interest.[19]

To explain how the first appropriate constant is obtained, we first note that (a) a 2×2 table has 1 degree of freedom for testing the null hypothesis of independence using the usual χ^2 distribution, and (b) the constant 1.96 (considered earlier herein) is the square root of the 95th percentile of the χ^2 distribution with 1 degree of freedom. The constant 1.96 is appropriate if the 2×2 table (with its 1 degree of freedom), which is to be tested for independence, was selected before the data were scanned, and if only this one 2×2 table is to be tested. If the 2×2 table is a subtable from a larger table (say a 3×3 table), and if it was selected by scanning the larger table, then the size of the larger table is relevant in determining the appropriate constant. If the larger table (from which the 2×2 subtable was selected) was a 3×3 table, then we note that (a) a 3×3 table has $2 \times 2 = 4$ degrees of freedom for testing the null hypothesis of independence using the usual χ^2 distribution, and (b) the constant 1.96 should be replaced by the square root of the 95th percentile of the χ^2 distribution with 4 degrees of freedom (rather than 1 degree of freedom).[20] This con-

---

[19] The second constant will depend upon the number of interactions that may be of possible interest, and it will increase as this number increases. In any particular case, if the second constant is larger than the first constant, then it can be replaced by the first constant since the first constant is appropriate even if an infinite number of interactions were of possible interest.

[20] The χ^2 distribution with four degrees of freedom is used here because the usual χ^2 statistic for testing the null hypothesis of independence in the 3×3 table has this as its large-sample distribution under the null hypothesis, and a modified form of this statistic (which has the same large-sample distribution under the null hypothesis) is related to the maximum value obtained when all possible interactions are calculated from the 3×3 table. For further details, see my article (1964b).

For the sake of convenience, the level of significance for each set of multiple tests presented herein will be the 5 percent level (or less), with the corresponding 95 percent level of confidence for the related simultaneous confidence intervals. For any given set of interactions to be analyzed, if all the interactions in the set are equal to zero for the population cross-classification table (i.e., if the corresponding null hypothesis is true for the population), then the probability is at least .95 that the standardized value of *all* the interactions in the set (calculated from the sample data) will be smaller in absolute value than the constant recommended here.

stant is 3.08. More generally, if the larger table (from which the 2×2 subtable was selected) was a $R \times C$ table, then we note that (a) a $R \times C$ table has $(R - 1)(C - 1)$ degrees of freedom for testing the null hypothesis of independence using the usual χ^2 distribution, and (b) the constant 1.96 should be replaced by the square root of the 95th percentile of the χ^2 distribution with $(R - 1)(C - 1)$ degrees of freedom.

To explain how the second appropriate constant is obtained, we first note that (a) a 2×2 table has at most one interaction of possible interest, and (b) the constant 1.96 (considered earlier herein) is the absolute value of the 2.5th percentile of the standardized normal distribution. The constant 1.96 is appropriate if the 2×2 table (with its one interaction of possible interest), which is to be tested for independence, is the only 2×2 table to be tested, and if it was selected before the data were scanned. If the 2×2 table is a subtable from a larger table, and if some of the other interactions in the larger table (corresponding to other subtables in the larger table) may be of interest, then the appropriate constant to be used should depend upon how many interactions in the larger table are of interest. If there are at most, say, twenty different interactions of interest in the larger table, then the constant 1.96 should be replaced by the absolute value of the (2.5/20)th percentile (i.e., the 0.125th percentile) of the standardized normal distribution (rather than the 2.5th percentile). This constant is 3.02. More generally, if there are at most K different interactions of interest in the larger table, then the constant 1.96 should be replaced by the absolute value of the $(2.5/K)$th percentile of the standardized normal distribution.

To facilitate the use of these constants, we give their numerical values in table 3, using the 5 percent level of significance.[21] This table gives both the first appropriate constant when the relevant number of degrees is 1, 2, 3, . . . , 35; and the second appropriate constant when the maximum number of interactions of interest is 1, 2, 3, . . . , 35. Note that the second appropriate constant, when the maximum number of interactions of interest is say twenty, is smaller than the first appropriate constant when the number of degrees of freedom is 4. Note also that the first appropriate constant to be used for ransacking a cross-classification table is smaller in one case than another if the number of degrees of freedom is smaller, and that the second appropriate constant is smaller in one case than another if the maximum number of interactions of possible interest is smaller. The research worker who has a specific set of, say, twenty interactions that are of interest, can use a smaller constant than can the research worker who has not specified, in advance of scanning the data, the set of interactions that may be of interest. In situations where both the first and second appropriate constants can be calculated, we use the smaller of the two constants when a bound on the level of significance is specified and when we would want to reduce the probability of errors of the second kind (of accepting the null hypothesis when it is false).

Let us now suppose that the cross-classification table under consideration

[21] See the second paragraph of footnote 20.

is a 3 × 3 table (say table 1). Since a 3 × 3 table has 2 × 2 = 4 degrees of freedom for testing the null hypothesis of independence, all interactions of possible interest in this table can be calculated directly from a basic set of four different interactions. Each of the four interactions can correspond to the interaction in a 2 × 2 subtable. One possible basic set of 2 × 2 subtables of table 1 is given in table 4. From these four subtables (tables 1A, 1B, 1C, 1D described in table 4), we can calculate the interactions corresponding to the nine possible 2 × 2 subtables formed from table 1 as indicated in table 5. Each of the nine different subtables of table 1 is de-

TABLE 3

CRITICAL CONSTANTS FOR SET OF MULTIPLE TESTS AT
THE 5% LEVEL OF SIGNIFICANCE

DEGREES OF FREEDOM OR NUMBER OF TESTS OF POSSIBLE INTEREST	CRITICAL CONSTANTS		DEGREES OF FREEDOM OR NUMBER OF TESTS OF POSSIBLE INTEREST	CRITICAL CONSTANTS	
	(a)*	(b)†		(a)*	(b)†
1.................	1.960	1.960	19.................	5.490	3.008
2.................	2.448	2.241	20.................	5.605	3.023
3.................	2.795	2.394	21.................	5.716	3.038
4.................	3.080	2.498	22.................	5.824	3.052
5.................	3.327	2.576	23.................	5.931	3.065
6.................	3.548	2.638	24.................	6.034	3.078
7.................	3.751	2.690	25.................	6.136	3.091
8.................	3.938	2.734	26.................	6.236	3.102
9.................	4.113	2.773	27.................	6.334	3.113
10.................	4.279	2.807	28.................	6.429	3.124
11.................	4.436	2.838	29.................	6.523	3.134
12.................	4.585	2.865	30.................	6.616	3.144
13.................	4.729	2.891	31.................	6.707	3.154
14.................	4.867	2.914	32.................	6.797	3.163
15.................	5.000	2.935	33.................	6.885	3.172
16.................	5.128	2.955	34.................	6.972	3.180
17.................	5.252	2.974	35.................	7.057	3.189
18.................	5.373	2.991			

* Appropriate when an unlimited number of tests about interactions might be made in a cross-classification table having a specified number of degrees of freedom.
† Appropriate when the number of tests of possible interest is specified.

scribed in table 5 by noting which two columns, and which two rows, are being compared in the subtable. The first four interactions in table 5 are calculated directly from the basic set of subtables (table 1A, 1B, 1C, 1D described in table 4); and the other five interactions in table 5 (pertaining to tables 1E, 1F, 1G, 1H, 1I) can be calculated by adding the corresponding interactions obtained from the basic set (or equivalently by multiplying the corresponding odds-ratios and taking the logarithm of the product): table 1E (interaction 1A plus 1B); table 1F (interaction 1C plus 1D); table 1G (interaction 1A plus 1C); table 1H (interaction 1B plus 1D); table 1I (interaction 1E plus 1F).

Again for those readers whose understanding is facilitated by the use of mathematical notation, we include table 6, which gives the interactions in

TABLE 4

A BASIC SET OF 2 × 2 SUBTABLES OF BRITISH SAMPLE

TABLE 1A			TABLE 1B		
FATHER'S STATUS	SUBJECT'S STATUS		FATHER'S STATUS	SUBJECT'S STATUS	
	U	M		M	L
U............	588	395	U...........	395	159
M............	349	714	M...........	714	447

TABLE 1C			TABLE 1D		
FATHER'S STATUS	SUBJECT'S STATUS		FATHER'S STATUS	SUBJECT'S STATUS	
	U	M		M	L
M............	349	714	M...........	714	447
L.............	114	320	L...........	320	441

TABLE 5

INTERACTION BETWEEN SUBJECT'S STATUS AND FATHER'S STATUS
IN EACH OF THE NINE 2 × 2 SUBTABLES OF THE
BRITISH SAMPLE

FATHER'S STATUS COMPARISON	SUBJECT'S STATUS COMPARISON		
	U Compared with M	M Compared with L	U Compared with L
U compared with M............	Table 1A: 1.11 (3.05)	Table 1B: 0.44 (1.56)	Table 1E: 1.56 (4.74)
M compared with L............	Table 1C: 0.32 (1.37)	Table 1D: 0.72 (2.05)	Table 1F: 1.03 (2.81)
U compared with L............	Table 1G: 1.43 (4.18)	Table 1H: 1.16 (3.19)	Table 1I: 2.59 (13.33)

NOTE.—Corresponding odds-ratio in parentheses.

TABLE 6

NINE INTERACTIONS IN TABLE 5 EXPRESSED IN TERMS OF THE LOGARITHM
g_{ij} OF THE OBSERVED FREQUENCY f_{ij} IN THE iTH ROW ($i = 1,2,3$) AND
jTH COLUMN ($j = 1,2,3$) OF THE 3 × 3 CROSS-CLASSIFICATION TABLE

FATHER'S STATUS COMPARISON	SUBJECT'S STATUS COMPARISON		
	U Compared with M	M Compared with L	U Compared with L
U compared with M.......	Table 1A: $g_{11} - g_{12} - g_{21} + g_{22}$	Table 1B: $g_{12} - g_{13} - g_{22} + g_{23}$	Table 1E: $g_{11} - g_{13} - g_{21} + g_{23}$
M compared with L.......	Table 1C: $g_{21} - g_{22} - g_{31} + g_{32}$	Table 1D: $g_{22} - g_{23} - g_{32} + g_{33}$	Table 1F: $g_{21} - g_{23} - g_{31} + g_{33}$
U compared with L.......	Table 1G: $g_{11} - g_{12} - g_{31} + g_{32}$	Table 1H: $g_{12} - g_{13} - g_{32} + g_{33}$	Table 1I: $g_{11} - g_{13} - g_{31} + g_{33}$

the nine 2×2 tables expressed in terms of the logarithms of the observed frequencies. Note that the interactions in table 6 corresponding to tables 1E, 1F, 1G, 1H can be obtained by direct calculation using the formulas in Table 6, or by adding the corresponding interactions obtained from the basic set of 2×2 subtables as noted in the preceding paragraph. For example, for table 1E we see that the corresponding interaction in table 6 is the sum of the interactions in table 6 pertaining to tables 1A and 1B.

Let us now suppose that the cross-classification table under consideration is a $R \times C$ table. Since a $R \times C$ table has $(R - 1)(C - 1)$ degrees of freedom for testing the null hypothesis of independence, all interactions of possible interest in the $R \times C$ table can be calculated directly from a basic set of $(R - 1)(C - 1)$ different interactions. Each of these interactions can correspond to the interaction in a 2×2 subtable. A basic set of 2×2 subtables can be obtained, for example, by selecting any given column (say, column C) and any given row (say, row R) of the $R \times C$ table, and then forming 2×2 subtables from the four cells that are in column C or in column j ($j = 1,2, \ldots, C - 1$) and in row R or in row i ($i = 1,2, \ldots, R - 1$). There will be $(R - 1)(C - 1)$ different subtables in the basic set, and from them we can calculate the interactions corresponding to the other 2×2 subtables formed from the $R \times C$ table. For the $R \times C$ table, we can compare each row with every other row (there are $R[R - 1]/2$ such comparisons), and each column with every other column (there are $C[C - 1]/2$ such comparisons), and so there will be $R(R - 1) \ C(C - 1)/4$ subtables; but all we need are the ones in the basic set (there were $[R - 1] \ [C - 1]$ subtables in the basic set) in order to determine the others.

THE VARIOUS INTERACTIONS BETWEEN THE COLUMN AND
ROW CLASSIFICATIONS

Note that each of the nine interactions presented in table 6 is of the following form:

$$G = \sum_{i=1}^{3}\sum_{j=1}^{3}a_{ij}g_{ij} , \qquad (7)$$

where g_{ij} is the logarithm of the observed frequency f_{ij} in the ith row and jth column ($i = 1, 2, 3; j = 1, 2, 3$), and where the a_{ij} are a set of constants that satisfy the following equations:

$$\sum_{j=1}^{3}a_{ij} = 0 , \qquad\qquad \text{for} \quad i = 1, 2, 3$$

$$\sum_{i=1}^{3}a_{ij} = 0 , \qquad\qquad \text{for} \quad j = 1, 2, 3 . \qquad (8)$$

Formula (8) states that if the constants a_{ij} are arranged as entries in a table of the form of table 1, then each row and each column of the table sums to zero.

As an example of formula (7), consider the interaction G calculated for table 2 (i.e., for table 1A of tables 4–6). From formula (1) or the corresponding formula in table 6, we see that this interaction is obtained by taking $a_{11} = a_{22} = 1$, $a_{12} = a_{21} = -1$, and $a_{13} = a_{23} = a_{31} = a_{32} = a_{33} = 0$. In other words, the interaction G calculated for table 2 is the interaction (between the column and row classifications of the 3×3 cross-classification table) that blanks out the entries ($f_{13}, f_{23}, f_{31}, f_{32}, f_{33}$) in the five cells of the third column and the third row of the table.

Any set of constants a_{ij} that satisfy the set of equations (8) can be used to define an interaction G based upon formula (7). We noted above that each of the interactions pertaining to the nine 2×2 subtables (table 6) is of the form (7). Furthermore, the sum, or the average, of several such interactions will be of this form. For example, the average of the four interactions pertaining to tables 1A, 1E, 1G, and 1I will be of this form. Since these four subtables are the only 2×2 subtables having interactions that are directly affected (in a positive way) by the number of U subjects whose fathers are also U (i.e., by the entry in the $[U,U]$ cell), we shall refer to their average interaction as the interaction pertaining to status inheritance of U status (i.e., interaction $[U,U]$).[22]

From the corresponding formulas in table 6, we see that the interaction (U,U) can be expressed as

$$g_{11} - [\tfrac{1}{2}(g_{12} + g_{13} + g_{21} + g_{31}) - \tfrac{1}{4}(g_{22} + g_{23} + g_{32} + g_{33})] . \qquad (9)$$

Thus, this interaction is obtained by taking $a_{11} = 1$, $a_{12} = a_{13} = a_{21} = a_{31} = -\tfrac{1}{2}$, $a_{22} = a_{23} = a_{32} = a_{33} = \tfrac{1}{4}$. Here none of the entries in the 3×3 cross-classification table are blanked out. If the average interaction is zero in the four 2×2 subtables that include the entry in the (U,U) cell, then the interaction (9) will be zero, and g_{11} will be equal to the quantity in brackets in formula (9). The interaction (U,U) measures the degree to which g_{11} differs from the bracketed quantity in (9). This bracketed quantity is a function of the entries in cells other than (U,U), and it could serve as a "predictor" of g_{11} under the assumption that there is no interaction in the 2×2 subtables that include the (U,U) cell. The extent to which g_{11} actually differs from this predictor can reflect "status inheritance" of U status.[23]

---

[22] An individual's status category refers here to the particular category into which his occupation is classified (upper, middle, or lower status categories), and "status inheritance" refers to the probability that his status category (U, M, or L) will be exactly the same as his father's. Other terms for this concept of status inheritance may in some respects be preferable and in other respects not. This concept does not necessarily refer to the inheritance of genetic characteristics, nor does it refer to the individual's literal inheritance of his father's specific occupation, except insofar as these phenomena, in conjunction with other phenomena (e.g., socialization, education), may lead to an increase in the probability that an individual's status category is the same as his father's. Of course, if the boundaries that are used to define the status categories are changed, then the categories will pertain to a different classification of occupations, and the magnitude of the status inheritance will depend upon the particular classification under consideration.

[23] Our attention is focused here on the entry in the (U,U) cell, and we judge its relative magnitude by comparison with a certain function of the entries in the other cells in the

Having noted that the interaction (U,U) is given by formula (9), we can now define the interaction (L,L) and the interaction (M,M) by the following formulas:

$$g_{33} - [\tfrac{1}{2}(g_{13} + g_{23} + g_{31} + g_{32}) - \tfrac{1}{4}(g_{11} + g_{12} + g_{21} + g_{22})], \qquad (10)$$

$$g_{22} - [\tfrac{1}{2}(g_{12} + g_{21} + g_{23} + g_{32}) - \tfrac{1}{4}(g_{11} + g_{13} + g_{31} + g_{33})]. \qquad (11)$$

Note that the interaction (L,L) defined by (10) is the average of the interactions pertaining to the four 2×2 subtables (tables 1D, 1F, 1H, 1I) that are directly affected (in a positive way) by the entry in the (L,L) cell. The relationship between the interaction (M,M) defined by (11) and the interactions pertaining to the four 2×2 subtables (tables 1A, 1B, 1C, 1D) that are directly affected by the entry in the (M,M) cell is more complicated because the effect of the entry in the (M,M) cell is positive in tables 1A and 1D but negative in tables 1B and 1C (see corresponding formulas in table 6). Because of the positive and negative effects, the interaction (M,M) defined by (11) is actually the average of the following four quantities: the interactions pertaining to tables 1A and 1D and the negative of the interactions pertaining to tables 1B and 1C.

The difference between any two interactions of the form (7) will also be of this form. For example, the difference between interaction (U,U) and interaction (M,M) is of this form. This difference can be used to compare the magnitudes of the status inheritance of U status and of M status. Similarly, we take the difference between interactions (M,M) and (L,L) to compare the magnitudes of the status inheritance of M status and of L status; and we take the difference between interactions (U,U) and (L,L) to compare the magnitudes of the status inheritance of U status and of L status.

Note that tables 1E and 1G are the only 2×2 subtables that are directly affected by the entry in the (U,U) cells and are not affected directly by either the (M,M) cell or the (L,L) cell. The tables 1A and 1I, which we used earlier (together with tables 1E and 1G) in defining the interaction pertaining to status inheritance of U status, are affected by the (U,U) cells, but they are also affected by the (M,M) cell and the (L,L) cell, respectively. Excluding now tables 1A and 1I, we calculate the average of the interactions pertaining to tables 1E and 1G. We shall refer to this average as the interaction pertaining to intrinsic status inheritance of U status.

From the corresponding formulae in table 6, we see that the interaction

---

cross-classification table. We could, of course, have written (9) in a form that would have drawn our attention to some other cell in the table or to some other phenomena that may be reflected in the table. We shall see later in this article that, in addition to status inheritance of U status, the interaction (U,U) given by (9) can reflect other phenomena as well. Because of this, we shall not be content with this measure, and shall introduce an alternative measure later in this section, namely, the interaction pertaining to the "intrinsic" status inheritance of U status.

pertaining to intrinsic status inheritance of U status can be expressed by the following formula:[24]

$$g_{11} - [\tfrac{1}{2}(g_{12} + g_{13} + g_{21} + g_{31} - g_{23} - g_{32})] . \tag{12}$$

Thus, this interaction is obtained by taking $a_{11} = 1$, $a_{12} = a_{13} = a_{21} = a_{31} = -\tfrac{1}{2}$, $a_{23} = a_{32} = \tfrac{1}{2}$, and $a_{22} = a_{33} = 0$. Here the entries in the cells (M,M) and (L,L) are blanked out. The interaction pertaining to intrinsic status inheritance of U status measures the degree to which g_{11} differs from the bracketed quantity in (12). This bracketed quantity is a function of the entries in the nondiagonal cells of the 3×3 cross-classification table, and it could serve as a "predictor" of g_{11} under the assumption that there is no interaction in tables 1E and 1G. The extent to which g_{11} actually differs from this predictor can reflect "intrinsic status inheritance" of U status.[25]

Having noted that the interaction pertaining to intrinsic status inheritance of U status is given by formula (12), we can now define the interactions pertaining to intrinsic status inheritance of L status and to intrinsic status inheritance of M status by

$$g_{33} - [\tfrac{1}{2}(g_{13} + g_{23} + g_{31} + g_{32} - g_{12} - g_{21})] , \tag{13}$$

and by

$$g_{22} - [\tfrac{1}{2}(g_{12} + g_{21} + g_{23} + g_{32} - g_{13} - g_{31})] , \tag{14}$$

respectively. The interaction (13) blanks out the entries in the cells (U,U) and (M,M), and it is the average of the interactions pertaining to tables 1F and 1H. The interaction (14) blanks out the entries in the cells (U,U) and (L,L), and it is the negative of the average of the interactions pertaining to tables 1B and 1C.

[24] Note that formula (12) can also be expressed as the logarithm of

$$f_{11}/[(\,f_{12}\,f_{13}\,f_{21}\,f_{31})/(\,f_{23}\,f_{32})]^{1/2} .$$

A similar kind of remark applies to the formulas (1), (7), (9)–(16) herein.

[25] A remark similar to that made in the first two sentences of footnote 23 would be in order here too. It should also be noted that, if there is "quasi-perfect mobility" (i.e., "quasi-independence" between the column classification and the row classification) when the three diagonal entries in the 3×3 cross-classification table are blanked out (see Goodman 1965b, 1968, and related comments later in the present article), then the only phenomenon measured by the interaction (12) is the degree to which g_{11} is larger than its predictor (in that case, we have "intrinsic status inheritance") or smaller than its predictor (in that case, we have "intrinsic status disinheritance"). As noted in the earlier articles cited above, the data considered here do exhibit this quasi-perfect mobility. (Our use here of the general concept of "quasi-perfect mobility" to assist with the interpretation of the interaction [12] could also have been employed in footnote 23 to assist with the interpretation of the interaction [9], but in that case the particular kind of "quasi-perfect mobility" that would have been relevant would have been for the case where only the entry in the (U,U) cell of the 3×3 table is blanked out. That particular kind of quasi-perfect mobility is contradicted by the data.)

The sum of the interactions (12)–(14) is

$$(g_{11} + g_{22} + g_{33}) - [\tfrac{1}{2}(g_{12} + g_{13} + g_{21} + g_{23} + g_{31} + g_{32})] . \qquad (15)$$

We shall call this sum the interaction pertaining to intrinsic net status inheritance of all statuses.[26] We would, of course, also want to compare the magnitudes of the intrinsic status inheritance of U status and of M status, etc. The difference between, say, the interactions pertaining to intrinsic status inheritance of U status and of M status (as defined by formulas [12] and [14]) is actually equal to $\tfrac{3}{4}$ of the difference between the interactions (U,U) and (M,M) (as defined by formulas [9] and [11]). Thus, the standardized value of the former difference is identical with the standardized value of the latter difference. A similar remark also applies when U status and L status are compared, and when M status and L status are compared.

Let us now consider the interaction defined as follows:

$$G = g_{12} + g_{23} + g_{31} - g_{13} - g_{32} - g_{21} . \qquad (16)$$

For this interaction, $a_{12} = a_{23} = a_{31} = 1$, $a_{13} = a_{32} = a_{21} = -1$, and $a_{11} = a_{22} = a_{33} = 0$. The three diagonal cells are blanked out. This interaction is not affected directly by the number of subjects who are in the same status categories as their fathers. This particular interaction could also be obtained by subtracting the interactions pertaining to tables 1B and 1C (or to tables 1E and 1G, or to tables 1H and 1F). If this interaction calculated by formula (16) is zero for table 1, then the interactions in tables 1B and 1C are equal, the interactions in tables 1E and 1G are equal, and the interactions in tables 1H and 1F are equal. Furthermore, if the interaction calculated by formula (16) is zero, then the model of quasi-perfect mobility, as defined in my earlier article (1965b), will fit table 1 when the three diagonal cells are blanked out.[27]

We can formulate still other interactions, which may be of interest in a particular context, by specifying the set of cells that are to be blanked out, and then determining the possible values of the a_{ij} for the cells that are not blanked out (see, for example, formulas [1], [12]–[14], [16]). This can also be done by considering the interaction obtained by subtracting any pair of interactions of interest, or by considering the interaction obtained by adding together (or by averaging) any set of interactions of interest. By these methods we obtain other sets of a_{ij} that satisfy (8), and thus other interactions between the column and row classifications of the 3×3 table. To illustrate the methods presented here, we shall confine our attention to the particular twenty interactions defined in the preceding paragraphs: namely, the interactions pertaining to the nine 2×2 subtables; the interactions (U,U), (M,M), and (L,L); the differences between interactions

---

[26] A remark similar to footnote 25 would apply here too.

[27] For a 3×3 cross-classification table in which the diagonal cells are blanked out, the definition of quasi-perfect mobility, as given in the article, is equivalent to the condition that the interaction (16) is zero for the corresponding population table; see my later article (1968) for further discussion of this point.

(U,U) and (M,M), between interactions (M,M) and (L,L), and between interactions (U,U) and (L,L); the interactions pertaining to the intrinsic status inheritance of U status, of M status, and of L status; the interaction pertaining to intrinsic net status inheritance of all statuses; and the interaction obtained by blanking out the diagonal cells.[28]

TABLE 7

STANDARDIZED VALUE OF 20 INTERACTIONS BETWEEN
SUBJECT'S STATUS AND FATHER'S STATUS IN
BRITISH SAMPLE

Interaction Due to	Standardized Value
U or M fathers and U or M subjects (table 1A)........................	12.08
U or M fathers and M or L subjects (table 1B)........................	3.96
U or M fathers and U or L subjects (table 1E).......................	13.59
M or L fathers and U or M subjects (table 1C).......................	2.49
M or L fathers and M or L subjects (table 1D).......................	7.49
M or L fathers and U or L subjects (table 1F).......................	8.10
U or L fathers and U or M subjects (table 1G)......................	11.26
U or L fathers and M or L subjects (table 1H).......................	9.68
U or L fathers and U or L subjects (table 1I)	18.70
Status inheritance of U status (interaction $[U,U]$)......................	19.45
Status inheritance of M status (interaction $[M,M]$).....................	3.69
Status inheritance of L status (interaction $[L,L]$)......................	15.32
Difference between interaction (U,U) and (M,M)......................	12.20
Difference between interaction (M,M) and (L,L).......................	-9.47
Difference between interaction (U,U) and (L,L)	3.24
Intrinsic status inheritance of U status (with blank $[M,M]$ and $[L,L]$).....	16.53
Intrinsic status inheritance of M status (with blank $[U,U]$ and $[L,L]$).....	-4.28
Intrinsic status inheritance of L status (with blank $[U,U]$ and $[M,M]$)....	11.64
Intrinsic net status inheritance of all statuses	20.19
Fathers and subjects with different statuses (with blank diagonal cells)....	0.78

The standard error of the interaction G defined by (7) can be calculated as follows:

$$S = \left(\sum_{i=1}^{3} \sum_{j=1}^{3} a_{ij}^2 \Big/ f_{ij} \right)^{1/2} . \tag{17}$$

If we divide the observed interaction G by its standard error, we get the following standardized value:[29]

$$Z = G/S . \tag{18}$$

For the data in table 1, the standardized values of the twenty interactions (between subject's status and father's status), described above, are given in table 7.

Each of the twenty interactions can be tested to see if it differs signifi-

---

[28] As we noted earlier, the standardized value of the difference between the interactions pertaining to intrinsic status inheritance of U status and of M status is equal to the standardized value of the difference between interactions (U,U) and (M,M). A similar remark also applies when U status and L status are compared, and when M status and L status are compared.

[29] See footnote 15.

cantly from zero. In each test, the absolute value of the corresponding Z would be compared with the constant 3.02 (rather than 1.96).[30] We see from table 7 that the largest standardized value pertaining to the 2×2 subtables is the one for table 1I (U or L fathers and U or L subjects), which is, however, smaller than the standardized values of the interaction pertaining to status inheritance of U status and of the interaction pertaining to intrinsic net status inheritance of all statuses. Furthermore, the interaction (U,U) is significantly larger than the interaction (L,L), which in turn is significantly larger than the interaction (M,M).

From table 7 we also see that, although the interaction (M,M) was positive, the interaction pertaining to intrinsic status inheritance of M status was negative, and that this negative value differed from zero in a statistically significant way. In the M status category, there was intrinsic status disinheritance, rather than status inheritance.[31] We shall return to this point in a later section.

Table 7 also shows us that the standardized value of the interaction obtained when the diagonal cells are blanked out is strikingly small.[32] This indicates that the model of quasi-perfect mobility fits the data in table 1 when the diagonal cells are blanked out. Although the method used here for studying quasi-perfect mobility is quite different from the method I used earlier (1965b), the conclusion concerning quasi-perfect mobility in table 1, which was arrived at in the earlier work, is confirmed by the present analysis.[33]

[30] See table 6 and related comments earlier in the present article. If the twenty interactions do not include all the interactions that may be of interest in the present context, then the constant 3.02 should be replaced by the appropriate constant which can be calculated once the total number of interactions of possible interest has been determined. If the total number of interactions of possible interest cannot be determined, then the constant 3.08 should be used instead of 3.02.

[31] Since the interaction pertaining to intrinsic status inheritance of M status (which we defined by formula [14]) was the negative of the average of the interactions pertaining to tables 1B and 1C, the negative value obtained in table 7 for the interaction pertaining to intrinsic status inheritance of M status describes the same phenomenon as the positive value obtained for the average of the interactions pertaining to tables 1B and 1C. The analysis presented herein will suggest that the data in table 1 reflect (a) quasi-perfect mobility for the nondiagonal entries, (b) status inheritance of U status and of L status, and (c) status disinheritance of M status. In particular we suggest that the data in tables 1B and 1C reflect (a) and (c). Although we "explain" the data in tables 1B and 1C by (a) and (c), other kinds of "explanations" of the data (which make use of other concepts) may also be possible; in which case, these other "explanations" of the data may also serve as "explanations" of the observed negative interaction pertaining to intrinsic status inheritance of M status (i.e., of the positive value obtained for the average interaction in the tables).

[32] Even if the constant 1.96 were used instead of 3.02, the observed value of Z would be strikingly small. Use of the constant 1.96 (rather than 3.02) would reduce the probability of errors of the second kind (of accepting the null hypothesis—that the corresponding interaction is zero—when it is false), but it would increase the probability of errors of the first kind (of rejecting the null hypothesis when it is true).

[33] With respect to the results presented in my earlier article concerning quasi-perfect mobility in the corresponding 3×3 table obtained from a sample of Danish males, the conclusions about these Danish data are also confirmed by the present method of analysis. In the next section, we shall compare the interactions in the British and Danish data.

We have discussed above the testing of a set of hypotheses concerning the various interactions between the column and row classifications of a cross-classification table. Formulas (7) and (17) can also be used to estimate the size of these interactions and to obtain simultaneous confidence intervals for them.[34]

COMPARING TWO (OR MORE) CROSS-CLASSIFICATION TABLES

To illustrate the methods presented in this section, we shall compare the British data (table 1) with the corresponding Danish data presented in table 8. This table is based upon data obtained by Svalastoga.[35] It provides a cross-classification of a sample of 2,391 males in Denmark according to each subject's occupational status category and his father's occupational status category.

TABLE 8

Cross-Classification of Sample of Danish Males according to Each Subject's Status Category and His Father's Status Category

Father's Status	Subject's Status		
	U	M	L
U............	685	280	118
M............	232	348	198
L............	83	201	246

Note.—This table referred to as Danish sample in following tables.

From table 8 we can obtain a basic set of four 2 × 2 subtables (as in table 4), and from these four subtables we can then calculate the interaction in each of the nine 2 × 2 subtables (as in table 5). The results corresponding to table 4 are given in table 9 for the Danish data. Each of the nine different subtables of table 8 (tables 8A–8I) are described in table 9 by noting which two columns, and which two rows, are being compared in the subtable. For the data in table 8, we can also calculate (as in table 7) the standardized value of each of the twenty interactions considered in the preceding section. These values are given in table 10.

Although there are some differences between the pattern of standardized values given in table 10 (Danish sample) and those given in table 7 (British

---

[34] The actual magnitudes of the interactions (or the corresponding generalized odds-ratios), and the simultaneous confidence intervals for the interactions in the population, will often be of more interest than the corresponding standardized values given here. See my article (1964b) for further details. For simplicity of exposition, we have confined our attention here to the standardized values.

[35] The upper-, middle-, and lower-status categories in table 8 correspond to the occupational status categories 1–6, 7, 8–9, respectively, as defined by Svalastoga (1959).

sample), the particular comments which were made in the preceding section concerning the results presented in table 7 would apply as well to table 10. Note the following: (*a*) the size of the standardized value for the interaction pertaining to table 8I compared with the standardized values for the interactions pertaining to status inheritance of *U* status and to intrinsic net status inheritance for all statuses; (*b*) the standardized values for the differences between the interactions (*U,U*), (*L,L*), and (*M,M*); (*c*) the standardized value for the interaction pertaining to intrinsic status in-

TABLE 9

INTERACTION BETWEEN SUBJECT'S STATUS AND FATHER'S STATUS
IN EACH OF THE NINE 2 × 2 SUBTABLES OF THE
DANISH SAMPLE

	SUBJECT'S STATUS COMPARISON		
FATHER'S STATUS COMPARISON	*U* Compared with *M*	*M* Compared with *L*	*U* Compared with *L*
U compared with *M*.............	Table 8A: 1.30 (3.67)	Table 8B: 0.30 (1.35)	Table 8E: 1.60 (4.95)
M compared with *L*.............	Table 8C: 0.48 (1.61)	Table 8D: 0.77 (2.15)	Table 8F: 1.24 (3.47)
U compared with *L*.............	Table 8G: 1.78 (5.92)	Table 8H: 1.07 (2.90)	Table 8I: 2.85 (17.21)

NOTE.—Corresponding odds-ratio in parentheses.

TABLE 10

STANDARDIZED VALUE OF 20 INTERACTIONS BETWEEN SUBJECT'S STATUS
AND FATHER'S STATUS IN DANISH SAMPLE

Interaction Due to	Standardized Value
U or *M* fathers and *U* or *M* subjects (table 8A)........................	11.76
U or *M* fathers and *M* or *L* subjects (table 8B)........................	2.12
U or *M* fathers and *U* or *L* subjects (table 8E).........................	11.52
M or *L* fathers and *U* or *M* subjects (table 8C)........................	3.08
M or *L* fathers and *M* or *L* subjects (table 8D)........................	5.88
M or *L* fathers and *U* or *L* subjects (table 8F).........................	7.80
U or *L* fathers and *U* or *M* subjects (table 8G)........................	11.98
U or *L* fathers and *M* or *L* subjects (table 8H)........................	7.34
U or *L* fathers and *U* or *L* subjects (table 8I).........................	17.63
Status inheritance of *U* status (interaction [*U,U*])....................	19.18
Status inheritance of *M* status (interaction [*M,M*])....................	3.40
Status inheritance of *L* status (interaction [*L,L*])....................	13.26
Difference between interaction (*U,U*) and (*M,M*).....................	11.13
Difference between interaction (*M,M*) and (*L,L*).....................	− 8.22
Difference between interaction (*U,U*) and (*L,L*).....................	3.49
Intrinsic status inheritance of *U* status (with blank [*M,M*] and [*L,L*]).....	16.06
Intrinsic status inheritance of *M* status (with blank [*U,U*] and [*L,L*]).....	− 3.49
Intrinsic status inheritance of *L* status (with blank [*U,U*] and [*M,M*])....	9.88
Intrinsic net status inheritance of all statuses.........................	18.30
Fathers and subjects with different statuses (with blank diagonal cells)....	− 0.91

heritance of M status; and (d) how small the interaction is when the diagonal cells have been blanked out.[36]

Each of the interactions calculated for the Danish sample could be compared with the corresponding interaction in the British sample. For an interaction G_1 in the British sample and the corresponding interaction G_2 in the Danish sample, we can calculate the difference

$$D = G_1 - G_2 . \tag{19}$$

The value of D is given in table 11 for the interactions pertaining to each of the nine 2 × 2 subtables of the 3 × 3 tables (tables 1 and 8). Note that

TABLE 11

DIFFERENCE BETWEEN BRITISH AND DANISH SAMPLES WITH RESPECT TO
THE INTERACTIONS* IN EACH OF THE NINE 2 × 2 SUBTABLES
OF EACH SAMPLE†

	SUBJECT'S STATUS COMPARISON		
FATHER'S STATUS COMPARISON	U Compared with M	M Compared with L	U Compared with L
U compared with M ..	Tables 1A and 8A: −0.18 (0.83)	Tables 1B and 8B: 0.14 (1.15)	Tables 1E and 8E: −0.04 (0.96)
M compared with L ..	Tables 1C and 8C: −0.16 (0.85)	Tables 1D and 8D: −0.05 (0.95)	Tables 1F and 8F: −0.21 (0.81)
U compared with L ...	Tables 1G and 8G: −0.35 (0.71)	Tables 1H and 8H: 0.09 (1.10)	Tables 1I and 8I: −0.26 (0.77)

NOTE.—Ratio of corresponding odds-ratios in parentheses.
* Interactions are between subject's status and father's status.
† Tables 1 and 8.

all but two of these differences are negative, which indicates that the interactions between subject's status and father's status in the Danish sample are somewhat larger on the whole than the corresponding interactions for the British sample. We shall gain some further insight into this matter later in the following section.

The standard error S_D of the difference D is calculated as follows:

$$S_D = (S_1^2 + S_2^2)^{1/2} , \tag{20}$$

where S_1 and S_2 are the standard errors of G_1 and G_2, respectively. As with formula (18), if we divide the observed difference D by its standard error, we get the standardized value

$$Z = D/S_D . \tag{21}$$

For the data in tables 1 and 8, the standardized value for the difference between the twenty interactions, which we considered earlier, are given in table 12.

[36] See footnote 33.

From table 12 we see that most of the standardized values are negative, and that none of them are statistically significant. Note that the three standardized values that are largest in absolute value pertain to various aspects of status inheritance of U status. (Table 1G is used in the calculation of the interactions pertaining to status inheritance of U status.) Thus, the interactions pertaining to status inheritance of U status are larger in

TABLE 12

STANDARDIZED VALUE OF DIFFERENCE BETWEEN BRITISH AND DANISH SAMPLES
WITH RESPECT TO 20 INTERACTIONS BETWEEN SUBJECT'S
STATUS AND FATHER'S STATUS

Interaction Due to	Standardized Value
U or M fathers and U or M subjects (tables 1A and 8A)................	−1.30
U or M fathers and M or L subjects (tables 1B and 8B)................	0.79
U or M fathers and U or L subjects (tables 1E and 8E)................	−0.25
M or L fathers and U or M subjects (tables 1C and 8C)................	−0.81
M or L fathers and M or L subjects (tables 1D and 8D)................	−0.29
M or L fathers and U or L subjects (tables 1F and 8F)................	−1.03
U or L fathers and U or M subjects (tables 1G and 8G)................	−1.79
U or L fathers and M or L subjects (tables 1H and 8H)................	0.50
U or L fathers and U or L subjects (tables 1I and 8I)................	−1.20
Status inheritance of U status (interaction $[U,U]$).....................	−1.60
Status inheritance of M status (interaction $[M,M]$).....................	−0.44
Status inheritance of L status (interaction $[L,L]$).....................	−0.73
Difference between interaction (U,U) and (M,M).....................	−0.86
Difference between interaction (M,M) and (L,L).....................	0.28
Difference between interaction (U,U) and (L,L).....................	−0.71
Intrinsic status inheritance of U status (with blank $[M,M]$ and $[L,L]$)......	−1.42
Intrinsic status inheritance of M status (with blank $[U,U]$ and $[L,L]$)......	0.08
Intrinsic status inheritance of L status (with blank $[U,U]$ and $[M,M]$).....	−0.39
Intrinsic net status inheritance of all statuses...........................	−1.41
Fathers and subjects with different statuses (with blank diagonal cells).....	1.20

the Danish study than in the British study, but the differences are not statistically significant.[37]

SOME RELATED METHODS FOR COMPARING TWO (OR MORE) CROSS-CLASSIFICATION TABLES

Table 12 is useful when we wish to examine the difference between each of the twenty interactions in the British sample and the corresponding interactions in the Danish sample in order to determine which (if any) are significantly different from zero. If we are interested simply in an overall test of the null hypothesis that all of these differences are zero for the cor-

[37] We shall see in a later section that, when the U status category is divided into three separate status categories (i.e., when each of the individuals in the U status category is reclassified into one of three different high status categories rather than grouped into a single U category), the difference between the social mobility patterns in the British and Danish studies is statistically significant with respect to status inheritance among those in the three high status categories.

responding population tables, we would reject the null hypothesis if any of the twenty standardized values were greater in absolute value than 3.02.[38]

But if we are interested in an overall test of the null hypothesis that all the interactions in the British population table are equal to the corresponding interactions in the Danish population table, it is actually not necessary to calculate the standardized value for the differences between each interaction in the British and Danish samples, as we did in table 12. Indeed, if we were interested in *all* the interactions (i.e., in the difference corresponding to each interaction in the 3 × 3 tables), it would not be sufficient to study by this method only the twenty differences considered in table 12, since there may be some other interaction in the 3 × 3 tables that would lead to a significantly large standardized value for the corresponding difference even though none of the twenty differences did. We provide below procedures that are suitable for testing the null hypothesis that all the interactions in the British population table are equal to the corresponding interactions in the Danish table.

As we noted earlier, all the interactions in a 3 × 3 table (with its 2 × 2 = 4 degrees of freedom) can be calculated from a set of four interactions that pertain to a basic set of four 2 × 2 subtables. Similarly, all the differences between the corresponding interactions in two different 3 × 3 tables can be calculated from a set of four differences that pertain to the differences between the corresponding interactions in the basic set of 2 × 2 subtables. Taking tables 1A, 1B, 1C, and 1D as the basic set (together with the corresponding tables 8A, 8B, 8C, and 8D), we see from table 11 that the basic set of four differences are −0.18, 0.14, −0.16, −0.05, respectively. It is possible to test whether the observed basic vector (−0.18, 0.14, −0.16, −0.05) differs significantly from the zero vector (0,0,0,0). The null hypothesis that the basic vector of differences between the two populations is the zero vector is equivalent to the null hypothesis that *all* the interactions in the British population table are equal to the corresponding interactions in the Danish population table. Applying the test of this null hypothesis presented in my article (1964c), we obtain a χ^2 value of 4.09.[39] Since we are studying the differences between two 3 × 3 tables (with 4 degrees of freedom in the 3 × 3 table), the χ^2 value obtained (4.09) should be compared with the usual percentiles of the χ^2 distribution with 4 degrees of freedom.[40]

[38] If we do not limit the number of possible interactions that we might investigate by this method, then the constant 3.02 would be replaced by 3.08, as we noted earlier.

[39] The same χ^2 value would have been obtained even if a different basic set of four subtables had been used. For example, the basic set obtained with tables 1D, 1F, 1H, 1I (and the corresponding tables 8D, 8F, 8H, 8I), or with tables 1A, 1E, 1G, 1I (and the corresponding tables 8A, 8E, 8G, 8I), could have been used instead of the set obtained with tables 1A, 1B, 1C, 1D (and the corresponding Tables 8A, 8B, 8C, 8D). Indeed, a basic set can be formed corresponding to the following lines from tables 7 and 10: the first (tables 1A and 8A), the fifth (tables 1D and 8D), seventeenth (intrinsic status inheritance of M status), and twentieth (fathers and subjects with different statuses). For further discussion of this test, see the article.

[40] Note that the observed basic vector has four entries in it corresponding to the 4 degrees of freedom. More generally, when comparing S different R × C tables, there will be $(R - 1)(C - 1)(S - 1)$ degrees of freedom for the test discussed here.

Thus, the observed basic vector does not differ significantly from the zero vector.

As we noted above, the test of whether the interactions in one of the 3 × 3 tables differs significantly from the corresponding interactions in the other 3 × 3 table is a test of the null hypothesis that the differences between the corresponding interactions are all equal to zero for the population tables. The two 3 × 3 tables (tables 1 and 8) can also be viewed as a single 3 × 3 × 2 table in which the rows, columns, and layers of the table denote the subject's status category of origin, status category of destination, and country of residence, respectively. The χ^2 test used in the preceding paragraph, which was presented in my article (1964c), is a test of whether there are no differences between the corresponding interactions in the two 3 × 3 population tables, and it can also be used to test the null hypothesis that

TABLE 13

CROSS-CLASSIFICATION OF BRITISH AND DANISH MALE
SAMPLES ACCORDING TO EACH SUBJECT'S STATUS CATE-
GORY AND HIS FATHER'S STATUS CATEGORY

FATHER'S STATUS	SUBJECT'S COUNTRY OF RESIDENCE	SUBJECT'S STATUS		
		U	M	L
U.............	Britain	588	395	159
	Denmark	685	280	118
M.............	Britain	349	714	447
	Denmark	232	348	198
L.............	Britain	114	320	411
	Denmark	83	201	246

all three-factor interactions in the 3 × 3 × 2 population table are equal to zero. We shall comment further below on the χ^2 test used in the preceding paragraph, and also on a different test of this hypothesis.

The 3 × 3 × 2 table can be rearranged as in table 13, in which we have a 2 × 3 table describing the pattern of mobility in Britain and in Denmark for those with U origins, and similarly two other 2 × 3 tables pertaining to those with M origins and those with L origins. The null hypothesis that all three-factor interactions in the 3 × 3 × 2 table are equal to zero is equivalent to the hypothesis that the interactions in the 2 × 3 table pertaining to origin U are equal to the corresponding interactions in the 2 × 3 table pertaining to origin M, which in turn are equal to the corresponding interactions in the 2 × 3 table pertaining to origin L.[41] For each 2 × 3 table (with its 2 degrees of freedom), we can obtain a basic set of two 2 × 2 subtables (e.g., by comparing subject's status U with status M and subject's status M with status L), and for each subtable in the basic set we can calculate the interaction between its column and row classifications. These

[41] Note that this hypothesis states that the corresponding interactions in the three 2 × 3 tables are equal to each other. This hypothesis is quite different from the hypothesis that the interactions in the three 2 × 3 tables are all equal to zero.

interactions are given in table 14.[42] From this table we see that the hypothesis to be tested is that the three vectors $(-0.50, 0.05)$, $(-0.31, -0.10)$, and $(-0.15, -0.05)$, corresponding to origin U, M, and L, respectively, do not differ significantly from each other. The χ^2 test used in the paragraph before the preceding one can be used to test this hypothesis. We noted there that a χ^2 value of 4.09 (with 4 degrees of freedom) was obtained, which is not statistically significant.

From table 14 we see that the interactions pertaining to origin L are larger than the corresponding interactions pertaining to origin M, which in turn are larger than the corresponding interactions pertaining to origin U (except in the comparison of subject's status M with status L, where the interaction pertaining to origin U is larger than the other two). It is because

TABLE 14

INTERACTION BETWEEN SUBJECT'S STATUS AND COUNTRY OF RESIDENCE
FOR EACH CATEGORY OF FATHER'S STATUS

FATHER'S STATUS	SUBJECT'S STATUS COMPARISON		
	U with M	M with L	U with L
U..................	$-0.50\ (0.61)$	$0.05\ (1.05)$	$-0.45\ (0.64)$
M..................	$-0.31\ (0.73)$	$-0.10\ (0.91)$	$-0.41\ (0.67)$
L..................	$-0.15\ (0.86)$	$-0.05\ (0.95)$	$-0.20\ (0.82)$

NOTE.—Corresponding odds-ratio in parentheses.

of this pattern in which the interactions decrease from origin L to origin M to origin U (with the exception noted above), that the differences presented in table 11 were all negative except in the comparison of subject's status M with status L, when the origin U is compared with the other two origins. Thus, the analysis of the data arranged as in table 13 sheds further light on the earlier analysis in which a different arrangement of the data was used.

As we have noted, the χ^2 test used here is a test of the null hypothesis that the three-factor interactions are zero in the $3 \times 3 \times 2$ table corresponding to tables 1 and 8 (or as described in table 13). A different method for testing this null hypothesis could be based upon the following procedure: First, estimate the frequencies that would be expected in the $3 \times 3 \times 2$ table under the assumption that the null hypothesis is true, and then compare these expected frequencies with the corresponding observed frequencies using the usual χ^2 goodness-of-fit statistic.[43] Applying this

[42] For the sake of completeness, we have also included in table 14 the interactions obtained when subject's status U is compared with status L, though these interactions are not part of the basic set. Note that each interaction pertaining to the comparison of subject's status U with status L is the sum of the corresponding interactions for the other two comparisons of subject's statuses.

[43] This procedure for testing the null hypothesis of no three-factor interaction, which we call the BFNRKLD test (for Bartlett-Fisher-Norton-Roy-Kastenbaum-Lamphiear-Darroch), is described in my article (1964c).

procedure to the data studied here, we obtain the expected frequencies given in table 15 and a value of 4.10 is obtained for the χ^2 goodness-of-fit statistic comparing the expected frequencies in table 15 with the corresponding observed frequencies in tables 1 and 8. This χ^2 value (4.10) should be compared with the usual percentiles of the χ^2 distribution with 4 degrees of freedom (as with the other χ^2 test used in this section).[44]

TABLE 15

PREDICTED MOBILITY PATTERN FOR BRITISH AND DANISH SAMPLES: INTERACTIONS BETWEEN SUBJECT'S STATUS AND FATHER'S STATUS IN BRITISH POPULATION ARE ASSUMED EQUAL TO THE CORRESPONDING INTERACTIONS IN DANISH POPULATION

FATHER'S STATUS	BRITISH SUBJECT'S STATUS			FATHER'S STATUS	DANISH SUBJECT'S STATUS		
	U	M	L		U	M	L
U...........	601.3	381.9	158.9	U...........	671.7	293.1	118.1
M...........	344.8	722.1	443.1	M...........	236.2	339.9	201.9
L............	104.9	325.1	415.0	L............	92.1	195.9	242.1

QUASI-INDEPENDENCE AND THE INTERACTIONS BETWEEN
THE COLUMN AND ROW CLASSIFICATIONS OF
A CROSS-CLASSIFICATION TABLE

If the column classification is independent of the row classification in a table (say, table 1), then all the interactions (between the column and row classifications of the table), as defined by formula (7) will be equal to zero, and vice versa. This relationship between the concept of independence in a cross-classification table and the interactions defined by formula (7) can be extended to a similar relationship between the concept of "quasi-independence" (or "quasi-perfect mobility"), as defined in my article (1965b), and a subset of these interactions.[45] For example, as we noted in an earlier section of the present paper, considering the 3×3 table (table 1) with the three cells on the main diagonal blanked out, if the column and row classifications are quasi-independent, then the interaction defined by formula (16) will be equal to zero, and vice versa (Note that the constants a_{ij} in formula [16] are equal to zero for the three blanked out cells.) Similarly, considering the 3×3 table (table 1) with the two cells (M,M) and (L,L) blanked out, if the column and row classifications are quasi-independent, then the interactions defined by formulas (12) and (16) will be equal to zero, and vice versa. (Note that the constants a_{ij} in formulas [12] and [16] are equal to zero for the two blanked out cells.) More generally,

---

[44] See second sentence of footnote 40.

[45] The term "quasi-perfect mobility" was used in my article to refer to this concept, rather than the more general term "quasi-independence," in order to emphasize its applicability to social mobility tables. As was noted in that article, the concepts and methods developed there can also be applied to other kinds of cross-classification tables.

considering a cross-classification table with a subset of the cells in the table blanked out, and the corresponding subset of the interactions defined by formula (7) for which the constants a_{ij} are equal to zero for the cells that have been blanked out, if the column and row classifications in the table are quasi-independent, then the corresponding subset of the interactions will be equal to zero, and vice versa.[46]

This equivalence between the concept of quasi-independence and the corresponding subset of the interactions defined by formula (7) can shed further light on both the analysis of quasi-independence and on the analysis of interactions. For example, let us consider the following two null hypotheses: (a) quasi-independence in table 1 with the three diagonal cells blanked out; and (b) quasi-independence in table 1 with the two diagonal cells (U,U) and (L,L) blanked out. For each of these null hypotheses, the χ^2 goodness-of-fit statistic comparing the observed frequencies with the frequencies that would be expected (under the null hypothesis) can be calculated, and the values obtained are 0.61 and 20.20, respectively, for hypothesis (a) and (b).[47] From the preceding paragraph, we see that the null hypothesis (a) states that the interaction is zero when only fathers and sons with different statuses are considered (i.e., that the interaction due to fathers and sons with different statuses is zero in the population), and the null hypothesis (b) states that, in addition (to null hypothesis [a] being true), the interaction pertaining to intrinsic status inheritance of M status is zero. Since null hypothesis (b) is a special case of null hypothesis (a), by subtracting the corresponding two χ^2 values (20.20 − 0.61), the difference obtained (19.59) provides us with a χ^2 value (with 1 degree of freedom) for testing the null hypothesis that the interaction pertaining to intrinsic status inheritance of M status is zero, when the null hypothesis (a) is true.[48] Thus, comparing the difference (19.59) with the usual percentiles of the χ^2 distribution with 1 degree of freedom, we reject the null hypothesis that the interaction pertaining to intrinsic status inheritance of M status is zero.[49]

[46] For further details, see my article (1968).

[47] These numerical results were given in my article (1965b). In addition to the χ^2 goodness-of-fit statistics, that article gave several other methods for comparing the expected frequencies with the observed frequencies. For the sake of simplicity and brevity, we shall not discuss these other methods here, though they are useful.

[48] As was noted in my article (1965b), the difference has 1 degree of freedom in the present context; it is the difference between a χ^2 value with 2 degrees of freedom and a χ^2 value with 1 degree of freedom. In the earlier article, the corresponding value based upon the likelihood-ratio statistics was used, rather than the goodness-of-fit statistics.

[49] Note that the difference obtained (19.59) is of the same order of magnitude as the square of the standardized value Z (in table 7) corresponding to the interaction pertaining to intrinsic status inheritance of M status. Note also that the value obtained (0.61) for the goodness-of-fit statistic for testing null hypothesis (a) is of the same order of magnitude as the square of the standardized value Z (in table 7) corresponding to the interaction pertaining to fathers and sons with different statuses. Under the null hypothesis (a), the value obtained for the goodness-of-fit statistic is asymptotically equivalent to the corresponding Z^2; and a similar remark applies to the difference obtained under the null

The preceding calculations were based upon the British data (table 1). A similar analysis of the Danish data (table 8) could be made. The conclusions obtained with the Danish data are similar to those presented above.

QUASI-HOMOGENEITY AND THE DIFFERENCES BETWEEN
THE INTERACTIONS IN TWO (OR MORE)
CROSS-CLASSIFICATION TABLES

As we noted in the preceding section, the concept of quasi-independence is a generalization of the usual concept of independence in the $R \times C$ cross-classification table which is suited to the situation where the entries in certain cells of the table are blanked out. It states that all the interactions (between the column and row classifications of the table), which are calculated from the cells that are not blanked out, are equal to zero. Similarly, the concept that two different $R \times C$ tables are homogeneous (with respect to the corresponding interactions in each table) can be generalized to obtain the concept of "quasi-homogeneity" of the two $R \times C$ tables. This concept is suited to the situation where the corresponding entries in certain cells of each table are blanked out.[50] It states that the differences between the corresponding interactions in each table are equal to zero, when we consider only those interactions which are calculated from the cells that are not blanked out. We shall now illustrate the application of this concept of quasi-homogeneity by reconsidering the comparisons of tables 1 and 8 presented earlier.

We noted in the section before the preceding one that the null hypothesis that the two population tables were homogeneous (with respect to the corresponding interactions in each table) could be tested by first calculating the frequencies that would be expected in the tables under the assumption that the null hypothesis is true (see table 15), and then comparing these expected frequencies with the corresponding observed frequencies using the usual χ^2 goodness-of-fit statistic. We obtained, by this method, a value of 4.10 for the χ^2 goodness-of-fit statistic (with 4 degrees of freedom). With this observed value, we would not reject the null hypothesis of homogeneity. Recall, however, that in our earlier analysis of the differences between the interactions in tables 1 and 8 (see table 12), when considering the three standardized values that were largest in absolute value, we found that all of these pertain to various aspects of status inheritance of U status. We shall now consider briefly the null hypothesis of quasi-homogeneity of tables 1 and 8 when the fathers and sons with the same U status (i.e., cell $[U,U]$) are blanked out.

With respect to this null hypothesis, the expected frequencies for the

---

hypothesis (b). As in the earlier analysis of the Z values, if all the interactions in table 1 were of possible interest, then the relevant percentiles in judging each Z^2 value (or the corresponding χ^2 values) are obtained from the χ^2 distribution with 4 degrees of freedom.

[50] The concept can also be applied in some situations where a different set of cell entries has been blanked out in each $R \times C$ table. For further details, see my article (1968).

British and Danish data (i.e., the frequencies expected under the null hypothesis) can be calculated using the methods described in my article (1968). These expected frequencies are given in table 16 herein. These are the frequencies that would be expected under the assumption that the British and Danish population tables are quasi-homogeneous (with respect to the corresponding interactions between the column and row classifications) when subjects with the same U status as their fathers are blanked out in each country. Note that by blanking out the cell (U,U) in both the British and Danish data, we are calculating the expected frequencies in the other cells without assuming that status inheritance of U status is the same in both countries (i.e., we are taking into account the actual status inheritance of U status in each country without assuming them to be equal).

TABLE 16

PREDICTED MOBILITY PATTERN FOR BRITISH AND DANISH SAMPLES: STATUS IN-
HERITANCE IN THE UPPER CATEGORY IN EACH SAMPLE IS TAKEN INTO AC-
COUNT AND THE INTERACTIONS* THAT DO NOT INVOLVE THIS STATUS IN-
HERITANCE IN BRITISH POPULATION ARE ASSUMED EQUAL TO THE CORRE-
SPONDING INTERACTIONS IN DANISH POPULATION

FATHER'S STATUS	BRITISH SUBJECT'S STATUS			FATHER'S STATUS	DANISH SUBJECT'S STATUS		
	U	M	L		U	M	L
U..........	588.0†	390.8	163.2	U..........	685.0†	284.2	113.8
M..........	354.2	715.4	440.3	M..........	226.8	346.6	204.7
L..........	108.8	322.8	413.5	L..........	88.2	198.2	243.5

* These interactions are between subject's status and father's status.

† These cells were blanked out when calculating the predicted mobility pattern for the cells that were not blanked out. The frequencies, which are given here in the cells that were blanked out, are the observed frequencies.

The value of 1.56 is obtained for the χ^2 goodness-of-fit statistic (with 3 degrees of freedom). Comparing this value (1.56) with the value of 4.10, which was obtained in the preceding paragraph, we see that the differences between the two countries (with respect to the interactions between subject's status and father's status) can be accounted for, to a rather large extent, by the difference in status inheritance of U status in these countries. In a later section, we shall see that a related difference between the two countries is even more pronounced.[51]

INTRINSIC STATUS INHERITANCE AND DISINHERITANCE

If the methods usually used to analyze social mobility tables (e.g., by calculating the usual mobility ratios) were applied to analyze tables 1 and 8, they would have left the impression that there was "status inheritance"

[51] See footnote 37.

in status category M. The index of immobility[52] for the M status category, which is based on the usual mobility ratio (i.e., it is the ratio of the observed frequency in cell (M,M) and the frequency expected under the assumption of perfect mobility), is greater than 1.00; namely, 1.16 and 1.29 for tables 1 and 8, respectively. In apparent agreement with this, the interaction pertaining to status inheritance (interaction $[M,M]$) is positive in both countries (see tables 7 and 10). But the mobility ratio and this particular interaction do not measure what they appear to measure; the magnitudes of the intrinsic status inheritance of the U and L statuses confound the meaning of this particular ratio and this interaction.[53] Because of this confounding, we introduced here the interactions pertaining to the intrinsic status inheritance of each status category, and we then found that it was negative for the M status category in both countries. Thus, there is actually an intrinsic status disinheritance (rather than inheritance) in the M status category of both countries.[54]

We noted above that the mobility ratio (and the corresponding index of immobility) did not measure what it appeared to measure, since it compared the observed frequency with an expected frequency that is affected by the relative magnitudes of the intrinsic status inheritance and disinheritance in the various status categories. This difficulty can be remedied by calculating a different set of "expected" frequencies by the following procedure: First, since the model of quasi-independence fit the data when the diagonal cells were blanked out, we use this model to calculate the "expected" frequencies in the cells that are not blanked out, and then from these "expected" frequencies (or, more directly, from the estimates of the parameters of the model from which the "expected" frequencies were calculated) we calculate the frequencies in the blanked cells that would make the pattern of "expected" frequencies conform to a pattern of independence (between the column and row classifications) in the entire cross-classification table. By a straightforward extension of the method I developed earlier (1965b), we obtain the "expected" frequencies in table 17.

[52] The terms "status immobility," "status inertia," "status stability," "status persistence," "status inheritance," "status association," which appear in the published literature, all refer to the same phenomenon; namely, the tendency for there to be a concentration of observations in the cells on the main diagonal (see, e.g., Rogoff 1953; Carlsson 1958).

[53] Since intrinsic status inheritance of the U and L status categories means that the observed frequencies in the cells (U,U) and (L,L) will be "too large" (in a certain specific sense), these larger frequencies will increase the column and row marginal totals pertaining to both the U and L status categories; and thus the size of the column and row marginals pertaining to the M status category will be decreased relative to the other status categories. With this relative decrease in the marginals pertaining to the M status category, we obtain a decrease in the expected frequency in the (M,M) cell (calculated under the assumption of perfect mobility); and thus the ratio of the observed to the expected frequency in the (M,M) cell is raised above 1.0. This should help to explain why the observed mobility ratio is greater than 1.0. The observed interaction (M,M) is positive for a similar kind of reason.

[54] See footnote 31.

By comparing the observed frequencies with the corresponding "expected" frequencies in table 17, we obtain a new set of "mobility ratios" which lead to quite different conclusions from the usual mobility ratios.[55] For example, confining our attention for the moment to the diagonal cells, these new ratios (which we shall call the "new indices of immobility" when they are calculated for the diagonal cells) are given in table 18. For both Britain and Denmark, the new index of immobility pertaining to status M

TABLE 17

PREDICTED MOBILITY PATTERNS FOR BRITISH AND DANISH SAMPLES: STATUS INHERITANCE (OR DISINHERITANCE) IN EACH STATUS CATEGORY IS TAKEN INTO ACCOUNT AND QUASI-INDEPENDENCE* IS ASSUMED

FATHER'S STATUS	BRITISH SUBJECT'S STATUS			FATHER'S STATUS	DANISH SUBJECT'S STATUS		
	U	M	L		U	M	L
U..........	131.1†	390.2	163.8	U..........	127.2†	284.7	113.3
M..........	358.8	1052.9†	442.2	M..........	227.3	509.1†	202.7
L..........	109.2	324.8	136.4†	L..........	87.7	196.3	78.2†

* This quasi-independence is between subject's status and father's status.

† These cells were blanked out when calculating the predicted mobility pattern for the cells that were not blanked out. The frequencies, which are given here in the cells that were blanked out, are the frequencies that would make the predicted mobility pattern conform to a pattern of "perfect mobility" for the entire cross-classification table.

TABLE 18

NEW INDEX OF STATUS IMMOBILITY FOR EACH STATUS CATEGORY IN BRITISH AND DANISH SAMPLES, AND CORRESPONDING INDEX OF IMMOBILITY BASED ON USUAL MOBILITY RATIO

STATUS CATEGORY	BRITISH SAMPLE		DANISH SAMPLE	
	New Index	Usual Index	New Index	Usual Index
U..............	4.48	1.71	5.39	1.51
M..............	0.68	1.16	0.68	1.29
L..............	3.01	1.67	3.15	1.97

[55] Although the usual mobility ratios are supposed to measure the degree of mobility in a way that is "independent," in a certain sense, of the effects of the column and row marginal distributions, we have noted that they do not do so in situations where the observed marginal distributions are themselves affected by other phenomena (e.g., by intrinsic status inheritance of L and U statuses). In these situations, the new mobility ratios presented here take into account (and adjust for) the effects of these phenomena as well as the effects of the column and row marginal distributions. The new mobility ratios are calculated by replacing the observed column and row marginals by "theoretical" column and row marginals that describe what the size of the marginals would have been in a hypothetical situation in which the effects of these phenomena are nil. The "theoretical" marginals are calculated (as in my article [1964a]) using only cell entries in the table that are not affected directly by the phenomena. We use a set of cells that exhibits quasi-independence between the column and row classifications.

is smaller than one, whereas the usual index is larger than one.[56] There are actually fewer individuals in the (M,M) cell of the cross-classification tables (tables 1 and 8) than would be "expected" in table 17, and more individuals in the (U,U) and (L,L) cells than would be "expected."

Since the sum of the "expected" frequencies in table 17 for the cells that had not been blanked out (i.e., the nondiagonal cells) is equal to the sum of the corresponding observed frequencies in those cells, we find that the sum of the frequencies in all the cells of this table will usually not be equal to the sum of the corresponding observed frequencies. Indeed, the relative difference between the totals (in all the cells) provides us with a measure of one aspect of the net amount of status "persistence" in the tables.[57] This measure tells us what proportion of the individuals in the observed sample would need to be added to the diagonal cells of table 17 in order to make the total of the frequencies in this table (with the added individuals) equal the observed sample size. Calculating this measure for the British and Danish samples, we obtain 0.11 and 0.24, respectively.

In addition to the usual calculation of the mobility ratios, various other measures, which are based upon a comparison of the observed frequencies with the usual expected frequencies (calculated under the assumption of perfect mobility), have been suggested by other writers.[58] Replacing the expected frequencies as usually calculated by the "expected" frequencies as calculated in table 17, we would now obtain a variety of new measures, analogous to those presented earlier, but capable of leading to entirely different conclusions (as was the case illustrated in table 18). We shall not go into these details here.

We shall now comment upon the relationship between the new index of immobility in table 18 and the interactions pertaining to intrinsic status inheritance which were introduced earlier in this article. Recall that the interaction pertaining to a given 2×2 subtable was calculated by taking the logarithm of the corresponding odds-ratio in the subtable, and that the interaction pertaining to intrinsic status inheritance of U status (in table 1) was obtained as the arithmetic average of the interactions in tables 1E and 1G. Thus, the interaction pertaining to intrinsic status inheritance of U status is equal to the logarithm of the geometric average

---

[56] In addition to this difference between the new index and the usual one, note also that the new index of immobility for the U status category is larger than for the L status category, but the usual index applied to the Danish data would have suggested the opposite to be the case.

[57] This relative difference is actually equal to the total difference between the observed and "expected" frequencies in the diagonal cells, divided by the total of all the observed frequencies in the cross-classification table. The difference between the observed and "expected" frequencies in the (U,U) cell, divided by the total of all the observed frequencies in the cross-classification table, we shall refer to as an index of status "persistence" of U status; and a similar definition would apply to the M status and the L status. This index is equal to 0.13, -0.10, and 0.08, for the U, M, and L status categories, respectively, in Britain; and 0.23, -0.07, and 0.07, respectively, in Denmark.

[58] See, e.g., Rogoff 1953; Glass 1954; Carlsson 1958; Svalastoga 1959.

of the odds-ratios in tables 1E and 1G.[59] If the model of quasi-perfect mobility (with the diagonal cells blanked out) were to fit the data perfectly, then this geometric average would equal the new index of immobility for U status as given in table 18.[60] A similar remark applies also to the M and L status categories. For the U, M, and L status categories, these geometric averages are 4.45, 0.68, and 3.00, respectively, for the British sample; and 5.42, 0.68, and 3.18, respectively, for the Danish sample. Note how similar these values are to the results obtained with the new index in table 18. (Since the interaction pertaining to intrinsic status inheritance of M status, as defined by formula [14], is the negative of the arithmetic average of the interactions in tables 1B and 1C, this interaction is equal to the logarithm of the geometric average of the reciprocals of the odds-ratios in tables 1B and 1C. Therefore, for the M status category, we actually use the geometric average of the reciprocals, rather than the geometric average itself, to obtain the numerical results presented above.)

From the results presented in tables 7 and 10, we see that all these values (i.e., the geometric averages corresponding to the interactions) differ from 1.00 in statistically significant ways. For the U and L status categories, these values are significantly larger than 1.00, and for the M status category, the values are significantly smaller than 1.00. Furthermore, we see that the values for the U status category are significantly larger than the corresponding values for the L status category, which in turn are significantly larger than the corresponding values for the M status category.

The interaction pertaining to intrinsic net status inheritance of all statuses, which was introduced earlier in this article, was the sum of the interactions pertaining to intrinsic status inheritance of U, M, and L statuses. Thus, this interaction is equal to the logarithm of the product of the three geometric averages referred to in the preceding paragraph. This product is equal to 9.13 and 11.65 for Britain and Denmark, respectively.[61] (Here too, for the M status category, we actually use the geometric average of the reciprocals, rather than the geometric average itself, in our calculations leading to the numerical results presented above.) From the results presented in tables 7 and 10, we see that these values are also significantly different from 1.00.

THE ANALYSIS OF CROSS-CLASSIFICATION TABLES OTHER THAN THE 3 × 3 TABLES

In the earlier sections of this paper, we used the 3 × 3 tables (tables 1 and 8) to illustrate the application of the various techniques of analysis pre-

[59] See also footnote 24.

[60] This relationship between the geometric average and the new index of immobility can be proved by calculating both of these quantities under the assumption that there is quasi-independence (i.e., quasi-perfect mobility), as defined in my article (1968), when the diagonal cells are blanked out.

[61] The calculation of this product leads also to the suggestion that the corresponding product be calculated for the values obtained with the new index of immobility given in

sented there. As we noted earlier, the general approach developed here could be applied more generally to cross-classification tables of any size, either square tables (e.g., 5 × 5 tables) or rectangular tables (e.g., 5 × 7 tables). In the present section, we shall illustrate how some of these techniques can be used with the larger tables.

Let us begin by considering the British and Danish data when five status categories (rather than three) are used. We shall use the same five status categories used earlier by Svalastoga (1959) for the comparison of the

TABLE 19

CROSS-CLASSIFICATION OF BRITISH AND DANISH
MALE SAMPLES ACCORDING TO EACH SUBJECT'S
STATUS CATEGORY AND HIS FATHER'S STATUS
CATEGORY

FATHER'S STATUS	A	B	C	D	E
	British Subject's Status				
A..........	50	45	8	18	8
B..........	28	174	84	154	55
C..........	11	78	110	223	96
D..........	14	150	185	714	447
E..........	0	42	72	320	411
	Danish Subject's Status				
A..........	18	17	16	4	2
B..........	24	105	109	59	21
C..........	23	84	289	217	59
D..........	8	49	175	348	198
E..........	6	8	69	201	246

British and Danish data, and later used by Levine (1967) and Mosteller (1968), but we shall reach somewhat different conclusions from those presented in the earlier work. The data are given in table 19.[62] The status categories A, B, and C in this table formed the U status category in tables 1 and 8; and status categories D and E in this table were the same as M and L, respectively, in the earlier tables.

---

table 18 for the U, M, and L status categories. This product would provide us with an index of net immobility.

[62] The entry in the (E,A) cell of the British table is 0 in the original data and here; but it was replaced by 3 in the tables used by Levine and Mosteller. Although there are situations in which a "smoothing" of the original data (or the replacement of a 0 value by, say, ½) might be a reasonable procedure to adopt (see, e.g., Gart and Zweifel 1967; Mosteller 1968), no justification is given for the replacement of a 0 value by 3 in the work by Levine and Mosteller. The mobility patterns in the British and Danish data are actually somewhat less similar when the original data are analyzed than when the 0 value is replaced by 3; but of course, in a study aimed at comparing the mobility patterns in the the two sets of data, this increased similarity would not provide adequate justification for this particular replacement of the 0 value.

Applying to table 19 the same method as used to calculate the expected frequencies given in table 15, we obtain a value of 43.40 for the χ^2 goodness-of-fit statistic (with $4 \times 4 = 16$ degrees of freedom) comparing the observed frequencies in table 19 with the corresponding expected frequencies. Comparing this value (43.40) with the usual percentiles of the χ^2 distribution with 16 degrees of freedom,[63] we reject the null hypothesis that the interactions between subject's status and father's status were the same in the populations represented by the British and Danish samples.[64]

Recall that we found earlier that the χ^2 value, which was obtained when the two 3×3 tables (tables 1 and 8) were analyzed to see if the interactions were the same in the British and Danish studies, could be accounted for, to a rather large extent, by the difference in status inheritance of U status in these countries. Since the U status category has been divided into the three high status categories A, B, and C, in the tables presently under consideration, we shall now examine whether the interactions (between subject's status and father's status) in the British and Danish studies are quasi-homogeneous when the observed status inheritance among the three high status categories A, B, and C, in each country is taken into account.

Applying to table 19 the same method used to calculate the expected frequencies given in table 16, blanking out the nine cells in table 19 that correspond to the (U,U) cell in table 1, we obtain a χ^2 value of 11.69 for the χ^2 goodness-of-fit statistic (with $16 - 9 = 7$ degrees of freedom) comparing the observed frequencies in table 19 with the corresponding expected frequencies.[65] Comparing this value with the value of 43.40, which was obtained in the paragraph before the preceding one, we now see that the differences between the two social mobility tables (with respect to the interactions between subject's status and father's status) can be accounted for, to a rather large extent, by the difference between the tables in the status inheritance among the three high status categories.

The difference between the two χ^2 values $(43.40 - 11.69)$ provides us with a value of 31.71, which can be treated as a χ^2 value (with $16 - 7 = 9$ degrees of freedom) for testing the null hypothesis that the British and Danish populations corresponding to table 19 are the same with respect to all interactions that are affected by the entries in the blanked out cells (i.e., the nine cells pertaining to status inheritance among the A, B, and C status categories), assuming that there is quasi-homogeneity with respect

[63] For example, the 95th percentile is 26.30. A question can be raised concerning the applicability of the usual large-sample χ^2 theory when one of the observed frequencies in the sample is zero; but we shall not pursue this point here.

[64] When considering the substantive meaning of this statistically significant difference, it should be noted that the British study included persons aged eighteen years and over, whereas the Danish study was limited to persons aged twenty-one years and over. For further details pertaining to the comparability of the British and Danish studies, see Svalastoga 1959.

[65] The 95th percentile of the χ^2 distribution with 7 degrees of freedom is 14.07.

to the interactions that are not affected by the entries in the blanked out cells. Comparing this value (31.71) with the usual percentiles of the χ^2 distribution with 9 degrees of freedom, we reject this null hypothesis.[66] By a comparison of the observed and expected frequencies in the test of homogeneity, or by some of the other methods described in the earlier sections, we find that there is, generally speaking, more status inheritance among the status categories A, B, and C in the Danish study than in the British study, except that status inheritance within the status category A is more pronounced in the British study.

As we noted earlier, the 5×5 cross-classification tables considered above differ from the 3×3 tables considered earlier in that the A, B, and C status categories above had been combined to form the U status category earlier.

TABLE 20

CROSS-CLASSIFICATION OF BRITISH MALE SAMPLE ACCORDING TO EACH SUBJECT'S STATUS CATEGORY

FATHER'S STATUS	SUBJECT'S STATUS				
	1	2	3	4	5
1............	297	92	172	37	26
2............	89	110	223	64	32
3............	164	185	714	258	189
4............	25	40	179	143	71
5............	17	32	141	91	106

Note that the observed frequency in each of the A, B, or C status categories is much less than in the D or E status categories. We shall now consider instead a 5×5 table (table 20) obtained by dividing the U status categories of the 3×3 table into two status categories (rather than three), and by dividing the L status category into two as well.[67] We shall use table 20 to illustrate the application (to tables other than the 3×3 tables) of some of the other techniques presented earlier in this article.

With the finer division into five status categories in table 20, we would expect that "status inheritance," as defined in my article (1965b), might affect not only the number of individuals who are in the same status category as their fathers but also the number of individuals who are in the

[66] The 95th percentile of the χ^2 distribution with 9 degrees of freedom is 16.92. Even if the χ^2 distribution with 16 degrees of freedom were used, in accordance with an analogous procedure based on one of the methods suggested earlier herein for the analysis of the corresponding Z^2 statistics, the null hypothesis would still be rejected.

[67] The British data are given in sufficient detail (and the sample is large enough) to make possible this particular 5×5 cross-classification. This could not be done with the Danish data. Even for the British data, it was not possible to divide the M status category into two subcategories. The particular 5×5 cross-classification (table 20) was considered earlier in my article (1965b).

status category immediately adjacent to their fathers.[68] Indeed, while the usual χ^2 test of the independence in the 5×5 table yields a χ^2 value of 780.47 (with $4 \times 4 = 16$ degrees of freedom), a χ^2 value of 1.31 is obtained (with $16 - 13 = 3$ degrees of freedom) for testing the null hypothesis of quasi-independence when those individuals who differ from their fathers by at most one status category are blanked out.[69] Comparing the two χ^2 values (780.47 with 1.31), we see that the dependence between subject's status and father's status in table 20 can be accounted for, almost entirely, by status inheritance within status categories and status inheritance among adjacent status categories.

TABLE 21

New Index of Status Immobility for Each Status Category in the British Sample Calculated by Two Different Methods

	NEW INDEX	
STATUS CATEGORY	Calculated by Method A*	Calculated by Method B†
1................	14.26	12.00
2................	2.00	2.62
3................	0.53	0.68
4................	3.13	3.15
5................	5.38	4.35

NOTE.—The cross-classification of the British Sample analyzed in the present table was presented in table 20, in which the five status categories (1, 2, . . . , 5) were used.

* Method A takes into account status inheritance within status categories and status inheritance among adjacent status categories.

† Method B takes into account status inheritance among status categories 1 and 2, status inheritance among status categories 4 and 5, and status inheritance in status category 3.

In view of the fact that table 20 was obtained by a division of the U and L status categories of table 1 into status categories 1 and 2 and status categories 4 and 5, respectively, of table 20, we might also expect that it would only be necessary to take into account status inheritance among status categories 1 and 2, status inheritance among status categories 4 and 5, and status inheritance in status category 3. Indeed, a χ^2 value of 7.86 is obtained (with $16 - 9 = 7$ degrees of freedom) for testing the null hypothesis of quasi-independence when those individuals in the four cells pertain-

[68] For the 5×5 tables in table 19, we would expect that "status inheritance" might affect the nine cell entries referred to earlier (pertaining to status inheritance among the A, B, and C status categories) and the two diagonal cells pertaining to status inheritance in the D status category and in the E status category.

[69] A total of thirteen cells were blanked out here: the five diagonal cells and the eight cells immediately adjacent to the diagonal cells.

ing to status inheritance among the status categories 1 and 2, the four cells pertaining to status inheritance among the status categories 4 and 5, and the diagonal cell pertaining to status inheritance in status category 3, are blanked out. Thus, we see that the data fit the model of quasi-independence quite well even when four of the thirteen cell entries, which were blanked out in the preceding paragraph, are not blanked out.

The numerical values obtained with the methods suggested earlier herein for calculating the new indices of immobility, and the various other measures introduced there, will depend upon which cells of the cross-classification table are blanked out. Thought must be given in each particular case to determining which cells should be blanked out. In the case considered above, the blanking out of the nine cells has the advantage that it blanks out fewer observations, while the blanking out of the thirteen cells has the advantage that it leads to a χ^2 value that is somewhat smaller in relative terms.[70] Table 21 compares the new indices of immobility, obtained by these two methods of blanking out. The results are quite similar. If an inappropriate set of cells had been blanked out in the 5 × 5 cross-classification (e.g., if only the diagonal cells had been blanked out in table 20), then quite different (and misleading) results would have been obtained.[71]

REFERENCES

Birch, M. W. 1963. "Maximum Likelihood in Three-Way Contingency Tables." *Journal of the Royal Statistical Society*, ser. B, 25:220–33.

Carlsson, G. 1958. *Mobility and Class Structure*. Lund, Sweden: Gleerup.

Duncan, O. D. 1966. "Methodological Issues in the Analysis of Social Mobility." In *Social Structure and Mobility in Economic Development*, edited by N. J. Smelser and S. M. Lipset. Chicago: Aldine.

Edwards, A. W. F. 1963. "The Measure of Association in a 2 × 2 Table." *Journal of the Royal Statistical Society*, ser. A, 126:109–14.

Fisher, R. A., and F. Yates. 1953. *Statistical Tables for Biological, Agricultural and Medical Research*. 6th ed. New York: Hafner.

Gart, J. J. 1962. "On the Combination of Relative Risks." *Biometrics* 18:601–10; 19:509.

Gart, J. J., and J. R. Zweifel. 1967. "On the Bias of Various Estimators of the Logit and its Variance." *Biometrika* 54:181–7.

Glass, D. V., ed. 1954. *Social Mobility in Britain*. Glencoe, Ill.: Free Press.

Goodman, L. A. 1961*a*. "Modifications of the Dorn-Stouffer-Tibbitts Method for 'Testing the Significance of Comparisons in Sociological Data.'" *American Journal of Sociology* 66:355–63.

———. 1961*b*. "Statistical Methods for the Mover-Stayer Model." *Journal of the American Statistical Association* 56:841–68.

———. 1963. "Statistical Methods for the Preliminary Analysis of Transaction Flows." *Econometrica* 31:197–208.

———. 1964*a*. "A Short Computer Program for the Analysis of Transaction Flows." *Behavioral Science* 9:176–86.

[70] In comparing the observed χ^2 values, the difference in their corresponding degrees of freedom can be taken into account by comparing the corresponding percentiles pertaining to the observed values.

[71] The inappropriateness of blanking out this particular set of cells was pointed out in my article (1965*b*). A similar point was also made by McFarland (1968).

Goodman, L. A. 1964b. "Simultaneous Confidence Limits for Cross-Product Ratios in Contingency Tables." *Journal of the Royal Statistical Society*, ser. B, 26:86–102.

———. 1964c. "Simple Methods for Analyzing Three-Factor Interactions in Contingency Tables." *Journal of the American Statistical Association* 59:319–52.

———. 1964d. "Interactions in Multidimensional Contingency Tables." *Annals of Mathematical Statistics* 35:632–46.

———. 1964e. "Simultaneous Confidence Intervals for Contrasts among Multinomial Populations." *Annals of Mathematical Statistics* 35:716–25.

———. 1965a. "On Simultaneous Confidence Intervals for Multinomial Proportions." *Technometrics* 7:247–54.

———. 1965b. "On the Statistical Analysis of Mobility Data." *American Journal of Sociology* 70:564–85.

———. 1965c. "On the Multivariate Analysis of Three Dichotomous Variables." *American Journal of Sociology* 71:290–301.

* ———. 1968. "The Analysis of Cross-Classified Data: Independence, Quasi-Independence, and Interactions in Contingency Tables with or without Missing Entries." *Journal of the American Statistical Association* 63:1091–1131.

Levine, J. H. 1967. "Measurement in the Study of Intergenerational Status Mobility." Ph.D. thesis, Harvard University.

McFarland, D. D. 1968. "An Extension of Conjoint Measurement to Test the Theory of Quasi-Perfect Mobility." Michigan Studies in Mathematical Sociology, Paper no. 3.

Miller, R. G., Jr. 1966. *Simultaneous Statistical Inference*. New York: McGraw-Hill.

Mosteller, F. 1968. "Association and Estimation in Contingency Tables." *Journal of the American Statistical Association* 63:1–28.

Pearson, E. S., and H. O. Hartley. 1954. *Biometrika Tables for Statisticians*. Vol. 1. Cambridge: Cambridge University Press.

Rogoff, N. 1953. *Recent Trends in Occupational Mobility*. Glencoe, Ill.: Free Press.

Selvin, H. C., and A. Stuart. 1966. "Data-Dredging Procedures in Survey Analysis." *The American Statistician* 20:20–23.

Stinchcombe, A. L. 1964. *Rebellion in a High School*. Chicago: Quadrangle Books.

Svalastoga, K. 1959. *Prestige, Class and Mobility*. London: William Heinemann.

White, H. C. 1963. "Cause and Effect in Social Mobility Tables." *Behavioral Science* 7:14–27.

APPENDIX C
Everyman's Model Building Apparatus: I
Multiplicative Models for the Analysis of Occupational Mobility Tables and Other Kinds of Cross-Classification Tables

This note shows how some specific models proposed by Duncan (1979), Goodman (1972), Haberman (1974), and Simon (1974), which turn out to be useful for the analysis of occupational mobility tables and other kinds of cross-classification tables, are related to models obtained by applying the general formulations of multiplicative models in Goodman (1972), Darroch and Ratcliff (1972), and Haberman (1974). It also shows how each model can be described in terms of its expected frequencies, or equivalently in terms of its pattern of odds-ratios, or equivalently in terms of its pattern of odds. In so doing, it provides (a) further insight into the meaning of some of the specific models, (b) greater flexibility in the possible interpretations of a wide range of potentially useful specific models included within the general class of multiplicative models developed for the analysis of cross-classification tables, and (c) improved methods for estimating the expected frequencies under some of the specific models.

In the analysis of occupational mobility tables describing, say, the cross-classification of son's occupational category and father's occupational category, we will usually find that the baseline model of perfect mobility (i.e., independence between son's occupational category and father's occupational category) will not serve as an adequate description of the observed data. A more adequate description can usually be obtained by modifying the baseline model in ways that can take account of the possible existence of, say, "occupational inheritance and/or disinheritance," "occupational immobility and/or persistence," "overall upward or downward occupational mobility," "occupational mobility inertia," "occupational mobility barriers," and other related phenomena, using models of the kind introduced in, for example, Goodman (1972).[1] With these models, which can take account of the possible existence of various relevant substantive phenomena, the statistical methods presented in Goodman (1972) can be used (a) to determine whether a satisfactory description of the observed data

[1] These models can be obtained from the baseline model with the introduction of appropriate multiplicative factors.

can be obtained by taking account of these phenomena, (b) to estimate the magnitude of the effects of these phenomena, (c) to determine which of these effects are statistically significant and which are not, and (d) to test various hypotheses about the effects of these phenomena.

These phenomena will affect various aspects of the observed data in various ways. They will affect (a) the pattern of the observed frequencies in the cells of the cross-classification table (i.e., the occupational mobility table); (b) the observed pattern of association between the column classification (i.e., son's occupational category) and the row classification (i.e., father's occupational category) as measured, say, by the pattern of the odds-ratios (i.e., cross-product ratios) calculated from 2×2 subtables of the cross-classification table; (c) the pattern of the observed odds that an observation will fall in column category j' rather than in category j'', (i.e., that the son will be in occupational category j' rather than in category j''), given that it was in row category i (i.e., given that the father was in occupational category i); and (d) the pattern of the observed odds that an observation would fall in row category i' rather than in category i'' (i.e., that the father would be in occupational category i' rather than in category i''), given that it is in column category j (i.e., given that the son is in occupational category j). Each of the models introduced in Goodman (1972) could be described in terms of its expected frequencies, or equivalently in terms of its pattern of odds-ratios, or equivalently in terms of its pattern of odds. The present note provides general formulae that show how a model expressed in terms of its expected frequencies can be reexpressed in terms of its pattern of odds-ratios or in terms of its pattern of odds; how a model expressed in terms of its pattern of odds-ratios can be reexpressed in terms of its expected frequencies or in terms of its pattern of odds; and how a model expressed in terms of its pattern of odds can be reexpressed in terms of its expected frequencies or in terms of its pattern of odds-ratios. (See formulae [19a]–[19c], [27a]–[27b], [28a]–[28b], [32], [33a]–[33b], [34a]–[34b] below.) These general formulae can be applied to a specific model originally described using one form of expression (say, in terms of its expected frequencies) in order to obtain descriptions (or interpretations) of the same model using other forms of expression. They can also be applied, in comparing specific models originally described using different forms of expression, in order to determine whether or not the models are equivalent, and if not in which respects they differ from each other. Application of these general formulae also can serve as a heuristic device to assist the research worker in his search for models that are particularly well suited to a given substantive area and in his examination of the possible interpretations and implications of these models.

The above remarks referring to the analysis of occupational mobility tables can be applied more generally to the analysis of other kinds of cross-classification tables as well. In the occupational mobility table there is a one-to-one correspondence between the classes of the row classification and the classes of the column classification, and the classes of the row (and column) classification can usually be ordered (from high to low). Although some of the specific models which will be considered here are particularly well suited to square contingency tables of this kind (in which there is a one-to-one correspondence and in which the classes of the row [and column] classification can usually be ordered), the general results presented in the present note and in Goodman (1972) can be applied also to rectangular tables (as well as to square tables), where there may or may not be some kind of correspondence between the classes of the row and column classifications and where the classes of the row (and/or column) classification may or may not be ordered. These results can also be directly extended to the analysis and comparison of two (or more) $R \times C$ cross-classification tables and to the analysis of multidimensional cross-classification tables.

For expository purposes, the general results will be presented near the end of this note. The note will consider first some simple specific models of the kind introduced in Goodman (1972). Although these models could be described for more general cross-classification tables, for simplicity of exposition our attention will be focused on, say, a 4×4 table with an observed count f_{ij} ($i = 1, 2, 3, 4; j = 1, 2, 3, 4$) in the ith row and jth column of the table and a corresponding expected count F_{ij} under a specified model. The observed and expected counts are displayed in tables 1 and 2. Under the standard baseline model of independence (or perfect mobility), the F_{ij} are of the simple multiplicative form

$$F_{ij} = \alpha_i \beta_j , \tag{1}$$

where the α_i and β_j are positive constants pertaining to the ith row and jth column, respectively (see, e.g., Goodman 1965). The expected counts under condition (1) are displayed in table 3.

As noted earlier herein, the expected counts under the baseline model of independence will usually not serve as an adequate description of an observed table of counts, and when they do not we can consider a wide range of modifications of the baseline model (see, e.g., Goodman 1969, 1972). These modifications introduce various multiplicative constants to take account of the various inadequacies of the baseline model as a description of the observed table of counts. It may even be possible sometimes to obtain an adequate description with the introduction of a single multiplicative constant, say, γ, to take account of the inadequacy of the baseline model. For example, if the inadequacy pertains primarily to the counts in the cells on the main diagonal, it may be possible to obtain an adequate description by introducing a single "inflation factor" γ, applied to the cells on the main diagonal, to take account of this inadequacy.[2] With the introduction of the multiplicative constant γ, formula (1) for the expected count F_{ij} is replaced by

$$F_{ij} = \begin{cases} \alpha_i\beta_j\,, & \text{for } i \neq j \\ \alpha_i\beta_j\gamma\,, & \text{for } i = j\,. \end{cases} \tag{2}$$

The expected counts under condition (2) are displayed in table 4. This model is a simple example of a model included within the general class of

Table 1

f_{11}	f_{12}	f_{13}	f_{14}
f_{21}	f_{22}	f_{23}	f_{24}
f_{31}	f_{32}	f_{33}	f_{34}
f_{41}	f_{42}	f_{43}	f_{44}

Table 2

F_{11}	F_{12}	F_{13}	F_{14}
F_{21}	F_{22}	F_{23}	F_{24}
F_{31}	F_{32}	F_{33}	F_{34}
F_{41}	F_{42}	F_{43}	F_{44}

Table 3

$\alpha_1\beta_1$	$\alpha_1\beta_2$	$\alpha_1\beta_3$	$\alpha_1\beta_4$
$\alpha_2\beta_1$	$\alpha_2\beta_2$	$\alpha_2\beta_3$	$\alpha_2\beta_4$
$\alpha_3\beta_1$	$\alpha_3\beta_2$	$\alpha_3\beta_3$	$\alpha_3\beta_4$
$\alpha_4\beta_1$	$\alpha_4\beta_2$	$\alpha_4\beta_3$	$\alpha_4\beta_4$

Table 4

$\alpha_1\beta_1\gamma$	$\alpha_1\beta_2$	$\alpha_1\beta_3$	$\alpha_1\beta_4$
$\alpha_2\beta_1$	$\alpha_2\beta_2\gamma$	$\alpha_2\beta_3$	$\alpha_2\beta_4$
$\alpha_3\beta_1$	$\alpha_3\beta_2$	$\alpha_3\beta_3\gamma$	$\alpha_3\beta_4$
$\alpha_4\beta_1$	$\alpha_4\beta_2$	$\alpha_4\beta_3$	$\alpha_4\beta_4\gamma$

Table 5

γ	1	1	1
1	γ	1	1
1	1	γ	1
1	1	1	γ

Table 6

1	δ	δ	δ
δ	1	δ	δ
δ	δ	1	δ
δ	δ	δ	1

[2] In the substantive context of social mobility analysis, if there is, in a certain specific sense, "status inheritance" in each of the cells on the main diagonal, then the multiplicative constant γ is an "inflation factor"; whereas if there is "status disinheritance" in each of the cells on the main diagonal, then the multiplicative constant γ is a "deflation factor." When the amount of status inheritance and/or status disinheritance differs in the different cells on the main diagonal, a different multiplicative constant can be applied to each cell on the main diagonal (say, γ_i pertaining to the ith cell on the main diagonal), and the usual model of quasi independence (or quasi-perfect mobility) is obtained (see, e.g., Goodman 1965, 1972). The multiplicative constants γ_i correspond to the "new index of immobility" in Goodman (1969, 1972).

multiplicative models introduced in Goodman (1972),[3] and the various statistical techniques presented in that article can be applied here.

Both models (1) and (2) include the multiplicative constants α_i and β_j pertaining to the ith row and jth column, respectively (for $i = 1, 2, 3, 4$; $j = 1, 2, 3, 4$); and all other models considered herein will also include these constants. Since these constants will be included in all of the models, it will be convenient for expository purposes to focus attention explicitly on the other multiplicative constants (if any) in the models, with the constants α_i and β_j included implicitly. Thus, instead of displaying the expected counts under model (2) as in table 4, for convenience we shall use table 5 for the display pertaining to this model.[4]

The introduction of a single "inflation factor" γ applied to the cells on the main diagonal, as in model (2), would actually be equivalent to the introduction of a single "deflation factor," say δ, applied to the cells that are not on the main diagonal. Thus, the expected counts under model (2) could also be expressed in the following equivalent form:[5]

$$F_{ij} = \begin{cases} \alpha_i\beta_j, & \text{for } i = j \\ \alpha_i\beta_j\delta, & \text{for } i \neq j. \end{cases} \tag{3}$$

Table 6 provides the display pertaining to this model.[6]

Model (3) is a special case of the usual "diagonals-parameter model" (applied to the full cross-classification table) where the same multiplicative

---

[3] Model (2) is included within the general case described in section 3 of Goodman (1972). This model can also be viewed as a special kind of "diagonals-parameter model" applied to the full cross-classification table (see sections 2.5 and 2.8 in the 1972 article) where the diagonals-parameter pertains only to the cells on the main diagonal. This model is also equivalent to a special case of the usual diagonals-parameter model (for the full cross-classification table) where all the diagonals-parameters, except for the parameter pertaining to the main diagonal, are set equal to one (or set equal to each other).

[4] Tabular displays of this general kind, corresponding to the various models considered herein and other models as well (see, e.g., tables 5–13), can serve as a heuristic device to assist the research worker in his search for models that are particularly well suited to a given substantive area. This device and others introduced later in the present note (e.g., the description of specific models using three different but equivalent forms of expression), can provide the research worker with a "machine" for building models that take account of relevant substantive phenomena. A wide variety of models can be examined in this way.

[5] The methods presented in Goodman (1972) for showing that two particular multiplicative models are equivalent can be applied directly here to show that models (2) and (3) are equivalent. Models (2) and (3) describe the "uniform inheritance model" and/or "uniform disinheritance model."

[6] The multiplicative constant δ in table 6 (i.e., in model [3]) is equal to $1/\gamma$, where γ is the multiplicative constant in table 5 (i.e., in model [2]). Table 6 can be obtained from table 5 by dividing each entry in table 5 by γ. (The constants pertaining to the rows and columns im model [3] are also related to but different from the corresponding constants in model [2]. More specifically, the α_i and β_j in model [3] are actually equal to $\alpha_i\gamma\nu$ and β_j/ν, respectively, for the α_i, β_j, and γ in model [2], with ν denoting any positive constant of proportionality.)

constant δ pertains to all cells that are not on the main diagonal.[7] In other words, in model (3) the diagonals-parameters are set equal to each other for all cells (i, j) where $|i - j| \neq 0$. When the diagonals-parameters in the usual diagonals-parameter model differ in the different diagonals, and the difference depends upon how far the diagonal is from the main diagonal, the diagonals-parameter pertaining to cell (i, j) will depend upon $|i - j|$. Table 7 provides the display pertaining to this situation. In this case, the

Table 7

1	δ_1	δ_2	δ_3
δ_1	1	δ_1	δ_2
δ_2	δ_1	1	δ_1
δ_3	δ_2	δ_1	1

Table 8

1	δ	δ^2	δ^3
δ	1	δ	δ^2
δ^2	δ	1	δ
δ^3	δ^2	δ	1

Table 9

1	δ_1	δ_1^2	δ_1^3
1	δ_2	δ_2^2	δ_2^3
1	δ_3	δ_3^2	δ_3^3
1	δ_4	δ_4^2	δ_4^3

Table 10

1	δ	δ^2	δ^3
1	δ^2	δ^4	δ^6
1	δ^3	δ^6	δ^9
1	δ^4	δ^8	δ^{12}

Table 11

1	1	1	1
1	δ	δ^2	δ^3
1	δ^2	δ^4	δ^6
1	δ^3	δ^6	δ^9

Table 12

1	δ	δ^2	δ^3
δ	δ^3	δ^5	δ^7
δ^2	δ^5	δ^8	δ^{11}
δ^3	δ^7	δ^{11}	δ^{15}

Table 13

1	1	1	1
1	ζ	ζ	ζ
1	ζ	ζ^2	ζ^2
1	ζ	ζ^2	ζ^3

[7] For related comments, see n. 3 above.

expected count F_{ij} can be expressed as follows:

$$F_{ij} = \alpha_i \beta_j \delta_k, \quad \text{for } k = |i - j| \tag{4}$$

where $\delta_0 = 1$. As already noted for the models considered earlier herein, model (4) is also a simple example of a model included within the general class of multiplicative models introduced in Goodman (1972), and the various statistical techniques presented in that article can be applied to the model.[8]

Comparing tables 6 and 7, we see that model (3) is a special case of model (4) in which the following condition is satisfied:[9]

$$\delta_k = \delta, \quad \text{for } k = 1, 2, 3. \tag{5}$$

Consider next the model obtained from model (4) when the δ_k satisfy the following condition (instead of condition [5]):

$$\delta_k = \delta^k, \quad \text{for } k = 1, 2, 3. \tag{6}$$

In this case, the expected count F_{ij} can be expressed as

$$F_{ij} = \alpha_i \beta_j \delta^k, \quad \text{for } k = |i - j|. \tag{7}$$

Table 8 provides the display for this model.[10] Condition (6) and the corresponding model (7) were mentioned in Goodman (1972), and the model is equivalent, in most respects, to the "fixed distance model" introduced by Haberman (1974).[11]

[8] In the context of social mobility analysis, the diagonals-parameter δ_k measures "status inertia" pertaining to a move from status category i to status category $i + k$ or $i - k$ (for $i = 1, 2, 3, 4$), i.e., a move of k status categories. The magnitude δ_k of "status inertia" (for $k = 1, 2, 3$) can be estimated using model (4) or more general models that include diagonals-parameters and other relevant parameters (see Goodman 1972), in the case where model (4) (or a more general model) is congruent with the observed data. The subscript k in model (4) pertains to the kth subset of the cells in the cross-classification table, when the cells are partitioned into subsets so that the cells included in the same subset are on the same diagonal. Formula (4) was also applied by Hauser (1978) with the cells partitioned into subsets so that the cells included in the same subset have expected frequencies that are at the same density level. As with model (4), the model applied in Hauser (1978) is an example of the kind of model included in the general class of multiplicative models introduced in Goodman (1972).

[9] In the context of social mobility analysis, condition (5) states that the magnitude δ_k of "status inertia" pertaining to a move of k status categories is equal for $k = 1, 2, 3$. To test whether the "status inertia" magnitudes are equal, we can compare the goodness-of-fit of model (4) (or a more general model that includes diagonals-parameters and other relevant parameters) and model (3) (or the corresponding more general model with condition [5] satisfied), in the case where the former model is congruent with the observed data.

[10] Model (7) is related to, but different from, the "uniform association model" in Duncan (1979). If the absolute difference $|i - j|$ in the formula for model (7) is replaced by the product ij, as in the formula for model (14) presented later herein, we then obtain a model that is equivalent to the "uniform association model."

[11] Model (7) is a special case of the "crossings-parameter model," introduced in Goodman (1972), in which all the "crossings-parameters" are equal in magnitude. In the context

Note how the multiplicative constant in the jth cell of the first row of table 8 is raised to higher powers as j increases (for $j = 1, 2, 3, 4$). Consider next the model obtained when this kind of pattern (observed in the first row of table 8) is applied to each row of the table, with a different multiplicative constant applied to each row. Table 9 provides the display for the model thus obtained. In this case, the expected count F_{ij} can be expressed as

$$F_{ij} = \alpha_i \beta_j \delta_i^{\,j-1} \, . \tag{8}$$

Model (8) is equivalent to the model that was presented in Simon (1974) and applied in Duncan (1979) to occupational mobility data.[12]

Consider next the model obtained from model (8) when the δ_i satisfy the following condition:

$$\delta_i = \delta^i \, , \quad \text{for } i = 1, 2, 3, 4 \, . \tag{9}$$

Table 10 provides the display for the model thus obtained. In this case, the expected count F_{ij} can be expressed as

$$F_{ij} = \alpha_i \beta_j \delta^{i(j-1)} \, . \tag{10}$$

Model (10) is also equivalent to the models corresponding to the displays in tables 11 and 12, and the corresponding expected count F_{ij} for these models can be expressed as

$$F_{ij} = \alpha_i \beta_j \delta^{(i-1)(j-1)} \tag{11}$$

and

$$F_{ij} = \alpha_i \beta_j \delta^{ij-1} \, , \tag{12}$$

respectively.[13] Indeed, models (10), (11), and (12) are all equivalent to the

---

of social mobility analysis, the "crossings-parameters" measure "status barriers" (or "distances") between adjacent status categories. The magnitudes of the "status barriers" (or "distances") can be estimated using the "crossings-parameter model" as in Goodman (1972), or the related "variable distance model" in Haberman (1974), or more general models that include crossings-parameters and other relevant parameters (see, e.g., Goodman 1972). To test whether "status barriers" (or "distances") between adjacent categories are equal in magnitude, we can compare the goodness-of-fit of the "crossings-parameter model" (or a more general model) and model (7) (or the corresponding more general model with all the crossings-parameters set equal), in the case where the former model is congruent with the observed data.

[12] See "formulation A" in Simon (1974) and the "row-effects model" in Duncan (1979). Further comments on model (8) are included later in the present note and in Goodman (1978).

[13] The methods presented in Goodman (1972) for showing that two particular models are equivalent can be applied directly here to show that models (10), (11), and (12) are equivalent. Table 11 can be obtained from table 10 by dividing each entry in the jth column of table 10 by δ^{j-1}, and table 12 can be obtained by multiplying each entry in the ith row by δ^{i-1}. (The constants pertaining to the rows and columns in model [10] are related to but different from the corresponding constants in model [11], which are in turn related to but different from the corresponding constants in model [12]. For example, the α_i and β_j in model [10] are actually equal to $\alpha_i \nu$ and $\beta_j / \delta^{i-1} \nu$, respectively, for the α_i, β_j, and δ in model [11], with ν denoting any positive constant of proportionality.)

models obtained when the expected count can be expressed as[14]

$$F_{ij} = \alpha_i \beta_j \delta^{(i-1)j}, \tag{13}$$

or as

$$F_{ij} = \alpha_i \beta_j \delta^{ij}, \tag{14}$$

or as

$$F_{ij} = \alpha_i \beta_j \delta^{(i-2.5)(j-2.5)}. \tag{15}$$

Models (10)–(15) are all equivalent to the "uniform association model" in Duncan (1979).[15]

Having noted above the equivalence of models (10)–(15), we comment next on the fact that the other models presented earlier herein can also be expressed in various equivalent forms. For example, models (2) and (3) (namely, the "uniform inheritance model" and "uniform disinheritance model") are equivalent, as we noted earlier (see tables 5 and 6). Similarly, the "fixed distance model" as described by model (7) (see table 8) is equivalent to the model corresponding to the display in table 13, and the corresponding expected count F_{ij} can be expressed as follows:[16]

$$F_{ij} = \begin{cases} \alpha_i \beta_j \zeta^{i-1}, & \text{for } i \leqq j, \\ \alpha_i \beta_j \zeta^{j-1}, & \text{for } i > j. \end{cases} \tag{16}$$

We may also note here that model (8) (see table 9) is equivalent to the models

[14] The remarks in n. 13 can be applied also to models (13), (14), and (15). It may also be worth noting that the equivalence of the models is not affected by replacing 2.5, which appears twice in the exponent in the formula for model (15), by any other specified numbers (e.g., by 1 in model [11] and by 0 in model [14]); and the specified numbers used in the two places in the exponent in the formula for model (15) can differ from each other (e.g., the 2.5 appearing first in the exponent in the formula for model [15] is replaced by 0 in model [10] and by 1 in model [13]; and the 2.5 appearing second in the exponent is replaced by 1 in model [10] and by 0 in model [13]). In some contexts, it may be convenient to use as the specified numbers $(R + 1)/2$ and $(C + 1)/2$, where R and C denote the number of rows and columns, respectively, in the cross-classification table.

[15] The formulation of this model presented in the present note will lead us later herein to an iterative estimation procedure that is different from the one used by Duncan (1979) to study this model. (On this topic, see also Goodman 1978.) Furthermore, because of the relationship between the "uniform association model" and the "fixed distance model" (model [7]) described in n. 10, the general iterative estimation procedure referred to later herein can be applied also to the "fixed distance model" (and other related models) as well as to the "uniform association model."

[16] The remarks in n. 13 can be applied also to models (7) and (16). The multiplicative constant ζ in table 13 (i.e., in model [16]) is equal to $1/\delta^2$, where δ is the multiplicative constant in table 8 (i.e., in model [7]). Table 13 can be obtained from table 8 by dividing each entry in the jth column of table 8 by δ^{j-1} and each entry in the ith row by δ^{i-1}. Models (7) and (16) might appear, at first sight, to be quite different from each other, but their equivalence will become more evident when we discuss the corresponding odds-ratios later herein. (Although table 13 might appear, at first sight, to resemble table 11 more closely than table 8, the model corresponding to table 13 is not equivalent to the model corresponding to table 11, but it is equivalent to the model corresponding to table 8.)

obtained when the expected count can be expressed as[17]

$$F_{ij} = \alpha_i \beta_j \delta_i{}^j , \qquad (17)$$

or as

$$F_{ij} = \alpha_i \beta_j \delta_i{}^{j-2.5} . \qquad (18)$$

Each of the models considered herein can be described in terms of its corresponding pattern of odds-ratios (i.e., cross-product ratios). In order to demonstrate this, we now shall consider the quantity Θ_{ij} defined as follows:

$$\Theta_{ij} = (F_{ij}F_{i+1,j+1})/(F_{i,j+1}F_{i+1,j}) \qquad (19a)$$

$$= (F_{ij}/F_{i,j+1})/(F_{i+1,j}/F_{i+1,j+1}) \qquad (19b)$$

$$= (F_{ij}/F_{i+1,j})/(F_{i,j+1}/F_{i+1\ j+1}) . \qquad (19c)$$

The above formulae define the odds-ratio (i.e., the cross-product ratio) Θ_{ij} in the following equivalent terms: (a) It is the cross-product ratio obtained from the expected counts (i.e., the F's) in the 2×2 subtable formed from the cells (i, j), $(i, j + 1)$, $(i + 1, j)$, $(i + 1, j + 1)$; (b) it is the ratio of the odds $F_{ij}/F_{i,j+1}$ that an observation will fall in column j rather than in column $j + 1$, given that it was in row i, and the odds $F_{i+1,j}/F_{i+1,j+1}$ that an observation will fall in column j rather than in column $j + 1$, given that it was in row $i + 1$; and (c) it is the ratio of the odds $F_{i,j}/F_{i+1,j}$ that an observation would fall in row i rather than in row $i + 1$, given that it is in column j, and the odds $F_{i,j+1}/F_{i+1,j+1}$ that an observation would fall in row i rather than in row $i + 1$, given that it is in column $j + 1$.[18]

By applying formula (19a) to model (1) (see table 3), we of course obtain

$$\Theta_{ij} = 1 , \quad \text{for all } i, j . \qquad (20)$$

Similarly, the odds-ratio for, say, model (7) (see table 8) can be expressed as follows:[19]

$$\Theta_{ij} = \begin{cases} 1/\delta^2 , & \text{for } i = j \\ 1 , & \text{for } i \neq i . \end{cases} \qquad (21)$$

[17] The remarks in n. 13 can be applied to models (8), (17), and (18). It may also be worth noting that the equivalence of the models is not affected by replacing 2.5, which appears in the exponent in the formula for model (18), by any other specified number (e.g., by 1 in model [8], and by 0 in model [17]). In some contexts, it may be convenient to use as the specified number $(C + 1)/2$, where C denotes the number of columns in the cross-classification table.

[18] For simplicity, only those odds-ratios that pertain to the cells in two successive rows (say, rows i and $i + 1$) and two successive columns (say, cols. j and $j + 1$) are considered here. All other odds-ratios pertaining to the cross-classification table can be calculated directly from this particular set of odds-ratios (see, e.g., Goodman 1969, 1978). This particular set can also be used to determine the formula for the expected counts F_{ij} under the model and the formulae for the corresponding odds (see formulae [32] and [33a]–[33b] below). Since this particular set can be used in determining the F_{ij} under the model, it can also be used to determine the corresponding tabular display (see, e.g., tables 5–13).

[19] The corresponding odds-ratio for model (16) (see table 13) is equal to ζ when $i = j$, and it is equal to 1 when $i \neq j$. This result helps to explain why models (7) and (16) are equivalent, with $\zeta = 1/\delta^2$.

More generally, the odds-ratio for model (4) (see table 7) can be expressed as

$$\Theta_{ij} = \begin{cases} 1/\delta_1{}^2\,, & \text{for } i = j \\ \delta_k{}^2/(\delta_{k-1}\delta_{k+1})\,, & \text{for } i \neq j\,, \end{cases} \tag{22}$$

with $k = |i - j|$ and $\delta_0 = 1$. (This odds-ratio for model [4] can, of course, also be written as

$$\Theta_{ij} = v_k\,, \quad \text{for } k = |i - j| \tag{23}$$

with $v_0 = 1/\delta_1{}^2$ and $v_k = \delta_k{}^2/(\delta_{k-1}\delta_{k+1})$, for $k = 1, 2, \ldots$.) In particular, for models (2) and (3) (see, e.g., table 6), we obtain the following:[20]

$$\Theta_{ij} = \begin{cases} 1/\delta^2\,, & \text{for } k = 0 \\ \delta\,, & \text{for } k = 1 \\ 1\,, & \text{for } k = 2, 3, \ldots \end{cases} \tag{24}$$

Consider next model (8) (see table 9). For this model, the odds-ratio can be expressed as follows:[21]

$$\Theta_{ij} = \delta_{i+1}/\delta_i\,, \quad \text{for all } i, j\,. \tag{25}$$

And for models (10)–(15) (see tables 10–12), we obtain[22]

$$\Theta_{ij} = \delta\,, \quad \text{for all } i, j\,. \tag{26}$$

Formulae (20)–(26) above describe the pattern of odds-ratios for each of the models considered herein. Each of these models can also be described in terms of its corresponding pattern of odds (rather than odds-ratios). In order to demonstrate this, consider now the quantities $\Omega_{ij}{}^{A\bar{B}}$ and $\Omega_{ji}{}^{B\bar{A}}$ defined as follows:

$$\Omega_{ij}{}^{A\bar{B}} = F_{ij}/F_{i,j+1}\,, \tag{27a}$$

$$\Omega_{ji}{}^{B\bar{A}} = F_{ij}/F_{i+1,j}\,. \tag{27b}$$

The above formulae define the odds $\Omega_{ij}{}^{A\bar{B}}$ and the odds $\Omega_{ji}{}^{B\bar{A}}$ in the following terms: (a) $\Omega_{ij}{}^{A\bar{B}}$ is the odds $F_{ij}/F_{i,j+1}$ that an observation will fall in column j rather than in column $j + 1$, given that it was in row i; and (b) $\Omega_{ji}{}^{B\bar{A}}$ is the

[20] Formula (24) can be calculated directly from table 6, and it also follows as a special case of formula (22), since $\delta_k = \delta$ (for $k = 1, 2, \ldots$) in models (2) and (3) as noted in formula (5). Similarly, formula (21) can be calculated directly from table 8 (or table 13), and it also follows as a special case of formula (22), since $\delta_k = \delta^k$ in model (7) as noted in formula (6).

[21] It was noted earlier that model (8) was equivalent to a model presented in Simon (1974) and Duncan (1979). In the latter article, the model is defined in terms of the odds-ratios; in the former, in terms of the odds. In the present note, the model is defined in terms of the expected counts F_{ij} since this definition provides further insight into the meaning of the model, and it will facilitate discussion below of iterative estimation procedures for this model and other related models. For further comments on this topic, see Goodman (1978).

[22] Formula (26) can be calculated directly from table 10 (or tables 11 and 12), and it also follows as a special case of formula (25), since $\delta_i = \delta^i$ in models (10)–(15) as noted in formula (9).

odds $F_{ij}/F_{i+1,j}$ that an observation would fall in row i rather than in row $i + 1$, given that it is in column j.[23] From (19b)–(19c) and (27a)–(27b), we obtain

$$\Theta_{ij} = \Omega_{ij}{}^{A\bar{B}}/\Omega_{i+1,j}{}^{A\bar{B}} \tag{28a}$$

$$= \Omega_{ji}{}^{B\bar{A}}/\Omega_{j+1,i}{}^{B\bar{A}} . \tag{28b}$$

By applying (27a)–(27b) to model 1 (see table 3), we of course obtain

$$\Omega_{ij}{}^{A\bar{B}} = \psi_j{}^B , \tag{29a}$$

$$\Omega_{ji}{}^{B\bar{A}} = \psi_i{}^A , \tag{29b}$$

with $\psi_i{}^A = \alpha_i/\alpha_{i+1}$ and $\psi_j{}^B = \beta_j/\beta_{j+1}$. Similarly, the odds for, say, models (10)–(15) (see, e.g., table 12) can be expressed as follows:[24]

$$\Omega_{ij}{}^{A\bar{B}} = \psi_j{}^B \xi^i , \tag{30a}$$

$$\Omega_{ji}{}^{B\bar{A}} = \psi_i{}^A \xi^j , \tag{30b}$$

where $\xi = 1/\delta$. More generally, the odds for model (8) (see table 9) can be expressed as[25]

$$\Omega_{ij}{}^{A\bar{B}} = \psi_j{}^B \xi_i , \tag{31a}$$

$$\Omega_{ji}{}^{B\bar{A}} = \psi_i{}^A \tau_i{}^j , \tag{31b}$$

where $\xi_i = 1/\delta_i$ and $\tau_i = \delta_i/\delta_{i+1}$. The other models presented earlier can also be expressed in similar terms, but these details will be left as an exercise for the interested reader.

We have now seen how each model can be described in terms of the pattern of odds-ratios (i.e., the Θ_{ij}), or equivalently in terms of the pattern of odds (i.e., the $\Omega_{ij}{}^{A\bar{B}}$ or the $\Omega_{ji}{}^{B\bar{A}}$), or equivalently in terms of the pattern of expected frequencies (i.e., the F_{ij}). For example, the "uniform association model" states that the odds-ratios Θ_{ij} are equal for all i and j (see formula [26]). And this model is equivalent to the model obtained by stating that the odds $\Omega_{ij}{}^{A\bar{B}}$ increase (or decrease) exponentially as row i increases (see

[23] For simplicity, only those odds $\Omega_{ij}{}^{A\bar{B}}$ that pertain to the cells in two successive columns (say, cols. j and $j + 1$) in a given row (say, row i), and those odds $\Omega_{ji}{}^{B\bar{A}}$ that pertain to the cells in two successive rows (say, rows i and $i + 1$) in a given column (say, col. j), are considered here. All other odds that pertain to the cells in any two columns (say, cols. j' and j'') in row i can be calculated directly from the $\Omega_{ij}{}^{A\bar{B}}$ (as the product of the $\Omega_{ij}{}^{A\bar{B}}$'s for $j = j', j' + 1, \ldots, j'' - 1$, when $j' < j''$); and all other odds that pertain to the cells in any two rows (say, rows i' and i'') in col. j can be calculated directly from the $\Omega_{ji}{}^{B\bar{A}}$ (as the product of the $\Omega_{ji}{}^{B\bar{A}}$'s for $i = i', i' + 1, \ldots, i'' - 1$, when $i' < i''$).

[24] Formulae (30a) and (30b) remain correct even if the exponents i and j are replaced by i minus any specified number and j minus any specified number, respectively. The relationship between $\psi_i{}^A$ and α_i/α_{i+1}, and between $\psi_j{}^B$ and β_j/β_{j+1}, will depend upon which exponents are used in formulae (30a) and (30b), and upon which of the models (10)–(15) is used.

[25] The remarks in n. 24 can be applied also to the exponent j in formula (31b) and the corresponding $\psi_i{}^A$. Formulae similar to (31a) and (31b) were used in Simon (1974) to define a model that is equivalent to model (8), as noted in n. 21.

formula [30a]); and the rate of increase (or decrease) is unaffected by the value of j, but the intercept of the corresponding exponential curve may be affected by the value of j.[26] And this in turn is equivalent to the model obtained by stating that the odds $\Omega_{ji}{}^{B\bar{A}}$ increase (or decrease) exponentially as column j increases (see formula [30b]); and the rate of increase (or decrease) is unaffected by the value of i, but the intercept of the corresponding exponential curve may be affected by the value of i.[27] And this in turn is equivalent to the model obtained by stating that the expected frequency F_{ij} is the product of a row factor α_i, a column factor β_j, and an interaction factor that increases (or decreases) exponentially as the product ij increases (see formula [14]).[28]

The equivalent descriptions in the preceding paragraph pertain to models (10)–(15). A similar set of equivalent descriptions can be obtained for, say, model (8) using formulae (25), (31a), and (31b). Similar results can also be obtained for each of the other models presented earlier herein.

For any model described in terms of the expected frequencies F_{ij}, formula (19) can be used to calculate the corresponding odds-ratios Θ_{ij}, and formulae (27a) and (27b) can be used to calculate the corresponding odds $\Omega_{ij}{}^{A\bar{B}}$ and $\Omega_{ji}{}^{B\bar{A}}$, respectively. For any model described in terms of the odds-ratios, we can calculate the corresponding expected frequencies from[29]

$$F_{ij} = \alpha_i\beta_j\prod_{s=1}^{i-1} \prod_{t=1}^{j-1}\Theta_{st} \; ; \tag{32}$$

and we can calculate the corresponding odds from

$$\Omega_{ij}{}^{A\bar{B}} = (\beta_j/\beta_{j+1}) \Big/ \prod_{s=1}^{i-1}\Theta_{sj} \; , \tag{33a}$$

[26] Expressed in terms of logarithms, formula (30a) can be used to describe the following linear relationship: The logarithm of the odds $\Omega_{ij}{}^{A\bar{B}}$ increases (or decreases) linearly as row i increases; and the slope of the increase (or decrease) is unaffected by the value of j, but the intercept of the corresponding straight line may be affected by the value of j.

[27] Formula (30b) can be used to describe a linear relationship for the logarithm of the odds $\Omega_{ji}{}^{B\bar{A}}$ in the same manner used in n. 26 to describe a linear relationship for the logarithm of the odds $\Omega_{ij}{}^{A\bar{B}}$.

[28] Expressed in terms of logarithms, formula (14) can be used to describe the following relationship: The logarithm of the expected frequency F_{ij} is the sum of a row factor ($\log \alpha_i$), a column factor ($\log \beta_j$), and an interaction factor that increases (or decreases) linearly as the product ij increases.

[29] The products

$$\prod_{s=1}^{i-1}\Theta_{st} \quad \text{and} \quad \prod_{t=1}^{j-1}\Theta_{st}$$

in formula (32) are clearly defined for the integer i (where $i = 2, 3, \ldots, R$) and the integer j (where $j = 2, 3, \ldots, C$), respectively; and when $i = 1$ or $j = 1$ the corresponding symbols can be defined as being equal to one.

$$\Omega_{ji}{}^{B\bar{A}} = (\alpha_i/\alpha_{i+1}) \bigg/ \prod_{t=1}^{j-1}\Theta_{it}, \qquad (33b)$$

where the α_i and β_j are the parameters used in formula (32). For any model described in terms of the odds, we can calculate the corresponding expected frequencies from[30]

$$F_{ij} = \alpha_i \bigg/ \prod_{t=1}^{j-1}\Omega_{it}{}^{A\bar{B}} \qquad (34a)$$

or

$$F_{ij} = \beta_j \bigg/ \prod_{s=1}^{i-1}\Omega_{js}{}^{B\bar{A}}, \qquad (34b)$$

and we can calculate the corresponding odds-ratios from formulae (28a)–(28b). It may also be worthwhile to note that the parameters α_i and β_j in formula (32) can be calculated in terms of the corresponding odds:

$$\alpha_i = \alpha_1 \bigg/ \prod_{s=1}^{i-1}\Omega_{1s}{}^{B\bar{A}}, \qquad (35a)$$

$$\beta_j = \beta_1 \bigg/ \prod_{t=1}^{j-1}\Omega_{1t}{}^{A\bar{B}}. \qquad (35b)$$

The general formulae presented above can be applied to the particular models presented earlier and to any other multiplicative models for the cross-classification table (e.g., the various models introduced in Goodman 1972).

Some of the results presented earlier in this note provide further insight into the meaning of some of the specific models considered herein. The general formulae presented above can be applied to a wide range of potentially useful specific models, and they will provide greater flexibility in the possible interpretations of these models. Let us turn now to a brief discussion of statistical techniques for the analysis of these models.

To estimate the expected frequencies under the "uniform association model" (as described in formulae [10]–[15], [26], [30a], or [30b]), Duncan (1979) used a trial-and-error search method in conjunction with the iterative procedure of the computer program ECTA (Everyman's Contingency Table

---

[30] The remark in n. 29 can be applied also to the products

$$\prod_{s=1}^{i-1}\Omega_{js}{}^{B\bar{A}} \quad \text{and} \quad \prod_{t=1}^{j-1}\Omega_{it}{}^{A\bar{B}}$$

in formulae (34b) and (34a). Formula (34a) calculates the expected count F_{ij} in terms of the parameters α_i (i.e., the row factors) and the set of odds $\Omega_{ij}{}^{A\bar{B}}$, whereas formula (34b) calculates the F_{ij} in terms of the parameters β_j (i.e., the column factors) and the set of odds $\Omega_{ji}{}^{B\bar{A}}$.

Analyzer).[31] This search method required the repeated calculation of "starting tables" for each successive application of the ECTA program. Instead of this trial-and-error search method, we can use a single iterative procedure that leads directly to the correct estimates.

For any model that can be described in terms of a tabular display that contains a multiplicative constant (say, δ or γ) but does not contain any higher powers of that constant (see, e.g., tables 5 and 6), the general iterative procedure presented in Goodman (1972) is available.[32] This iterative procedure can also be applied when the tabular display for the model contains various multiplicative constants (say, δ_1, δ_2, δ_3) but does not contain any higher powers of those constants (see, e.g., table 7). When the tabular display for the model contains a multiplicative constant (say, δ or ζ) and higher powers of that constant (see, e.g., tables 8, 10–13), the iterative scaling process in Darroch and Ratcliff (1972) is available.[33] This procedure can also be applied when the tabular display for the model contains various multiplicative constants (say, δ_1, δ_2, δ_3, δ_4) and higher powers of those constants (see, e.g., table 9).

The procedures referred to above can be applied to tabular displays for the full cross-classification table, and they can be modified in a straight-forward way in order to make them applicable to tables in which some of the cells are omitted (see, e.g., Goodman 1968, 1972, 1978). For the sake of brevity, the present note will not go into these matters.

REFERENCES

Darroch, J. N., and D. Ratcliff. 1972. "Generalized Iterative Scaling for Log-linear Models." *Annals of Mathematical Statistics* 43 (October): 1470–80.

Duncan, O. D. 1979. "How Destination Depends on Origin in the Occupational Mobility Table." *American Journal of Sociology* 84 (January): 793–803.

Goodman, L. A. 1965. "On the Statistical Analysis of Mobility Tables." *American Journal of Sociology* 70 (March): 564–85.

[31] The ECTA computer program, prepared by R. Fay and the present author, is available from the author.

[32] The iterative scaling process in Darroch and Ratcliff (1972), and the modified Newton-Raphson method in Haberman (1974), could also be applied, but the procedure in Goodman (1972) is simpler when it is applicable. The cyclic iterative process in Darroch and Ratcliff (1972) reduces to the simpler iterative procedure in Goodman (1972) when the latter procedure is applicable. Although the modified Newton-Raphson method will usually require fewer iterations, the iterative procedure in Goodman (1972) is easier to apply; and even when the iterative procedure requires many iterations, the actual cost of using the procedure (i.e., the cost of a run applying a given computer program on an electronic computer) will usually be small. The modified Newton-Raphson method and the iterative scaling process in Darroch and Ratcliff (1972) can be used for all of the models presented in this note.

[33] In particular, the iterative scaling process is available for models (10)–(15). For these particular models and some other related models, an alternative iterative procedure was introduced and applied in Goodman (1978). This alternative procedure is relatively easy to apply, and it converges more rapidly than the Darroch-Ratcliff procedure in many cases.

* ———. 1968. "The Analysis of Cross-classified Data: Independence, Quasi-Independence, and Interactions in Contingency Tables with or without Missing Entries." *Journal of the American Statistical Association* 63 (December): 1091–131.

* ———. 1969. "How to Ransack Social Mobility Tables and Other Kinds of Cross-Classification Tables." *American Journal of Sociology* 75 (July): 1–39.

* ———. 1972. "Some Multiplicative Models for the Analysis of Cross-classified Data." Pp. 649–96 in *Proceedings of the Sixth Berkeley Symposium on Mathematical Statistics and Probability*, edited by L. Le Cam, J. Neyman, and E. L. Scott. Berkeley: University of California Press.

* ———. 1978. "Simple Models for the Analysis of Association in Cross-Classifications Having Ordered Row Categories and Ordered Column Categories." Unpublished paper.

Haberman, S. J. 1974. *The Analysis of Frequency Data*. Chicago: University of Chicago Press.

Hauser, R. M. 1978. "A Structural Model of the Mobility Table." *Social Forces* 56 (March): 919–53.

Simon, G. 1974. "Alternative Analyses for the Singly-ordered Contingency Table." *Journal of the American Statistical Association* 69 (December): 971–76.

A CAUTIONARY ADDENDUM

Formulae (32) and (33) should remind the reader that we have considered here only models for F_{ij} that include α_i and β_j, only models for $\Omega_{ij}{}^{A\bar{B}}$ that include $(\beta_j/\beta_{j+1}) = \psi_j{}^B$, and only models for $\Omega_{ji}{}^{B\bar{A}}$ that include $(\alpha_i/\alpha_{i+1}) = \psi_i{}^A$.

APPENDIX D
Everyman's Model Building Apparatus: II
Some Multiplicative Models for the Analysis of Cross-Classified Data

1. Introduction and summary

In the present article, we shall present some multiplicative models for the analysis of $R \times C$ contingency tables (that is, contingency tables with R rows and C columns), and shall apply these models to cross classified data in ways that will lead to a more complete analysis of these data than has heretofore been possible.

For the $R \times C$ contingency table, the usual model of "independence" in the table (that is, independence between the row classification and column classification of the table) is a simple example of a multiplicative model. For short, I shall call this model (that is, the model of independence between the row classification and column classification of the table) the I model. The model of "quasi-independence" in the $R \times C$ table, which was introduced and developed in my earlier work, and which I shall comment upon again later, is another example of a multiplicative model (see, for example, Goodman [9], [10], [12], [13], Caussinus [4], Bishop and Fienberg [2]). For short, I shall call this model the Q model. The various multiplicative models which I shall present here can be viewed as modifications or generalizations of the I model and/or the Q model.

To illustrate the application of these models, we shall analyze a 5×5 contingency table (Table I) in which there is a one to one correspondence between the five classes of the row classification and the five classes of the column classification, and in which the classes of the row (and column) classification can be ordered (from high to low). Although some of the particular models, which we shall consider herein (see Section 2), are particularly well suited to square contingency tables of this kind (in which there is this one to one correspondence and in which the classes of the row (and column) classification can be ordered), we wish to draw the reader's attention to the fact that the general class of multiplicative models presented in this article (see Sections 3 and 4) also includes a variety of models that can be applied more generally to rectangular contingency tables (as well as to square tables), where there may or may not be some kind of correspondence between the classes of the row and

TABLE I

CROSS CLASSIFICATION OF BRITISH MALE SAMPLE ACCORDING TO EACH SUBJECT'S STATUS
CATEGORY AND HIS FATHER'S STATUS CATEGORY, USING FIVE STATUS CATEGORIES

		Subject's Status				
		1	2	3	4	5
	1	50	45	8	18	8
	2	28	174	84	154	55
Father's	3	11	78	110	223	96
Status	4	14	150	185	714	447
	5	0	42	72	320	411

column classifications and where the classes of the row (and/or column) classifications may or may not be ordered.

Although the models presented here are described in different terms from the models in Haberman's fundamental work [20], it can be shown that the general theory and methods developed by Haberman are applicable to the various models considered herein. In most respects, the class of models considered by Haberman is broader than the class considered here; but by adopting a somewhat different perspective here and by confining our attention to a more limited class of models, we shall obtain some new results.

We shall formulate the models for the case where a random sample of n observations is drawn from the population cross classification table (the case where the sample size n is fixed), but the methods that we shall present here can also be applied to the case where a sample of $n_i.$ observations is drawn from the ith row, $i = 1, 2, \cdots, R$, of the population table (the case where the row marginals are fixed), or where a sample of $n_{.j}$ observations is drawn from the jth column, $j = 1, 2, \cdots, C$, of the population table (the case where the column marginals are fixed). The analysis in the case where the row marginals or the column marginals are fixed is similar, in most respects, to the analysis in the case where only the sample size n is fixed; but there are differences in the way some of the parameters of interest are defined in these cases, and there also are differences in the way these parameters are estimated. These differences will be discussed later (see Section 5).

The table that we shall use for illustrative purposes (Table I) presents data on intergenerational social mobility in Britain, which were collected by Glass and his coworkers [6]. The data in this table were obtained by a kind of stratified random sampling, but for our present exposition we view this table as a contingency table; that is, as if simple random sampling had been used. Table I was used earlier by Svalastoga [25], Levine [22], Mosteller [24], and Goodman [14] for purposes of comparison with a comparable 5 × 5 table (Table II) describing social mobility in Denmark, and it is a condensation of a 7 × 7 British table (Table III) that used a more detailed set of classes (status categories). Table I was formed from Table III by combining status category 2 with 3 and status category 6 with 7 in Table III, in order to make the status

TABLE II

CROSS CLASSIFICATION OF DANISH MALE SAMPLE ACCORDING TO EACH SUBJECT'S STATUS
CATEGORY AND HIS FATHER'S STATUS CATEGORY, USING FIVE STATUS CATEGORIES

| | | Subject's Status | | | | |
		1	2	3	4	5
Father's Status	1	18	17	16	4	2
	2	24	105	109	59	21
	3	23	84	289	217	95
	4	8	49	175	348	198
	5	6	8	69	201	246

TABLE III

CROSS CLASSIFICATION OF BRITISH MALE SAMPLE ACCORDING TO EACH SUBJECT'S STATUS
CATEGORY AND HIS FATHER'S STATUS CATEGORY, USING SEVEN STATUS CATEGORIES

| | | Subject's Status | | | | | | |
		1	2	3	4	5	6	7
Father's Status	1	50	19	26	8	18	6	2
	2	16	40	34	18	31	8	3
	3	12	35	65	66	123	23	21
	4	11	20	58	110	223	64	32
	5	14	36	114	185	714	258	189
	6	0	6	19	40	179	143	71
	7	0	3	14	32	141	91	106

categories more comparable to the corresponding categories in the Danish
5×5 table. For expository purposes, when illustrating the application of the
models and methods presented here, we shall focus our attention on the
analysis of Table I; but for the sake of completeness, we shall present corresponding results for Tables II and III as well, and shall also comment briefly
upon these results (see Sections 6 and 7); which will further enrich our understanding of the data.

The main part of this paper will be concerned with the development of models
and methods for the analysis of a given $R \times C$ table (or a given set of R or C
multinomial populations). We shall also comment briefly in the final section
(Section 8) on the extension and application of the models and methods presented to the analysis and comparison of two (or more) $R \times C$ cross classification tables, and to the analysis of multidimensional cross classification tables.

2. Some examples of multiplicative models

For expository purposes, we shall begin by considering first the usual model
of "independence" between the row classification and the column classification
in an $R \times C$ cross classification table (the I model), then the model of "quasi-
independence" in the $R \times C$ table (the Q model), and then various modifications
or generalizations of these models.

2.1. *The model of independence (the I model).*   We shall now define the usual model of "independence" between the row classification and the column classification in an $R \times C$ population cross classification table. This model can be defined in various ways, and for our present development of the subject we shall proceed as follows. Let $\pi_{i,j}$ denote the probability that an individual in the $R \times C$ population table will fall in cell (i,j) of the table (that is, in the ith row and jth column), for $i = 1, 2, \cdots, R$, and $j = 1, 2, \cdots, C$. Then the row and column classifications are defined as "independent" if the probability $\pi_{i,j}$ can be written as

(2.1.1) $\pi_{i,j} = \alpha_i \beta_j$ for $i = 1, 2, \cdots, R$; $j = 1, 2, \cdots, C$,

for a set of positive constants α_i and β_j, for $i = 1, 2, \cdots, R$, and $j = 1, 2, \cdots, C$. When (2.1.1) is satisfied, α_i can be interpreted as the probability that an individual will fall in the ith row of the population table (when the α_i have been scaled so that $\Sigma_i \alpha_i = 1$), and a similar interpretation can be given to the β_j. If some of the rows or columns are empty, we consider the table consisting of the nonempty rows and columns.

For a sample of n individuals, let $f_{i,j}$ denote the number of individuals that fall in cell (i,j) of the table, and let $\hat{f}_{i,j}$ denote the maximum likelihood estimate of the expected number that would fall in cell (i,j) under a given model. Under the usual model of independence between the row classification and the column classification of the table, the $\hat{f}_{i,j}$ can be written as

(2.1.2) $$\hat{f}_{i,j} = \frac{f_i^\alpha f_j^\beta}{n},$$

where f_i^α and f_j^β denotes the ith row marginal and jth column marginal, respectively, in the table of the $f_{i,j}$. From (2.1.2) we see that the $\hat{f}_{i,j}$ can be written in the form

(2.1.3) $$\hat{f}_{i,j} = a_i b_j,$$

where the a_i and b_j are such that

(2.1.4) $$\sum_j \hat{f}_{i,j} = f_i^\alpha, \qquad \sum_i \hat{f}_{i,j} = f_j^\beta.$$

Conditions (2.1.4) can be rewritten as

(2.1.5) $$\hat{f}_i^\alpha = f_i^\alpha, \qquad \hat{f}_j^\beta = f_j^\beta,$$

where the $\hat{f}_i^\alpha$ and $\hat{f}_j^\beta$ denote the ith row marginal and jth column marginal, respectively, in the table of the $\hat{f}_{i,j}$. Thus, the row and column marginals of the $\hat{f}$ fit the corresponding observed quantities.

Although the number of the a_i and the b_j in (2.1.3) is $R + C$, we can ignore one of these quantities (say, a_1) since $\hat{f}_{i,j}$ is unaffected by scaling the a_i and the b_j so that $a_1 = 1$; that is, by replacing a_i and b_j by $\tilde{a}_i = a_i/a_1$ and $\tilde{b}_j = a_1 b_j$, respectively. Similarly, although the number of restrictions described by (2.1.5) is $R + C$, we can ignore one of these restrictions (say, the first restriction), since if $f_j^\beta = f_j^\beta$ for $j = 1, 2, \cdots, C$, then $\Sigma_{i,j} \hat{f}_{i,j} = n$; and thus, if also $\hat{f}_i^\alpha = f_i^\alpha$ for $i = 2, 3, \cdots, R$, then $\hat{f}_1^\alpha = f_1^\alpha$. Thus, to calculate the degrees of freedom for testing the model of independence, we subtract $R + C - 1$ from $R \times C$, obtaining thereby the usual quantity, namely, $(R - 1)(C - 1)$.

2.2. *The model of quasi-independence* (*the Q model*). The model (2.1.1) in the preceding section applies to all $R \times C$ cells (i, j) for $i = 1, 2, \cdots, R$, $j = 1, 2, \cdots, C$. Now we shall consider a subset S of these cells; for example, the subset consisting of the cells that are not on the main diagonal of the table (that is, the cells (i, j) with $i \neq j$). For a given subset S, the row and column classification is defined as "quasi-independent" (with respect to S) if the probability $\pi_{i,j}$ can be written as

$$(2.2.1) \qquad\qquad \pi_{i,j} = \alpha_i \beta_j \qquad \text{for cells } (i, j) \text{ in } S,$$

for a set of positive constants α_i and β_j.

Since we are not concerned here with the cells that are not in S, we can assign zero probability to those cells. Thus, (2.2.1) can be rewritten as

$$(2.2.2) \qquad \pi_{i,j} = \delta_{i,j}^S \alpha_i \beta_j \qquad \text{for} \quad i = 1, 2, \cdots, R; \qquad j = 1, 2, \cdots, C,$$

where

$$(2.2.3) \qquad\qquad \delta_{i,j}^S = \begin{cases} 1 & \text{for cells } (i, j) \text{ in } S, \\ 0 & \text{otherwise.} \end{cases}$$

Letting $f_{i,j}$ denote the observed number of individuals that fall in cell (i, j), the maximum likelihood estimate $\hat{f}_{i,j}$ of the corresponding expected number (under model (2.2.1)) can be written as

$$(2.2.4) \qquad\qquad \hat{f}_{i,j} = \delta_{i,j}^S a_i b_j,$$

where the a_i and b_j are such that

$$(2.2.5) \qquad\qquad \hat{f}_i^\alpha = f_i^\alpha, \qquad \hat{f}_j^\beta = f_j^\beta,$$

and where now f_i^α and f_j^β are defined as

$$(2.2.6) \qquad\qquad f_i^\alpha = \sum_j \delta_{i,j}^S f_{i,j}, \qquad f_j^\beta = \sum_i \delta_{i,j}^S f_{i,j},$$

and the $\hat{f}_i^\alpha$ and $\hat{f}_j^\beta$ are defined similarly (with the $f_{i,j}$ in (2.2.6) replaced by the corresponding $\hat{f}_{i,j}$). Methods for calculating the $\hat{f}_{i,j}$ were discussed in, for example, Goodman [10], [13], and we shall return to them later herein.

To facilitate our understanding of matters that will be discussed later, we now introduce some new terminology. For each cell (i, j), let $\Lambda_{i,j}$ denote the set of parameters that appear in the formula for $\pi_{i,j}$ under a given model (see, for example, (2.2.1)). Thus, for the Q model, $\Lambda_{i,j}$ contains α_i and β. if cell (i, j) is in S, and $\Lambda_{i,j}$ is empty if (i, j) is not in S. With this terminology, we can rewrite (2.2.6) as

$$(2.2.7) \qquad\qquad f_i^\alpha = \sum_{g,h} \delta_{g,h}^{\alpha_i} f_{g,h}, \qquad f_j^\beta = \sum_{g,h} \delta_{g,h}^{\beta_j} f_{g,h},$$

where

$$\delta_{g,h}^{\alpha_i} = \begin{cases} 1 & \text{if } \alpha_i \in \Lambda_{g,h}, \\ 0 & \text{otherwise}, \end{cases}$$

(2.2.8)

$$\delta_{g,h}^{\beta_j} = \begin{cases} 1 & \text{if } \beta_j \in \Lambda_{g,h}, \\ 0 & \text{otherwise}. \end{cases}$$

Note that (2.2.7) states that f_i^α is the sum of the $f_{g,h}$ for cells (g, h) for which $\alpha_i \in \Lambda_{g,h}$; and that f_j^β is the corresponding sum for cells (g, h) for which $\beta_j \in \Lambda_{g,h}$. A similar statement applies to the $\hat{f}_i^\alpha$ and $\hat{f}_j^\beta$ (with the $f_{g,h}$ in (2.2.7) replaced by the corresponding $\hat{f}_{g,h}$).

To calculate the degrees of freedom for testing the model in this section, we consider first the case where the set S includes at least one cell from each row and column of the table, and where S is "inseparable" in the sense that it cannot be partitioned into two mutually exclusive (and exhaustive) subsets S_1 and S_2 that have no rows and no columns in common (see, for example, Goodman [13], Caussinus [4]). Note that S would be separable if the subsets S_1 and S_2 had no parameters in common; in other words, if the set of parameters that are contained in S_1 (that is, in $\Lambda_{i,j}$ for one or more of the cells (i, j) in S_1) and the set of parameters that are contained in S_2 (that is, in $\Lambda_{i,j}$ for one or more of the cells (i, j) in S_2) were mutually exclusive. For the case where S is inseparable, the remarks in the final paragraph of Section 2.1 can be directly applied; and in the present case, the degrees of freedom are obtained by subtracting $R + C - 1$ from $R \times C - V$, where V is the number of cells in the $R \times C$ table that are not included in S. Thus, as in the earlier literature on "quasi-independence," we find that there are $(R - 1)(C - 1) - V$ degrees of freedom.

In cases where entire rows and/or entire columns are not included in S, the above formula for the degrees of freedom can still be applied, except that "R" and "C" in that formula should be taken as the number of rows and columns, respectively, that contain at least one cell from S, and similarly the quantity V should be calculated for this (modified) "R" $\times$ "C" table. For cases in which S is separable, the results presented above can be applied separately to each subset that is itself not separable. A separable set S can always be partitioned into such subsets.

2.3. *The QO model, the QP model, the QN model, and the QPN model.* The results in the preceding section pertain to the case where S is any given subset of the cells in the $R \times C$ table. Consider now the case where the cross classification table is square (that is, $R = C$), where there is a one to one correspondence between the ith class of the row classification and the ith class of the column classification for $i = 1, 2, \cdots, R$, and where S is the set of cells that are not on the main diagonal (that is, the cells (i, j) with $i \neq j$). Since S consists of the off diagonal cells, we shall call the model of quasi-independence (with respect to this set S) the QO model. The remarks in the preceding section can be applied directly to the QO model. Note, for example, that the number of degrees of freedom for testing this model will be $(R - 1)(R - 1) - R = R^2 - 3R + 1$.

Consider now the case where the classes of the row (and column) classification in the $R \times R$ table can also be ordered from 1 to R, and where S is the set of cells (i, j) with $i > j$. For each cell in S, the difference $i - j$ is positive, and so we shall call this particular model of quasi-independence the QP model. From the remarks in the preceding section, we see that the number of degrees of freedom for testing the QP model will be $(R - 2)(R - 2) - [(R - 1)(R - 2)/2] = (R - 2)(R - 3)/2$. Note that the degrees of freedom are zero for $R = 3$; we shall be concerned here mainly with models for cases where $R > 3$.

Consider now the case where S is the set of cells (i, j) with $i < j$. For each cell in S, the difference $i - j$ is negative, and so we shall call this particular model of quasi-independence the QN model. As in the preceding paragraph, the number of degrees of freedom for testing the QN model will be $(R - 2)(R - 3)/2$.

Consider now the model in which the probability $\pi_{i, j}$ can be written as

$$(2.3.1) \qquad \pi_{i, j} = \begin{cases} \alpha_i \beta_j & \text{for} \quad i > j, \\ \alpha_i' \beta_j' & \text{for} \quad i < j. \end{cases}$$

This model states that both the QP model and the QN model are true, and so we shall call it the QPN model. Note that this model is not the same as the QO model, although both models pertain to the cells (i, j) with $i \ne j$. The QO model is a special case of the QPN model in which

$$(2.3.2) \qquad \begin{aligned} \alpha_i' &= \Delta \alpha_i & \text{for} \quad i = 2, 3, \cdots, R - 1, \\ \beta_j' &= \Delta^* \beta_j & \text{for} \quad j = 2, 3, \cdots, R - 1, \end{aligned}$$

and in which

$$(2.3.3) \qquad \Delta^* = \frac{1}{\Delta}.$$

The QPN model is not, strictly speaking, an example of a model of quasi-independence as this term was defined in the preceding section. Nevertheless, the methods developed earlier for the quasi-independence model (see, for example, Goodman [13]) can be applied to the QPN model, by analyzing separately the subsets S_1 and S_2, where S_1 is the set of cells (i, j) with $i > j$, and S_2 is the set of cells (i, j) with $i < j$; and applying the corresponding models (the QP and QN models) to those sets. Note that, although the sets S_1 and S_2 do have rows and columns in common, these sets are separable for the QPN model, since the set of parameters in S_1 (the α_i and β_j) and the set of parameters in S_2 (the α_i' and β_j') are mutually exclusive.

The number of degrees of freedom for testing the QPN model is the sum of the degrees of freedom for testing the QP model in S_1 and the QN model in S_2. Thus, there are $(R - 2)(R - 3)$ degrees of freedom for testing the QPN model. Note that the difference between the degrees of freedom for the QO model and the QPN model is $2R - 5$, which corresponds to the sum of the degrees of freedom associated with testing condition (2.3.2) and condition (2.3.3) (namely, $2(R - 3)$ degrees of freedom for (2.3.2) and one degree of freedom for (2.3.3)).

We now extend the concept of "quasi-independence" to include models of the kind described by (2.3.1). Let $S_1, S_2, \cdots, S_K$ denote mutually exclusive subsets of the cells (i, j) in an $R \times C$ cross classification table. The model of "quasi-independence" (with respect to the subsets S_k, for $k = 1, 2, \cdots, K$) is defined by the condition that the probability $\pi_{i,j}$ can be written as

(2.3.4) $\pi_{i,j} = \alpha_i^{(k)} \beta_j^{(k)}$ for cells (i, j) in S_k,

for $k = 1, 2, \cdots, K$. The sets $S_1, S_2, \cdots, S_K$ are separable for the model defined by (2.3.4), since the set of parameters in S_k (namely, $\alpha_i^{(k)}$ and $\beta_j^{(k)}$) and the set of parameters in $S_{k'}$ (namely, $\alpha_i^{(k')}$ and $\beta_j^{(k')}$) are mutually exclusive for $k \neq k'$. To analyze this more general model of "quasi-independence," we can apply the methods developed earlier for the more usual quasi-independence model, by analyzing separately the sets $S_1, S_2, \cdots, S_K$, applying the corresponding model of quasi-independence to each set.

2.4. *The triangles parameter model (the T model).* We return again to the square contingency table $(R = C)$ in which there is a one to one correspondence between the classes of the row and column classification, and in which the classes of the row (and column) classification are ordered from 1 to R. Consider now the special case of the QPN model in which condition (2.3.2) is satisfied (but condition (2.3.3) may or may not be satisfied). This special case of the QPN model is equivalent to the model in which the probability $\pi_{i,j}$ can be written as

(2.4.1) $\pi_{i,j} = \alpha_i \beta_j \tau_k$ for cells (i, j) in S_k,

for $k = 1, 2$, where S_1 is the set of cells (i, j) with $i > j$, and S_2 is the set of cells (i, j) with $i < j$. For cell (i, j) in S_k, under model (2.4.1) the set $\Lambda_{i,j}$ contains α_i, β_j, and τ_k; and $\Lambda_{i,j}$ is empty if (i, j) is not in S_1 or S_2. The model (2.4.1) differs from the QO model in that it introduces an additional set of parameters τ_k that pertains differentially to the triangular subsets S_k, for $k = 1$ and 2, and so we call this model the triangles parameter model (the T model).

Note that the sets S_1 and S_2 are not separable for the T model defined by (2.4.1) since the set of parameters in S_1 (namely, α_i, β_j, and τ_1) and the set of parameters in S_2 (namely, α_i, β_j, and τ_2) are not mutually exclusive—the parameters α_i for $i = 2, 3, \cdots, R - 1$ and β_j for $j = 2, 3, \cdots, R - 1$ are included in both sets. Although the T model is not an example of a quasi-independence model as defined in Section 2.2 (nor of the more general model of "quasi-independence" defined by (2.3.4)), the remarks in Section 2.2 can be directly extended to the T model. By direct extension of (2.2.4) to (2.2.8), we find that the estimate $\hat{f}_{i,j}$ under the T model can be written as

(2.4.2) $\hat{f}_{i,j} = a_i b_j t_k$ for cells (i, j) in S_k,

for $k = 1$ and 2, where the a_i, b_j, and t_k are such that

(2.4.3) $\hat{f}_i^\alpha = f_i^\alpha, \qquad \hat{f}_j^\beta = f_j^\beta, \qquad \hat{f}_k^\tau = f_k^\tau,$

where the f_i^α and f_j^β are defined by (2.2.7), and f_k^τ is defined by

(2.4.4) $$f_k^\tau = \sum_{g,h} \delta_{g,h}^{\tau_k} f_{g,h},$$

where

(2.4.5) $$\delta_{g,h}^{\tau_k} = \begin{cases} 1 & \text{if} \quad \tau_k \in \Lambda_{g,h}, \\ 0 & \text{otherwise}; \end{cases}$$

and with the $\hat{f}_i^\alpha$, $\hat{f}_j^\beta$, $\hat{f}_k^\tau$ defined similarly (with the $f_{g,h}$ in (2.4.4) replaced by the corresponding $\hat{f}_{g,h}$).

Although there are two t_k in (2.4.2) (namely, t_1 and t_2), we can ignore one of them (say, t_1) since $\hat{f}_{i,j}$ is unaffected by scaling the t_k (and the a_i) so that $t_1 = 1$; that is, by replacing t_k and a_i by $\tilde{t}_k = t_k/t_1$ and $\tilde{a}_i = a_i t_1$, respectively. Similarly, although there are two restrictions described by the third condition of (2.4.3) for $k = 1$ and 2, we can ignore one of these restrictions (say, the first restriction) since if $\hat{f}_i^\alpha = f_i^\alpha$ for $i = 1, 2, \cdots, R$, then $\Sigma \hat{f}_{i,j} = n$ (where the $\hat{f}$ are summed over the off diagonal cells and n is similarly calculated for the f); and thus, if $\hat{f}_2^\tau = f_2^\tau$, then $\hat{f}_1^\tau = f_1^\tau$. Since there is one more parameter in the T model than in the QO model, the number of degrees of freedom for testing the T model will be $R^2 - 3R = R(R - 3)$, for $R \geq 3$.

2.5. *The diagonals parameter model* (*the D model*) *and related models.* Consider now the model in which the probability $\pi_{i,j}$ can be written as

(2.5.1) $$\pi_{i,j} = \alpha_i \beta_j \delta_k \qquad \text{for cells } (i, j) \text{ in } S_k',$$

where S_k' is the set of cells (i, j) with $i - j = k$, for $k = \pm 1, \pm 2, \cdots, \pm(R - 1)$. The model (2.5.1) differs from the QO model in that it introduces an additional set of parameters (the δ_k) that pertains differentially to the minor diagonals S_k for $k = \pm 1, \pm 2, \cdots, \pm(R - 1)$, and so we call this model the diagonals parameter model (the D model).

The T model (see (2.4.1)) is a special case of the D model in which the following condition is satisfied:

(2.5.2) $$\delta_k = \begin{cases} \delta^* & \text{for} \quad k = 1, 2, \cdots, R - 1, \\ \delta^{**} & \text{for} \quad k = -1, -2, \cdots, -(R - 1). \end{cases}$$

The remarks about the analysis of the T model in the preceding section can be extended directly to the D model. For example, under the D model, the $\hat{f}_{i,j}$ can be written as

(2.5.3) $$\hat{f}_{i,j} = a_i b_j d_k \qquad \text{for cells } (i, j) \text{ in } S_k',$$

for $k = \pm 1, \pm 2, \cdots, \pm(R - 1)$, where the a_i, b_j and d_k are such that

(2.5.4) $$\hat{f}_i^\alpha = f_i^\alpha, \qquad \hat{f}_j^\beta = f_j^\beta, \qquad \hat{f}_k^\delta = f_k^\delta,$$

where the f_i^α and f_j^β are defined by (2.2.7) and f_k^δ is defined similarly to (2.4.4) and (2.4.5), with δ replacing τ in those formulae. (The corresponding $\hat{f}$ are defined similarly.)

Although there are $2(R - 1)$ statistics d_k in (2.5.3) $\big($namely, d_k for $k = \pm 1$, $\pm 2, \cdots, \pm(R - 1)\big)$, we can ignore two of them (say, d_k for $k = \pm 1$) since $\hat{f}_{i,j}$ is unaffected by transforming the d_k (and the a_i and the b_j) so that $d_k = 1$ for $k = \pm 1$; that is, by replacing d_k by

$$(2.5.5) \qquad \tilde{d}_k = \frac{d_k d_*^{k-1}}{d_1} \qquad \text{for} \quad k = \pm 1, \pm 2, \cdots, \pm(R - 1),$$

with

$$(2.5.6) \qquad\qquad d_* = \left(\frac{d_{-1}}{d_1}\right)^{1/2},$$

and replacing a_i and b_j by

$$(2.5.7) \qquad\qquad \tilde{a}_i = \frac{a_i d_1}{d_*^{i-1}}, \qquad \tilde{b}_j = b_j d_*^j,$$

respectively. Thus since there are $2(R - 2)$ more parameters in the D model than in the QO model, the number of degrees of freedom for testing the D model will be $R^2 - 5R + 5$, for $R \geq 4$. There will be zero degrees of freedom for testing the D model in the case where $R = 3$.

Consider now the special case of the D model in which the following condition is satisfied:

$$(2.5.8) \qquad \delta_k = \delta_{k*} \qquad \text{for} \quad k^* = -k, \text{with } k = 1, 2, \cdots, R - 1.$$

In this case, the parameter δ_k pertains to the pair of minor diagonals S_k' and S_{k*}' with $k^* = -k$; that is, to the cells (i, j) for which the absolute value $|i - j|$ is equal to k. We shall call this case the DA model. The earlier remarks about the analysis of the D model can be directly extended to the DA model, where now δ_k pertains to the paired minor diagonals, for $k = 1, 2, \cdots, R - 1$. The DA model has $R - 2$ more parameters than the QO model for $R \geq 4$, and so the number of degrees of freedom for testing the DA model will be $R^2 - 4R + 3 = (R - 1)(R - 3)$, for $R \geq 4$. For $R = 3$, the DA model is equivalent to the QO model, so that in this special case there will be one degree of freedom for testing the model. Note that the difference between the degrees of freedom for the DA model and the D model is $R - 2$ for $R \geq 4$, which corresponds to the degrees of freedom associated with testing condition (2.5.8), for $k = 2, 3, \cdots$, $R - 1$ (with $\delta_k = 1$, for $k = \pm 1$).

Consider now the special case of the D model in which the following condition is satisfied:

$$(2.5.9) \qquad\qquad \delta_k = 1, \qquad \text{for} \quad k = -1, -2, \cdots, -(R - 1).$$

In this case, the parameter δ_k pertains only to the minor diagonals S_k' for which k is positive; that is, to the cells (i, j) for which $i - j = k$ is positive. We shall call this case the DP model. The condition (2.5.9) is actually equivalent to the following condition, which might appear (at first sight) to be more general;

namely,

(2.5.10) $\delta_k = \delta^k$ for $k = -1, -2, \cdots, -(R - 1)$,

for some positive constant δ. Conditions (2.5.9) and (2.5.10) are equivalent because the $\pi_{i,j}$ of (2.5.1) is unaffected by replacing δ_k, α_i, and β_j by

(2.5.11) $\tilde{\delta}_k = \dfrac{\delta_k}{\delta^k},$ $\tilde{\alpha}_i = \alpha_i \delta^{i-1},$ $\tilde{\beta}_j = \dfrac{\beta_j}{\delta^{j-1}},$

respectively. When the parameters are transformed so that $\delta_k = 1$ for $k = \pm 1$, the condition (2.5.10) is replaced by the following condition:

(2.5.12) $\delta_k = (\delta')^{k+1}$ for $k = -1, -2, \cdots, -(R - 1)$,

for a positive constant δ'.

The earlier remarks about the analysis of the D model can also be directly extended to the DP model, where now δ_k pertains to the minor diagonals S'_k for which k is positive for $k = 1, 2, \cdots, R - 1$. The DP model has $R - 1$ more parameters than the QO model (namely, the δ_k for $k = 2, 3, \cdots, R - 1$; and δ' from (2.5.12)), and so the number of degrees of freedom for testing the DP model will be $R^2 - 4R + 2$, for $R \geq 4$. There will be zero degrees of freedom for testing the DP model in the case where $R = 3$.

Consider now the special case of the D model in which the following condition is satisfied:

(2.5.13) $\delta_k = 1$ for $k = 1, 2, \cdots, R - 1$.

We shall call this case the DN model. By modifying in an obvious manner the remarks (pertaining to the DP model) in the preceding two paragraphs, they can be applied to the DN model.

2.6. *The crossings parameter model (the C model).*   We return again to the QPN model, and consider the special case where the following condition is satisfied:

(2.6.1) $\alpha_i \beta_i = \alpha'_i \beta'_i$ for $i = 2, 3, \cdots, R - 1$.

This special case of the QPN model is equivalent to the model in which the probability $\pi_{i,j}$ can be written as

(2.6.2) $\pi_{i,j} = \alpha_i \beta_j \gamma'_{i,j}$ for $i \neq j$,

where

(2.6.3) $\gamma'_{i,j} = \begin{cases} \displaystyle\prod_{u=j}^{i-1} \gamma_u & \text{for } i > j, \\ \displaystyle\prod_{u=i}^{j-1} \gamma_u & \text{for } i < j. \end{cases}$

The model (2.6.2)–(2.6.3) differs from the QO model in that it introduces an additional set of parameters, namely, the γ_u, for $u = 1, 2, \cdots, R - 1$, that pertains differentially (and multiplicatively) to each crossing between adjacent classes (from class u to $u + 1$ or from class $u + 1$ to u). In this model, the parameter γ_u pertaining to the crossing from class u to $u + 1$ is equal to the parameter pertaining to the crossing from $u + 1$ to u. We shall call this model the crossings parameter model (the C model). Note that the symbol C will be used to refer to this model and also, as earlier, to the number of columns in a rectangular contingency table; the meaning of the symbol will be clear in either case.

The remarks in the preceding section about the analysis of the models considered there can be directly extended to the C model. Under the C model, the $\hat{f}_{i,j}$ can be written as

$$(2.6.4) \qquad \hat{f}_{i,j} = a_i b_j c'_{i,j},$$

where

$$(2.6.5) \qquad c'_{i,j} = \begin{cases} \prod_{u=j}^{i-1} c_u & \text{for} \quad i > j, \\ \prod_{u=i}^{j-1} c_u & \text{for} \quad i < j, \end{cases}$$

and where the a_i, b_j, and c_u are such that

$$(2.6.6) \qquad \hat{f}_i^\alpha = f_i^\alpha, \qquad \hat{f}_j^\beta = f_j^\beta, \qquad \hat{f}_u^\gamma = f_u^\gamma,$$

where f_i^α and f_j^β are defined by (2.2.7), and f_u^γ is defined similarly to (2.4.4) and (2.4.5) with τ replaced by γ in those formulae. The corresponding $\hat{f}$ are defined similarly.

Although there are $(R - 1)$ statistics c_u in (2.6.4) and (2.6.5) (namely, c_u, for $u = 1, 2, \cdots, R - 1$), we can ignore two of them (c_1 and c_{R-1}) since $\hat{f}_{i,j}$ is unaffected by setting $c_1 = c_{R-1} = 1$; that is, by replacing these two c_u by $\tilde{c}_1 = \tilde{c}_{R-1} = 1$ and by replacing a_1, a_R, b_1, b_R by $\tilde{a}_1 = a_1 c_1$, $\tilde{a}_R = a_R c_{R-1}$, $\tilde{b}_1 = b_1 c_1$, $\tilde{b}_R = b_R c_{R-1}$. Since there are $R - 3$ more parameters in the C model than in the QO model, the number of degrees of freedom for testing the C model is $R^2 - 4R + 4 = (R - 2)^2$. Note that the difference between the degrees of freedom for the C model and the QPN model is $R - 2$, which corresponds to the degrees of freedom associated with testing condition (2.6.1).

From (2.6.2) and (2.6.3) we see that the factor $\gamma'_{i,j}$ associated with a change from the ith class (with respect to the row classification) to the jth class (with respect to the column classification) was a product of the γ_u parameters pertaining to successive one step changes (crossings) from class i to j. Thus, the crossings parameter model (the C model) could also have been called the "one step Markov" model. (This terminology is appropriate, in a certain sense, since the parameter γ_u pertaining to an individual's one step change from class u to $u + 1$ depends only upon the class u and not upon the earlier history of changes that may have led to the individual's presence in class u. On the other hand, the terminology is not quite appropriate since the direction of change (from

class u to $u + 1$ or from class u to $u - 1$) does depend upon this earlier history.)
Although the models in Haberman [20] are described there in different terms
from the models presented here, it can be shown that the C model (see (2.6.4)
and (2.6.5)) is equivalent, in most respect, to the "variable distance" model
applied by Haberman. With the present formulation of the C model, some of
the parameters and their estimates will be defined and calculated differently
from the corresponding definitions and calculations that were applied to the
"variable distance" model (see, for example, the related comments at the end of
Section 7).

Let us suppose now that we wished to generalize the C model by replacing
(2.6.3) by

$$(2.6.7) \qquad \gamma'_{i,j} = \begin{cases} \displaystyle\prod_{u=j}^{i-1} \gamma_u^* & \text{for } i > j, \\ \displaystyle\prod_{u=i}^{j-1} \gamma_u^{**} & \text{for } i < j. \end{cases}$$

This model distinguishes (at first sight) between the parameter γ_u^* pertaining to the
crossing from the uth row class to the $(u + 1)$th column class and the parameter
γ_u^{**} pertaining to the crossing from the $(u + 1)$th row class to the uth column
class. Actually, this model is equivalent to the C model (with $\gamma_u^* = \gamma_u^{**}$) since the
$\pi_{i,j}$ defined by (2.6.2) and (2.6.7) are unaffected by replacing the γ_u^* and γ_u^{**} by
$\tilde{\gamma}_u = (\gamma_u^* \gamma_u^{**})^{1/2}$, and by replacing α_i and β_j by $\tilde{\alpha}_i = \alpha_i \gamma'_{i-1}$ and $\tilde{\beta}_j = \beta_j / \gamma'_{j-1}$, with

$$(2.6.8) \qquad \gamma'_i = \begin{cases} 1 & \text{for } i = 1, \\ (\gamma_i^*/\gamma_i^{**})^{1/2} & \text{for } i = 2, 3, \cdots, R - 1. \end{cases}$$

Note, in particular, that the special case of the model defined by (2.6.2) and
(2.6.7), in which $\gamma_u^{**} = 1$ for $u = 1, 2, \cdots, R - 1$, is equivalent to the C model
as defined by (2.6.2) and (2.6.3). A similar remark applies for the special case of
the model defined by (2.6.2) and (2.6.7) in which $\gamma_u^* = 1$ for $u = 1, 2, \cdots, R - 1$.

2.7. *The diagonals crossings parameter model (the DC model) and other
combined models.* Consider now the model in which the probability $\pi_{i,j}$ can
be written as

$$(2.7.1) \qquad \pi_{i,j} = \alpha_i \beta_j \gamma'_{i,j} \delta_k \qquad \text{for cells } (i,j) \text{ in } S'_k,$$

where S'_k is defined as in (2.5.1), and $\gamma'_{i,j}$ is defined as in (2.6.3). The remarks in
Sections 2.5 and 2.6 can be directly extended to apply to this model (the DC
model).

The DC model differs from the D model in that it includes an additional set of
parameters (namely, the γ_u, for $u = 1, 2, \cdots, R - 1$). We noted earlier that γ_1
and γ_{R-1} could be ignored in the C model, and now for the DC model we also
find this to be the case and that, in addition, this model is unaffected by a change
in scale for the γ_u (with corresponding changes made in the other parameters).
Thus, there are $R - 4$ more parameters in the DC model than in the D model,
and so the number of degrees of freedom for testing the DC model will be
$R^2 - 6R + 9 = (R - 3)^2$.

The C model can be combined in a similar way with the other models in Section 2.5, obtaining thereby the DAC model, the DPC model, and the DNC model. In these cases too the number of degrees of freedom for the models are obtained by subtracting $R - 4$ from the number for the corresponding model in Section 2.5. Thus, for the DAC model, we obtain $R^2 - 5R + 7$ degrees of freedom; and for the DPC and DNC models, we obtain $R^2 - 5R + 6 = (R - 2)(R - 3)$ degrees of freedom. For $R = 3$, the DAC model is equivalent to the DA model and the QO model. In addition, the T model of Section 2.3 can be combined with the DA model, the C model, and the DAC model. The number of degrees of freedom for these combined models are obtained by subtracting one from the number for the corresponding (uncombined) model. Thus, the degrees of freedom for the DAT model, the CT model, and the DACT model are $R^2 - 4R + 2$, $R^2 - 4R + 3 = (R - 1)(R - 3)$, and $R^2 - 5R + 6 = (R - 2)(R - 3)$, respectively. The latter two formulas apply for $R \geq 3$, while the first formula applies for $R \geq 4$. For $R = 3$, the DAT model actually has zero degrees of freedom, as do the other models (discussed in the present section and in Section 2.4) that include the triangles parameter τ_k.

All of the models considered in the present section and in Sections 2.4 to 2.6 are special cases of the DC model. For models that do not include the crossings parameters, we have

(2.7.2) $\gamma_u = 1$ for $u = 2, 3, \cdots, R - 2$,

in (2.7.1) (see (2.6.3)). For models that do not include the diagonals parameters, we have

(2.7.3) $\delta_k = 1$ for $k = \pm 1, \pm 2, \cdots, \pm (R - 1)$,

in (2.7.1). For models that include the triangles parameter (but not the parameter pertaining to the paired minor diagonals), the δ_k in (2.7.1) will satisfy condition (2.5.2). Similarly, the δ_k in (2.7.1) will satisfy condition (2.5.8) for models that include parameters pertaining to the paired minor diagonals (but not the triangles parameter), and they will satisfy the following condition for models that include both the parameters pertaining to the paired minor diagonals and the triangles parameters:

(2.7.4) $\delta_k = \tau' \delta_{k*}$ for $k* = -k$, with $k = 1, 2, \cdots, R - 1$.

Furthermore, the δ_k in (2.7.1) will satisfy condition (2.5.9) for models that do not include parameters pertaining to the "negative" diagonals, and they will satisfy (2.5.13) for models that do not include parameters pertaining to the "positive" diagonals.

2.8. *The DC Model for the full table (the DCF model) and related models.* The models in Sections 2.3 to 2.7 were concerned with the analysis of the off diagonal cells, and were extensions of the QO model. Now we shall present models for the analysis of the full table—models that are extensions of the *I* model.

Consider the model in which the probability $\pi_{i,j}$ is given by (2.7.1), except that now we also apply (2.7.1) to the set S'_0 (that is, the cells (i,j) with $i - j = 0$), as well as to the sets S'_k as defined in (2.5.1) for $k = \pm 1, \pm 2, \cdots, \pm(R - 1)$; and we set $\gamma'_{i,j} = 1$ for $i = j$. This model (the DCF model) differs from the DC model in that the R cells on the main diagonal are now included in the analysis, an additional diagonals parameter δ_0 is included, and two additional crossings parameters γ_1 and γ_{R-1} are also included. Although the probability $\pi_{i,j}$ for the DC model is unaffected by ignoring the parameters γ_1 and γ_{R-1} (that is, by setting $\gamma_1 = \gamma_{R-1} = 1$ and making corresponding changes in $\alpha_1, \alpha_R, \beta_1, \beta_R$), this is not so for the DCF model; the $\pi_{i,j}$ for the DCF model would be affected by ignoring γ_1 and γ_{R-1}. Therefore, the number of degrees of freedom for the DCF model can be obtained by adding $R - 3$ to the number for the DC model, thus obtaining $R^2 - 5R + 6 = (R - 2)(R - 3)$.

The relationship between the DC model and the DCF model, which we noted in the preceding paragraph, can be extended to other models. To each of the models introduced in Sections 2.4 to 2.7 for the analysis of the off diagonal cells, there is a corresponding model defined for the full table. The number of degrees of freedom for the model for the full table can be obtained by adding $R - 3$ to the number for the corresponding model (for the analysis of the off diagonal cells) if that model includes both diagonals and crossings parameters; by adding $R - 1$ to the number for the corresponding model if that model includes diagonals parameters but not crossings parameters, by adding $R - 2$ to the number for the corresponding model if that model includes crossings parameters but not diagonals parameters. (In the special case where $R = 3$, the above calculation is modified slightly if the corresponding model is one of those models for which the particular formula given earlier herein for the degrees of freedom does not apply when $R = 3$.) A similar calculation can be made when the model also includes the triangles parameter. Alternatively, the degrees of freedom for the models for the full table could be calculated directly using the same methods that were applied in Sections 2.4 to 2.7 (but without first calculating the results for the models for the off diagonal cells and then adding the appropriate quantities). The number of degrees of freedom for testing each of the models considered herein is given in Table IV.

3. The general case

We return now to the general $R \times C$ table. Let $\pi_{i,j}$ denote the probability that an observation will fall in cell (i,j), let $f_{i,j}$ denote the observed frequency in cell (i,j) for a sample of n observations, and let $\hat{f}_{i,j}$ denote the maximum likelihood estimate of the expected frequency under a given model. We shall now denote the parameters in the model as $\lambda_1, \lambda_2, \cdots, \lambda_W$ (with $\lambda_w > 0$ for $w = 1, 2, \cdots, W$), and we let Λ denote the full set of parameters; that is, $\Lambda = \{\lambda_1, \lambda_2, \cdots, \lambda_W\}$. For each cell (i,j) in that table, let $\Lambda_{i,j}$ denote a given subset of Λ. Consider now the model in which the probability $\pi_{i,j}$ can be

TABLE IV

THE DEGREES OF FREEDOM FOR TESTING VARIOUS MODELS
APPLIED TO THE RECTANGULAR $R \times C$ TABLE AND TO THE
SQUARE $R \times R$ TABLE (FOR $R \geqq 3$)

*The asterisk indicates that the formula does not apply for $R = 3$.
For this special case, see comments in article.
**For the case of quasi-independence, see further details in the article.

Model	Degrees of Freedom
Independence	$(R - 1)(C - 1)$
Quasi-Independence	$[(R - 1)(C - 1) - V]$**
QO	$R^2 - 3R + 1$
QP (or QN)	$(R - 2)(R - 3)/2$
QPN	$(R - 2)(R - 3)$
T	$R(R - 3)$
D	$(R^2 - 5R + 5)$*
DA	$(R - 1)(R - 3)$*
DP (or DN)	$(R^2 - 4R + 2)$*
C	$(R - 2)^2$
DC	$(R - 3)^2$
DAC	$R^2 - 5R + 7$
DPC (or DNC)	$(R - 2)(R - 3)$
DAT	$(R^2 - 4R + 2)$*
CT	$(R - 1)(R - 3)$
DACT	$(R - 2)(R - 3)$
TF	$R^2 - 2R - 1$
DF	$(R - 2)^2$
DAF	$(R - 1)(R - 2)$
DPF (or DNF)	$R^2 - 3R + 1$
CF	$(R - 1)(R - 2)$
DCF	$(R - 2)(R - 3)$
DACF	$(R - 2)^2$
DPCF (or DNCF)	$(R - 1)(R - 3)$
DATF	$R^2 - 3R + 1$
CTF	$R(R - 3)$
DACTF	$(R - 1)(R - 3)$

written as

$$(3.1) \qquad \pi_{i,j} = \prod_{\Lambda_{i,j}} \lambda_w,$$

where $\Pi_{\Lambda_{i,j}}$ denotes a product over the indices w for which $\lambda_w \in \Lambda_{i,j}$ with the
product defined as zero when $\Lambda_{i,j}$ is empty.

Let f_w^λ and $\hat{f}_w^\lambda$ be defined by

$$(3.2) \qquad f_w^\lambda = \sum_{g,h} \delta_{g,h}^{\lambda,w} f_{g,h}, \qquad \hat{f}_w^\lambda = \sum_{g,h} \delta_{g,h}^{\lambda,w} \hat{f}_{g,h},$$

where

$$(3.3) \qquad \delta_{g,h}^{\lambda,w} = \begin{cases} 1 & \text{if } \lambda_w \in \Lambda_{g,h}, \\ 0 & \text{otherwise.} \end{cases}$$

Then for the model (3.1), it is easy to show that $\hat{f}_{i,j}$ can be written as

$$(3.4) \qquad \hat{f}_{i,j} = \prod_{\Lambda_{i,j}} \ell_w,$$

where the ℓ_w are such that

$$(3.5) \qquad \hat{f}_w^\lambda = f_w^\lambda \qquad \text{for} \quad w = 1, 2, \cdots, W.$$

To calculate the $\hat{f}_{i,j}$ defined by (3.4) we can proceed by the following iterative scaling method. At the initial step we define

$$(3.6) \qquad \hat{f}_{i,j}(0) = \begin{cases} 0 & \text{if} \quad \Lambda_{i,j} \text{ is empty,} \\ 1 & \text{otherwise.} \end{cases}$$

Then we set $v = w$ in the following formula, and we use (3.7) to calculate $\hat{f}_{i,j}(v)$ for $w = 1, 2, \cdots, W$:

$$(3.7) \qquad \hat{f}_{i,j}(v) = \begin{cases} \hat{f}_{i,j}(v-1) f_w^\lambda / [\hat{f}(v-1)]_w^\lambda & \text{if} \quad \lambda_w \in \Lambda_{i,j}, \\ \hat{f}_{i,j}(v-1) & \text{otherwise,} \end{cases}$$

where

$$(3.8) \qquad [\hat{f}(v-1)]_w^\lambda = \sum_{g,h} \delta_{g,h}^{\lambda, w} \hat{f}_{g,h}(v-1).$$

This is the first cycle of iterations. For the second cycle, we set $v = W + w$ in (3.7), and we use (3.7) to calculate $\hat{f}_{i,j}(v)$ considering again $w = 1, 2, \cdots, W$. For the third cycle, we set $v = 2W + w$ in (3.7), and we proceed as in the preceding cycle of iterations. The cycles of iterations are continued until the $\hat{f}_{i,j}(v)$ satisfy condition (3.5).

The above method is a generalization of a corresponding procedure that was used earlier to calculate the maximum likelihood estimate $\hat{f}_{i,j}$ under the quasi-independence model and under other related models (see, for example, Caussinus [4], Bishop and Fienberg [2], Goodman [13], [17]). This method (as described above) does not provide estimates of the parameters λ_w. To calculate the ℓ_w in (3.4) we can proceed by any of the following three methods.

(1) After calculating the $\hat{f}_{i,j}$ by the iterative procedure given above, equation (3.4) can be solved for the ℓ_w. Explicit expressions for the ℓ_w as functions of the $\hat{f}_{i,j}$ can be obtained for the models of Sections 2.2 to 2.8. See the Appendix where such expressions are given.

(2) Instead of calculating the $\hat{f}_{i,j}$ by the iterative method (3.6) to (3.8), the ℓ_w in (3.4) can be calculated by a direct extension of the iterative procedure that was used earlier by Goodman [10], [13] to estimate the parameters in the quasi-independence model. To do this, we first note from (3.4) and (3.5) that

$$(3.9) \qquad \hat{f}_w^\lambda = \ell_w \sum_{g,h} \delta_{g,h}^{\lambda, w} \prod_{\Lambda_{g,h,w}} \ell_u,$$

where $\Lambda_{g,h,w}$ is the set consisting of all those λ in $\Lambda_{g,h}$ except λ_w, and where $\Pi_{\Lambda_{g,h,w}}$

denotes a product over the indices u for which $\lambda_u \in \Lambda_{g,h,w}$. We can rewrite (3.5) as

$$(3.10) \qquad \ell_w = \frac{f_w^\lambda}{\sum\limits_{g,h} \delta_{g,h}^{\lambda,w} \prod\limits_{\Lambda g,h,w} \ell_u}.$$

To start the iterative procedure for calculating ℓ_w, we define

$$(3.11) \qquad \ell_w(0) = 1 \qquad \text{for} \quad w = 1, 2, \cdots, W.$$

For the first cycle of iterations, we use the following formula to calculate $\ell_w(v)$ for $v = 1, 2, \cdots, W$:

$$(3.12) \qquad \ell_w(v) = \begin{cases} f_w^\lambda / \sum\limits_{g,h} \delta_{g,h}^{\lambda,w} \prod\limits_{\Lambda g,h,w} \ell_u(v-1) & \text{if} \quad v = w, \\ \ell_w(v-1) & \text{otherwise.} \end{cases}$$

For the second cycle of iterations, we replace the condition that $w = v$, which appears on the right side of (3.12), by the condition that $w = v - W$, and then apply (3.12) for $v = W + 1, W + 2, \cdots, 2W$. For the third cycle, we replace the condition that $w = v$ by the condition that $w = v - 2W$, and then apply (3.12) for $v = 2W + 1, 2W + 2, \cdots, 3W$, and so on.

(3) Instead of calculating the ℓ_w in (3.4) by the methods described under (1) or (2) above, they can be determined by the following formula, making use of the terms $f_w^\lambda / [\hat{f}(v-1)]_w^\lambda$ calculated in the iterative scaling method described by (3.6) to (3.8):

$$(3.13) \qquad \ell_w'(T) = \prod_{t=0}^{T-1} \left\{ \frac{f_w^\lambda}{[\hat{f}(tW + w - 1)]_w^\lambda} \right\}$$

where $\Pi_{t=0}^T$ denotes the product of the term in braces for $t = 0, 1, \cdots, T$; with $\Pi_{t=0}^0$ denoting the term in braces for $t = 0$. If the iterative scaling method is completed when T cycles of iterations have been carried out, then $\ell_w'(T)$ can be used as the ℓ_w in (3.4).

The following formula describes the relationship between the $\ell_w'(T)$ defined by (3.13) and the $\ell_w(v)$ defined by (3.12):

$$(3.14) \qquad \ell_w'(T) = \ell_w(v) \qquad \text{for} \quad v = (T - 1)W + w.$$

Formula (3.14) can be proved by mathematical induction on T. (For some related (but different) results on the relationship between the iterative scaling method described by (3.6) to (3.8) and the iterative method described by (3.11) and (3.12), see Goodman's article [13] on the model of quasi-independence, and Haberman's work [20] on more general models.)

It should be noted that, for a particular model, the ℓ_w in (3.4), which we can calculate by any of the methods described under (1), (2), or (3) above, may still need to be scaled (transformed) in order to obtain maximum likelihood estimates of the corresponding scaled (transformed) parameters. (The λ_w in (3.1) and the ℓ_w in (3.4) may not be uniquely defined until they have been scaled (transformed) in a suitable manner.) Thus, for a particular model, if the $\hat{f}_{i,j}$ are unaffected by setting, say, $\ell_1, \ell_2, \cdots, \ell_U$ equal to one (where $U < W$) and by transforming $\ell_{U+1}, \ell_{U+2}, \cdots, \ell_W$ accordingly so that the transformed ℓ are uniquely defined, then these transformed quantities are the maximum likelihood estimates of the corresponding transformed parameters. (Actually, since (3.1) pertains to the probabilities $\pi_{i,j}$ whereas (3.4) pertains to the expected frequencies $\hat{f}_{i,j}$, the particular transformations that are used will determine whether a given transformed ℓ is an estimate of the corresponding transformed λ, or whether it is an estimate of the corresponding transformed λ multiplied by the sample size n.) For further comments on the transformed estimates, see Sections 4 and 7, and the Appendix.

When $f_{i,j} > 0$ for all cells (i, j) for which $\Lambda_{i,j}$ is not empty, then the results of Haberman [20] can be applied to show that the iterative procedures described here will converge to quantities that can be used to obtain the maximum likelihood estimates (that is, the $\hat{f}_{i,j}$ and the transformed ℓ). For cases where $f_{i,j} = 0$ for one or more cells (i, j) for which $\Lambda_{i,j}$ is not empty, the iterative procedures can still be used to obtain the maximum likelihood estimates, so long as the iterative procedures converge to a solution with $\hat{f}_{i,j} \neq 0$ when $\Lambda_{i,j}$ is not empty. The modified Newton-Raphson method, which was applied by Haberman [20] in his numerical example, has a more rapid convergence rate than do the iterative procedures described here (see Haberman [20]); but for data analysis in which a number of different models (of the kind presented here) are applied, the procedures described here have the advantage of being easier to program for a computer.

Before closing this section, we shall give an example of a multiplicative model that is not included within the class of models defined by (3.1), and that cannot be analyzed using the methods presented above. Consider again the QPN model in the special case where

$$(3.15) \qquad \begin{aligned} \alpha_i' &= \Delta\alpha_i\phi^i && \text{for} \quad i = 2, 3, \cdots, R-1, \\[2mm] \beta_j' &= \frac{\Delta^*\beta_j}{\phi^j} && \text{for} \quad j = 2, 3, \cdots, R-1. \end{aligned}$$

This special case of the QPN model is equivalent to the special case of the DAT model in which the additional condition

$$(3.16) \qquad\qquad\qquad \delta_k = \delta^k,$$

where $\delta = 1/\sqrt{\phi}$, is imposed. Although the DAT model, as defined earlier, can be analyzed by the methods presented in the present section, different methods are required for the special case in which condition (3.16) is imposed. The modified Newton-Raphson method presented in Haberman [20] can be applied to this special case. (The "fixed distance" model, which was applied in Haberman [20], is equivalent, in most respects, to the special case of the DA model in which condition (3.16) is imposed. In the present paragraph (see (3.15)) we have been considering the more general DAT model, rather than the DA model, in the special case where condition (3.16) is imposed.)

4. Unrestricted and restricted multiplicative models

The model defined by (3.1) was "intrinsically unrestricted" in the sense that no restrictions (or conditions) were imposed upon the parameters λ_w for $w = 1, 2, \cdots, W$, except for the fact that these parameters were such that

$$(4.1) \qquad \sum_{i, j} \pi_{i, j} = 1.$$

(Of course, since the parameters λ_w were used in (3.1) to form the probabilities $\pi_{i, j}$ for the cells (i, j) where $\pi_{i, j} > 0$, we also assumed that $\lambda_w > 0$ for $w = 1, 2, \cdots, W$.) Formula (3.1) can also be written as

$$(4.2) \qquad \pi_{i, j} = \left[\prod_{\Lambda_{i, j}} \lambda_w \right] \left(\sum \right)^{-1}$$

where Σ denotes the summation of the $\Pi_{\Lambda_{i, j}} \lambda_w$ over all cells (i, j) in the $R \times C$ table. Expressing the model in the form (4.2), we see that the λ_w in (4.2) are even unrestricted in the sense that the condition (4.1) does not impose any restrictions upon them.

For the various models introduced in Sections 2.1 to 2.8, we noted that the $\pi_{i, j}$ were unaffected by scaling (transforming) some of the λ parameters in certain ways. The parameters as described in formulas of the form (3.1) or (4.2) (see, for example, (2.1.1), (2.2.1), (2.3.1), and so on) were not uniquely defined until certain kinds of restrictions were imposed upon them (for example, the restriction that $\alpha_1 = 1$ in formula (2.1.1)). For each of the models in Sections 2.1 to 2.8, in order to calculate the degrees of freedom for testing the model, we described restrictions that could be imposed upon the λ parameters that (a) would uniquely define these parameters, and (b) would not affect the $\pi_{i, j}$. In some of the earlier sections, these restrictions were imposed upon the corresponding estimates of the λ parameters, but they could as well have been imposed upon the λ parameters. Since these particular kinds of restrictions did not affect the $\pi_{i, j}$, the models obtained when the restrictions were imposed were equivalent to the unrestricted models. This was the case for each of the models considered in Sections 2.1 to 2.8.

In addition to introducing restrictions upon the λ parameters that did not affect the $\pi_{i, j}$ (in order to calculate the degrees of freedom for testing the model or to uniquely define the parameters), we also introduced certain kinds of restrictions upon the parameters that did affect the $\pi_{i, j}$. For example, conditions (2.5.8), (2.5.9), and (2.5.10) were restrictions imposed upon the parameters that changed the D model into the DA model, the DP model, and the DN model, respectively. Despite the fact that these particular restrictions did affect the $\pi_{i, j}$, the models obtained when these restrictions were imposed could also be expressed in the general form (3.1) or (4.2), and so these models were also equivalent to unrestricted models. On the other hand, we noted at the end of Section 3, that if condition (3.16) were imposed upon the parameters of the DAT model (or the DA model, the DAC model, or the DACT model), the model obtained thereby would not be within the class of models defined by (3.1).

We shall call a model "intrinsically unrestricted" if it can be expressed in the general form (3.1) or (4.2). (Thus, the DA model, the DP model and the DN model are intrinsically unrestricted in this sense, despite conditions (2.5.8), (2.5.9), (2.5.10); whereas, the modification of the DAT model, which is obtained when condition (3.16) is imposed, is not unrestricted.) We shall now describe some of the kinds of restrictions that can be imposed upon a model of the general form (3.1) which are such that the modified models obtained thereby would also be intrinsically unrestricted.

Let H denote a given model of the form (3.1). The model H can be described by the set of parameters $\Lambda = \{\lambda_1, \lambda_2, \cdots, \lambda_W\}$, and by the subsets $\Lambda_{i,j}$ that are defined for each cell (i, j) in the table (see Section 3). Let Λ' be a given subset of the set Λ, and let H' denote the modification of model H that is obtained by imposing the condition

$$(4.3) \qquad\qquad \lambda_u = 1 \qquad \text{for} \quad \lambda_u \in \Lambda'.$$

Despite the fact that this modification (that is, the model H') is a special case of model H that satisfied condition (4.3), it is also intrinsically unrestricted. Model H' can be expressed in the form (3.1) simply by deleting from Λ and from each set $\Lambda_{i,j}$ any λ_u that are included in Λ'. (For some examples of the modification H', note that the QO model and each of the models in Sections 2.4 to 2.7, except the models that include the paired minor diagonals parameters and/or the triangles parameter (for example, the DA model, the DAT model, and so forth), can be formed from the DC model by this type of modification.)

Now let $\Lambda_1^*, \Lambda_2^*, \cdots, \Lambda_K^*$ denote mutually exclusive subsets of the parameters in Λ; and for each parameter λ_w in Λ, let S_w^λ denote the set of cells (i, j) for which $\lambda_w \in \Lambda_{i,j}$. Consider the modification of model H that is obtained by imposing the conditions

$$(4.4) \qquad\qquad \lambda_u = \lambda_{u'} \qquad \text{for all } \lambda_u \text{ and } \lambda_{u'} \in \Lambda_k^*,$$

for $k = 1, 2, \cdots, K$. This modification will be called a H'' type of modification if each Λ_k^* is such that the sets S_u and $S_{u'}$ are mutually exclusive for all λ_u and $\lambda_{u'}$ in Λ_k^*, for $k = 1, 2, \cdots, K$ (that is, if all λ_u and $\lambda_{u'}$ in Λ_k^* are "separable"). For some examples of the H'' type of modification, note that the QO model can be formed from the QPN model by this type of modification, and the models that include the paired minor diagonals parameters or the triangles parameter can also be formed from the corresponding models that include the diagonals parameters, by this type of modification. The model obtained by the H'' type of modification is also intrinsically unrestricted. It can be expressed in the form (3.1) by removing from Λ and from each $\Lambda_{i,j}$ any λ that are included in Λ_k^*, and by replacing each of these λ by a single parameter, say λ_k^* for $k = 1, 2, \cdots, K$.

The modification described by (2.7.4) might appear (at first sight) to differ from a H'' type of modification, but the change from the DC model to the DACT (or from the D model to the DAT model), which is described by the condition (2.7.4), can also be expressed in the following equivalent way. Without affecting the probabilities $\pi_{i,j}$ in the DC model (or the D model), the triangles parameters could be included in the expression (2.7.1) (or the expression (2.5.1)) for the $\pi_{i,j}$ (as a multiplicative factor of the kind appearing in (2.4.1)); and with the inclusion of these parameters in the model, the change from the DC model to the DACT model (or from the D model to the DAT model) can be expressed by condition (2.5.8) (rather than (2.7.4)), which is obviously a condition of the H'' type. A similar kind of remark can be made about the change from the QPN model to the T model, the change from the QPN to the C model, and the change from the QPN model to the CT model.

For a given model H of the form (3.1), we noted in Section 3 that the estimate $\hat{f}_{i,j}$ of the expected frequency satisfied condition (3.5). For the modification H' of H obtained by imposing condition (4.3), the estimate $\hat{f}_{i,j}$ of the expected frequency under model H' will satisfy the following modification of (3.5):

$$(4.5) \qquad \hat{f}_w^\lambda = f_w^\lambda \quad \text{if} \quad \lambda_w \notin \Lambda'.$$

For the modification H'' of H obtained by imposing condition (4.4), the estimate $\hat{f}_{i,j}$ of the expected frequency under model H'' will satisfy the following modification of (3.5):

$$(4.6) \qquad \begin{aligned} \hat{f}_w^\lambda &= f_w^\lambda \quad \text{if} \quad \lambda_w \notin \Lambda_k^* \quad \text{for} \quad k = 1, 2, \cdots, K, \\ \sum_{\Lambda_k^*} \hat{f}_u^\lambda &= \sum_{\Lambda_k^*} f_u^\lambda \qquad\qquad \text{for} \quad k = 1, 2, \cdots, K, \end{aligned}$$

where $\sum_{\Lambda_k^*}$ denotes summation over the indices u for which $\lambda_u \in \Lambda_k^*$.

We noted earlier that all of the models in Section 2.4 to 2.7 can be obtained from the DC model by using modification H' and/or H''. We shall now show how the models of Section 2.8 can be obtained from the DC model by using these kinds of modifications.

The DC model (as defined by (2.7.1)) was concerned with the analysis of the off diagonal cells, and so for simplicity we could set $\pi_{i,i} = 0$ in (2.7.1). On the other hand, we need not have imposed this restriction on the $\pi_{i,i}$, and could instead have defined the DC model by writing the probability $\pi_{i,j}$ as

$$(4.7) \quad \pi_{i,j} = \begin{cases} \alpha_i \beta_j \gamma'_{i,j} \delta_k & \text{for cells } (i,j) \text{ in } S'_k (k = \pm 1, \pm 2, \cdots, \pm(R-1)), \\ \pi_{i,i} & \text{for cells } (i,i) \text{ in } S'_0. \end{cases}$$

The $\pi_{i,i}$ on the right side of (4.7) can be viewed as "intrinsically unrestricted" λ parameters, as can the parameters α_i, β_j, γ_u, and δ_k. If the condition

$$(4.8) \qquad\qquad \pi_{i,i} = \alpha_i \beta_i \delta_0$$

is imposed upon the $\pi_{i,i}$ in (4.7), the DC model will be changed to the DCF model. To express condition (4.8) in the form (4.4) (that is, as a modification of the H'' type), we first note that the $\pi_{i,i}$ in (4.6) can be written as $\alpha'_i \beta'_i \delta_0$ (where the α'_i, β'_i, δ_0 are intrinsically unrestricted λ parameters) without affecting the probabilities in the DC model (see 4.7); and we then impose the condition

(4.9) $\alpha_i = \alpha_i'$, $\beta_j = \beta_j'$ for $i = 1, 2, \cdots, R; j = 1, 2, \cdots, R$,

to change the DC model to the DCF model.

All of the models in Section 2.8 can be obtained from the DCF model by using modifications H' and/or H'' in the same ways that these modifications would be used to obtain the corresponding models of Sections 2.4 to 2.7 from the DC model. Since we noted in the preceding paragraph that the DCF model can be obtained from the DC model using a modification of the H'' type, we now see that all of the models in Section 2.8 can also be obtained from the DC model by using the modifications H' and/or H''. Furthermore, each of the models in Section 2.8 can be obtained from the corresponding model in Sections 2.4 to 2.7 by using a modification of the H'' type in the same way that it was used above to obtain the DCF model from the DC model.

As we noted earlier, the present article is limited to multiplicative models of the general form (3.1), that is, models that are intrinsically unrestricted. These include all the models of Sections 2.1 to 2.8 and many others as well, but they do not include "restricted" models of the kind referred to at the end of Section 3.

5. The ratio index and the relative difference index for the cells on the main diagonal

Consider again the DC model for the off diagonal cells, and the corresponding model for the full table (that is, the DCF model). For the DCF model (as defined in Section 2.8), the probability $\pi_{i,j}$ can be written as

(5.1) $\mu_{i,j} = \alpha_i \beta_j \gamma_{i,j}' \delta_k$ for cells (i, j) in S_k',

for $k = 0, \pm 1, \pm 2, \cdots, \pm(R - 1)$, with $\gamma_{i,j}' = 1$ for $i = j$. Thus, for both the DCF model and the DC model, the probability $\pi_{i,j}$ can be written as

(5.2) $\pi_{i,j} = \alpha_i \beta_j \gamma_{i,j}' \delta_k \mu_{i,j}$ for cells (i, j) in S_k',

for $k = 0, \pm 1, \pm 2, \cdots, \pm(R - 1)$, where the $\mu_{i,j}$ satisfy condition

(5.3) $\mu_{i,j} = 1$ for all cells (i, j),

for the DCF model, and condition

(5.4) $\mu_{i,j} = \begin{cases} 1 & \text{for } i \neq j, \\ \pi_{i,i}/(\alpha_i \beta_i \delta_0) & \text{for } i = j \end{cases}$

for the DC model. Note that the $\pi_{i,j}$ defined by (5.2) and (5.4) are equivalent to the $\pi_{i,j}$ defined by (4.7).

In view of (5.4), the quantity

(5.5) $$\mu_i = \frac{\pi_{i,i}}{\alpha_i \beta_i \delta_0}$$

is of interest. We shall call μ_i the ratio index for the ith cell on the main diagonal.

(This index was defined earlier in Goodman [14] for the model of quasi-independence, and it was called there a "new index of immobility.") For models that do not include diagonals parameters (or the triangles parameter), we set $\delta_0 = 1$; for the other models of Section 2.4 to 2.7, the parameter δ_0 cannot be estimated from the data without introducing some additional assumptions (which we shall discuss in Section 7); for the models of Section 2.8, we set $\mu_i = 1$ for $i = 1, 2, \cdots, R$, and the parameter δ_0 (and the other δ_k) in (5.1) can be estimated from the data.

In models that include crossings parameters for the analysis of the off diagonal cells (for example, the C model or DC model), we noted earlier (see Sections 2.6 and 2.7) that the probability $\pi_{i,j}$ is unaffected by setting $\gamma_1 = \gamma_{R-1} = 1$, and by making corresponding changes in $\alpha_1, \alpha_R, \beta_1, \beta_R$. On the other hand, instead of setting $\gamma_1 = \gamma_{R-1} = 1$, the $\pi_{i,j}$ would also be unaffected by making some other assumptions about γ_1 and γ_{R-1} (with corresponding changes made in $\alpha_1, \alpha_R, \beta_1, \beta_R$); and with these assumptions (which we shall discuss in Section 7), the data could be used to estimate γ_1 and γ_{R-1}. These assumptions about γ_1 and γ_{R-1} will affect $\alpha_1\beta_1$ and $\alpha_R\beta_R$; and they thereby will affect μ_1 and μ_R.

For the DC model for analyzing the off diagonal cells, the remarks in the preceding two paragraphs indicate that there is an element of arbitrariness about μ_1, μ_R and δ_0 (that is, the additional assumptions, to which we referred in those paragraphs, will affect these quantities). This was not the case for the DCF model (see Section 2.8). Note that the difference between the degrees of freedom for the DCF model and the DC model is $R - 3$, which corresponds to the degrees of freedom associated with testing the hypothesis

$$(5.6) \qquad \mu_i = \mu \qquad \text{for} \quad i = 2, 3, \cdots, R - 1,$$

where μ is unspecified. A similar kind of remark can be applied to the difference between the degrees of freedom for each of the models in Section 2.8 and the corresponding model from Sections 2.4 to 2.7. For the models in Section 2.8 that do not include crossings parameters, replace (5.6) by the same condition applied for $i = 1, 2, \cdots, R$ (rather than for $i = 2, 3, \cdots, R - 1$); and for models that do not include diagonals parameters (or the triangles parameter), replace the unspecified quantity μ in (5.6) by one.

Let us now denote $\alpha_i\beta_i\delta_0$ by $\pi_{i,i}^*$, and let $\pi_{i,j}^* = \pi_{i,j}$ for $i \neq j$, with the $\pi_{i,j}$ satisfying condition (4.7) for the DC model. With this notation, the index μ_i defined by (5.5) can be written as

$$(5.7) \qquad \mu_i = \frac{\pi_{i,i}}{\pi_{i,i}^*}.$$

Instead of this ratio index, consider now the quantity

$$(5.8) \qquad \mu_i^* = \frac{(\pi_{i,i} - \pi_{i,i}^*)}{\pi_{i\cdot}},$$

where $\pi_{i\cdot} = \Sigma_{j=1}^R \pi_{i,j}$, which we shall call the relative difference index for the ith cell on the main diagonal. This index was defined earlier in Goodman [16] for the model of quasi-independence, and it was called there the "index of persistence."

Let $\tilde{\pi}_{i,j}$ and $\tilde{\pi}_{i,j}^*$ denote $\pi_{i,j}/\pi_{i\cdot}$ and $\pi_{i,j}^*/\pi_{i\cdot}^*$, respectively, where $\pi_{i\cdot}^* = \Sigma_{j=1}^{R} \pi_{i,j}^*$. From (4.7) and (5.8) we find that $\tilde{\pi}_{i,j}$ can be written as

$$(5.9) \qquad \tilde{\pi}_{i,j} = \begin{cases} (1 - \mu_i^*)\tilde{\pi}_{i,j}^* & \text{for } i \neq j, \\ \mu_i^* + [(1 - \mu_i^*)\tilde{\pi}_{i,j}^*] & \text{for } i = j. \end{cases}$$

Because of (5.9), the index μ_i^* can be interpreted as the proportion of "stayers" among those individuals who are in the ith row in the population. This interpretation would apply when $\mu_i^* > 0$.

For the case where $\mu_i^* < 0$, we can rewrite (5.9) as

$$(5.10) \qquad \tilde{\pi}_{i,j} = \begin{cases} \tilde{\pi}_{i,j}^*(1 + v_i) & \text{for } i \neq j, \\ \tilde{\pi}_{i,i}^* - v_i(1 - \tilde{\pi}_{i,i}^*) & \text{for } i = j, \end{cases}$$

where $v_i = -\mu_i^*$. Because of (5.10), the index v_i (that is, the index $-\mu_i^*$) can be interpreted (when $\mu_i^* < 0$) as the proportion of individuals who have a "second chance" to move out of the ith row class among those individuals who are in the ith row in the population. This interpretation can be applied when $\tilde{\pi}_{i,i}^* > v_i$. The interpretations presented in the present paragraph, and in the preceding one, are extensions of the interpretations introduced in Goodman [16] for the model of quasi-independence.

From (5.7) and (5.8), we see that μ_i and μ_i^* are related as follows:

$$(5.11) \qquad \mu_i = \frac{\tilde{\pi}_{i,i}}{\tilde{\pi}_{i,i} - \mu_i^*}$$

$$\mu_i^* = \frac{\tilde{\pi}_{i,i}(\mu_i - 1)}{\mu_i}.$$

In addition, the index μ_i^* can be rewritten as

$$(5.12) \qquad \mu_i^* = \frac{\tilde{\pi}_{i,i} - \tilde{\pi}_{i,i}^*}{1 - \tilde{\pi}_{i,i}^*}.$$

Thus, the index μ_i^* measures the difference $(\tilde{\pi}_{i,i} - \tilde{\pi}_{i,i}^*)$ relative to the difference $(1 - \tilde{\pi}_{i,i}^*)$.

From (5.12) we see that the index μ_i^* can be expressed as a function of $\tilde{\pi}_{i,i}$ and $\tilde{\pi}_{i,i}^*$ (rather than $\pi_{i,i}$ and $\pi_{i,i}^*$), whereas the corresponding ratio index μ_i was a function of $\pi_{i,i}$ and $\pi_{i,i}^*$. (Compare (5.12) with (5.7).) Note that $\tilde{\pi}_{i,j}$ is the conditional probability that an individual will fall in the jth column class of the population table, given that he is in the ith row class; and $\tilde{\pi}_{i,j}^*$ is the corresponding conditional probability obtained by replacing $\pi_{i,i}$ by $\alpha_i\beta_i\delta_0$. The conditional probabilities $\tilde{\pi}_{i,j}$ and $\tilde{\pi}_{i,j}^*$ are particularly relevant when the data to be analyzed have been obtained from a sample of n_i individuals drawn from the ith row class for $i = 1, 2, \cdots, R$ (that is, when the row marginals are fixed), rather than from a sample of n individuals drawn from the population cross classification table. It is in this context that the index μ_i^* (rather than the index μ_i) is particularly relevant.

When a sample of n individuals is drawn from the population cross classification table, the index μ_i may be viewed as one of the parameters of the model, since the $\pi_{i,j}$ can be expressed by (5.2) with the parameter $\mu_{i,j}$ in (5.2) set equal to μ_i for $i = j$ (see (5.4) and (5.5)). This remark can be applied to any of the models of Sections 2.4 to 2.7; and for the models of Section 2.8 the parameter μ_i is set equal to one. Similarly, when a sample of n_i individuals is drawn from the ith row class for $i = 1, 2, \cdots, R$, the index μ_i^* may be viewed as one of the parameters of the model, since the $\tilde{\pi}_{i,j}$ can be expressed by (5.9).

Note that the index μ_i is "symmetric" in the sense that it is invariant when the row classes are interchanged with the column classes. Of course, this will not be the case for the index μ_i^*. In addition to the index μ_i^* defined herein for the case where the row marginals are fixed, there is the relative difference index that would be defined in a directly analogous way for the case where the column marginals are fixed.

Applying the general methods of estimation described in Section 3 to the DC model, we can calculate the estimate

$$(5.13) \qquad \hat{f}_{i,j} = \begin{cases} a_i b_j c'_{i,j} d_k & \text{for} \quad i \neq j, \\ f_{i,i} & \text{for} \quad i = j, \end{cases}$$

of the expected frequency under the model. (Compare (5.13) with (4.7).) Note that d_0 does not appear in (5.13), and the corresponding δ_0 did not appear in (4.7) or (2.7.1). For models that do not include diagonals parameters (or the triangles parameter), we set $d_0 = 1$; for models that do include these parameters, the value of d_0 will be estimated from the data after we introduce some additional assumptions (which we shall discuss in Section 7). Denoting $a_i b_i d_0$ by $f_{i,i}^*$, and letting $f_{i,j}^* = \hat{f}_{i,j}$ for $i \neq j$ (with $\hat{f}_{i,j}$ defined by (5.13)), we can estimate the index μ_i, which was defined by (5.7),

$$(5.14) \qquad m_i = \frac{f_{i,i}}{f_{i,i}^*}.$$

Similarly, the index μ_i^*, which was defined by (5.8), can be estimated as

$$(5.15) \qquad m_i^* = \frac{f_{i,i} - f_{i,i}^*}{f_{i\cdot}}.$$

where $f_{i\cdot} = \Sigma_{j=1}^R f_{i,j}$. Formulae that are directly analogous to (5.11) and (5.12) can be obtained for m_i and m_i^*, by replacing μ_i, μ_i^*, $\tilde{\pi}_{i,i}$, and $\tilde{\pi}_{i,i}^*$ in (5.11) and (5.12) by m_i, m_i^*, $f_{i,i}/f_{i\cdot}$, and $f_{i,i}^*/f_{i\cdot}^*$, respectively, where $f_{i\cdot}^* = \Sigma_{j=1}^R f_{i,j}^*$. The estimates m_i and m_i^* can be calculated for the QO model and for each of the models in Sections 2.4 to 2.7.

6. The comparison of observed frequencies and expected frequencies under the various models

The usual chi square goodness of fit statistic for comparing the observed frequency $f_{i,j}$ with the corresponding estimate $\hat{f}_{i,j}$ of the expected frequency under a given model, can be written as

$$(6.1) \qquad \sum \frac{(f_{i,j} - \hat{f}_{i,j})^2}{\hat{f}_{i,j}},$$

and the corresponding chi square statistic based upon the likelihood ratio criterion can be written as

$$(6.2) \qquad 2\sum f_{i,j} \log\left(\frac{f_{i,j}}{\hat{f}_{i,j}}\right),$$

where the summation in (6.1) and (6.2) is taken over the off diagonal cells for the QO model and for the models of Sections 2.4 to 2.7, over all the cells in the table for the model of "independence" and for the models of Section 2.8, and over the set (or sets) of cells that are to be analyzed for a given model of quasi-independence of the kind described in Section 2.2 and 2.3. Both the statistic (6.1) and the statistic (6.2) have an asymptotic chi square distribution under the given model, with the degrees of freedom equal to the number of parameters in the model (calculating this number after the parameters have been uniquely defined). In certain contexts, the statistic (6.2) has some advantages over (6.1) (see, for example, Bahadur [1], Good [7], Goodman [13], [15], [17], [19], and Hoeffding [21]). We shall give in Table V the numerical values of both (6.1) and (6.2), for various models applied to the British 5×5 table (Table I), the Danish 5×5 table (Table II), and the British 7×7 table (Table III); but, for the sake of simplicity, when we discuss Table V later in the present section, we shall confine our attention to the numerical values of the statistic (6.2).

Since the estimate $\hat{f}_{i,j}$ of the expected frequency under each of the models considered here can be expressed in the general form (3.4), we see that the statistic (6.2) can also be written as

$$(6.3) \qquad 2\left[\sum f_{i,j} \log f_{i,j} - \sum_{w=1}^{W} f_w^\lambda \log \ell_w\right],$$

where the first summation sign $\sum$ in (6.3) has the same meaning that it did in (6.1) and (6.2); namely, the summation over all cells (i,j) for which $\Lambda_{i,j}$ is not empty. Note that formula (6.3) provides a method for calculating the statistic (6.2) using the W terms ℓ_w for $w = 1, 2, \cdots, W$ without calculating the $\hat{f}_{i,j}$ terms.

Now let H denote a given model of the form (3.1), and let H^+ denote the modified model that is obtained by applying to H a given modification of the H' and/or H'' type (see Section 4). As we noted in Section 4, the model H^+ is also "intrinsically unrestricted." Let $[H^+|H]$ denote the hypothesis that H^+

TABLE V

COMPARISON OF THE OBSERVED FREQUENCIES AND THE EXPECTED FREQUENCIES
UNDER VARIOUS MODELS APPLIED TO THE BRITISH AND DANISH 5 × 5 TABLES, AND THE
BRITISH 7 × 7 TABLE

| | | British and Danish 5 × 5 Tables | | | |
| | | British Sample | | Danish Sample | |
Model	Degrees of Freedom	Goodness of Fit Chi Square	Likelihood Ratio Chi Square	Goodness of Fit Chi Square	Likelihood Ratio Chi Square
Ind	16	1199.4	811.0	754.1	654.2
QO	11	328.7	249.4	270.3	248.7
QP	3	8.5	12.6	6.9	7.4
QN	3	1.3	1.4	2.4	2.5
QPN	6	9.9	14.0	9.4	9.9
T	10	313.1	242.3	269.3	248.5
C	9	11.9	15.4	12.2	12.8
DA	8	15.9	19.1	6.7	6.9
CT	8	10.2	14.1	12.1	12.7
DAT	7	14.4	17.8	6.6	6.8
DP	7	10.3	10.6	6.8	7.0
DN	7	18.6	23.8	10.3	10.9
DAC	7	8.6	11.1	6.4	6.6
DACT	6	7.2	10.0	6.4	6.5
DPC	6	2.2	2.2	6.6	6.9
DNC	6	9.5	13.4	10.0	10.5
D	5	9.0	9.5	4.7	4.8
DC	4	1.5	1.6	4.4	4.5
DCF	6	6.7	6.9	6.3	6.3
DPCF	8	7.6	7.7	8.2	8.3
DACF	9	13.8	16.7	8.1	8.4
DF	9	52.1	50.4	10.1	10.2
DAF	12	59.5	60.6	12.2	12.4

is true assuming that H is true. Since H^+ is a modification of H in which some given conditions of the type (4.3) and/or (4.4) are imposed, the hypothesis $[H^+|H]$ states that the given conditions are true, assuming the H is true. Let $\chi^2(H)$ and $\chi^2(H^+)$ denote the statistic (6.2) with $\hat{f}_{i,j}$ calculated under H and H^+, respectively. The statistics $\chi^2(H)$ and $\chi^2(H^+)$ can be used to test the models H and H^+, respectively, and the following statistic can be used to test the hypothesis $[H^+|H]$:

$$(6.4) \quad \chi^2(H^+|H) = \chi^2(H^+) - X^2(H)$$

$$= 2 \sum f \log \left[\frac{\hat{f}}{\hat{f}^+} \right] = 2 \sum \hat{f} \log \left[\frac{\hat{f}}{\hat{f}^+} \right],$$

where $\hat{f}$ and $\hat{f}^+$ are the estimated expected frequencies under H and H^+, respectively. The final equality in (6.4) holds because the $\hat{f}$ satisfy (3.5) and

TABLE V (Continued)

Model	Degrees of Freedom	British 7 × 7 Table Goodness of Fit Chi Square	Likelihood Ratio Chi Square
Ind	36	1361.7	897.5
QO	29	523.0	408.4
QP	10	9.4	13.4
QN	10	7.4	7.5
QPN	20	16.7	20.9
T	28	517.8	404.1
C	25	20.6	24.6
DA	24	20.1	22.1
CT	24	19.9	24.1
DAT	23	19.5	21.6
DP	23	21.3	22.3
DN	23	19.3	23.6
DAC	21	15.1	17.1
DACT	20	14.6	16.6
DPC	20	14.6	15.8
DNC	20	13.8	18.0
D	19	13.6	14.6
DC	16	8.4	9.4
DCF	20	25.0	26.3
DPCF	24	38.8	39.7
DACF	25	31.7	33.8
DF	25	54.2	54.8
DAF	30	59.8	61.9

the $\hat{f}^+$ satisfy conditions of the form (4.5) and/or (4.6). The statistic (6.4) is the chi square statistic based upon the likelihood ratio criterion for testing the hypothesis $[H^+|H]$. This statistic has an asymptotic chi square distribution under the hypothesis $[H^+|H]$, with the degrees of freedom equal to the difference between the corresponding number of degrees of freedom for testing H^+ and H, respectively.

Let us now examine the numerical values of $\chi^2(H)$, which are given in Table V for each of the models in Sections 2.3 to 2.7, and for some of the models in Section 2.8, applied to Table I. For the DC model, we see that $\chi^2(DC) = 1.6$ with 4 degrees of freedom, which indicates that this model fits the data very well. Comparing the D model with the DC model using the statistic (6.4), we obtain $\chi^2(D|DC) = 7.9$ with one degree of freedom, which indicates that the crossings parameter makes a statistically significant contribution. In other words, assuming that the DC model is true, a test of the null hypothesis (2.7.3) would lead to rejection of the hypothesis. Comparing the C model with the DC model, we obtain $\chi^2(C|DC) = 13.8$ with 5 degrees of freedom, which indicates that the diagonals parameters make a statistically significant contribution. In other words, assuming that the DC model is true, a test of the null hypothesis (2.7.2) would lead to the rejection of the hypothesis.

Comparing the CT model, the DAC model, and the DNC model with the DC model, we obtain $\chi^2(\mathrm{CT}|\mathrm{DC}) = 12.5$, $\chi^2(\mathrm{DAC}|\mathrm{DC}) = 9.5$, and $\chi^2(\mathrm{DNC}|\mathrm{DC}) = 11.8$, with 4, 3, and 2 degrees of freedom, respectively. Thus, assuming that the DC model is true, a test of each of the null hypotheses (2.5.2), (2.5.8), and (2.5.13) would lead to their rejection. A similar result is obtained comparing the DACT model with the DC model. Comparing the DCF model and the DPC model with the DC model, we obtain $\chi^2(\mathrm{DCF}|\mathrm{DC}) = 5.3$ and $\chi^2(\mathrm{DPC}|\mathrm{DC}) = 0.6$ each with 2 degrees of freedom. Thus, assuming that the DC model is true, a test of the null hypothesis (5.6) would lead to rejection of the hypothesis at the 10 per cent level of significance, and a test of the null hypothesis (2.5.9) would lead to acceptance of that hypothesis. Indeed, the DPC model fits the data very well.

Having noted that the DPC model fits the data well, we now compare various models with the DPC model. Comparing the DP and the C models with the DPC model, we obtain $\chi^2(\mathrm{DP}|\mathrm{DPC}) = 8.4$ and $\chi^2(\mathrm{C}|\mathrm{DPC}) = 13.2$, with 1 and 3 degrees of freedom, respectively, which indicates that both the crossings parameters and the parameters pertaining to the "positive" diagonals in the DPC model make a statistically significant contribution. Comparing the DPCF model with the DPC model, we obtain $\chi^2(\mathrm{DPCF}|\mathrm{DPC}) = 5.5$ with 2 degrees of freedom. Thus, assuming that the DPC model is true, a test of the null hypothesis (5.6) would lead to rejection of the hypothesis at the 10 per cent level of significance.

The preceding comments pertained to the results given in Table V for the analysis of Table I. The corresponding results, which are given in Table V for the analysis of Tables II and III, do not lead to conclusions that are as clear cut as those obtained for Table I. We shall now comment briefly on the results for Tables II and III without presenting a full analysis of them.

As was the case for Table I, the DC model fits the data very well for Table III; and it fits the data rather well for Table II, but not as well as for Tables I and III. Among the models that fit the data well (or rather well), we find the DA model for Table II and the DAC model for Table III. Comparing the models for the analysis of the full tables with the corresponding models for the analysis of the off diagonal cells, we find that a test of the null hypothesis (5.6) would lead to rejection of the hypothesis for Table III and acceptance of the hypothesis for Table II. Comparison of the QP and QN models indicates that the QN model fits the data better than the QP model for Tables II and III (and also for Table I).

For each chi square statistic, the corresponding number of degrees of freedom can be obtained from Tables IV and V. These tables give the degrees of freedom of the corresponding asymptotic distribution under the null hypothesis. This is the appropriate number of degrees of freedom to use in testing the hypothesis *if* the hypothesis were decided upon before the data were studied. On the other hand, if a set of hypotheses were tested simultaneously (or if the particular hypothesis that was tested was contained within a larger set of hypotheses that were studied), the degrees of freedom could be adjusted in a similar way to the adjustment made in calculating simultaneous confidence intervals and simultaneous tests in the present context (see Goodman [11], [14], [19]). This adjustment will limit the risks of rejecting hypotheses that are true, even when the hypotheses are suggested by the data. Of course, the risks of accepting false hypotheses are also affected if the hypotheses are suggested by the data.

The various hypotheses and models that we have tested and compared here could also have been assessed by adapting to the present context some of the concepts that arise in stepwise regression (for example, some of the concepts of backward regression and/or forward regression). For a discussion of this kind of adaptation, and for an example of its application, the reader is referred to Goodman [18].

7. The estimated parameters and indices

In this section we shall comment briefly upon the estimates of some of the parameters, and of the ratio and relative difference indices, which are obtained when some of the models of Section 2 are applied to Tables I, II, and III. These estimates will be presented in Tables VI to X later in this section.

For the models that included the triangles parameters τ_k for $k = 1$ and 2 (see, for example, (2.4.1)), we noted earlier that these parameters were not uniquely defined until one restriction was imposed upon them. This restriction could be expressed in several different ways; for example, as (a) the condition that $\tau_1 = 1$ (as we did in Section 2.4), or as (b) the condition that $\tau_2 = 1$, or as (c) the condition

$$(7.1) \qquad\qquad \tau_1 \tau_2 = 1.$$

For our present purposes, it is convenient to impose condition (7.1), and to take τ_1 as the uniquely defined triangles parameter τ. From (7.1), we see that τ can also be expressed as

$$(7.2) \qquad\qquad \tau = \left(\frac{\tau_1}{\tau_2}\right)^{1/2}$$

(In contexts where condition (7.1) is replaced by one of the other conditions given above, the quantity defined by (7.2) would also be replaced as the triangles parameter.)

Table VI gives the maximum likelihood estimate t of τ obtained under the four models that include the triangles parameter; namely, the T model, the CT model, the DAT model, and the DACT model. Note that the estimate t is less than one for each of the cases considered in Table VI, which indicates that, aside from the effects of the other parameters in the model, the estimated triangles parameter will diminish the estimated expected frequencies for the cells in set S_1 (where $i - j > 0$) relative to the estimated expected frequencies for the cells in set S_2 (where $i - j < 0$). For each of the three mobility tables

TABLE VI

THE ESTIMATE OF THE TRIANGLES PARAMETER UNDER VARIOUS MODELS
APPLIED TO THE BRITISH AND DANISH SAMPLES

	Models			
	T	CT	DAT	DACT
British 5 × 5 Table	0.855	0.935	0.935	0.937
Danish 5 × 5 Table	0.970	0.981	0.980	0.983
British 7 × 7 Table	0.904	0.966	0.966	0.968

(Tables I, II, and III), this would indicate that the estimated τ parameter has the direct effect of introducing "downward mobility" (as expressed in the fact that $(\tau_2/\tau_1)^{1/2}$ is estimated as being larger than one), over and above the indirect effects (with respect to upward or downward mobility) that are due to the other parameters. The effect of t appears to be more pronounced for the T model (particularly for Table I), and it becomes less pronounced as more parameters (for example, the crossings parameters and/or the parameters pertaining to the paired minor diagonals) are included in the model. To test whether $\tau = 1$ in, say, the DACT model applied to Tables I, II, and III, we compare the DAC model with the DACT model using the results given in Table V, and we find that the τ parameter does not have a statistically significant effect when the other parameters are included in the model.

With respect to the diagonals parameters (Table VII), we note that d_k decreases as $|k|$ increases in all cases, except for d_4 for Table II under the DPC, D, and DC models. This would indicate that aside from the effects of the other parameters in the model, generally speaking the estimated diagonals parameters diminish the estimated expected frequencies in a progressively more pronounced way for cells that are on minor diagonals that are further away from the main diagonal. In other words, the estimates d_k have the direct effect of introducing "status inertia" in the mobility table. With respect to Table II, it is worth noting (see Table V) that the modifications of the DA model and the DAC model that are obtained by distinguishing diagonals parameters on the "positive" diagonals from those on the "negative" diagonals (for example, the D model, the DC model, and the DPC model) did not improve the fit markedly. Note also that the difference in Table VII between d_k and the corresponding d_{-k} is, generally speaking, smaller for Table II than for the other tables. When comparing the DA model with the DAC model (or the D model with the DC model), we find that the effect of d_k is somewhat more pronounced in the former model than in the latter one (which included the crossings parameters as well). To facilitate the comparison of models in Table VII, condition (2.5.12) was used, rather than the equivalent (2.5.9), in the DPC model; and condition (7.3) below was used in the DAC, DPC, and DC models.

With respect to the crossings parameters (Table VIII), for models that include both the γ_u and δ_k parameters, we noted earlier that the γ_u, for $u =$

TABLE VII

THE ESTIMATE OF THE DIAGONALS PARAMETERS UNDER VARIOUS MODELS
APPLIED TO THE BRITISH AND DANISH SAMPLES

| | Models | | | | | | | |
| | DA | DAC | DPC | | D | | DC | |
British 5 × 5 Table	$d_k = d_{-k}$	$d_k = d_{-k}$	d_k	d_{-k}	d_k	d_{-k}	d_k	d_{-k}
$k = 1$	1.00	1.00	1.00	1.00	1.00	1.00	1.00	1.00
$k = 2$	0.59	0.64	0.74	0.54	0.68	0.52	0.73	0.56
$k = 3$	0.26	0.32	0.39	0.29	0.32	0.22	0.39	0.28
$k = 4$	0.08	0.13	0.00	0.16	0.00	0.11	0.00	0.17
Danish 5 × 5 Table								
$k = 1$	1.00	1.00	1.00	1.00	1.00	1.00	1.00	1.00
$k = 2$	0.48	0.51	0.52	0.45	0.49	0.47	0.52	0.50
$k = 3$	0.15	0.16	0.14	0.20	0.13	0.16	0.14	0.17
$k = 4$	0.11	0.12	0.17	0.09	0.15	0.06	0.17	0.06
British 7 × 7 Table								
$k = 1$	1.00	1.00	1.00	1.00	1.00	1.00	1.00	1.00
$k = 2$	0.65	0.70	0.69	0.61	0.64	0.65	0.69	0.70
$k = 3$	0.34	0.40	0.51	0.38	0.41	0.28	0.49	0.34
$k = 4$	0.20	0.26	0.30	0.23	0.21	0.18	0.28	0.25
$k = 5$	0.08	0.11	0.08	0.14	0.05	0.09	0.08	0.13
$k = 6$	0.03	0.04	0.00	0.09	0.00	0.04	0.00	0.06

TABLE VIII

THE ESTIMATE OF THE CROSSINGS PARAMETERS UNDER VARIOUS MODELS
APPLIED TO THE BRITISH AND DANISH SAMPLES

| | Models | | | |
	C	DAC	DPC	DC
British 5 × 5 Table				
c_2	0.40	0.46	0.45	0.46
c_3	0.60	0.64	0.63	0.64
Danish 5 × 5 Table				
c_2	0.46	0.51	0.48	0.51
c_3	0.43	0.47	0.46	0.48
British 7 × 7 Table				
c_2	0.54	0.60	0.55	0.60
c_3	0.52	0.58	0.53	0.58
c_4	0.60	0.67	0.61	0.66
c_5	0.64	0.70	0.65	0.70

$2, 3, \cdots, R - 2$, were not uniquely defined until one restriction was imposed upon them—a restriction that has the effect of fixing the scale of the γ_u. This restriction could be expressed in several different ways; for example, as (a) the condition that

$$(7.3) \qquad\qquad \max_k \gamma_k = 1 \qquad \text{for} \quad 2 \leq k \leq R - 2,$$

which is equivalent to replacing the γ_u by $\tilde{\gamma}_u = \gamma_u/\gamma^*$, where $\gamma^* = \max_k \gamma_k$ for $2 \leq k \leq R - 2$; or (b) the condition that

$$(7.4) \qquad\qquad\qquad \delta_2 \delta_{-2} = 1,$$

which will also have the effect of fixing the scale of the γ. For models that included the δ_k parameters, we noted earlier that the restriction that $\delta_1 = \delta_{-1} = 1$ would uniquely define the δ_k; this restriction together with condition (7.4) would uniquely define the δ_k and γ_u for $u = 2, 3, \cdots, R - 2$, in models that included both sets of parameters. In order to facilitate comparison between the crossings parameters for the C model (for which the γ_u for $u = 2, 3, \cdots, R - 2$, are uniquely defined without imposing any restrictions upon them) and the corresponding parameters in models that also include the δ_k parameters, the restriction (7.4) was used in calculating the results presented in Table VIII. To make the c_u in Table VIII consistent with the corresponding d_k in Table VII for a model that includes both sets of parameters (for example, the DAC, the DPC, and the DC models), it is only necessary to divide each of the c_u in Table VIII by $\max_k c_k$ for $2 \leq k \leq R - 2$, for the given model (see condition (7.3)). The estimates c_u in Table VIII have the direct effect of introducing "status barriers" in the mobility tables. Comparing the results in Table VIII for the 5×5 tables (that is, Tables I and II), we note that the effect of c_2 is more pronounced than that of c_3 for Table I, and the reverse is true for Table II. For Table III, the effect of c_u becomes more pronounced as u decreases, except for $u = 2$. From Table VIII we see that the relative difference between the c is less for Table II than for Table I. From Table V we also take note of the fact that the modification of the various models (for example, the DA, the DP, the D models) that is obtained by including the crossing parameters (thus obtaining the DAC, the DPC, and the DC models) did not improve the fit markedly for Table II, but it did for Table I. Finally, we note that the corresponding c_u in Table VIII are very similar for the DAC model and the DC model.

With respect to the ratio index and the relative difference index (Tables IX and X), we first note that the numerical values obtained for the QO model (which did not fit the mobility tables well) are grossly misleading. For models that fit the data well, the numerical values obtained for these indices can differ greatly from the values obtained with models that do not fit the data. Note also that the corresponding values for the DA model and the D model are very similar, and so are the corresponding values of the DAC and the DC models. With the introduction of the additional parameters (for example, the δ_k and/or the γ_u) into the QO model, the effect of the m_i diminishes (see Table IX).

TABLE IX

THE ESTIMATE OF THE RATIO INDEX FOR THE CELLS ON THE MAIN DIAGONAL OF THE $R \times R$ CROSS CLASSIFICATION TABLE, UNDER VARIOUS MODELS APPLIED TO THE BRITISH AND DANISH SAMPLES

	Models					
	QO	DA	DAC	DPC	D	DC
British 5 × 5 Table						
m_1	34.5	3.8	4.6	4.5	3.8	4.5
m_2	4.0	0.9	0.6	0.6	0.9	0.6
m_3	1.7	1.0	1.0	1.0	1.0	1.0
m_4	1.0	0.7	0.8	0.7	0.8	0.8
m_5	2.9	0.9	1.1	1.1	0.9	1.1
Danish 5 × 5 Table						
m_1	13.8	1.1	1.2	1.2	1.1	1.2
m_2	4.8	0.9	1.0	1.0	0.9	1.0
m_3	1.8	0.8	0.8	0.8	0.8	0.8
m_4	1.2	0.7	0.7	0.7	0.7	0.7
m_5	3.4	0.7	0.8	0.7	0.7	0.8
British 7 × 7 Table						
m_1	35.0	2.4	2.6	2.4	2.4	2.6
m_2	8.6	1.5	1.3	1.2	1.5	1.3
m_3	2.2	0.7	0.6	0.5	0.7	0.6
m_4	1.7	1.0	1.0	1.0	1.0	1.0
m_5	1.2	0.8	0.8	0.7	0.8	0.8
m_6	2.3	1.3	1.4	1.3	1.3	1.4
m_7	2.9	0.7	0.8	0.7	0.7	0.8

TABLE X

THE ESTIMATE OF THE RELATIVE DIFFERENCE INDEX FOR THE CELLS ON THE MAIN DIAGONAL OF THE $R \times R$ CROSS CLASSIFICATION TABLE UNDER VARIOUS MODELS APPLIED TO THE BRITISH AND DANISH SAMPLES

	Models					
	QO	DA	DAC	DPC	D	DC
British 5 × 5 Table						
m_1^*	0.38	0.29	0.30	0.30	0.29	0.30
m_2^*	0.26	−0.05	−0.23	−0.24	−0.04	−0.22
m_3^*	0.09	−0.01	0.00	0.00	−0.01	0.00
m_4^*	−0.01	−0.17	−0.16	−0.16	−0.16	−0.14
m_5^*	0.32	−0.04	0.05	0.04	−0.04	0.05
Danish 5 × 5 Table						
m_1^*	0.29	0.02	0.06	0.04	0.02	0.06
m_2^*	0.26	−0.02	0.01	−0.01	−0.02	0.01
m_3^*	0.18	−0.09	−0.09	−0.13	−0.09	−0.09
m_4^*	0.08	−0.16	−0.16	−0.19	−0.16	−0.16
m_5^*	0.33	−0.22	−0.15	−0.20	−0.21	−0.14
British 7 × 7 Table						
m_1^*	0.38	0.23	0.24	0.23	0.23	0.24
m_2^*	0.24	0.09	0.06	0.05	0.09	0.06
m_3^*	0.10	−0.07	−0.11	−0.17	−0.07	−0.12
m_4^*	0.09	0.01	0.01	−0.01	0.00	0.01
m_5^*	0.08	−0.14	−0.12	−0.20	−0.14	−0.12
m_6^*	0.17	0.06	0.08	0.08	0.06	0.08
m_7^*	0.18	−0.14	−0.06	−0.09	−0.14	−0.06

To test hypotheses about the μ_i, we return to our earlier discussion of (5.6). As we noted there, for a given model that does not include crossings parameters (but does include diagonals parameters or the triangles parameter), the hypothesis that the relative differences among the μ_i are nil for $i = 1, 2, \cdots, R$, can be tested by comparing the corresponding model for the analysis of the full table with the model for the analysis of the off diagonal cells (for example, comparing the DF model with the D model, or the DAF model with the DA model). Also, for a given model that does include crossings parameters (and also diagonals parameters and/or the triangles parameter), the hypothesis that the relative differences among the μ_i are nil for $i = 2, 3, \cdots, R - 2$, excluding $i = 1$ and $i = R$, can be tested by a similar kind of comparison (for example, the comparison of the DCF model with the DC model, or the DPCF model with the DPC model, or the DACF model with the DAC model). Examination of the corresponding relative magnitudes in Table IX shed further light on the results obtained by comparing the corresponding chi squares given in Table V. Recall, for example, that the comparison of the DCF model with the DC model indicated that the relative differences among the μ_i were statistically significant for Table III; they were not as statistically significant for Table I (but they were significant at the 10 percent level); and they were not statistically significant for Table II.

We remarked in Section 5 that, in calculating the m_i and m_i^* for models that include diagonals parameters and/or the triangles parameter, we must first make some assumptions about δ_0. For the calculations in Tables IX and X, we have assumed that

$$(7.5) \qquad \frac{\delta_0}{\delta_1''} = \frac{\delta_1''}{\delta_2''},$$

where δ_k'' is defined as

$$(7.6) \qquad \delta_k'' = (\delta_k \delta_{-k})^{1/2}.$$

Denoting δ_0 by δ_0'', condition (7.5) states that $\delta_k''/\delta_{k+1}''$ is constant, for $k = 0$ and 1. Although there is an element of arbitrariness in this way of defining δ_0, there are good reasons for using (7.5) here. (An alternative procedure would be to set $\delta_0 = 1$, which would yield the same result as obtained with (7.5) in cases where the model does not include diagonals parameters (and/or the triangles parameter), and also in cases where the model includes both the crossings parameters and diagonals parameters (and/or the triangles parameter) when the parameters are uniquely defined by condition (7.4) together with the condition that $\delta_1 = \delta_{-1} = 1$. In addition, for models that include both γ_u and δ_k (and/or τ_k), the m_i for $i = 2, 3, \cdots, R - 1$, would be the same when $\delta_0 = 1$ as the corresponding quantities obtained when the parameters are uniquely defined by condition (7.3) together with the condition that $\delta_1 = \delta_{-1} = 1$.) Since we set $\delta_1 = \delta_{-1} = 1$ in all models that include diagonals parameters, condition (7.5) can be simplified to

(7.7) $$\delta_0 = \frac{1}{\delta_2''}.$$

In order to calculate m_1 and m_R (and also m_1^* and m_R^*) in Tables IX and X, we have set $\gamma_1 = \gamma_{R-1} = \gamma^*$, where $\gamma^* = \max_k \gamma_k$ for $2 \leq k \leq R - 2$. This procedure provides a way of calculating m_1 and m_R (and also m_1^* and m_R^*) that is conservative in the sense that, while it acknowledges the possible existence of the crossings parameters γ_1 and γ_{R-1}, it estimates their effects as being equal to the least pronounced estimated effects among the γ_u for $u = 2, 3, \cdots, R - 2$. (In his analysis of the "variable distance" model, Haberman [20] made the assumption that $\mu_1 = \mu_R = 1$ (that is, that $\log \mu_1 = \log \mu_R = 0$), and under this assumption he then estimated parameters corresponding to γ_1 and γ_{R-1} (namely, $\log \gamma_1$ and $\log \gamma_{R-1}$). In contrast to this, in the present article the μ_1 and μ_R (and also the μ_1^* and μ_R^*) are estimated from the data as indicated in the first sentence of this paragraph. Also, in contrast to the earlier analysis of the "variable distance" model, the parameters μ_i^* for $i = 1, 2, \cdots, R$, introduced here provide an additional index of interest (see Section 5).)

8. Extensions and applications to the analysis of two (or more) cross classification tables, and to the analysis of multidimensional tables

The results presented in Sections 3 and 4 for the general case of the $R \times C$ table can be directly extended to the analysis of two $R \times C$ tables (that is, to the analysis of the $R \times C \times 2$ table), to the analysis of G such $R \times C$ tables (that is, to the analysis of the $R \times C \times G$ table), and more generally to the analysis of multidimensional contingency tables. Indeed, the results presented in those sections can be applied directly to the multidimensional table simply by replacing each reference to the cells (i, j) of the $R \times C$ table throughout those sections by a corresponding reference to the cells of the multidimensional table.

I shall give here only a few examples (although there are many) of the possible extensions of the particular models introduced earlier to the analysis of three way tables (or to the analysis of contingency tables of higher dimensions). Suppose we applied, say, the DC model to G different $R \times R$ tables and found that the model fit the data for each of these tables. For the gth table, $g = 1, 2, \cdots$, the parameters $\alpha_i^{(g)}$, $\beta_j^{(g)}$, $\delta_k^{(g)}$, $\gamma_u^{(g)}$ could be estimated by the methods described earlier, and we could consider various hypotheses of the following kind:

(8.1) $\delta_k^{(g)} = \delta_k$ for $g = 1, 2, \cdots, G,$

(8.2) $\gamma_u^{(g)} = \gamma_u$ for $g = 1, 2, \cdots, G,$

(8.3) $\delta_k^{(g)} = \delta_k$ and $\gamma_u^{(g)} = \gamma_u$ for $g = 1, 2, \cdots, G.$

Each of these hypotheses can be expressed as an "intrinsically unrestricted" model for the $R \times C \times G$ table, since the restrictions (8.1), (8.2), and (8.3) are of the H'' type (as defined in Section 4). Thus, the method presented earlier could also be used to analyze the model H'' obtained by modifying the DC model for each of the G tables by imposing conditions of the kind described above (that is, (8.1) to (8.3)).

Let H_g denote a given model (for example, the DC model) that will be applied to the gth $R \times R$ table for $g = 1, 2, \cdots, G$, and let H denote the hypothesis (model) that states that the H_g are true for $g = 1, 2, \cdots, G$. Let H'' denote the model obtained by modifying H by imposing a given condition (for example, a condition of the kind described under (8.1) to (8.3)) that still permits H'' to be expressed as an "intrinsically unrestricted" model for the $R \times C \times G$ table. Let $\chi^2(H_g)$, $\chi^2(H)$, and $\chi^2(H'')$ denote the chi square statistic based upon the likelihood ratio criterion for testing H_g, H, and H'', respectively. Each of these statistics can be calculated by the methods presented earlier applied to the G different $R \times R$ tables (for calculating $\chi^2(H_g)$) and to the $R \times R \times G$ table (for calculating $\chi^2(H)$ and $\chi^2(H'')$). Note that

$$(8.4) \qquad \chi^2(H) = \sum_{g=1}^{G} \chi^2(H_g).$$

Letting $[H''|H]$ denote the hypothesis that H'' is true assuming that H is true, we see that $[H''|H]$ states that the given condition, which was used to modify H to form H'', is true assuming that H is true. The following statistic is the chi square statistic based upon the likelihood ratio criterion for testing $[H''|H]$:

$$(8.5) \qquad \chi^2(H''|H) = \chi^2(H'') - \chi^2(H)$$
$$= 2 \sum f \log \left[\frac{\hat{f}}{\hat{f}''} \right] = 2 \sum \hat{f} \log \left[\frac{\hat{f}}{\hat{f}''} \right],$$

where $\hat{f}$ and $\hat{f}''$ denote the estimated expected frequencies in the $R \times C \times G$ table under H and H'', respectively. Note that the $\hat{f}$ pertaining to the gth $R \times R$ table can be calculated separately for each of the G tables, but the $\hat{f}''$ need to be calculated from the $R \times R \times G$ table (if H'' is a hypothesis of the kind described by (8.1) to (8.3)).

The statistic (8.5) has an asymptotic chi square distribution under the hypothesis $[H''|H]$, with the degrees of freedom equal to the difference between the corresponding number of degrees of freedom for testing H'' and H, respectively. The degrees of freedom of $\chi^2(H''|H)$ can also be calculated from the number of restrictions on the parameters (calculating this number after the parameters have been uniquely defined). Thus, for example, for testing hypotheses (8.1), 8.2), and (8.3), the corresponding number of degrees of freedom will be $G - 1$ multiplied by $2(R - 2) - 1 = 2R - 5$, $(R - 3) - 1 = R - 4$, and $2(R - 2) + (R - 4) = 3R - 8$, for hypotheses (8.1), (8.2), and (8.3), respectively.

We shall now comment briefly on the relationship between hypotheses of the kind considered above for the three way table (or for tables of higher dimension) and the usual hypothesis H_0 of zero three factor interaction in the three way table (or the corresponding kind of hypotheses for the table of higher dimension) (see, for example, Goodman [15], [17]). The usual hypothesis H_0 in the three way $R \times C \times G$ table states that the probability $\pi_{i,j,g}$ can be written as

$$(8.6) \qquad \pi_{i,j,g} = \alpha_i^{(g)} \beta_j^{(g)} \theta_{i,j}$$

$$\text{for } i = 1, 2, \cdots, R, \quad j = 1, 2, \cdots, C, \quad g = 1, 2, \cdots, G.$$

For the $R \times R \times G$ table, consider now the hypothesis H that states that the DCF model holds true for the gth $R \times R$ table, $g = 1, 2, \cdots, G$, and let H'' denote the modification of H obtained by imposing condition (8.3) on model H. The model H'' can be expressed as

$$(8.7) \qquad \pi_{i,j,g} = \alpha_i^{(g)} \beta_j^{(g)} \gamma_{i,j}' \delta_k \quad \text{for cells } (i, j, g) \text{ for which } (i, j) \text{ is in } S_k',$$

for $k = 0, \pm 1, \pm 2, \cdots, \pm(R - 1)$; and with $\gamma_{i,j}'$ defined by (2.6.3), with $\gamma_{i,j}' = 1$ for $i = j$. To test the hypotheses H_0, H, and H'' in the $R \times R \times G$ table, the corresponding number of degrees of freedom will be $(R - 1)^2 (G - 1)$, $G(R - 2)(R - 3)$, and $G(R - 1)^2 - (3R - 5)$, respectively. Since there are $(R - 2)(R - 3)$ degrees of freedom for testing the DCF model (see Table IV), the corresponding number of degrees of freedom for the H model will be $G(R - 2)(R - 3)$. Note also that the degrees of freedom for the H'' model can be calculated by subtracting from GR^2 the number of estimated parameters under the model (namely, $G(2R - 1) + (3R - 5)$) or by adding $(G - 1)$ $(3R - 5)$ to $G(R - 2)(R - 3)$, since condition (8.3) actually imposes $(G - 1)$ $(3R - 5)$ restrictions upon the parameters of H. The hypothesis $[H'' | H]$ states that condition (8.3) is true, assuming that H is true; and the hypothesis $[H'' | H_0]$ states that the following condition is true, assuming that H_0 is true:

$$(8.8) \qquad \qquad \theta_{i,j} = \gamma_{i,j}' \delta_k \qquad \text{for} \quad (i, j) \text{ in } S_k',$$

for $k = 0, \pm 1, \pm 2, \cdots, \pm(R - 1)$, where the parameters in (8.8) are defined by the expressions (8.6) and (8.7). To test the hypotheses $[H'' | H]$ and $[H'' | H_0]$, the corresponding number of degrees of freedom will be $(G - 1)(3R - 5)$ and

$$(8.9) \qquad (R - 1)^2 - (3R - 5) = R^2 - 5R + 6 = (R - 2)(R - 3),$$

respectively.

Note that the same number of degrees of freedom are obtained for the hypothesis $[H'' | H_0]$ as for the DCF model in the $R \times R$ table. The hypothesis $[H'' | H_0]$ states that the parameters $\theta_{i,j}$ in (8.6) will satisfy condition (8.8); and the DCF model states that the probabilities $\pi_{i,j}$ can be written as

$$(8.10) \qquad \qquad \pi_{i,j} = \alpha_i \beta_j \theta_{i,j}',$$

where the $\theta_{i,j}'$ are of the form

$$(8.11) \qquad \qquad \theta_{i,j}' = \gamma_{i,j}' \delta_k \qquad \text{for cells } (i, j) \text{ in } S_k',$$

for $k = 0, \pm 1, \pm 2, \cdots, \pm(R - 1)$. Similarly, each of the hypotheses considered in Sections 2.1 to 2.8 states that the probabilities $\pi_{i,j}$ can be written as

(8.10) where the $\theta'_{i,j}$ are subject to certain specified conditions. For example, the DC model states that the $\theta'_{i,j}$ are of the form

$$(8.12) \qquad \theta'_{i,j} = \begin{cases} \gamma'_{i,j}\delta_k & \text{for cells } (i,j) \text{ in } S'_k \text{ for } k = \pm 1, \pm 2, \cdots, \pm(R-1), \\ \mu'_i & \text{for cells } (i,i) \text{ in } S'_0, \end{cases}$$

where μ'_i is an "intrinsically unrestricted" parameter.

For the usual hypothesis H_0 of zero three factor interaction in the $R \times C \times G$ table (see (8.6)), the probabilities $\pi_{i,j,g}$ can be rewritten as

$$(8.13) \qquad\qquad\qquad \pi_{i,j,g} = \alpha_{i,g}\beta_{j,g}\theta_{i,j}.$$

In the present section, we have considered hypotheses about the form of the $\theta_{i,j}$ in the $R \times R \times G$ table. It should also be noted that the general methods presented in Sections 3 and 4 can be directly applied to any given hypothesis about the form of the $\alpha_{i,g}$, $\beta_{j,g}$, and/or $\theta_{i,j}$ in the $R \times C \times G$ table, as long as the corresponding model is "intrinsically unrestricted" in the three way table.

The methods presented here can be directly applied not only to models for the three way table that are formed by imposing conditions on the parameters in (8.13), but also more generally to any hypothesis about the probabilities $\pi_{i,j,g}$ in the three way table (or in a table of higher dimension), as long as the corresponding model is intrinsically unrestricted. As an example of such models (that is, intrinsically unrestricted models) that are not formed by imposing conditions on the parameters in (8.13), see Goodman [13], [14] where the hypothesis of zero three factor interaction is extended to the case where a given subset of the cells in the three way table are deleted. These models for the three way table can be further extended in the same ways as we have here extended the model of quasi-independence in the two way table. For example, in the same way that the T model was formed by introducing the triangles parameters into the QO model, we could also introduce the three dimensional analogues of the triangles parameters (considering now parameters pertaining to certain triangles and tetrahedra in the three way table) into the models for the three way table considered in Goodman [13] (that is, into models of zero three factor interaction applied to a given subset of the cells of the table). In the same way that the triangles parameters are introduced in order to describe a particular kind of two factor interaction (between the row and column classifications) in the two way table, the three dimensional analogues of the triangles parameters can be introduced in order to describe a particular kind of three factor interaction in the three way table. For three way tables that do not conform to the usual hypothesis H_0 of zero three factor interaction, we can now provide a wide variety of multiplicative models (that is, the three dimensional analogues of the models in Sections 2.2 to 2.8) that can be used to analyze the data. In addition, for three way tables that do conform to the usual hypothesis H_0, we noted earlier in the present section that the general methods presented here can be used to test given hypotheses about the form of the parameters in the H_0 model (that is, hypotheses about the form of the two factor interactions in the three way table).

The preceding remarks can be directly extended to the multidimensional contingency table. We noted earlier that the usual hypothesis H_0 of zero three factor interaction in the three way table could be expressed as an intrinsically unrestricted multiplicative model, and similarly each of the hierarchical hypotheses described in Goodman [17] for the multidimensional table can also be expressed as an intrinsically unrestricted multiplicative model. The various extensions and modifications of H_0, which we described earlier in the present section for the analysis of the three way table, can also be directly extended in order to provide further extensions and modifications of the hierarchical hypotheses that were considered in the earlier literature on multidimensional contingency tables. Since these extensions and modifications are directly analogous to those already presented in the present article, we need not discuss this further here.

Before closing this section, we return for a moment to the models of Sections 2.3 to 2.8. Note that (2.3.4) can be viewed as a model for an $R \times C \times K$ table (R rows, C columns, K layers) that describes conditional quasi-independence between the row and column classifications, given the kth layer classification, $k = 1, 2, \cdots, K$, when certain cells (i, j, k) have been deleted, namely, the cells (i, j, k) for which the (i, j) is not in S_k (see, for example, Goodman [13], [17]). In particular, (2.3.1) is a model that describes conditional quasi-independence in the $R \times R \times 2$ table, where one layer pertains to positive $(i - j)$ and the other layer pertains to negative $(i - j)$. Similarly, (2.4.1) is a model for quasi-mutual independence in the $R \times R \times 2$ table (that is, a model of "complete independence" among the three variables in the three way table when certain cells have been deleted); and (2.5.1) is a model of quasi-mutual independence in an $R \times R \times [2(R - 1)]$ table. The other models in Sections 2.3 to 2.8 can also be viewed as models in three way or multi-way tables.

APPENDIX

Explicit Formulae for the Estimates of the Parameters in the Models

For any given model of the kind described in Sections 2.2 to 2.8, we shall now show how the maximum likelihood estimates of the parameters in the model can be expressed explicitly as functions of the estimates $\hat{f}_{i,j}$ of the expected frequencies under the model. Other ways to calculate the maximum likelihood estimates of the parameters were described in Section 3. The results, which we shall now present, will provide (a) further insight into the meaning of the parameters (expressed explicitly as functions of the probabilities $\pi_{i,j}$), and (b) a method for calculating the maximum likelihood estimates of the parameters (after the estimates $\hat{f}_{i,j}$ have been calculated as described in Section 3) which some readers may find easier to apply than the other methods that were described in Section 3 for estimating the parameters.

For simplicity, let us first consider the QO model (see Section 2.3). For this model, the maximum likelihood estimate $\hat{f}_{i,j}$ can be written as follows (see (2.2.4)):

(A.1) $\qquad\qquad\qquad\qquad \hat{f}_{i,j} = a_i b_j \qquad$ for $\; i \neq j.$

As we noted earlier (see Sections 2.1 to 2.3), the $\hat{f}_{i,j}$ in (A.1) will be unchanged if a_1 is set equal to one (and the other a_i and b_j in (A.1) are changed accordingly). With $a_1 = 1$, we see from (A.1) that the b_j can be written as

(A.2) $\qquad\qquad b_j = \begin{cases} \hat{f}_{1,j} & \text{for} \quad j = 2, 3, \cdots, R, \\ \hat{f}_{3,1}\,\hat{f}_{1,2}/\hat{f}_{3,2} & \text{for} \quad j = 1. \end{cases}$

Similarly, having calculated b_1 from (A.2), we obtain the following formula for the a_i

(A.3) $\qquad\qquad\quad a_i = \begin{cases} 1 & \text{for} \quad i = 1, \\ \hat{f}_{i,1}/b_1 & \text{for} \quad i = 2, 3, \cdots, R. \end{cases}$

If we are interested in the a_i after they have been scaled so that $\Sigma_i \, a_i = 1$, then a_i of (A.3) can be replaced by $\tilde{a}_i = a_i/\Sigma_{h=1}^{R} a_h$. The $\tilde{a}_i$ are the maximum likelihood estimates of the scaled parameters $\tilde{\alpha}_i = \alpha_i/\Sigma_{h=1}^{R} \alpha_h$, which can be interpreted (for the QO model) as the hypothetical proportion of individuals in the ith row class in the hypothetical population in which none of cells on the main diagonal needs to be deleted, and there is independence between the row and column classifications in the table (see Goodman [13], [14]). A similar comment applies to b_j and to the corresponding $\tilde{b}_j$ and $\tilde{\beta}_j$. For the QO model, we find that

(A.4) $\qquad\qquad \tilde{\beta}_j = \tilde{\pi}^{*}_{i,j} \qquad$ for $\; i = 1, 2, \cdots, R, \quad j = 1, 2, \cdots, R,$

where $\tilde{\pi}^{*}_{i,j} = \pi^{*}_{i,j}/\pi_i.$ is the hypothetical conditional probability defined in Section 5. Thus, by applying the mover-stayer interpretation described by (5.9) to the QO model, we see from (A.4) that $\tilde{\beta}_j$ can be interpreted as the hypothetical probability that a "mover" will be in the jth column class (see, for example, Goodman [16]). By interchanging the row and column classifications, and then applying the mover-stayer interpretation described by (5.9), we see that the $\tilde{\alpha}_i$ can be interpreted in a similar way to the above interpretation of the $\tilde{\beta}_j$. (Analogous kinds of interpretations of the $\tilde{\beta}_j$ and $\tilde{\alpha}_i$ can be obtained when (5.10) is applicable, rather than (5.9).)

Consider now the QP and QN models (see Section 2.3). For each of these models, the parameters can be estimated by formulae similar to (A.2) and (A.3), based upon the fact that the b_j are proportional to the $\hat{f}_{R,j}$ for $j = 1, 2, \cdots,$ $R - 1$, and the a_i are proportional to the $\hat{f}_{i,1}$ for $i = 2, 3, \cdots, R$, for the QP model, and upon the fact that the b$_j$ are proportional to the $\hat{f}_{1,j}$ for $j = 2, 3, \cdots, R$ and the a_i are proportional to the $\hat{f}_{i,R}$ for $i = 1, 2, \cdots, R - 1$, for the QN model. More generally, for any model of quasi-independence for an inseparable set of cells (or for the inseparable subsets of a separable set of cells), the parameters can also be estimated by formulae similar to (A.2) and (A.3).

Now consider the DC model (see Section 2.7). For this model, the maximum likelihood estimate $\hat{f}_{i,j}$ can be written as follows (see (2.7.1)):

$$(A.5) \qquad \hat{f}_{i,j} = a_i b_j c'_{i,j} d_k \qquad \text{for cells } (i,j) \text{ in } S'_k,$$

for $k = \pm 1, \pm 2, \cdots, \pm (R-1)$, where

$$(A.6) \qquad c'_{i,j} = \begin{cases} \displaystyle\prod_{u=j}^{i-1} c_u & \text{for } i > j, \\ \displaystyle\prod_{u=i}^{j-1} c_u & \text{for } i < j. \end{cases}$$

We shall let v_i, w_i, y_i, and z_i denote the quantities

$$(A.7) \qquad v_i = \frac{(\hat{f}_{i,i+2}\hat{f}_{i+1,i-1})}{(\hat{f}_{i,i-1}\hat{f}_{i+1,i+2})} \qquad \text{for } i = 2, 3, \cdots, R-2,$$

$$(A.8) \qquad w_i = \frac{(\hat{f}_{i,1}\hat{f}_{2,i+1})}{(\hat{f}_{2,1}\hat{f}_{i,i+1})} \qquad \text{for } i = 3, 4, \cdots, R-1,$$

$$(A.9) \qquad y_i = \left[\prod_{j=1}^{i}\left(\frac{\hat{f}_{j,j+1}}{\hat{f}_{j+1,j}}\right)\right]\left[\left(\frac{\hat{f}_{i+1,1}}{\hat{f}_{1,i+1}}\right)\right] \qquad \text{for } i = 2, 3, \cdots, R-1,$$

$$(A.10) \qquad z_i = \begin{cases} \dfrac{(\hat{f}_{R,1}\hat{f}_{R-1,2})}{(\hat{f}_{R-1,1}\hat{f}_{R,2})} & \text{for } i = 1, \\[3mm] \dfrac{(\hat{f}_{1,R}\hat{f}_{2,R-1})}{(\hat{f}_{1,R-1}\hat{f}_{2,R})} & \text{for } i = -1. \end{cases}$$

(For simplicity, we shall first assume that $\hat{f}_{i,j} > 0$ for $i \neq j$.) From (A.5) to (A.10), we find that

$$(A.11) \qquad v_i = \frac{c_i^2 d'_2}{d'_1} \qquad \text{for } i = 2, 3, \cdots, R-2,$$

$$(A.12) \qquad w_i = \frac{d'_{i-1}\left(\displaystyle\prod_{j=2}^{i-1} c_j^2\right)}{d'_1} \qquad \text{for } i = 3, 4, \cdots, R-1,$$

$$(A.13) \qquad y_i = \left(\frac{d_{-1}}{d_1}\right)^i\left(\frac{d_i}{d_{-i}}\right) \qquad \text{for } i = 2, 3, \cdots, R-1,$$

$$(A.14) \qquad z_i = \begin{cases} \dfrac{d_{R-1} d_{R-3}}{d_{R-2}^2} & \text{for } i = 1, \\[3mm] \dfrac{d_{-(R-1)} d_{-(R-3)}}{d_{-(R-2)}^2} & \text{for } i = -1, \end{cases}$$

where d'_i is defined by

$$(A.15) \qquad d'_i = d_i d_{-i}.$$

As we noted earlier (see Section 7), the c_u in (A.5) and (A.6) can be defined uniquely for $u = 2, 3, \cdots, R - 2$, either by introducing a restriction to be imposed directly upon them (for example, that the maximum c_u be set equal to one) or by introducing an additional restriction to be imposed upon the d_k (for example, that $d_2' = 1$, in addition to the restriction that $d_1 = d_{-1} = 1$). The former kind of restriction would be appropriate when the DC model is viewed as an extension of the D model, and the latter kind of restriction would be appropriate when the DC model is viewed as an extension of the C model. If the maximum c_u is equal to one for $u = 2, 3, \cdots, R - 2$, then from (A.11) we obtain the following formula for the c_u,

$$(A.16) \qquad c_u = \left(\frac{v_u}{v^*} \right)^{1/2} \qquad \text{for} \quad u = 2, 3, \cdots, R - 2,$$

where

$$(A.17) \qquad v^* = \max_i v_i \qquad \text{for} \quad 2 \leqq i \leqq R - 2.$$

If instead of the above restriction on the maximum c_u, we set $d_2' = 1$ (in addition to setting $d_1 = d_{-1} = 1$), we see from (A.11) that c_u would be calculated by a modified form of (A.16) in which v^* is replaced by one. Since the $\hat{f}_{i,j}$ in (A.5) are unaffected if d_1 and d_{-1} are set equal to one (and the a_i, b_j, and other d_k are changed accordingly), we see from (A.12) that the d_i' can be calculated by

$$(A.18) \qquad d_i' = \frac{\overset{i}{w}_{i+1}}{\prod_{j=2}^{i} c_j^2} \qquad \text{for} \quad i = 2, 3, \cdots, R - 2,$$

where the c_j are calculated from (A.16). From (A.13) and (A.15), we see that the d_i can be calculated as

$$(A.19) \qquad d_i = \begin{cases} (d_i' y_i)^{1/2} & \text{for} \quad i = 2, 3, \cdots, R - 2, \\ (d_i'/y_i)^{1/2} & \text{for} \quad i = -2, -3, \cdots, -(R - 2), \end{cases}$$

where d_i' is calculated from (A.18). From (A.14) we obtain the following formulae for d_{R-1} and $d_{-(R-1)}$:

$$(A.20) \qquad d_i = \begin{cases} z_1 d_{R-2}^2 / d_{R-3} & \text{for} \quad i = R - 1, \\ z_{-1} d_{-(R-2)}^2 / d_{-(R-3)} & \text{for} \quad i = -(R - 1). \end{cases}$$

We next consider

$$(A.21) \qquad \hat{f}_{i,j}' = \frac{\hat{f}_{i,j}}{d_k c_{i,j}'} \qquad \text{for cells } (i, j) \text{ in } S_k',$$

for $k = \pm 1, \pm 2, \cdots, \pm(R - 1)$, where the d_k are calculated from (A.19) and (A.20) and the $c_{i,j}'$ are calculated from (A.6), with c_u calculated from (A.16). From (A.5) and (A.21), we see that

(A.22) $$\hat{f}'_{i,j} = a_i b_j \qquad \text{for} \quad i \neq j.$$

Since the $\hat{f}'_{i,j}$ are of the same form as described by (A.1), the a_i and b_j can be calculated from (A.2) and (A.3) by replacing $\hat{f}_{i,j}$ by $\hat{f}'_{i,j}$ in these formulae. Thus, by applying the methods described in the present and preceding paragraphs, all of the parameters in the DC model can be estimated.

In the preceding discussion of the DC model, we assumed that $\hat{f}_{i,j} > 0$ for $i \neq j$. In cases where this assumption is not true, the above methods require some modification. For example, if $f_{R,1} = 0$ (as is the case for Tables I and III), then $\hat{f}_{R,1} = 0$ and $d_{R-1} = 0$ when the DC model is applied to these tables, and $\hat{f}'_{R,1}$ will be undefined. In this case, the $\hat{f}'_{i,j}$ that are well defined will have the same form as (A.22), and the methods described earlier for estimating the parameters in the model of quasi-independence can be applied to this set of $\hat{f}'_{i,j}$.

The methods described in this section can be applied, either directly or indirectly, to estimate the parameters in any of the models of Sections 2.2 to 2.8. For example, with the DPC model, by a direct application of the above formulae, we would obtain, among other things, the estimate d_k of the δ_k that satisfy (2.5.12). By an indirect application, we would first set $d_k = 1$ for $k = -1, -2, \cdots, -(R-1)$, in accordance with condition (2.5.9), and then from (A.11), (A.12), and (A.15), we would obtain

(A.23) $$d_1 = \frac{v_2}{y_2 c_2^2},$$

with c_2 calculated from (A.16). (For the DPC model, if the d_k are set at one for $k = -1, -2, \cdots, -(R-1)$, then d_1 will not be set at one.) To calculate d_k for $k = 2, 3, \cdots, R-1$, for this model, we then obtain, from (A.12) and (A.15),

(A,24) $$d_i = d_1 d'_i, \qquad \text{for} \quad i = 2, 3, \cdots, R-2,$$

with d_1 and d'_i calculated from (A.23) and (A.18), respectively. The value of d_{R-1} can be calculated from (A.20), using the d_i, for $i = R-2$ and $R-3$, calculated from (A.24).

In cases where the given model includes the triangles parameter (for example, in the DACT model), the parameter τ can be expressed as

(A.25) $$\tau = \left(\frac{\delta_k}{\delta_{-k}} \right)^{1/2} \qquad \text{for} \quad k = 1, 2, \cdots, R-1,$$

where $\tau = \sqrt{\tau'}$, for τ' defined by (2.7.4). From (A.13) and (A.25) we would obtain the following formula for the maximum likelihood estimate t of τ:

(A.26) $$t = \frac{1}{\sqrt{y_2}}.$$

If the model includes both the triangles parameter and the parameters pertaining to the paired minor diagonals, then after introducing the τ parameter explicitly into the model, the model will be unaffected by setting $\delta_k = \delta_{-k}$ for $k = 1, 2, \cdots, R - 1$. With the parameter τ estimated by (A.26), we can estimate $\delta_k = \delta_{-k}$ by

$$(A.27) \qquad d_k = \sqrt{d'_k} \qquad \text{for} \quad k = 2, 3, \cdots, R - 2,$$

where d'_k is calculated from (A.18). We can set $d_1 = d_{-1} = 1$ in this model, and d_{R-1} can be calculated from (A.20), using d_i for $i = R - 2$ and $R - 3$ calculated from ($A.27$).

For the QO model or for any of the models described in Sections 2.4 to 2.7, the ratio index μ_i and the relative difference index μ_i^*, which we defined in Section 5, can be estimated by the corresponding quantities m_i and m_i^* (see (5.14) and (5.15)), with the a_i and b_j calculated as described in the present section, and with d_0 as described in Section 7. For the models described in Section 2.8, we set $\mu_i = 1$, and therefore

$$(A.28) \qquad \hat{f}_{i,i} = a_i b_i d_0 \qquad \text{for} \quad i = 1, 2, \cdots, R.$$

With the $\hat{f}_{i,j}$ calculated by the iterative scaling method (for all cells (i,j) in the $R \times R$ table under the models of Section 2.8), we can calculate d_0 from

$$(A.29) \qquad d_0 = \frac{\hat{f}_{i,i}}{a_i b_i},$$

with the a_i and b_i calculated as described earlier in the present section.

For any given model of the kind described in Section 2.8 (for example, the DCF model), an alternative method for calculating d_0 can be based upon the fact that

$$(A.30) \qquad d_0^2 = d'_1 c_i^2 u_i,$$

where

$$(A.31) \qquad u_i = \frac{(\hat{f}_{i,i} \hat{f}_{i+1,i+1})}{(\hat{f}_{i,i+1} \hat{f}_{i+1,i})} \qquad \text{for} \quad i = 1, 2, \cdots, R - 1,$$

with the c_i calculated as earlier for $i = 2, 3, \cdots, R - 2$. Formula ($A.30$) can be used to calculate d_0 (applying the formula for any given value of $i = 2, 3, \cdots, R - 2$), and then c_1 and c_{R-1} can be calculated by rewriting (A.30)

$$(A.32) \qquad c_i = \frac{d_0}{(d'_1 u_i)^{1/2}}.$$

Now for all cells (i, j) in the table, we can consider

$$(A.33) \qquad \hat{f}'_{i,j} = \frac{\hat{f}_{i,j}}{d_k c_{i,j}} \qquad \text{for cells } (i, j) \text{ in } S'_k,$$

for $k = 0, \pm 1, \pm 2, \cdots, \pm(R - 1)$. (Compare (A.33) with (A.21).) The $\hat{f}'_{i,j}$ will be of the form

$$(A.34) \qquad \hat{f}'_{i,j} = a_i b_j \qquad \text{for all cells } (i, j)$$

(see (A.22)), and so the a_i and b_j can be calculated here by the same methods used to estimate the parameters in the usual model of independence between the row and column classifications. For the models of Section 2.8, the method just described provides an alternative to the method described following (A.22) for calculating a_i and b_j. It should also be noted, as we did earlier, that in cases where the assumption that $\hat{f}_{i,j} > 0$ is not met for all cells in the table (under a given model of Section 2.8), the above methods require modifications of the kind which we described in the paragraph following (A.22).

The results of the present section can be applied to any of the models in Section 2.2 to 2.8 whenever the maximum likelihood estimate $\hat{f}_{i,j}$ exists. For comments concerning the existence of the $\hat{f}_{i,j}$, see Section 3 herein and Haberman [20].

REFERENCES

[1] R. R. BAHADUR, "Rates of convergence of estimates and test statistics," *Ann. Math. Statist.*, Vol. 38 (1967), pp. 303–324.
[2] Y. M. M. BISHOP and S. E. FIENBERG, "Incomplete two-dimensional contingency tables," *Biometrics*, Vol. 25 (1969), pp. 118–128.
[3] I. BLUMEN. M. KOGAN. and P. J. McCARTHY. *The Industrial Mobility of Labor as a Probability Process*, Cornell Studies in Industrial and Labor Relations, Vol. 4, Ithaca, Cornell University, 1955.
[4] H. CAUSSINUS, "Contribution à l'analyse statistique des tableaux de corrélation." *Annales de la Faculté des Sciences de l'Université de Toulouse*, Vol. 29 (1965). pp. 77–182.
[5] S. E. FIENBERG. "Quasi-independence and maximum-likelihood estimation in incomplete contingency tables." *J. Amer. Statist. Assoc..* Vol. 65 (1970) pp. 1610–1616.
[6] D. V. GLASS (editor), *Social Mobility in Britain*. Glencoe. Free Press, 1954.
[7] I. J. GOOD, "Saddle-point methods for the multinomial distribution," *Ann. Math. Statist.*, Vol. 28 (1957), pp. 861–881.
[8] L. A. GOODMAN, "Statistical methods for the mover-stayer model," *J. Amer. Statist. Assoc.*, Vol. 56 (1961), pp. 841–868.
[9] ———, "Statistical methods for the preliminary analysis of transaction flows," *Econometrica*, Vol. 31 (1963), pp. 197–208.
[10] ———. "A short computer program for the analysis of transaction flows." *Behav. Sci.*, Vol. 9 (1964), pp. 176–186.
[11] ———. "Simultaneous confidence limits for cross-product ratios in contingency tables," *J. Roy. Statist. Soc., Ser. B*, Vol. 26 (1964), pp. 86–102.
[12] ———, "On the statistical analysis of mobility tables," *Am. J. Sociology*, Vol. 70 (1965), pp. 564–585.
*[13] ———, "The analysis of cross-classified data: Independence, quasi-independence, and interactions in contingency tables with or without missing entries," *J. Amer. Statist. Assoc.*, Vol. 63 (1968), pp. 1091–1131.
*[14] ———, "How to ransack social mobility tables and other kinds of cross-classification tables," *Am. J. Sociology*, Vol. 75 (1969), pp. 1–40.
[15] ———, "On partitioning χ^2 and detecting partial association in three-way contingency tables," *J. Roy. Statist. Soc., Ser. B*, Vol. 31 (1969), pp. 486–498.
[16] ———, "On the measurement of social mobility: An index of status persistence," *American Sociological Review*, Vol. 34 (1969), pp. 832–850.
[17] ———, "The multivariate analysis of qualitative data: Interactions among multiple classifications," *J. Amer. Statist. Assoc.*, Vol. 65 (1970), pp. 226–256.
[18] ———, "The analysis of multidimensional contingency tables: Stepwise procedures and

direct estimation methods for building models for multiple classifications," *Technomet.*, Vol. 13 (1971), pp. 33–61.

[19] ———, "A simple simultaneous test procedure for quasi-independence in contingency tables," *J. Roy. Statist. Soc., Ser. C*, Vol. 20 (1971).

[20] S. HABERMAN, "The general log-linear model," Ph.D. thesis, University of Chicago, 1970.

[21] W. HOEFFDING, "Asymptotically optimal tests for multinomial distributions," *Ann. Math. Statist.*, Vol. 36 (1965), pp. 369–408.

[22] J. LEVINE, "Measurement in the study of intergenerational status mobility," Ph.D. thesis, Harvard University, 1967.

[23] N. MANTEL, "Incomplete contingency tables," *Biometrics*, Vol. 26 (1970), pp. 291–304.

[24] F. MOSTELLER, "Association and estimation in contingency tables," *J. Amer. Statist. Assoc.*, Vol. 63 (1968), pp. 1–28.

[25] K. SVALASTOGA, *Prestige, Class and Mobility*, London, William Heinemann, 1959.

A Note on Computer Programs

Because the greater part of this book is concerned with association models, I shall first comment on computer programs that can be used to apply these models, and then on programs that can be used to apply some of the other models considered in the book.

The class of association models introduced in Chapters 4, 5, and 6 can be applied using the Analysis of Association program (ANOAS) based upon iterative procedures of the kind described in Appendix B of Chapter 4, and extensions thereof. (The iterative procedure in Appendix A of that chapter can be replaced by the kind of iterative procedure described in Appendix B there, by obtaining trial values for $\log \gamma_i$ and $\log \delta_j$ (rather than for γ_i and δ_j) using iterations of the general kind described in Appendix B (replacing the iterations [5.3c]-[5.3d] of Chapter 4), with σ_j^* and ρ_i^* in Appendix B replaced by σ_j and ρ_i from [5.3c]-[5.3d].) People interested in the ANOAS program should write to Leo A. Goodman, Department of Statistics, University of Chicago, 1126 East 59 Street, Chicago, Illinois 60637. A somewhat similar program for the analysis of the models in Chapters 4, 5, 8, and 9 of this book can be obtained from Clifford C. Clogg, 504 Liberal Arts Tower, Pennsylvania State University, University Park, Pennsylvania 16802.

The models that are log-linear can be applied using various procedures. For example, the diagonals-parameter symmetry models discussed in Chapters 1 and 2 can be applied using elementary methods and calculations done by hand, when the data are rearranged as described earlier (see, for example, Table 5 in Chapter 1). The ECTA program (Everyman's Contingency Table Analyzer) can also be used with these models, and with some of the other log-linear models (see, for example, Duncan and McRae, 1978). People interested in the ECTA program should write to Leo A. Goodman at the address given in the preceding paragraph.

All of the log-linear models presented in this book can be applied using computer programs for general log-linear models (for example, GLIM in Baker and Nelder, 1978; FREQ in Haberman, 1979; Loglinear in Nie, 1983). However, if GLIM is used to apply the log-linear models in this book, there are small discrepancies between the generalized Pearson chi-square values obtained with GLIM and the corresponding goodness-of-fit chi-square values presented here. The Pearson goodness-of-fit chi-square values presented in this book were obtained with the usual formula [viz., the sum of the (observed-fitted)^2/fitted] and are essentially the same as those obtained by computing the sum of the squared standardized residuals; but they are slightly different from the generalized Pearson chi-square values obtained with GLIM. The GLIM manual states that the generalized Pearson chi-square is the sum of the squared standardized residuals, but this statement is, strictly speaking, incorrect as a description of the "generalized Pearson chi-square" actually calculated with GLIM. The generalized Pearson chi-square calculated with GLIM needs to be corrected in order to conform to the description given in the manual, or the description of this quantity in the manual needs to be changed and the discrepancy described here needs to be noted. (For further details, see the final paragraph of Section 4 in Chapter 3 of this book.)

All of the association models in Chapters 4, 5, and 6 (both the models that are log-linear and those that are not log-linear) can be applied using the ANOAS computer programs mentioned earlier, the association models that are log-linear can also be applied using programs for general log-linear models, and the association models that are not log-linear (for example, model II in Chapter 4 and the equivalent RC model in Chapters 5 and 6, or the more general association models in Chapter 6) can also be applied by extending the log-linear procedure, first viewing the parameters pertaining to row scores as specified in order to estimate the corresponding parameters pertaining to column scores, then viewing the estimated parameters thus obtained pertaining to column scores as specified to estimate the corresponding parameters pertaining to row scores, and proceeding in this alternating fashion until convergence is achieved (see, for example, the antepenultimate paragraph in Section 5 of Chapter 4).

All of the models in Appendix D can be applied using the ECTA program by viewing each of these models in its equivalent form as a simple log-linear model (for example, a conditional quasi-independence model or a quasi-mutual-independence model) in a three-way or multi-way table (see the last paragraph in Section 8 of Appendix D). Computer programs for general log-linear models can also be used here. A single program (FACTAB) for the analysis of the models in Appendix D can be obtained from Thomas Pullum, Department of Sociology, University of Washington, Seattle, Washington 89195.

References

Baker, R. J., and J. A. Nelder (1978), *The GLIM System, Generalised Linear Interactive Modelling Manual,* Release 3, Oxford: Numerical Algorithms Group.

Duncan, O. D., and J. A. McRae (1978), "Multiway Contingency Analysis with a Scaled Response or Factor," in K. F. Schuessler, ed., *Sociological Methodology 1979,* San Francisco: Jossey-Bass, 66–85.

Haberman, S. J. (1979), *Analysis of Qualitative Data, Vol. 2: New Developments:* New York: Academic Press.

Nie, N. H. (1983). *SPSS^x User's Guide.* New York: McGraw-Hill.

Index

409